I0649474

Letters to Elizabeth Toldridge
and
Anne Tillery Renshaw

THE HIPPOCAMPUS PRESS LIBRARY OF THE
COLLECTED LETTERS OF H. P. LOVECRAFT

VOLUME 6

───────────

H. P. LOVECRAFT

LETTERS TO
ELIZABETH TOLDRIDGE
AND
ANNE TILLERY RENSHAW

EDITED BY
DAVID E. SCHULTZ AND S. T. JOSHI

Hippocampus Press

New York

Copyright © 2014 by Hippocampus Press
Introduction and editorial matter copyright © 2014
by David E. Schultz and S. T. Joshi

The letters of H. P. Lovecraft, and Elizabeth Toldridge's previously unpub-
lished poems, are published by permission of the Estate of H. P. Lovecraft and
the John Hay Library, Brown University. Toldridge's letters and other unpub-
lished poems are published by permission of the Manuscripts and Archives Division, New York Public Library, Astor, Lenox, and Tilden Foundations.

Published by Hippocampus Press
P.O. Box 641, New York, NY 10156.
http://www.hippocampuspress.com

All rights reserved.
No part of this work may be reproduced in any form or by any means
without the written permission of the publisher.

Cover design and Hippocampus Press logo by Anastasia Damianakos.
Cover production by Barbara Briggs Silbert.

First Edition
1 3 5 7 9 8 6 4 2

ISBN 978-1-61498-059-9

Contents

Acknowledgments

The editors are grateful to the following for assistance in preparing this volume: Michael Abolafia, Rosemary Cullen of the John Hay Library, Phillip A. Ellis, Kenneth W. Faig, Jr., Taylor Fleet, Kathy Frymark of the Salzmann Library of St. Francis de Sales Seminary, Milwaukee, WI, Derrick Hussey, Donovan K. Loucks, Terence McVicker, Christopher O'Brien, J.-M. Rajala, and Peter Ruber.

Abbreviations

AHT	Arkham House transcripts of Lovecraft's letters
ALS	autograph letter, signed
ANS	autograph note, signed
CE	Lovecraft, *Collected Essays* (2004–06; 5 vols.)
D	Lovecraft, *Dagon and Other Macabre Tales* (1986)
DH	Lovecraft, *The Dunwich Horror and Others* (1984)
HPL	H. P. Lovecraft
JHL	John Hay Library, Brown University
LL	S. T. Joshi, comp., *Lovecraft's Library: A Catalogue* (rev. ed. 2012; numbers refer to entries)
MM	Lovecraft, *At the Mountains of Madness and Other Novels* (1985)
RHB	R. H. Barlow
SL	Lovecraft, *Selected Letters* (1965–76; 5 vols.)
WT	*Weird Tales*

Introduction

H. P. Lovecraft, though once briefly married, was an inveterate bachelor. His friends and correspondents were primarily men, mostly writers of one stripe or another: aspirants, amateurs, professionals, poets, clients. He had no women friends in Providence (so far as we know), but he was not averse to the company of women, and a not inconsiderable portion of his correspondents were female. His letters to women were mostly to his aunts—written to apprise them of his day-to-day activities when he travelled, for he lived near or with either aunt following his permanent resettlement in Providence in 1926. But other female correspondents, like the males, shared an avid interest in writing: C. L. Moore was a professional writer, Natalie Woolley a poet, and Margaret Sylvester, Hazel Heald, and Zealia Bishop clients and aspiring writers.

Lovecraft's correspondence with the poet Elizabeth Toldridge of Washington, DC, shed light not only on his relationships with women but also on a particularly personal, intimate aspect of himself. Early on Lovecraft had considered himself a poet. Indeed, he remained one throughout his life, though his late mode of expression was chiefly prose. He averred he was more of a "metrical mechanic" than an actual poet, one quick to correct faulty scansion or errant rhymes in the verses of poets less technically capable than himself. In time he realized that rhyme and meter alone do not poetry make.

Although Lovecraft had virtually abandoned poesy by 1924, he was around that time enlisted as judge for a poetry contest. A note in *Tryout* informs us: "We also doff our hats to Mr. Lovecraft, as a poet. That is why he was selected to act as judge in a $25.00 poetry contest for the League of American Pennocnen [i.e., Penwomen]."[1] Perhaps at the suggestion of a mutual colleague, an amateur journalist, or a member of the League itself (an organization of professional women artists, composers, and writers founded in 1897), someone asked Lovecraft to judge the contest and he acceded. The contest was his first brief brush with the Elizabeth Toldridge, who around that time was becoming active in the American Poetry Circle, founded by Leacy Naylor Green-Leach in Baltimore in 1923, which published her verse in their magazine. The contest had long-reaching effects. Toldridge wrote Lovecraft about the contest in 1928, and in 1930, from New York, Lovecraft explained to his aunt, about mail received in his absense: "Those Virginia pictures probably came from some member of that Poetry Circle branch in Washington (i.e., Toldridge's friend Florence Radcliffe, also of the Circle)—whose personnel persistently & rather inanely address me as 'Judge' because I judged a poetry contest of theirs six years ago."[2]

---

1. [C. W. Smith], "Around the Circle," *Tryout* 9, No. 2 (February 1924): [n.p.]
2. HPL to L. D. Clark, 20–21 May 1930; ms., JHL.

How Toldridge, four years after the fact, found Lovecraft is not known. As noted, she and Miss Radcliffe continually addressed Lovecraft as "Judge," to his chagrin. Unlike Ambrose Bierce, who bristled at being addressed "Dear Master" in letters from George Sterling, Lovecraft did not admonish his correspondents. Toldridge's observation that she had misplaced Lovecraft's comments on her work and hoped to reread them sparked a lively correspondence that spanned some nine years and more than one hundred letters by each, most discussing particulars of poetry or containing Lovecraft's suggestions to Toldridge for improving her verses. In his first letter to her, Lovecraft revealed:

> At the time [of the contest], I might have been more prone to side with the technical sticklers; but latterly I have been paying less & less attention to form, & more and more to imaginative content—so much so that my published criticisms in the old magazines of the United Amateur Press Association now strike me as somewhat absurd & pedantic.

Those familiar with Lovecraft's "Department of Public Criticism" columns and other essays from his heyday in amateur journalism will scarcely believe that the "metrical mechanic" had so radically rethought his approach to poetry. And yet Lovecraft's new poetry, mainly in *Fungi from Yuggoth,* bear out his new precepts. Lovecraft always said that his work on a book of poetry appreciation for Maurice W. Moe caused him to take up poesy again, but it is clear that his correspondence with Toldridge strongly influenced his attempts to avoid artificial diction and to cultivate greater expression of imagery and emotion, all while loosening his former draconian strictures of versification.

Elizabeth Augusta Toldridge (1861–1940) was the daughter of Barnet Toldridge and Elizabeth Broadbent, a graduate in 1880 of the Maryland State Normal School at Towson (now Towson University), and long a clerk in the U.S. Treasury. She published two books—*The Soul of Love* (1910), a collection of prose poems, and *Mother's Love Songs* (1911), a poetry collection—long before encountering Lovecraft.[3] She published no other books, but placed poems here and there, sometimes signing her work—verse and fiction—"Barnet Toldridge," her father's name. Around 1929, she prepared a manuscript for a book to be titled *Winnings.* It was not published, but its contents are preserved among the papers of Alfred A. Knopf, to whom she entrusted the manuscript.

In that first letter to Toldridge, Lovecraft also wrote: "I regret to learn that you have sustained an accident, & hope that the effects of it will be very quickly & completely eradicated." The accident, its severity, and when it occurred we may never learn. Lovecraft described her as "crippled & shut in."[4] Toldridge

---

3. About the latter title, H. L. Mencken wrote: "MOTHER'S LOVE SONGS, by Elizabeth Toldridge (*Badger*), suffers from monotony of theme, for every song celebrates a daughter's love for her mother, but here and there a fine line keeps one reading on." "A Novel of the First Rank," *Smart Set* 35, No. 3 (November 1911): 158.
4. HPL to RHB, 1 September 1934; *O Fortunate Floridian* 175.

lived at the Farragut in Washington, DC, for three decades, then was forced late in life to move to the La Salle. Lovecraft met her in 1929. He had planned merely to telephone her, suspecting that "(though learned & interesting in letters) [she] is probably a bore, but who would naturally be offended if she heard of my passing through without a word on the wire."[5] When he called, "she cordially insisted that I pay at least a brief call in person. She is a somewhat stately & intelligent gentlewoman living amidst family portraits & reliques in a pleasant apartment-house." The visit proved "less boresome than . . . anticipated."[6] At Lovecraft's urging, R. H. Barlow visited her in 1934 when he was in Washington for medical treatment, and in 1936 en route to Providence to see Lovecraft.

Lovecraft always addressed familiar correspondents with friendly or humorous names, once it was clear formality was no longer required, and signed his letters E'ch-Pi-El, HPL, even Howard; but although he referred to Toldridge in letters to R. H. Barlow as "Aunt Lizzie," he always addressed her as "Miss Toldridge" and always signed himself "H. P. Lovecraft." It is difficult to conceive them maintaining a lively correspondence for nine years. After all, Lovecraft favored weird literature, and Toldridge more pedestrian topics. Lovecraft's mechanistic-materialistic stance did not complement Toldridge's pious, religious leanings. And yet his interest in her work seems genuine. His papers contain dozens of drafts of her poems (see Appendix; it is well known that he rarely kept letters by others because of lack of space to store them, or lack of interest in content). He wrote highly of her work to persons seeking material to publish in their amateur journals: "I am at present in touch with a nice old lady (a truly gifted poetess, at that!)";[7] "there is a lot of fine material (poetry) available from an old lady in Washington, D.C.";[8] "To that list of names I sent, another really ought to be added—*Miss Elizabeth Toldridge* . . . an old lady of great poetic accomplishment, some of whose wistful, delicate lyrics you may have encountered in the various poetry magazines."[9] Lovecraft and Barlow got Toldridge into the N.A.P.A., and the Bibliography shows that her poems were published in journals where their own work appeared.

Toldridge, despite her rather tame literary interests, followed Lovecraft's published work, which during the time of their correspondence was primarily his horror fiction. He tried to dissuade her from purchasing the magazines in which his work appeared, but she ignored his advices and he lent her manuscripts of others. Indeed Toldridge scoured the newspapers for interesting articles to fuel the imagination of her correspondent.

*   *   *

---

5. HPL to L. D. Clark, 6 May 1929; ms., JHL.

6. HPL to L. D. Clark, 7 May 1929; ms., JHL.

7. HPL to Richard E. Morse, 24 December 1933; ms., JHL.

8. HPL to Hyman Bradofsky, 23 July 1935; ms., JHL.

9. HPL to Lloyd Arthur Eschbach, 3 April 1935; ms. in private hands.

Anne Vyne Tillery Renshaw was an amateur journalist from Mississippi and early associate of Lovecraft. She was born c. 1890 in North Carolina and married to Joseph W. Renshaw (1877–1920) of Tennessee. Her father was L. F. Tillery, former mayor of Rocky Mount, North Carolina. She taught English, speech, and sociology in colleges and was said to have been a student of psychology in Europe with Dr. Alfred Adler of Vienna.[10] The date of her death is unknown, but the *Rocky Mount Evening Telegram* refers to her in an article dated 26 September 1953 as "the late Mrs. Anne Tillery Renshaw."

J. W. Renshaw, himself an amateur journalist, was co-editor with Anne of *Ole Miss'*. A well-known amateur in the 1910s, she published many poems (the radicalism of which Lovecraft chided in "Metrical Regularity" and "The Vers Libre Epidemic"). She edited the *Pinfeather* (for which Lovecraft wrote "To the Members of the Pin-Feathers . . ."), *Ole Miss'* ("Systematic Instruction in the United" and "A Mississippi Autumn"[11]), the *Symphony* ("The Smile"; Lovecraft wrote about the journal in "Symphony and Stress"), the *Looking Glass*, and the *United Amateur* for September 1919 (with "The Dead Bookworm." In her early amateur journalist days, Renshaw wrote a brief article on Lovecraft, "Our Friend, the Conservative," and Lovecraft published her poem "The Horizon of Dreams" in his own journal.

Lovecraft began corresponding with Renshaw c. 1914. Few of her letters to him survive, but those that do reveal a vivacious personality who, even in her business letters, seems flirtatious. Of the industrious Renshaw, Lovecraft wrote: "When I was V.P.[12] my work was overshadowed by the 2nd V.P. department, then under the direction of that incredibly energetic recruiter Mrs. Renshaw; & I did little save follow up the multitudinous prospectives she unearthed." She fancied herself a poet, but Lovecraft was not impressed with her method. He wrote: "Mrs. Renshaw is so imbued with nonsense concerning 'Poetic Spontaneity', that I doubt if her work will ever appeal to many. . . . Miss [Louise Imogen] Guiney followed vaguer literary deities, of whom the Miltonic spirit Chaos seems to be the leader. And Mrs. Renshaw appears to be a sister-worshipper at the same shrine."[13] However, he did find merit in some of her work.[14]

---

10. "Business and Professional Women To Hear Guest Speaker Tomorrow," *St. Petersburg Times* (3 January 1943): 13.

11. "'A Mississippi Autumn' was written as prose by Mrs. Renshaw, and set in heroic verse without change of ideas by the present critic. The metaphor is uniformly lofty and delicate, whilst the development of the sentiment is facile and pleasing. It is to be hoped that the original thoughts of the author are not impaired or obscured by the technical turns of the less inspired versifier." *CE* 1.105.

12. HPL was first Vice President in 1915–16, at which time he wrote the recruiting pamphlet, *United Amateur Press Association: Exponent of Amateur Journalism* (1916?).

13. HPL to Rheinhart Kleiner, 2 February 1916; *Letters to Rheinhart Kleiner* 30.

14. Of Renshaw, HPL wrote: "Our fellow-amateur Mrs. Renshaw, a superlatively good poet despite radical theories, has recently composed a piece of apparent vers libre which is really a well-defined iambic composition with variation in the length of the lines. The

Lovecraft was Renshaw's assistant editor for the *Credential,* which published the work of new amateurs; only the April 1920 issue is known to have appeared. In late 1916, Lovecraft, Renshaw, and a Mrs. J. G. Smith formed the short-lived Symphony Literary Service. In 1919 Lovecraft supported Renshaw's successful candidacy for Official Editor of the UAPA.[15] He met Renshaw, previously head of the English department at Research University in Washington, DC, at the time teaching at the Curry School of Expression,[16] for the first time in Boston on 17 August 1921:

> . . . I at last met in person the celebrated leader of United affairs whom I have known by letters for seven years—Mrs. Anne Tillery Renshaw of Rocky Mount, N.C., & Washington, D.C. In aspect stout & homely, she is in conversation pleasant, cultivated, & intelligent; with all the force of mind & speech becoming a philosopher, poet, & professor of English, drama, & public speaking. . . . At the School of Expression the only amateurs were Mrs. Renshaw & her travelling companion Miss Crist—a colourless young woman who acts as her secretary, typist, & general caretaker; reminding her when she leaves her handbag behind or fails to put on her hat—for Mrs. R. has all the absentmindedness of genius. . . . The conversation consisted almost exclusively of philosophical argument, in which Mrs. R. has all the facility & urbanity of James F. Morton Jr. . . . Mrs. Renshaw, who had evidently acquired some of that flattering tendency which is inherent in the air of country villages like Boston, insisted that I ought to write a text-book on English—offering to see to its publication & introduce it in classes at Research University. . . . This rather reminded me of the high-flown pipe-dreams of Alnaschar—but another of her commercial suggestions was really practical so far as appearances go. This latter was a plan for me to correct & criticise by mail a number of English themes each week—the exercises of Mrs. R's classes at the University. . . . Plans with financial features usually fall through, so I am not yet planning what make of automobile I shall purchase with the fortune gained from text book authorship & associate professorship![17]

On 11 April 1925, Renshaw drove Lovecraft, George Kirk, and Edward L. Sechrist around Washington, DC, on a sightseeing tour. Lovecraft seems to have been doing further revisory work for Renshaw during the late 1920s. We know that he was in touch with her c. 1930, for he wrote to a correspondent:

---

innate poet has unwittingly triumphed over the radical theorist! We may, then, safely trust to time to bring the really gifted experimenters within the fold again" (*CE* 2.20).

15. "For Official Editor—Anne Tillery Renshaw," *Conservative,* July 1919.

16. "It's a good idea to give 'eloquence' a black eye. . . . God, if somebody could only drown half the teachers of elocution! This *Curry System* that James Ferdinand and Ma Renshaw dote so beatifically upon gives me dull, boneless ache betwixt the shoulderblades." (HPL to Maurice W. Moe, [March 1931?]; AHT).

17. HPL to Annie E. P. Gamwell, 19 August 1921; ms., JHL.

. . . our old-time fellow-amateur Mrs. Renshaw has reappear'd on the horizon with a lot of overflow theme papers from her school to be criticis'd and graded. All this means cash for coach-drivers, of course but it also means *work*—and nothing repels and discourages me more than the latter.[18]

Little more is heard of Renshaw until early 1936. Now running her own school of speech, she asked Lovecraft to revise the manuscript for her book *Well-Bred Speech*. Lovecraft described the project in a letter to his aunt:

> I now made an attempt to go on with the one revision job which I have not yet returned—in the hope that I might be able to perform at least part of it & receive remuneration therefor. Results remain doubtful, since the more original parts will need leisure & concentration. It is a text-book on English usage . . . & most of my time today was spent in straightening out historical & mythological errors in the section where certain familiar allusions are explained.[19]

Lovecraft's revision was extensive, even to writing entire chapters (see Appendix). Because he was slow in completing the book (because of increasingly bad health, and because of a month-long visit from R. H. Barlow), Renshaw rushed the book into print, omitting much of Lovecraft's work. Lovecraft guiltily lowered his meager fee of $150 to $100. The final chapter, "What Shall I Read?", was published years later as "Suggestions for a Reading Guide." Early the next year, Renshaw published *Salvaging Self Esteem: A Program for Self-Improvement.*

Lovecraft's correspondence with Toldridge and Renshaw reveals many sides of his personality not generally seen in his letters to male cronies. The sensitive poet and critic of poetry; the cosmic philosopher who was also concerned with the social, political, and economic trends of his day; the diligent revisionist and careful student of the English language; the frugal but extensive traveler—all these and other traits of Lovecraft's variegated personality emerge in these letters. But above all we find the courteous and courtly gentleman whose formality of expression does not conceal the abiding fondness and respect he exhibited toward these and other women colleagues, who no doubt returned those sentiments to the full.

—DAVID E. SCHULTZ
S. T. JOSHI.

A Note on the Text

The text of Lovecraft's letters to Elizabeth Toldridge derives entirely from handwritten manuscripts preserved at the John Hay Library. A few surviving letters to Anne Tillery Renshaw are at the John Hay Library in manuscript, but others derive from transcripts made by Arkham House.

---

18. HPL to Frank Belknap Long, March 1930; AHT.
19. HPL to Annie E. P. Gamwell, 29 March 1936; ms., JHL.

Letters to Elizabeth Toldridge

Barret Toldindge

Letters to Elizabeth Toldridge

1928

[1]   [ALS]

10 Barnes St.,

Providence, R.I.,

Octr. 16, 1928

Dear Mrs. Toldridge:—

Yours of the 12th has just been forwarded from my former address,[1] & I was interested in hearing an echo from that long-distant poetry competition, which—as involving my only judicial experience of the kind—I recall very well.[2] I regret to learn that you have sustained an accident, & hope that the effects of it will be very quickly & completely eradicated.

My memories of the entries in the contest are very indistinct, but I remember that I liked "In the Woods" & spoke of it at some length. It is certainly very gratifying to know that you found my remarks encouraging, & I regret that my report was mislaid before you could re-read it. If you would care to let me see the sonnet again, I would be glad to comment on it once more—the intervening 4½ years, & my forgetting of my own former words, giving my new report something of the nature of a fresh opinion. I am sorry that a lack of literal conformity to any of the conventional sonnet forms deprived the poem of a first award. At the time, I might have been more prone to side with the technical sticklers; but latterly I have been paying less & less attention to form, & more and more to imaginative content—so much so that my published criticisms in the old magazines of the United Amateur Press Association now strike me as somewhat absurd & pedantic.[3]

Regarding the nature & publication possibilities of your work in general, I would not be inclined to consider its lack of "modernism" a barrier to success. So far as I can see, the importance of the radical forms has been greatly exaggerated—indeed, it seems to me that there is already a tendency to return to modes closer to the main stream of tradition. Of course, the details of poetry must always change slightly from generation to generation, as a culture's philosophic outlook & sense of emotional values change, & as specific words, forms, ideas, & images gain & lose certain associational overtones through the added experience & changing environment of the race. But these details need not involve any such spectacular structural innovations as are found in the chaotic products of the "advanced moderns"—T. S. Eliot, E. E. Cummings, Gertrude Stein, & so on. When all anchors of inheritance & all traditional feelings & associations are eliminated, a great part of the finest essence of beauty is destroyed; so that the result is more a concoction of impressionistic philosophy & scientific psychology than a work of art. Authentic poetry, I feel certain, will continue to represent the major patterns bequeathed by Chaucer & the Elizabethans & the classicists & the romantic revivalists, & others who have kept to a certain progressive homogeneity of attitude & manner. It will be coloured & modified by the changes of the time, as it has been by earlier changes; but I do not believe it will dissolve into the grotesque chaos represented by "The Waste Land" and "Tender Buttons".[4]

If my opinion regarding your work will be of any value & encouragement to you, I shall be very glad to look over any verses you may wish to send, & give them such comment as might prove helpful. In these latter years I have done more with prose than with verse, (my own creative work is now almost exclusively weird fiction in the manner of Poe, Arthur Machen, Algernon Blackwood, &c) but I still fancy I know an iambus from an anapaest, & a true poetic image from a pompous rhetorical vacuum. There is no need of typing the MSS.—years of professional revision have made me almost a handwriting expert!

Awaiting, then, some representative samples of your work, & hoping that your recovery from the injury will prove swift, I am

Yrs very sincerely,

H P Lovecraft

Notes

1. HPL had lived at 10 Barnes since April 1926, after a two-year stay in New York City, where his last residence was 169 Clinton Street.
2. HPL had served as a judge for a poetry contest held by the Baltimore Circle of Bookfellows c. April 1924.
3. HPL refers to such items as "Department of Public Criticism" (21 columns, 1914–19) and other articles criticizing amateur writing. They are gathered in *CE* 1.
4. *The Waste Land* (1922) is a long poem by Eliot, *Tender Buttons* (1914) a prose-poetic work by Stein.

[2]   [ALS]

10 Barnes St.,
Providence, R.I.,
Novr. 20, 1928

Dear Mrs. Toldridge:—

I deserve censure for my delay in acknowledging your several consignments of verse; but as chance would have it, they found me in the midst of one of the severest avalanches of excessive work which my history records. The poems pleased me immensely, & I made marginal annotations from time to time to guide me in my reply. Now I shall endeavour to render some sort of a report—meanwhile thanking you for the anthology;[1] which I surely welcome, & for which I should certainly have asked had its kind transmission not anticipated the request.

Pray feel entirely at liberty to quote my opinions of your weird sonnet—& of the other poems as well—whenever & wherever you choose. Such pronouncements may not have much weight, for as a matter of fact I am an absolutely unknown quantity in the larger world of bards & reviewers; but if you think they would serve as helpful bits of corroborative detail now & then, do not hesitate so to employ them.

Now as for the poems—they are indeed delightful & meritorious productions; not one touched with crudity or awkwardness, & many of them possessing really exceptional excellence. As you point out, they reflect in general the characteristic moods & expression of the nineteenth century; but this to my mind calls for no changes in text, except perhaps in two or three instances where the flexibility of the medium would tend to make archaisms, poeticisms, or artificialities stand out in unduly strong relief. All of them exhibit what seems to me a genuine & keenly sensitive poetic vision coupled with unusual skill in selecting symbols & capturing images—& I find, too, an apt & delicate command of language, & a sense of *phonetic & musical* values which I was never able to achieve myself in those days when I aspired to Parnassian bays. Decidedly, they all live up to the promise of "In the Woods", & I surely think they deserve preservation in book form if you could ever arrange for such a thing.

Concerning professional markets—I presume you already realise that the *remunerative* disposal of poetry is, & always has been, a matter of the vastest difficulty; in which it would seem that chance & influence are not entirely absent. I think it would do no harm to try the standard magazines—*Harper's, Century, Scribner's* &c—once in a while, even though many rejections might precede an acceptance. But a more fruitful field—albeit a slightly humbler one—can be found in certain *newspapers* of high grade, which use verse on their editorial pages or literary pages, or in their Sunday supplements. Some of these papers pay, (though not munificently) & some do not; but in any case they maintain decently high standards, so that one may feel it a genuine honour & pleasure to be represented in one of them. When the regular editorial department does not accept verse, it is often acceptable with the special "columnists" who provide a daily variety of wit, wisdom, & beauty. None of these columnar acceptances, however, involve cash. For work of a definitely *pious* cast, such as I note amongst your recent assortment, I think the *religious press* would be the most hospitable & appropriate haven. These magazines pay relatively little—& more often nothing—but many of them have gratifyingly high literary standards.

Not having explored the poetry field for many years, my memory is a trifle hazy regarding the best places to send material; but I might fuse together my own distant recollections & the more recent experiences of friends into a brief series of suggestions.

The following are standard newspapers open to verse contributions:

Boston Evening Transcript (pays, I think)
New York Times (pays)
Springfield (Mass.) *Republican*
Honolulu (Hawaii) *Star-Bulletin* (I don't know conditions, but it has a good literary page & a Lit. Ed.—Clifford Gessler—very favourable to poets. He is a poet himself)[2]
Providence Journal (address the editor[3] of the Wednesday page called "These Plantations[']") (pays)
Chicago Tribune (address "R.H.L."'s[4] column—"A Line O' Type or Two")

It might pay to try almost *any* newspaper of settled & conservative standing. You doubtless know the best ones in Washington, & are familiar with many others by name—such as the Baltimore *Sun,* Philadelphia *Public Ledger,* New York *Evening Post* & *Herald-Tribune,* Albany *Knickerbocker Press,* Worcester *Telegram,* Hartford *Courant,* Cleveland *Plain Dealer,* St. Louis *Globe-Democrat,* Kansas City *Star,* Detroit *Free Press,* &c. &c. By noting the sources of reprinted poems in the *Literary Digest* you can get many valuable suggestions. If you know anything of the state of *Vermont,* or have any material bearing thereon, your contributions would be welcomed by a little magazine called *Driftwind,* published by a friend of mine—Walter J. Coates, North Montpelier, Vt. (no pay, however)

As for religious publications—I have heard that the following are open to verse contributions:

Christian Advocate (Nashville Tenn. I think)
Christian Endeavour World, 41 Mt. Vernon St., Boston.
Christian Herald, Bible House, N.Y. City
Commonweal (Catholic—might like your St. Francis) 1950 Grand Central Terminal, New York City
Congregationalist, 14 Beacon St. Boston
Presbyterian Advance (can't recall address, but can find out)
Watchman (Baptist—can find out address)
Wellspring—14 Beacon St Boston

I regret that I can't furnish ampler information, but I am sadly rusty in these matters—since I have no verse of my own to place, & since my revision business does not involve placing. If I think of other markets I'll add them.

About a *book* of poetry—that is not difficult to secure if one is able &

willing to assume the financial responsibility; & I believe I could direct you to publishers who, for a small volume, could considerably if not spectacularly underquote the "$400.00 to $1000.00" whose tasteless & out-of-place presence in the anthology preface so justly irritates you.[5] One friend of mine in particular—who has handled the publishing end of many books which I have edited—could give extremely advantageous figures if he could find an opportunity to undertake the work. A year ago he brought out a sumptuously de luxe 86-page poetry volume for $500.00, & he is now undertaking a less elaborate second edition of the same work for $350.00 or $375.00—I am not sure which. These editions, I believe, are of from 250 to 300 copies each. He has handled very small books as low as $125.00—that is, thin affairs of 32 pages or so. His work is of very high quality, & of phenomenal typographical accuracy. If you like, I will ask him about his terms for any size & style of book you may wish; or you could write him yourself. He is *W. Paul Cook, Box 215, Athol, Mass.*[6]

Now about the poems, individually considered—as I suggested earlier in this letter, the formal sonnets & other specimens which follow a highly technical pattern do not need any change in style. They fulfil the conditions of their form & conception, and & thereby constitute adequate & satisfactory units. In cases, however, where the verse-form is of a flexible type approaching the conversational, the informal, or the narrative, it seems to me that the deletion of a few archaisms, inversions, stock poeticisms, & the like would be of considerable benefit. Accordingly I am returning "The Poetry Path" & "When Souls Strike Fire" with a few suggested emendations & marginal comments—which you may or may not find helpful. The former, which I hope was favourably received in the competition you mention, would be a good thing to send to any of the newspapers I have listed. The latter—which really shews a remarkable delicacy of vision & emotional analysis—ought to be welcomed by one or another of the religious magazines. "Unmothered" is another of the less formal & more conversational poems—but in this you have *not* leaned toward inversions & poeticisms as in the two preceding. It is very delightful, & the only technical flaw I find is the rhyming of two *secondary* accents in the final stanza, where *anti"-pho-nies'* & *mem"-o-ries'* are paired off. At least one of these should be replaced with something in which a primary or sole accent falls on the final *-eeze* syllable. This point, however, is a very minor one—equal liberties being found in much of the accepted & recognised work of the day. I would recommend the sending of the verse to some good newspaper. An appreciative reading is often secured in this way, & poems so published have an excellent chance of favourable reprinting.

In leaving the subject of poetic artificialities, let me enclose a typical modern specimen (i.e., conservatively modern, & not "modernistic") produced by the very youngest creative generation. In this sonnet sequence the young author has rejected all artificialities of form,[7] & has adopted the straightforward syntax of daily speech even though not sinking to its general slipshodness & colloquialism. This, I think, is really the wisest thing to do. The exaltation of the poetic mood need not be discarded or debased, yet the suggestion of hollowness or sentimentality can be almost wholly eliminated. Straightforwardness need not mean the absolutely literal reproduction of daily conversation, (although John V. A. Weaver[8] & others have tried it) but rather an approximation to the customary grammatical structure & dominant vocabulary of such conversation—excluding the trivial or irrelevant, the undignified or inharmonious. It is—or ought to be—neither "poetic language" nor neighbourhood & family gossip, but a kind of greatest common denominator of the two. Let me add that my sagaciously mouthed precepts are wholly of an objective nature—& sadly unsustained by my personal example. If you are by instinct a Victorian, I myself am an even more remotely obsolete being— to wit, a powdered & periwigged Queen Anne's man or Georgian of the formal & artificial 18th century. The eighteenth century is my natural spiritual home. I learned the art of "poetick numbers" at the age of six from a schoolbook (pub. in 1797) of my great-great-grandfather's,[9] used the "long f" in penmanfhip until yᵉ Difciplines of School broke up yᵉ Habit, & rhymed for long years in the heroick metre & manner of Dryden & Pope, Johnfon & Goldfmith. Here is the beginning of one of my youthful effusions— "Autumn"—& I fancy you will smile in comparing it with the "straightforward diction" sermons which I now preach at such great length:

> ARCADIAN Goddefs! whose fond pleafing Reign
> Enchants the Foreft, and delights the Plain;
> O'er vernal Scenes a gentle Magick pours,
> And glads the Flow'rs that bloom on fummer Shoars:
> To Days lefs bright thy potent Charm extend,
> Nor fcorn the fad Vertumnus as thy Friend.[10]

Returning to your poems—"Life" & "Death" are both very fine, & I would recommend your trying them on the very best of the papers I have listed—say the *Boston Transcript, Providence Journal,* or *N.Y. Times.* In "Death" I would suggest a little clarification of the 8th stanza—possibly by the substitution of *"One"* for "A" at the beginning of line 2. I would also suggest an elimination of some of the numerous *-ee* rhymes in the latter half of this poem. The same rhyme ought not to be repeated too often in a brief composition. All the poems in the sprightly Gallic forms are piquant & pleasant, & worthy of publication in a good medium. Of these I think the rondel "The Robe" is perhaps the best— although on a fresh survey I might easily prefer one of the others. In these highly artificial forms it would be absurd to object to a moderate amount of artificial diction, so I will not even suggest the removal of *bedight* or cognate expressions. (*'broidered,* &c) "Dawn", in the anthology, is a splendid little poem; &

I would recommend its newspaper re-publication. There is real glamour in it—glamour, & the power of visual evocation. All in all, however, I think your *sonnets* are your best work; & would be inclined to deem the sonnet your most natural medium of expression. This form is perhaps the best adapted of all to catch the overtones of delicate reflection & symbolic association which seem characteristic of your work; & I would not, if I were you, permit any anti-sonnet sentiments of contemporary critics or judges to alienate you from this literary channel. "Sweet Francis" is an ineffably appealing poem, & I do not wonder at the London commendation it received. All these pieces are full of truly original & graphic turns of idea, imagery, & expression—they are real poetry, in that they speak sincerely & straightforwardly of adequate things in the adequate language of symbol & song. "The Gathering Years" struck me especially favourably—lines like "A shadowy upper sea without a shore" being vividly pictorial & imaginatively stimulating. "Stars" is another outstanding success—with haunting lines like "On wild invisible winds the shadows chase". I would surely try "The Gathering Years" & "Stars" on periodicals of the *Century* grade—yes, & the others, too. Then, if they are rejected by these Olympian havens, you could approach the better-class newspaper field. About "In the Woods"—I would not change it too extensively. When a poem is as nearly perfect as that, it would be a pity to sacrifice spontaneity to cater to any merely technical minutiae. The substitution of *even* for *e'en* is a good thing—it is more typographical than really linguistic anyway. But I would not try to change *yon* to *that.* Let the sonnet stand as printed in the anthology. About sonnet-forms—as I said, many variations are, by long & illustrious precedent, permitted in the sestette. A glance over the sonnets of all the representative poets will quickly establish this fact. Note, too, that the sequence I am enclosing employs three

different patterns—
$$\left\{\begin{array}{ll}\text{efg} & \text{egf} \\ \text{eff} & \text{eef} \\ \text{efg} & \text{efg}\end{array}\right. .$$

Altogether, I think, you have reason to take a genuine satisfaction in your work as a whole. It is unmistakably the fruit of an authentic poetic gift, & to me the demands of expression seem to be met with encouraging adequacy. To recommend elementary manuals of technique at this stage would be like carrying coals to Newcastle, though I might suggest that no one could peruse Brander Matthews' "Study of Versification", Gummere's "Handbook of Poetics", or Prof. Raymond's "Poetry as a Representative Art" without enlightenment & profit. A friend of mine in Wisconsin has written a book which I would like to recommend beside these—but alas! it is not quite finished, although accepted (from a survey of the uncompleted MS.) by the Macmillan Co. This will be "The Gateway to Poetry" by Maurice Winter Moe.[11]

Incidentally—if you are interested in literary groups—I wonder if you have been in touch with the well-known "Bookfellows" of Chicago? This circle, I think, would be highly congenial to you. It is conducted by a Mr. & Mrs.

Seymour,[12] whose address I think I can find you if you are interested. I might remark that the A.P.C anthology seems to contain a vast amount of excellent material. I have heard of several of the contributors, & have briefly met two of them—Mrs. Ada B. Stevens & Harold Vinal[13]—in person. I note that one poet—Samuel Heller[14]—hails from my own not over-extensive commonwealth of Rhode Island; though I do not know anything about him. These anthologies are very good things, I think. The Bookfellows have one, & still another more specialised one has been issued by the Dean Publishing Co. of New York. The Quill Club of London also issue—or did issue—an excellent one. That, by the way, is a group worth joining. There is an American branch—of which you might learn by inquiring of *Adam H. Brown, 127 Howland Ave., Toronto, Canada*, the only surviving member whose address I recall.

I am glad that you did not find "Dagon" hopelessly boresome. As I re-read it, it sounded rather stilted & artificial to me—I think my style has improved in the eleven years since I wrote it. Tales based on the old Atlantis & Lemuria legends are not new, but I relied on atmosphere to provide the equivalent of novelty. Yes—I saw that newspaper item about the medallion found off the coast of France, but don't take much stock in it. I fancy the thing was either Phœnician or Greek—if not early Gallic under Greek or Punic influences. These "resemblances" to Central American styles are easy to imagine, but not many of them will bear analysis. Extravagant theorists like Lewis Spence try to prove that both Europe & America were peopled by migrations from a sunken Atlantis,[15] but I greatly doubt if any mid-Atlantic continent has existed since ages vastly anterior to man. If any vast inhabited land areas have sunk, it has been in the *Pacific*. I have used the sunken-land motif often in fiction—it fascinates me prodigiously. As for sending another tale—since you're not fond of horrors, the range of choice is relatively scant; but I will slip an item or two in this epistle. "The Silver Key" is one of those non-popular fantasies which I can get the editor to print only by "holding out on him"—not sending any of the tales *he* likes until he prints one of *my* favourites! I will also send another typical horror—"The Call of Cthulhu"—which is about to be reprinted in a new anthology of unusual tales. This will be my second appearance between cloth covers, one other anthology having used a tale of mine a year ago.[16] Very soon one of my tales will appear as a miniature book, & later on the publishers of *Weird Tales* intend to issue a collection of [what they consider] my best stories in book form. As to a strange-planet tale—I have thought of writing one, & shall do so eventually. In the "Eyrie" attached to "Cthulhu"[17] you will get a hint of the manner in which I would approach such an undertaking. By the way—one of my yarns has just gained me a "three star" or Roll of Honour mention in Edward J. O'Brien's "Best Short Stories of 1928." If you come across that volume at the library or in a bookstall you will find me alphabetically listed—with a short biographical note.[18] ¶ Thanking you again for the anthology, congratulating you upon your verse, & hoping that the foregoing remarks may prove helpful, I remain

Yrs most sincerely,

H P Lovecraft

P.S. [on envelope:] I forgot to say that "Poe" is magnificent! The last three lines are a triumph. "The Sea" is good, but I would advise you to stick to *metrical* verse.

Notes

1. The *American Poetry Circle Anthology* (New York: Leacy N. Green-Leach, 1928; *LL* 24).

2. Clifford Gessler (1893–?), poet, journalist (chiefly for the *Honolulu Star-Bulletin*), and author of travel books about Hawaii and Polynesia.

3. Probably W. Chesley Worthington (1903–), who may have published five of HPL's *Fungi from Yuggoth* in 1930.

4. Richard Henry Little (1869–1946).

5. Leacy Naylor Green-Leach, *American Poetry Circle Anthology* (1928) p. 4: "Moreover for very many poets who are unable to get together from $400.00 to $1000.00 to have a collection of his (or her) poems published, anthologies in which he (or she) can appear at different times of the year at $6.00 per page and 3 copies of the book—are a godsend."

6. W. Paul Cook published Samuel Loveman's *The Hermaphrodite: A Poem* (1926), then under the imprint of the Recluse Press published Frank Belknap Long's *The Man from Genoa and Other Poems* (1926), John Ravenor Bullen's *White Fire* (1927), Donald Wandrei's *Ecstasy and Other Poems* (1928), and printed (but was unable to publish) HPL's *The Shunned House* (1928).

7. HPL refers to Donald Wandrei. Twelve of his *Sonnets of the Midnight Hours* appeared in *WT* between May 1928 and 1929. His sonnets employ the many different rhyming patterns HPL describes below.

8. John V[an] A[lstyne] Weaver (1893–1938), assistant book editor of the *Chicago Daily News*, author of five volumes of verse, two novels, and a play before going to Hollywood to write dialogue for the movies. H. L. Mencken edited his *Collected Poems*.

9. Abner Alden's *The Reader* (actually dating to 1802). HPL owned a 3rd ed. (1808). HPL's great-great-grandfather was Stephen Place, Jr. (1783–1849).

10. Ll. 1–6 of "Autumn" (1917).

11. Referred to below, and in letters to others, as *Doorways to Poetry*. Moe's book apparently was never published, for later HPL lamented "I wish some publisher had the nerve to issue Moe's own textbook" (letter to Edward H. Cole, 31 January 1934; ms., JHL). Its contents may have been used in highly truncated form in *Imagery Aids* (Wauwatosa, WI: Kenyon Press, 1931).

12. George Steele Seymour (1878–) and Flora Warren Seymour (1888–1948). The Bookfellows issued an annual poetry anthology. HPL had one in his library, a gift from Frank Belknap Long.

13. Ada Borden Stevens published three volumes of poetry in the 1930s as well as the periodical *Decimal: A Modicum of Verse* (1932–35). Harold Vinal (1891–1965) founded

the poetry magazine *Voices,* which he edited throughout his life. His first book of poems, *White April* (1922), was published by Yale University Press.

14. Samuel Heller published three volumes of poetry between 1930 and 1949.

15. Lewis Spence (1874–1955), Scottish journalist, poet, and occult scholar, wrote *The Problem of Atlantis* (1924), *Atlantis in America* (1925), *The History of Atlantis* (1927), and *The Occult Sciences in Atlantis* (1943).

16. HPL refers to the previous appearance of "The Horror of Red Hook." He ignores several minor books by others that contained material by him.

17. HPL presumably refers to his letter to Farnsworth Wright of 5 July 1927 (*SL* 2.149–51), part of which was published in "The Eyrie" for February 1928, the same issue that contained "The Call of Cthulhu."

18. See "[Autobiographical Notice]" in the Bibliography.

1929

[3]   [ALS]

10 Barnes St.,

Providence, R.I.,

Feby 21, 1929.

Dear Mifs Toldridge:—

   The three envelopes safely arrived, & I have since been reading the poems with keen appreciation—jotting down notes about them from time to time as before. I enclose these notes herewith, though urging you to consider them merely as *suggestions* rather than as the authoritative pronouncements of an Olympian authority. You surely have no reason to feel hesitant about the merit of this assortment, & I trust that many of the verses will ultimately find permanence between cloth covers. As for your reluctance to "claim credit" for passages which are altered—bless my soul! but if authors applied that theory a vast number of the world's classics would wear a woefully different aspect. Acceptance of suggestions for various lines & passages is universal throughout the writing world. Pope supplied innumerable lines for Thomson's "Seasons", including the notable passage in "Autumn", whilst some of the most striking passages in Goldsmith's "Traveller" & "Deserted Village" were interpolated by Dr. Johnson. One could extend such a list ad infinitum—at any rate, it is clear that no one need demur at profitting by critical advice when such advice seems sound. As for certain passages you mention in the preceding assortment of poems—let me again urge you not to accept my opinions as inflexible judgments when they tend to run counter to your own artistic sense. In truth, no one critic is competent to put a poem into ideal form, so great is the element of latitude in personal taste. A poet really desiring the most thorough critical judgments of his work can do nothing better than place it in many diverse hands, obtaining in the end a symposium of opinions amidst which his own aesthetic faculty will generally be able to strike a golden mean. That is what one poet actually did with our gang when he wished to issue a smaller & better selected second edition of his collection. He gave five or six of us copies of the bulky first edition, & we all picked a list of what we thought worthy of preservation—supplying revisions where necessary. We refrained from comparing notes in order to preserve the impartiality of our respective judgments.[1] Returning to concrete instances—I hereby repeal my suggestion regarding the

Garlanded over the dark—Deeps of the dusk that mark

passages. There was no real error in any case, & if the original wording expressed any particularly vivid image or impression on your part it would be sheer vandalism to change it. Freshness & spontaneity are the prime desiderata—that is why it is always best to learn one's rules & crystallise one's methods at the very outset, then forgetting all about them & singing freely from sheer lyrical impulse. In short, please consider that metamorphosis of the "Garlanded . . . . deeps . . ." passage as cancelled, forgotten, & unsaid! About the other point—there is a great deal of ambiguous opinion about the use of *none* (literally *no one* or *not one*) as a plural, & it really must be admitted that contemporary usage is sanctioning it more & more. My suggestion was probably absurdly pedantic, & I hereby withdraw it officially—leaving the question entirely to your own judgment. As for the *hath*—it was, of course, the definitely & intentionally archaistic cast of the poem which made this expression whimsically appropriate. As I have said, there is certainly a place for a moderate amount of pseudo-archaism in verse; & that place is work of a frankly artificial, whimsical, or lightly traditional cast—something removed from daily life, profound seriousness, & intimate poignancy. I am filing the recent set of poems—about whose merit you are altogether too modest—with the others received; so that when your book plans are taken up for development there will be a rather representative collection of your work to draw on. At that time I shall be very glad to help in the selection of the contents, though I would advise you to obtain other opinions as well, & exercise your own preferences very freely. You might pass this set around, for selective opinions, among those whose judgments you have found most reliable. When you wish to do this, I can return the MSS. for that purpose after giving my own opinions. I don't know whether Mr. Cook would demand typing or not in case of his handling the order. It might be avoided—especially since his proofs are very carefully read. In any case, don't have anything typed until you know exactly what's going into the book—let the selections be made from MSS. The first step would be to decide how large a book you wished. It is usual to have no more than one poem to a page, even if the specimen is only a quatrain or a fragment carried over from a preceding page. I should think that something of from 50 to 100 pages, size 5 × 7 or somewhat larger, would be an excellent size to plan for. Cook would, however, undertake something even smaller;—i.e., thinner—as you may see by the two specimens of his Recluse Press craftsmanship which I am sending for your inspection.

Speaking of these specimens—they form 2/3 of a trio of "gang" products which I thought might be of poetic interest. I am sorry that these small volumes—my only copies—can be only a loan; but at least there is no hurry whatever about their return. The Long & Loveman books are of Cook's printing, & would seem to me to illustrate very much the style of volume which would best suit your work. Long is my favourite "adopted grandson"—a brilliant, bookish small boy of nearly 27 who will never grow up if he lives to be 127. He has the pure aesthete temperament to a phenomenal degree, & shews a freshness & vitality of the most delightful sort; even though—like others of our circle—he tends to have a wider experience in literature than in life. Loveman is a remarkable lyrist whose short poems have never seen book publication; but this longish "Hermaphrodite" reveals his astonishing spiritual kinship with the ancient world, & his spontaneous mastery of a wistful, Hellenistic sort of beauty, better than anything else except his hymns to Dionysus & Apollo—which I have somewhere in MS. & will send you if this specimen interests you. I have already mentioned Smith as a singular poet-painter. "The Star-Treader" is his first book, published years ago before he was out of his 'teens. His work is still much the same—indeed, so cosmic a soul seems quite independent of the time-spirit. Smith records in verse much of the weirdness & extra-terrestrial atmosphere which I cumbrously & laboriously strive to capture in prose. Don't bother to read all this material if it seems to promise boredom rather than interest. Actually, I suppose the gang represents an aesthetic tradition very different from that in which you chiefly work. We belong to the wholly aesthete-pagan tradition of Keats, Poe, Swinburne, Walter Pater, Oscar Wilde, Baudelaire, & so on, hence may seem a trifle bizarre from the standpoint of the milder Tennyson–Browning–Matthew Arnold &c. tradition to which your own poetry seems to adhere in a majority of cases. Art for art's sake only is our motto—yet we appreciate whatever *is* art, no matter what its source & mood & purpose may be. If this stuff is of interest, I can send more of it later on—especially Clark Ashton Smith material, & Loveman odes & lyrics in MS. form.[2] We are certainly a gallery of anachronisms. Long as a poet obviously belongs to the aesthetic 'nineties, whilst Loveman really forms part of the romantic movement of a century ago—being akin to Keats & Walter Savage Landor. Smith is, in all but race & language, a French symbolist or Parnassian of the middle 19th century—closer to Baudelaire than any other American I know. He has translated Baudelaire into English prose, & also writes poems in French which have been substantially praised even by French critics. One Paris editor told him he could scarcely believe that French was not his mother-tongue. Smith's drawings & paintings range from realistic subjects with an aura of strangeness about them to the very peaks & depths of livid nightmare, hasheesh-ecstasy,

& polychromatic madness. I'll shew you 2 or 3 of his small sketches when I can find them. I am glad you found my own horrors—"Red Hook" and "Rats"—moderately endurable, despite the places where wading through seemed difficult. Doubtless I am the sort of shock-purveyor condemned by critics of the accepted urbane tradition as decadent or culturally immature; but I can't resist the fascination of the *outside's* mythical shadow-land, & I really have a fairly respectable line of literary predecessors to back me up. The history of horror fiction is scarcely less interesting to me than the product itself, & I have prepared a sketch of some of the salient points which I will send as soon as Cook lets me have an extra copy—it being included in his privately printed magazine *The Recluse*.[3] No—I have not read the novels you mention. Indeed, my laxity in absorbing latter-day fiction is quite reprehensible—I never seem to keep up with much except the weird & the bizarre. It was only a couple of weeks ago that I got around to the wildly acclaimed "Bridge of San Luis Rey",[4] which everyone was supposed to know by heart at least a year & a half ago! I respect honest realism in fiction, but don't seem to get wholly fascinated till phantasy enters in. My favourite living authors are Arthur Machen, Algernon Blackwood, Walter de la Mare, & Lord Dunsany, all of whom you would probably find highly interesting in various ways. Dunsany does not deal much in horror, but weaves a strangely potent fantastic beauty which has its roots in primitive myth & folklore. I know of no other writer who so magically opens up the enchanted sunset gates of secret & ethereal worlds. He influenced me overwhelmingly about a decade ago—my "White Ship" period—& if you liked that, you would like Dunsany himself still better. I'd be inclined to advise you to read his "Gods of Pegana"[,] "A Dreamer's Tales", "The Sword of Welleran", "The Book of Wonder", & "Time & the Gods." It is sheer music, colour, ecstasy, & dream. The Modern Library has very economical editions—Dreamer's Tales & Sword of Welleran bound under the former title, & Book of Wonder containing also Time & the Gods. But one ought to see the standard edition also on account of S. H. Sime's marvellous fantastic illustrations. All in all, I think Dunsany represents about the high-water mark in verbal magic. With me, at least, it doesn't wear thin with the years; & I can enjoy his early work as much today as when I first stumbled on it in 1919. His one-act plays are quite famous, but the tales come first in my personal estimation. His recent work—novel-length phantasies— seems less closely packed with breathless unreality than the early products; yet there is surely no dearth. The latest thing of his is "The Blessing of Pan", which appeared about a year ago. "Chronicles of Rodriguez", in the picaresque manner, is also worth a leisurely perusal.

And now I must gratefully mention how much I enjoyed "The House of the Isles",[5] which swept my imagination along with a kind of feudal pageantry all the more potent because it was real family history, & written by one of the characters of the pageant itself, as it were. There was the joy of literary old acquaintance, too, for I so well recalled the descriptions of Sir Alexander Macdonald & his seat at Arundale in Skye, contained in Johnson's & Boswell's books on the Hebrides. "Bozzy's" account of the visit is most amusing, for it so naively reveals the cockneyish impertinence of both guests—leviathan & satellite alike—in their conversations with one who disappointed them by being a scholar & gentleman instead of a barbarian chieftain. With ideas of the Scots gained wholly from ballad & legend, Dr. Johnson could not envisage any Highland or Hebridean chief as other than a black-browed warrior amidst his men-at-arms. "Sir," he rumbled, "The Highland chiefs should not be allowed to go farther south than Aberdeen. A strong-minded man, like Sir James Macdonald, may be improved by an English education; but in general, they will be tamed into insignificance." Two days later the Great Bear could not resist reopening the attack—though not without the incitement of his bounderish little fellow-traveller. "Were I in your place, Sir," he thundered to the polite though no doubt inwardly amused lord of the manor, "in seven years I would make this an independent island. I would roast oxen whole, & hang out a flag as a signal to the Macdonalds to come & get beef & whiskey!" Warming to his attack, he bore down all of the host's mild remonstrances in his typical roughshod way. "Nay, Sir!" he exploded, "if you are born to object, I have done with you! Sir, I would have a magazine of arms." When Sir Alexander thoughtfully suggested that such a ponderous arsenal might rust, the Great Cham of Letters detonated violently & climactically—"Let there be men to keep them clean. Your ancestors did not use to let their arms rust!" Boswell's closing remarks on this episode sum up a delicious study in comparative good-breeding. "We attempted in vain to communicate to him (Sir A.) a portion of our enthusiasm. He bore with so polite a good-nature our warm, & what some might call Gothick, expostulations, on this subject, that I should not forgive myself, were to record all that Dr. Johnson's ardour led him to say. This day was little better than a blank."[6] Much as this incident always amused me, I did not until reading this book realise that the modern Macdonald baronets were actually the dominant heirs & representatives of the mediaeval Lords of the Isles; whose state was little short of royal, & who must have been second only to the Kings of Scotland as self-sufficient powers (for Norway's overlordship was doubtless very shadowy even at its strongest) north of the Solway, the Cheviots, & the Tweed. It is certainly a vivid & dramatic chronicle, & gripped my imagination strongly enough to send me more than once to histories & reference works for parallel background-material & scenic colour. Certainly, it is especially felicitous to have this stirring tale unfolded by one of the line itself—& I am sure that Lady Macdonald's second volume[7] must be an equally absorbing document. In spite of the prime importance of the early sections, there is particular interest in the dramatic loss & regaining of the title by the direct line, as here related. All the material for a novel is in an episode like that—& aside from the spectacular interest one must really admire the present baronet prodigiously for the courage with which he has rectified a woeful legal wrong & secured for his posterity their true ancient heritage. He could prove to Dr. Johnson that a Scottish chief can still be relied on to assert his rights, even without "a magazine of arms" in his stronghold! The long pedigree is certainly a matter of the keenest interest—both the actually historic portion, which may be taken as extending back to the generations just preceding Somerled, & the earlier parts in which legendry & oral tradition blend gracefully into an increasing twilight of poetic narrative. It is certainly phenomenally ancient & brilliant, & much longer in its authentic record than the average pedigree among even the oldest group of landed & noble houses. I surely regret that not even the most liberal stretching & myth-making process will enable me to find a personal ancestor among this brilliant company—at least, with any data in my own library—& shall have to see some time whether my 137th King of Ireland, Baudoin Ui Niall, connects up in any way with the posterity of Japhet, Scota, & the other epic figures. Probably he does, since I fancy nearly all Celtic lines claim the picturesque roots of this tree in common; but in my present hazy ignorance of early Gaelic legend I shall have to push the linkage back a few generations to the Garden of Eden. That is always a safe plan—& has the illustrious precedent set by Lord Chesterfield, who in gentle satire on the inflation of ancestral scrolls placed among his family portraits the faithful likenesses of those first progenitors—*Adam de Stanhope* & *Eve de Stanhope*. Analogously, many a retrospective citizen of imperial Rome, not content with linking himself to the Claudii, Cornelii, Valerii, & Fabii of the early republic, started off the array of niche-enshrined masques in his atrium with the likenesses of Auchises, Venus, Æneas, & Iulus. But anyway, as I have said, I am very grateful for the loan of "The House of the Isles", & would be glad to see the subsequent volume some time if it be of convenient mailing proportions. I am sure the authoress must be a correspondent of infinite graciousness & charm, & am glad you are favoured with such a living & tangible bond with the concrete reality of the heroic age & its heritage. I imagine that the position of Sir Alexander among his tenants must be that of the old-time squire at his best—a noble relationship which seems all too inevitably on the decline, destined to fall before the stultifying levelling processes of the machine age. The picture of Thorpe House shews a delightful edifice—of early 18th century date, I should say at a guess—& I fancy the Macdonalds take an even greater pride in the ivied remnants of the Duntulm. I can well understand the fascination which this stately elder life & its monuments possesses for you; for truly, there is nothing more provocative to the imagination than the solid foundations—both material & imponderable—upon which a great civilisation is built. In actual detail, the period of romantic mediaevalism contained repellent amounts of crudeness. There is little doubt but that neither Somerled nor Baudoin Ui Niall could write his own name, & both probably ate half-cooked meat with unassisted hands, wiping their greasy fingers on their garments. But taken in its entirety, with all its proud, violent feelings & ruthlessly energetic deeds, it has the inestimable quality of typifying concretely & dramatically those basic thoughts, feelings, attitudes, & motive-patterns from which the whole fabric of Aryan life has flowered, & which have characterised the experience of the race during the longest part of its history. It is a symbol of the utmost potency, & has a natural hold on the deepest hidden psychological process of the European personality. The ending of a stream of experience based upon the approximately similar conditions which have always surrounded us hitherto, & which have thus become the indispensable background & reference-points of our habitual thoughts & feelings, is tremendously to be regretted. It is a tragedy because it deprives us of that reservoir of precedent which has so much to do with our sense of the value & significance of things—throwing us back to the beginning, as it were, & placing before us the task of founding a whole new tradition based on the newer conditions of living.[8] And yet it cannot be avoided. Mechanical invention has, for better or for worse, permanently altered mankind's relationship to his setting & to the forces of nature generally; & has just as inevitably begun to produce a new type of organisation among his own numbers as a result of changed modes of housing, transportation, manufacture, agriculture, commerce, & economic adjustment. Our familiar bases of intellectual & emotional reliance are suddenly removed from the sphere of actual life & relegated to the domain of the traditional & the aesthetic only. Lucky is he whose temperament & opportunities permit him to live largely in historic imagination—as is likewise he who happens to be placed where the processes of change are most gradual & least noticeable. Fortunately a good deal of the traditional still survives in isolated instances—Europe has its feudal oases both material & mental, just as America has its vestigial fragments of the colonial past. Old Providence's restful hill & Georgian lanes & doorways form a typical specimen of such a material survival—just as Annapolis does in your part of the world. But of course the far older survivals in Europe pale all cisatlantic cases to insignificance. I imagine with envy the charm of dwelling amongst reliques extending back a thousand years & more, & representing every separate blood & culture stream in one's composite heritage—even the stream of classic civilisation as lingering in Hadrian's Wall, the ruins at Caerleon, Bath, & elsewhere, the rutted lengths of Watling-street, Ermine-street, Icknald-street, & the Fosse-way, the great Roman north gate of Lincoln, & the Roman lighthouse now fused into the bulk of Dover Castle. Roman Britain has always particularly enthralled me because I am a devoted enthusiast on the subject of Rome. The Roman dominion of the consuls & the Caesars is my second country—as I go back through history I find my sympathies, loyalties, sense of placement & point of view transferred instinctively to the banks of the Tiber as soon as I reach a point where Anglo-Saxon England does not exist. This being so, it is easy to imagine the peculiar fascination I experience when considering the one point where the two great streams—Roman & British—actually & concretely met & became one for a time. Some day I am going to construct myself a fictitious genealogy linking one of my Welsh lines with the Roman colonists of that region. It is perfectly possible that I do actually derive a drop of genuine Roman blood from such a source—just as any descendant of any Welsh ancestor has a chance of doing—& that my love of Rome comes from a true fragment of the imperious germ-plasm of the eagle-nosed, broad-browed, tight-lipped followers of the conquering eagles, as represented by A. Plautius, P. Ostorius Scapula, T. Flavius Vespasianus, Cn. Julius Agricola, Suetonius Paullinus, Lollius Urbicus, Claudius Albinus, & the clanking legions that clustered around their glistening standards. S.P.Q.R.! Alala! And shall I disown the possibility of harbouring such blood merely because I possess no objective record of it? Mehercule! Non esse consuetudinem Romanorum sic fato adverso victum esse![9] Rather shall a reality be made certain by a symbol, & a truth live in the aether of a dream. So I shall some day certainly mould for myself an authentic pedigree from some haughty patrician praefectus of the Second Augustan Legion whose marble villa may have stood on the vine-clad slopes above the Usk, near the imperial camp & the civil capital of Britannia Secunda—proud Isca Silurum, with its baths, amphitheatre, tessellated pavements, & Tuscan-columned Temple of Diana—that noble, forgotten city (now sunk to a small village, & threatening to be engulfed as a suburb of the grimy industrial metropolis of Newport, Wales) whose "splendid palaces", according to Geoffrey of Monmouth & Giraldus Cambrensis, "with their gilded roofs once rivalled the grandeur of Rome." Arthur Machen, whose fantastic tales I have mentioned as forming one of my chief literary admirations, is a native of this once-Roman Gwent region, & has woven its archaic magic & classical heritage into his work with poignant & haunting skill. You really must read his "Hill of Dreams"—which includes a magnificent dream-life episode in which the hero transports himself back through the centuries & dwells in spirit among the marble walls & columns of Roman Isca Silurum. The later name of this town is Caerleon-on-Usk,* & Machen in most of his novels changes it to "Caermaen"—I know not why. Incidentally—it is now held by certain ethnologists like Sir Arthur Keith & Arthur Weigall that we inherit a greater proportion of the blood of Roman Britain than was formerly thought probable. This, however, does to really help out my wish to be descended from the Julii & Marcelli & Pompeii & Lucretii, since by the time extensive Roman colonisation took place, the Roman stock itself had become as vitiated & mongrelised as the American people now threaten to be. The legions of the later generals & praefects who clustered around Eboracum (York) & its imperial palace, & witnessed the death of Constantius & the accession of Constantinus the Great,

---

*It is often held to be the seat of King Arthur

were not Italic Romans in any true sense; but merely foreigners from every part of the empire, covered with a varying veneer of the Latin language & institutions. Beside the altars to Apollo & Diana, & to the Romanised-Celtic Silvanus Cocidius (a sort of British Pan) which are often excavated near the Roman camp-hillocks & town-sites, we find cryptic altars to Mithra & the strange eastern gods brought in by the exotic legionaries who may have been recruited in Asia Minor, Egypt, or the decaying realms beyond the Tigris. Sadly enough, it was a far from Roman race-stock which settled "Roman" Britain. We are reminded of Juvenal's fling at the composition of the Roman urban mob of his day—"Jampridam Syrus in Tiberim defluxit Orontes, et linguam et mores et cum tibicine chordas obliquas nec non gentilia tympana secum vexit . . . ." or as Gifford translates it—or rather paraphrases it—

> "Long since, the steam that wanton Syria loves
> Has disembogued its filth in Tiber's waves;
> Its language, arts; o'erwhelm'd us with the scum
> Of Antioch's streets, its minstrel, harp, & drum."[10]

Therefore I shall go back to the earlier Roman conquerors for my ancestor, choosing or inventing somebody about 60 or 70 A.D. (coins as far back as Otho—soon after Nero—are found at Caerleon) & giving him a good ancient name derived from the equestrian order of the original Roman people. I think a sturdy provincial house from the Sabine hills or the plains of Etruria would serve me very well—something like L. Caelius Rufus, M. Helvius Murena, Q. Opsitius Tanus, P. Vargunteius Minor, or Cn. Pomponius Falco. There's a wealth of material for such adaptation & adoption amongst the consular fasti in Dio Cassius; & once I get my ancestor, I can trace his line through a delectable series of absorptive steps—half-Celtic Roman provincials & early Cambrian bards & scholars—until I arrive at a full-fledged Welshman. As you see, I am by no means insensible to that fondness for distant times & scenes which you yourself harbour—indeed, I design to compose a tale some day based upon Roman Britain & the dark Druid secrets preceding Roman Britain; a tale in which both lonely Stonehenge & the colonnaded forum of Londinium shall be glimpsed against a background of stark cosmic *outsideness*. This reminds me—I shall be glad to look over the tale you mention, "A Psychological Accident", especially if it deals with unexplained singularities of time & space.

Your ancestral notes proved highly interesting—especially the link with Lord Saye & Sele, since an early baron of that line is glimpsed in New England's history. In 1634, apprehensive of the spread of the New-Netherland Dutch into New-England & wishing to preserve the latter region for Puritan theocracy, the Presbyterian & pro-Puritan Lords Saye & Sele, & Brooke, became the patentees of a new colonial outpost in Connecticut, & sent settlers to found the town which has ever since borne their joint names in the form of *Saybrook*. They would have emigrated themselves, had they been able to induce the General Court & Assembly of the Massachusetts-Bay to grant their posterity hereditary seats based on their titles. Lacking this privilege, they stayed in England; though assisting their colony in every possible way. Behold how the affairs of mankind are linked! Had the stiff-necked group of peak-hatted Puritans in Boston been a little less democratic in their legislation, the Barons of Saye & Sele would have become typical nasal-voiced Yankees & Harvard or Yale men, & your ancestor the Colonel would have had to look elsewhere for a bride! Saybrook lies at the mouth of the Connecticut River, about half way between Providence & New York. In early days it possessed a fort for defence against the Dutch & the Pequot Indians, & it was to this spot that Cromwell, Hampden, & other Puritan leaders once thought of emigrating—before they decided to precipitate the Civil Wars & stain their hands with regicide. The college of Yale was here founded in 1701, remaining for 15 years in a one-story building 80 feet long & producing 60 graduates before its removal to New Haven, farther west. In 1708 a band of clergymen here prepared a special "confession of faith" which received the name of the *Saybrook Platform*. I have never been off the train at Saybrook, but have always intended to explore it some day; since it is said to be very quaint & typical of early New England, & to contain a striking sepulchral antiquity in the form of an historic tomb. This tomb, a heavy affair of a pattern unique in New England & compared by one writer to a Druid monument, is of the Lady Anne Butler, wife of Col. George Fenwick—who was a co-patentee of Lord Saye & Sele in the colonising venture, & who superintended the settlement from 1639 till 1644, when the patentees sold their grant to the Connecticut Colony. Upon Lady Fenwick's death in 1648, her husband reared this striking tomb in the village burial-ground; leaving financial provisions for its perpetual care* when he returned to England. He was later one of the regicide judges, & was the officer who besieged Hume Castle for Cromwell in 1650—the occasion on which the governor of the fortress bravely defied him (though soon compelled to surrender) with the stout Caledonian couplets:

> "I, William of the Wastle,
> Am now in my Castle:
> And aw the dogs in the town
> Shanna gar me gang down."[11]

---

*Later artisans, in re-tracing the inscription, reverently added a *Cross*—which, ironically enough, would have horrified the austere Puritan & his lady, since their sect held the cross to be a wicked Popish device!

Col. Fenwick died before Dunkirk—killed in action—in 1658, his last request being to be buried therein. He lies there today, in that strange old French seaport which has known the sway of England, Spain & France; whilst his wife still sleeps in the old burying-ground beside the Connecticut, an hundred miles from Providence. She has not, however, rested undisturbed; for when the railway was put through Saybrook in the 19th century it carved off a corner of the ancient necropolis & necessitated the removal of the tomb to another site near by. When this was done, the skeleton of Lady Fenwick was found almost intact, with a heavy braid of auburn hair still resisting the two centuries of interment. With typical peasant irreverence, the villagers of Saybrook annexed the gruesome relique & parcelled it out amongst themselves as souvenirs—some local families being said to retain their charnel allotment to this very day! The removed tomb—which I certainly mean to see before long—is situate near the entrance of the old cemetery, surrounded by the gaunt & time-ravaged headstones of worthies dating downward from Col. Fenwick's own time. I shall not find many inscriptions, though, for the years & the storms have worn them away; & all the leaden coats-of-arms attached to the grey slate slabs were wrenched off during the revolution to be melted into bullets. Time & change . . . . . . time & change . . . . . . but such, anyway, is the Saybrook which your noble kinsman's will & patent brought into being!

It is interesting to hear that your friend Mifs Radcliffe[12] is among the numerous posterity of Cambria's native monarchs! Yes—Llewellyn is the last of them. Poor soul! Edward the First was determined to provoke him into a fight wherein he might be conquered, & the rising came at last. Llewellyn had his victories, but was slain in battle at last—slain by surprise, unarmed & defenceless—& subsequently his head was set for public derision on the Tower of London, circled by a wreath to imitate a *coin* in reference to the legendary prophecy of Merlin, which had precipitated the final rising, 'that when English money should become round, [and Edward had just abolished cut pence, therefore making all English money round] a Prince of Wales would be crowned in London'. That was in 1282. Later (a tradition saith) King Edward promised to give the Welsh a Prince born in their country & speaking no other language—then presenting as his choice his own infant son, just born in the castle of Carnarvon, in Wales, & certainly *speaking* the language of no other country. I haven't kept track of all my own Welsh princes, because the various alleged lines of linkage are so conveniently & comfortably left to oral tradition except in one case—the very case where the written record strikes me as weakest! They include Owen Gwynedd, Prince of North Wales, who is claimed as a forbear by the Parry line, Rywallon ap Conwyn, Prince of North Wales, 11th in descent from Cadwallader, last King of Britain, & another Prince—this time of South Wales—who is supposed to hook up somewhere on the same line— a Carew branch. Incidentally, I trust that Miss Radcliffe will persevere in her idea of having a book, & that she will entrust its publishing to the able & conscientious W. Paul Cook. You might shew her the two Recluse Press products sent under separate cover—fair specimens (except for one hideous misprint in the Loveman book, due to an 11th hour text change & not really Cook's fault) of Athol typography & workmanship. As to my 'not being interested in her poetry'—I'm sure there's nothing in the two printed specimens I have seen to warrant such a prophecy. I would be glad to see more, if you have any easily transmissible copies; though as I have previously pointed out, I am no authority whose verdict can be considered of any ultimate value. There are scores of points of merit in verse which my relatively mediocre taste might fail altogether to grasp—so that I always prefer to be one of many in offering suggestions; one of a jury rather than a sole magistrate.

I trust the books—including "The House of the Isles"—will reach you safely within a week. Don't be alarmed if they fail to arrive simultaneously with this letter, since 3d class mail always moves more slowly, & the package (which has to be taken to the P.O.) may not get started at once anyway. After "Red Hook" & "The Rats", I don't know whether you'll ever wish to see any more of my cosmic nightmares, but I'll enclose one more anyway—my latest, which will not appear in *Weird Tales* till next month.[13] Don't read it if it sounds too menacing at the outset—for I fancy it's worse than the other two in its crawling terror & ultimate explosion. The local colour is fairly realistic—just an exaggeration of the decadent backwoods of central & western Massachusetts, speech & all. The natives there believe all sorts of things—the whippoorwill superstition is genuine folklore, & no invention of mine.

Meanwhile I trust you will find the comments on your verses at least fairly helpful. They are only suggestions, so don't feel constrained to accept them all if they contradict some well-defined image expressed by your original text. ¶ I trust the injuries of your friend who was run over did not prove permanently disabling. ¶ With best wishes, & apologising for the rambling tediousness of the present epistle, I remain

Your most obt Servt

H P Lovecraft

Notes

1. HPL to Lillian D. Clark, 9 October 1925 (ms. JHL): "The meeting was very fair, Morton . . . imposing upon us the task of reading a dull book of poems by the amateur James Larkin Pearson, who wants help in selecting the best ones for a smaller volume. He asked Morton's aid, & Jacobus Ferdinandus wants us all to submit a symposium of verdicts. Anything to please—but I do dread wading through those 400-odd pages!"

2. HPL's transcriptions of Loveman's (spoken) verse still exist at JHL and are printed in *Out of the Immortal Night*.

3. HPL refers to "Supernatural Horror in Literature."

4. By Thornton Wilder.

5. By Lady Macdonald, a correspondent of Toldridge.

6. See James Boswell, *The Journal of a Tour of the Hebrides with Samuel Johnson, LL.D.* (1785), under the dates 2 and 4 September [1773].

7. *The Fortunes of a Family (Bosville of New Hall, Gunthwaite and Thorpe) through Nine Centuries.*

8. HPL articulated these concepts later that year in certain of his *Fungi from Yuggoth.*

9. "It is not the custom of the Romans, with fate going against them in this way, to be defeated." HPL's adaptation of Caesar's statement *Non esse consuetidinem populi Romani accipere ab hoste armato condicionem* (It is not the custom of the Roman people to accept terms from an armed enemy): *Gallic War* 5.41 (attributed to Cicero).

10. From William Gifford's translation (1802) of Juvenal, *Satires* 3.62–65.

11. HPL probably found this quotation in Thomas Carlyle's *Oliver Cromwell's Letters and Speeches* (1845).

12. Florence Radcliffe of Washington, DC. Several of her letters and manuscripts are in the Lovecraft collection at JHL.

13. "The Dunwich Horror."

[4]   [ALS]

10 Barnes St.,
Providence, R.I.,
March 8, 1929.

Dear Mifs Toldridge:—

I am very glad to hear that you found my comment on your verses helpful—though as I said before, one person's opinion ought never to be taken save as part of a wide & representative array of critical advice. Equally competent persons who read my tales give vastly different verdicts regarding the same specimen, & I have learned from experience that the only reliable guide to absolute merit is an intelligent synthesis of as many opinions as possible. I rather thought a line had been omitted in transcribing "Poor Little Pictures," & believe that yours, as now quoted, needs no change. Use my substitute in any later poem you wish; for as I have said, the custom of incorporating others' lines now & then has always been quite general. Once, many years ago, Samuel Loveman *dreamed* a single line of verse—"The golden cuckoo cries the early dawn"—& awaked before anything else came to him. Having no inclination to evolve more from it, he turned it over to our "gang" as common property; & two or three of us wrote separate poems around it. I do not think any of these have been preserved, but the incident illustrates the commonness of the practice. I am glad you find "Helmsman" suitable where I put it. It usually pays to try all sorts of circumlocution, substitution, & calculation before accepting a word which does not fit the image in mind with absolute perfection—a perfection extending to associational overtones & symbolisms as well as to technical prosodic value & dictionary meaning. One ought to have the feeling of Gautier, Flaubert, & de Maupassant for the *inevitable word*. As for the matter of reading the masters of literature—this, I think, ought to be done gradually, & without any sense of effort or duty. All representative types ought to be included, though not with any view to imitation. It would be a great mistake to become overawed by the perfection of the best writers, or to allow their modes of utterance to influence one's own style unduly. Each person has a style of his own which is natural to him, & his business as a poet is simply to sing what is in him in his own way—without paying any attention to what others have done before him. The world is full of things both naturally great & naturally small, & the existence of the greater does not in any way detract from the value of the lesser in its own field. My fiction can't be compared with Poe's or Machen's, but I take no less pleasure in writing it on that account. The masters of art are not to 'bow down before', but to enjoy rationally & with a proper appreciation. They influence one best when he tries *least* to be influenced—& the best kind of stimulus they give is a subtle & imperceptible sort which makes the novice do better *in his own way* rather than reflect *their* moods, subject-matter, & mannerisms. There is no need of indulging in the emotional attitude of *humility* merely because one does not attain the standard of the eminent. Far wiser it is to regard one's relative insignificance as simply an *impersonal fact*—which has no bearing on one's modest & spontaneous efforts at self-expression. Just as it is unwise on the one hand to fancy that one can even approximate the abnormal genius of Keats or Milton or Chaucer, so is it equally unwise to let the fact of the existence of such geniuses cow one into silence or imitativeness. Each person has his own niche, & does best by staying in it & ignoring what is going on outside. Or rather, by ignoring the outside *consciously,* though subtly & unconsciously imbibing that mellowing & maturing influence which familiarity with good literature always gives. I can give this advice with especial sincerity because my own poetic possibilities were wrecked by following the opposite course. In my metrical novitiate I was, alas, a chronic & inveterate mimic; allowing my antiquarian tendencies to get the better of my abstract poetic feeling. As a result, the whole purpose of my writing soon became distorted—till at length I wrote only as a means of re-creating around me the atmosphere of my 18th century favourites. Self-expression as such sank out of sight, & my sole test of excellence was the degree with which I approached the style of Mr. Pope, Dr. Young, Mr. Thomson, Mr. Addison, Mr. Tickell, Mr. Purnell, Dr. Goldsmith, Dr. Johnson, & so on. My verse lost every vestige of originality & sincerity, its only care being to reproduce the typical forms & sentiments of the Georgian scene amidst which it was supposed to be produced. Language, vocabulary, ideas, imagery—everything succumbed to my one intense purpose of thinking & dreaming myself back into that world of periwigs & long ſ's which for some odd reason seemed to me the normal world. Thus was formed a habit of imitativeness which I can never wholly shake off. Even when I break away, it is generally only through imitating something else! There are my "Poe" pieces & my "Dunsany" pieces—but alas—where are any *Lovecraft* pieces? Only in some of my more realistic fictional *prose* do I shew any signs of developing, at this late date, a style of my own—though some have been so good as to say that my epistles have a certain originality within the limits of the 18th century tradition; as Cowper's differ from Walpole's, or Gray's from Swift's. In verse, I have cheated myself of a style by copying the styles of others. Now of course I am an extreme case, but what has harmed me greatly might easily harm everyone a little, in proportion to the extent they practiced the imitative principle. Therefore I invariably warn all bards—in the slang of the day—to *be themselves;* saying what they wish to say as they wish to say it, & allowing the masters to influence them only indirectly—broadening their sensitivenesses & capacities for imaginative experience rather than affecting their habits of utterance. Walter Pater writes in prose, but much of what he says is equivalent to poetry. "Marius the Epicurean", "The Renaissance", & "Greek Studies" will give the cream of his genius—especially the first named. Of Swinburne the earlier work is the best. Wilde's poems are exquisite, but somewhat impaired by imitativeness. I think he is at his best—aside from his wit-&-comedy side—in "The Picture of Dorian Gray" & the delicate fairy tales, especially "The Fisherman & his Soul." Baudelaire is best absorbed through the selection of translations in one of the inexpensive "Modern Library" volumes. About the semi-amateur poetry magazines—I suppose one might become bored with them, but they surely contain a great deal of excellent matter & no doubt open up many fruitful avenues of comment & criticism. Professional periodicals are, of course, a more rigorous test of merit; & I trust you will in time get a few more pieces in shape to submit to some of them. But a book is naturally the most satisfying of all, & this is what your best work really deserves as a definitive embodiment. Incidentally—don't for a moment regret that your natural medium is poetry instead of prose! Rather ought you to congratulate yourself on this point; for there is no question but that poetry, with its tightly-packed symbolism, inclusive imagery, & union of sound with language, is a far more concentrated & undiluted essence of the beauty & wonder of things than any form of prose could possibly be. Almost no one would be a prose-writer if he could write poetry. We wielders of ponderous periods & rhymeless rhetoric are frankly dealers in the second-best! Still—don't let this deter you from writing occasional tales *in addition* to your verse. I am sure you underrate the sketches you describe. Even if they lacked *plot,* they lost nothing of art thereby; for plot is essentially an artificiality, & not at all necessary to good writing despite the arbitrary insistence on it practiced by conventional editors. Personally I despise it—atmosphere & characterisation being what I respect in a piece of fiction. The happy-ending superstition is of course a wretched type of puerility, & I am glad you decided to defy it in the final version of your "Psychological Accident."

What you say of my stories pleases me greatly—especially as regards that air of *realism* which I am making increasing efforts to achieve in such specimens as are not pure phantasy. It delights me even more, though, to hear that my nameless cosmic monsters have an air of originality about them! Shapeless, unheard-of creatures are not original with me; for although Poe did not use them, they figure quite widely in minor horror-writing since his time. Usually they tend to be exaggerations of certain known life-forms such as insects, poisonous plants, protozoa, & the like, although a few writers break wholly away from terrestrial analogy & depict things as abstractly cosmic as luminous protoplasmic globes. If I have gone beyond these, it is only subtly & atmospherically—in details, & in occasional imputations of geometrical, biological, & physico-chemical properties definitely outside the realm of matter as understood by us. Most of my monsters fail altogether to satisfy my sense of the cosmic—the abnormally chromatic entity in "The Colour Out of Space" being the only one of the lot which I take any pride in. As for sketches with sheer beauty rather than horror as a nucleus—I used to write many, but seemed to find them less distinctive than the horror specimens. They tended to become mere imitations of Dunsany, or to have that suspicion of mawkishness & namby-pambyness which is the death of all art. In my actual imaginative contact with life, I am vastly more responsive to beauty than to horror—indeed, I never experience real cosmic horror except in infrequent nightmares. However, when I come to record my various imaginative experiences, I generally find that only the horror items have any uniqueness or originality. Others have seen the same beautiful things that I have seen, & have sung them more nobly. Dunsany, indeed, has said exquisitely almost everything I could possibly wish to say; so that when I indulge in sheer phantasy I can do no more than imitate him. Thus horror alone is left as my peculiar kingdom, & in it I must hold my lowly reproduction of a Plutonian court. I shall, though, no doubt make further experiments in the non-macabre—seeing what I can do without copying Dunsany on the one hand, & without falling into insipid sentimentality & affectation on the other hand. This latter pitfall is hard to avoid—in fact, Dunsany is the only fantaisiste I know who consistently succeeds in keeping clear of it. Algernon Blackwood, fine as he is in horror, becomes insufferably puerile & twaddlesome when he tries to spin whimsical phantasies about nice, pretty things! Roman Britain has been a favourite theme with weird writers—especially Machen—so that I shall have to exercise discrimination when I treat of it. It would be more convincingly realistic to abstain from all prophetic symbolism, & to enter thoroughly into the actual life & feelings of the time & place as far as history & anthropology can indicate them. The Druids are indeed a fascinating subject—meriting indeed a story all their own, & extending back *before* Roman times. They were, as you doubtless know, inexorably opposed to Roman rule; & the instigating influence in all Celtic revolts against Rome. On this account the e   mperor Claudius ordered them all suppressed—especially in Britain, which was, rather than Gaul, their headquarters—whilst the general Suetonius Paullinus destroyed their most sacred oaken grove on the island of Mona. (Anglesea) The Druids were far more mystical & cosmic than the adherents of either the Graeco-Roman or Teutonic religions, & were compared to the disciples of Pythagoras by the Roman & Greek writers who first knew them. Their menhirs & rocking-stones have a curious analogy to the hieratic monuments of many primitive races—including, by the way, the earliest Indian tribes in Rhode Island, many of whose sun-&-moon boulders still remain hereabouts in lonely countrysides with an eastern vista. In point of cruelty the Druids were about the average—their sacrifices being mostly bullocks, but occasionally a human being, usually a condemned criminal. Prior to the Druids, & to the Aryan races which evolved them, Western Europe was undoubtedly inhabited by a squat Mongoloid race whose last living vestiges are the Lapps. This is the race which bequeathed the hideous witch-cult to posterity, & which lingers in popular folklore in the form of *gnomes* & *kobolds,* evil fairies & the "little people." There is no archaeological evidence to prove that this stock ever crossed into the British Isles, but writers like Arthur Machen love to imagine that they did, & to base fantastic & horrible tales upon certain influences emanating from them. They would fit well into any Romano-Britannic tale—as a sinister background already fabulously ancient when the first Roman galley hove in sight of Dover's chalky cliffs. As for my Roman genealogy—it has been so long since I first planned its preparation, that I fear it will long remain a future prospect. Your choice of L. Caelius Rufus as the direct ancestor is rather a coincidence, insomuch as that is the only name which I did *not* get from the consular tables in Dio Cassius. L. Caelius Rufus was the name borne by myself in the most realistic Roman dream I ever had—a dream of a year ago last October, in which I was a propraetor of Hispania Tarraconensis, with a villa at Calagurris, on the Iberus. In this incredibly vivid dream I was appealed to by the praefectus urbi of Pompelo, a small village near the Pyrenees, to save the town from a hideous mountain doom—the curse of a dark, strange race who burned fires on the hilltops & demanded human sacrifices from the Celtiberian tribes & Roman colonists. There were all sorts of technicalities in the way, & I had repeated conferences with M. Aelius Varus, trubunus militum in command of the XIIth legion whose camp was just outside the walls of Calagurris. Finally I sent a messenger to the proconsul in Tarraco—P. Scribonius Libo—& he came in person & authorised the march of the legion to Pompelo & into the hills beyond. The journey north was incredibly vivid, & I can still see the frightened village of Pompelo with its crude buildings, single temple of Mercury, & crowded forum. At sunset we marched into the hills with a native guide—a boy of half Roman & half Celtiberian blood. Then the fires blazed out on the peaks, & the dream became a nightmare from which I awaked in terror. I have preserved this dream in detail through letters written to young Long & to another fantaisiste I know—a delightful young Irishman named Dwyer— when the impression was very fresh. They still have the letters, & I mean some day to borrow them & make a story of the dream—supplying what plot & motivating elements are lacking.[1] But anyway, there is where the name L. Caelius Rufus came from! Incidentally—it is not difficult to find books giving one a familiarity with Roman life, places & personalities. Aside from elementary textbooks & manuals of Roman antiquities, there are two delightful novels by a fellow-Marylander of yours which carry one with uncanny closeness to the heart of Rome as it was in the later Antonine age. They are—to be read in the order named—"The Unwilling Vestal" & "Andivius Hedulio", by Edward Lucas White; who is, I believe, a classical teacher in some boys' school in or around Baltimore. All other allegedly Roman novels—like "Quo Vadis" or "A Friend of Caesar"[2]—are psychologically false, reading modern emotions into Roman characters. White alone has escaped this pitfall, giving us Romans that are Romans. Incidentally—if getting to the library is difficult, I can lend you all the Machen & Dunsany items & "Andivius Hedulio" by mail. Let me know if this would be more convenient for you than bibliothecal extraction.

I am enclosing some of my less horrible things—mostly MSS. rejected by the magazines—for your leisurely perusal & ultimate (though not hurried) return. As for "poetry" of mine—there is nothing worth serious consideration, & I have thrown away most of the voluminous rhyming of former days. Merely for your amusement, though, I will send an envelope full of the assorted junk still cluttering up my files—to be returned in the end. You will see evidences of all my various metrical stages—pure 18th century imitation, pseudo-Poe-etry, & halting attempts at emancipation which don't get far from the standard models. Nowadays I write no verse except when forced to it by demands for elegies, birthday lines, & so on, which I cannot civilly refuse. Among the enclosed the latest item is an elegy on a delightful rural poet whose rich personality I valued highly, & who lived to be 96. I used to celebrate each of his birthdays in rhyme, & had hoped to write an ode for his living centennial.[3] In all these verses you will note with ironic amusement that I freely use all the archaisms, inversions, & poeticisms against which I so constantly warn others! This is because I do not try at all to be a poet in any serious sense. My verse is simply antiquarianism & nothing more. And to other bards I give the time-honoured advise—"Do as I *say*, not as I *do*"!

I am glad that you find the Long-Loveman-Smith work of interest, but hope that you will not allow it to give you a lesser idea of your own work. Loveman is indeed what one might call "half arrived", although the persistently archaistic nature of his verse will never permit him to receive the recognition he deserves. Much the same may be said of Smith, though on the Pacific Coast his obscurity is perhaps a little less dense. In general, obscurity may be said to form the keynote of our gang. We are all persons with not quite enough sheer genius to come to the surface—a condition to which I wish all my fellow-members could be as reconciled as I am. Personally, I am too much of a cynic to care whether I amount to anything or not, or whether my work be known or unknown to the fame-creating public. I felt sure you would find the workmanship of Cook's volume pleasing. He could make a smaller book if requested, I think, though the present size appealed to the especial authors represented. He has sometimes attended to the distribution & marketing of the books he prints, although he does not always do so. I think he could be induced to accept such a responsibility if he published your verse.

March 9

Your note & enclosure of the 6th arrived yesterday, & I looked with interest over the amended version of "The Palace of the Lord." The rhyming of secondarily accented syllables (bal"co*ny'*-shad"o*wy'*-ver"i*ly'*) is well eliminated; but I note that you have gone to the length of removing *all* such syllables instead of simply removing *all but one,* in order to destroy *all rhymes founded on a pair of such.* I trust you realise that what is considered bad technique is *not* the use of *any* secondarily accented syllables in rhyming, but simply *the founding of a rhyme on more than one of such.* Thus you may rhyme *lee* & *mel"ody'* or *bill"owing'* & *sing,* but **not** *air"ily'* & *mel"ody'* or *bill"owing'* & *mur"muring'.* In a word—you *may* use a secondarily accented syllable as a line-ending *whenever it is not meant to rhyme with* **another** *secondarily accented syllable.* Now the effect of this principle on the present poem is, that you may retain if you wish *either one* of the two endings, *balcony* or *shadowy.* You can't have *both,* for that would form a rhyme of secondarily accented syllables; but you *can* have *either one.* In my suggestions of last week I think I provided for the retention of *balcony;* but since you give signs in your recent note of regretting the loss of *shadowy* much more, I will amend my suggestion & recommend that you eliminate *balcony* as the new version, thus making possible the restoration of *shadowy.*

Of course this makes the barest suggestion of a clash with *mystery* in the middle of the next line, but I do not think the defect a fatal one. The prime object, of course, is to keep the entire piece as close as possible to the actual visual imagery behind it. Probably the best version *intrinsically* would be one without an [—"—y'] ending of the line before that containing *mystery;* but when any basic question of the author's instinctive imagery or sound-sense is concerned, it is always preferable to strain a point in favour of non-alteration. All told, I suppose the really best version of these lines is what you now have,—*galleried lea* & *splendour-free*—since with this arrangement no *possible* clash with *mystery* can be felt. But I thought I ought to make it clear that, so far as the matter of secondary accents goes, you are really at liberty to restore either *balcony* or *shadowy*—one or the other, but not both. I do not think that *galleried lea* is too strained, for one of the definitions of *gallery* is "any long passage".

Of course, in ecclesiastical architecture* the term really does mean the raised floor above the aisles; but the existence of the other definition saves the situation well enough. Besides—in symbolic language a part often serves to represent the whole, so that the *pillars* of a gallery may very properly be taken as representing the gallery itself. The boughs of a forest, one may say, make enough of a gallery floor to justify the viewing of the tree-trunks as gallery pillars, & the regarding of the whole wood as *galleried*. At all events, this term is *infinitely* better than the laboriously archaistic *asilèd*. But turning from the endings to the beginnings of lines—I must say regretfully that I don't see how the newly-inserted *you* & *nay* can be retained. These self-conscious archaisms are conspicuous enough at best; (the *you* in your prize weird poem just "gets by" because of its harmony with the bizarrerie of the whole & its normal syntactical position in the line) but when they are given positions of especial prominence as here, & when one of them (you) is cast in a highly artificial phrase, they become virtually inadmissible. Indeed, it would really be the safest policy to drop them in *all* cases; for they are to all practical intents & purposes unsuitable for *serious* poetic expression—i.e., expression untinged by whimsicality or by the large-scale reproduction of an Elizabethan or Chaucerian mood. Just consider that there are no such words as *you* or *nay!* In line 3 I would advise the restoration of *behold,* just as you had it at first. In line 1, if you wish to eliminate the faintly colloquial impartations of "A stable, this?" you might at least experiment with the effect of "A stable, here?" But in any case banish *you* & *nay!!!* Coming down to line 8, I realise that *These* cannot be quite so strong as *Rare*—yet still think that the stock phrase *Rare poems* is weaker in itself than the plainer version could possibly be. Why not let the adjective express the physical magnitude of the "poems" rather than their poignancy of inspiration? The selfsame idea is really suggested through symbolism, though perhaps not as directly as one might desire. In such a case you could say *"Vast* poems". But anything is better than a hackneyed phrase. In the next line—the first of the sestette—the new version is less powerful than the old because it involves the cumbrous & "poetical" attempt to lumber along without a verb where a verb is clearly needed. I can see why you might have found something prosaic about *no great gift*—but that is not so bad as a verbless line. Verbs are like wheels—one can't move a phrase without them except by a sadly dragging and scraping kind of locomotion. In considering this line I have come to the conclusion that the word *meet* is not yet too obsolete & archaic for use in a text as essentially stately & solemn as this, hence I am recommending the use of *"is no meet gift".* This, I think, concludes all the suggestions that can be made regarding the poem; & I hope my remarks may prove helpful rather than confusing. As I said before, the sonnet is really very powerful & beautiful; & I hope sincerely that it may meet with an encourag-

---

*assuming that you wish to convey an image of a cathedral or temple of night ing reception in the prize contest. However, pray don't be discouraged if it doesn't—for as I have said repeatedly, one person's opinion—or even one set of judges' opinions—means comparatively little as a definite determinant of absolute merit. Still, I know that an obscure shewing in a competition must have its irritating side. I have never done any competing myself, since I don't take my effusions very seriously or have much confidence in their worth. Send along the Christmas, Easter, & other verses you mention whenever you happen to have available copies. I am sure they can't be as poor as you think! Incidentally—I hope this epistle will reach you in time to allow you to decide on a definitive "Palace of the Lord" version for the contest. Regarding your verse in general—I don't see why you need to wish for a style any different from your own, since the existing style has both distinction & charm. Simplicity is the greatest virtue poetry can have—& the atmosphere of scholarship ought to be sedulously shunned. Poetry is not academic & intellectual, & when it becomes so it ceases to be poetry. What it really is, in essence, is song & symbolism—& an atmosphere of complex erudition is antagonistic to both of these things. Yes—I think the word *avatar* isn't at all bad as a poetic ingredient. About *gyre*—oddly enough, I don't recall using the word in your poetry, although I may perhaps have done so once or twice. What it means, is a *circular motion;* or in particular, *an orbit,* or *circular* (or rotatory—or elliptical—or anything like reeling, spinning, curving, or whirling) *path described by a moving object.* You can find it in Stormonth's Dictionary. If the word occurs in this sense in any revisions, it is all right. If not, look again & see if my nefarious chirography is not responsible for some misreading. It is curious that I can't recall using it. I wouldn't recommend so unfamiliar a word for frequent use, but there are places (especially where cosmic things & celestial vortices are concerned) where it would be very felicitous & appropriate. As for "The Rosebush" & the other—don't hurry about the copying, or even try to make other copies if the existing ones are legible in any way. I am not particular about niceties of calligraphy—I can't be, on the principle of the glass house dweller & the art of petrean ballistics! Simply send them along in any old form whenever it may be convenient. I don't envy you the task of finishing off & typing your various verse specimens, but know that such ordeals are necessary before any work can be brought before the public. Once in a while I rebel at such a task, especially if it be inordinately long. Thus I wrote two semi-novels a couple of years ago—one of 110 pages & the other of 150 pages—& was so appalled at the thought of typing them that they still lie idle & unread![4] By the time I get the nerve to approach the torture, I shall probably be unable to decipher the text myself . . . . . for if you think my epistolary MSS. are bad, you ought to see the MSS. of my formal literary productions, with their interlineations & deletions, re-castings & substitutions!!! Oh, yes—& you need not hesitate to send specimens of Mifs Radcliffe's work when you have some on hand; although as always, I must not be regarded as any supreme authority or final arbiter of merit. If suggestions will assist, well & good—but I can't guarantee the insight & acumen of my suggestions! Incidentally, I am sure that Miss R's recent depreciation of all her work is based on modesty rather than on impersonal analysis. In the matter of the last line of "Love", she is entirely in the right; for so far as I can see, the editor's substitution produced a wholly false, & unintended, & peculiarly meaningless implication—i.e., an implication *that the answer to life is the fact that he who loves knows that answer!* Puzzle—find the sense! In the original, the idea is clear—*that love provides an answer to life because the process of loving provides a sense of the adequacy of living.* In other words, the editor's unwarranted liberty placed the substance of the last line in the position of *being the answer referred to in the line preceding;* whereas the poet's intention was obviously to have it form *the reason for the condition referred to in that preceding line.* So much hinges on one apparently insignificant conjunction! But I have known errors in mere punctuation to produce almost equally great distortions of meaning.

It was very interesting to learn of your ancestral connexion with New Hampshire—though I am less acquainted with its history than with that of southern New England, hence did not know of Provost-Marshal Broadbent. 1681 was surely a turbulent time up there, for the colony had but lately (July 1679) been separated from the Massachusetts-Bay & made into a separate royal province—the first royal province, with Governor appointed by the Crown, in America. There was great dispute regarding land titles, since much land was claimed by irregular Massachusetts settlers against the lawful title of John Mason, the patentee whose complaints at length secured the new province government. The governor, Edward Cranfield, had a hard time indeed, & in Jany. 1683 was forced to dissolve a session of the provincial assembly—an act which certain colonists disputed as illegal, & which one recalcitrant soul, Edward Gove, opposed so violently that he was arrested, taken to England, & confined for a time in the Tower of London. I can well imagine the position of a cholerick litigious gentleman—whatever side he may have been on—in the midst of these doings, & doubt not but that Provost Joshua was abundantly glad to see Old England's great oaks & misty green hedges again. New Hampshire afterward prospered, & enjoy'd a line of royal governors—the Wentworths—whose direct line remain'd loyal to His Majesty's lawful authority during the troubles of 1775–83. Sir John Wentworth, Bart., last of those governors, went to Nova Scotia after the loss of his province & later became governor there. His predecessor Benning Wentworth, whose rambling mansion at Little Harbour, near Portsmouth, I have seen, is the hero of Longfellow's poem "Lady Wentworth", (one of the "Tales of the Wayside Inn") wherein his second marriage to one of his serving-maids (albeit a girl of good ancestry) is picturesquely described. My publisher-friend W. Paul Cook is a lineal descendant of Gov. Benning Wentworth by his first wife; whilst another friend of mine—the novelist Mrs. Miniter of Wilbraham, Mass.—is descended from Benning & wife #2. It is after this gentleman that the town of Bennington, in Vermont (then known as the New-Hampshire grants) was named. One wonders what connexion these N.H. Wentworths may have with the Bosvilles' Wentworth relations. By the way—I presume you noted that the Bosvilles have a link with the *other half* of Saybrook, Conn., insomuch as the second Godfrey—the Roundhead Colonel—was a stepson of one of the Grevilles, the husband of another, & a recipient of the influence of Fulke Greville, *Lord Brooke*. Thus you & Lady Macdonald, between you, manage to have a shadowy symbolic linkage in a sleepy old New England town by the banks of the Connecticut!

Apropos of this—I did indeed enjoy "The House of the Isles", & surely have no objection to your telling the gifted authoress so, although such commendation cannot mean much from an obscure person without literary standing. As for Maurice MacNeill—even if I would have hard work claiming him through Ireland's 137th monarch, I have a friend who ought to hail him as a kinsman; for the naive & beloved dean of our gang, a justly appreciated writer of historical fiction for boys, is none other than one *Everett McNeil*, scion of stern Caledonia by way of New York State & Wisconsin, & now a denizen of Brooklyn, N.Y. In one of the accompanying envelopes I will enclose an account of "Mac's" latest book[5]—which you can insert in "The House of the Isles" as a supplement if you wish! Another interesting albeit remote Scottish connexion is provided by the home town of the faithful Cook—*Athol*, in the Province of the Massachusetts-Bay. This settlement, made in 1735 under the name of *Pequoig*, soon had amongst its proprietors a certain Col. John Murray, cousin of the Duke of Atholl in Scotland; who became highly influential, & in 1762 cause the town (after a brief trial of the name *Paxton*) to adopt the designation of his titled relatives, albeit in a slightly misspelled form. He claimed that the region reminded him of the family seat in Perthshire—Blair Atholl, with its Blair Castle—near fateful Killiekrankie, where Claverhouse fell in 1689 in his hour of victory. Blair Atholl is said to be very beautiful, & the poet James Hogg—"The Ettick Shepherd"—has celebrated the stirring sound of the Atholl pipes in a passage of much vividness & merit. When the unfortunate revolt of 1775–83 came, Col. Murray remained loyal to our rightful Sovereign & transferred his residence to St. John's, in New-Brunswick. The town of Athol, however, always retained an affectionate regard for its Scottish godmother; & has frequently exchanged courtesies with the Dukes at Blair Castle. During the celebration of an anniversary some years ago, the town made a prominent display of the Murray plaid—indeed, one of the view cards in my possession has a border formed of this picturesquely traditional design. What an appropriate place for the publication of a book of poems by a descendant & admire of the Scottish Chiefs! As for "Bozzy"—I knew that his line was descended from the ancient de Bosvilles, though of course the amount of blood which he had in common with his contemporaries, the Bosvilles of Gunthwaite, was really quite negligible. Biology does not stress remote connexion as visibly & significantly as does heraldic romance! What I quoted of his conversation with Sir Alexander Macdonald at Armidale comes from his book on his tour of the Hebrides with Dr. Johnson—a volume I should think you would enjoy reading. "Bozzy" was a queer combination—not the utter fool & intellectual parasite that Macaulay makes him out to be, but a man of really sound scholarship & keen & versatile intellect; handicapped by an unfortunate amorphousness of temperament, or emotional immaturity, which removed from his thought & conduct that element of taste, balance, & proportion which prevents most men of equal birth & education from making fools, boors, nuisances, & coxcombs of themselves. He was, & will remain in history, an essentially ridiculous figure; but for all that he had a sharp, active mind, & a set of talents in one direction approaching sheer genius. Poor Bozzy! I hope he duly secured his loan from the fourth Godfrey Bosville.

March 10

It is almost needless to say that I enjoyed "The Fortunes of a Family" exceedingly—indeed, I do not know of any family chronicle more genuinely animated & interesting, & more happily free from the monotonously statistical atmosphere into which such accounts are too often prone to fall. The Bosville-Macdonald line is surely fortunate in having both of its sides so ably, attractively, & succinctly set forth for the benefit of a posterity which would otherwise have to delve laboriously among original sources in order to achieve any comparable degree of dramatic ancestral perspective. It is curious that this valuable work should be done by one who is a Bosville-Macdonald by marriage rather than by birth, & who claims only a few of the lines & forbears described as an actual blood heritage. Naturally, since it depicts a quiet & representatively English house, this second book has not the close connexion with colourful legend & exciting barbarism that its predecessor has. Here we find no massacres, royal defiances, viking voyages, or enemies immured in subterraneous dungeons; but in place of these there is a delightful reflection of the slow, profound current of that solid Anglo-Saxon life which has gradually reëstablished the old Roman concept of order, & has brought its possessors to an unchallengeable place as heirs of Rome's supremacy. The whole work, with its very judicious choice of anecdotes, reproduced documents, & the like, serves admirably to bring the whole poetic pageant of old English life close to the modern reader. Entire chapters of feudal history & old-world law & custom are evoked by the various glimpses of manorial accretion, division, & inheritance—glimpses which include the familiar use of vanishing technical terms & the frequent mention of rent periods & assizes based on Saints' Days already obsolete & half-forgotten in America, & perhaps destined for obsolescence in the democratic, half-socialised or small-freehold England of the future. There are rich volumes of poetry in such things as the picturesque nominal rents paid by certain tenants to the lord of the manor—a thwittle, a pair of broad arrows "well hedyd & barbyd ardrly", a left-hand glove, a snowball at midsummer & a red rose at Christmas, a peppercorn, & so on. What echoes of mediaeval chivalry do these bits of legalistic naivete recall! What vestiges of knightly custom, fealty, vassalage, & lordship are here preserved in symbolic form to leaven the prosaic corpus juris civilis of a monotonously exact & exasperatingly unimaginative aera! There are too few of these survivals in America—too few survivals even from the early colony times, though of the latter Old Providence has a very decent share. As a whole, though, I think that "The Fortunes of a Family" reaches its apex of charm in its reflections of 18th century life. There is an added vividness about a picture of this period which comes not from the point of view of formal history or illustrious biography & memoirs, but from the angle of a private household with all its intimate inward vicissitudes & homely domestic details. It is this species of chronicle which best enables us to live the sprightly epoch over again in our own persons; & to apprehend as daily reality what would be mere abstract history if viewed only in connexion with hackneyed figures & events that everybody knows. Affairs at Gunthwaite & Thorpe, & echoes of a vivacious Georgian London, acquire for us a highly convincing nearness; till we can scarce refrain from feeling an actual kinship with the Bosville household whose members arise so naturally before our eyes. The fourth Godfrey—he of the memoirs—is to me an exceedingly attractive figure; a typical 18th century 'squire of the more intelligent sort, with a taste for liberal letters, a regard for the amenities of rustic proprietorship, & a lively care for the dignities & antiquities of his family—despite the injudicious documentary holocaust he authorised in youth! The family's enjoyment of a borrowed *telescope* is typical of the 18th century's increasing scientific spirit—& especially interesting to me because I have a mounted telescope myself, & was an ardent amateur astronomer in youth. In Georgian times, it was the mark of a man of taste (as distinguish'd from a mere town fop on the one hand, & from a vegetative Will Wimble or 'Squire Western on the other hand) to possess a small telescope, a microscope, & a set of globes. (terrestrial & celestial) Providence was rather backward in acquiring a citizenry who enjoyed these things, insomuch as *Newport* was anciently the chief town of the colony; but in 1746 there came hither a Mr. John Merritt, a gentleman merchant of England who had previously stay'd a while at Newport, who quickly set the example for local cultivation by having the first coach-&-six, the first telescope, & the first really good library of the classicks, that the townsfolk had ever seen at close range. After that, as Providence began to outdistance Newport in the race for supremacy, other cultural leaders appeared; especially Mr. Joseph Brown (an architectural & scientific dilettante who designed the finest church* & mansions* in the village, & who ended up as professor of natural philosophy in the

---

*all still in good condition

college) & Governor Stephen Hopkins—whose modest house, built in 1742, has just been renovated & opened to the publick as a colonially furnish'd museum. These men founded the first circulating library in town, (still in existence) & imported a fine reflecting telescope from London with which to view the transit of Venus in 1769. I have seen that telescope—which is still in fine condition, & preserved at the Ladd Observatory of Brown University. Aye, & I have frequently meditated beside John Merritt's grave, with its column & urn, in the hidden hillside churchyard of old St. John's[6]—formerly King's Church.[7]

Yes—I noticed the name *Gervas*—which is a frequent one in old families with a Norman tradition. It comes originally from the French St. Gervais, a sort of Gallic St. Swithin whose day is June 19th. If it rain on St. Gervais's day, say the French, it will rain for 40 days thereafter! The exact spelling of the name is quite immaterial—it is all the same thing. Several bearers of it have earned a moderate celebrity—such as the 12th century monkish writer Gervaise of Canterbury, the 13th century Anglo-Latin chronicler Gervas of Tilbury, & the later well-known Jervaise Markham, author of "Country Contentments", "The Gentleman's Academie", & other rural treatises of squirearchical appeal. The name had some foothold in early America, but is less met with now; although Samuel Loveman has a young friend named Gervaise Butler—known to his intimates as "Jerry." Incidentally—you will find the name *Dudley* also amongst the Bosville connexions, thus completing the linkage with the unhappy Jervas Dudley of my tale.[8] The Dudleys of New England spring from an early governor of the Massachusetts-Bay who was of the family of the celebrated Elizabethan Earl of Leicester. But enough of rambling! Again I thank you sincerely for the loan of the volume—which I shall mail back tomorrow or Tuesday.

The cuttings enclos'd in your letter all prov'd of interest. I had seen the Dunsany poems, but am glad to have these versions on better paper for my scrap-book. I heard Dunsany lecture in Boston in 1919—he seems as delightful in person as on paper, & only my disgust for intrusiveness prevented me from seeking an introduction to him after his reading, when autograph-mad throngs nearly swept him off his feet. He, by the way, attended Cheam School in early youth—that school where more than one little Bosville went. I must read that "Destiny Bay"; for I know Byrne's style,[9] & the moon-magical extract seems very promising. There is nothing quite like the Celtic imagination! Glad to know that the Ui Niall banshee is still faithful—perhaps it will give a solo when I pass out; for though the blood is strained rather thin, the antiquarian spirit is still strong! The item on early Irish ethnology impels me to add one more to the unwieldy bulk of tales I am sending—hence please find enclos'd (for ultimate return) "The Moon-Bog", in which I recall certain vague legends of rather less scientific value than the new data of Dublin University. "The Cheerful Cherub"[10] seems full of pleasantly optimistic & appropriate reflections—it seems to me I've met him once or twice before, although he isn't syndicated in the local daily I take. I shall send the Newman misprint cutting to an amateur publishing friend (*not* Cook!)[11] who appears badly in need of some such reminder, & shall return the Magna Charta item herewith, since its reference to Lord Saye & Sale makes it appropriate for your genealogical files. I have seen the idea of that paragraph expressed before— even to the extent of the assertion that almost any Englishman can claim Charlemagne as an ancestor. But why stop at Charlemagne? I prefer the boldness that goes beyond prosaic probabilities, & applaud such feats as that of Albert Gallatin, the Swiss-American statesman of the early 19th century who traced his line back to the Roman Dictator & Consul of B.C. 249—A. Atilius Calatinus, who fought in Sicily during the 1st Punic War, & was the first Roman Dictator to command an army outside continental Italy. S.P.Q.R.! Ave Roma Immortalis! I also recall my childish admiration for the elaborate hypothetical lineage of Admiral Dewey as given by effusive biographers in the days of his glory. The newspaper-kings-at-arms had him comfortably traced back to Constantine the Great—who, if not of the old Italian hawk-nose stock, was at least a Roman emperor, mighty warrior, & celebrated figure generally! That Shapley lecture must have been very interesting, & I hope it will be repeated in Providence. Shapley is probably the foremost living American astronomer, & I have read his small book "Starlight" with great interest. One has to read constantly & alertly to keep up with the newest celestial developments, for what was the frontier a year or two ago become "old stuff" before one realises it. This, of course, does not apply to the solar system; but to the sider[e]al & nebular universe, its construction & dimensions. All that I learned of this field a quarter of a century ago is as obsolete as the Ptolemaic theory today!

But again I must put a stop to senile rambling! I trust my suggestions anent "The Palace of the Lord" may prove helpful; & hope, as I said before, that the sonnet may achieve distinction in the competition. Let me add that the avalanche of prose & verse accompanying this envelope does *not* carry with it any obligation of hasty perusal. Read the stuff as gradually as you please—or not at all, which would probably be much wiser!

Your oblig'd obt Servt

H P Lovecraft

Notes

1. HPL's account of the dream (as recorded in a letter to Donald Wandrei) was published posthumously as "The Very Old Folk." Long printed a verbatim transcript of the letter to him containing the dream in his novel *The Horror from the Hills* (1931).

2. By Henryk Sienkiewitz and William Stearns Davis, respectively.

3. HPL wrote annual birthday odes to amateur poet Jonathan E. Hoag (1831–1927) from 1918 to 1927, followed by the elegy "Ave atque Vale" upon Hoag's death. The first six were published in *The Poetical Works of Jonathan E. Hoag* (1923), edited by HPL.

4. *The Dream-Quest of Unknown Kadath* (1926–27) and *The Case of Charles Dexter Ward* (1927). Neither was published in HPL's lifetime.

5. Either *The Shadow of the Iroquois* (New York: Dutton, 1928) or *The Shores of Adventure* (New York: Dutton, 1929).

6. St. John's Episcopal Church (1810) at 275 North Main Street.

7. HPL derived most of this information on colonial Providence from Gertrude Selwyn Kimball's *Providence in Colonial Times* (1912), which he read at the New York Public Library in 1925. He used some of this information in *The Case of Charles Dexter Ward.*

8. "The Tomb."

9. Donn Byrne, pseudonym of Brian Oswald Donn-Byrne (1889–1928), Irish novelist.

10. "The Cheerful Cherub" was a series of illustrated poems written by Rebecca McCann and purportedly spoken by a male baby (hence HPL's reference to "him"). They were first syndicated in newspapers and later collected in several volumes.

11. Probably Charles W. "Tryout" Smith.

[5]   [ALS]

10 Barnes St.,
Providence, R.I.,
March 15, 1929

Dear Mifs Toldridge:—

Both envelopes & the book package safely arrived, & I have just read "The Rosebush" with keen interest & admiration. It is in truth a very captivating piece of writing; virtually compounded of poetic images, & having a delicate underlying verbal cadence which well sustains the fragile, Dresden-China atmosphere of the phantasy. Of course, there is no need to point out that the story as a story is of a type definitely artificial & in line with a well-marked sentimental convention. It is, undoubtedly, consciously so; like the paintings of a Watteau or a Fragonard, or the fairy-tales & prose-poems of Oscar Wilde. The appeal lies not in resemblance to life, but in the airy emphasis of certain aspects of dream. It is in essence poetry, & must be judged by the canons thereof. The dominant mood seems to me admirably sustained in every part, both by language & by imagery; & there is almost nothing which one would wish changed. In a place or two there might be a slight shortening—or rather, division—of very long sentences, & twice I caught a *like* were where *as* ought to be; but aside from such minutiae I don't see how it could be improved. As I say, the artificial emotionalism is wholly legitimate according to the spirit of dream-decoration; & the only concession to naturalism one could possibly suggest would be a somewhat greater informality in the speeches addressed to honest black Tawm. Altogether, I think you have reason to take the highest pride in this achievement—an achievement which constitutes poetry despite its prose mould—& I fancy you might find some editor receptive toward it if you tried a sufficient number. You handle prose very well—with an adequate ear for its subtle rhythms & atmospheric balance as well as an adequate regard for the visible rules of rhetoric. Such gifts ought to make you a successful fantaisiste—or a successful fictionist if you employ your prose style on more realistic & disillusioned material. I shall look forward to the perusal of your other story with additional eagerness. Moreover, I would be delighted to see some ghostly material from your pen. If you lack plots, I will copy some suggestions for you from my common-place book, which contains more ideas than I shall ever have time to exploit. Even now that book is lent to a young author who claims a similar dearth of plot-ideas—none other than my "adopted grandson" Frank Belknap Long, who can spin magnificent horrors when given a suitable start. The only thing you may not like about the plot-germs is that they are all sombre & terrible. I never base my lighter fantasies on anything solid enough to write down in advance—for I have too much of the scientifically disillusioned realist in me to treat life or human events in a romantic or sentimental spirit. When I deal in ethereal dream, it is *all* dream—all a matter of grotesque pictorial patterns & non-human & non-terrestrial scenes & laws. But if horror-ideas will be of any use to you, you are welcome to a selection of them as soon as "Little Belknap" returns my notebook. Incidentally, I have just turned over to him that Hispano-Roman dream of mine which I described in my last letter. I have been considering it so long that it has lost interest & freshness for me, whereas my "grandchild" thinks so well of it that he plans to base a novel on it![1]

I trust "The Palace of the Lord" reached you in time for submission to the competition. I see by your later note that you wish to retain *Night's balcony*—which I trust you have done, since it is altogether permissible if all *other* secondarily accented rhyme-syllables are eliminated. All this I have explained in my former epistle. It is really better to retain *balcony* than *shadowy*.

And let me thank you most appreciatively for the delightfully felicitous though all too undeserved lines on my work which you enclosed![2] Really, I shall have to concoct something of merit in order to justify them! They are inimitably graceful, & with a genuine sense of spatial vastness & outer voids. If you will retitle the piece "Lord Dunsany" & submit it to some paper, I'll wage you might get it published! It would surely fit that inspired weaver of dream! *Galaxies of stars* is not, in its net effect, tautological. One has to use individual taste in dealing with such phrases, & in this case the effect is—at least, so far as my ear goes—much the same as that of the universally sanctioned *crowd of people*, or *dreamed a dream*. Again, abundant thanks & modestly deprecating obeisances!

I am glad you enjoyed the Long-Loveman-Smith volumes. Yes indeed, Long surely is a member of the gang, & one of the most important of all! I was sure that I had mentioned him, though possibly I took him so much for granted that I fancied he didn't need verbal mention. He is, though nearly twelve years my junior, probably the closest of all my friends—a disillusioned cynic with a contempt for life & its conventions & commonplaces much like my own, & with a love of phantasy & art for art's sake which still further enhances the resemblance. Though we have not actual blood in common, it was because of a very genuine mental family resemblance that I "adopted" the little imp as an aesthetic grandson & heir a decade ago, when I first noted the nature of his work & saw my own youth repeated in him. We are very different on the surface, however; for "Sonny" pretends to like modern ways & professes a vast boredom anent his old "Grandpa Theobald's" perennial Georgian antiquarianism. At other times, though, he claims to be a greater antiquarian than the old gentleman; & to hark back to the Renaissance for his intellectual & emotional sources. He likes to link himself up with the Mediterranean tradition, & to consider himself the reincarnation of some cinquecento Florentine nobleman or Castilian hidalgo! A great boy—& he'll never grow up!

I looked over the Radcliffe poems with keen interest, & am returning them under separate cover with a few designedly constructive comments. You can give these to Miss R—or if she is sensitive about critical comment, you can re-phrase the suggestions yourself & transmit them in the most tactful way. There is not, however, any vast need for tact; for the work is all excellent, & at least two of the poems ("Trysting-Place" & "Lost Ideals") of really distinguished merit. Most certainly do I consider her work eminently worthy of continuance & preservation for publication, & I am sure that W. Paul Cook would be glad of the opportunity to print a book of it. At the same time there is no need for you to deprecate your own work in comparison. Miss R. shews a tendency to greater abstraction of theme & toward rhetorical antitheses in the handling of ideas, but this circumstance does not lessen the value of good work in another vein. Don't mistake differences in kind for differences in degree! Yes—I agree with you in singling out "Lost Ideals" as a particularly notable specimen.

The new Poetry Circle Anthology, though started now, may not appear till a year after its predecessor—is not the idea to publish annually? I think it will be no mistake to send some of your best specimens for inclusion, since the audience cannot help containing an unusual number of really appreciative & aesthetically competent readers. Your selection as judge in the sonnet contest is indeed a very genuine compliment, & I trust you will harbour no qualms about serving. All your work proves you to possess both the requisite degree of taste & the necessary amount of technical knowledge, & I am sure the various competitors are quite safe in your hands. As for the amount of interest in the Circle as a whole—undoubtedly all such things please more acutely at first than later, yet they have a certain residuum of permanent appeal, & would probably be missed more or less if abandoned. Have you ever heard of an "International Writers' League" with headquarters somewhere in

Kentucky? It seems to be rather like your Circle, & issues an annual anthology. A friend of mine in New Mexico[3] has just joined, & seems to find it highly congenial—indeed, he means to insert three or four of his poems in the 1929 anthology. The Bookfellows of Chicago are another group of the same sort. Long has had something in their anthology once or twice.[4] These circles are useful, sometimes, in acquiring a set of poetic friends to whom one can shew one's work, & who can be made to form a sort of background for one's poetic efforts. Comments & suggestions from varied sources always have a mellowing & maturing effect on one's work—I know I owe a great deal to the impartial comments of different critics & fellow-writers in the old United Amateur Press Association, whose evaporation I still regret. But for these steadying influences, I would still in all probability be aping the minutest mannerisms of Mr. Pope & Dr. Johnson as I used to do. A book, though, is very satisfying in addition to membership in a congenial group; & I surely hope you can ultimately manage to have one.

And now let me express my sympathy regarding your recent capsizing in the tempest! Truly, that is no pleasant experience under any circumstances; & when one is only just recovering from an accident it is doubly alarming. I am glad to hear that the result in the present case did not prove serious, & hope you will be alertly on your guard hereafter—heeding all storm-signals of the weather bureau, & remaining safely at anchor in the harbour of the Farragut when the savage whirlwinds rage! I know how vicious winds can be—especially in cities where tall buildings produce concentrations & violent currents. There are places in downtown Providence where I sometimes have to hold on to myself as well as to my three-cornered Georgian hat & carefully powdered tie-wig! By this time I trust that all effects of the disaster have vanished.

I note the cuttings with interest & thanks. A laureate on the radio would be even more unusual in America than in England, & I fear that all too many honest "fans" would soon cut off "this Plato guy" in favour of Paul Whiteman or Graham McNamee or Roxy[5] or some other purveyor more in accord with their cosmic yearnings. As to the Spillway's disappointment in Ireland— of course it is an anticlimax to see the ould place at peace. Had it been so in 1642, the parents of little Tommy Casey would never have been murthered, & I would have had to rely on Wales & Cornwall for all my Celtic mysticism! It will be interesting to see how the Free State will really affect Irish letters. I hope the *Gaelic* fad won't be carried too far; for English is really the natural tongue of the Hibernian writers, & any reversion to another would snap the main line of a tradition which has produced the greatest poet alive today— Yeats. The Irish have a peculiar charm in the use of English, which could never be duplicated in another language. Moreover, a change would lose them most of their present audience. Authors with obscure native tongues— Icelandic, Polish, &c—often voluntarily turn to French or English in order to secure a better hearing.

With best wishes, & thanks for the glimpses of "The Rosebush", I remain

Your Moft Ob^t Servt

H P Lovecraft

P.S. Wednesday was so delightfully warm that I made my first woodland excursion of 1929, taking my work out to the ancient countryside north of the town & spending the afternoon atop a great rock overhanging a still-unmelted forest pool. There were still patches of snow on the shady slopes, but spring's awakening was near, & I heard the stirring of fauns in the thickets. In summer I seek the fields & groves every afternoon, taking my reading & writing along in a black leatherette case.

Notes

1. See letter 4, n. 1.
2. HPL refers to Toldridge's poem "H. P. Lovecraft"; see Appendix.
3. HPL probably refers to Eugene B. Kuntz of Clovis, NM.
4. G. S. Seymour, *A Bookfellow Anthology* (12 vols., 1925–36). HPL had only Vol. 1 (1925). It includes a poem by Frank Belknap Long ("A Sonnet for Seamen," p. 93).
5. Paul Samuel Whiteman (1890–1967), American bandleader and orchestral director. Graham McNamee (1888–1942), a pioneering American broadcaster, the first color commentator on baseball games. Samuel Roxy Rothafel (1882–1936), American impresario nicknamed "Roxy."

[6]   [ALS]

c/o Vrest Orton

Odell Farm

283 Odell Avenue

Yonkers, New York

April 15, 1929

Dear Mifs Toldridge:—

Your interesting letters with enclosures were duly forwarded to me at my present visiting address, & I am glad to hear that you found pleasure in the books &c. which I sent before my departure. No haste about their return—nor any need for special delay, either, since my aunt will receive them safely if they come whilst I am still absent. I may be away for two weeks more—one week here, & the next with my grandson Frank Belknap Long in New York. Meanwhile I suppose my letters will be fragmentary & inadequate, since various engagements crowd me so closely during my sojourn near the metropolis. It is a curiously ironic circumstance that the numerical majority of my friends live in & near New York—a town I detest so heartily! This place, however, is on the very rim of the metropolitan zone;

hence is exempt from all the Manhattanese characteristics I hate. The countryside is picturesque & hilly, & as yet but little impaired by real-estate "developments." Orton's house is an early 19th century farmstead; white & rambling, & with the small-paned windows, steps up & down from room to room, low ceilings, broad floor-boards, & mantled fireplaces which bespeak the genuine old-American home. The grounds are ample & lovely; with great elms, numerous peach trees now in pink blossom, a rambling brook, a sunken garden, & a series of grape-arbours, flower-beds, & climbing rose vines which will give an even greater exquisiteness to the scene later in the season. Activities are of a sort congruous with the setting—yesterday we changed the course of a tributary to the brook, built two stone footbridges, pruned the fruit trees, & trained the vines on a new home-made trellis. New York, though a whole hemisphere away in atmosphere & spirit, is only 40 minutes distant by train, & 2 hours by the more inexpensive combination of surface-car & subway elevated which I generally employ. I have seen a good part of the old "gang", & expect to see the rest before my return. Wednesday night there will be a regular meeting of the bygone kind at George Kirk's—& next Friday–Saturday–Sunday Orton & I expect to take a motor trip to Athol to see Cook. Truly a dizzy round for an ancient Georgian recluse!

Naturally I have revisited most of my favourite museums & antiquarian haunts—noting with regret that the quaintness of Greenwich-Village is rapidly passing. Whole blocks of colonial houses have come down since I knew the place; & now the more placid but less ancient Chelsea-Village to the north of it is menaced. Famous "London Terrace" in West 23d St.—where a friend of mine[1] has lived all his life—is to come down shortly to make room for a wretched apartment skyscraper. But of course a good deal of the old material is still left—especially such houses as are preserved as museums. Very soon I intend to take a couple of young fellows over my principal antiquarian route, shewing them a side of N Y which they never knew despite birth lifelong residence there.

Glad you found "The Outsider" worth reading. It is this which will probably be chosen as a title-story for a book of mine if *Weird Tales* ever decides to issue that long-contemplated collection. I am not overfond of the thing myself—its "punch" is too obviously mechanical.

I've heard more from the Boston witch-descendant,[2] who likewise turns out to be a lineal scion (through the Massachusetts Eastys, who were originally D'Estes of Ferrara, Italy) of Lucrezia Borgia & Pope Alexander the Sixth! Likewise, her forbears were intimately acquainted with Old Diamond & Moll Pitcher of Marblehead, about whom I told you some time ago. She has not yet related any specific dark tales transmitted down her family line, but still promises to do so. Meanwhile "The Dunwich Horror" has elicited *another* letter from a New England inquirer who wishes to know what guarded secrets of diabolism I can reveal, & what dark books on forbidden rites & arcana I can recommend! This one is a naive old fellow in rural Maine, who says he has studied "occultism" since 1893, & who promises not to put any information I may give him to malign use!!

Trust you will thoroughly enjoy both of the Machen books. "The Hill of Dreams" is a remarkable work of art—an imaginative autobiography which cannot but take a permanent place in English literature. "The House of Souls" runs more strongly to intense horror-material.

As for my philosophic attitude—yes, it is indeed as completely pagan & cynical as I have stated; although of course it requires interpretation, as all philosophic attitudes do. I believe in nothing—am a mechanistic material-ist—but enjoy practicing ancestral attitudes & gestures, & increasing my slen-der sense of importance by occasionally encouraging other literary amateurs. My position is the result of a most careful consideration of just what man's knowledge of the universe is, & involves a very searching analysis of the ulti-mate basis of commonly accepted standards & values. I have argued endlessly over this position, though it is really an immaterial matter what anybody be-lieves. Unlike you, I do *not* like to find an apparent "meaning" in things; be-cause I do not believe that *anything* has any meaning, & therefore consider the assumption of such a thing bad science & defective art.

About poetic technique—when I say that the language of ordinary con-versation ought to be used, I do not mean that the usual banalities & transient colloquialisms are to be included. I merely mean that forms obviously differ-ent from common speech are to be excluded. When the subject-matter is un-usual, unusual words & forms are less obtrusive; but in familiar lyrics & conventional sonnets it is fatal to be recherché & high-flown. I'd like to see your weird poem "Laocoön" when it is done.

The cuttings were very interesting—those lines on cherry blossoms re-mind me of the peach-blossoms right here where I am visiting! I must see the cherry-blossom display in Washington some time. The only spring trip thither I ever made was in 1925, just too late for the phenomenon. The lines of Wil-liam Sharp (who, by the way, has written some remarkable weird material un-der the pseudonym of "Fiona MacLeod") are highly potent despite their simplicity. I have followed the draining of Lacus Nemorensis with great inter-est, though without much hope that anything valuable will be discovered on Caligula's galleys.[3] Too many divers have explored the sunken ships to leave any probability that detachable material remains. However, the draining of the lake will be almost certainly worth while, because the floor is undoubtedly covered with articles thrown in as votive offerings to Diana, to whom the spot was sacred. This lake & its temple form a highly peculiar shrine—dating from immemorial antiquity, & during classic times being notable for the sin-gular conditions attaching to its priesthood. The priest of this temple was re-quired by custom to be a *runaway slave*, & to gain his office by challenging the existing incumbent & killing him in single combat. Thus he was always compelled to meet challengers whenever they might appear—& in the end to fall at the hands of a younger or stronger man. Macaulay, in his "Lays of Ancient Rome," speaks of him as

> "The priest who slew the slayer
> And shall himself be slain."[4]

Very interesting details about the shrine & lake can be obtained from Frazer's monumental anthropological work, "The Golden Bough." The programme of the Society of Women Geographers is indeed ambitious—especially that of Mrs. Adams, whose courage after so dire an accident is surely miraculous. I'd like to see that Delphic festival. Greece is the third in order of European nations which I would enjoy visiting—England & Italy being the other two. Greece contains some remarkable survivals of classic myth among the peasantry—I heard a highly illuminating lecture on the subject a year ago by Sir Rennell Rodd, a lifelong student of neo-Hellenic folklore. Much remains to be excavated in Greece—indeed, it is possible that art will receive a new stimulus from what archaeology will unearth during the next 10 or 20 years. The membership of Miss Morrow in your poetry Circle must be very interesting for the members to consider. Her work has real merit—though one cannot tell how much of a literary career she will care to follow.

There was some very good material in your last set of verses, & I'm sure some of the Easter & Christmas pieces would do very well for a book. That volume certainly must materialise some day!

With best wishes, & profound apologies for the hasty & prosy letter which the haste of guesthood compels this to be, I remain

Yr moft obt hble Servt

H P Lovecraft

Notes

1. A person named De Kay—first name unknown.
2. HPL's correspondent (never named in any of his letters and otherwise unidentified) claimed to be a direct lineal descendant of the Salem witch Mary Easty, who was hanged on Gallows Hill on 19 August 1692.
3. HPL refers to "The Lake of Nemi," a poem by Scottish writer William Sharp (1855–1905) included in his poetry volume *Sospiri di Roma* (1891). The poem is about Lake Nemi (Lacus Nemorensis in Latin). Sharp also wrote weird tales under the pseudonym Fiona Macleod, notably "The Sin-Eater" (1895).
4. From Thomas Babington Macaulay's "The Battle of the Lake Regillus" (*Lays of Ancient Rome,* 1842), ll. 175–76.

[7]   [ALS]

Home addrefs,

10 Barnes St.,   Beach in Libby Hill Park,

Providence, R.I.,   Richmond, Va., C.S.A.,

May 4, 1929

Dear Mifs Toldridge:—

If my Yonkers epistle was a surprise, I fancy a note from the sun-swept bluffs of stately *Richmond* will be still more of one—yet to such an aestival clime has my antiquarian zeal led me! I meant to visit Old Philadelphia only; but a timely cheque empowered me to go farther, so I decided to pay my long-intended visit to the cradle of American civilisation—the banks of the York & James. Nor have I been disappointed in my expectations, for I have found here a wealth of colonial material rivalling that in my own New England—& in the Annapolis & Alexandria which gave me my first tantalising taste of Southernism. Fredericksburg is a treasure-house—Richmond seems like a second home-town—Williamsburg is an ecstacy of architecture rivalling even my favourite Marblehead—Yorktown is almost equal to Fredericksburg—& *Jamestown* is one of the most powerful imaginative stimuli I have ever received. To stand upon the soil where Elizabethan gentleman-adventurers first broke ground for the settlement of the western world is to experience a thrill that nothing else can give. Here has been a continuous civilisation since 1607— thirteen years before the landing of the Pilgrims on Plymouth Rock—& here developed a stately & mellow culture which at its ante-bellum apex may fairly be said to have eclipsed any other in the nation. The lone church tower,* the Gothic walls of the ruined Ambler house, the various foundation stones visible here & there, & the tree-grown churchyard with its crumbling walls, all combine to produce an atmosphere which induces conversation in awed whispers. I have never seen anything like it before.

Williamsburg—now under careful restoration to its colonial state—was of course the architectural high spot. I spent much time in the Wythe house & Old Bruton Church & churchyard, & duly examined all the other notable buildings & sites—the gaol where Blackbeard's men were kept before their trial & hanging, the college hall designed in person by Sir Christopher Wren, the 1769 Courthouse, the foundations of the vanished colony house, & so on. All told, I came to know Williamsburg rather well in a single afternoon; & am now anxious to visit it 3 or 4 years hence, when the restoration will be complete.[1]

In Richmond the chief object of interest for me is the Poe Shrine—an old stone house with the two adjoining houses connected as wings & used as a storehouse of Poe reliques. Here I have spent much time examining the objects associated with my supreme literary favourite—to say nothing of the marvellous model of Richmond in 1820, housed in one of the wings. On my

---

*now attached to a modern reproduction of the old church

final days in the town I am idling about the parks & getting my accumulated revision & correspondence done. Tomorrow or the next day—my cash being nearly exhausted—I shall face northward again; picking up accumulated mail at Long's in N.Y., & making one final side-trip up the Hudson to see Bernard Dwyer if I find any revision-cheques awaiting me. If I don't, I shall have to head directly for home! If I have a chance to stop in Washington I shall probably greet you over the telephone—though I am not yet sure whether my financial-transportational programme will permit of a stop. I would, if I did stop, also call up my old friend Edward L. Sechrist of the government beekeeping dept.—a delightful aesthete & poet with a predilection for primitive life, who has spent much time in Africa & the South Sea Islands.

My Yonkers idyll was succeeded by a week of Manhattanising as the guest of my little grandson Frank B. Long, Jun., during which I saw much of the gang & did considerable colonial exploring. But I can't like New York—& am incredibly glad to be out of it again & on the road amidst traditional scenes. Too bad I must re-cross through it—but Long is still receiving my mail, & I've left my overcoat & one valise with him! None of us hear anything from Cook, & we are beginning to get somewhat worried about him—though inexplicable silences are not altogether novel phenomena on his part. If I am able to go home via the Mohawk Trail route I shall probably stop off in Athol & see what the trouble is—I have already asked a friend there for information.

As for my philosophy—it does not argue youth, for I shall be 39 next August; but it does argue impersonal scientific observation—free from emotions such as hope or will—of the evidence presented to our perceptive apparatus by such portions of the external world as impinge upon it. I believed—or disbelieved—as I do, long before there was any such thing as a "younger generation" or "post-war disillusion"—indeed, I can be regarded as a product of the old line of sceptics beginning with the Greek atomists & Epicureans & linked to the present by such figures as Hobbes, Voltaire, Diderot, Hume, & the later groups centreing in Schopenhauer & Nietzsche, Huxley, & Haeckel. But I don't bother much about philosophy in my old age—I merely let it slide as a matter which at best must deal only with fragments or probabilities. It is simply one probability among others that the cosmos is a blind, impersonal vortex eternally seething from nowhere to nowhere—simply that such an assumption is the least improbable of many, & that there is not a shred of evidence or likelihood of any other state of things. It really means nothing to anybody—all one can do is to go about his business & custom & nature direct, obeying the rules imposed by common sense, habit, & aesthetics. Nothing really matters. Imagination is an amusement which one may draw from many sources—from all the reservoir of images & illusions deposited by the massed fancies of the race & the dreams & experiences of the individual. It is a pleasant sort of psychological rearrangement, but has not relation to truth or to the actual structure & motivation of the universe.

I am glad you enjoyed "The Hill of Dreams"—which is a striking work of art. It reflects the possible fate of many a sensitive dreamer under unfortunate environmental influences. In "The House of Souls" the best tale is probably "The White People" & the *worst* without question "The Inmost Light." "The Great God Pan" is perhaps the most famous & superficially brilliant, but it depends too much on *coincidences* to be art of the first quality. I can't agree that my style is favourably compared to Machen's. He has a rhythm & music which I could never achieve—& which I could not even imitate without the cure of affectation.

Glad the cat-&-dog sketch proved amusing.[2] I had a chance to prove my feline devotion last week at Little Belknap's, for the Child has lately secured a dog—a black Scotch Terrier—& all the family have combined to render it homage & neglect their regal & magnificent coon-cat Felis. I lost no opportunity to shew my unshaken preference for Felis, though at all times treating his canine rival with amiable civility. Felis is still Grandpa's boy—& I took pains to let everyone know it.

Pardon change of paper-size at this point—& good riddance to that small-sized pad!

The Boston witch-lady & the Maine wizard prove rather interesting—the latter in a somewhat amusing way. I decided not to make fun of him, but told him of such weird books as I know about—& he has just replied with the most ridiculous conceivable barrage of undigested esoteric jargon. He is quite a type—a dupe of the theosophists & kindred cults to judge by his epistolary allusions.

The experience of your Washington circle with the apostles of modernism must have been somewhat disconcerting, though the visitors seem to have been quite characteristic of their type—the self-conscious Greenwich-Village aesthetes. Such persons do not *shock* me, because I recognise their right to follow their standards as I follow mine; but they do make [me] ineffably tired with their affectations & superficialities & backgroundless aesthetic drifting. This Harrison is rather a well-known public nuisance—a loud-mouthed, assertive self-advertiser with a shrewd eye for good business.[3] I have never met him, though many of "the gang" have. Such people are well described as the "submerged truth" of the arts—a group with scant natural gifts, but with a mania for aping the startling iconoclasm of greater artists with whom iconoclasm is only a side-issue. One need not, however, worry about appearing in *The Troubadour*.[4] Poems by everybody can appear anywhere without injury, & a well-defined piece of work speaks for itself whatever its environment. I doubt if the publishers are actually dishonest, or of such a nature as to injure the standing of their contributors.

The "Garden" you speak of as finding in "The Hill of Dreams" rather puzzles me—is it an old piece of typed MS. under my name or a pseudonym?[5] I dimly recall grinding out such a piece in 1916 or thereabouts, but it is such stereotyped hack work that I've never counted it among my literary permanencies. I didn't know any copy was still in existence—if indeed the verses you mention *are* that piece. Your own poem of similar theme was undoubtedly much better.

The Radcliffe note was duly forwarded, & I was glad to learn that Miss R. found my comments helpful. I am acknowledging it this afternoon—with many apologies for any delay in so doing. She appears to share your excessive modesty concerning the merit of her work—& speaks most admiringly of yours.

Your *storm* had its echoes in the North, but was more spread out—as the most rainy & dismal April on record. I don't know how it is there now—but it surely is a welcome relief to bask beneath the summer-like sun of Richmond. I left a raw world of half-budded boughs behind on Wednesday morning, & have since revelled in the full summer greenery of a more genial clime. If I were not so strongly attached to the scenery & architecture of New England I would certainly live in the south—even farther south than this, say Charleston or New Orleans.

I liked both "The Birth of Eros" & "Pandora's Gift" very much, & am honoured at the fact that my work suggested them. The few archaisms seem quite permissible in view of the themes—though perhaps the last line of "Pandora" might bear a change. Would it spoil the sense to substitute *could* for *did?*

The cuttings were very interesting—especially the picture of Sir Alexander Macdonald & his rival chieftains. Their pacific mode of settling precedence was very civilised, though I fear poor Bozzy & Dr. Johnson would condemn it as unworthy of the proud scions of Somerled, Donald Gorm, & such-like ruthless warriors.

But I have rambled long enough, & the sun is getting low over the yellow band of the James & the green Virginia plains outspread before me. Best wishes—& I'll call on you on the wire if I pause at all in Wash'n en route north.

Yr ob^t Servt

H P Lovecraft

Notes

1. See letter 101.

2. "Cats and Dogs."

3. HPL elsewhere referred to the publisher Henry Harrison as "sometimes straight & sometimes racketeering" and as a "racketeering vanity-publisher," a "shark."

4. *Troubadour* (San Diego: Artemesia Press, 1928–32), a poetry magazine.

5. "A Garden," AMS (signed "L. Theobald, Junr."), TMS (JHL); *Vagrant* [Spring 1927]: 60. Included in a letter to the Kleicomolo (April 1917 [AHT]; *RK* 91); HPL erroneously dates the poem to 1918 at *SL* 1.59. The issue of the *Vagrant* was long delayed and should have emerged as early as 1923.

[8]   [ALS]

10 Barnes St.,
Providence, R.I.,
May 29, 1929

Dear Mifs Toldridge:—

Your note with enclosure, & the returned "cat & dog" MS., arrived just as I was about to drop you a line & send you the long-promised loan books—"Andivius Hedulio" & two Dunsany volumes. My variegated odyssey, protracted beyond all expectations, ended only last week when W. Paul Cook brought me down in his car from Athol; & I have since been lost to the world in an effort to wade through a nearly two months' accumulation of papers, magazines, & unforwarded 2nd & 3d class mail. Now, however, I am beginning to see daylight again—& shall mail the bundle of books on my first trip out to the post office.

I am, naturally, delighted to learn from Lady Macdonald's letter that she was pleased with my remarks on the two books; & shall of course be enormously grateful for permanent copies of the volumes in question. It is highly generous of her to offer to send them, & she many be sure that they will both form valued & appreciated additions to my library. As I said last winter, traditional material of this sort is always of the keenest interest to me, & it is indeed an unexpected pleasure to be able to look forward to the twofold & unusual enrichment of my shelves. Please tell Lady M. that I shall prove an eager & thankful recipient! Incidentally, I am glad to note from her letter that a second & public edition of the books is planned. They certainly ought to be thus available for the generality of antiquarians, genealogists, & tradition-lovers of every kind. I shall be interested to note the new links with New England & the Province of the Mafsachusetts-Bay which the second edition of the Bosville history will supply . . . . . . & incidentally, I surely envy the source of this information his ancient Essex priory & its cloisters! Let me thank you for sending me Lady M.'s interesting letter—which I herewith return.

It is almost needless to repeat how much I enjoyed my call at the Farragut three weeks ago, & I can only hope that my incessant loquacity was not a bore. I shall surely drop around again the next time I am in Washington, & would be glad to meet the rest of your poetry group—although I would hesitate to fatigue them with any oration on the Pierian art! Lectures & speeches of every kind seem to me the sheerest nonsense, since one can never declaim a set of facts half so adequately & comprehensively as it can be written. I never attend a lecture except when I absolutely can't obtain the equivalent text in printed form. Incidentally—in case you wish to do some recruiting for your circle—I will give here the name & address of the interesting Washington friend (bee expert, poet, African & Polynesian traveller, &c) of whom I spoke, & who will probably be my host on future sojourns of mine in the capital. He is *Edward Lloyd Sechrist, 923 Dorset Ave., Chevy Chase.* This is his office address—a bee station in Somerset, Md.—since he will not have a permanent home address till July. I have just heard from him, & he has been thoughtful enough to send me an excellent photograph of the prehistoric Zimbabwe bird-idol which so greatly aroused my imagination when I saw it in his collection.

My trip after leaving Washington proved as interesting as the preceding southerly portion, & spun itself out to an unforeseen length. I first paused in Philadelphia, always a favourite town with me, & went over my customary colonial haunts—besides inspecting the magnificent new art museum near the edge of Fairmount Park. This majestic Hellenic Acropolis, crowning an elevation & forming the apex of a long parkway vista, is positively the most impressive piece of contemporary architecture I have ever seen—a vast colonnaded temple of tinted marble, set high above broad flights of steps flanked by waterfalls & enclosing a tessellated courtyard at whose centre a many-jetted fountain plays. Silhouetted against the western sky it is one of the most stupendous & dream-exciting structures that the fancy can picture—a veritable gateway out of reality & into a timeless region of myth & beauty. The interior is not yet finished, but the one habitable wing houses a highly remarkable series of English Georgian & Colonial panelled rooms—including the only Pennsylvania-German specimens I have ever seen. Some of the rooms from England are from houses of the same style & period as Tharpe Hall.

From Philadelphia I proceeded to New York, where my young grandchild Frank B. Long & his parents gave me a motor lift up the Hudson shore to Kingston—the ancient town harbouring my artist-fantaisiste friend Bernard Austin Dwyer, whom neither Long nor I had ever met in person before, despite long & interesting correspondence. Dwyer turned out to be as genial & pleasant in person as on paper, & I stayed at his house several days— though Long had to move on & collaborate with his father in a trout-fishing excursion (which turned out absolutely fruitless!). Kingston itself interested me prodigiously, for it is a highly venerable & historic place full of reliques of the past. The present city is a fusion of two once separate villages—Kingston proper, where my host lives & which is about a mile inland from the Hudson's west bank, & the river-port of *Rondout* on the hilly bank itself, where the ferry from Rhinebeck lands & which is now a somewhat picturesque slum. The two were fused about 50 years ago when a municipal form of government was adopted.

The history of the region goes back to the decade of 1620–30, when the Dutch built a fort (*ronduit*) at the mouth of a creek on land called by the Indians *Ponckhockie*. The fort became the centre of a settlement called *Roundout*, & the creek received the name of Rondout Creek. About 1652 Kingston proper—the land then called Atkarkton, northwest of Rondout & inland along Esopus Creek,—was settled by Dutchmen & Englishmen from Reusselaerwyck, farther up the river, after disputes regarding land titles had driven them from the latter place. In 1655 serious Indian wars convulsed the locality, & in 1658 the Atkarkton settlers appealed to the Dutch governor Petrus Stuyvesant for aid. He granted their petition on condition that they form their holdings into a palisaded village, & this requirement was at once complied with. The resulting stockaded town, which was chartered by Gov. Styvesant in 1661 under the name of *Wiltwyck,* corresponds quite closely to the present west end & main business district of Kingston; even the original street-lines being largely preserved. Solid stone houses were built, some of which remain to this day, & which formed the characteristic architecture of the region. After the transfer of New-Netherland to the British crown as the Province of New-York, the name of Wiltwyck was changed to *Kingston;* & the village prospered exceedingly. In 1695 the Rev. John Miller, Chaplain of his Majesty's forces & aide to the Governor of New-York, published a book with maps descriptive of the province & therein spoke of Kingston as a town of the same area as Albany, but with half as many houses—i.e., 6 furlongs in circumference, & with 100 buildings. Many of those buildings are still standing today. Severe Indian warfare harassed the town throughout its early history—incidents not improved by the high-handed seizure of lands & arbitrary & cruel treatment of Indians by the Dutch settlers. By the time of the Revolution Kingston had 200 houses, a market & brew house, a church, an academy (still standing) a courthouse, & two schools. As a storehouse & source of supplies for the rebel armies operating in its vicinity, it was a highly dangerous menace to His Majesty's forces; so that in the autumn of 1777 its destruction by fire was found needful. Most of the rebel inhabitants, being forewarned, fled to the village of Hurley & other points, & the regular troops entered without opposition, setting fire to all the edifices save those belonging to loyal subjects of our rightful sovereign. This process consumed only the wooden dwellings, leaving the walls & beams of the great stone houses scarcely damaged. Accordingly the returning rebels later rebuilt their houses, so that large numbers of the early structures still stand despite the holocaust. At this time, Oct. 16, 1777, the rebel senate of New-York was meeting at the Ten Broeck house in Kingston, (now pointed out as the "Senate House" & becoming a public museum—see accompanying postcard) & adjourned its sessions to the Van Deusen house in Hurley when the former was burnt. The city of New York was then the legal capital of the province, but it was not at that time in the lands of the rebels—hence their sessions at Kingston, which was the third town in importance in the colony, Albany being second. In the compact part of Kingston not more than one or two houses were left undamaged by flame. Today the Van Steenbough house (hardly in the village according to the boundaries of 1777) is pointed out as the only one which was not touched. For this exemption various reasons are assigned—the political loyalty of the owner being the most probable one. The tenure of Kingston by His Majesty's forces was not of long duration, since powerful rebel armies under Genl.

George Clinton (a native of the region, & later Governor of NY State for 21 years) were observed to be advancing toward the town. Having destroyed all possible rebel supplies, the army evacuated without pursuit of the fleeing villagers; & did not again enter. The rebel army soon arrived, & with its aid the townsfolk quickly reëstablished themselves in their accustomed haunts. Local progress was by no means retarded, & in 1783 Kingston (being used to harbouring a legislative body) offered itself as a possible capital for the United States—which offer was declined, since your own Federal City of Washington was planned for the purpose. After the Revolution Kingston remained a very important town, though it did not grow as rapidly as many—Albany & NY City monopolising the activity along the Hudson. At the Bogardus Tavern many persons of the first importance were entertained; & it was there that Aaron Burr, observing the clever chalk drawings of a stable-boy on a barn door, resolved to send the lad to Europe for an art education, & thus produced the eminent painted John Vanderlyn. As the 19th century wore on, Kingston was more & more rivalled by the river settlement of *Rondout,* on the Hudson at the mouth of the creek, which naturally obtained a great share of the region's trade. By the 1840's Rondout was greater than Kingston in population, & was heavily built up along its narrow hilly streets, in contrast to Kingston's struggling houses, broad streets, & level terrain. At the same time it was less select in population & less rich in traditions—a hive of trader & bargemen rather than a settled domain of hereditary agricultural magnates. In the 'fifties Rondout applied for a city charter, & seemed for a while about to get it—but vested & dignified Kingston subtly intervened with legislative influence, & finally succeeded in disposing of its rival by engulfing it—i.e., securing a combined city charter for the villages of Kingston & Rondout *under the name of Kingston.* Thus Kingston became, by one sudden act, a city & a river port, with two distinct settled areas separated by a sparsely populated zone. So it has remained to this day; save that the sparse zone is gradually filling up with public & private buildings including the railway station, P.O., public library, city hall, hospital, & Y M C A. Kingston proper (or "uptown") has retained its social supremacy, & there may be found all the leading dwellings & shops. Hilly Rondout on the river has become a sort of declassé section largely given over to foreigners, from whom Kingston proper is almost wholly free. The city is distinguished by a reposefulness highly pleasant to observe, & scarcely changes in population from decade to decade—lingering for the past thirty years around 25,000 to 30,000. It has a single street-car line from the steamboat wharf through Rondout & Kingston proper—which still remains wholly two-man, still uses small single-truck cars, & still has *open cars* in season. Motor coach service also exists—both local, & to other towns including N Y City. It must be a delightful place to live, save for its coldness in winter—for it has all the freshness, charm, & simplicity of a small village.

Other places in the Kingston region which I visited were the famous colonial villages of Hurley (abt. 3 m. N W of Kingston) & New Paltz (16 m. S.). The road to Hurley lies through an extremely fine rolling countryside; with green cultivated fields in a very unspoiled & un-modern state, & the foothills of the Catskills as an eternal dominating background. (These hills also form part of certain vistas in Kingston itself.) In general, this territory is unchanged since the colonial period; being still owned & farmed by the descendants of the original Dutch & Huguenot settlers. Hurley was not in any way a disappointment. It is a straggling hamlet of ancient stone houses stretched along the highroad, with plenty of trees & diverging lanes, & the green fields & blossoming orchards stretching off on either side to where the purple mountains loom mystically. The houses are of Dutch masonry construction, some of them with wooden attics & lean-to's, & a few with projecting porches. All have the horizontally divided Dutch door with iron knocker & hinges to match, & the average date is from about 1700 to 1730. (Kingston's houses extend from abt. 1670 to 1720 or 1730) It is noteworthy that none of these later Co. Dutch houses ever developed the gracefully curving roof-line or the gambrel arrangement so characteristic of the Dutch Colonial architecture of southern New York. In this up-river region the plain peaked-roofed tradition always persisted; so that the architectural atmosphere is absolutely distinct from the architectural atmosphere of Manhattan, Long Island, Staten Island, & Rockland County. The houses of Hurley have seen very little change in the more than two centuries of their existence, for the place is delectably slow & sleepy, with true Catskill conservatism. All the dwellings are tenanted by the same old families who built them—an Elmendorf still runs the single village store & post office—& the ancient Dutch Reformed Church still ends the vista at the bend of the road. The town is very famous among antiquarians—models of the houses being in the N.Y. Hist. Soc., & a large space being devoted to them in H. D. Eberlein's volume "The Architecture of Colonial America." Hurley, at first called merely the "New Village", was founded about 1660 by the overflow population of Wiltwyck, (Kingston) who desired to expand in the fertile untimbered lowlands. A large proportion of the settlers were French Huguenots, though the Dutch element was very numerous. Land grants were made by Gov. Petrus Stuyvesant without consent of the Indians who formed the original population; a circumstance which paved the way for considerable warfare & general harassment. On June 7, 1663, Hurley was burned to the ground by savages, & all the women & children were carried away into captivity. It was not until September that the pursuing forces of the Dutch succeeded in locating the prisoners—who had not been ill-treated, although they were later to have been burned alive in revenge for certain Indians who had been captured by the whites & sold as slaves to traders from Curaçao. In the years that followed, Hurley prospered exceedingly, perhaps occupying a more important position in the life of the region than it does today. Its cheeses, milk, cakes, & other products were famous throughout the

New-Netherland region, & formed the subject of more than one bit of Dutch doggerel folklore—of which the following translation is typical:

> "What shall we with the wheat bread do?
>   Eat it with the cheese from Hurley.
> What shall we with the pancakes do?   ⎤ *
>   Dip them in the syrup of Hurley.   ⎦
> What shall we with the corn-meal do
>   That comes from round about Hurley?
> Johnnycake bake, both sweet & brown,
>   With green cream cheese from Hurley."

It was from Hurley that the settlement of New Paltz was made by Huguenots in 1617; & to Hurley that the fleeing people of Kingston repaired just a century later, when the torches of the royal forces menaced their homes. On that latter occasion the state senate also fled to Hurley, conducting its deliberations in the old Van Deusen house (built 1723) which is still standing & colonially furnished with a view to antique-selling. I entered & thoroughly explored the Van Deusen house, & found little change since the 18th century. The graceful panelling & staircase strike the eye at once, & all the quaint old hardware remains. The oldest house in the village is the Elmendorf store, dating from about 1700. All told, it is hard to find a better living specimen of old New-Netherland than sleepy Hurley. A Dutch diplomat, visiting the place not long ago, declared that as a whole it is more typically & historically Dutch than anything now left in Holland!

My other sub-pilgrimage was to New Paltz—which lies about 16 miles south of Kingston, but the Wallkill & Shawangunk Creeks, & in the eternal shadow of the lordly & lovely Shawangunk Hills. It is a thriving village with shops, hotels, banks, a normal-school, & a newspaper, quite in contrast to the scattered & somnolent Hurley; but the modern (i.e., post-Revolutionary) town lies some distance from the heart of the ancient settlement. This has tended to preserve the original area in its pristine, early Hurley-like state; so that we may still see the place as it was in the early 18th Century. To reach the old town from the modern town one has to walk a considerable distance, descending a steep hill & crossing the railway track. The countryside between Kingston & New Paltz is as splendidly unspoiled as that between Kingston & Hurley—a typical sample of the quiet Dutch milieu so well exploited by Washington Irving. Any one of these drowsy old villages might well have been the abode of Rip Van Winkle. On this particular route lovely valleys

---

*The original of this couplet, illustrating the Dutch of the district, runs:
    "Wat zullen wij met die pannekoeken doen?
    Doop het met die stroop van Harley."

abounded, & bends of streams in the lee of mountains produced a scenic effect hard to surpass. I saw at least one old-fashioned *covered bridge,* a type of survival usually associated nowadays with Vermont or western Massachusetts. At length the coach ascended a hill & delivered me at the principal tavern of New Paltz—the "modern" part, although even that is as quaint as Georgetown or Annapolis, & far more untainted as to original population. There are virtually no foreigners in this idyllic backwater, nearly all the inhabitants being descended from the first Huguenot settlers. Making judicious inquiries, I soon found my way down to the ancient section—Huguenot St.—& there revelled in the sparse line of old stone dwellings which has given the town so great an historical & architectural fame. There are not many—perhaps a half-dozen at best—but their fine preservation & isolation from modern influences give them a magnified charm. One of them (see accompanying postcard) is fitted as a museum & open to the public; others remain private dwellings, mostly in the hands of the families that built them more than two centuries ago. The museum—which is the old Jean Hasbrouck house built in 1712—is a large stone house of one full story & two attic stories under the immense sloping roof—an ideal storehouse for grain or other rural commodities. It is a fine type of early colonial construction under Dutch influence, (though Frenchmen built it) & I examined it with the utmost thoroughness & interest; visiting the attic & noting the massive exposed beams. It is called the "Memorial House", & a boulder monument to the town's founders stands on the small triangular green opposite it. Nearby is the quaint burying-ground housing those 'rude forefathers of the hamlet.'[1] The other houses—of varied types, & having features as unique as transoms with double rows of lights—stretch southward along a broad shady street reminiscent of the main street of Deerfield, Mass., or Duke of Gloucester St. In Williamsburg, Virginia. All of these—the DuBois, Elbing, Abraham Hasbrouck, Freer, &c. houses—are of about the 1700 period, as can be well seen from every detail of their construction. The interior of the "Memorial House" has some highly primitive features such as the great plank doors—some unpanelled & some single-panelled. Oddly enough, there is just one of the ancient stone houses in the "modern" village—now used as a public library. In the old times it must have been an isolated farmhouse on a lonely hill.

New Paltz was settled by French Huguenots who had undergone a long & singular course of persecution & migration. Emigrating originally from France, they had settled at Pfalz or Paltz in the Protestant Rhineland; but had eventually been so harassed by French troops from across the border in their Catholic homeland that they reëmigrated to Holland. There, affected by that longing for a new world which sent so many religious refugees overseas, they took part in the general Dutch migration to New-Netherland—though sedulously retaining their French language & customs, a Gallic trait which we can see even today exemplified in their French-Canadian communities of Rhode-

Island. Preferring the rural reaches of the upper Hudson to the crowded & cosmopolitan New-Amsterdam, this band of Huguenots (led by one Louis DuBois, a pioneer of the utmost solidity & ability) selected Wiltwyck (Kingston) as an abiding place; but later transferred themselves to the "Nieuw Dorp" (Hurley), which they considered more favourable to their retention of French speech & ways than the rather uncongenial Dutch trading-post within the palisade. After the burning of Hurley in 1663, Louis DuBois was much impressed by the lovely countryside south of Roundout Creek, which was made familiar to him during his participation in the search for the Indian captives—amongst whom were his own wife & three sons. Especially did he relish the idyllic valley of the Wallkill, nestling amidst the Shawanguncks & cut off from the bustling world which had treated him & his band so ill. During the next fourteen years—a span marked by the transfer of the colony from the Holland States-General to the authority of His Britannic Majesty—duBois interested many of his fellow-Frenchmen in a project for securing land-patents & founding a new Huguenot village in the Shawangunk country; a project finally carried through with the aid of Abraham Hasbrouck, a young Huguenot having influence with the Governor Sir Edward Andros—the same official who was so much hated in New England because of his arbitrary exercise of power. Arrangements were also made to purchase the land lawfully from the Indians—a step which would have delighted Roger Williams, Rhode-Island's founder—for the patentees were not insensible of the hostility created by the high-handed seizures of the Dutch. In May 1677 the Indians formally ceded the land in exchange for much assorted merchandise, & 4 months later His Majesty's government granted the legal patent to the settlers—Louis, Abraham & Isaac DuBois, Jean & Abraham Hasbrouck, Andries & Simon Le Fevre, Pierre Days, Louis Bevier, Antoine Crispell, & Hugo Frére, ancestor of the *Freer* family whose taste & generosity have given your city one of the finest art galleries. Homes were built the following spring—rude cabins on the site of the stone houses built during the next generation—& a few other settlers were admitted, including at least one Dutch family. A little stone Huguenot church, with services in French, soon adorned the village green—& the village was named *New Paltz* in honour of that place in Germany which had first given the wanderers a haven. With the years New Paltz attained a very comfortable agricultural prosperity, though remaining in that unspoiled state which best suited the founders' wishes. Every effort was made to preserve the traditional piety & French ways of the forefathers, yet in the course of time the influence of the surrounding Dutch population could not help being felt. It became harder & harder to secure French-speaking schoolmasters & clergymen, & in the end the younger generation fell into the habit of speaking Dutch. Naturally the elders protested, & there is a well-known tale of a child sent to a relative's house to borrow some kitchen utility, & refused it because she could not speak its name in French. This transition period was likewise marked by ecclesiastical schisms—some church-members wishing to adhere to the Reformed Dutch Church fabric whilst others clung to a French Huguenot independence. Between 1730 & 1750 Du[t]ch definitely displaced French as the daily language of New Paltz, & in 1752 the church commenced the official use of that tongue. The village was now predominantly a part of the Dutch Hudson Valley, (whose language & manners the British government did not interfere with) though still remembering in its different traditions. Some of the pathos of the linguistic change is reflected in the will of Monsieur Jean Tebenin, the local schoolmaster who flourished in the early 18th century. He saw the gathering clouds; & when he left his French Bible to the church, provided for its sale for the benefit of the poor if the French language should ever cease to be used thereabouts. New Paltz in its Dutch-speaking period enjoyed a steady growth, & that happy immunity from striking events which marks a peaceful community. Branches of its Huguenot stock were represented in the Revolution, yet that war itself left the town serene & unravaged. As the 18th century drew to its close, time took its revenge upon the once conquering Dutch language by pressing it to extinction as French had formerly been pressed—the latest conqueror being the all-engulfing English. Signs of Yankee progress became manifest as an Anglo-Saxon population filtered in, but the newer element built on the hill above old Huguenot St.; shifting the villages centre of gravity & leaving the ancient part undisturbed to this day. In 1833 an academy was founded, which survives at present as a state normal school. I was forced to survey New Paltz in somewhat drizzly weather, yet the sightseeing was extremely enjoyable. After the study of three such representative places as Kingston, Hurley, & New Paltz I feel that I have some knowledge of the southerly New-Netherland. An ascent to Albany completed my present canvass of the Dutch terrain—for after a brief glance at that none-too-interesting town I proceeded to still uglier Troy & took the Boston & Maine train for the Hoosac Tunnel & my native New England.

This ride was not at all dull, for the landscape of northern N Y State is very fine & includes many mountain vistas. Then the hills grew wilder & greener & more beautiful—yet less luxuriant in foliage as the course ran northward into an earlier & earlier spring. I was at last concluding my foreign travel, & approaching the sacred & familiar soil of rock-bound New England! No more would I encounter strange tongues, histories, & heritages—the scene was to shift in an instant from the exotic to the accustomed. The pillared doorways of Manhattan, the marble steps & keystones of Philadelphia, the steep roofs & dormers of the South, & the old stone dwellings of the Esopus Valley—all these, & the centuried echoes of those who have known them, were about to vanish as if snapped off by an electric switch. In an instant my eyes were to be filled with known & neighbouring things—the eternal hills & stone walls of my native land, the oft-rehearsed legends of familiar tribes & settlements, the homely accents of Puritan speech, the white steeples & farmhouse gables of New-England's countryside, the loved, ancient names & known places which look back only to English dreams & memories—Pownal, Williamstown, North-Adams, Zoar, Shelburne Falls, Greenfield, Orange, & *Athol*—for it was to this Massachusetts town that I was proceeding for a visit with my friend Cook before making my final descent on Providence. Near North-Adams (the west end of the Mohawk Trail, over which I had planned to go by coach, but which I found was closed to traffic) the Berkshire Hills loomed up in monstrous impressiveness, & I regretted bitterly that I was to go under them instead of over them. Then came the Hoosac Tunnel, & after that occasional exquisite glimpses of mountain & valley—Charlemont, Shelburne Falls, & so on. The landscape grew best near the end of the Berkshire region, when the lovely valley of the Deerfield River opened up in full sunny expansiveness. Then came Greenfield & the picturesque run along Miller's River through Orange to Athol—where I once more set foot upon my native Novanglian sod. *Home!* . . . . for the first thing I saw upon quitting the station was a motor-truck with a *Rhode Island* license-plate—belonging to the Tar Products Corporation of *Providence!*

Cook was a good host—my anxiety about his silence having been unfounded. Mere pressure of business was responsible, as I learned from a letter whilst re-crossing through N Y City. He took me out at once to his new farm near the town—a place which most unfortunately he must soon sell because his wife's health requires the comforts of urban life. The countryside proved exquisite—the very quintessence of ancient New England—rolling, stony hills, narrow, winding, rutted roads, stone walls, archaic apple-orchards in white bloom, & sparsely scattered white farmhouses. Cook's place is one of the latter—set on high ground with one of the most magnificent rural landscape effects conceivable—both foreground & far horizon of hills beyond hills. At one point a blue lakelet glistens among tall pines. No other house is in sight—just stone walls, green fields, distant hills, & the scattered buildings of the venerable farm. Here I stayed for some time; occasionally taken on motor trips by Cook or by our young friend H. Warner Munn, whose weird stories have been so well received of late. Once we went up to Vermont to see the poet Arthur Goodenough in that rapturously beautiful Brattleboro region which so enthralled me on my first sight of it in 1927. (I think I sent you my printed rhapsody on that region—entitled "Vermont—a First Impression"—did I not?) Another time we visited Westminster, where I spent the summer of 1899 with my mother, & which I remembered in all its details though I had not seen it all the intervening thirty years. Finally I decided to conclude my two months of varied wandering, & had Cook bring me down to Providence in his car—traversing the territory described in my "Dunwich Horror". It was surely good to see old Rhode Island again—& Providence never looked lovelier than when I glimpsed its sun-sparkling spires & domes from a high point on the Lonisquisset Pike as we sped southward through my favourite Quinsnicket or Lincoln Woods country. At last we entered the well-remembered streets, & turned into the shady & village-like neighbourhood I am fortunate enough to inhabit. 10 Barnes was still there, & my aunt was on hand to give us a royal welcome. Here have I tarried ever since—immersed in back numbers of papers & getting readjusted, & I shall soon be at my regular work. It was a great trip—from early in April to the last of May—yet I am glad to be home again. Providence is exquisite in the late spring, & nearby are the woods & fields of my childhood; still unchanged, & welcoming me on every warm, pleasant afternoon when I take my work out to the open. There is no place like it—at least, for the native into whose fancy its image has sunk deeply. God Save His Majesty's Colony of Rhode-Island & Providence-Plantations!

But so much for travel—this extended account of which I fear has proved sadly tedious reading. Let me thank you again for sending Lady Macdonald's letter—& again assure you how glad & grateful I shall be to receive copies of "The House of the Isles" & "The Fortunes of a Family." Likewise let me reaffirm how much I enjoyed my call upon you this month—& how pleasant I found Washington in general on this trip. I regretted that my purse would not permit of a longer stay in Washington & the south, & shall be glad when my visit to Sechrist allows me a more leisurely opportunity to digest the district & its various atmospheric phases. "Andivius" & the Dunsany books have been wrapped for some time, & will enter the mails as soon as I can get down to the post-office—which probably means that they will follow this epistle in a day or two.

With best wishes, I remain yr most obt Servt,
H P Lovecraft

Notes

1. From Thomas Gray, *Elegy in a Country Churchyard,* l. 16.

[9]   [ALS]

10 Barnes St.,
Providence, R.I.,
June 10, 1929.

Dear Mifs Toldridge:—

No—there is not the least haste about returning the books recently sent; indeed, I would advise you not to skim them too rapidly—especially the Dunsany volumes, where so much depends upon a leisurely absorption of the rhythm & colouring. I thought you would find Dunsany enjoyable. Later on, if you wish, I can send a good deal more of his work—sketches, brief plays, & his phantasies of novel length. To my mind very few authors either dead or living equal Dunsany in conjuring up really tangible & convincing worlds of dream-splendour. He has virtually created a new field—&, I am sorry to say rather exhausted it himself; insomuch as his later material lacks the concentrated power & substance of these early things. Edward L. White is a dreamer of a widely different school—one in whom archaeological accuracy triumphs over all else. "Andivius Hedulio" as a novel is a rather improbable, unwieldy, & at times childishly naive piece of work; but as a potent & accurate evocation of the Imperial Roman world it is without a peer. It is perhaps the only novel which successfully re-creates Rome from the true Roman point of view. Rambling though it is, it succeeds in giving a faithful picture of almost every phase of life in the Antonine period— country life, Rome, the provincial towns, the road, the sea, Gaul, North Africa—all the region most strongly under the influence of the dominant civilization. The only two phases of Imperial life which it does not exploit are the frontiers of the barbarous West & the vast decadent world of the East, where Hellenic culture blended with Asiatic influences & excluded the spread of Latin speech & thought. Some time White may treat of these phases, for he knows them well. He is, I believe, a classical teacher in a boys' school near Baltimore. In the original edition of "Andivius Hedulio" White had a long postscript in which he made the claim of having *dreamed* the whole story in a single night. This sounded so improbable that the publishers deleted it from later editions—rather at the cost of certain picturesqueness, however. White must have written a dozen or more books.

Yes—my trip indeed turned out to be a marvellously varied & pleasant Odyssey. It is not hard to find traces of the past, & of an appreciation of the past, if one knows where to look. America possesses all the elements of a stable & adequate imaginative background, though in urban regions this heritage tends to be lost through intrusive foreign influences & the spread of hasty, mechanised ways without roots or sources in history. I wish I might see the *Gruyeres* whose cheese I have so long relished & whose atmosphere is so well described in the cutting you kindly sent. Such a town seems almost too good to be true in 1929, even in the quietest European backwater; & I hope its quaintness may not lead to its exploitation, popularisation, & aesthetic annihilation.

I shall, as I said, be extremely grateful for the Macdonald & Bosville books; & am indebted to you for motivating their transmission. The second edition of "The Fortunes of a Family," I imagine, will treat of more *collateral* Bosville branches than were touched upon in the original version. Considering how a line multiplies in the course of a few centuries, it can be seen that there is virtually no limit to the proper territory of a family history, provided information is available. I have just been looking over an old New England genealogy with some curious linkages in the past & present—that of the line which produced John Carter, Providence's colonial printer, & publisher of the Providence Gazette & Country-Journal before, during, & after the revolution. His old shop & office, the Sign of Shakespear's Head, in Gaol-Lane, is still standing[1] in good condition notwithstanding the sinking of the neighbourhood to slumdom. It is a large square house on a steep hill, with fanlighted doorway & the double flight of railed steps so typical of colonial Providence. Carter was a son of a younger son of the Virginia Carters, & was born in Philadelphia in 1745. In youth he served as an apprentice in the printing shop of Benjamin Franklin, & in 1767 he came to Providence as an assistant to the publisher Wm Goddard, whose business & whose newspaper he purchased for himself in 1768. From that time till his death in 1814 he was the leading printer & publisher of Providence, & the manner in which his descendants reached the highest places of aristocracy is worthy of a novel—or of treatment in some such work as Lady Macdonald's. John Carter himself married Amy Crawford of Providence, a descendant of the Earls of Crawford in Lanarkshire, Scotland, & more immediately of the ship-owning Crawfords of Rhode Island. Their daughter Ann, born in 1770, married Nicholas Brown of the great Providence line of marine merchant princes for whom Brown University is named; & her descendants in turn represent the present dominant patrician caste of Providence. One of these descendants in 1911 married Ralph Francis Julian Stonor, Baron Camoys, holder of a title created in 1383— whose young son, the Hon. Ralph Robert Watts Sherman Stonor, born in 1913, thus represents a completion of the circle from nobility through Yankeedom back to nobility. Another daughter of John Carter—the youngest child, as Ann was the eldest—was Elizabeth Ann, born in 1790, who married a Danforth (later a Mayor of Providence) & inherited the old house in Gaol Lane (renamed "Meeting St." from the Quaker Meeting House at the bottom of the hill) which had been the Sign of Shakespeare's Head. This Walter Raleigh Danforth was own cousin to the father of my elder aunt's husband, & I now have his copy of Johnson's Dictionary. Their daughter married Richard Bowen Allen of Newport & became the mother of Crawford Carter Allen, born in 1861 & a close friend of my uncle & aunt. He, in 1909, married Maude D'Arc Corsi, daughter of Count Corsi of Rome, Italy by an English mother—a Caulcott of Chester & Kensington—thus linking the Carter line once more to a noble house. Unfortunately he died in 1917 without issue, so that the actual blood blending did not occur. His widow—who was educated in England & does not strongly reflect the Italian strain—still lives in Newport, albeit in reduced circumstances, & sometimes comes to see my aunt. I am not yet certain whether Carter's Virginia forbears, whose provenance was upper Norfolk, were related to the famous Carters of Shirley. This transposition of a Virginia line to New England always affected my fancy strongly— hence my frequently recurrent fictional character "Randolph Carter". No one has yet written a book on the Carter line, though a great-great-grandson, John Carter Brown Woods, has prepared an interesting & accurate illustrated brochure for private circulation.[2] Efforts of descendants to obtain a presumable likeness of John Carter, who had no portrait painted in his lifetime, are somewhat amusing in their circuitousness. In 1853 Mr. Danforth—a son-in-law—sought a memory-sketch from the Providence artist Thomas F. Hoppin, who had known Carter in the latter's last days; & this sketch being made, it was elaborated into an oil portrait by a collateral descendant—Samuel Brown, then an art student in Rome. My aunt's friend Mrs. Corsi-Allen now owns this portrait, but it is universally admitted to be idealised out of all true resemblance. The real clue to Carter's aspect probably lies in a very different direction; through a case of *striking resemblance* which was widely remarked during his lifetime. In those days Carter was hailed as the exact double of a Unitarian clergyman of Boston—one John Murray, who attained a considerable degree of eminence. Now Dr. Murray *did* have a portrait painted from life, hence present Carter descendants feel that an important guide to their ancestor's features is still in existence. The author of the brochure—J. C. B. Woods, has arranged for a copy of this portrait—checked up by comparison with the Hoppin memory-sketch of 1853—& in all human probability this will be the closest possible record of the old publisher's features. I pass in sight of the ancient Carter house every time I walk down town—& the neighbourhood is still much as he knew it in 1770 & thereabouts. Across the street an old brick schoolhouse built in 1769 is still serving its original purpose, whilst at the foot of the hill the Old Quaker Meeting House (1745) still broods beside its deserted wagon-sheds. Up the hill from the house is the venerable arsenal; & still higher the street becomes so precipitous that it has to change to a quaintly arched-over flight of stone steps. A little to the left is the ancient Golden Ball Inn where Washington, Lafayette, & Jefferson have stopped; whilst beyond the 1769 schoolhouse one can see the ancient brick colony-house (1760) through the trees. There is another very strange old house nearby which houses some distant relatives of mine, & which I have made the scene of a sombre horror-tale. This tale is to be issued as a small book by W. Paul Cook, & you will later see a copy. It is called "The Shunned House." As I have intimated, the neighbourhood is now sadly declining; & very recently there have been signs of a ruthless demolition of landmarks which will sweep away all the old-time atmosphere. It began, indeed, a full decade ago, when the old Updike house below Shakespear's Head was torn down. This place was in colonial times owned by Capt. John Updike*, Carter's brother-in-law, but not inhabited by him. A curious situation once arose when a tenant of this house opened a rival printing office—next door to the established Shakespear's Head! Capt. Updike did not care to harbour his brother-in-law's business enemy as a tenant, yet what was he to do as an honourable landlord bound by lease? Much friction ensued, & I do not know

---

*The origin of this Rhode Island name is curious. It is of remote *Dutch* derivation—Op Dyck—the family having filtered into western R.I. from Long Island & the New Netherlands.

how the matter eventuated! In this rough sketch, the left-hand house higher up the hill is Shakespeare's Head, whilst the right-hand one is the ancient Updike place, how demolished. This represents their aspect in my youth. The tiny low building between—now a stone mason's shop—used to harbour physician's offices—my own uncle-in-law Dr. Clark (the cousin of Allen, Carter's descendant) having practiced there for a time. But now the old days & ways are going slowly & insidiously. The Updike house is down, & the old Quaker meeting-house is for sale. And just now—& heard the news only yesterday, a thing which caused me to get out the Carter booklet again, & which therefore precipitates this bit of reminiscent rambling—a still further change is to befall the ancient neighbourhood. At the corner of Benefit St., across from the Arsenal & just below the point where Gaol-Lane breaks into a flight of steps, there has hitherto been a bit of *actual country* remaining—field, gardens, cottages, orchards, & an old stone greenhouse—a bit of real colonial village days, & saved from encroachment by the extreme steepness of the hill. Now, however, I am told that *all this is to go within a fortnight;* a wretched ultramodern *apartment-house* with all urban sophistications being on the brink of erection there! Imagine my sensations! A modern brick apartment-house in ancient Gaol-Lane beneath the flight of steps & above the 1769 Schoolhouse, the 1760 colony-house, the Golden Ball, the Quaker Meeting House, & the Sign of Shakespear's Head! It is enough to send an Old Gentleman to his archives to read over data on the days & ways & faces that were—the days & ways & faces of 1770, when John Carter each Wednesday issued (with the Royal Arcus at the head) the Providence Gazette & Country-Journal, Containing the Frefheft Advices, both Foreign & Domeftick. By the way—I shall have a chance in a few days to give one of the appreciative members of "the gang" a last look at the doomed neighbourhood, for I expect the genial James F. Morton (curator of the Paterson Museum—I've mentioned him before, I think) to spend half a week in Providence before his Harvard commencement. He will mourn with me.

As for the poem you mention wishing to have looked over—don't hesitate to send it along whenever you come across it. It'll be no bore, I assure you. Your present new poem—"Divinity"—seems to me highly effective & well-written, with a commendable freedom from artificial "poeticisms" & inversions. The reference to electrons is not erroneous, but on the other hand quite apt. As an argument, the lines surely have a gracefulness beyond dispute, & a generous panegyrical quality—which no mundane opponent is likely to merit; yet I doubt if they shake very heavily the stern probabilities of science. There is nothing to take real exception to in the statement that a given group of human tendencies springs from the natural collocation of material particles operating automatically without the intervention of an external consciousness. Such a statement does not imply in any way the action of *chance* (for a cosmos of mutually interacting parts is *all law & no chance*, albeit the law is not *conscious*) or the creation of something out of nothing. Nothing is created from nothing, because there can be no nothingness. The whole cosmos is, always has been, & always will be a limitless field of force composed of alternately combining & dispersing electrons. They work in fixed ways, none of which need explanation by any hypothetical "spiritual" world apart from that whose laws they obey. Our subjective notions of these forces—i.e., our arbitrary & artificial classification of them into "wonderful" & "common," "good" & "evil", "beautiful" & "ugly", &c. &c.—are based wholly on local perspectives & relative personal standards due to our own perceptive & emotional apparatus, & having no relation to absolute truth, absolute values, or the actual motive-power of infinite entity. These local human feelings, perspectives, preferences, wishes, & aspirations are quite clearly & adequately accounted for by modern psychology—materially accounted for in a way which proves them absolutely valueless & supremely irrelevant in the task of interpreting the phenomena around us. Everything that exists or happens, exists or happens because the balance of forces in the cosmic pattern makes it inevitable. Whatever ethical or preferential qualities we seem to see in anything are sheer fictions of our minds & emotions—fictions based on a body of race-legendry originated when mankind was unable to conceive of external nature as apart from the anthropomorphic & the anthropocentric.

However—all this means nothing in the organisation of society & government. In a cosmos without absolute values we have to rely on the relative values affecting our daily sense of comfort, pleasure, & emotional satisfaction. What gives us relative painlessness & contentment we may arbitrarily call "good", & vice versa. This local nomenclature is necessary to give us that benign illusion of placement, direction, & stable background on which the still more important illusions of "worth-whileness", dramatic significance in events, & interest in life depend. Now what gives one person or race or age relative painlessness & contentment often disagrees sharply on the psychological side form what gives these same boons to another person or race or age. Therefore "good" is a relative & variable quality, depending on ancestry, chronology, geography, nationality, & individual temperament. Amidst this variability there is *only one anchor of fixity* which we can seize upon as the working pseudo-standard of "values" which we need in order to feel settled & contented—& that anchor is *tradition,* the potent emotional legacy bequeathed to us by the massed experience of our ancestors, individual or national, biological or cultural. Tradition means nothing cosmically, but it means everything locally & pragmatically because we have nothing else to shield us from a devastating sense of "lostness" in endless time & space. Nowadays we can't believe as our forefathers did, but we can share some of their instinctive feelings toward the daily scenes around them, so that a sort of comfortable placement in the invisible cosmic pattern will seem (falsely—but what of it?) to be provided for us. Those who can feel tradition most strongly are the luckiest just now, for amidst the jumbled impression & radically changing experiences of a machine age there is but little sense of fixity or satisfaction to be gained from an adjustment to immediate reality. It will take generations for the machine age to build up enough stable illusions to found a new fabric of satisfying tradition. Yet the change must come—& we don't yet know just how much comfortable illusion & perspective we can carry over from the now dying age into the nascent age ahead. All this is admirably discussed in an article in the June *Current History* magazine—"Forces That are Destroying Traditional Beliefs", by Prof. John Herman Randall, Jr., of Columbia.[3] Randall—a Baptist clergyman's son—is an old family friend of my young "grandchild" Frank Belknap Long Jr. He is only 28 years old, but was an "infant prodigy" & has been a recognised philosophical author & teacher for years. However—don't let me drag all this discussion to a boresome length. It really doesn't matter, except to himself, what anybody believes; & if anyone can get more contentment out of the old faith than out of the new facts, I'd be the last to wish so useless a thing as his actual emotional disillusionment. All I ever do is to state my own position clearly, in order that I may not hypocritically seem to be other than I am; giving only enough argument to shew that my attitude is a maturely thought-out one & not a mere accident or freak of irresponsible caprice.

I'm sorry you find it so difficult to get to the library, & wish there were a more easily available branch you could use. But possibly the journey & the steps will seem a trifle less formidable when you are further recovered from your accident. As for the Poetry Circle—I'm sure Sechrist would enjoy a meeting if he is in town when you convene. He is sent on tours quite frequently by the government, (when I tried to look him up in Wash'n last July I found he was in

Laramie, Wyoming!) but of course has long stretches of non-travelling work during which he would be able to participate in local activities.

Yes—that Kingston–Hurley–New Paltz region is very unusual & refreshing. The Sleight house—now owned by the D.A.R. & open as a museum—is a very fine specimen.[4] I had some views of the interior, but unfortunately lost them before leaving Kingston.

As for the Labour Party's victory[5]—it is of course depressing to contemplate the enthronement of a group pledged to work against the social order which produced our characteristic civilisation with its gentle, leisurely folk-ways; yet after all there is no great reason for alarm. British labour is more moderate in act than in speech, & has a healthy unconscious reverence for stable institutions which offers pretty good assurance against anything like Bolshevism. If the Labourites ever influence England deeply, it will not be without a reciprocal influence which Old English ways & heritages will exert over them. They will level themselves up as they level the country down—not that such a levelling is as pleasant & poetically satisfying as the old order, but that it is about the best thing we can expect in the course of historic evolution. Oddly enough, it is really *not* socialist politics which is chiefly abolishing the beloved old semi-feudal order. It is doing its share, of course, as its economic system makes the large tenure of land more & more costly & difficult; but there are stronger & subtler influences at work—a cultural old age of the nation, & an insidiously novel set of satisfaction-standards introduced by machine-bred luxuries, whereby the descendants of the old families themselves are finding former adjustments to society inadequate, & are demanding a more urbanised life—on a smaller & more intimate scale—with less dignity & ceremony & more purely physical luxury. The motives for maintaining traditional country life on a manorial scale are operating more feebly with the younger generation than with their elders. Only the other day I learned that Eden Hall in Cumberland—the Musgrave seat whose fairy-cup legend I described to you[6]—has been sold, & that the magic cup is now in the S. Kensington Museum![7] Of course the change from a feudal rustic society to a half-socialised system of urban luxury & economic-mindedness will be very gradual at most—& perhaps never complete. The old tradition is strong & beautiful & will die hard—as with the Dukes of Norfolk mentioned in your cutting. But mutation is in the air, & there is certain to be a vast shifting of the political & social balance. England can never be *governed* by its squires again. One thing I'll say for labour; & that is, that it isn't as offensive as the corresponding mutatory force which now threatens culture in America. I refer to the force of *business* as a dominating motive in life, & a persistent absorbing of the strongest creative energies of the American people. This intensive commercialism is a force more basically dangerous & anti-cultural than labour ever has been, & threatens to build to an arrogant fabric which it will be very hard to overthrow or modify with civilised ideas. Yet like socialism, it is one of the inevitable results of the equally inevitable discovery of machinery. There's nothing to do but grin & bear it!

    With best wishes—

             Yrs sincerely,

             H P Lovecraft

P.S. That cutting about the Iroquois epic interested me intensely. There is a vast art-potentiality in the Indian mind, & all of the native legends would re-pay critical & intelligent study.

Notes

1. The John Carter House (1772), 21 Meeting Street. The *Providence Gazette and Country Journal* (est. 1762) was published by William Goddard in a shop marked by the sign of Shakespear's Head on North Main Street. John Carter joined the paper in 1767 and by 1768 was sole proprietor. He and his wife moved the business into the house they built on Meeting Street.

2. HPL apparently refers to John Carter Brown Woods, *John Carter of Providence, Rhode Island: July 21, 1745–August 19, 1814, and His Descendants, a Brief Narrative* (Providence, 1918; reprinted from *Rhode Island Historical Society Collections* 11, No. 4 [October 1918]).

3. John Herman Randall, Jr., "Forces That Are Destroying Traditional Beliefs," *Current History* 30, No. 3 (June 1929): 355–62.

4. The Henry Sleight House (built before 1695) at 3 Crown Street in Kingston.

5. On 5 June 1929, the British Labour party, led by Ramsey Macdonald, won the parliamentary election, ruling until 1931, when it joined with other parties to form a coalition National Labour government (ruling until 1935).

6. Possibly told orally when HPL visited Toldridge. See *SL* 4.392.

7. The "S. Kensington Museum" is the Victoria and Albert Museum. Much of HPL's information regarding his paternal ancestry cannot be confirmed and is now suspect.

[10]   [ALS]

                            10 Barnes St.,

                            Providence, R.I.,

                            [July 1, 1929]

Dear Mifs Toldridge:—

             Yrs. of the 21st & 23d both arrived, & I was glad to look over the verses enclosed. I am sending herewith a sheet of comment which I trust may prove helpful. Don't feel obliged to follow any of these recommendations literally, for independence in artistic creation ought never to be sacrificed. Merely take my remarks as *suggestions*—which is all they are intended to be. What is more, don't unduly minimise the value of your work or fancy that you have not written real poems. Virtually all of your products contain very generous quantities of the authentic poetic element—which is more than any metrical attempt of my own ever succeeded in capturing! The best way to write real poetry is not to care whether you write it or not—to banish such ulterior objects as fame or approval or the world from consideration & pay attention only to the moods or images you record. To my mind, the prime essential of aesthetic effort is to repudiate mankind & the world, & stand alone in the cosmos, face to face with the revelation of beauty which one desires to crystallise & perpetuate.

I have received *The Troubadour* & have read it with much interest. As a semi-amateur medium it is very good, containing many really fresh & vitalised reactions to beauty & to the contemporary scene. Most of the poems seem slightly immature—as if the bards needed to cultivate a grace & roundedness of expression to match their poignancy of perception. Some of the stuff is frankly mediocre, but poets like John Lee Higgins[1] are factors to be reckoned with. I'd like to look him up when I'm in Wash'n again. It is indeed a provoking thing that your "Unmothered" was so badly mutilated, & I cannot see why the editor chose to take such a causeless & disastrous liberty. It seems to be an intentional change, since the surviving fragments of stanzas 2 & 3 are clumsily (and unintelligently) fitted into a single stanza of the dominant pattern. The only way one could account for the deletion as a pure typographical error would be to assume that the copying was done hastily & interruptedly; so that the copyist, in finishing out an incompletely written stanza, mistook #2 for #3. But this is rather a far-fetched theory—& implies a carelessness almost as inexcusable as the poor taste of deliberate deletion. Certainly, the incident is highly regrettable, & I can sympathise very profoundly from having had my writings similarly mangled by editors & compositors—the last such case occurring no longer ago than March of the present year.[2] There isn't much to be done about it once it occurs—though one can take precautions by always telling editors in advance that one's work must appear unaltered or not at all. I would write the editor if I were you, asking why the mutilation occurred, & pointing out the flagrant loss of sense & impairment of form involved. He might, if properly impressed by the gravity of the error, consent to publish the correct version.

There is no reason for not wishing work to appear in *The Troubadour;* for as I have said, the magazine is really rather good of its kind. The social & political opinions of its editors & contributors have nothing to do with its aesthetic merit, & this latter is all that concerns you as a poet. Incidentally—there's nothing about "anarchists" to be afraid of! Most aesthetic radicals are *not* anarchists but advocates of some socialistic or communistic system—yet in any case, be they socialists, bolsheviks, or anarchists in truth, they are very harmless folk. Such people are simply idealists without a balance-wheel—people who see the crudity & absurdity of our present social-political order, but who fail to see that any other order is certain to be equally crude & absurd, & even more unsatisfactory because ungrounded in natural evolution. They are as sincerely well-meaning as any other reformers, & like all such are at once comic & pathetic because of their belief in human perfectibility. Despite their bold talk they are timid & ineffectual creatures, most of whom would not hurt a fly if they could. I know many of them by correspondence—delightful persons when kept off the subject of their hobby. As a matter of fact, all benevolent persons have the instincts of socialists & anarchists; whilst the Christian religion, literally interpreted, is communistic in every particular. Social & political conservatism are the products of hard common sense & stern experience & of the practical & cynical side of mankind, whereby he recognises realities instead of chasing illusions. I myself am a conservative because I am a cynic & a pagan. You may have heard the epigrammatic saying "If a man isn't a socialist *before* he's 25, he has no heart; & if he *is* a socialist *after* 25 he has no head!" The real trouble with Greenwich Village "radicals" isn't any real radicalism, but a slovenly insincerity & cheap posing habit which merely uses the guise of radicalism as an easy way of attracting attention. Such radicals aren't *dangerous,* but merely *wearisome*—& occasionally disgusting when their manners too repeatedly contravene the inconspicuous average. Once in a while real talent crops out amongst them, so that they can't be dismissed en masse; but in general they are charlatans who thump tubs & kettles because they can't play violins. Cheap & pitiful—but scarcely formidable!

I have read Miss Radcliffe's "Manifestation" with much interest & pleasure, & consider it a very fine piece of work. Imagination, sound, & cadence march hand in hand & with commendable unity—& I think the slight irregularity in the final stanza (ultimate plan) is quite permissible in view of the dominant metrical plan. This type of rhythm always holds great potentialities of flexibility. Yes—the poem is really remarkably good, & I trust it may achieve publication in some suitable medium.

The cuttings you enclosed are of unusual interest—especially the one pertaining to interplanetary navigation. I seriously think the moon will be reached by some human device (such as a rocket capable of registering its arrival by a flare or smoke display) before many years, although I have my doubts concerning the presence of any living passenger on the vehicle. Beyond the moon, prospects are very doubtful, though there is no theoretical impossibility about the transmission of a projectile. Much depends on the developments of future science regarding gravity & intra-atomic force—I wouldn't be surprised if before the end of the existing civilisation some wholly new principle might enable men to reach the moon, & possibly Mars & Venus. One couldn't live on the moon without a diving suit to supply air & regulate temperature, though Mars & Venus might possibly support life in an uncomfortable way for a while. Mercury is too near the sun to be considered—it would burn one to a crisp—& the outer planets (Jupiter, Saturn, Uranus, & Neptune) are probably not solid in constitution. With diving & heating apparatus one might possibly explore the satellites of the outer planets. As for the realms beyond the solar system—the spaces involved are so great that it may be doubted if any possible advances in technology could make them accessible to men or to man-sent missiles. Imagination is likely to remain our only supplement to the spectroscopes, camera-telescope, & micrometer in plumbing the deeps of the galactic & nebular universe!

The cave discovery in New Mexico is also highly interesting & important, forming a new link in the chain of facts concerning the lost cultures of the western world. The last two or three years have certainly upset a good many established anthropological hypotheses—especially as regards the remote primitive periods of which bones & flint implements, embedded in rock & gravel, are the only surviving relics. Recent discoveries of fully developed human remains in very ancient geological strata push back the date of man's evolution astonishingly—making the existence of the race a matter of *millions* of years instead of the scant 500,000 assumed by conservative biologists of the last quarter-century. Also, the *distribution* of early man seems vastly wider than at first conjectured—including Africa & America as well as Asia. Biologists are now beginning to think that before the glacial ages several different human species or genera (too distinct for intercrossing) existed, our own among others; & that the hard economic competition imposed by the sudden ordeal of glacier-dodging brought about a struggle for survival from which only our species & the Neanderthaloid species (annihilated in Europe & Africa about 30,000 B.C.) succeeded in emerging. Our species seems to have been fully developed & distinct in its mental superiority over a million years ago—so that its own infancy must extend back into the age of the great mammals. We seem to be the oldest of all the biped stocks which sprang from the ground-apes—having a head start over our rivals which enabled us to annihilate them all before the dawn of recorded history. All the undeveloped semi-human skulls that have been dug up are not those of our ancestors, but of other races which existed when our species was much as it is now. Somewhere in the bleak steppes of Mongolia, under vast layers of sand & earth & other fossils, we shall probably find in the future the skeletal vestiges of the immensely remoter dawn-man who really were our lineal forbears. The account of the lineage of the children's songs is very interesting. Only since the era of the great philologists—Max Müller & the brothers Grimm— have we realised the vast antiquity of our commonest juvenile folklore. Now we realise that the greater part of our popular jingles & fairy-tales belongs to the very oldest fabric of Aryan myth; so that the prototypes of many a well-known rhyme or legend of today may be found in the most primitive Sanscrit literature of India. Another interesting item is the succession of the uncouth Alberta farmer to the Earldom of Egmont. The new peer must be a highly picturesque figure—though if he intends to ruin his estate by turning it all to farm land, I rather hope the rival Australian claimant will succeed in displacing him! The succession of a peer from a remote colonial or American line is by no means unprecedented, though it seldom involves quite so grotesque a figure as the dour Perceval. Once a mulatto from Rhodesia almost inherited a peerage, being debarred only at the last moment by a technicality regarding his legitimacy according to English law. The case of the Earls of Fairfax is well known—the head of the Virginia Fairfaxes going to England to take the title in the 19th century, despite 250 years of continuous American heredity.

My curatorial friend Morton has been & gone, & we had some exceedingly pleasant trips during his sojourn. Most of our antiquarian explorations were down the west shore of Narragansett Bay, to the quaint old colonial seaports of East Greenwich & Wickford. The former is a prosperous village with many narrow, ancient streets running up the steep hill from Coresett Bay, & several old public buildings of distinction. It has a famous academy—still surviving—which my mother, elder aunt, grandfather, & great-aunt attended; & a 1750 courthouse of admirable design. (see card) Wickford—further south—is quainter still, being five miles off the railway. Here we have a perfect & unspoiled example of a pure Yankee colonial town—with giant elms, Georgian houses, & churches, & original hereditary population. There are absolutely no foreigners in the place, & its leisurely atmosphere takes one back two centuries. Since Morton's visit I have had a pleasant call from W. Paul Cook & the young weird writer H. Warner Munn—the two motoring down from Athol in Munn's new Graham-Paige.

I am returning *The Troubadour* under separate cover. Again accept my sympathy anent the mangled poem!

With best wishes—

    Yr obt hble Servt

        H P Lovecraft

[P.S. on envelope:] I have just received my copies of "The House of the Isles" & "The Fortunes of a Family"—welcome additions indeed to my library!

[Enclosures]

Notes

1. Author of *Old Wharves and Other Poems* (1921). *Troubadour* 2, No. 1 (July 1929) contained "The Wild Geese Cry" (p. 14), "Desolation" (p. 15), and "Enlightenment" (p. 16).
2. The only work HPL published in March 1929 was a letter, "Retain Historic 'Old Brick Row,'" *Providence Sunday Journal* (24 March 1929): A5.

[11]   [ALS]

                    10 Barnes St.,

                    Providence, R.I.,

                    July 1[, 1929]

Dear Mifs Toldridge:—

Just as my earlier letter goes into the mail, I am in receipt of yrs. of the

28th. Don't feel hesitant about sending the verse queries—am glad if I can assist, & congratulate you on the typing opportunity. As to the additional points:

Life—*scrollèd* is not as good as *scrolls of*—not so poetical in a *true* sense, because not so simple & natural; but it is not a very bad artificiality, & may well remain if you feel it essential to spontaneity.

¶ Fancy's *tapestry* is much better—better by far—than the strained & artificial *broidery*.

¶ *You* is an affected word which really ought to be ruled out of all verses except those which are frankly imitative of mediaevalism. It means nothing in the living language of the existing period, & has meant nothing for 300 or more years. However, in a ballad of quasi-archaic cast it is less frankly impossible than elsewhere; hence I wouldn't call its use here absolutely prohibited. It is weaker & less effective—more artificial & unnatural—than the word *that* would be; but can be retained if it is felt to be essential to spontaneity.

¶ "Yet life is *'ware*" is very bad. This needs removal more than any other of the archaisms, because it is more of a purely gratuitous distortion—with less justification in the usage of any period. It would be an excellent thing if you could gradually work out of the idea that this kind of stilted & artificial language is "poetical" in any way; for truly, it is *not*. It is a drag & hindrance on real poetic feeling & expression, because *real* poetry means spontaneous expression in the simplest & most poignantly vital *living* language. The great object of the poet is to get rid of the cumbrous & the emptily quaint, & buckle down to *the plain, the direct & the vital*—the pure, precious stuff of actual life & human daily speech. No—*'ware* is almost impossible by any sound contemporary canon, although I hesitate in giving any strong piece of advice single-handed. Ask others about it. I would advise the line "Yet Life *well knows* he shall not be." In the same stanza I'd advise eliminating the artificial word *darksome* also. I ought to have suggested this before—pardon the omission. Better say *night-black* enemy—or anything direct & belonging to a living vocabulary.

Death—You can safely keep the line "Eh, but his quarry's fair."

¶ "As leans he" is pretty bad from a contemporary standpoint & one ought not to think of using such a distortion in writing a new poem. I would say "As he leans to—&c"[.] However, in a ballad whose general form has archaic roots, some latitude is perhaps allowable. Minor inversions are sometimes tacitly tolerated, hence I suppose this major one might "get by." The *cadence* in this line is better in your version, so perhaps you might let it be; although if there were plenty of time I'd advise searching for a fresh version with equally good cadence yet without the awkward inversion. I think though, that it would be better to sacrifice cadence in the interest for powerful & simple diction—hence I advise "*As *he leans to* &c" as a hastily revised version. Inversions & artificialities drain the poetic power out of a piece of verse quicker than anything else I know. It is the primary step in a good technical training to shed all allegiance to such tawdry external embellishments, & to form a state of mind which automatically revolts from them & rejects them. It must be the job of the earlier 20th century to repair the harm done by the middle 19th.

¶ *Did probe* is so extreme as to be almost automatically ruled out—the question is not so much *whether* to get rid of it as *how* to get rid of it. ". . . *shall probe* . . . . *spoil* . . . ." is the best alternative I can think of just now, although time & reflection would probably yield better. The real time to avoid these pitfalls is *before the poem is written*—so that of course the problem of revising them is rather perplexing. The most important thing is to get the mind out of the habit of depending on such devices in the first place. It is not so important to weed out the artificialities in older material as to avoid incorporating such things in future work.

¶ In the next stanza discussed, I ought to have advised you to eliminate the artificial device *"Yon angel dread"*. Say, instead,

"the dreaded angel smiles: these charms—"

In line 3, I prefer *his* to *those*.

¶ In the stanza after this—

"where	match	his	lonely
	mate	such	power"

I think *his* is in every way stronger, more direct, & more graphic than such. I would also prefer match to mate. remember that the real standard of vital, poignant language is resemblance to what would be used in current & emotionally sincere conversation.

¶ The expression "there *be*" is always less preferable than "there is". It is artificial & uncalled-for. In this line I would say

"Yet there *is* mightier than he,
One silent stern, & grand"

(About that *one* see other letter)

¶ *Wingèd* is tolerated more widely than most archaisms. No great harm in keeping it. You don't need to accent-mark the *e* of *lidded*, for it *couldn't* be pronounced any other way. The mark is used only to avoid ambiguity, as between *wingèd* & *wing'd*.

¶ "all secrets guess" will do.

Now as I said before—don't accept all my dicta as irrevocable pronouncements. Seek other opinions & collate them all. I simply state matters as *I* understand them; but in questions of taste like these there is considerable latitude, so that one person's opinion is a mere drop in the bucket—one vote in a general election! I certainly hope the poems will appear some day in a medium worthy of their excellence.

The cuttings are highly interesting. Smithson's story has always seemed rather dramatic to me. His half-brother Lord Percy is very favourably remembered in New England, for even when he played the part of military foe to the rebel colonists his conduct was marked by conspicuous gallantry & magnanimity. As for letter writing as a waning art—I suppose it is, although I belong to an older generation which adhered to it. Come to think of it, the young fellows are getting briefer & briefer as they mechanically click out their laconic phrases on staccato Remingtons & Coronas! But I shall never outlive the leisurely methods & standards of the 18th century. For me, periwig & goose-quill for ever!

Trusting that the foregoing notes may be of some assistance in your revisory task, I remain

Yr most obt Servt

H P Lovecraft

[12]   [ALS]

July 17[, 1929]

Dear Mifs Toldridge:—

Many thanks for the London newspaper extracts, which I read with the keenest interest. The King's recovery certainly occasioned one of the most impressive public demonstrations of modern times, & I hope that the recent additional operation will not entail any relapse of such seriousness as to make the rejoicing seem premature. The Times account is gracefully written, & the pictures cover the ground well.

I have not so far received the boorish letter (from *The Troubadour*, I infer), which you mention, but will leave this envelope unsealed until it comes—when I will return it with any comment it may call for. It is unfortunate that ordinary courtesy & consideration seem to be lacking from the psychology of the typical modernist, but this deficiency seems always to attend radical innovators & those involved in sweeping & spectacular repudiations of the past. There is no reason why it should, since courtesy is really not an empty decoration of traditional manners, but a practical application of the very principles of kindliness & good will which radicals might be expected to revere; but we generally find, in practice, that these radicals feel the traditional associations of the quality more acutely than they feel its basic essence, hence regard it with hostility & distrust & refuse to practice it. Later, if their system of things were ever established, they would probably regain their urbanity; for it is unsettledness & transition which chiefly breed the present lack. However—if I were you I wouldn't bother about the *Troubadour* matter one way or the other, since the discourtesy merely proves the editor's crudeness without affecting you in the least.

Regarding the points in the recent "Life & Death" revision—I think "*With* scrolls of bloom & bud" has a clearness & directness which "*In*" lacks, although both are equally acceptable as poetry. I'd say *"That* upper sea he would explore". In the case of a word to replace *darksome,* I think I'd say *lethal* rather than *deadly.* It has fewer commonplace associations without being any less plain & contemporary, & gives you a good alliterative effect with its context. In the next case I'd choose "He *bears* a golden lyre." And in the next one *"shall* probe" strikes me as adequate. About "The all of *joyance* & of woe"— whilst *joyance* is not quite so natural & idiomatic as *pleasure,* it surely is a highly melodious & prepossessing word, & might not be out of place in a ballad of this type. I think you may safely retain it if it appeals to you.

I trust your birthday festivities proved duly sparkling & congenial—permit me to join your guests in wishing you the traditional many happy returns! You had a delightful day for the occasion if Washington & Providence weather were parallel. I spent the whole afternoon in the woods & fields, whither I take my work in a leatherette case on all warm & sunny summer days.

With best of wishes, & hoping that the enclosed verse suggestions may prove useful,

I remain yr ob^{dt} h^{ble} Servt

H P Lovecraft

6 p.m. Same day—

Gray's letter to you has just arrived, & I really am astonished at the bald, insensitive rudeness of its tone. It certainly goes beyond even the average of modernistic bad manners! However, that need not disturb you. All the thing is, is a naive proof of its churlish writer's coarseness & underbreeding!

[13]   [ALS]

July 31, 1929

Dear Mifs Toldridge:—

Yrs. of the 25th & 29th duly arrived, & I am enclosing the revision-notes with such comment as I feel competent to give. I trust it may prove of some aid—though you must not fail to remember that it carries no authority beyond one person's opinion. The two new poems are delightful, & I feel greatly complimented by your suggestion that my stories may have inspired them. They are poignant & delicate & vivid, & so free from artificialities of language that I have no changes of text to suggest on that score. The only single detail I could possibly question, is the phrase *hither dwell* in l. 6 of "I Know A Forest." The word *hither* signifies *direction—motion toward* something rather than *position in or at* something—so that the conception of *'dwelling hither'* is very hard to form. I think you can very neatly cut the Gordian knot of the difficulty by saying *'herein* dwell' instead of *hither;* though of course you may have some apter alternative to supply.

As for a book of your poems—I have said several times before, I see no reason for hesitancy on your part whenever you find it possible to make the financial arrangements. You are surely aware, from the titles & authors advertised in the small poetry magazines, that no one thinks of waiting for a Shelleyan or Coleridgian afflatus before embarking between cloth covers. Books of poems in every way far inferior to yours issue from the presses every day—nor is there any reason to bemoan the fact, since any reasonably good poet deserves the comfort of seeing his best material in compact & permanent form for the benefit of his friends if he can afford it. It is needless to say that a judicious collection of your best work would form a highly pleasing & meritorious volume for which no excuses need be made. As for future work—in referring to it I surely had no intention of minimising that which you have already done! Moreover, you have no need to worry because you are not producing material at a swifter rate. Naturally one does not try to keep up a factory-like flow of uniform quantity-production, for sheer spontaneity is the essence of all superior work. It is perfectly natural—& wholly wise—to slow up just now & devote your time to the job of getting your previous work into definite shape—catching up & squaring things to date, as it were. Then, when your accumulated material is in a state reasonably satisfactory to you, you will find yourself once more turning out new material at your usual rate, in the same spontaneous way that you turned out the earlier pieces. There is certainly no reason for you to wish to do your work in a hurry—fortunately you are not a commercialised Edgar A. Guest, bound to grind out a verse a day for an inexorable syndicate! One ought not to want to write poems merely for the sake of having a large number on hand. The only raison d'etre for a poem is a necessity on the author's part to capture some mood or image in a certain way—& when that necessity comes, the poem is written irrespective of external circumstances. If it doesn't write itself in that way, there's no need of regretting that it doesn't exist—for of what use is a poem except to fulfil the poet's imaginative & emotional needs? Some of the best poets—Poe, Gray, Coleridge, Wilde, Collins—have produced a very slender amount of material, quantitatively reckoned.

As for the archaisms & inversions whose elimination I am advising—I really do not think you will miss them as much as you imagine. Certainly straightforward verse will soon come to *'feel like poetry'* to you; since the poetic essence is not a superficial thing of outward trappings, but a deeply-seated type of patterned & symbolic vision whose force is all the greater for simple & unbedizened formulation. So much more effective will you find this sincere way of writing, that in time it is the artificial & inverted sort of thing which you will consider ineffective & unpoetic. The revolt against artificiality of diction began very far back, but was slow in gaining headway. Wordsworth violently attacked the pseudo-classicism of 18th century verse, & made great headway against inversions. Indeed, despite the crop of new & still tawdrier affectations which Victorianism produced, we may still give the Victorian bards credit for improving on the Georgians in the one matter of *inversions*. In

a numerical count, it is clear that Tennyson, Browning, Arnold, Morris, Swinburne &c. assay far fewer inversions per 100 lines than Addison, Pope,
Young, Thomson, & Goldsmith. They undeniably came measurably *closer*—
though not very close, alas—to the living speech of cultivated people. Another thing you will notice is that the sheer *aesthetic instinct* of the greater Victorians saved them from the most excessive affectations of their period. Even
when artificialities were freely permitted, some inward prompting of sensitive
taste prevented bards of the *very first rank* from overindulging in them beyond
very moderate limits. To use a paradox, Tennyson was not half so Tennyson-
ian as his lesser imitators! All that one needs to do to prove this point is to
look over a volume of the really great Victorians—& then compare it with
the inferior magazine verse of the same period. Beside the orgy of rococo affectation in the *minor* material, even Rossetti or Kingsley or Whittier or Longfellow sounds highly "modern" & straightforward. This really proves that
inversion & artificiality form a *basic & intrinsic weakness*—since it shews that
really capable poets *naturally & unconsciously* react against such "licence" even
when it is a popular & universally sanctioned custom. Artificial "poetic diction" is a direct departure from that spontaneous reflection of real life & feeling which constitutes true poetry. Essentially, it doesn't mean anything. The
final revolt against artificiality seems to have begun in those chaotic & transitional 'nineties when all extremes met. Some of the bards—like Wilde &
Dowson—clung rather belatedly to the outworn languors of the hothouse
school, but Kipling was an immeasurably healthy influence in breaking the
spell. Gradually we see that serious poets begin to drop the affected archaisms & inversions almost instinctively—before any formal critical precepts on
the subject are formulated. Francis Thompson & A. E. Housman have very
few. As the 20th century gains headway, we find the practice of straightforward diction conscious & triumphant, so that virtually no major work since
1910 has had any dominant idiom other than that of natural & living conversation. Textbooks now begin to enunciate the precept, & teachers caution
their classes against the use of baroque phraseology—a very necessary action,
since of course the final change is of such recency that the bulk of the models
in any curriculum must necessarily belong to the ages of artificiality. You can
find an excellent summary of the whole thing in one of those convenient little
five-cent Haldeman-Julius Blue Books—No. 514—Clement Wood's "Hints
on Writing Poetry." I think that booklet would interest you—as would other
booklets of the series. You ought to send to the Haldeman-Julius Co., Girard,
Kansas, for a catalogue of their 5¢ publications. Incidentally—the revision job
I am doing now is on a splendid poetical handbook—a treatise on the appreciation of poetry—by a Wisconsin high-school teacher. You would undoubtedly enjoy it, & I shall probably be able to send you a complimentary copy
when it is published. I never saw a clearer & more graphic study of the es-

sence of poetry than this volume—which will be called "Doorways to Poetry." The author, M. W. Moe, is one of my old "amateur journalistic" circle.

I'm glad you found Dunsany of interest, & assure you that there's no hurry whatever about the return of the books. Dunsany is profoundly original & poignantly beautiful, & his cosmic perspective makes him especially fascinating to me. He influenced my writing profoundly in 1919 & 1920—perhaps impressing me more than any other one writer save Poe. Glad you found the Newport cards & descriptions of interest—I've been too desperately busy to make any explorations since then, although I manage to get out to the woods & fields with my work in my usual way. Thanks very much for the cuttings, all of which are of much interest. The only papers I see regularly are the Prov. Journal & Bulletin & N Y Times, so that aside from universally duplicated A.P. or syndicate matter, anything in Wash. or Balt. papers would be likely to be new to me. This Muscovite Aristeaus[1] is quite picturesque-looking—& I'm sure Sechrist must have heard of him. Sechrist, by the way, would probably make a good speaker for your Circle meetings. His poetry is only semi-modernistic—& is somewhat coloured by the Polynesian folklore which he greatly admires & of which he is a thorough student.

I don't agree with that defence of the Middle Ages, which seems based on a biassed & romanticised conception. Of course no one claims that all civilisation was dead, for Gothic architecture & many fine examples of handicraft remain as reliques of such culture as there was. But when we compare the general mentality & aesthetic feeling of the period with those of the periods preceding & following, we find a falling-off so vast that "barbarism" is none too harsh a term to describe it with. Such Latin as was spoken was a debased jargon. All learning & art—even all literary—had retired into the monasteries. All healthy & independent *thought* was extinct, even in the monasteries. The wreck was so complete that almost nothing of the past was preserved. In the 11th & 12th centuries Virgil was commonly thought to have been a mighty sorcerer! Had Europe been obliged to depend on herself for reviving influences, not enough would have survived to bring about the Renaissance. Fortunately the *Arabic* civilisation saved what we could not have—& it is from the Saracenic writers that we derived that renewed contact with Hellenism which gave the world a true civilisation once more.

The astronomical items are interesting. The solar system undoubtedly arose through a "near-collision" of stellar bodies which wrenched off the substance of the planets from one of them—& it is quite probable that an actual collision in the future will prove the end of it. As for the moon—the Fisher theory[2] is important, & surely suggests quaint possibilities to the fantastic writer. I shall file the item with my weird data.

I note the colonial house items, & am sorry that an old Alexandria mansion is to be moved away. Despoiling an ancient region of its houses is a regrettable procedure, for building & environment need to be together in order to produce a really authentic effect. Alexandria is exquisite just as it is—& fortunately, it will have plenty of Georgian buildings left even after the removal of this one. Another thing I hate is the dismantling of an old house to furnish panelling, mantels, &c. for other houses or museums. This practice is on the increase—I saw a sign indicating such material for sale on the finest brick house in Falmouth, just across the Rappahannock from Fredericksburg. Stratford, thank heaven, is safely assured of a suitable future. I must see it some time. Glad to note that Switzerland is learning to check vandalism. As to the prediction of a distinctive American architecture—I am still in doubt. The special forms necessitated by a few overgrown cities can hardly evolve into general national types. Anyway, the architectural expression of a uselessly speeded-up age of aimless commerce & machinery can hardly contain any beauty comparable to that of older architectures.

With best wishes, & hoping that the enclosed comments may be helpful,
    I remain
          Yr most obt Servt
              H P Lovecraft

Notes

1. Aristaeus was the Greek god of bee-keeping and cheese-making. The Russian apiarist is unknown.
2. Ormond Fisher (1817–1914), a British geologist and geophysicist, conjectured that the Pacific Ocean was the formed when the moon broke off from the earth. HPL refers to this theory in *At the Mountains of Madness* (MM 66). The theory is no longer accepted.

[14]   [ANS postcard][1]

                        [Postmarked Providence, RI,
                               11 August 1929]

I learn with regret in a note from Mifs Radcliffe that you have been suffering somewhat with the prevailing warm weather. Here is a view which ought to serve as a sort of counteractive—but which I trust finds you already much improved. Don't take the strength to reply to my recent letter until you are thoroughly recovered, for there's nothing like rest in shaking off an indisposition. ¶ This Fairbanks house—which I saw last week—is the oldest building in New England & the oldest frame edifice of English construction in North America. Built in 1636, the year Providence was founded, it is still in good shape & open as a museum. The interior as quaint & fascinating as the exterior—rambling, shadowy, & full of reminders of vanished days. I also visited the Red Horse Tavern in Sudbury—built in 1686 & famous as Longfellow's 'Wayside Inn.' I had never seen either of these places before, notwithstanding their relative nearness to Providence. Later this week I may spend a few days on Cape Cod with my young poet-friend Frank Belknap Long, Jr. Meanwhile

I trust Washington will have cooler weather, & that you will soon be fully back to usual health. ¶ With best wishes, Yr obt Servt H P Lovecraft

Notes

1. *Front:* Fairbanks House, Dedham, Mass. Built 1636.

[15]   [ALS]

Onset, Cape Cod,
Aug. 14, 1929

Dear Mifs Toldridge:—

Your letter with enclosures arrived just as I was leaving the house for my Cape Cod trip, hence I am enabled to reply amidst the comparative leisure of "hookey-playing" from the piled-up revision work at home. I met young Long & his parents in ancient New Bedford, & we all did that quaint old port rather fully. The waterfront streets are still ineffably quaint despite the decline of the whaling industry, & the little Seaman's Bethel on Johnnycake Hill described in Melville's "Moby Dick"[1] is absolutely unchanged in every particular. Of chief interest, perhaps, is the great whaling museum with its vast rotunda containing a perfect copy of an old-time New Bedford whaler—an absolute fac-simile in every respect save reduced size, & open for the inspection of visitors. Nothing has ever given me so perfect a glimpse of old-Yankee maritime colour as this unusual exhibit—though there is a *real* whaling ship open as a museum some distance from New Bedford; a thing I must see some time. From New Bedford we came north through the very picturesque old seaport villages of Mattapoisett, Marion, & Wareham, & are now stopping at Onset, at the base of Cape Cod. With this as a base we hope to explore most of the Cape's scenic & antiquarian regions in the Long motor. Then Providence—where I speed my hosts upon their New-Yorkward way. It bids fair to be a phenomenally pleasant outing.

I was glad to learn from your letter that your indisposition is now a thing of the past—& trust your culinary providers will be more cautious about ingredients in future! You will doubtless welcome cooler weather, too.

Your new poems are all delightful, & I perused the three with a genuinely acute interest & pleasure. Not one but would appear to advantage in a book. The "Laocoön" one appealed to me tremendously, & I can easily & poignantly visualise the scene on which it is based. I think the extra syllables—*as of, as if* will do very well as they are. "Long Years" is splendid. You *might* say "Twinkling bright bubbles", justifying your usage by some vague word-association principle, but I think you were wise not to do so. What you have is excellent. Also—the *upon-dawn* rhyming is justified by good precedent. In line 6 I cannot decipher anything before the word *morning*—an erasure without replacement evidently having been made. "A Failure" is excellent. I think it is well to say *bravely* rather than *grandly* in the final line. You have reason to congratulate yourself on these recent poems—they surely augur well for your future work. Don't unduly depreciate what you write. Work like yours represents a degree of insight & craftsmanship needing no apology. And there is no reason at all for your not signing the prospective volume with your own name. Just go ahead & write to please yourself in the manner which best pleases you & which is most characteristic of you. Don't bother to worry about whether the result is good or not, or what anybody thinks of it, or whether anybody sees or reads it. Write for self-expression only, & let the rest take care of itself. View the whole matter coolly & impersonally—casually & indifferently. Excessive humility is as futile as egotism.

Moe's "Doorways to Poetry" is surely going to be a good thing, & I shall see that you receive a copy. He puts his finger more exactly on the difference between true & false poetry than I ever saw anyone else do.

Take all the time you wish with Dunsany. As for his influence on me—of course I had the same general cosmic attitude before, for that is why his discovery was such an event to me. But I couldn't even begin to formulate my attitude in artistic prose till I had him to follow as a model. "Polaris" represents my closest approach to the Dunsanian style before I knew of Dunsany. As you say, Dunsany is unlikely to appeal to more than a narrow special circle; hence he will always be regarded as a minor writer by general literary critics. To those who share his mood, however, he will always bulk very importantly.

No—I haven't written anything lately, since revisory work has left me with no time. Whenever the pressure does abate, I am so fatigued that I feel less like writing than getting out to the woods & field & ancient places. Hence my present carefree jaunt! By autumn or winter I hope to get around to some writing. Incidentally, the anthology with my "Call of Cthulhu" is out. It is called "Beware After Dark" & is issued by the Macaulay Co. I shall also have a tale—"Pickman's Model"—reprinted in the new British anthology of weird tales published by Hutchinson & Co., London.

The cuttings you enclosed are all of interest. I did not realise that Villiers de l'Isle Adam, whose tales I admire exceedingly & who is a kind of idol to many of "the gang", had any kind of connexion with Thomas A. Edison![2] The primitive Cro-Magnon pictures on the cave walls of France & northern Spain are indeed remarkable, & shew a grade of artistic development far beyond what the savage or pastoral mode of life of the creators would lead us to expect. It is this race which met & combated the repulsive "Neanderthal" race of semi-humans & won Europe finally for the highly developed human species to which we belong. I have read some of John Buchan's books, & find them indeed lively & interesting, though not accurate in antiquarian colour or realistic in psychology & motivation. Of those I have seen, I prefer "Witch Wood". As for the Rev. Eleazar Williams' claim to be the lost Dauphin—there is really nothing to it, any more than there is to the similar claim of the Russian Naundorff,[3] whose descendants still live in Paris. In the excitement of the French royalist restoration of 1815 the tale of the unfortunate child was so widely circulated & popularised that almost any man of unknown parentage & of an age like the Dauphin's either honestly believed or pretended that he was indeed the tragically vanished boy grown up. The archaic Swedish fort is indeed interesting, insomuch as we have very little data on the life & customs of the northern races during the Roman imperial period. Nor is the later Scandinavian fortress of Elsinore without keen interest. This rocket business is certainly highly important, & ought to lead to striking atmospheric discoveries even if it never makes connexions with the moon.

Aug. 16

My Cape Cod sojourn is turning out to be wholly delightful. Wednesday we made a circuit of the lower arm of the cape; taking in Sandwich, Barnstable, Yarmouth, Orleans, Chatham, & Hyannis, & seeing many ancient dwellings & windmills. Of all the towns, Sandwich is the most fascinating—with its old white steeple, colonial houses, spreading common, old mill & brook, & general air of well-preserved survival. Yesterday we went to Woods' Hole & explored the U.S. govt. marine museum. Tomorrow we shall edge toward Providence—where, alas, the Longs can stop but briefly.

With all good wishes, & hoping that your delightful new verses may achieve worthy publication, I remain

Yr most obt Servt

H P Lovecraft

Notes

1. In Chapter 6 (The Sermon).
2. Jean-Marie-Mathias-Philippe-Auguste, comte de Villiers de l'Isle-Adam (1838–1889), French Symbolist writer known for his *contes cruels*, wrote the science fiction novel *L'Ève future* (1886; tr. as *The Future Eve;* also as *Tomorrow's Eve* and *The Eve of the Future*), which popularized the term *android*. Edison is the fictional main character.
3. Karl Wilhelm Naundorff (1785?–1845), a German clock- and watch-maker, who claimed to be Prince Louis-Charles, or Louis XVII of France.

[16]   [ALS]

[c. late August 1929]

Dear Mifs Toldridge:—

Back from Onset into a devastating whirl of work—including a speeding-up of the Moe poetry book. I enclose a typical section to shew you what is like—& will see that you get the whole book when it's published.

Glad Dedham was of interest to you. Very shortly I'll send you a carbon of a "travelogue" I wrote about that trip.[1] The Onset excursion ended up with a sort of climax—my first aëroplane ride. Quite an exhilarating experience, which I want to repeat. In a hydro-aëroplane, which ascended high over the head of Buzzard's Bay & gave one a sense of cosmic independence from the map-like world & blue & green beauty outspread below. Very little sensation of *motion,* merely an impression of *wind.*

Found anthology "Beware After Dark" awaiting me on return. Very prepossessing. I am in good company, with E. F. Benson, Arthur Machen, Hawthorne, Lafcadio Hearn, Ellen Glasgow, Irwin S. Cobb, Robert Louis Stevenson, &c. among others represented. My story in there is "The Call of Cthulhu."

Pardon disjointed note form of ensuing comment, but thought you'd like to have these points touched upon before I have time to pen an actual epistle. Am in a desperate race against time to get that poetry book done, & don't know when I'll get to the surface!

Decent weather since Monday's rain—hope to get out in the open this afternoon with such of my work as is portable.

Best wishes—

Yr most obt Servt

H P Lovecraft

Notes

Laocoön of Wood

1st line sestette

Probably original "He stood at bay" is more powerful, yet there does remain an undeniable obscurity for the less discerning reader. After all, I imagine your final compromise-line is best—

He stood at bay with saplings he had bred

—for the word *saplings* provides the needed key without impairing the dramatic effect.

Poem would be stronger, by the way, if in l. 7 *hath* were changed to *has.*

Subject-Matter of Poetry

Forms of visible beauty, dramatic change & contrast, wonder, mystery—anything of the sort is suitable. Never worry about material, but simply write what asks to be written. Never take art seriously—it ceases to be art when one does. Poetry is by nature simply an elegant amusement. When, by chance, it strikes a high level of art, all well & good—but it doesn't hurt anybody if it doesn't. Nothing in existence is important enough to merit anxiety. A large number of your poems are good enough for book publication—don't be so particular about confining such publication to the two or three *very* best. There is always some difference of individual opinion about exact quality anyway.

Long Long Yrs.
I don't think the 2 *ings* conflict. I prefer *wondering* to *listening.*

Mood of Verses
Never lack confidence in your own "vagaries"—for *all* poetry comes from the spontaneous "vagaries" of the poet. Set purpose & intentional choice of mood are fatal to art. At the same time, don't get the idea that your early material isn't of adequate quality. It is indeed very fine—for no matter what your *theories* were, a large proportion of your products undoubtedly arose from spontaneous mood. Avoid self-consciousness—try not to think about the writing process or your status in art. Forget about everything except the pleasure of celebrating beauty for its own sake. The quality of your work will take care of itself.

Beauty—
A very fine poem. I don't see anything to change in it.

Cuttings—
Shocked to hear of death of Scott—just as I was reading admiring reviews of his second series of Boswell papers.[2] ¶ China is a great garden country. I have always had curious dreams of Chinese gardens, derived from a picture seen in infancy. ¶ Century had to go[3]—too many high-grade monthlies. Atlantic is getting soft. Scribners affected. Harpers holds the serious lead.

Joint Publication
I don't think it's well for two bards to write in one book unless both have a strong community of theme & mood. In other words, each poet's expression is a highly individualised thing, & ought to be kept distinctive. One might say that joint publication is not advisable unless the resultant book can reflect a single mood stronger than the individuality of either of the poets who present it. But don't get the idea that your poetry is inferior to Miss Radcliff's, or that you ought to cultivate "thought." "Thought" is not the proper subject-matter for poetry—which ought to deal wholly in *moods* & *imagery.* Save *thought* for prose essays & treatises.

Books—
I've no idea when Cook will find & distribute my thin, short story "The Shunned House." He is frightfully busy. It's all printed, & has been for over a year, but I'm in no hurry. As for a collection of my junk—such has often

been broached, but has never eventuated, & I don't care greatly whether it ever does or not. A book of sketches by you might have great appeal if you would eschew artificial conceptions of life & emotion & work with the real, stern, prosaic material of human psychology & motivation.

Notes

1. "An Account of a Trip to the Antient Fairbanks House . . ."
2. Geoffrey Scott (1884–1929), British scholar and poet, had been retained as an editor of the papers of James Boswell. He died on 14 August of pneumonia.
3. HPL refers to the *Century Magazine* (1870f.), which ceased as a monthly with the issue of August 1929. It continued as a quarterly until Spring 1930. The other magazines referred to are the *Atlantic Monthly*, *Scribner's*, and *Harper's*.

[17]   [ALS]¹

Septr. 3[, 1929]

Dear Mifs Toldridge:—

I had to solve the congestion problem by telling my textbook client that I simply *couldn't* deliver on the designated date, & offering him a choice between delay & non-performance. He chose delay, & was quite amiable about it—so I have managed to create a sort of artificial & temporary breathing spell. The book, though, will surely have to be in shape by the end of September. It will form about the best analysis of what is & what isn't poetry that has ever appeared in print—& I can truly say that it has proved the most satisfactory & agreeable revision job I have ever tackled on a professional basis. The section you saw is a fair sample of the text—yet an even more valuable feature is the unique battery of tests & specimens, whereby the student is given concrete glimpses of verse (& prose as well) of different degrees of excellence, & taught to select the best, with an intelligent knowledge of *why* he selects it. You will be interested in the section where Moe treats of the old-time artificialities, archaisms, & inversions. He is very clear & helpful on that theme, & means to include a good-sized array of selections shewing the artificial affectations of the past as contrasted with the straightforward diction of the present.

About the nature of poetry—I surely did not mean to belittle it by calling it 'simply an elegant amusement', because I believe that nothing in existence is more important than elegant amusement. What I wished to recommend was that you beware against making a *burden* of the art; for if you do that, you make it fail of its purpose, which is to amuse the creator. I wished to make it clear that the fun & function of poetry are all comprised within the process of creating it, & that it is needless & unwise to worry about what happens to it once it is written. Its importance resides in the pleasure it gives you during the writing—the mental & emotional satisfaction of self-expression. Once it has given you this, it has fully & adequately performed its function; & there is no need to bother about who else sees it—although it is of course pleasant to have others see one's work, so that there can be criticism & helpful discussion about it. And as I say, this does not imply any triviality on the part of the art; for is not emotional satisfaction the only supreme goal of any intelligent life? The cosmos contains nothing of greater importance for the negligible atoms called human beings than the condition of being elegantly amused. It is only mental laziness & artificial convention which can lead us to measure "accomplishment" by the approval of others. All these things mean nothing. The very idea of "accomplishment" is basically an artificiality & an illusion. However, if we need a set of empirical working-standards—protective illusions, as it were— we can very logically say that *the satisfaction of our own emotions* is the one solid thing which we can ever get out of life; the only thing we have any rational right to call "success" or "accomplishment" in a quasi-absolute sense. Each thinking person is really a solitary entity facing the formless & illimitable cosmos. None of the other entities really count except as minor decorative factors. Naturally "success" & "accomplishment" cannot be the same for any two persons, since each individual has a distinct set of emotional needs wholly peculiar to himself. The only constant & homogeneous element behind the verbal abstractions is that of *emotional equilibrium*—a subjective state of satisfaction. If we can attain this, we have "success" & "accomplishment"— but it doesn't matter how we do it so long as we attain it somehow, & each person's particular "success" is a different objective entity or condition from any other person's "success." Certainly, life can have no greater gift than emotional contentment during the aimless years from nothingness to nothingness again! However—this is not to imply that the business of acquiring contentment is an easy or frivolous matter. Only the psychology of Victorian illusion & hypocrisy tries to invest trivial & meaningless things with the insipid glamour of a pretended jollity & happiness. In stern fact, the restless demands prompted by our glandular & nervous reactions are exceedingly complex, contradictory, & imperious in their nature; & subject to rigid & intricate laws of psychology, physiology, biochemistry, & physics which must be realistically studied & familiarly known before they can be adequately dealt with. So real & fixed is this state of things, that we may easily see how futile it is to expect anything to produce emotional satisfaction—or to pretend that it does—unless all the *genuine* laws of emotion & nerve-reaction are recognised & complied with. False or insincere amusement is the sort of activity which does not meet the real psychological demands of the human glandular-nervous system, but merely affects to do so. Real amusement is the sort which is based on a knowledge of real needs, & which therefore hits the spot. *This latter kind of amusement is what art is*—& there is nothing more important in the universe. You may clearly see that there can be no frivolity in this element, because it implies a close knowledge of real psychological demands, & a strict adherence to them. As soon as the artistic expression diverges from the sphere of natural demand, it becomes trivial, insincere, & artificial—ceasing in fact to be artistic at all. This means exactly the same thing that you mean when, using the older conventional terminology, you speak of art as "the very language of the soul". What used to be called the "soul" in the days of religious myth, is in fact simply the fixed sum total of human instincts & emotions, as motivated & directed by sense-impressions, gland-secretions, & nerve-reactions. Art is, surely enough, the one authentic language of this sharply-patterned, exacting, & complex congeries of natural processes; & as such is as serious as anything else in life. But life itself is not very serious—not even worth counting in a general survey of the cosmos—so we must not make ourselves ridiculous by imputing too grave an importance to anything we do or feel. And as I have said, the fact that art is the natural language of the "soul" or sense-gland-nerve system, does not by any means imply that it depends for its effectiveness upon an audience. It is a serious matter as such things go—but its only true province is to satisfy its producer's emotions. And when its producer takes it too seriously, he defeats its purpose by annulling its possible satisfying effect through a fresh load of worry! As for art's relation to "prophecy & truth"—not much can be said for that. Truth is something which can't be got at except by a slow piecing-together of data, little by little, through the gradual, cautious operation of those rigid cognitive processes whereby we know that two & four are different things, & that black & white are not the same. Any other use of the word is elliptical, figurative, relative, or emptily meaningless—though we often employ it to express the real conformity of a work of art to the emotions it is designed to satisfy. This "truth to the emotions" of a work of art of course has nothing to do with the actual, absolute *truth* as a delineator of what is or isn't so in the domain of reality. What it is "true" to is merely the emotional demands of the average sense-gland-nerve system of average people—& these demands have no relation to the absolute facts of the universe. A work of art must be "true" to human feeling, but it need not be at all *true* to actual objective fact. This sounds like ambiguity until we stop to consider that we use the word "*true*" to express two antipodally different things—a circumstance which leads me to condemn the use of the word except in its literal sense of objective, scientific reality. "Prophecy" is the business of the scientist & philosophic historian—not of the poet. All the poet can do is to guess, absorb other people's conclusions, & set forth his feelings in symbolic form. Naturally he is quick to absorb impressions—the quality that makes him a poet gives him this facility—& sensitive in his reaction to them; so that when he sets them forth symbolically he is usually reflecting a section of current opinion in a more than commonly graphic & poignant way. This makes his voice more clearly audible than the average, & gains him the reputation of "prophet" when he happens to touch upon the territory generally covered by the conception of "prophecy". But there is no exactitude, authority, or close cerebration in what he "prophesies"—& he is in truth more often wrong than right, since he is always led by unreliable sympathies & caprices rather than by coolly intelligent analysis of the events concerned, & a calmly rational estimate of the probable result of their interaction. It is never the glowing bard, but always the steel-cold man of intelligence, who gets closest to the *truth*—the question of *what is & what isn't*—& has the best chance of constructing a sound forecast of what will be. Poetry & art for *beauty*—but science & philosophy for *truth*. It was a glowing, misty-minded young poet, & not a sober man of analytical intellect, who muddled matters by fastening a false linkage of truth & beauty upon the popular consciousness![2] However—this isn't to say that poets & artists are less important than men of science, for in hard fact we must admit that *truth* is nothing of any intrinsic importance. It doesn't actually matter a hang whether we know anything about anything or not, so long as we can be contented. If we can happily do it, we might just as well believe in Santa-Claus, God, a green-cheese moon, fairies, witches, good & evil, unicorns, ghosts, immortality, the Arabian Nights, a flat earth, &c. &c., as learn the real facts about the universe & its streams & patterns of eternal & alternately evolving & devolving energy. Truth becomes important *only when it is necessary to establish our emotional satisfaction.* Emotional satisfaction is the one big thing; & the greatest person is the one who can create the thing most emotionally satisfying, whether or not it has any relation to truth or prophecy. On the whole, I think that beauty is more often satisfying than truth; so that the poet & artist are really somewhat ahead of the scientist & philosopher as factors in a sound & exquisite culture. It is certain that the human personality never attained a greater height of satisfying realisation than in the age of Pericles—yet we know that Periclean Athens was in many respects childishly naive & ignorant in its conception of the universe. The present age, though, has its natural emotional demand for truth very keenly developed; so that no classic parallel will work very exactly. Successful emotional adjustment or equilibrium today undoubtedly requires a far greater proportion of realistic fact-comprehension than an equally successful adjustment in the Hellas of 400 B.C.—or even in our own mutable civilisation a generation or two ago. This does not imply any especial *advance,* but merely a *change.* We can't regulate our emotional demands, & there is no reason to prefer any one set to any other. All we can do is to note their slow, automatic, deterministic change, & to meet them as best we may in the art-forms & folkways of each new generation. There is nothing more to life than that.

Art, then, is really very important—perhaps the most all-inclusive & important single element in life—though it abrogates its function & ceases to be art as soon as it becomes self-conscious, puffed with illusions of *cosmic* significance, (as distinguished from local, human, emotional significance) or burdened with ulterior considerations & worries based on its possible reception by the world & its effect on its creator's position. There is an old epigram which defines a gentleman as 'a man who doesn't give a damn whether he's a gentleman or not'—& I would extend its principle to other arts than that of living, by averring that an artist is one who doesn't give a damn whether he is creating art or not, but who succeeds through not trying to succeed; who aims simply to express himself, & only incidentally finds himself creating real beauty. We may describe the successful aesthete in a very free paraphrase of Waller—

"He sought content, & fill'd his arms with bays."[3]

Certainly, all true poetry comes out of experience & emotion; for we cannot have an authentic urge for expression unless we have really lived or felt what we want to say. This does not mean that every poem must describe some specific objective incident in our history, but merely that it must adhere to territory with which we are sufficiently familiar to harbour *really profound & poignant* feelings concerning it.

Your sonnet, "The Surgeon", is a very fine piece of work—I am reën-closing it, together with the other requested comment. You have no need to fear for the quality of your work—just keep on writing what you feel like writing, in the way you want to write it, & you will continue to produce a body of work with very high genuine poetic content. Just keep what you write in good, legible shape, & you can feel assured of having the goods safely ready whenever a book-publishing opportunity comes along. I am glad Mifs Radcliffe has found my occasional comments helpful, & would be glad to give other items of hers a gradual survey & comment if she isn't in any hurry about them. So Washington has some new poetry magazines! Of course, these semi-amateur ventures are necessarily uneven, but if I were you I wouldn't condemn them all without a hearing. They are liable to include something very good now & then—& I think there's a great deal to this young fellow John Lee Higgins. Amusingly enough, I came very close to serving as *temporary editor* of one of these small ventures last month. The *Am. Poetry Mag.*, published in Wauwautosa,[*sic*] Wis., was in heavy arrears to its printer; & he had a plan for seizing it by legal attachment & running it himself until the editor (one Clara Catherine Prince Homan) settled up. In this case, he wanted me to act as editor during his tenure. I half-agreed, though really dreading the task in view of the Moe work—but I haven't heard anything of it since. Presumably Mrs. Homan "came across" with the $900.00 when faced with the actual imminence of a court seizure for debt.

The cuttings you enclosed are indeed highly interesting—especially the one relating to southwestern Indian poetry. The poetic fancy & myth-making genius of the red man is of course nothing new to any student of his legendry; but these lyrics surely approach more closely to the standard European idea of poetry than anything else I ever beheld. They hold an almost Dunsanian sense of phantasy—with the added advantage that their naivete is actual & not assumed. Young races & nations usually produce the soundest &

most vital art. The great vigour & merit of all Indian art-remains, produced at a very early stage of social evolution, proves that the race had very great aesthetic potentialities which might have flowered strangely & marvellously had not its cultural progress been cut abruptly short by European conquest. Had no white men come to America, there is little doubt but that the civilisations of Peru & Mexico would eventually have spread throughout the two continents; taking different forms among different tribes, & developing into a series of great cultures as powerful & as utterly distinctive as those of Egypt, the Tigris-Euphrates valley, Crete, India, or China. There would have been something quasi-Oriental about it, since the Indians are Mongoloids with instincts modelled on the Eastern rather than the European Aryan plan. I shall send the cutting on to others of "the gang."

The brief paragraph on August reminds me of my one recent outing—taken when I temporarily cut the Gordian knot of my work-congestion problem. It was a trip to the exquisite & unspoiled countryside of Western Rhode Island, where all my maternal ancestors immediately came from; & involved a sight of some of the loveliest pastoral scenes the imagination can depict. As you are aware, I am more responsive to peaceful rural landscapes than to any other form of beauty; so you can well imagine the delightfulness of the excursion. My specific purpose was to look up some old family homesteads & burying grounds, for I have a wish to include the *epitaphs* of all my ancestors in my genealogical records. As usual, I wrote up my expedition in travelogue form for my young poet-"grandchild" Frank B. Long Jr.—& I think I'll enclose a carbon of it for you to read—asking that you ultimately (tho' in no haste) return it. Since it alludes so often to a former travelogue of 3 yrs. ago, I guess I'll enclose a carbon of that also; making one two-chapter narrative of the whole business.[4] I mean to make more of these rural-ancestral expeditions; eventually covering all the New-England areas represented in my maternal heredity.

With best wishes for all your work & interests, I remain

Yr most ob^t Servt

H P Lovecraft

Notes

1. The letter was published in part as "Poetry and the Artistic Ideal."
2. HPL refers to Keats's celebrated statement "Beauty is truth, truth beauty—that is all / Ye know on earth, and all ye need to know" ("Ode on a Grecian Urn," ll. 49–50).
3. Edmund Waller (1606–1687), "The Story of Phœbus and Daphne, Applied": "Like Phœbus thus, acquiring unsought praise, / He [Thyrsis] catch'd at love, and fill'd his arm with bays" (ll. 19–20).
4. The travelogue of 1926 is published in *Letters to James F. Morton,* pp. 94–108. Regarding the more recent trip, see *SL* 3.15–20.

[18]   [ALS]

10 Barnes St.,

Providence, R.I.,

Septr. 16, 1929.

Dear Mifs Toldridge:—

I read with interest yours of the 9th, with enclosures, & must congratulate you on the charm & excellence of "Ships", which seems to me full of a quiet, dreamlike beauty not unmixed with wonder. When I began reading it I was all ready to advise the deletion of the much-used phrase *"thing of beauty"*, but upon continuing I saw that this is balanced by several later phrases of parallel cast—*"thing of dream"*, *"thing of wonder"*, &c—hence rescinded my provisional verdict & decided that the parallelism makes the first phrase admissible—by the same psychological principle which allows any trite phrase a place, if it be used as a *text* around which to weave a new & original fabric. Again let me congratulate you upon a highly successful sonnet.

Your revision of "New York" is all, I am sure, in the direction of improvement. I am wondering, though, whether *peeping towers* did not convey an image of *brooding curiousness*—a curiousness almost malign, & hinting at a half-sentience on the part of the steel-&-concrete monsters—which scarcely resides in the idea of *watch-towers?* The truth probably is, that the poet *did not intend* such an image—her attitude toward the metropolis being favourable—hence your emendation was quite in order. But to me, with my unfavourable attitude toward Manhattan, the peeping tower image seemed very apt & graphic. Poetry must avoid the quality of unctuousness or saccharinity in the interest of specific power & genuine vitality.

The books safely arrived, & I am glad you found them of interest. If any of the other volumes I have mentioned from time to time sound interesting, pray let me know, & I shall be glad to send them along for an indefinite period. I regret that I don't own the other Roman novel by Edward Lucas White—"The Unwilling Vestal." Some time soon, if it would be of any interest, I will send a volume which will interest you more *as a publication* than as a work of art—namely, the finest product ever struck off by Cook's Recluse Press. It is the poetry of a deceased amateur poet—the late John Ravenor Bullen of Canada, a member of the "amateur journalism" circle whose verses I posthumously arranged & edited at the request of his family. The poems are occasionally pretty, but generally tame & Victorian & emotionally unoriginal; so that in writing a preface I had to fall back on friendly memory more than on authentic enthusiasm as a stimulus—for Bullen was an admirable person. The book was financed by a wealthy friend of Bullen's in Chicago, hence the typographical lavishness. The copy I shall send—if you wish it—need not be returned, since I have almost a dozen extras.

Glad the travelogue to "Little Belknap" proved of interest. I am so overwhelmed with things to do just now that I don't know whether I can take that third trip to the Foster country this autumn. No—the Tyler in my line is not of Virginian derivation; in fact, there are virtually no southern streams entering the older Rhode Island stock—or so few that they form notable exceptions like the case of the John Carter which I cited some weeks ago. That is rather a source of regret to me, since my esteem for the Southern civilisation is exceedingly high. The Foster Tylers came from the Mafsachusetts-Bay about 1720.

Your choice of "Winnings" as a book-title is really a stroke of genius! It is tremendously apt & original, & has precisely the sort of piquant distinctiveness which a book-title ought to have. I could never have thought of so vivid a caption in a whole lifetime of cogitation; since I belong, mentally, to the period when "Poems, on feveral Occafions" was the characteristic heading for a versifier's collected works! The title-page or introductory quatrain is extremely good & suitable, & I am sure the collection will be a splendidly tasteful item when it eventually appears.[1]

The cuttings you enclosed are all interesting. That Roman coin in the Indian grave could be used fictionally to sustain a notion on which I've have been ruminating for years—a forgotten colony of Rome on American soil, including a city of Roman architecture with temple-crowned citadel, columned forum, & marble arenas & baths. I would have it come in conflict with the representatives of some native civilisation—Maya, Aztec, &c—& perhaps suffer extirpation in a desperate battle, or sink amidst an earthquake. The Malaysian temple item also has fictional possibilities—for a story could connect it with the unknown & primordial Pacific-island culture whose Cyclopean masonry & colossi are found in places like Ponape, in the Carolines, or Easter Island. I suppose you have seen the Easter Island images in the National Museum of your city—the only specimens in the United States. They formed a high spot of my last spring's visit, for I had never seen them before. Few objects are so imaginatively provocative.

Had a call from one of "the gang" a week ago yesterday, when George Kirk & his wife passed through Providence on the last lap of a long New England motor tour. I took him to the ancient & unchanged fishing village of Pawtuxet, down the bay. Very shortly I may have another & longer-term visitor in the person of one of the "gang's" youngest members—Donald Wandrei of St. Paul, Minn., who turned 21 this summer. He has been working for a year in the advertising dept. of Dutton's in New York—& receiving very good remuneration for one of his age & inexperience—but the unimaginative cheapness of commercialism so preyed on his nerves that he has just resigned in disgust, & resolved to turn back to his own natural field of weird poetry & prose fantasy, even though he starve in the process. He has just begun what he calls 'a novel of age-old horror',[2] & wants a quiet environment to develop it in—hence his idea of visiting Providence for a time, & taking an attic room in this house, as he did during the summer of 1927. I shall be very glad indeed to have him here, if he so decides, for he is one of the most pleasing & bright of all my "adopted grandsons"! ¶ With best wishes—

Yr most obt Servt

H P Lovecraft

P.S. When you read that second travelogue, written from memory, take into account the following errata according to data I have since looked at. (a) James Phillips Sr. died *1746,* not 1753. (b) Michael Phillips died *1686,* not 1689. (c) seat of Norfolk Phillipses is *not* Raymond (an error started by Cotton Mather in the Magnalia) but Rainham St. Martin's, in the hundred of Gallow.

Notes

1. For the apparent contents, see Appendix. The ms. held at the New York Public Library is untitled, though Toldridge refers to it as *Winnings* in her letters to Knopf. It comprises various individual poems (i.e., the typescript is not numbered through).
2. Initially titled *Dead Titans, Waken!,* it was first published as *The Web of Easter Island.*

[19]   [ALS]

10 Barnes St.,

Providence, R.I.,

Octr. 1, 1929.

Dear Mifs Toldridge:—

I was glad to hear that the Foster travelogue did not prove boresome. It would be rather pleasant to write a longer thing of the kind, as you suggest—a sort of family history, with plenty of local atmosphere & folklore—although most readers would be likely to find it a bit tame. Life in old Rhode Island lacked the scale, spaciousness, & diversification of the corresponding phases of British life, since the exigencies of pioneering toned it down to a sort of tranquil Arcadian simplicity. Still—that is the stuff idylls are made of!

As for more stories of mine—I rather feared that too extensive doses of my macabre subject-matter might be a bit strong for your taste, but here goes with one more instalment of three. These are all rather early specimens, & possess extravagances & crudities which I hope are absent from my later stuff. "The Lurking Fear" is the poorest technically, because it was written *to order* for a cheap magazine (the enclosed W.T. version being a reprint) which laid down laws of quantitative proportioning & sub-climaxes that took all the spontaneity away. Indeed, it was my disgust at the mechanical nature of this piece which made me swear off the practice of writing to order. "The Statement of Randolph Carter" is an almost literal transcription (plus a slight framework to give raison d'etre), of an actual dream which I had on the night of Dec. 29, 1919. In the dream I was "Randolph Carter", while the poet

Samuel Loveman played the part of the story's "Harley Warren". In that final sentence substitute the name "Loveman" for "Warren", & you will have the exact words which were ringing in my ears as I started awake from the nightmare. I wrote the dream out the next day in a letter to Maurice W. Moe, (the chap for whom I'm now revising the poetry book) & he has always insisted that my rough account to him was better than the finished story as here given. I have my doubts about that, though.[1]

The cuttings you enclosed are all of interest. I am glad to know that Arlington will be restored, since it has always been an object of my admiration. I went through it—or as much of it as was publicly open—in 1925, but it was then totally unfurnished. Even then, though, I could appreciate its architectural excellence. That item about the 2500-year-old lily-seed goes at once into my weird files—although I have my doubts about the actuality of the germination. Similar tales used to be told about wheat-grains from Egyptian tombs, but scientific opinion has shewn them all to be apocryphal. That Quincy House item—which had appeared in my local paper—was indeed melancholy news; for I had often stopped at the old tavern, & the amateur press associations used often to hold conventions there. It was on the site of the ancient Brattle St. church—which in early colonial times displayed its Puritan zeal by refusing the gift of an organ—which it termed "an ungodly chest of whistles." The organ went to St. John's in Portsmouth, N.H., where it still remains in good condition. The Quincy is the second old Boston hotel to go this year—the old U.S. Hotel, built in 1826 (& where Loveman & I stopped only last January) having closed down about a month ago. Only one or two of the famous old hostelries are left now. As for Dr. Hridlicka—he leaves the Indian origin question about where it was before.[2] Asiatic navigation is a virtual certainty, though details & technical confirmations are still to be secured. It is also still an open question as to whether any non-Indian stocks had a foothold in America in prehistoric times. That article on bell-ringing reminds me of my frequent wish to master some of the quaint terminology of the vanishing craft. The late John Ravenor Bullen knew it fluently, & used it in one of his tales. It would be a pity if the nomenclature & the art were alike to die out, & I hope some Henry Fordlike person will intervene to save them—if only in a museum way. America never had this bit of colour, for Puritan steeples generally boasted only a single bell. Still—even those unvarying peals sound highly picturesque & attractive across a rural valley through the haze of summer or over the crisp Christmas snows. In the second lot of cuttings I note one item which reveals a temperament enviably dissimilar to my own—namely, the statement of Mr. Temple Thurston[3] that writing is something which can be done at *any* time. It may be so with him but I must regretfully say that it is not so with me. Of course, I can write straightforward prose on any given subject at any time—plain essay prose, which simply relates facts already formulated in my mind. But when it comes to fiction, or anything calling upon the creative imagination, I find that my mind is not always equally in shape. It pays to make the most of spells of particular ability when they come, & to save the dull periods for hack work. That autumn idyl by D. C. Peattie[4] is exceedingly appealing. I am very fond of gardens—in fact they are among the most potent of all imaginative stimuli with me.

I regret to hear that you have no copyist now available, but fancy one will turn up presently. Surely there is no haste needed about the MSS. I'll send that Bullen book in a day or two—& will also slip in one or two good astronomical volumes. In astronomy it is best to begin with something absurdly simple like Bayne's "Pith of Astronomy" & then follow up with a general treatise of wider scope—such as Newcomb's "Astronomy for Everybody". Good parallel reading is furnished by some book treating of the *constellations* & their mythological background—a subject of the utmost poetical fascination, though of course not a part of scientific astronomy, since the apparent arrangement of the stars in our sky is nine-tenths a mere effect of perspective, unrelated to the actual structure of the universe. To astronomers, the constellations mean no more than a set of convenient empirical landmarks—for the easy identification of stars, & as a working background for the observation of motions within our solar system. Constellation-study must not be confused with real astronomical research, though as I have said, it is a thing of eternal interest for the poet, aesthete, anthropologist, & antiquarian—a liberal education, as it were, in mythology. The Bullen book is for you to keep; the astronomical volumes can be returned at your convenience—retain them as long as you like, & when they come back I'll send others.

About the idea of a Roman colony in America—it was new to me when I thought of it, but I later saw a fantastic use of it in connexion with some curious sunken pavements (really French, no doubt) along the northern coast of Maine. Moreover—there have been several novels about surviving Roman colonies in *Africa*. As for the Easter Island images—bless me! but they are *colossal* . . . . the heads alone must be 6 to 8 feet high! They are unbelievably impressive—you really ought to get around to the Smithsonian to see them. What Sechrist had—& of which he sent me a photograph—was a little *bird* idol only six inches or so long, from the ruins of the mysterious African jungle city Zimbabwe. Easter Island is a lonely spot in the South Pacific Ocean.

I have finished the Moe book at last, but don't know when it will be published. He'll try it on Macmillan first—& I wish him luck! Just now I am neck deep in a new job—a long professional attack on free clinics by a Chicago physician.[5]

I agree that *doorways* are always fascinating things—you are aware of my fondness for the Georgian colonial type so prevalent in Providence & elsewhere. In this connexion you'll be interested to see my new bookplate—a thing with which I am prodigiously pleased. The designer is a young writer & newspaper man, but his artistic skill is certainly far above the amateur grade.[6]

I may not be able to get in my Foster trip this autumn after all; since every day is incredibly rushed, & the weather does not seem to promise any such warm geniality as that of last October. Still, I shall probably secure many less ambitious rural afternoon outings—my work going along with me. Young Wandrei's visit is still doubtful, for he has temporarily found something to do in N Y—less oppressive than the Dutton work.

With best wishes, & hoping that the enclosed tales will not prove a bore, I remain

Yr most obt Servt

H P Lovecraft

Notes

1. HPL refers to the account of the dream that he included in a letter to the Gallomo (a round-robin correspondence group including Alfred Galpin, HPL, and Maurice W. Moe) dated 11 December 1919 (*SL* 1.94–97). HPL's dating of the dream to 29 December is clearly an error; it probably occurred on 9 December.
2. Aleš Hrdlička (1869–1943), Czech anthropologist who lived in the U.S., was the first scientist to document the theory of human colonization of the American continent from east Asia 15,000 years ago.
3. Ernest Temple Thurston (1879–1933), prolific Anglo-Irish poet and playwright.
4. HPL refers to the nature writer Donald Culcross Peattie (1898–1964). Although HPL professes admiration for Peattie's work, he told August Derleth he found Peattie's writings "relatively lifeless & pedantic" (*Essential Solitude* 641).
5. This was apparently Lee Alexander Stone, who later never paid his revision bill (see *SL* 3.170–71).
6. HPL's bookplate was designed by Wilfred B. Talman.

[20]   [ALS]

10 Barnes St.,

Providence, R.I.,

Octr. 25, 1929.

Dear Mifs Toldridge:—

I am glad to hear that you found the Bullen book of interest. Don't mistake the contents for great poetry, though—& don't use the verses as models, for Bullen had all the archaisms, inversions, &c., which it is so necessary for the contemporary poet to get rid of. Incidentally—I trust you did not think I wrote that sonnet toward the close of the preface. It is an anonymous bit which Bullen's mother found in a Canadian paper, & no one to whom I shewed it seems to have any idea as to the authorship.[1] Keep the astronomies as long as you like—reading the Bayne book first. Later I will send others—including some which deal with the traditional & mythological lore connected with the constellations. All this, ultimately, should be supplemented by some work dealing with the nature & dimensions of the larger universe as a whole, as revealed by the discoveries of the last 20 years. I don't own such a book, but can enthusiastically recommend the small popular treaties entitled "Starlight", by Prof. Harlow Shapley.

Glad you found the stories readable. I'll send three more this time, which can be returned at your leisure. Hope I can snatch the time to write some more during the coming winter, although the congestion of revision seems to increase rather than decrease. It is possible that I shall have the job of doing all (or as much as I handle of it) the revision for a new publishing house in Wisconsin,[2] which will specialise in pedagogical books; & if so, my extra time will be sorely limited indeed!

The cuttings proved exceedingly interesting—especially the one about Fredericksburg, which I explored so thoroughly last May. The town fascinated me tremendously—even more so than Williamsburg, since its archaism is a natural survival rather than a self-conscious restoration—& I'm sure I'd choose it as a residence if I were ever to settle outside New-England. It has some fine old doorways—with rectangular transoms more often than semicircular fanlights—whose details are highly esteemed by architects; & across the Rappahannock is the still older & quainter hamlet of Falmouth, which retains much charm despite its slum decadence. Fredericksburg contains the mansion of Kenmore, long the home of Genl. Washington's sister, & the cottage where his mother spent her last days.

The article about place-names is exceedingly interesting, & could be carried to still greater lengths by the inclusion of Indian names—which tell much of the aboriginal tribes. I like the nomenclature of New England best of all, & wish the population were correspondingly all-British! I had not before realised the stark grotesqueness of names in the poor-white regions of Kentucky & Tennessee.

The Poe observances must have been interesting. I saw his grave in the yard of Westminster Presbyterian Church during my trip of 1928, but did not have time to stop off at Baltimore last spring. I am about to purchase the best recent biography of Poe—the 2-volume "Israfel", by Hervey Allen. I already possess the Ingram & Woodberry biographies.

Many thanks for sending the poetry magazine—which I am safely returning herewith. It seems to me a particularly delightful venture—less cumbered with mediocre & inferior material than any other semi-amateur verse periodical I have ever seen—& I surely wish it a long & prosperous life. Of the various items in the contents, I seem to find most real vision & originality in the short unassuming "Stone Wall" on page 9. But every piece has more than ordinary merit. I trust you will contribute to it later on.

I hope you may not find the Christmas card work a burden—I surely envy anyone who can draw or paint. Young Talman, who designed my bookplate, often draws his own Christmas cards; & usually with very felicitous results.

Weather hereabouts has not been as genial as in Washington, so that I have not had so many woodland writing sessions as I had last autumn. At prevailing temperatures, one has to keep moving outdoors. I hope, however, to get a few good walks before the foliage is all gone. It is in the spring & fall, I imagine, that the difference in latitude between R.I. & D.C. becomes most manifest. Last spring I found Washington very mild at a time when the north was still uncomfortable. The best days here have been Oct. 20–21, when I had glorious afternoons amidst the gay leafage & rustic & village vistas of the Quinsnicket region. All this makes me especially appreciative of the October landscape items in the latest batch of cuttings. There is one place in Quinsnicket—on the side of a hill—where I could sit for hours gazing at the landscape without being bored. The road spirals down to an eastward valley with a glassy mere at its bottom— beyond which rises another hill, now gay with autumn splendour—on which the idyllic gables & spires of the village of Saylesville can be seen in the distance. On the right are rolling meadows with quaint stone walls, & the forested edge of a deep, brook-traversed ravine; whilst on the left are terraced uplands with frequent outcroppings of rock & at present dotted with the corn-sheaves of harvest time. At the rim of these uplands the ancient roofs of two farmhouses—one built in 1670 & the other in 1732—can be glimpsed through the scarlet & gold of gnarled orchard-trees. A place like this makes me regret, more than anything else, my inability to draw & paint. It looks something like this:

I can appreciate, too, the editorial on "White Moon's Wizardry", since the Hunter's Moon last week was exceptionally fine. I took several walks to get the benefit of the mystic moonbeams on particular bits of landscape & architecture—river reflections, &c—& would well appreciate the expression "burning moonlight"—used by Flecker in the last act of his "Hassan."[3]

Other cuttings of much interest are those connected with extinct cultures. I had seen a short item about the Esquimau discovery before, but this account is much ampler. Lost Arctic & Antarctic civilisations form a fascinating idea to me—I used it once in "Polaris", & expect to use it again more than once. The Maya question is absorbingly interesting, too. Le Plongeon[4] is hardly to be taken seriously, yet even without his chimerical notions the history of the ancient culture, with its sudden shift from Central America to Yucatan about 500 A.D., is dramatic & mysterious enough. The origin of the Mayas is almost indisputably Asiatic, & their art will be found, on analysis, much closer to that of India & Indo-China than to any art-stream of Africa or Western Asia. It is very doubtful whether an inhabited Atlantis ever existed, although vast areas in the Atlantic have undoubtedly sunk at one time or another. It seems likely that the classic Atlantis of Plato was in North Africa, on the shores of a lagoon now dried up. The fabled Poseidonis was in all probability somewhere near the later Tunis. But a sunken land is a great theme for fiction, & I always like to read Atlantean tales. There is a new one by A. Conan Doyle just out—"The Maracot Deep"—which I want to read as soon as possible.

Apropos of former discussions anent hackneyed "poetical" words—I am enclosing a delectable melange which Moe lately sent me, & which I must ask to be returned for my scrap-book. The compiler has hit upon a marvellous number of characteristically outworn & over-used "beautiful" words— though it would be easy to add dozens more to the index expurgatorius . . . . *Samarcand, Arcady, star-dust, recompense*, &c. &c. &c. Freshness of poetic appeal is best secured by using as few as possible of these venerable standbys, & striving to get the image to the reader in a more direct way.

With best wishes, & trusting that you will be neither bored to death nor jolted into nervous prostration by the enclosed three hair-raisers,

I have yᵉ honour to fubfcribe myfelf,

Yr moft obᵈᵗ hble Servt

H P Lovecraft

Notes

1. Apparently an untitled sonnet by one Alice Roger Collins in the Toronto *Globe*.

2. Presumably The Kenyon Press.

3. The phrase "burning moonlight" does not occur in James Elroy Flecker's *Hassan* (1915), but the phrase "blazing moonlight" is found in a scene description in Act 5, sc. 2.

4. Augustus Le Plongeon (1826–1908), author of *Vestiges of the Mayas* (1881), *Sacred Mysteries among the Mayas and the Quiches, 11,500 Years Ago* (1886), and other works. He proposed a now discredited theory that the Maya had been in touch with the lost continent of Atlantis and were ancestral to Ancient Egypt.

[21]   [ALS]

10 Barnes St.,
Providence, R.I.,
Novr. 26, 1929.

Dear Mifs Toldridge:—

The tales duly came back, & I am glad they did not prove wearisome. I shall send some more as soon as I can go over the unclassified main section of my archives & find new specimens. Yes—"The Temple" (the undersea tale about the German commander) was printed in *Weird Tales* over four years ago. I am getting the tail end of my miscellaneous revision in shape now,[1] & hope to get time to write some more stories before the bulk of the new work descends upon me. That book firm, by the way, is *not* a large one; but a very modest concern just starting in. Besides myself, they will have my young friend Long—& also two or three U. of Wis. professors to handle the specialised pedagogical revision.

Yes—everything pertaining to the Mayan & Aztec civilisations is interesting, & I fancy I shall use the theme more than once. Indeed—my next revision job will give me a chance to practice, since it will require the introduction of this theme in such as a way as to involve wholly original composition on my part.

Glad to hear that you have secured a chance to have your poetry typed—& I'm sure you need have no hesitancy in letting Mr. Norr handle the job. With the many facilities of his office it could hardly form any imposition on your part. And don't feel that the typing debars you from future revision of the verses in question. It is easy to make legible minor corrections in letters carefully printed with pen & ink.

"Israfel" turned out to be a splendid piece of biographical writing—the best study of Poe I have ever seen, & the only one to include the new light shed on Poe (all favourable to him & adverse to his penurious & hypocritical guardian Allan) through the discovery of the Poe-Allan letters in the Valentine Museum at Richmond in 1925. The book not only presents Poe with marvellous vividness, but gives a striking picture of his general period—that grotesque age of decline when the Georgian culture of America was breaking down under the impacts of the rich & ignorant parvenu element, & giving place to the nightmare of sentimental barbarism known as the Victorian age. Even more than Meade Minnegerode's well known "Fabulous Forties",[2] "Israfel" presents a devastating picture of the intellectual & aesthetic bankruptcy of the Andrew Jackson–Polk–Harrison–Tyler period. Of all the prominent literati, Poe was the only one to glimpse the futile absurdity of the pompous & finical cultural abyss into which the nation was plunging. It was not for nothing that he had lived in Georgian Richmond & gone to school at Stoke-Newington in London.

The outings were good while they lasted, but November temperatures & barren trees make the woods & fields less alluring now than last month. Probably the desolation has been less rapid in Washington—the ten or so degrees of difference in latitude make considerable climatic difference, as I found last spring when I descended from a very bleak New York into a very genial & vernal D.C. & Va. I trust you may distribute your card-illuminating work in such a way as to avoid the extremes of fatigue—& that your aunt's health may improve under the influence of the Indian-summer you mention.

The cuttings all proved of interest. Your Poetry Circle meeting must have been very pleasant & interesting, & I hope you managed to attend it. One of the old United Amateur group in Milwaukee—Edward F. Daas—informs me that he has become president of a new literary club, which contains a poetical subdivision—a group within the main group, with a separate director. Later on he might enjoy getting in touch with your group—exchanging publications, if his organisation decides to issue one. He once led a literary group in Washington—the Pen & Ink Club—when he was doing war work in the capital in 1917–19.

The various nature-items are all pleasant & timely—D. C. Peattie has an unusual facility in capturing the changing charm of the seasons. And that "Dusk in the Mountains" is delightfully graphic—I am putting that in my permanent files. The article on quaint *rants* in England is also very pleasing. A whole volume could be written on such things—& these are only a few of the multitude of ancient symbolic ceremonies which still manage to preserve some poetry in the daily life of Great-Britain. The loss of corresponding quaintnesses on this continent is generally to be deplored.

The article on Washington by Mr. Perry—the British journalist—especially interested me because he stayed some time with the Providence Journal & Bulletin. He seemed to think well of Rhode Island, & declared that the city reminded him more of an English town than any of the other American urban centres he had seen—its narrow, curving streets, old Georgian houses, quiet manners & absence of Western "push" & effusiveness, &c. He seems to be right about Washington—the capital is undoubtedly destined to become the most intrinsically beautiful city in America.

The Smithsonian quest for the universe's "Mother Stuff" promises to be a merry chase—& yet how much nearer we are even than in 1801, when Dalton discovered the atom![3] It seems very certain that the actual "mother stuff" (or *protyl,* as Haeckel used to call the hypothetical basic substance) will prove to be something wholly alien to our ideas of *substance,* & closely allied to what we recognise as *energy.* Before its nature can be grasped, our whole notions of *entity* will have to undergo a revision & clarification. The clearest picture we can devise of the cosmos is that of an infinite & eternal fixed condition—a basic reality that simply *is, always has been, & always will be;* something fundamental & boundless & static as a whole, & utterly outside the realm of such things as time, space, direction, purpose, or consciousness. One of the fixed conditions of this infinite & eternal entity is *pattern* or *rhythm*—certain regular relationships of part to part within the fabric of the unchanging whole; & specialised aspects of this rhythm appear to be the basis of our notions of time, space, motion, matter, & change.

We may say that these things—time, space, &c.—are *proximate realities,* because they depend on a fixed & particular perceptive apparatus—i.e., the senses of a certain sub-phase of entity which is well-defined though transient, insignificant, & accidental; to wit, the animal organism called man. But we may *not* call these proximate realities *ultimate;* since all their familiar aspects are due wholly to our own accidental structure & position. Even the world of a cat is highly different from ours, while the world of a beetle is abysmally different from either. The world of an organism on another planet—especially one in another galaxy—is so different from anything we can conceive that we would probably have difficulty in identifying any of its attributes beyond the simplest abstractions of time, space, & change. And it is wholly conceivable that registering consciousnesses exist, in which the conceptions of time & space, matter & motion, energy & change, cause & effect, are wholly or largely absent. Truly, we approach strange realms of thought & imagination when we embark upon Mr. Rollins' quest,[4] or consider my own lifelong & similarly-intentioned query, "what is anything?" Anybody with simple or stereotyped ideas about the universe has a lot of disillusioning reading before him nowadays—Bertrand Russell's "Our Knowledge of the External World", Eddington's "Nature of the Physical World", Sir James Jeans' "Universe Around Us", Krutch's "The Modern Temper", &c. No wonder one of our gang likes to abridge my question "what is anything?" into the more basic & sceptical question "*Is* anything?"

    With best wishes, & trusting your holiday work will not prove too confining & exhausting,
    I remain
        Yr most obt Servt
           H P Lovecraft

[P.S.] Speaking of my stuff—I enclose another recent specimen illustrative of my efforts to practice what I preach regarding direct and unaffected diction— a sort of irregular semi-sonnet, based on an actual dream.[5]

Notes

1. Among other possible projects, HPL was working on the ghostwritten tale "The Mound" (December 1929–January 1930), for Zealia Bishop.
2. Meade Minnigerode (1887–1967), American writer born in London, author of *The Fabulous Forties: 1840–1850* (1924), an account of New York in the time of Dickens.
3. British chemist John Dalton (1766–1844) established a rudimentary theory about the atom in a series of papers delivered in 1801; he later published the first table of relative atomic weights.
4. HPL refers to *The Pack of Autolycus,* ed. Hyder Edward Rollins (Cambridge, MA: Harvard University Press, 1927), reprinting broadside ballads of strange occurrences from 1624 to 1693.
5. The poem "Recapture," later incorporated into *Fungi from Yuggoth.*

[22]   [ALS]

[December 19, 1929]

Dear Mifs Toldridge:—

I must not delay longer in thanking you for the 1929 anthology, which duly came, in addition to the returned astronomies. It is truly an excellent volume, & perhaps strikes a higher average than its predecessor of 1928. The misprints, omissions, early form-closings, &c. &c. are naturally very regrettable, but probably do not exceed those encountered in connexion with other annuals of the kind. Real care in such matters is a rare thing to find. I have looked the book through & found many items of great interest & merit besides your own contributions. One of the best poets—as judged in a cursory survey—is on the very last page; one Franklin N. Wood[1] of Florida. The worst poet, without a particle of doubt, is one Cora Smith Gould of New York. Again let me thank you for the anthology, which I shall shortly explore with greater thoroughness.

I am glad that all your MSS. have been copied so neatly, & hope that they may eventually encounter an hospitable publisher. Certainly the Frederick A. Stokes Co. is a thoroughly reliable firm, & one need not hesitate about submitting anything to them. It would be pleasant if your prose could be published in time, although I would pay prime attention to the verse ventures if I were you. A collection of poems—titled, as you so aptly suggested, "Winnings"—is clearly the logical book to concentrate primary efforts upon.

Glad the astronomical works proved interesting. To my mind an elementary knowledge of the nature & workings of the universe is a really essential part of any artist's or thinker's background. It is the greatest clarifier of perspective I know of, & is a whole imaginative education in itself because of the stupendous magnitudes & distances it brings up for attention. But all the distances described in the two books I lent you are as nothing compared with the nearly unthinkable chasms envisaged by modern astronomy. To get a hint of these things one must read some very recent treatise—the smallest & clearest of which, I think, is "Starlight" by Prof. Harlow Shapley.

Glad my recent verse attempts did not seem too feeble. Weird Tales—which prints most of my fiction—has accepted "The Ancient Track" & "Recapture", but rejected "The Outpost" as too long. In these new efforts I try to practice what I preach about vital & conversational diction—though I no doubt slip up occasionally. Enclosed is still another metrical outburst—together with an illustrated article on the event which occasioned it.[2] I spoke of these old warehouses once before, I think, & tried to sketch what they look like. The accompanying data will tell a great deal more. Their doom is a source of the greatest pain & disgust to me, although I well know that it cannot be averted. [*passage cancelled by HPL*] The verses are to be returned, although there is not the least hurry about them. I have sent them to the Prov. Journal—but without much expectation of their being accepted. Also—could you please return the illustrated article? I find I can't get the duplicates I expected.

Speaking of the Journal—the enclosed cuttings from the literary column, "The Side Show", conducted by Bertrand K. Hart, the literary editor, shew how some of the members of my "gang" have recently secured local notice through a discussion anent the weirdest story in all literature.[3] By a coincidence, B.K.H. discovered my "Cthulhu" just at this time, although I had not told him I wrote original fiction. It is surely odd that he once lived where I laid one of the Cthulhu scenes![4] There were one or two more of these columns devoted to the weird tale discussion, but I can't find them just now. (Or if I come across them before sealing this, I'll enclose them.) The whole batch can be kept as long as you like, though I must ask its eventual return. You'll notice in one of the cuttings the information that I've gained in a 3-star or Roll of Honour rating in the O'Brien anthology for a second consecutive year—this time with "The Dunwich Horror". It is rather gratifying to repeat the 1928 honour—I hardly expected it this year. O'Brien also cites my "Silver Key" in his one-star class—& the same story receives an equivalent mention in the O. Henry Memorial Prize Story annual for 1929—the one that cited "Pickman's Model" last year. I don't value the O. Henry Memorial mention much, since the principle of selection is rather popular & conventional; but I do prize O'Brien's mention, because he is a real artist who judges by purely aesthetic standards.[5]

Many thanks of the cuttings—& pray don't apologise for their meagreness. Never bother to look for items which don't happen along of themselves—there are so many topics of interest that one couldn't begin to keep track of all of them. That St. Louis mound item is of especial interest to me just now, insomuch as my current job is the weaving of a tale around a similar thing in Oklahoma. The alleged author intended to let the story go as a simple tale of a haunted mound, with a couple of Indian ghosts around it; but I decided at once that such a thing would be insufferably tame & flat.[6] Accordingly I am having the mound turn out to be the gateway of a primordial & forgotten subterranean world—the home of a fearsomely ancient & decadent race cut off from the outer earth since the prehistoric sinking of fabulous Atlantis & Lemuria. In the course of the tale I introduce a man who descends into the abyss—a Spaniard of Coronado's expedition of 1541—& another, in the present age, who *begins* a descent but *very hastily returns* to the upper air after *seeing a certain thing*.

Dec. 20

The delightful cards & additional cuttings arrived yesterday—truly, the delicate paintings are exquisite, & I am sorry you did not feel able to do more of them. Let us hope you will have better luck next year—I am sure that the remuneration for such exquisite work must be fairly substantial—though even so, scarcely adequate for work of so high a grade. Again let me thank you for the delightful specimens—that Georgian doorway is so attractive that I hardly fancy I'll send it away! At least, no further than the aunt who dwells within the walls of 10 Barnes.

That revision job—which really amounts to original composition—is proving to be rather an incubus, for the idea is spinning itself out into a veritable novelette. Nevertheless I have had to spare time enough to do something about the acute problem of excess books—& have just secured 4 new small cases (cheap unpainted affairs) to set on top of other furniture in the absence of additional floor space. The work of rearranging classes, & absorbing the surplus volumes which were scattered around promiscuously, proved considerable—& even in the end I found the congestion only partly alleviated. Not an inch of shelf space to spare, & several of the older cases still crowded!

The cuttings all proved highly interesting—admirably chosen, & redolent of that sense of space & strangeness which gives escape from the monotony of commonplace existence. The dating of the pueblos by tree-rings is surely a remarkable feat—would that there were some analogous way of dating the vastly more ancient stone Aztec-Maya ruins to the southward! Another interesting thing was the allusion to Kafirs in Afghanistan. This & other phenomena are last reliques of the great Dravidian culture—wholly non-negroid—which once stretched up out of Africa & across Asia into India; a culture which *may* have been responsible for ruins like Zimbabwe, though others attribute such things to outposts of Semitic traders—Arabs or Phoenicians.

You are to be envied the good weather Washington is enjoying. After some excruciating cold, we have settled down to a sort of rainy season—although from my point of view that is infinitely better than the cold.

With best wishes, & renewed thanks for the cards & the Anthology, I remain

Yr moft oblig'd obt Servt

H P Lovecraft

[P. S. on envelope:] Your latest verses, with clever accompanying comment, just arrived. They are splendid, & as I read them I can't think of any correction to suggest. The idea is very well put. Of course, all natural beauty is accidental so far as its quality as beauty is concerned. The various meteorological, geographical, botanical, geological, &c. phenomena which we recognise as "beautiful"—sunsets, landscapes, flowers, &c.—are the products of blind & chance forces in which no element of the aesthetic as such could figure. When they began to take form there was no certainty that any creature would ever exist, who would like them & place them in a class called "beautiful" apart from other phenomena. When later accidents developed the animal called man, he formed these likings for a variety of reasons—most of them associated with his early experiences & symbolisations, & some based on their relationship to the quality of rhythm or symmetry, of which he is fond.

That he considers them "beautiful" is wholly accidental. Nothing has any "beauty" except in his imagination. Apart from this subjective accident, the aesthetic has no existence. All that the cosmos recognises is whirling energy.

[P.P.S. on envelope, above return address:] I think the plural of *sheen* is admissible.

Notes

1. Author of *Florida and Other Poems* (1925) and *The Alchemy of Words* (1929).
2. *Netopian* 10, No. 5 (November 1929) contained "The Passing of Some Hundred-Year-Old Waterfront Landmarks" (7, 10–11) and "In the Path of Municipal Progress" (8–9). HPL's poem was "The East India Brick Row."
3. B. K. Hart, "The Sideshow," *Providence Journal* 101, No. 280 (23 November 1929): 2; 101, No. 281 (25 November 1929): 2; 101, No. 286 (30 November 1929): 10.
4. Hart once lived in the Fleur-de-Lys building at 7 Thomas Street, where HPL had placed the artist Henry Anthony Wilcox in "The Call of Cthulhu."
5. Blanche Colton Williams (1879–1944), ed., *O. Henry Memorial Award Prize Stories* (Garden City, NY: Doubleday, Doran, 1928). HPL's "Pickman's Model" was awarded a third-rank rating.
6. See letter 21, n. 1.

1930

[23]　　[ALS]

[8 January 1930]

Dear Mifs Toldridge:—

　　　　　　I appreciated yours of the 27th with enclosures, & am glad you found the "Brick Row" lines worth reading. If the thing appears in print* I'll send a pair of copies for you & Mifs Radcliffe. It is indeed one redeeming thing, as you say, that the old row was well covered by artists before the days of its menace. One of these etchers—Henry J. Peck—has similarly drawn most of the ancient byways of the town, so that the elder scenes need never be forgotten. The only trouble is that the pictures are all scattered now. I saw them in an exhibition a year ago, & wished they might all be reproduced in a single volume.[1]

　　Thanks exceedingly for the holiday greetings—though you really ought not to have spared so many of those exquisitely coloured cards. Three of them have performed valuable service in furnishing "Quick comebacks" for cards received from unexpected sources! I note with interest the item touching on the history

_____

*It *has* appeared—this morning. Copies enclosed.

of Christmas cards—a wholly new thing to me, since I had shared the popular delusion that Victorian England was responsible for them. They run a curious aesthetic gamut—from surprising heights of beauty & appropriateness in design & words alike, down to the very nadir of tawdriness & banality.

Your current enclosures certainly are a prize-winning lot—even fantastic fiction this time! That tale, "The Moon-Slave",[2] is really marvellously effective, & will probably cause me to investigate more fully an author whom I have hitherto slighted because of the insipidity of some of his material. The astronomical cuttings are very interesting—that Henry[3] article on the origin of the solar system sums up the now accepted planetesimal hypotheses better than any other popular article I have seen. In my early astronomical days the old hypothesis of Laplace—postulating a solar nebula which contracted & left behind rings which broke up into planetary fragments—was still unchallenged, & I grew so used to it that I had hard work readjusting myself to the newer conception when Profs. Chamberlin & Moulton (of the U. of Chicago) first promulgated it.[4] But the solid evidence was there—so I had to come around in the end. Another tremendously absorbing thing is that idea of draining the North Sea—which offers all kinds of openings for fantastic fictional treatment. Strange Cyclopean ruins & foundation walls crusted with barnacles & tangled seaweed . . . . . . I'd hate, though, in all truth, to see the familiar face of the globe thus distorted. Modern industry is apparently resolved to leave nothing on earth to which anybody is accustomed—& no doubt it will begin on the moon & nearer planets as soon as the Goddard or Oberth rockets enable men to penetrate outer space![5] As a contrast, the archaic ceremonials of Japan are refreshing! After all, as much as the modernisation of Japan is destroying, it may be that the innate aestheticism of the Japanese mind will manage to salvage more from the past than the western world can.

Glad to hear that you had such a pleasant Christmas. I've never had a radio—in fact, I like to have as few modern inventions as possible about me. Probably my musical craving is not strongly developed—my mind is, at bottom, predominately visual. I celebrated Christmas by getting my convalescent aunt down town (it was only to an uptown restaurant Thanksgiving) for the first time since June 1928—an experience which, I was glad to note, proved more of a tonic than a tax. Of late my relapse into rhyming has become quite marked. At all-too-rare moments I am grinding out a sort of sequence of weird sonnets—"Fungi from Yuggoth"—of which I'll enclose specimens later on. I have about 16 or 17 done.[6]

With best wishes—

Yr most obt Servt

H P Lovecraft

P.S. No—it's hard to the point of impossibility to find publishers to take poetical book MSS. on royalty basis. ¶ I think one would give a very *faint* K sound to the C in Cthulhu—it is seldom pronounced *on earth!* ¶ No—I shan't be mentioned in connexion with "The Mound". ¶ Interested to hear that Lady Macdonald has published another volume.[7] ¶ Trust your aunt will recover after all, despite the incidents which tend to retard the process.

Notes

1. Henry J. Peck (1880–1964), *Glimpses of Providence: From Crayon Drawings, with Notes* ([Warren, RI: Henry J. Peck, n.d.]). See HPL to Maurice W. Moe, 13 December 1928 (ms, JHL): "I had the honour of meeting him in person, & told him, I wou'd not be satisfy'd till he had publisht a book of his collected urban sketches."
2. Barry Pain, "The Moon-Slave," in *Stories in the Dark* (1901).
3. Thomas R. Henry (1893–) science writer for the *Washington Evening Star* and press writer for the Smithsonian Institution from 1931 until the mid-1960s.
4. In 1905, Thomas Chrowder Chamberlin and Forest Ray Moulton propounded a theory of the creation of the solar system substantially different from that of Laplace's nebular hypothesis. The theory was discarded by the late 1930s and is now no longer accepted.
5. For Goddard, see letter 93, n. 1. Hermann Julius Oberth (1894–1989), Austro-Hungarian-born German physicist and engineer, considered a founding father of rocketry and astronautics.
6. By early January 1930, HPL had drafted thirty-five sonnets in the sequence. For several years, he circulated a typescript of only the first thirty-three, presumably because, as he said (see letters 24 and 26), he intended to write more, and so left the final two aside to serve as the coda to the ultimate sequence. "Recapture," written in early December 1929, was added to the sequence in 1936, when it was made No. 34, and then "Evening Star" and "Continuity" were finally appended as the penultimate and ultimate pieces.
7. *All the Days of My Life.*

[24]   [ALS]

[January 1930]

Dear Mifs Toldridge:—

Your letter with the interesting cuttings duly arrived, & I am glad to hear of your plans for the classification of your poems. Surely I would be glad to offer suggestions regarding arrangement, &c. If the verses in question are those of which I already have copies, you need not bother to send me the typed pieces. Merely *list the titles* you have chosen—& if there are any which I haven't here, I'll let you know so that you can send them. Or possibly the existing version has changes not incorporated in the MSS. I have—in which case it might be better to let me see the definitive text. As for being a custodian of your poetry & prose books in case your own custodianship were unfeasible—surely I'd esteem it an honour, though I feel certain you will have no need to provide for any such change of tenure in the present epoch!

Regarding the inclusion of your father's poetry in a book of your own—

of course it would be possible, although it would tend to impair the unity of a small volume. The same question came up when I edited the late Mr. Bullen's poetry—some of the family wished to include verse by the poet's father & brother, but others advised against it & finally prevailed. It would really be better if your father's work could appear in a small book by itself.

As for your own verse—I wouldn't worry if I were you about the changes incident to a readjustment to the contemporary scene. The essential quality of poetic vision does not depend on period or perspective or theme; & after your view is re-focussed to the values & proportions now recognised as sound, you will find yourself reacting to them just as richly & naturally as you formerly reacted to the values & proportions of the preceding age. This does not involve any loss or impairment of personality or individual nature. The individual quality is not a matter of theme, but is simply the manner in which one responds to any theme that one does respond to. The history of poetry is full of cases of writers who have lived from one age into another & changed their styles accordingly. Byron, for instance, first wrote in the Georgian manner & then wholly recast himself in the mould of the romantic revival—as did many another poet who lived in the early XIX century. And in a later age, Amy Lowell discarded the late XIX century tradition for the imagistic thought of the early XX century. In neither case was the poet's essential personality changed. They merely continued to express in their own respective ways the impressions which impinged upon them. The change was not in them, but in the impinging impressions.

I will send along my "Fungi from Yuggoth" as soon as I get them back from young Long—if they come today, I'll enclose them herewith. They seem to be very uneven, & I'm not at all enthusiastic about them. Essentially, I am a prose writer. However—"Brick Row" seems to have been favourably received, & won me a very pleasant letter from the editor.

Don't hesitate about opening your poetry package. It can't bite you—& if there are any stenographic errors you can correct them easily & inconspicuously with pen & ink. It never pays to take things heavily—what can there be in a typescript, whose contents you know, to get excited about? I shall be interested to learn the result of your definitive selections for the future book.

Many thanks for the kind loan of Lady Macdonald's book, of which I shall be very careful. Certainly, she exhibited a great deal of courage, ability, & determination in straightening out the matter of her husband's title. Indeed— the Bosville-Macdonalds ought all to be grateful to her for her skilled & graceful services as historian of their line. The present book is a mine of graceful anecdote, & of genuine source-material in the historical envisagement of a period & milieu now definitely obsolescent. Lady Macdonald has certainly enjoyed a very smooth & pleasant life, & I trust it may remain unbrokenly so for the balance of her days. This glimpse of her career & family comes very interestingly after one has read her other books. I shall presently return the volume, & trust it may reach you in prime condition.

Returning to the matter of poetry—I am sure that your absence of the joy-motive, as mentioned in your second letter, is merely temporary; or perhaps a maturer observation & expanded perspective are transmuting the relatively naive & illusory phenomenon of *joy* into the equally gratifying but more solid & intelligently enduring phenomenon of *interest*. I think, on the whole, that *interest* & *appreciation*, plus a sense of adventurous expectancy which clearly recognises its phantasmal & unrealisable nature, are perhaps more important than more unreasoning *joy* in the poetic motivations of experienced & sophisticated poets. However, the distinction is too slight to be worth bothering about. The right attitude is simply to take what pleasure one can in the visible beauty of the moment, & let everything else in the cosmos go hang.

Yes—it is unfortunate that books of verse are not publishable on a royalty basis, but I think you will find almost as much amusement in *arranging* one as in having it published. Then, when the opportunity does come, the MS. will be all ready at short notice. Personally, I don't give a rap whether anything of mine ever gets between book covers or not. My pleasure is in weaving images, & it's all one to me what becomes of them after they're done. Incidentally—my "Fungi" have just come back, & I am enclosing them herewith. There are 33 here, but I shall probably grind out a dozen or so more before I consider the sequence concluded. I shall re-use a good many of the ideas in later short stories. You will notice throughout the series my effort to break away from tawdry & artificial "poetic diction" & write in the living language of normal utterance. Probably I haven't fully succeeded, but this junk at least implies a start in the right direction. As for a Providence book—it would be interesting to compile, but I fear the demand would not be great enough to make the undertaking feasible.

"Lilt & Lure" is a delightfully lyrical piece, & certainly deserves a prominent place in the prospective volume. I'm sure you need have no qualms about its inadequacy—& it is an altogether unmerited compliment to me to fancy I could do better with the theme. The fact is, I probably couldn't do half so well; for my fund of poetic images is very meagre & one-sided. I am sensitive only to certain phases of life—phases involving the play of the imagination close to the borderline of the unreal & the unknown. As for the poem itself—I wouldn't call it too light; for although it doesn't try to express the whole of life, with all the pains, frustrations, & monotonies forming a great part of that phenomenon, it surely does express very adequately one side of life—a side which is made no less real by the existence of others. The metre is highly appropriate, & I can think of very few needed improvements in the wording. The phrase ". . . and the—— of it", recurring in each first line, is perhaps a trifle more artificial & mannered than one would recommend on first consideration, but further analysis tends to shew that its artificiality &

mannerism are not obtrusive *when the determinant word is a noun.* It is only when this word becomes an *adjective* that the shadow of artificiality seems to descend. Possibly you can see what I mean by comparing two specific instances—"and the *joy* of it" (noun) & "and the *strange* of it." (adj.) Of these phrases, the first sounds pretty normal, whereas the second bears the unmistakable stamp of Victorian unnaturalness & effect-seeking. Acting on this principle, I have taken the liberty to introduce the following changes in the MS:

Stan. II, l. 1—for *strange* read *spell*
Stan. VI, l. 1—for *sweet* read *zest*

The only other change I would suggest is the following:

Stan. VI, l. 2—for *Immortal* read Never-stilled
This is for the sake of the dactylic metre, which demands a line with a '—˘˘—' beat (accent strong on the first syllable & weak on the next two) instead of such a beat as the word *Im mor´ tal* could provide. I think you can easily see the reason why *Nev-er-still'd breath* is a better dactylic line than the obviously iambic *Im-mor-tal breath*[.] I might suggest that the poem's last line would be stronger if a key-word—a noun—fell on the strongly accented first syllable instead of the adjective *glad;* but a second reading convinces me that this point is a minor one, & that this line may very well be left as it is. Again let me congratulate you upon the excellence of this verse, & express the hope that it may achieve publication both in periodical & book form.

The new batch of cuttings contains some highly interesting material—certainly, your papers must average a higher percentage of intelligent contents than ours up here do. I'd like to see that revived *Virginia Gazette*—as indeed I shall the next time I get down to Williamsburg.[1] The town itself will probably be twice as fascinating in a year or so—when the restoration is further advanced—as it was last May when I explored it. Another tremendously absorbing item was that about Zimbabwe. I had never before seen a *picture* of any part of that cryptic city of primordial ghosts, & was correspondingly fascinated by the view accompanying the article. Clearly, this forgotten metropolis represents a lost Semitic civilisation that once stretched down the East African coast—but it must have differed curiously from all others, as the nature & workmanship of all its surviving artifacts (including the bird-idol owned by Sechrist) prove. The item on India is very graphic—I agree with you in your high estimate of the Nevinson articles.[2] India is one of the toughest problems & most discouraging messes of the modern world—& is at the same time one of the most interesting of ethnological & archaeological problems. Till recently it was thought to represent a stratified fusion of *two* races—conquering Aryan & conquered Dravidian—but lately ethnologists have professed to trace a *third*—a reddish-Caucasian stock like that of ancient Egypt, which survives as the nucleus of the Rajput element & next the highest caste.

I trust that by this time you have begun the correction & classification of your typed MSS. Let me know if I can assist in any way—but don't take my word, or that of any other one critic, as a final arbiter. Hope the suggested changes in "Lilt & Lure" will meet your approval.

Sorry to hear your aunt's health does not improve, though glad it is not further declining.

With best wishes, & renewed thanks for the loan of the Macdonald book,

Yr obt h^{ble} Servt

H P Lovecraft

[P.S.] The cuttings all proved entertaining. I have a vast respect for your neighbour Justice Holmes. ¶ As for the word "Nanny"—a family I knew in youth had a delightful nurse whom they called "Nana".

Notes

1. The *Virginia Gazette* (1736–81) was a weekly paper published in Williamsburg. It was revived in 1930 by Edwin McDonald, running until 1971.
2. Henry Woodd Nevinson (1856–1941), *The New Spirit in India* (1908).

[25]   [ALS]

[11 February 1930]

Dear Mifs Toldridge:—

I was pleased to hear in your letter of the 25th that you found my Yuggothian Fungi worth reading. No haste about their return—but don't make the mistake of overrating them. At best they are a by-product—a side line—of one whose principal medium is prose. Thanks for the two magazines—which I shall duly return. The appearance of an obsolete text of "The Eagle" must be rather provoking, but after all it does not really matter so long as you have the corrected text on file for later use. It can't be very bad if it has brought you the invitation you mention—which I trust you'll accept. I have seen some of the Hartsock's verse & think very highly of it.[1] He is a genuine & poignant poet, & am sure you will enjoy meeting him. As for the matter of the award for a poem not really yours—that surely is rather disconcerting at first, but undoubtedly a letter of explanation will help to straighten it out & secure the honour for whomever is the actual author of the verse. These small semi-amateur magazines are carelessly edited, on the whole—yet they fill a definite need, & deserve all the encouragement they can get.

Thanks exceedingly for the cuttings, which as usual contain a high percentage of glamourous & vista-opening material. The Greenlaw dictum is one which can be endorsed, in substance, by all friends of civilisation; but it would be easy to carry it over the borderline into the realm of sentimentality & absurdity. As for the naval parley—what it really is, is an attempt to get rid of some of the current expense of battleship building.[2] All this talk of universal peace is empty—there will always be wars as long as human beings exist, though their increasing frightfulness will probably tend to make the more intelligent nations slightly more cautious about entering into them.

Glad you found my comments on your new poems reasonably helpful. Regarding the nouns in the first lines of the dactylic piece—you don't need to use the exact ones I suggested for these, like other corrections of mine, are wholly tentative. I merely wished to shew approximately the sort of change required—the elimination of the artificial-sounding adjective use. As for the bulk of current small-magazine verse—of course one will find all the minor rules transcended now & then. An occasional liberty or two doesn't usually spoil a good poem, & many of the best poets slip up occasionally, but it's a good idea to try to be as correct as possible. Copy the excellences, rather than the faults, of the great! About *"Immortal"* at the beginning of a dactylic line— of course such wrenching of accents is often allowed, but in this especial case it seemed to halt the swing of the lines more than usual. I don't think you'll make any mistake in adopting *"Never-still'd."*

The Circle, as usual, is interesting in contents; the two best pieces, I think, being yours & Mr. Higgins's. *The Carillon*[3] certainly has an impressive list of recognised literary figures as contributors—if it keeps this up it will be a leading organ of American poetry! The best item, I think—or rather, the one I like the best—is the very first, by David Morton.[4]

Later

Thanks for the second envelope with its interesting contents & flattering comment on "Yuggoth". It pleases me to note the analytical reading on which your opinion of the verses is based, & in most cases I think I can agree with your preferences among them. There was no hurry at all about their return—& of course it was entirely all right to copy those which you did. Heaven knows I have no pose or affectations or palpitations about such truck as I grind out—I don't give a hang who sees it or what becomes of it. The fun is in the writing—& beyond that my only interest is in shewing it to a few tolerant & appreciative readers. Most of these sonnets represent odd moods & images which have been flitting around in my head for ages—& in several cases I intend to use the themes over again in prose fiction. Oh, yes—aside from the introductory three they are meant for independent publication. I am letting the Prov. Journal have a first chance at them, & what they return I shall send to *Weird Tales*. The residue after this will go to *Driftwind* (a Vermont magazine which comes close to the domain of the *Circle* & *Carillon* class, & which uses the work of many of these groups) & what they don't want I shall dump on the amateur press.

It is interesting to know that your father was an early devotee of Poe—a circumstance highly appropriate in a Baltimorean, in view of Poe's long residence & burial in the city. Possibly you know of the neighbourhoods (now declined, of course, & even then declining) where he lived with his aunt & cousins—first in Milk St. (now Eastern Ave.) near the S.W. corner of Patterson Park in the Falls' Point district, & later in Amity St., west of Fremont Ave. He was in Baltimore for a time in 1829, prior to his entrance to West Point, & again from 1831 to 1835, at which time he went to Richmond to take the editorship of the Southern Literary Messenger. It was in Baltimore that he obtained his first literary recognition, as a result of the publication of his prize-winning tale—"Ms. found in a Bottle"—in the Baltimore Saturday Visiter.[5] I have not looked up the Poe houses or localities in Baltimore, but mean to do so some time. That city ought really to have more of a claim to him than Fordham, (now absorbed in N Y City) where so much is made of his cottage. Richmond, however, is really the authentic "home town"—where all the formative influences of youth had their sway. My own taste for Poe preceded the wave of popularity beginning with the 1909 centenary. I came upon him at the age of 7—back in 1897—& was imitating his tales in 1898. Two of my products of that year—"The Mysterious Ship" & "The Secret of the Grave"—are still knocking about the house somewhere.[6] Too bad your father's library was dispersed. It was lucky for me that my old home did not dissolve till I was 14, & able to exert my will toward the preservation of such parts of the Lovecraft & Phillips family libraries as I desired to keep. These units still form a third to a half of my books, for lack of wall space has made me perforce a slow & cautious collector. Your grandmother must indeed have been interesting & delightful—I always liked courtly old people whose experience reached back to the pre-Victorian age before the Georgian tradition had quite expired—or at least, to periods still coloured by memories of those older days. My paternal grandmother was dead long before I was born, but I can well recall my maternal grandmother, who died when I was five. I often wished my line had a greater longevity, so that in youth I might have had more direct living links with Georgian times. One of my friends, now 33, has only just lost his maternal grandmother[7]—an inexhaustible repository of old Vermont lore with whom I conversed interestedly when I visited him in Yonkers last spring.

No hurry about arranging your verses—& as I said, I shall be glad to look them over & make suggestions as to selection & arrangement when they are tentatively assembled. The offer of the Harbour Press sounds alluring—I can tell more about it when I see a prospectus—but of course you realise how keen the competition must be for a place on their necessarily limited publishing programme. No harm in trying—but with conditions as they are, one ought not to count very heavily on success. There are only a few winners in any one lottery! As I remarked once before, there are a very large number of good poets writing at present, so that the presentation of all of them in suitable media—save at their own expense—is a virtual impossibility. With all its defects, this is an age of very widely diffused general taste—so that good & correct poets are not the rarities they were in Poe's day, or even fifty years ago.

Anent "Lilt & Lure"—I think

"Gay tryst with death"

is an excellent & appropriate last line. The strong accent on the adjective is *desirable* rather than otherwise, insomuch as the theme makes this word the emphatic & determinant element of the line. The second version suggested—

"—keeping gay

"Trysting with death."

does not seem to me so good. For one thing, it involves a superfluity of participles—a plethora of *"-ings"*. As for a separation of light & serious verses in different books—that is not really necessary, as you will see from an analysis of most small volumes of verse. One might make separate sections within the same book—but more than that is seldom imperative. Often there is a sort of unity or continuity of mood, point of view, & style in an author's work which persists amidst all his varieties of theme & spirits, & which binds light & heavy verse together in a large, inclusive way. It strikes me, cursorily, that this is the case with your work.

Sorry to hear that Hartsock's dealings with his fellow-poets & encouragers have been marked by insolence & poor taste—yet this is often the case with aesthetes whose art-feeling is restricted to a single medium or a few media rather than extended to the whole field of life & tradition. It is paradoxical but true that no one can be a more conspicuous bounder than a certain type of self-conscious & egocentric poet or artist—& of course this tendency is intensified when the subject is a Jew or other cultural alien (as I had not suspected Hartsock to be, either from his work or from his surname!) upon whom the moods & memories & loyalties & inhibitions of the native main stream have only a nominal hold. However—one can't expect to be suited by every side of every person, & a little poor taste doesn't make Hartsock any the worse artist. The fact remains that he does possess an authentic poetic sensitiveness & a delicate knowledge of how to use it. He is no less a poet even though he may be crude & offensive to the last degree in manners & personal dealings. It amuses me, though, to think that this tuneful lyrist whom I had pictured as a highly-bred Southerner may, after all, be merely one of the unctuously arrogant Semitic types whose cumulative preponderance makes New York so repellent a place nowadays!

I am glad to hear that your aunt's health is shewing at least a slight upward trend, & hope that rapid progress in the same direction may ensue.

The new batch of cuttings is piquant & varied. Surely that Turkish village must be a pathetic & even sinister place! I wonder if Wells knew of it when he wrote his "Country of the Blind"?[8] I wish I could see that display of Fredericksburg pictures at the Congressional Library. Evidently these architectural &

antiquarian exhibits are a regular thing—they were shewing photographs of old Virginia parish churches when I was there last spring. Fredericksburg is one of the most fascinating places I have ever seen—archaic & Georgian, yet not self-conscious or museum-like. I'm not sure but that I'd rather live there than anywhere else except Providence. I saw Fredericksburg pretty thoroughly last May—thanks to a lucky meeting with a splendidly intelligent old gentleman who knew just what to point out in an historic & architectural way. By the way—the same magazine that published the Brick Row article & pictures has just published an illustrated article on Benefit St., in Providence,[9] which I will shew you when I get a duplicate. It gives an excellent sidelight on the elder Providence. One of the oldest parts of Benefit St. is only 2 blocks from 10 Barnes St.

    With best wishes—

                    Yr obt Servt
                    H P Lovecraft

Later

    Y[rs] of the 7th has now arrived, & I note with great interest your choice of poems for the future volume. It seems to me that your choices are eminently sound—so sound that hardly any outside suggestions are necessary—but I will presently go over it more minutely, with the actual verses before me, & see if I have any additional opinions to offer. Your choice of opening & closing poems strikes me as ideal. Of the doubtful verses at the end of your list I would perhaps recommend "Smoke" & "In Hospital" for inclusion—but I will speak more conclusively of that later on. The volume, I know, will be a highly pleasing & creditable one; & I hope it can eventually be brought out in an attractive format. You have no reason to think disparagingly of the contents—& especially, it is wholly needless to regret the relatively non-voluminous output of your pen. That is really a virtue in a poet—look at the slender poetry produced by such masters as Poe & Gray & Collins! It is the mediocre bard who mechanically grinds out lines by the ream, lacking the self-critical faculty to limit his utterance to things he really *needs* to say. I can attest this from weary experience with many a verbose & prolific bardling! As for my Fungi—those are only a special instance in a single vein, & I may never write another metric line in months. Your general poetic work attains a level far higher than any general poetic work of mine could possibly approach. Which reminds me—there is no reason to think the newspaper press would not welcome your recent verses. I had not heard of the Williamsport column, but it sounds very promising & I advise you to try it.

    Thanks in advance for the booklet which you mention, & which I shall appreciate upon its arrival. Anything about an old house is interesting to me, & from your description this promises to be a very notable item.

    The new cuttings are highly edifying. I must read the Summers & Kittredge books on witchcraft & vampirism. Summers is a rather eccentric but deeply scholarly man whose work is destined to become classic in its field. The Peattie article is delightful, as usual, though I am less in sympathy with the scene than with the scenes of spring, summer, & autumn. Winter is the one enemy against which I have no defence but flight; & much as I love old New England I fear I shall have to shift my headquarters southward some day—since I shall never have the means to maintain two homes or spend the winters in travel. I may yet end up among the colonial antiquities of Charleston, Savannah, St. Augustine, or New Orleans—or perhaps Bermuda or Jamaica. As for "The Day of Doom"[10]—I think my friend Morton can recite most of it from memory. It is an amusing old thing—especially where old Wigglesworth deals with the Calvinistic damnation of innocent but unbaptised infants. He hates to condemn them to everlasting fire, but cannot get rid of his notion of "original sin"—therefore writes as follows:

> "You Sinners are, and fuch a Share
>   As Sinners may expect;
> Such you fhall have, for I do fare
>   None but mine own Elect.
> Yet to compare your Sin with their
>   Who liv'd a longer Time,
> I do confefs yours is much lefs
>   Tho' ev'ry Sin's a Crime.
> A Crime it is, therefore in Blifs
>   You may not hope to dwell;
> But unto you I fhall allow
>   The eafieft Room in Hell."

That snow scene must be unusual for Washington—I wish such scenes were unusual everywhere! Today, though, is relatively mild & decent, hence I think I'll try to get some outdoor air before the prisoning cold shuts down again.

More anent the poems later.

   Yr obt Servt

      H P Lovecraft

P.S. Am enclosing the Benefit St. article herewith. Would like to see it again ultimately, but no hurry. These old houses begin only two blocks down the hill from where I am—Jenckes St. being a continuation of Barnes.

Notes

1. Probably Ernest Hartsock (1903–1930), author of the poetry collection *Romance and Stardust* (Saugus, MA: Charles A. A. Parker, 1925). HPL was acquainted with the publisher.

2. HPL refers to the London Naval Conference (21 January–22 April 1930), in which the US and four other nations agreed to a five-year moratorium on capital ship construction and other measures.

3. The *Circle* (Baltimore, 1924–38), edited by Lacey N. Green-Leach. HPL refers to 7, No. 1 (January–February 1930), containing "The Eagle" by Toldridge p. 20) and "Winter" by John Lee Higgins (p. 14). The *Carillon* (Washington, DC, 1929–33).

4. David Morton (1886–1957) was a widely published American poet, critic, and editor. See his *Poems 1920–1945* (1945).

5. Published 19 October 1833.

6. "The Secret of the Grave" is apparently HPL's error for "The Mystery of the Grave-Yard." Both stories are in *MW* (11–16).

7. HPL's paternal grandmother was Helen (Allgood) Lovecraft (1821–1881); his maternal grandmother was Robie Alzada (Place) Phillips (1827–1896). Vrest Orton's grandmother was a Teachout.

8. H. G. Wells, "The Country of the Blind," *Strand Magazine* (April 1904); in *The Country of the Blind and Other Stories* (1911).

9. *Netopian* 10, No. 7 (January 1930) contained "Looking Backward Through the Years on Benefit Street" (7, 10–11) and "On Benefit Street, Providence, May Be Found Some of Rhode Island's Most Characteristic Colonial Architecture" (8–9).

10. Michael Wigglesworth (1631–1705), a Puritan minister, wrote *The Day of Doom* (1662), a religious poem that was a best-seller in New England for a century after it was published.

[26]   [ALS]

[10 March 1930]

Dear Mifs Toldridge:—

I am glad to hear that the views of Benefit St. proved of interest. It is a delightful old thoroughfare, & I only wish the extreme northern & southern ends could be kept in as good condition as the choice section just south of College Hill. So far it has defied time admirably, but I fear that change will some day overtake it. Its first apartment house is now under construction—on an historic corner near the old Court House (1761), Golden Ball Inn (1784), Sign of Shakespeare's Head (home of Prov. Gazette 1763), First Baptist Church, (1775) Quaker Meeting-House (1745) & Meeting St. brick school, (1769)—& the coming of this intruder makes one fear for the safety of many of these centuried neighbours! I hope the Netopian (which is a trade magazine published by one of our local banks)[1] will present illustrated articles on other ancient Providence localities—the supply of such picturesque regions being well-nigh inexhaustible. The John Brown house is one of many notable mansions constructed by members of an opulent sea-trading family. John's brother Joseph built a house of very original design in South Main St. in 1774; which is still standing in perfect shape, & whose curved pediment & general outline have been copied in one of our newest business blocks.

Thanks exceedingly for the cuttings—especially the one about London street-names. Providence, thank heaven, has avoided the stultifying custom of numbering—our only numbered streets being ten obscure ones in the north end of the town. Our principal business thoroughfare is called *Westminster St.;* that of next importance being *Weybosset St.*—the Indian name for "place of landing." The junction of the two is known as *Turk's Head,* after the sign on one of the old shops there. I recall the old colonial building at Turk's Head—in fact, my barber had his shop there—but it has now given way to a 16-story office structure. Around the waterfront we have streets as picturesquely named as *Gold St., Silver St., Doubloon St., Guilder St., Bullion St.,* &c., & on the ancient hill the Quaker influence is manifest by such names as *Benevolent St.* But for the most part old local family names predominate—& sometimes old individual names. Thus we have a *Brown St.,* a *Chad Brown St.,* & a *Moses Brown St.* Our *Broadway* was once a splendid residential street, a mile long & lined with mansions, but is now sunk to a slum & is rapidly being engulfed by the vast Federal Hill Italian colony. Two or three of the ancient families, however, still cling to their old homes—odd oases amidst a desert of Sicilian squalor & Neapolitan noisomeness! Many of the colonial street names have disappeared—Back St. becoming Benefit St.; Gaol-Lane changing successively to King St. & Meeting St.; Presbyterian-Lane to Rosemary-Lane & later to College St., North-Baptist Lane to Thomas St., (scene of the B.K.H.–Call of Cthulhu coincidence) & so on. But it will take many more generations to drain all the quaintness out of Old Providence. Incidentally—that #10 cutting amused me. I thought of Downing St. when I moved here, but Stratton St. is a new one! By the way—enormous thanks for that Georgetown view. I have seen the house many times, & have ordinary postcard views of it; but nothing catches the spirit so well as this etching. Swann seems to have something of the sympathetic antiquarian feeling of Providence's Henry J. Peck.

The second batch of cuttings is phenomenally rich in interesting material. I shall file the Dunstanborough legend in a book of old family legends which I have, & the Roman art item will go in a work on Graeco-Roman art. That is one of the ways I keep track of cuttings—though it is a woefully unsystematic one. When I consider my files as a whole, I feel marked sympathy with De Quincey's method—as so opportunely mentioned in one of the cuttings in this lot!

That crocus picture is alluring in the extreme! We have not yet reached that stage of vernality up here, though the past week has indeed given us a fair imitation of April in temperature. One day it was 68° & another day 64°—I have made several walking expeditions, & on one occasion induced my aunt to make a brief excursion to the outer world. However, there is unfortunately much opportunity for frigid weather between now & the real spring. The Peattie article brings out much of the charm of winter, but I had much rather enjoy that charm on paper from the safe distance of Charleston or St. Augustine or New Orleans! The idea that Washington was once an In-

dian manufacturing centre is highly interesting—indeed there is much material for absorbing speculation in the whole pre-European ethnology of America. Rhode Island undoubtedly had a long & colourful Indian history, for the
artifacts & ceremonial rocks of at least one unknown pre-Algonquin race are
discernible in several localities. They call it the "red pottery race" after its
characteristic product. The false path in the Egyptian tomb is another archaeological fact of great piquancy. And speaking of Egypt—the literal news
of the day furnishes one item as good as any weird fictional plot yet written.
Have you seen the item of the suicide of Lord Westbury last Friday? He was
the father of one of the explorers of Tutankhamen's tomb, & his rooms in
London were full of strange Egyptian objects. On Friday he leapt from a 7th
floor window, leaving a note in which he said "I really cannot stand any more
horrors."[2] This is no product of imagination, but a literal bit of fact from the
day's news! I wish I could see that Viking house reconstruction in Iceland—
indeed, I have always wanted to see Iceland under appropriate summer conditions. There is a provocative imaginative fascination about "Ultima Thule"
which has affected me profoundly since childhood. I suppose Reykjavik has
much modern architecture, but even so, I fancy there must be a great deal of
the mediaeval left in it. The Georgetown article was also of interest. It pleases
me to hear that the beauty of this section is beginning to be appreciated,
though I fear that, as in the case of Providence, a large amount of destruction
as well as preservation will attend the exploitation & development.

Regarding your poems—in "Lilt & Lure", if I were you, I would make an
effort to find some compromise word—a noun—to bridge the gulf between
zest & *sweet*. The latter has overtones of sentimentality & triteness which
greatly lessen its desirability, although of course its presence would not greatly
harm the poem as a whole. Too bad the typed verses have so many misprints,
but ink-&-eraser will do much toward annulling the damage. As for book-
selections—I am carefully retaining your title-list, & will correlate it with the
MSS. I have on hand at the first adequate opportunity. In the matter of the
sentimental "epic"—I would advise caution in offering anything to the public
which would tend to suggest moods grounded in exploded fallacy. If I recall
the verses aright, they perpetuate the myth of two "souls" which are "destined" for each other—or something to that effect; a temporary decorative
idea so plainly contrary to all fact that in this honest age it has implications of
humour rather than of seriousness. There is an air of unreality about 19th century material of this sort which one can't get away from, & which becomes
glaringly obvious the moment one gives human influences & relationships a
serious & open-minded study. It may have had a poetic appeal during the
brief period—say 1830–1890—when people deliberately detached reason &
observation from their aesthetic life, but it is too far out of the main stream
of vital expression to have a permanent significance. There is no such thing as
"love" as Victorians understood—or pretended to understand—it; & the too-

ponderous treatment of the mere congeniality which comprised the non-erotic side of the nearest corresponding reality is an aesthetic mistake involving the fatal fault of emotional inappropriateness—i.e., the adoption of a manner & medium not adapted to the given material. It is a pity that so much violent "de-bunking" has to be done today—but the chief fault is with the Victorian concocters of the original "bunk" rather than with the modern truth-seekers who have the thankless task of exposing & destroying it!

I did write two more of the Yuggothian fungi, but have not typed them as yet. [*Insert:* Weird Tales has just accepted 10 of these—making 15 placed so far.] Poetry is only a side-line with me—what I want to get at is a batch of new stories, but revision gets in the way whenever I try. As for "evil" poets—don't be deluded by the myth that artistic merit has anything to do with the artificial & changeable folkway-fashions which we naively call "good" & "evil". Art—including poetry—is simply the language of the imagination raised to the highest degree of poignancy, & it makes no difference whether the imagination contains what a particular age & race may consider "good", or whether it contain what that age & race happens to group as "evil". The greatest of all French poets was the thorough Satanist Baudelaire—the very title of his principal collection being "Les Fleurs du Mal". Of all the great poets of the world, a full majority have been unspeakable scoundrels—indeed, most of the bards I chiefly admire, I'd hate to have inside my house! Not that I have any cosmic prejudice against any form of so-called "evil", but that one naturally feels somewhat uncomfortable talking to people whose basic emotions & customs are too widely different from what one's own may happen—through accidents of heredity & environment—to be.

The Washington visit of Mrs. Green-Leach[3] must have been interesting—& her connexion with the Somerled-founded house of the Isles no doubt appealed particularly to you. I can imagine the pleasure of the Washington circle as a whole at learning how well it compares with all the other local subdivisions of the national circle. As for the 1930 anthology—I don't see why you don't wish to be represented in it, for some of the material is sure to be at least reasonably good, & there is no question that it helps to get your work before audiences of genuine appreciativeness. As such anthologies go, the Green-Leach one is distinctly above the average—you ought to see the absurd mess issued by the International Writers' League![4]

Just now I am awaiting the arrival of a rather interesting gift from my fellow-fantaisiste Clark Ashton Smith—a bit of *dinosaur bone* about 500,000,000 years old. The original possessor was a being some 20 feet high which lumbered about the tropical palm & fungus groves of California until death overtook him. Then he slept through the ages until the steam-shovels of a railway cutting brought him again to the light of day. The skeleton still remains visible in the side of the cut—glimpsed by travellers from car windows, but largely undisturbed because it is too fragmentary to be of museum value, & too remote from any settlement to invite frequent souvenir-hunters. Smith himself visited it on a camping trip, & took several souvenirs for himself & his fantastically inclined friends. It certainly will be quite an imaginative stimulus! Smith is writing a great deal of weird prose nowadays—something of a departure from his usual poetry & painting.

> With best wishes,
> Yr most obᵗ hble Servt
> H P Lovecraft

Notes

1. Published by the Rhode Island Hospital Trust Co.
2. Richard Luttrell Pilkington Bethell, 3rd Baron Westbury (1852–1930).
3. Leacy Naylor Green-Leach (1862–1936) established the Baltimore literary group, the American Poetry Circle, and also founded and edited the Baltimore-based literary magazine, the *Circle*, which ran from 1923 until 1938. She was also the publisher of the *American Poetry Circle Anthology*.
4. Ethel Brooks Koger, ed., *Florida Poets* (Newport, KY: International Writer's League, 1930f.).

[27]   [ALS]

[mid-March 1930]

Dear Mifs Toldridge:—

I note the new & the revised poems with much interest, & am sure that all four are eminently suitable for the future book. I don't see anything to revise in "Crusade" & "The Convert"—& virtually no flaws in the other two. However, in "The Other Things" I believe I'd change two singular nouns to plural toward the end—*arabesques* & *reflections*. This rendering appears to me to make for greater idiomatic smoothness. As for the queries—I think the existing "all these beauties" is much better than "these loved beauties" would be. "Dim etchings" is vastly—*infinitely*—preferable to "rare sketches." The word *rare* is so poetically hackneyed as to be almost taboo in good verse. In the "cloud" line, the existing *arabesques* version has the clearer image-value, though the alternative version "flower & leaf & cloud" has a compensating suggestion-value which makes choice difficult. It would not harm the poem to use either. In "Ships", my advice would be to stick to "she is bound" for l. 6. The inverted idiom is wholly meaningless, & detracts from the poem because it calls attention to itself as a mechanical & unmotivated device. This unnatural language suggests the inflated, romantic, unnatural 19ᵗʰ century approach to poetry. With the restoration of normal sincerity to verse, there must come likewise a restoration of sincere & direct diction. In the 9ᵗʰ line I fancy "for the many" would be better, after all, than "for a many." All these poems are highly attractive, & well worthy of inclusion in a published collection.

The illuminated card is a delightful piece of work, & I am very grateful for the opportunity of adding it to my files. Your skill in this delicate artistic medium is extremely enviable, & I trust it meets appropriate recognition—both aesthetic & financial—in the proper quarters. Again let me thank you for the pleasing specimen.

Considering the mediocre & uncritical nature of the accepting media, I don't think the acceptance of some of my "Fungi" argues very much for their quality. I have just dumped four more on *Driftwind* & six others on W. Paul Cook's *Recluse*—these being unremunerative publications. Am still stalled on page 26 of my new story,[1] since imperative revisory matters have wholly engulfed me.

Thanks for sending *The Circle*, which I will return safely. The activities of the group must be highly interesting, & I am sure you ought to enter all the various contests. The excitement of competing must be far from negligible, & you really have excellent chances of winning prominent awards—perhaps first awards—in any of the classes. It is too bad that Mrs. Green-Leach is so careless about attending to changes in poems, but possibly a few lessons like the recent "Eagle" incident will serve as at least a partial corrective. Meanwhile it would pay poets to be very careful not to send in anything for *The Circle* until they feel sure it is in its final & best possible form. There is always a temptation to send a thing prematurely—to secure a place for it, as it were, no matter how many changes are contemplated in the text. But obviously, this is a policy one cannot safely follow in the case of *The Circle*.

About correcting your MSS.—you don't need to be punctiliously artistic about it so long as you take pains to be perfectly *legible*. It doesn't take so very much time & effort to go over a bunch of MSS. in this way—I did a MS. of 92 pages (i.e., going over it for bad typing & correcting the errors in ink) in a single evening a couple of weeks ago. I don't believe it would do any harm to insert a sentence in "The Rosebush" with ink. The better grade of editors are not sticklers in such matters—in fact, the only editorial group I know of that *would* object to pen-&-ink inserts, is one so sensational & low-grade that your MSS. would never fit them anyway. . . . I refer to the Macfadden group.

Glad to hear that Mifs Radcliffe has secured a prize. Not long ago I received from her a magazine with a very appealing poem about the Great Falls of the Potomac, which I believe are imperilled by some miserable mechanical water-power project. I am sorry to learn that your aunt's health does not improve, but trust there is still room for a turn toward the better.

As for "When Souls Strike Fire"—the only reason I suggest the postponement for some later volume is that it might puzzle the reader accustomed to contemporary conceptions of values, & impair the acceptance of the purely lyrical items in the book. This might not be true if it were shorter in proportion, but its length would single it out for especial notice. As I believe I said when surveying it a year or so ago, it is excellent as a poem, but

rather obviously reflects a philosophy based on a completely exploded conception of the universe & of the basic sources, bearings, linkages, & operation
of human emotions. Since the pioneering work of Freud & the still more analytical work of his successors—Pavlov, Jung, Adler, Watson, &c. &c. &c. we
have come to see that there is no such thing as "love" in any unified, permanent, or important sense; & recognise that the earlier notions of such matters
were due to sheer lack of scientific knowledge & to certain well-defined poetic
or religio-mystical delusions. To speak of the "immortality" or cosmic significance of anything as mythical or illusory as "love", is today essentially meaningless; so that serious poetry can no longer continue to echo the mediaeval-
Victorian way of handling such themes. It is notable that the extremely sentimental treatment of "love" has been almost wholly confined to ages of either great ignorance (such as the romantic & squalid Middle Ages) or great
affectation & self-delusion. (such as the Victorian age.) Even in the absence
of technical psychological scholarship, all the more rational ages of the past—
Greece, Rome, the Elizabethan era, the 18th century—had a healthy instinctive perspective & sense of solid reality which withheld them from the most
attenuated & insipid forms of romantic extravagance. Their treatment of
amatory themes was robust & lifelike & honest—with a saving sense of nor-
mality which always kept clear of spinning illusory cobwebs of cosmic significance about the mating phenomena of mankind. Such is the main line of
major poetic tradition, to which the 20th century has very healthily returned.
The moonstruck rhapsodisings of the mediaeval sentimentalists, & the similar
extravagances of Victorians who assiduously cultivated the mediaeval mood,
are distinct variants from the major stream. Most certainly, it would pay the
poet to beware of weaving intense ecstasies around things which do not exist—around artificial ideas & delusions which have no counterparts in the
world of normal phenomena. The one exception, perhaps, concerns the
myths & unrealities of religious faith, whose profound inculcation into the
now dying cultural cycle has given them a sort of unity & coherence & spurious life. But even these myths will have to be excised from the poetic field in
a century or less, when religion will have ceased to be believed by any people
who think at all. It is more than probable, too, that my own type of phantasy
will cease to be aesthetically significant when the habit of normal perception
& appraisal becomes general & instinctive among the western races. I am sure
that the changes in your poem must all be in the right direction, & believe
that in any but an important first book it would be pleasantly acceptable as an
echo of older attitudes which we all recall, or have heard of, even though we
no longer share them.

The cuttings you enclosed are of extreme interest—that about the "star
jelly" being absorbingly & superlatively so. No idea has ever fascinated me so
much as that of the wafting of alien life across space, & I have enjoyed reading about these doubtful phenomena in books like Charles Fort's eccentric

"Book of the Damned" and "New Lands." It is really improbable that any matter in the condition we recognise as "organic" could manage to get from one orb to another under the strenuous conditions of meteoric flight, though these occasional reports certainly do have their puzzling aspects. I have used the idea once—in "The Colour Out of Space"—& may yet use it again in a different way. In fact, I am suggesting it in the Vermont tale now half-completed. This cutting contains a number of points I had not encountered before, & goes at once into my choicest files. Incidentally—you have no doubt read reports of the discovery of the new trans-Neptunian planet . . . . a thing which excites me more than any other happening of recent times. Its existence is no surprise, for observers have long known that one or more such worlds probably exist beyond Neptune; yet its actually finding carries hardly less glamour on that account. Keats (thinking no doubt of Herschel's discovery of Uranus in 1781, or perhaps of the finding of the earlier asteroids) caught the magic of planetary discovery in two lines of his Chapman's Homer sonnet,[2] & that magic is surely as keen today as then. Asteroidal discovery does not mean much—but a major planet—a vast unknown world—is quite another matter. I have always wished I could live to see such a thing come to light—& here it is! The first real planet to be discovered since 1846, & only the *third* in the history of the human race! One wonders what it is like, & what dim-litten fungi may sprout coldly on its frozen surface! I think I shall suggest its being named "Yuggoth"![3] Reports make it smaller than Uranus & Neptune, but larger than the earth. I shall await its ephemerides & elements with interest. Probably it will receive a symbol & be treated of in the Nautical Almanack—I wonder whether it will get into the popular almanacks as well? Probably the future 200-inch reflector to be set up in California will tell more about it—& perhaps even help in locating still more distant planets. There is still quite a bit of interest in the limited solar system despite the diversion of astronomers' chief notice to the larger problems of the stellar universe. Another thing that pleases me is that the newcomer came to light at the Lowell Observatory, & from Lowell's own calculations. Poor chap! His better known observations & speculations never fared well in the scientific world; but now, thirteen years after his death, it is possible that his calculations may win him a major place among astronomers.

The lost city in Queretaro is another fascinating theme—& still more so is the exploration of the Carlsbad Caverns. This tremendous underground world almost paralyses the imagination—there is no telling what gulfs beyond gulfs the adventurers may not find as they penetrate farther & farther toward the earth's core. One is reminded of Jules Verne's tale of a journey to the centre of the earth. The loss of "Abingdon" is indeed a tragedy—& a warning to those who postpone historic restorations till too late. From the picture, though, I judge that the old house had been badly malformed & modernised at some time during the barbarous neo-Gothic period—say 1830–1850. The Bridges material is interesting. Without doubt "The Testament of Beauty["][4]

is a very tedious & Victorian thing as a whole—full of arid sententiousness & tawdry artificialities—yet equally without doubt it must rise at times to heights of genuine vision & authentic beauty.

Later

　　The Circle & your second letter have now arrived, & I am highly grateful for the generous array of material enclosed. The magazine has some very good stuff in it, though I cannot understand the allotment of the "page of honour" to that screamingly ridiculous burlesque on bad verse entitled "A Song of Life."[5] Unless it is a joke, the only reason I can think of for such a "howler" in a distinguished place is that of commercial "pull"—for I notice that the *Circle*'s editor is also the publisher of a book of alleged "poems" by the perpetrator of this monstrosity. But be it a joke or a business trick, it's a bad thing for the prestige of the magazine!

　　There were some very interesting things among the cuttings—& I note the stained glass item. There is indeed a singular aesthetic & imaginative appeal in painted windows, as most old-world travellers attest—though I am myself not so sensitive to Gothic & mediaeval arts as to things of the Graeco-Roman tradition. Many of the older New England churches inserted stained glass during the Victorian age, but they are now removing them very largely in the interest of architectural harmony—since small plain panes are what go with Georgian architecture. Trinity in Newport is the latest church to plan such colonial restoration. On account of your interest in the subject I am reënclosing the item—for you may wish to file it yourself. The Irish "history" is interesting, though Father Dwyer has obviously allowed himself to get a bit ahead of the probable facts amidst his laudable ancestral patriotism. The "Milesians" are probably pure myth[6]—although of course many waves of prehistoric migration brought various races of Mediterranean, Nordic, & Alpine race-stock over both of the British Isles. In the early historic period the peoples of Britain & Ireland were very much alike—& very much like the Gauls of the Continent. Ireland probably surpassed Britain in settled folkways & arts, but the condition was hardly what one could call an actual civilisation. It probably parallelled the advanced barbarian-cultures of Gaul & Spain—which of course included settled town-dwelling & considerable artistic craftsmanship. The new-planet data, naturally, interested me greatly; & I appreciated the references to Poe memorials in Baltimore. The Peattie nature articles, too, are perennially full of charm. I could appreciate that reference to the artificial spring & summer obtainable in florists' shops, because in childhood I used to haunt such places about February, when the strain of hated winter became unbearable. I liked to walk through the long greenhouses & imbibe the atmosphere of warm earth & plant-life, & see the vivid masses of green & floral colour. One of my early doggerel attempts was a description of an hypothetical glass-covered, furnace-heated world of groves & gardens in which one might spend a decently painless winter!

The dinosaur bone-fragments have come—crumbling bits of organic phosphate with whispers of palaeogean antiquity around them. But I must have been half-asleep in saying they are *five hundred million* years old! I am getting careless with ciphers, I fancy, in my old age! The approximate period of the great reptiles was *50,000,000*—*fifty-million*—years ago—the Cretaceous age. *500,000,000* years would carry one back to the time of the protozoa! Yes—a dinosaur skeleton surely *would* be worth crossing a continent to see; but I don't have to do it, since there are several excellent specimens— mounted, & with missing bones carefully supplied in plaster—in the American Museum of Natural History in N.Y.

"Rue & Ruin" would be a good title for a poem. No need of worrying about subject-matter—whatever exists in the surrounding world is appropriate for poetic treatment, one thing as much as another. Don't let the explosion of Victorian myth & humbug disturb you. There was no real value in the "da-da-da" namby-pamby pretences & fashions of that amusing era. What fun or benefit could anybody get from swallowing a whole scale of milk & water falsities & values—for the most part pitifully sterile, thin, & unimaginative—when there is enough real, pagan, visual beauty in the world to keep any poetic mind busy without them? I can't see that the passing of such sickly lies as the "twin soul" bunk &c. leaves existence especially barren. Not more than a third of the intelligent population ever believed the old stuff anyway—I know I didn't, & I was born far back enough—1890—to catch its death-rattles—& there are too many absorbing realities—colour, form, rhythm, wonder—which nothing can destroy to make one need to mourn a temporary bit of cheap "hokum". In my chosen 18th century people got on very well without the mawkish insincerities & delusions of the age that followed. Plenty of time to choose an anthology poem—I am sure it would be pleasant to be represented. And I'd send poems to the London Poetry Review,[7] too, if I were you. My own stuff wouldn't be likely to fit there—although I might shoot on a few items if I wrote another batch.

What you say about Providence is certainly correct, & I well know that no other town could fit me so naturally. If cold weather ever does force me to transfer my base southward, I shall probably choose not Bermuda but some place like Charleston, which presumably has more resemblances to my native milieu. As for transitions—the advent of machinery is making the present one more violent than most, but I guess there'll be enough of the older world left standing to last me out.

Clark Ashton Smith's stories are very good—some of them notably so— though they scarcely equal his verse. About half, so far, have landed in *Weird Tales*. Young Long flourishes unabated—I shall see him next month when I take my trip. I still hear from the witch-descendant, but have not received any dark inner hereditary legends as yet. Most such legends have a tendency to evaporate & turn pale when reduced to concreteness & visibility.

With best wishes, & renewed thanks for all the material sent,
    I remain
            Yr moft oblig'd ob^t Servt
                H P Lovecraft

P.S. Heard a good lecture on modern French art last week by Prof. Sachs of Harvard. Providence is having a notable exhibition of this material—Cezanne, Gauguin, Van Gogh, Degas, Seurat, Picasso, Matisse, &c. &c.—at the art museum, so that a whole group of lectures is clustering around it.[8]

Notes

1. "The Whisperer in Darkness."
2. HPL refers to Keats's sonnet "On First Looking into Chapman's Homer" (October 1816), which tells of the author's astonishment at reading Homer as freely translated by the Elizabethan playwright George Chapman. HPL specifically refers to ll. 9–10: "Then felt I like some watcher of the skies / When a new planet swims into his ken . . ." Neptune was discovered in 1846.
3. "XIV. Starwinds" contains the lines "This is the hour when moonstruck poets know / What fungi sprout in Yuggoth . . . " (ll. 9–10).Venetia Burney (1918–2009), an eleven-year-old schoolgirl in Oxford, England, interested in classical mythology and astronomy, suggested to her grandfather Falconer Madan, a former librarian at the Bodleian Library, that the planet be named *Pluto*. Her suggestion was cabled to colleagues in the United States. The object was officially named on 24 March 1930 (in preference to Minerva and Cronus), and the name was announced on 1 May.
4. A long philosophic poem (1929) by Robert Seymour Bridges (1844–1930).
5. Marianne Clarke, "A Song of Life," *Circle* (March–April 1930). The book was *Miss America* (New York: Leacy Naylor Green-Leach, 1929).
6. In Irish mythology, the Milesians were the descendants of Míl Espáine, the final invaders of Ireland who defeated and displaced the semi-divine Tuatha Dé Danann.
7. *Poetry Review* (London, 1912f.), still being published.
8. HPL refers to Paul J. Sachs (1878–1965), professor of fine arts at Harvard and director of the Fogg Museum (1923–45) there. Cf. HPL to Frank Belknap Long, 14 March 1930 (ms., JHL), "Last Wednesday night [c. March 5 or 12?] my aunt dragged me to a lecture on this exhibition by Prof. Sachs of Harvard, so that I have acquired at least a vague idea of what these queer foreign monkeys were trying to do when they scatter'd their paint around so promiscuously."

[28]   [ALS]

                                                [24 April 1930]

Dear Mifs Toldridge:—
            Before starting on the long trip—beginning with a visit of a week or two at young Long's in N.Y.—which will constitute my annual hibernation-breaking, I must express my thanks for the recent batch of

enclosures. They surely include some tremendously interesting items—especially the account of surviving old London houses & the glimpse of pirate tradition on Cape Cod. It pleased me, too, to see the Georgian style hailed as the typical architecture of America; & I hope that this point of view will be retained in the future, despite what the coming Chicago Exposition will do to popularise the modernistic conception of a machine architecture based on the mere balancing of bleak and barren masses. Glad that the floods spared Carcassonne—a place I wish very much to see along with Nuremburg, Ratsibon, Rothenburg, & other European towns where the mediaeval order of things remains virtually unchanged by the centuries. The number of such unspoiled reliques grows less year by year. It is a pity, by the way, that the Roman bridge at Treves—the ancient Augusta Trevirorum—will have to be enlarged. I wish it could be let alone, & a vehicular tunnel be bored under the river to supply increased traffic needs. The Abyssinian cat item interested me greatly, since cats are my favourite living things. I rather prefer the present European breed, though, to the primitive African type with large ears & pointed muzzle. Of all cats, I like the Siamese type the least, & the common black type—with large yellow eyes—the most. I note the item about Hart Crane's new poem with much interest, since Crane is a friend of my friend Samuel Loveman. He comes from Cleveland, & when sober—as he is once or twice a year—is an admirably attractive chap. I have met him several times, for he lived in Brooklyn when I did—having a room in an old house on the harbour side of Columbia Heights, within sight of the spidery arc of Brooklyn Bridge, which formed the subject of his then-nascent chef-d'oeuvre.[1] If he doesn't die of delirium tremens before another decade is over, he will form one of the standard figures in the poetry of the younger generation. He is part of the semi-Greenwich-Village crowd which includes E. E. Cummings, Waldo Frank, John Dos Passos, & other well-known modernists.

I shall be on the road in a very few days now, for the weather is getting decently civilised. After my sojourn with Long & the "gang" in N.Y., my aim is to get as far south as my cash will take me—utilising motor "lifts", of which Long & his parents will give me the first, to cut down coach fare. I don't know even remotely how chance will arrange my programme, but I hope to make Charleston at least. I'll have to take some work along, but I can perform it more readily in a genial climate. From all accounts, Charleston must be one of the most fascinating old Georgian cities in the United States, & I hope I can afford to stop there at least a week. Whether I shall be able to manage a site-trip to Savannah is yet problematical.

Thanks very much for *The Carillon*, which I shall return safely. Its contents represent a high degree of inspiration & accomplishment, & I certainly hope it will prove a successful & permanent venture. The Sarrett & Bellamann pieces strike me most poignantly of all the contributions—both authors have been favourites of mine for many years.[2] Thanks for permission to retain the magazine, but I really think you ought to retain a complete file yourself, since your own connexion with poetry is so much more active & continuous than mine. Accordingly I will send the copy along before I start on my trip.

Special thanks are due you for the delightful & timely assortment of cards which recently came. I appreciate the greeting exceedingly, & shall use the extras to much advantage—especially the birthday one, which by coincidence comes just in time for my elder aunt, who turns 74 on the 20th of this month.

The poem on the tree-toads is delectable, & really ought to go into your future volume. I feel sure that time & reflection will bring to light a perfect *-eace* rhyme in l. 6 to replace *trees*. Have you thought of *fleece*—perhaps in connexion with the idea of wave-tips? If I had more time just now I'd try to devise an alternative—perhaps I shall think of one later on. But the piece is delightful just as it is. Enclosed is a cutting on some more northerly spring chirpers—which need not be returned.

The second batch of cuttings includes some highly interesting material. I was particularly glad to learn about the location of that Key homestead, for which I have twice looked in vain as a result of vague guidebook directions. The geographical & anthropological items are interesting—photography of unknown Thibet mountains recalls the native legends of the mysterious "Mi-Go", or "Abominable Snow Men" who dwell on the inaccessible peaks of that region. The Florida excavations may be of distinct value to science—& the lately traced links betwixt Japan & Polynesia are of the utmost significance. The cyclopean effigies on Easter Island are still a tremendously alluring challenge to archaeology.

The third shipment also held some fascinating items—& I was interested at getting my first glimpse of the Charleston stamps. I hope to be in Charleston within three weeks. Thanks for the alluring illustrated booklet. Tropical echoes always please me, for I haven't your ability to enjoy the allegedly temperate zone except in May, June, July, & August. All the rest of the year is a total loss to me. If I had cash I'd spend the residual nightmare-months in Jamaica or somewhere—possibly in Argentina or Australia, where summer coincides with the northern winter. For as a matter of fact, I really like the scenery of a temperate zone in summer better than the scenery of the tropics. The ideal plan would be to follow the temperate summer around the globe. As for arctic climate in past ages—despite the recent Berry conclusions I think the question must still be considered an open one. The same problem exists in the Antarctic also, geologists of the Byrd expedition having found many fossils indicating a tropical past. The study of the earth's remote history must still be regarded as in its infancy. The architectural "doo-dad" article interested me—it really contains a vast amount of truth. That State, War, & Navy building represents the lowest level to which human taste can sink—a vicious taste that infected America like a plague from 1850 to 1900. Providence has some hideous specimens left from that period—including the City Hall & the Old Superior Court House—but thank heaven the latter is now in the hands of the wreckers. However—it is possible to overdo the matter of objecting to ornamentation. Each of the really fine traditional forms of architecture has its natural decorative elements, naturally evolved through considerations of structural support or harmonious balance of design. These elements, confined to their proper place, are certainly not to be grouped in the "doo-dad" class—which answers your query about Gothic columns so far as structures of true Gothic conception & design are concerned. The Washington cathedral, I might remark, is developing into a splendid work of art—which I think will surpass New York's rival cathedral of St John the Divine in the end. The trouble is that many builders—especially in the Victorian age—have not confined their use of traditional design to its correct traditional functions & proportions. Even the modern packing-box architecture is better than ornament of a tawdry, out-of-place, excessive, or misproportioned sort. Washington, on the whole, has been very fortunate architecturally. Most of the northern cities have ten times as much structural ugliness cluttering up their streets—downtown Boston being an especially depressing example. New York until about 1910–20 was a hideous nightmare, but now the skyscrapers have saved it by giving it (at a distance) an exotic & fairylike appearance. The only really lovely places in America—architecturally speaking—are certain old villages which progress has left behind. Luckily Rhode Island has a goodly quota of these—the drowsy little seaport of Wickford, on the west shore of Narragansett Bay, being my nomination for first prize. The Harrow article greatly interested me. It is my opinion that the liberal education of the old public school ought certainly to be retained—to train high-grade minds in the art of getting as much as possible out of the experience of living—despite the spread of industrial & mechanical interests amongst the majority. Even in a politically & economically socialistic state—the inevitable state of tomorrow—it seems to me that it might be possible to maintain a tradition of genuine cultivation & aesthetic sensitiveness among a more or less limited circle of appreciative & reflective persons. Still—the moods & knowledge of today certainly demand a marked variation from the over-conventionalised curriculum of the public school as hitherto known.

I am glad you have found my remarks on your verse helpful—but don't regret your inability to write in modern style. Sincere & artistic expression of visible beauty, if plainly & straightforwardly recorded without extravagances or tawdry mannerisms, is always of genuine value, whether or not it is shaped in the mould of any particular period. The best art is timeless—independent of any one age, but reduced to such simplicity & plainness that it belongs to all. Many of the typical mannerisms of our present moderns are just as cheap & artificial in their way as the older Victorian mannerisms against which I constantly preach. It is the best policy to steer clear of them all—to cling to the main stream of plain, vital language & reasonable coherence, eschewing whatever savours of the local, the transient, & the affected. This applies equally to the Victorian *oh's* & *ah's* & *haths* & *erewhiles,* & to the ultra-modern jazz & chaoticist effects. Much of the new stuff will be laughed at in 1980 as heartily as 1880 stuff is laughed at now—& will still be laughed at then. What will escape laughter is the plain recording of images & moods genuinely experienced—whether in 1380, 1580, 1680, 1830, 1880, 1930, or any other time!

That art exhibition was vastly interesting historically, although my personal taste does not incline toward the newer schools of painting. I fully comprehend & appreciate the moderns in an objective way—sympathising with their efforts to reduce all art to rhythmic & decorative principles—but my own aesthetic sense demands the coherent patterns of older & less abstract ages. Providence indeed has a fair quota of aesthetic advantages—museums, lectures, institutions of learning, & so on. In fact, three of its treasures are the foremost of their kind in the world—the John Carter Brown Library's collection of early Americana, the Annmary Brown Memorial Library's collection of books printed before 1500, & the Pendleton Collection of Georgian furniture.[3]

My Vermont story is stalled on page 32—rush of work at this pre-voyage season having left me not a moment of leisure to write on it. I may take it along with me to do in Charleston—as I shall have to take a certain amount of revisory work. The scenes of this tale are entirely on the earth—in the wild hills of Vermont—although not all of the living characters originated on the earth.

As for philosophic matters—my remarks ought not to have much novelty or shock-effect in 1930, since most of the idols I ridicule have been virtually dead for a third of a century. I think you would find your perspective greatly clarified by a coherent knowledge of the course of human thought since the earliest times—a knowledge which would shew you that the phase of delusion just overthrown has never been a deeply seated or universal thing. Actually, the moderns think much as Democritus did in 450 B.C., as Lucretius did in 65 or 70 B.C., as Spinoza did in the 17th century, & as La Mettrie, Diderot, Helvetius, Hume, & dozens of others did in the supremely rational 18th century. You ought most emphatically to read "The Story of Philosophy" by Dr. Will Durant, which has just been added to the list of "Star Dollar Books"— obtainable at any bookshop or Liggett drugstore for a dollar. This is a simple layman's introduction to the subject, & reads as easily, straightforwardly, & fascinatingly as a novel. I don't know of anything which gives a better idea & perspective of the way the various ages have inquired into the nature of things. You can also get this work in separate parts in the Haldeman-Julius Blue Books—a list of which I enclose. The Blue Books include scores of items which you would find most enlightening. If, after reading Durant, you want a fuller idea of the way intelligent contemporaries regard the cosmos & its illusions of value, you can't do better than to read the works of the greatest living philosopher (who is a poet as well)—George Santayana. Begin with his "Scepticism & Animal Faith", & then proceed to the five-volume "Life of Reason". A shorter, harsher, & more typically American angle is afforded by Joseph

Wood Krutch's "The Modern Temper." This "love" business is pretty well disposed of by the psycho-analysts—Freud, Jung, Adler,—& the behaviourists of Dr. John B. Watson's school. But the notion of "immortality" has been dead among serious thinkers for an even longer time—no first-rate philosopher in the world's history has ever had a great deal of use for it, & for fully fifty years no high-grade thinker of any sort has taken it as more than a poetic dream. Even the professed Christian believers of today—save for a pathetic residue of yesterday's age of orthodoxy—regard a "hereafter" as merely an allegorical crystallisation of an ancient human wish. There is absolutely nothing in the idea of personal immortality—it the deadest notion in the whole ash-heap of burned-out delusions. But nobody need mourn about it. Even an ordinary life-span gives most people all the boredom they can stand, & if they had immortality they would eventually find it unendurable. It is significant that the only living race who still *really* believe in future lives—the Hindoos—conceive as their highest final reward a "Nirvana" which implies the ultimate extinction of consciousness after many reincarnations. I'm sure I don't want anything more than non-existence when I round out a few decades more. I had it before I was born—through all the aeons prior to Aug. 20, 1890—& I don't see why it will suit me any less after I die—through all the aeons subsequent to 1960 or 1970 or so. I've no complaint to enter about the way the cosmos treated me in the pre-1890 days when I didn't exist, & the thought of other such days to come doesn't disturb me in the least. On again, off again! And while I do exist—though it be but for a brief moment—I utilise my mind & aesthetic sense in such a way as to gather in all the pleasure & beauty I can. Eat, drink, & be merry—for tomorrow doesn't exist!

By the way—I can't agree that the habit of *normal perception & appraisal* would cause imagination to whither away. The proper province of imagination is wholly removed from the world of objective phenomena which perception & appraisal cover, & I have found that the force of an imaginative image is even *heightened* by juxtaposition with objective images realistically treated. In a word, imagination does not need to *contradict* truth, but preferably reaches out into the abyss of the unknowable & *supplements* truth. Romantic *contradictions of known truth* are always ridiculous; but fantastic *excursions beyond truth* or *excrescences upon truth* are not necessarily so. Thus whilst I cultivate *phantasy*, I laugh at & am sickened by mere *romance*. If one must weave cobwebs of empty aether, let them not constitute puerile denials of what we know to be fact, but rather let them supply a decorative element to those cosmic spaces which would otherwise be an ambiguous & tantalising void. Thus the best religions are toys or soporifics which do not visibly clash with the recognised phenomena of life. Dumas & Walter Scott bore me, but Dunsany, the Bible, Grimms' Fairy Tales, & the Arabian Nights interest & delight me. No—I shan't give up writing phantasy, although I think I shall have fewer & fewer readers as time passes. Fortunately I don't give a hang whether or not anybody reads what I write.

About "When Souls Take Fire"—yes, as I said before, it has some splendid imagery & phraseology, & surely makes the most of its subject. It is good & powerful work—& would be perfectly all right in any but a first book. Undoubtedly effective treatment can cause a fallacious subject or point of view to "get by" now & then—especially if the author was sincere & intense in his delusion at the time of writing. Thus Dante & Milton still rank near the top of the poetic ladder, even though their basic conceptions of man & the cosmos now rank among the world's waste paper & standing jokes.

But speaking of poetry—your new piece, "Horse Chestnut", is an absolutely magnificent little lyric; full of delicately vivid images & haunting overtones of cosmic mystery & beauty. I'd rank it even a trifle above "The Magic Charms"—& I surely hope it will see appropriate print in the course of time. The only emendation I could possibly suggest is in the third line of the third stanza, where the syllables seem crowded despite the most heroic efforts at rhetorical elision. Fortunately this matter can be remedied with the most extreme simplicity, & without any sacrifice of sense. Simply leave off the word *Its* & you have a perfect line

In-ex´-pli-ca-ble dreams

which harmonises with all the other corresponding lines—

Triumphant to the spring
Swaying above the curb
—&c.

Surely this is an Easter card de luxe! Don't fail to send it to *The Circle* or some other suitable repository.

No—there hasn't been any spring to speak of in Providence as yet. It's surprising what a difference three degrees of latitude can make. We've had a few flowers, but the buds on the trees shew no haste to burgeon forth into foliage. It's never any good in R.I. till May. Well—I hope to be in a warmer clime shortly. In a few days I shall be in N.Y. with Long, & after that my programme is indeterminate. But the general motto is "Charleston or bust!"

Best wishes—yr obt h^{ble} Servt

H P Lovecraft

Notes

1. Hart Crane's *The Bridge* appeared in 1930.

2. Lew Sarett (1888–1954), a professor at Northwestern University, was the author of *Many Many Moons* (1920), *The Box of God* (1922), *Slow Smoke* (1925), and *Wings Against the Moon* (1932). Henry Bellamann (1882–1945), American novelist, poet, and music instructor, published the poetry volumes *Cups of Illusion* (1923) and *The Upward Pass* (1928). *Carillon* 1, No. 3 (April 1930): Sarett, "April Rain" (p. 3); Bellamann, "Windy Day" (p. 5).

3. The Pendleton Collection is held at the Rhode Island School of Design.

[29]   [ALS]

En route—
Kingston, N.Y.,
June 5, 1930

Dear Miss Toldridge:—

Your three envelopes were forwarded to me in New York, & I am very grateful of the varied & interesting contents. The cuttings were all of interest—though I was sorry to learn of the destruction of Bassett Hall in Williamsburg, which I saw in May 12—only 4 days before the fire. Oddly enough, I passed through Danville on the very day after that meteor was found—though I did not know of it till I read of it in the Richmond papers on the following day.

The verses are all delightful, & the Holmes tribute has a timely & appropriate ring. "Magic Charms" is splendid, & I think the form *musics* is quite permissible. The only changes I suggest are (a) line 2, where the expression "heart-stirrings" takes its accents awkwardly, (heart´-stir̆-rings´ (could you say

˘ – ˘ – ˘ – ˘ – ˘

As gentle as a murmur born of peace?)

(b) line 4—"flag is furled" sounds trite—but perhaps it is all right for this once.
(c) line 8—for *be* read *is*. (colloq. pref.)
(d) line 12—redundant syllables. Could you say "Echoes of wonders in her oldest wood"?

"Ephemera" is magnificent—I can't think of anything which ought to be changed in it.

As for sonnet competitions—thanks exceedingly for the circular, but I fear my stuff has not the qualities looked for in anything of this sort. I am retaining the prospectus, insomuch as the contest appears to be open until next year. However, most of my effort just now will go into fiction—one specimen of which I have been modelling in odd moments on my trip, & which I shall try to whip into final shape when I get home. I have a letter from the publishers Simon & Schuster encouraging me to submit a novel, & I may do it if all turns out well.[1] There is no guarantee of acceptance, but it would at least get a decent editorial reading & a mature verdict.

As for the sonnets you mention as being wrong in the sestette—surely you have no reason to be discouraged about them unless they happen to violate the arbitrary rules of some particular contest. There is always a certain amount of latitude permissible in the sestette of a sonnet, & many if not most of the standard poets have taken advantage of this fact to produce very varied types. I myself never bother about arbitrary rules—in fact, I adopt all sorts of arrangements, & invariably end in a couplet. Young Frank B. Long goes to still further extremes of liberalism, & introduces original variations even in the octave. You are right in considering "In the Woods" among your best sonnets, & I am sure it ought to fare well in any contest wherein it may be entered.

Concerning possible changes in public demand as applied to poetry—I can hardly give an expert opinion, since I make no attempt to follow verse seriously or keep track of contemporary trends. On a guess, however, I would say that what is wanted is simply a sincere & straightforward symbolisation of actual human moods & feelings—taken from real life & experience rather than reflecting literary backgrounds. This principle ought not to militate against regular & traditional verse if it is poignant & sincere, but I suppose in practice most judges tend to question the subconscious first handness of sentiments which too much resemble the artificial or frequently-exploited sentiments of familiar standard verse. It would take a really profound critic to glimpse the touch of sincerity in poetry whose exterior is thoroughly conventional & seemingly derived from orthodox literary sources. That is the inevitable handicap of the traditionalist today. Don't try to write to order, though. No verse is effective unless it is spontaneous. The thing to do is to cultivate an independent outlook toward the external world; avoiding all traces of artificiality, conventionality, & traditional sentimentality. What then comes out naturally in the way of poetry is likely to be the real stuff. Certainly—I'll be glad to look over your book MS. when it is complete, & surely hope it can get into type sooner or later.

I was very sorry not to be able to stop off at Washington on my return trip, but my stay in Richmond was so prolonged that all my cash was gone except my return fare. In New York I found cheques which gave me a financial "second wind" for my wanderings; hence after a 2-weeks' visit with Frank B. Long & frequent meetings with others of the "old gang" I have ascended the Hudson to ancient Kingston—that town of old stone houses in the idyllic Catskill region which I think I described last year—to visit the gifted artist Bernard Dwyer. We are spending every day in the open country—weather having been kind to us—& Dwyer has just presented me with a splendid pencil sketch of our favourite landscape spot—a lonely knoll with a great rock, a giant elm, & a vista of distant rolling plains & purple mountains which could scarcely be duplicated—in point of quiet pastoral beauty—anywhere on the globe. The north is surely lovely enough when summer does come—but the trouble is that this elusive season arrives provokingly late & departs tantalisingly early. From here I shall cross the Mohawk Trail to Athol, have a look at W. Paul Cook, & then descend to Providence via Worcester. Another week will probably see me at my own hearth after an absence of a month & a half.

Charleston not only equalled but surpassed my brightest expectations. It is a marvellous 18th century survival, & probably preserves more of the colonial architecture & spirit than any other place in the United States. The climate is ideal—I would move there for good in a moment if my attachment to Rhode Island were less strong. Houses date from 1730 to about 1810 in the old section below Broad St., & include many types unknown to the north. Most of them are of stuccoed brick, with steep tiled roofs which give them a sort of continental aspect. Piazzas on all three stories, opening on walled gardens with magnificent wrought-iron gates, (see enclosed card) testify to the outdoor mode of life worked out by the colonists after they had become thoroughly assimilated in this exotic geographic milieu. In cultural tone Charleston is not excelled by any city on this continent. [Its re]lative isolation, & the long seasons spent in it by neighbouring planters whose estates became malarial in summer, made it a peculiarly independent & vigorous centre of taste & learning, & it is today a veritable last stronghold of our dying elder civilisation. I arrived too late to see the gardens at their best, but what I did see was amply enough for one trip![2]

In Richmond I looked up various sites & objects connected with Poe, & did a good deal of writing in the exquisite Maymont Gardens of which I enclose a descriptive folder. The Japanese section of this marvellous place surpasses in exotic glamour anything I have ever seen before—I get almost maudlin whenever I try to describe it. It is a direct embodiment of a type of dreamlike scene which I have always envisaged as a sort of imaginative phantom—"The Gardens of Yin", as it were[3]—but which I hardly expected ever to see objectively exemplified on this planet. I hated to return north, & found New York detestably chilly & depressing; but Kingston has given me some delectably warm weather, & has served nobly in taking the taste of Manhattan out of my mouth.

With best wishes, & trusting you have been enjoying the mellow late-spring weather, I remain

Yr most obt hble Servt

H P Lovecraft

Notes

1. On 20 May, HPL received a letter from Clifton Fadiman of Simon & Schuster asking him to submit a novel for consideration. HPL did not realize that the letter was a mimeographed form letter sent to all the authors on the "Honor Roll" of Edward J. O'Brien's *Best Short Stories of the Year*. HPL replied that he had no novel at hand, but wondered if a volume of short stories would be of interest. Fadiman did not express much enthusiasm.

2. HPL wrote a travelogue following this trip, titled "An Account of Charleston, in His Maj^ty's Province of South-Carolina."

3. A sonnet from *Fungi from Yuggoth*.

[30]   [ALS]

Boston—
July 3, 1930

Dear Miss Toldridge:—

    This appears to be my touring year; but I take work & writing materials along with me, so that my wanderings don't spell utter gaps in my accustomed programme. From Kingston I went to Albany & over the glorious Mohawk Trail to Athol, where I was sorry to find Cook in rather poor health. He recovers slowly from his breakdown, & is also troubled with chronic appendicitis. He has a new Recluse in press, but there's no telling when it will be out.[1] Finally reaching home, I was at once engulfed in accumulated work—amidst which I received a pleasant visit from James F. Morton; a visit involving interesting side trips, including one to historic Newport. Now I have gone on to Boston for the convention of the Natl. Amateur Press Assn.—which Morton is also attending. I shall be here, probably, 4 or 5 days—attending some convention sessions but mainly seeing historic & antiquarian sights.

    Many thanks for *The Poetry Review,* which I return herewith. I especially enjoyed the article on Pope's use of heroics, & that on Virgil's influence in English poetry.[2] The magazine is a very solid & meritorious one. Thanks also for the cuttings, which assayed high in interest. That Poe enthusiast certainly carried his veneration to heroic extremes—would that the typographical integrity of lesser poets could be safeguarded even a fraction as well! I surely hope Temple Bar can be saved & restored to a London setting. Too much of Old London is daily becoming hopelessly lost. The item about Washingtonian headquarters is very interesting. In Providence there are several houses which Genl. W. has entered. I also noted with amusement the article on "ghost writers"—among whom a good part of my labours groups me. About a poem for the Circle Anthology—almost any of your leading pieces, as mentioned, would do. "Poe" would be a very good choice. Nor would "The Magic Charms" be amiss. The new version of this is very fine, & I don't see but what it can stand just as it is. In line 13 I think *Her prophecy* is preferable to *A prophecy.*

    Glad to hear you found the travel cards interesting. Charleston is truly a marvellous place—the most perfectly preserved bit of the urban past I have ever seen. Colonial life flows down to the present in an unbroken stream, & the place & its inhabitants are so perfectly integrated that I am tempted to call it the only fully civilised city in the U.S. Richmond is fascinating, though. The Maymont folder may be retained, since I have nearly half a dozen extras. This park is not in the heart of the city but on the outskirts—on the high bluffs overlooking the James west of the settled section. It is contiguous to—& an adjunct of—extensive Byrd Park.

    As for poetic revisions—I think your change to "Above his golden lyre" in "Death" is good. Keep the new version. In the other poem I think I advised you to keep "Twinkling bright bubbles" as it is—the force of the phrase atoning for its vagueness of syntax. At any rate, I now advise this retention. In "Unmothered" I think your change is good, & advise you to use the latest version. As for a lyric contest, I am sure that either "Ships" or "Ephemera" would do admirably for it. I don't know, really, which of the two I prefer. "Birth of Eros" & "Lilt & Lure" would also do—though I fancy brevity is a desideratum.

Glad some of your pieces landed in good old Charleston. Calhoun is one of the principal cross streets—very good in parts—& is a kind of intangible line separating the modern from the fairly old section to the southward.

About the reading-chances of a poem in an anthology as compared with one in an author's own collection, I agree that the anthology is more likely to be shelved & forgotten, or perhaps overlooked. Yet anthologies still flourish—& they do have a very substantial value.

As for *mimeographing* & *multigraphing*—I understand that they differ somewhat in mechanical principle, but just how, I do not know. Multigraphing, I think, is the better & more expensive process; requiring larger machines, producing a clearer typography, & yielding more copies when desired. In the mimeograph there is a wax stencil from which copies are directly "pulled", but there is some further detail in the multigraph. I surely hope that your friend Mr. Norr will be able to produce a complete a legible MS. of your collection as you may finally decide to have it. About the publication of paper books—I doubt if the Boni company would be a market for light reading. Their new paper book series is designed to present distinctly solid & contemporaneously vital literature in reasonably priced form. I don't know just what firm would be the most likely to handle material of the sort you have in mind.

Regarding the nature of contemporary poetry—the sincere & straightforward symbolisation of actual human moods & feelings—& I think that this really represents what must form the nucleus of all genuine or serious poetry. The element of music is a valuable addition, but it must not contravene the facts & proportions of the actual life which forms its subject-matter. Otherwise it becomes irrelevant & meaningless, as so much 19th century writing is. Any notion that the worlds of "poetry" & of "life" are separate or different is a false & artistically ruinous one. The form—whether or not in accord with previous habits & traditions of writing—is largely immaterial. Certainly there is no more real harm in being traditional in *manner* than in being radical in manner. The only harm is in being conventional in *ideas*—this being harmful because convention is often meaningless & unrelated to genuine life. Excessive simplicity of outlook is of course an obstacle, but it is something which can generally be surmounted. It is not necessary to depend wholly on one's own moods for material, since observation & psychological study tell much of the typical moods & emotional nuances of others, & of the part these things play in the collective life of the existing civilisation's main stream.

My story remains in abeyance, awaiting reconstruction on a somewhat improved & less diffuse plan. I don't think that novel scheme amounts to much—it is probably part of a general attempt to stir up possible MSS for consideration, though the number actually accepted will be slight.

Whether Cook could consider book publication just now seems slightly problematical. His health & energy are at a very low ebb, & he can scarcely attend to his daily routine as it comes along—to say nothing of the *Recluse* he has under way. But with a turn for the better I am sure he will be wanting to resume his publishing programme again.

Have visited one fine old house here—the early 19th century work of the architect Bulfinch—& hope to study others before I return home. The Mass. Tercentenary has given Boston quite an antiquarian spirit this year.

With best wishes, & hoping that your MS. & poetry placements may develop favourably,

I remain

Yr most obt hble Servt

H P Lovecraft

Notes

1. Cook had set several pieces in type and even printed them, but no issue of *Recluse* No. 2 ever appeared. HPL had contributed several sonnets from *Fungi from Yuggoth* and "The Strange High House in the Mist."
2. *Poetry Review* 21, No. 3 (May–June 1930) contains Michael Roberts, "Pope and English Classicism" (161–70) and Federico Olivero, "Virgil in XVII and XVIII Century English Literature" (171–92).

[31]   [ALS]

Quinsnicket Woods—6 m.
north of Providence
[early August 1930]

Dear Mifs Toldridge:—

I am very grateful for the two cargoes of interesting cuttings, several of which have gone into my files, whilst others (those on the antiquity of man in the New World) are playing a part in an anthropological controversy with my young friend Long. The Boston cutting was especially appropriate in view of my recent sojourn there. The N.A.P.A. convention was less dull than I had expected, & drew forth an unusual array of old-timers. During my stay in the Hub area I made side-trips to my favourite Salem & Marblehead, & also a first trip to Quincy, where I saw (in addition to the other historic houses) that delightful Adams mansion of which you so kindly sent me a descriptive booklet last year. Upon returning home after a week, I found a monstrous turmoil of piled-up work awaiting me, & am only just beginning to get it straightened out. One of the convention delegates—the Official Editor—stopped here on his way home to Indiana,[1] & I took him on a side-trip to ancient Newport—a far quainter town than either Boston or Providence, & in man ways comparable to Salem & Charleston.

The recent mild weather suits me exactly, & I have accomplished more in the last month than in all last winter & spring combined. I am at my best between 80° & 90°—or even higher—& am no good at all under 75° or so. Every sunny afternoon—& that means virtually every afternoon of late—I take my work to the woods & fields & river-banks in a bag & perform it in the open. I dread the thought of autumn, & wish I could make for Charleston about the first of October!

My aunt has had another acute spell lately, & is helped by a nurse each day. She has, however, just secured a new physician who is to administer some ray treatments about which he is highly optimistic. I am glad to hear that your aunt is at least comfortable & semi-active, but regret to hear that her complete recovery is not looked for. I'm sorry, likewise, to learn that Miss Radcliffe's health continues to be so unsatisfactory. Cook has been to the hospital & emerged again—but without the appendicitis operation which he really ought to have. He seems to have just enough energy to drag along in his daily routine without doing anything else, & will evidently need much recuperation before he can resume his old-time publishing activities. His cloth-bound edition of my "Shunned House" has been held up in ¾ complete form for nearly a year.

Glad to hear that some of your work has gone to contests & anthology, & hope it will all receive high honours. It is indeed too bad that Cook cannot handle the book at present, but possibly other publishers might—at least, if some financial advance were possible. Another friend of mine—Vrest Orton, c/o Tuttle Co., Rutland, Vermont—is now connected with a firm publishing books at the author's expense,[2] & still another publisher—Kenyon Press Publishing Co., Wauwatosa, Wisconsin—is about to undertake this business—with some sort of easy-payment plan annexed. This latter is the outfit for which I shall probably do more or less regular revision if it ever gets its programme started.

Regarding "The Rosebush"—it is hard telling just what publisher would be best. I doubt if there would be much use writing before submitting MS., since one can scarcely judge a thing by descriptions. Markets are poor just now—especially for naive or traditional material—so that success ought not to be looked for too confidently. No harm in trying Little, Brown, Dutton, Century, Simon & Schuster, & other standard publishers for this & the other tale.

Concerning poetry—I don't think that lack of rhyme & metre is really the criterion of "new" verse. It is something often found in connexion with modern poetry, but does not form its essence. What makes poetry "new" or otherwise is its basic psychology—its plan of emotional selectiveness & system of emphases & cosmic perspectives. It is true that only "new" poetry can successfully use irregular forms, but not true that it *needs* them, or even that these forms are the best possible ones for it. Some of the most contemporary & original verse appears in the ordinary English rhythms & is the better for so doing. And most certainly, unless one be exceedingly contemporary & disillusioned in imaginative substance, one ought to let "free verse" severely alone. In 8 cases out of 10 it is merely an indolent device for side-stepping the delicate process of creating good metre.

You have no need of worrying about the quality of your verse. In looking about for an improved perspective, the thing to do is not to try, positively, *to be unconventional;* but to try, negatively, *not to be conventional*—a distinction which, though perhaps subtle & confusing at first sight, has great significance when closely examined. The idea is not to avoid anything consciously, but merely to see that one accepts as important only what is genuine & spontaneous—nothing which gains its prominence solely through previous literary use or popular belief, & which has no actual basis in experience. Some sort of scientific understanding of the vastness & impersonality of the cosmos, & of the insignificance & negligibility of the human atom therein, is a necessary preliminary to the straight thinking & sincere feeling demanded of a contemporary poet. This enables one to envisage, roughly, a scale of emotional values graded according to poignancy & sincerity—a scale which gives the very primitive & directly instinct-based emotions a high place, closely rivalled by the emotions of wonder & beauty, & by the feelings of wistfulness & pathos bred from the disparity betwixt illusion-born wishes & the inflexible actualities of the universe. The real poet writing out of the knowledge of today is frequently impassioned & occasionally ecstatic; but always over *real* things & impressions, & never over imaginary values, situations, & ideals. He never assumes more than really is—never gets worked up about nothing. If he expresses sorrow, it is over a direct infraction of his personal adjustments, & never over some vague world-evil which people pretend to lament but really don't give a hang about. If he rejoices at the presence of beauty, it is always some *real* beauty, as of a sunset, person, landscape, or object of art, & never the pretended theoretical beauty of "goodness" & other myths. In a word— he knows what things really are, & how little anything means, & tries not to slop over. More often we find him in a mood of wistful pathos or bitterness—the natural result of contemplating a cosmic order which coincides only occasionally with the illusions & volitional inclinations of the species. The prevailing tendency is toward *subjectiveness*—toward the very minute analysis of the emotions themselves rather than of the external objects with which these emotions are concerned; but whether this tendency is a permanent one, or merely a transient phase of the disillusioning process of this age, it is yet too early to say. My own junk is neither traditional nor modern, but of a special type never very popular, & as close to the new or to the old psychology—

namely, the recording of the illusory phenomena of the mind, as such, & without any attempt at correlation with reality. Probably it is, if anything, more fundamentally ancient than modern; though it often becomes modern in its recognition of the unreality of aspirations & fulfilments.

I enclose something about the period wing of the Boston museum, which I revisited last month. No—I couldn't afford to stop at the Hotel Thos. Jefferson in Richmond. I was nearly broke except for coach fare to N.Y., & had to be content with a $1.50 room in the annex of Murphy's Hotel.

With best wishes—

Yr most oblg'd obt Servt

H P Lovecraft

Notes

1. Helm C. Spink, the man who published *Further Criticism of Poetry.*
2. Presumably The Stephen Daye Press. The only work HPL did for the operation was *History of Dartmouth College* (1932) by Leon Burr Richardson. See letter 41.

[32]   [ALS]

Providence

[late August 1930]

Dear Mifs Toldridge:—

I found yrs. of recent date on my return from a week in the Cape Cod region, spent with young Long & his parents. Very pleasant—but not warm enough for me. Thanks exceedingly for the interesting cuttings, all of which I perused with great pleasure.

Sorry there has been so much trouble & technicality regarding your anthology poems, but am glad the matter is getting settled. For my part, I think the objection against two Poe tributes was very trivial—& I have no patience, either, with insistence on meaningless niceties of typing. Surely, it will be a pleasing contrast to have a book some day, with contents chosen in accordance with your own taste.

I get out to the woods each warm afternoon, but the coolness toward evening drives me to shelter at an earlier hour than formerly. In midsummer I stay till the last beam of daylight fades. My aunt seems much better than in July—due largely to a new physician who gives ultra-violet ray treatments. A nurse, however, is still necessary. Regret to hear that your aunt's course is toward greater weakness rather than greater strength.

Am beginning to get my revision under control, & hope to snatch time for some tales of my own before long. The coming week-end I shall take advantage of a cheap excursion to the quaint & ancient town of *Quebec*—which I have wished to see all my life, & which after all is not so very far from New England. This city, founded in 1608, is perhaps the most traditional & old-world-like place on the American continent, & I look forward to a marvellous time there. It will mark my first excursion outside the territorial limits of the U.S., & my first treading of the soil of that British Empire to which my spirit has never ceased to be loyal despite the secession of the Rhode Island colony on May 4, 1776. Will continue this letter after my return, enclosing any good Quebec views I may happen to come across. Long has just been there, & says it will surpass my fondest expectations—except that I'll find it too French for my ingrainedly English soul.

Later

And it *did* surpass all my fondest expectations! Never have I seen another place like it! All my former standards of urban beauty must be abandoned after my sight of Quebec! It hardly belongs to the world of prosaic reality at all—it is a dream of city walls, fortress-crowned cliffs, silver spires, narrow, winding, perpendicular streets, magnificent vistas, & the mellow, leisurely civilisation of an elder world. The enclosed gives hardly more than a hint of the actuality. Horse vehicles still abound, & the atmosphere is altogether of the past. It is a perfectly preserved bit of old royalist France, transplanted to the New World with very little loss of atmosphere. My stay was perforce tragically brief, but in 3 days (from early morning till pitch dark) I managed to see about everything there was to see (aside from interiors) by keeping constantly on the move. I feel as if I had lived there for years—though I must go again & at greater length in order to absorb impressions to a really satisfying degree. The oldest house (vide enc.) was built in 1674, but most of the buildings date from the early or middle 18th century. All architecture is French—mostly brick & stucco—& the buildings strongly suggest those of Charleston, S.C.—perhaps because of the strong French Huguenot influence in the latter town. The 400-foot perpendicular cliff with its staircases & steep ascents, the massive & almost perfectly preserved city wall, the dominating citadel, & the strange, ancient tangled streets, all combine to make Quebec an almost unearthly bit of fairyland. Everything I have seen before seems tame in comparison. The only side trip I took was to the great falls of the Montmorency river—on the upper level of which stands the old house in which the Duke of Kent (Queen Victoria's father) lived whilst in military service here in the late 1790's. The countryside has some moderately quaint villages dominated by curious French churches, but is too much modernised to be really colourful. The real charm is all concentrated in Quebec City. I imagine, though, that parts of Nova Scotia (as described in the cutting you sent) must retain a quaintness which rural Quebec has lost. On my return trip I stopped off at Boston for the all-day boat trip to Provincetown, at the tip of Cape Cod—which I did not reach during the Cape Codding of the previous month. I found the town nothing notable, but the water journey (my first sail out of sight of land) was highly impressive. Approaching Boston Harbour in the sunset from the open sea was an utterly novel experience—to see the gray headlands & lighthouses & islands rise out of misty nothingness was to be brought close to the gates of phantasy. I was so pleased that I did not stop to enquire, like the young voyager in the cutting from John O'Ren,[1] whether this sort of thing was really necessary.

Incidentally—I am much obliged for the cuttings, all of which I perused with much interest. Glad to hear you have enjoyed some pleasant visitors. My aunt, though still having a nurse, is enormously better at present, & gets around the house without difficulty.

I note the Bobbs-Merrill letter, & hope they will accept your "Rosebush" even though the letter's limited length makes such acceptance problematical. As for poetry—while, as I said, the essence of modernity is in psychological substance rather than form, you have no need to regret any slowness you may have in catching the contemporary mood. Modernity, in the main, is an *amplification* rather than *negation* of the past, & there is still an enormous field in which the poet may continue to function in accustomed ways. It is only a certain segment of earlier thought & feeling which has become definitely obsolete—a segment chiefly covered by the hollow, artificial, & affected verses of the 19th century. It is mainly the Victorian mood & perspective which good sense has outlawed & cancelled. Elizabethan & 17th century poetry—& a good deal of the pre-Victorian work of the early XIX & later XVIII century—can still stand on its own feet.

There's no need of your hurrying about the collection of poems—the more time you take, the better & more careful the result. I'll let you have any further news of Recluse & Kenyon Presses. Poor Cook—I can't get a word out of him, & some of his clients—especially one in Canada—are becoming angrily impatient about his silences & delays. I haven't had time to do anything to my new story—for as soon as I got caught up with my work I made the Quebec trip & allowed another accumulation of stuff to pile up on me. Probably I shan't really settle down to original writing till the weather is too cold to let me escape to the scenic outdoors!

With best wishes—

I remain

Yr obt hble Servt

H P Lovecraft

P.S. Additional material just recd. Thanks for extra cuttings. Sorry B-M couldn't use Rosebush—yes, I think a gift-book form would be highly appropriate. Hope you have luck in Poetry Review contest.

As for contemporary fiction—stories serialised in newspapers aren't always representative of the standard article. However, the contemporary tendency is toward the abrupt & staccato. Some aspects of this tendency are psychologically justified; others more a mere matter of fashion.

[P.P.S.] Had an echo of marine adventure the other day in the form of a letter from New Zealand. Stampless, watersoaked, & marked with a rubber stamp

Salvaged from S.S. Tahiti
Lost at sea.

[P.P.P.S. on envelope:] Just before mailing this, new envelope of enclosures arrived. Many thanks—cuttings are all of interest. Hope the book MSS. come along satisfactorily. Sorry you find the warm weather oppressive. I like it tremendously—never felt better in my life! I am at my best around 90°—no good at all under 75°. I can't bear to think of chilly autumn ahead. But I know others don't find my kind of weather comfortable, & suppose it's hard on the crops. Am out in the open every day, & am getting my work cleaned up as far as possible in the hope of getting at my story-writing before cold weather paralyses my energy. I really ought to live in a subtropical climate like the West Indies.

Notes

1. A columnist for the Baltimore *Sun*.

[33]   [ALS]

[24 October 1930]

Dear Miss Toldridge:—

Many thanks for the cuttings, all of which were interesting. The situation in Rome—where *moderately* ancient buildings have to be demolished to make way for *really* ancient restorations—is surely perplexing; but I think the present course is the right one, since nothing can compare in value with the genuine remnants of classical, Latin-speaking Rome. It may be, however, that the upheaval will proceed too far; causing the wreckage of many old houses for modernisation purposes as well as for archaeological revival. Those Salish Indian myths are especially interesting, & many points in them ought to be good for weird fictional treatment—particularly the legends of hidden races of beings, & the "land & water mysteries" which cause the early death of all who glimpse them. Another very interesting thing is the account of the origin of certain British place-names.

Yes—that Quebec journey was surely a notable event for me, & one which I must manage to repeat at greater length. Nowhere else on this continent, I feel sure, can so much of the Old World have managed to survive; & I certainly hope that no rash modernisation will spoil the perfect beauty of the town as it is. By all odds, Quebec & Charleston are the two most fascinating places I have ever seen; & I wish I could divide all my time between them & Providence.

I have just learned from H. Warner Munn of Athol that Cook is resting at his sister's home near Lake Sunapee, N.H. Whether his relinquishment of business ties is permanent or only temporary, & whether his health is improving or declining, I have not yet been able to ascertain; but I shall endeavour to gain more news.

Thanks very much for the *Poetry Review*, which I enjoyed greatly, & am returning under separate cover. The references to Lord Dunsany especially appealed to me, since of all contemporary authors he most closely expresses my own moods & point of view. I have long been hoping to get hold of his "Fifty Poems", & mean to do so when I find time to look around the library. Much of the contents, of course, I have seen from time to time in magazines.

The second lot of cuttings contains some exceedingly interesting material. I wish I might have heard "Æ".[1] He lectured in Providence a year or two ago, but I was unable to attend. As for the origin of bull-fighting—I am sure I can't add anything to what is generally known. The bull fight is a lineal descendant of the Roman sports of the arena—which were as common in Spain as in any of the Latin-speaking provinces of the Empire—& its association with religious festivals is simply due to the early custom of honouring such occasions with choice performances of the favourite national amusement.

Naturally my outdoor reading & writing sessions are not very frequent now that October is here, but I hope to take a few purely recreational woodland walks before the splendour of autumn foliage has departed. I can well imagine how you must wish for some glimpses of the rural landscape, & hope you can arrange to get a few now & then. If memory serves me correctly, Washington is close to some particularly good scenery—south of the Potomac, in the Fairfax C.H. & Falls Church regions.

As for quoting my random remarks on poetry—surely I have no objection, though I am not enough of an authority on the subject to make my views worth much. Incidentally, I note in this latest *Poetry Review* some very illuminating remarks on the difference between older & newer methods. Concerning quatrains—I think myself that they are too brief for the adequate expression of any important image according to the Anglo-Saxon manner. The Sino-Japanese type of poetic expression—a purely pictorial & singularly symbolic & associative type, depending on a long & sharply differentiated cultural heritage—naturally lends itself to extreme brevity; but in the western world it takes forcing to achieve parallel effects.

I'm sure I wouldn't worry about the placement of the small book MSS. Of course, it is pleasant to appear in print, & there is always a chance of stumbling on the right publisher; but most writers have far more unplaceable than placeable MSS. I don't expect to land more than a quarter of the stuff I have ground out or will grind out. The real satisfaction of creative art is the process of creation itself—or the sight of one's own completed product, crystallising permanently & tangibly what was formerly only an elusive vision. Whether anyone else ever sees the product or not, is a wholly secondary matter.

As for my spectrally affiliated New England correspondents—I have not again heard from the grotesque Maine person, but hear frequently from the old lady descended from Salem witches. She sent several moderately gruesome legends lately, but in general I find it more natural to invent cosmic horrors of my own than to utilise actual folklore incidents. I use actual local colour in treating of geography & customs; but when it comes to actual incidents & types of unreal phenomena, I have so far preferred to invent rather than adapt. I don't see any reason why you couldn't write a weird tale. The magazine *Weird Tales* (840 N. Michigan Ave., Chicago, Ill.) is relatively easy to break into—any writer being welcome if his ideas have a modicum of originality. Indeed, a good part of the stuff it uses does not seem to have even that modicum! The chief thing is to break away from the saccharine & the conventional. From a commercial standpoint the worst drawback about writing for W.T. is that if they reject a MS., it is not likely to be placeable anywhere else—since the magazine is alone in its field. *Ghost Stories* is hardly to be considered, since its especially low-grade appeal has not yet been altered despite its change from Macfadden to Hersey ownership. If a story's weirdness, however, be due to scientific imagination (voyages to other planets by mechanical means, creation of metal men, &c) instead of downright supernaturalism, it has at least a half-chance with the "scientifiction" magazine—Amazing, Astounding, & Wonder Stories. Clark Ashton Smith is now "going over big" with *Wonder Stories*, & has been asked to write a whole series of tales (interplanetary voyaging in an atomic-energy space-ship) for it. If anyone has a knack at this kind of thing, there is really an excellent & increasing market open to him. I fear I'm not much in this line myself, but nevertheless believe I'll try a few specimens & see how they are regarded by editors. I have just finished a 69-page novelette which W.T. has accepted for $350.00—to use as a 2-part serial in the June & July issues.[2]

The latest lot of cuttings is of great interest. Too bad Kinfuss Castle must be sold, & I can well imagine the feelings of Lady Macdonald concerning the matter. Economic readjustments, however, are inevitable all over the world; & are the direct, logical results of the invention of large-scale productive machinery; a thing which could not have been avoided. The resulting type of social organisation—when it shall have finally taken shape—will be more monstrous than the dying order, & probably less aesthetically fruitful; but there is no reason to think it will be complete barbarism. The one important thing to avoid is a sudden revolutionary explosion extensive enough to establish full bolshevism throughout the western world. Among the other cuttings I note with interest that about Dean Forest & the Verderers.[3] Good fictional material. The pronunciation of place-names also offers much of interest. I think R.I. adheres to the original pronunciation of debatable names—

Warwick, Greenwich, &c—better than any other part of the U.S. Another very absorbing item is that concerning the 4th dimensional model. I intend to use the idea of multiple dimensions in some tales later on—my friend Long has already done so, especially in a novelette to appear shortly in W.T.

My aunt's health is decidedly better, & she no longer requires the nurse. The coming of furnace heat & its dryness is a good thing for her, I think.

With best wishes, & thanking you again for the cuttings & Poetry Review, I remain

Yr most ob^t h^{ble} Servt

H P Lovecraft

Notes

1. The pseudonym of George William Russell (1867–1935), an Irish nationalist, writer, editor, critic, poet, and painter.
2. In fact, "The Whisperer in Darkness" appeared in its entirety in the August 1931 issue.
3. The Verderers in the Forest of Dean in Britain have been in existence since c. 1218. They are charged with protecting the vert and venison (i.e., vegetation and habitat) of the Forest.

[34]   [ALS]

Nov. 23[, 1930]

Dear Miss Toldridge:—

I am very glad indeed to hear that your sonnet won the prize, & am sure the honour was amply deserved. Such recognition is encouraging, even if not very substantial financially. It will, I am sure, be repeated in connexion with many other specimens of yours.

It is very kind to think of sending the Dunsany piece, but you really ought not to deface your file of the Poetry Review. The magazine is so excellent that it ought to be kept intact. Anyway—the piece was more important for quotations than for text, & I'll get all these passages when I buy the Dunsany volume—as I certainly shall. But let me thank you just the same.

Am in touch with Cook at last, & am pleased to find he is physically better, though very seedy in a nervous way. He has left Athol for good, & plans to settle shortly in Clarendon, Vermont, where in conjunction with another publisher he expects to found "The Parsonage Press"—so called because their quarters will be a former parsonage. The quality of the stuff turned out will certainly be of the highest, but I'm afraid Cook can't offer quite such good terms as he used to do when conducting the old Recluse Press alone. His partner will be Vrest Orton—whom I think I once recommended as a possible publisher in connexion with his present enterprise, the Tuttle Co. of Rutland, Vt.

Thanks exceedingly for the cuttings—a vast lot of Roman material is surely coming to light these days as a result of the Fascist policy. This is really quite an age of archaeology—in Greece & the Tigris-Euphrates region as well as Italy. Little by little, many blank spaces in the antique record can probably be filled in before long. The item about "ghost writing" was very amusing to me, inasmuch as I have done a vast amount of it. It is not as trying as actual revision, but has none of the zest of creative composition because of the prescribed nature of the subject in most cases. I know that old Alexandria drugstore, & have had ice-cream there; a thing probably unavailable in Genl. Washington's time. There is an older shop of the sort in Charleston—dating from the 1780's—but it is not now in its original location, & has given its ancient fixtures to the Charleston Museum. The quotation from Walpole about the "six best books" seems to me so silly & arbitrarily dogmatic that I doubt its serious authenticity very much. It looks to me as if some reporter had tried to make a literal statement out of some epigrammatic utterance which the context would utterly change in purport.[1] As for the absence of cats in Angora—it may be so, but if it is, I shall never visit the capital of Mustapha Kamal's domain.[2] No region devoid of cats is civilisation to me!

Yes—I was glad of the $350.00 sale, although it has really ceased to be of any interest to me whether anybody reads my junk or not—that is, outside of the discriminating minority to whom I can send the MS. if a thing doesn't make type. I want the fun of writing it, & the cash if I can get it—but what other people read & like is no business of mine. I have long ago graduated from the naive system of false, artificial values which made 19th century people care about the effect of their products on others. By the same token, don't worry about "The Rosebush". It is very good, & it will be very pleasant if it doesn't get published; but publication is no such vast desideratum that one need be impatient about it. Public & editorial taste are no criterion of merit—it doesn't make a MS. better to have it published, or worse to leave it unpublished! As for the *fourth dimension*—you will find that excellently treated in a serial by my young friend Long, shortly to begin in *Weird Tales*—"The Horror from the Hills." I may get around to that theme myself later on. There are plenty of subjects available—the only trouble is to get time to do them justice in good prose.

Sorry to hear that Miss Radcliffe's recovery is so slow. I received a note from her the other day, & am now answering it. It seems that she has a number of verses collected & ready for inspection. Cook seems to be getting stronger, & I fancy his new firm will be ready to talk business in the spring.

Sino-Japanese poetry belongs in a tradition all its own, reflecting the essentially contemplative & tranquil character of the high-grade Mongolian mind. I saw an excellent article on it not long ago, though I can't recall exactly where. It may possibly have been in one of those issues of *The Poetry Review*— it would pay you to glance through the file & see if any such thing has appeared during the past year. A typical kind of Chinese poetry is that of simple description—especially of landscape or atmospheric effects—in which the aspect of the scene presented generally suggests some mood on the writer's part. *Brevity* is the keynote of all such efforts; it being apparently thought that all impressions as fleeting as those of poetic feeling ought to have an embodiment correspondingly elusive & glancing, lest the effect be one of incongruous heaviness. The typical Japanese *hokku* is limited to 17 syllables, usually divided into 3 lines of 5, 7, & 5 syllables each. The following specimen—taken from an essay on the subject by Lafcadio Hearn—is quite typical:

> Tsurigaué ni
> Tomarité nemuru
> Kochō kana!

[Perched upon the temple-bell, the butterfly sleeps.]

This is a complete poem. It presents a definite image which, to a cultivated mind charged with the traditions of Japanese life & art, evokes a long train of imaginative associations in a sort of visual pageantry. Such brevity seems affected among Anglo-Saxons, but in Japan it is perfectly adequate & appropriate. We can catch the beauty ourselves with a little reflection & objective analysis. Occasionally the Japanese grow more abstract & sententious, as in the following:

> Owarété mo,
> Isoganu furi no
> Chochō Kana!

[Ah, the butterfly! Even when chased, it never seems to be in a hurry.]

> Chō wo oü
> Kokoro-mochitashi
> Itsumadémo!

[Would that I might always have the spirit to chase butterflies!]

The prevalence of the *butterfly* in Sino-Japanese verse is an indication of the delicate atmosphere of colour & scenic loveliness which pervades the whole tradition. Many persons—especially Witter Bynner[3]—have tried to reproduce the spirit of far Eastern verse in English; & although the task is difficult, I do not think they have been entirely unsuccessful. But if they emulate Oriental brevity, they must emulate the Oriental mood & subject matter as well. It is certainly true that a single quatrain is too short to give an English poet any proper leeway *in the accustomed Occidental manner*.

What you say of misprints is only too true—they often exasperate me beyond words—yet there seems to be no way of getting rid of the nuisance. Only the very highest priced magazines can afford to have proofreading of the most careful sort; & without this the possibilities of error are infinite. The worst sort of error, as you point out, is the tricky kind which makes the author seem illiterate rather than the kind whose true nature is easily recognisable.

The Nobel Prize award to Lewis[4] is not as bad as it might be—although I'd have picked Dreiser, while others would have chosen O'Neill, Cabell, Cather, or even Wilder. Lewis is more a man of ideas than an aesthete, but his novels are sound in craftsmanship even if possessed of an ulterior intellectual purpose. He has punctured the pitiful shams & inanities of conventional American life as few others have; & certainly deserves a prize for social service, whether or not he merits one for sheer artistic craftsmanship. Thanks to him, no adult will ever again take seriously the vacuous pretences & hypocrisies of the Victorian-bred & commercial-minded middle class—a class whose stultifying stupidity & mendacity once dominated American life & threatened to engulf its literature & destroy its taste.

As for politics—no, I don't pay any attention whatever to them, since I am perfectly well aware that the visible political machinery is not the real force which shapes American policies & acts. Behind the mask the pressure of vested economic interests is absolutely omnipotent, & always has its way no matter what the masses vote or want to vote for. By manipulating primaries, circulating propaganda, fighting laws in the courts, bribing & wrecking officials, &c. &c., the large industries of the country are in complete & unshakable control. This is so in all nominal democracies, & is not as bad as it seems. One industry checks another, & all fear the physical power of the mob.

Just recd. the envelope of the 16th with enclosures. The poems are truly excellent, & contain little which suggests a need of change. "Lightnings & Thunders" is indisputably the best of all; containing genuine images & being uttered in the pictorial language which is the true medium of poetry. This certainly ought to land to advantage somewhere—in the Circle, the Anthology, or some more professional medium. "Earth Speaks" is another splendid specimen, even though the last two lines contain an artificial inversion. On the whole, I don't think this pair call for any change. Even the aforementioned inversion is a relatively mild one. "Jan & Lorna" is good, too. I read the Blackmore novel in childhood,[5] & thought many parts of it fairly interesting. Too bad the last of the Ridds is leaving his ancestral country—but that is a very natural phenomenon of any age of sharp social transition like the present. In the poem, I am making only one change, to eliminate the stock phrase "world in thrall." The stanza, as I would suggest, might well be recast to have l. 2 read "The bravest maid we know", & l. 4 "Has charmed our fathers so." The poem originally entitled "Mead" is also excellent, though here I think a little alteration would help. In the first place, the title seems rather stagey & artificial, & not altogether applicable. "Toll" looks to me vastly preferable. In st. 2, the phrase "birds cease their roundelays" is exceedingly trite & artificial, & requires change. I suggest

> "The birds wing songless away"

—with a change of l 7 to

> "and clouds muffle night & day."

Toward the end some change also seems desirable. The phrase "true love" is fiendishly hackneyed, but might "get by" for once. The italicisation &c in this line, however, seems somewhat needless. But the most important change is in the final two lines, whose original form seems extremely bald, stilted, prosaic, & didactic. I am changing (for the sake of the rhyme) l. 2 to read "where true love lights up the soul", & providing the following final couplet—

> "For at every gate on the winding road
> The keeper must have his toll."

I hope that, as you suggest, you are on the brink of another period of intensive poetic productivity; for it is certainly a comfort to get stray images & impressions chained down in preservable & recallable form. I shall read the Quatrain number of *The Circle*[6] with interest—many thanks in advance. I haven't written anything since my long story, but hear that my old "Rats in the Walls" is to be reprinted in the new issue of the British "Not at Night" anthology.

Many thanks for the cuttings, which include some things of keen interest. The existence of the unicorn as a reality would certainly be a highly striking discovery, & a great provocation for weird fiction! The matter of a new cosmic unit is likewise of the greatest interest—& even more importance. More will certainly be known of the internal construction & motions of the galactic system when the new 200-inch reflecting telescope is completed. It is meanwhile exciting to watch the progress of the debate between Jeans & Millikan regarding the 'one-wayness' or 'two[-]wayness' of the known cosmos. Lay opinion here is wholly worthless. The existing cosmos was built up somehow, but it may easily have been by a temporary or even accidental process not now operating in space. Very possibly the normal condition of infinity is simply electronic emptiness traversed by slow pulses of unmodified wave-energy.

My aunt, I am glad to say, seems to continue her improvement; & I hope to be able to drag her out to a good Thanksgiving dinner at the nearest restaurant. Sorry to hear that your aunt does no more than hold her own.

Latest word from Cook seems to indicate a likelihood of his spending the winter with the editor of *Driftwind* in North Montpelier, Vt. This editor— Walter J. Coates—seems to be dipping more & more into book publishing; so some time you might make arrangements with him if Cook does not reëstablish a press.

Best wishes, & congratulations on the excellent new verses.

Yr ob^t Servt

H P Lovecraft

P.S. Trust you will not find the Christmas card work too arduous.

P.P.S. That Macmillan Junior Reader (#2) with an extract from my "travelogue" on Sleepy Hollow is out. Instead of using the the [*sic*] thing as a footnote, the publishers gave it place as a regular selection.

Notes

1. In November 1930, British novelist Hugh Walpole (1884–1941) made a list of the six best books of the year. He had been preparing such lists since at least 1922.

2. Angora is the historic name of Ankara, Turkey. Mustafa Kemal Atatürk (1881–1938), army officer and revolutionary statesman, was founder of the Republic of Turkey and its first president.

3. Harold Witter Bynner (1881–1968), American poet, writer, and scholar, author of *The Jade Mountain* (1929), translations from the Chinese, with Kiang Kang-hu.

4. Sinclair Lewis won the Nobel Prize for literature in 1930.

5. R. D. Blackmore, *Lorna Doone: A Romance of Exmoor* (1869).

6. *Circle* (November–December 1930) contains Toldridge's quatrain, "S.O.S."

[35]   [ALS]

[20 December 1930]

Dear Miss Toldridge:—

Thanks very much for the recent material—of which I am returning the interesting Poetry Review. Too bad your quatrain was misprinted, & wish a way could be found to stop such carelessness. The current *Circle* is quite interesting, though the quatrain form hardly permits the contributors to display their full powers.

It is exceedingly thoughtful of you to set aside some Christmas cards to send, & I can assure you that early arrival is no liability from my point of view. The only trouble is that you ought not to expend trying labour on items bringing in no return! If I had more cash I'd order all my cards from your select, hand-painted stock; but stern necessity forces me to confine myself to one-cent Woolworth specimens (the plainer ones are not all absurd or obtrusive) except for a few which go to more or less fastidious or supercilious destinations. Certainly, all the cards of yours which I have seen have been eminently choice & usable—but it isn't very profitable to donate what might be advantageously marketed! At any rate, pray accept my most genuine thanks. The set arrived safely, & I found all of splendid tastefulness. As you say, verses don't generally live up to pictures—a dilemma I usually solve by getting cards without verse. It's always safe to choose plain & dignified prose variants of the "Merry

Christmas & Happy New Year" cliché. By the way—my aunt wishes to express her appreciation of the delightful card intended for her, & I must express my own for the corresponding envelope marked for Yuletide opening.

Thanks, too, for the recent cuttings. I am sending the one about the standing stones to a writer deeply interested in Celtic antiquities, & have filed the one about the arctic lizard in my own weird archives. This latter, if it does not turn out to be a false report, will certainly create a stir among palaeontologists.

Long's story begins in the Jany. *Weird Tales,* now on the stands, & will run to 3 parts. The magazine, however, is about to retrench soon & become a bi-monthly—so that my "Whisperer in Darkness" will appear as a complete novelette next summer. I am glad of this, since serials are always clumsy & bothersome. My Yuggoth sonnets have been appearing right along for months—there are two in the current issue.[1] I don't think it would pay for you to get the magazine, though, for you would certainly find it uninteresting.

Chesterton has just lectured here, but I did not attend his performance. He is a likeable character, but not to be taken seriously in an intellectual way. There is something almost pathetic in his attempt to defend obsolete values & conceptions of the universe—for much as one may love tradition, it is silly to deny actually discovered facts. G K C is clever & entertaining—but the real brains of the modern world lie in characters like George Santayana, Bertrand Russell, H G Wells, or men of science like Einstein, Eddington, Jeans, Keith, Millikan, G. Elliott Smith, & so on. Chesterton would be less out of place if he would stick to aesthetics & literature & keep clear of philosophy—whose modern developments he cannot grasp, & which he therefore treats in a spirit rendered frivolous, irrelevant, & meaningless by the knowledge of today.

You would probably like Wilder's "Bridge"—which is clever though overrated. I admire Sinclair Lewis intensely, for he has the artist's capacity to apply appropriate emotions to the objects he treats. To regard the contemporary American scene & its childish ideas without satire would be impossible for any keen & honest intellect. I agree with Lewis thoroughly, though am somewhat bored by his spirit of propaganda & by the journalistic commonplaceness of his style.

As for world-politics—the present age surely presents a spectacle of chaos & absolute unpredictability hardly to be found since the fall of the Roman Empire; & there is little doubt but that the cause, operating through a complex chain of social & economic consequences, is the high development of machinery during the 19th & 20th centuries. At a stage like the present, history may take any one of many widely divergent courses; & only a charlatan would venture to guess which one it will be. It is well to count both Russia & India out of the main stream of civilisation. What happens within them is of small importance so long as it does not react on the Western World—but this contingency makes them constant dangers. Russia is the more active danger, because communism really is the logical form of government toward which a machine age heads, unless checked in time by very dramatic methods (as repugnant, unfortunately, to thoughtless conservatives as to the communists themselves) which will ensure a more widespread diffusion of the means of life without interrupting the existing civilisation & the arts founded on individual thought & feeling. The principle of *Fascism* is the one which looks best to me. Democracy is simply a joke.

Thanks exceedingly for thinking of sending the new Circle Anthology—but if you have to pay for copies it's really an unwarranted extravagance! I've absolutely cut out all generosity in these latter years of poverty, & never spend a cent except for my own pleasure—books & antiquarian travel. These annuals sometimes have excellent material—it would be interesting to look over old ones to see how many of the contributors have or haven't drifted into general recognition. Glad my remarks on the recent verses proved helpful. Yes—if I were you I surely would send the lightning poem to the Poetry Review.

As for Einstein—there can be no doubt but that his fame is solidly founded. Whatever future mathematicians & physicists may discover regarding the widest working out of his principles, it seems certain that the general facts of relativity & curved space are unshakable realities, without considering which it will be impossible to form any sort of true conception of the cosmos. There is no point in this archaic attitude of questioning how the ordered cosmos 'was evolved out of nothingness', for we realise now that there never was or can be such a thing as nothingness. The cosmos always existed & always will exist, its order being a basic & inseparable function of the mathematical entity called Space-Time. There is no sense in talking about the "creation" of something which never needed to be "created". Such things as "wonder", "glory", &c. are merely subjective reactions of the nervous system of a particular kind of organisation, & the newer of psychology of Freud, Adler, Watson, Pavlov, &c. has caused these reactions to be very well understood. It is merely a vestige of primitive ignorance to supply the idea of conscious personality & purpose to the eternal & impersonal congeries of regular forces & motion-patterns which forms the totality of entity. No—I'm the last person on earth to be a good astronomer, for I can't compass the absolutely necessary mathematics. Mathematics are 0.9 of modern astronomy. I hoped to be an astronomer when a boy, but saw the foolishness of the idea—in view of my mind & temperament—by the time I was well into the 'teens. But of course I still take an active interest in all such astronomical developments as laymen can understand, & am very eager to see the completion of the 200-inch reflector. Nothing even approaching that size in my day. Planets beyond Pluto may conceivably be discovered. I am using Pluto in my new story. Yes—I shall probably use a rocket voyage sooner or later.

The Radcliffe material arrived recently, & I shall be glad to look it over gradually—as my programme clears up a bit. There will certainly be no charge, & I trust that whatever comments I append may prove useful to Miss R. Sorry to hear that her recovery is so slow.

  With best holiday wishes—

Your most oblig^d ob^t Servt

H P Lovecraft

P.S. That view about Poe is by no means an uncommon one. His *style* was undoubtedly touched by the crude bombast & cheap romanticism of the American 1830's, so that many Frenchmen declare they cannot read him except in Baudelaire's & Mallarme's translation. At the same time, it is going rather too far to minimise the unique imaginative content of his work. Huxley probably takes his cue from the late W. C. Brownell—who disparaged Poe from another critical angle.[2]

Notes

1. "Nyarlathotep" and "Azathoth."
2. W. C. Brownell (1851–1928), a leading American critic of the day, wrote disparagingly of Poe in his study *American Prose Masters* (1909). British novelist and essayist Aldous Huxley criticized Poe's poetry in the essay "Vulgarity in Literature" (*Saturday Review of Literature*, 27 September 1930).

1931

[36] [ALS]

10 Barnes St.,

Providence, R.I.,

Jany. 25, 1931.

Dear Miss Toldridge:—

    Your recent letters duly arrived, & I must thank you for the additional Christmas cards, which will be choice items of my 1931 outgoing batch. I believe I have already expressed my gratitude for the anthology, which has among its contents some excellent material. Let me add my appreciation of your new sonnet, "Locusts & Wild Honey"; which impresses me as particularly excellent, & which I am sure will be welcomed in print. I can think of no necessary or even advisable change, & must congratulate you upon a graphic & delightful piece of imagery. No need to worry about the future of poetry—the type of psychological action involved in its production is too fundamental to permit of its extinction, though naturally its forms & themes vary as ideas & environments vary. Of course, its relative prominence among other forms of mental activity is different in different civilisations, & at different periods in the same civilisation; but we seldom find it wholly absent from the lore of any race at any time.

No—Providence does not have any public merrymaking on New Year's Eve, though at the hotels & restaurants there are various programmes of artificial gaiety, while I believe most of the theatres have midnight performances. New Year's is not a native New England festival—any more than Christmas used to be; (in 1650 celebration of Christmas was illegal in the Massachusetts-Bay Colony) & though we have adopted Christmas, we have been less ready to welcome its follower. Large-scale New Year celebration is distinctly a Dutch custom—developing in New York so far as this continent is concerned, & spreading thence to whatever other American regions have adopted it.

Sorry to hear of the accident to your aunt, but glad she is recovering from it. My aunt shews no signs of any recurrence of the acute trouble of last summer, though of course she cannot undergo much exertion, or make trips outside except on special occasions. Cook's improvement continues, though he has given up the idea of the publishing partnership at Clarendon. However, there are plenty of places one can get a book printed. If one is tolerant of a slight ruggedness or provincialism in format, one could very profitably investigate the rates & facilities of the Driftwind Press—Walter J. Coates, N. Montpelier, Vt.—where, incidentally, Cook is now visiting. Another good place is the Kenyon Press Pub. Co.—L. J. Sweet, 291 Kenyon Ave., Wauwatosa, Wis.

There were some highly interesting things among the cuttings—the cat items being especially welcome to a veteran ailurophile. The lost oasis city is a fruitful weird theme, as is the lost meteorite of 1908. I can testify to the truth of that *gate* article from a knowledge of both Salem & Charleston. The Poe stamp ought certainly to be issued—whether or not the honoring of a literary figure forms an innovation. America is curiously backward in its tributes to aesthetes. We hear of Jany. 19 as Lee's birthday, yet not one person in a hundred realises that it is also Poe's.[1] Incidentally—objections to certain stylistic qualities in Poe do not by any means invalidate his claim to a virtual leadership among American authors. In sheer genius—uniqueness of mood & perspective, & ability to crystallise that mood in words—he excels virtually all of the more polished & disciplined writers who win critical approval. Only the school of Brownell is against him as a whole—& even this school has less authority in the light of the newest psychology. Poe's main faults were simply those of his age—the occasional bombast & tinkle of the shoddy 1830's & 1840's—but he had, behind these, a solid genius shared by no other American then or since with the very possible exception of Whitman & Melville, & the less certain exception of Mark Twain. To gain a full idea of the utter & abysmal banality of the 1830's & 1840's in America, one must glance over some typical anthology of the period like Griswold's "Poets & Poetry of America." Fully 90% of the poems & authors represented are utterly forgotten now. Who but antiquarians today have ever heard of the idols of that time—James G. Percival, Fitz-Greene Halleck, Maria Brooks, John Pierpont, Joseph Rodman Drake, Hannel F. Gould, &c. &c. &c? Mrs. Sigourney is still known by name as a sort of byword for dull inanity.[2] As for Weird Tales—it is hardly worth buying, & I doubt if it would have anything of interest to you. If you want to see what a "Yuggothian Fungus" looks like in print, I'll hunt up a duplicate of one of the recent issues and send it along. I have one somewhere, though I can't lay my hands on it now. The magazine, it now appears, will return to its monthly schedule in June.

As for civilisation—there is no reason for mourning the passing of the present western world; for all cultures peter out in the end, & I don't think this has been a very notable one except in the single field of scientific achievement. The civilisations of Egypt, Persia, Greece, & Rome undoubtedly excelled ours—in fact, virtually everything of value in ours was borrowed or inherited from Greece & Rome, so that it is really a prolongation of the Graeco-Roman stream rather than a new & separate affair. Probably the next civilisation will be a sort of continuation of this as this is of the Graeco-Roman. One cannot yet tell whether a stable machine-culture will grow out of contemporary life without an intervening break, or whether the present fabric will explode & give place to a wholly new growth beginning with pastoral & agricultural barbarism amidst which the machine will be forgotten except as a subject of magical tales. It doesn't greatly matter in the end. As for the idea of "liberty"—a good deal is pure sentimentality & hokum . . . . a matter of more pompous language without any underlying reality. Perfect freedom never has existed & never can exist. When individualism goes too far, it cancels itself & produces chaos. Then comes disintegration, & a choice betwixt the two forms of control represented by fascism & communism. Between these, the logical choice is fascism; for this retains the stratification & cultural traditions of the past, whereas communism diligently wipes all these things out. Democracy in a complex industrial civilisation is a joke—since it means nothing but the concentration of all resources in the hands of a few capable plutocrats, & the subterranean rule of this group under the outward forms of democracy. Concerning unemployment—the present wave is the worst yet because it combines a new & permanent element with the recurrent depression-element which always comes at intervals in unregulated commercial nations. This new & permanent element is what we have come to call *technological unemployment*, & is the result of a very simple but profoundly important effect of mechanised industry—namely; that under all conditions, & to a constantly increasing degree as invention advances, *it now requires only a few persons, comparatively speaking, to produce all the materials which the total consumption of the world can possibly demand*. This is because of the infinite multiplying-power of the machine. Once make a pattern, & the apparatus to construct a given article from it, & there is no limit to the *number of such articles* which a mere handful of machine-tenders can produce. If more than the world's normal supply are made, there will be no one to buy them. Obviously, the old system of unregulated individual industry breaks down here. The manufacturer, under the traditional system, seeks to produce as much as possible with as little expenditure as possible; & therefore installs labour-saving machinery, discharging all but the few men needed to run it, & keeping these busy for as much time as he can in the face of labour-union pressure. This formerly gained him a good profit, but now he finds that after his cheap, easy & inexhaustible producing mechanism has turned out a certain amount of goods, there is no market whatever for any more. People can use only a certain amount of any one thing, hence beyond that limit articles of the sort are useless. The so-called "saturation-point" has been reached, despite all artificial devices like style changes & "high-pressure salesmanship." Moreover—the manufacturer *has restricted his own market* by trying to produce more & more cheaply—like the dog with a bone in his mouth who lost the bone through reaching for its reflection in the water. In discharging men & installing machines, he so swelled the pauper class that the remaining solvent elements, capable of forming a market, was materially decreased. If men can't be employed, they can't get money; & if they can't get money, they can't buy goods. Thus the manufacturer is caught in his own trap. By trying to produce goods more cheaply, he stripped so many people of their money that there are no longer enough solvent people to buy his goods! The eternal vicious circle—& a fine piece of grim cosmic irony. Then he closes down altogether & lives on his accumulated surplus while the masses live on charity or starve to death. Virtually no goods are produced. Prices fall, & eventually the few people who are not on charity manage to use up the existing stock of goods. This ends the *temporary* depression & gives the manufacturer a market once more. He reopens his factory & begins to produce again. *Formerly*, this brought safe prosperity, since the fresh start of industry required enough employed men to redistribute money, rescue the poor from charity, & expand markets once more. *But this recovery is less & less complete as the machine age advances, because the fresh start of industry & the virtually unlimited production of goods requires fewer & fewer employees.* The residue of the *permanently unemployed & unemployable* increases rapidly, & we have at last to face the situation that *all the possible business of the world can be performed by only a fraction of the world's population*—the rest remaining absolutely superfluous & without any natural function, whereby they can lay claim to food, clothing, & shelter. It is no longer a fact that there is always work for willing hands. The hands may be willing, but all the work that needs doing has been done. No matter what the size of a population, there is work for only a fraction of it so long as those in control of the power & industrial machinery are allowed to map out their own employing conditions & operate on the principle of minimum outlay. Those who have money will get more & more of it. The very brightest of those without money will get the few available jobs & receive whatever wages the owners will wish to pay. And the rest will starve or accept an increasingly impatient charity. The result of this unsupervised & unmodified drift is, of course, inevitable social revolution. No vast horde of people will endure long starvation if they have the physical force to seize food; & when the masses of the starving are large & desperate enough they will have the force & will use it. Then communism & chaos. *But*—the manufacturers know all this as well as anybody else, & will undoubtedly look for compromise-courses. Their goal is *greatest ultimate profit,* & when they see that *immediate* economy only restricts their market & imperils the whole system whereby they enjoy privilege, they will realise that good business demands less economy at the start. Better a costlier "overhead" & a sounder market & future. Thus you will see the moneyed groups making grudging concessions to the mob. Knowing that people can't buy things unless they have money, they will employ *more people for shorter hours* in the expectation that most of the money they pay will come back in the form of expanded markets. This will work a while, but not far enough. The extent of voluntary concession, as conditioned by visible profits, will not be enough to give permanent employment to enough people to remove the revolutionary menace due to starvation. If the existing social order is to last, more money must be distributed in some way or other, regardless of normal principles of profit. Socialistic measures like those already in force in England—old age pensions & unemployment insurance—the so-called "dole"—will be as necessary as fire-engines at a fire. As time passes, vested capital will have to "shell out" more & more in order to survive. It will be a painful thing for the plutocrats to yield up the latent surpluses which have hitherto given them absolute political power, but they will of course do this rather than sacrifice the social order which at least allows them enough profit to live in personal luxury & preserve the continuous traditions of the civilisation. Besides, if they are shrewd they can continue to rule as absolutely as at present—since they represent the sharpest brains, & will not be interfered with by a well-fed majority. All political administration in a machine age is so complex as to be beyond the comprehension of the common layman, & in time even the masses will come to realise this & be glad not to meddle in the business. Fed, clothed, housed, & amused, they will be content to leave bothersome problems to those better able to understand & deal with them. If social evolution gets this far without an explosion—as of course many doubt—the result will not be anything which one need lament. Of course, all familiar things & relationships—travel, housing, architecture, working conditions, social & family organisation, politics, &c—will have changed so greatly that the present generation would find them bewildering & meaningless; but to those of the future they are likely to be as familiar & acceptable as earlier conditions have been to earlier generations. The amount of leisure possessed by all classes will necessarily—in view of the little work to be done by human agency—be prodigious; & it is barely possible that this enforced leisure, plus the collapse of the profit principle &

the substitution of a production-for-use-only policy, will help to recreate the now-dying moods, perspectives, codes, & art-forms of non-commercial aristocracy among the governing classes. The gradual rise of the best brains to these classes will make them potentially very choice—& will leave the permanent masses correspondingly stupid & docile. The rebirth of the old paternalistic social order—ruling aristocracy & obedient proletariat—through a fruition of the very socialistic principle which moneyed reactionaries now decry, would be one of the richest ironies in the whole cosmic joke & muddle called life! But it does not do to be optimistic. Almost any trivial circumstance might throw a monkey-wrench in the whole works. A little delay in plutocratic disgorging will mean a communist revolution. A good-sized world war with modern inventions would mean tremendous mutual annihilations, ending in a series of revolutions completely destructive of civilisation. In any case, general world-weariness will sooner or later cause the complex burden of civilisation to become too much for the race—so that most of it will be gradually dropped (as the refinements of Roman civilisation were generally dropped toward the end) through the simple realisation that the game isn't worth the candle. But all this is perfectly natural, & need occasion no regret. At any rate, what I look for in America during the next 25, 50, or 100 years is a gradual giving-in of the moneyed groups on matters of surplus capital, employing conditions, immediate profits, & government supervision; together with a compensating recognition of the actual governing supremacy of these groups. A communist revolution is possible, but I fancy the financial leaders will be too wise to let things get that far. A shelling-out of surplus profits will be the palliative for unemployment—doles, pensions, better wages, shorter hours, & larger totals of employes—& with care the general order of things can be kept going. All told, it is undoubtedly worth keeping at virtually any cost; at least, for the next few centuries.

As for relativity—since only the profoundest professional mathematicians have any real conception of it, I can hardly hope to be very clear on the subject. I will, though, send along one of the Haldeman-Julius booklets on the subject when I can find it—a thing giving several reasonably comprehensible hints.[3] The crux of course is that all entity is so bound up in the elements of *time & motion* that even *size* depends on position & velocity. A yardstick at a certain speed in one part of the universe may be of a size wholly different from its size at another speed in another part of the universe. Nor is space a mere empty abstraction. Straight lines do not exist, nor does *theoretical* infinity. What seems infinite extension is simply part of an inevitable returning curve, so that the effect of proceeding directly away from any given point in space is to return at length to that same point from the opposite direction. What lies *ultimately* beyond the deepest gulf of infinity is *the very spot on which we stand.* As for the religious myth—or more especially, the "immortality" delusion—it simply does not belong to adult contemporary thought. The "losses" entailed by the hard fact are merely sentimental moods & perspectives, for which modern psychology fully accounts. Of course existence "means" nothing. It simply *is*. Organic entity is merely a temporary fact, but the absence of cosmic implications does not, to a mature & disillusioned mind, militate against the enjoyment of such pleasurable processes as the working of senses, imagination, & intellect provide for.

 With best wishes—

Sincerely yrs

H P Lovecraft

[P.S. on envelope:] Latest just recd. Yes—I'll be glad to look over the poems when they're done. Thanks for glimpse of Circle—I'll return it shortly. The prize poems aren't especially notable, yet some are far from bad. I'd almost wager that some very subtle misprint is responsible for those flaming & carolling leaves & wings. The verse as a whole seems of higher grade than would allow for such a slip. Still—one can't tell. That is probably the poem for the $5.00 prize. #3 is pretty good, but #1 is rather poor—really undeserving of Hon. Mention. Glad to see Cherry Blossoms—it ought to have taken a prize.[4] ¶ Glad to hear of your enjoyable trip to Alexandria—a great old town, one of my favourites. ¶ Thanks for additional cuttings—all interesting.

[P.]P.S. Too bad about prizes—but I wouldn't let such matters worry me. These things mean nothing—I never tried for one in my life.

[P.P.P.S.] Thanks for permission to retain Circle

Notes

1. Robert E. Lee was born in 1807, Poe in 1809.
2. Lydia Huntley Sigourney (1791–1865), a popular American poet during the early and mid-19th century, known as the "Sweet Singer of Hartford."
3. Possibly *An Introduction to Einstein's Theory of Relativity* by William F. Hudgings (1922).
4. Toldridge's poem was "Cherry Bloom." The prize-winning poems were "Where Four Leaf Clovers Grow" by Grace Turner Smith and "After the Storm" by Margaret Laurie Seaman.

[37] [ALS]

March 23, 1931

Dear Miss Toldridge:—

    I have delayed reprehensibly in acknowledging & returning *The Poetry Review*, but tasks piled up on my programme to such an extent that everything else had to lie dormant for a time. At present I am taking one last despairing look at the circumambient world before plunging into the abyss of a job calling for *100* pages of typing—the nadir of martyrdom from my point of view.[1] Meanwhile I am indebted to you for other material—including the interesting *Circle,* which I return herewith with much gratitude after an appreciative perusal, & the delightfully coloured Easter cards—concerning whose workmanship I am sure you are too modest. You really ought not to spare so many of these potentially profitable items. I never acquired the custom of sending Easter cards—though one would think a warmth-enthusiast like myself would be the first to celebrate a festival whose real origin is equinoctial & whose name is derived from the Saxon spring-goddess Eastre!—but my younger aunt (not the one at 10 Barnes—whose present health is very encouraging) has always done so, & will be exceedingly grateful for these specimens—which, however, she will feel rather guilty in accepting gratuitously. At any rate, pray accept my sincerest thanks! I must likewise express my gratitude for the cuttings—which included much of keen interest. The crossing of Arabia Deserta vastly stirred my imagination, since this region has always been a centre of mystery & picturesque superstition. It is reputedly haunted by daemons, & contains the ghost or wraith of the primal bygone Irem, the City of Pillars.[2] Too bad you missed seeing the Poe relative. I shall read that book when it becomes available at the library, though I hardly think it will rival the probably definitive biography by Hervey Allen. That sculptured memorial will be very appropriate—I have seen pictures of it, off & on, since its completion nearly a decade ago; & shall be glad to see the actual thing in place after its dedication. The sculptor's conception—scrolling the subject's head with raven-wings—is a very apt one; & does not carry the principle of grotesqueness to the extent of affectation.

By the way I must express thanks for that agreeable vernal harbinger which came last month, & which expanded very gracefully under aqueous influence. It was very ably seconded by one of the Peattie articles among the cuttings. He really sustains a surprising level of interest & diversity in view of his inexhaustible yearly repetitions.

Let me congratulate you sincerely upon your recent sonnet, "Her Silence", & upon the prize it very deservedly won. It is truly a splendid piece of work, & ought to take a substantial place in any collection of yours. In l. 8, I think *quiet* is rather preferable to *stillest.*

As for poetry in general—as I said before, it is no more likely to become extinct than painting or music or any other rhythmical, symbolic, & expressive manifestation of the race's nervous reactions, glandular functionings, & psychological association-patterns. It is nothing to get sentimental about—no "higher" a form of expression than prose or mathematics or any other basic response of the brain to impinging stimuli—but it is just as characteristic & permanent as any other form. It has a different relative importance in different times & places, but can hardly be totally absent from any social order. Modern America is of course an unfavourable environment as such things go—but naturally, no comprehensive student will judge the civilisation as a whole by the temporarily dominant element of loud-mouthed commercialists & utilitarians. There is no law against practicing the arts, even though the persons who fill the daily headlines care little about them. As for civilisation in general—the transiency & insignificance of mankind are understood more & more thoroughly in each new generation, so that the older sense of human importance will soon become less & less absurdly manifest in literature & the arts. Younger people today do not harbour either intellectually or emotionally the delusions of the earlier modern world; but are returning very perceptibly to the more rationally proportioned conceptions of the best ages of classical antiquity. The exaggerated & ridiculous seriousness of the 19th century, with its absurd notions about the deep significance & ponderous importance of the things, is a sensation which the present generation can understand only through antiquarian study—though of course the lower orders retain most of the exploded attitudes so far as outward form is concerned, while the cheaper & more immature forms of conventional art & literature continue to function vacuously & insincerely on the same basis. As for democracy—it has never been a really possible form of government on a large scale, never can be, & never could have been. It is simply a pose or attitude or catchword so far as any actual national policy is concerned—a myth fostered by politicians for their own immediate advantage. The only conditions under which anything approaching it can function, are those of a very small, very homogeneous, very new, & mainly agricultural community such as the New England of the 17th & 18th centuries, the New Zealand of the 19th century, or Switzerland at various stages of its history. The moment a people becomes heterogeneous, or the moment it adopts forms of involved commerce or mechanised industry, the condition of democracy becomes as automatically impossible as unrestricted traffic on a busy city intersection or Homeric military tactics on a modern battlefield of tanks & poison gas. If the forms & pose are kept up, that is merely so much sham & hokum which deceives nobody save the simple—just as the Emperor Augustus rejected the title of "king", kept alive the fiction of the Roman "republic", & had himself solemnly "elected" every year to all the various offices—consul, praetor, quaestor, &c—whose powers his actual position included. But there is no reason to mourn the absence of democracy—because it is a sheer illusion which never existed on a national scale. There is no reason to attach any merit to it—indeed, its worship is generally a purely unintelligent acquiescence in a type of theory long ago proved irrelevant & unsound. If anything is truly lamentable, it is the extent to which 19th century people naively swallowed the democratic hoax—thereby strengthening the popular adherence to a meaningless fetish incapable of contemporary application. Today all government involves the most abstruse & complicated technology, so that the average citizen is absolutely without power to form any intelligent estimate of the value of any proposed measure. Only the most highly trained technicians can now have any real idea of what any governmental policy or operation is about—hence the so-called "will of the people" is merely a superfluity without the least trace of value in meeting & dealing with specific problems. Any sort of successful government must be administered by specialists working in coördination & able to plan over long time-intervals without fear of interference or overturn. This is as true in communistic as in fascist government—for of course modern Russia is ruled by a very small group of men who, despite a low origin & lack of general culture, are nevertheless highly trained in their particular respective lines according to the dominant ideology. The cause of modern conditions is, of course, the invention of machinery capable of establishing new rhythms of economic & social life & organisation—a purely impersonal & inevitable phenomenon which could not have produced any different results. That is why there is no use in getting indignant about things, no matter how much one may naturally regret the cultural losses & dying traditions incidental to a profound readjustment. It couldn't have been any different. All that one needs to bother about in government is actual results in terms of daily life. High-sounding theories & principles are *words*—just that & no more. What a government may reasonably be expected to guarantee to the individual is relative security, a chance to obtain the surroundings & impressions which harmonise with one's background, abilities, or appreciative capabilities, a freedom to express intellectual opinion & aesthetic personality without restriction, a general atmosphere favourable to the creation of art & the search for truth for their own sakes, & a continuity of folkways sufficient to promote a sense of congenial placement & to create the illusions of interest, direction, & value in the otherwise meaningless phenomena of conscious existence. It is not to be expected that these things can be achieved with any degree of perfection by *any possible* sort of government—but the important thing is to realise that *these alone are the things that count*—these, & not such mythical, futile, & irrelevant *word-conceptions* as "equality", "prosperity", "justice", "opportunity", "property", "democracy", "independence", "self-sufficiency", "self-government", "responsibility", & kindred blah-blah. It doesn't matter an infernal rap *how* a nation achieves a reasonably civilised & orderly condition, so long as it *does* achieve such. King, oligarchy, fascist dictator—it's all the same in the end. One method is as good as another *provided it works*. Even communism would be all right *if* it would work for civilised ends—but so far there does not seem to be evidence that it can effectively do so.

About Einstein—that Seares cutting which you enclosed gives about as simple, graphic, & effective a way of grasping the general space idea as I have yet seen.[3] As Seares says, the way to clear one's mind of hampering preconceptions & give the problem a fresh approach is to get rid of the purely arbitrary notion of space *as an entity* & begin to regard it as *a set of provisional working rules.* Einstein has indeed received new data causing modifications of certain details of his field theory, & may have more to say shortly about quantum mechanics—the recent principle so closely connected with the operation of cause & effect in certain minute cases. The general effect of such discoveries is certainly to impose limits on the predictability of certain types of phenomena, though this recognition of limits is itself really an extension of our general knowledge of the cosmos.

I was glad to see your vivid & delightful poem in its Charlestonian setting; & am herewith returning the cutting, since its inscribed nature seems to stamp it as an only copy. Too bad obstacles have developed in some of the contests—but these things are really not worth bothering about. Contests are subject to all sorts of irrational caprices, & their only use anyway is to give one a sort of renewed assurance that one's stuff has merit. You no longer need such added assurances; since the almost uniformly favourable criticism given your work in widely different places & by widely different persons has undoubtedly proved to you impersonally & objectively that you indeed reach a rare level of genuine & skilful poetic expression.

With best wishes—

Yr most ob^t Servt

H P Lovecraft

P.S. Have lately finished an antarctic horror that which comes to novelette length—but which I haven't yet had time to get in shape for professional submission. ¶ Poetry Review is highly interesting. That article on Poetic Innovation ought to answer a good many of your questions as to what constitutes the contemporary mood in verse.[4]

Notes

1. HPL was typing the recently completed *At the Mountains of Madness.*

2. See entry 47 in "Commonplace Book."

3. The clipping probably referred to Frederick Hanley Seares (1873–1964), American astronomer.

4. Michael Roberts, "Poetic Innovation," *Poetry Review* 22, No. 1 (January–February 1931): 3–16.

[38]   [ALS]

10 Barnes St.,
Providence, R.I.,
April 29, 1931

Dear Miss Toldridge:—

I am late in thanking you for the extremely tasteful & highly appreciated Easter greeting, but this spring my programme has been such a feverish rush to get varied things attended to that letters are piling up mile high. In addition to my regular activities, I was fairly driven into a general sorting of my files—whose chaotic condition had begun to destroy their usefulness—& so great did their disorder prove, that the work of rectification took nearly a week. I am not sorry, however, to get the job over with; for it has been hanging over my head like a nightmare for the last three years! At present I am trying to get things in shape for a trip of perhaps a month or more—starting with New York & probably extending in various radial directions from there, with its culmination up the Hudson Valley. During the summer I shall have a period of book-editing work in Brattleboro, Vermont, but I don't know whether I shall join this on the present trip or make a separate jaunt of it with a home period between. That antarctic thing is a new production—not the one I mentioned as having been accepted. I am still floundering around with the typing, but am resolved to get the wretched business over with before I start travelling. It is very doubtful whether I can get any editor to take this; for my style is not a popular one, & long stories are drugs on the market. But this particular tale could not have been done in less than 35,000 words, so I have nothing to regret about the composition. I like this better than the last one.

I regret exceedingly to hear of your aunt's death, & extend my sincerest sympathy. Such events are always melancholy & unnerving to those who survive, but one has to reflect that they form part of the natural & expected order of cosmic organisation. For a time, though, one is more conscious of the immediate sense of loss than of the cosmic inevitability. I am sorry likewise to hear of Miss Radcliffe's continued indisposition, & hope that rest & interesting activities may bring about a decided improvement. In time I am sure that both you & she can issue your respective collected verse, even though a resumption of Cook's enterprises seems unfortunately unlikely. When in Vermont I shall inquire further into the conditions & prices of the Stephen Daye Press—Orton's venture, which I think I mentioned to both you & Miss R. Last week I returned Miss Radcliffe's book of manuscripts for safety's sake; since my room is likely to be upheaved by a wholesale cleaning during my absence, & I don't want any important items to be lost or mislaid.

As for book-publication in general—there's no need to feel discouraged about rejections, since for every volume published hundreds are turned down. A book is a hard thing to place, & many friends of mine have had splendid prose & verse items repeatedly turned down. I don't really expect to have any published collection of my junk. Last month the Putnam firm asked to see some of my MSS., & I sent such as were lying around loose (36 in all)—but I have so little expectation of any favourable result that I would not copy anything out of my files for the purpose. The Dutton firm is not especially good to deal with; as was attested by my old friend, the late Everett McNeil, whose juvenile historical novels they published. They drove very sharp bargains with him, & he always said that they did not take sufficient pains in advertising & marketing his books—preferring to concentrate on their best sellers. The head of the firm is a Mr. Macrae—& his son is now an important figure in the business.[1] I hope the new firm you speak of will prove hospitable toward "The Rosebush" & other items of yours. By the way—Cook's failure (financial as well as physical) probably means the total loss of my small 60-page book, "The Shunned House", which was to have appeared long ago. The loose sheets of the whole edition are tied up in a Boston bindery, & nobody seems to know how to finance their extrication—or, for that matter, what to do with them if they were extricated.

I am grateful for the cuttings—& was especially interested by the notes on local Baltimore pronunciations. The "aow" sound—as in "daown", "raound", &c.—seems once to have been common all the way along the Atlantic coast, & especially in New England. It has now, however, vanished from these immediate parts; though it lingers in Vermont & (less emphatically) in rural Western Massachusetts. Going south, it is absent in N Y City & New Jersey, but reappears in full strength in Pennsylvania—including Philadelphia. Baltimore is the logical southward continuation of this belt, but the widely recruited population of Washington causes an interruption there. In the south the "aow" sound—though with an intonation softer & more musical than its northern rendering—is quite universal except in Charleston; which, because of its isolation from a populous hinterland & its early ease of communication with England, never picked up the broadest characteristics of southern dialect. With the course of time, use of the radio will probably standardise pronunciation to a quite universal urban model.

As for the status of poetry—I'm sure there's nothing to worry about! Whatever art or activity gives one satisfaction is a perfectly adequate one, no matter what its abstract status may be—though so far as that goes, there is certainly no art or activity which can be sensibly held as surpassing poetry. Poetry can express more phases & details & shadings of any given thing than any other aesthetic medium when handled by a master, hence surely deserves a place among the very foremost of human phenomena.

About space—I don't see that it need be any the less interesting when regarded simply as a set of working rules. If anything, such a conception adds the drama of mystery & uncertainty to the cosmos as it seethes on behind its veil of subjective aspects. It is mistaken to become too attached to any particular set of ideas or intellectual conventions. The true philosopher knows how delusive everything is, hence doubts all things from the very start. Then when new revelations come, he has nothing to lose.

As for democracy—it has had brief periods of real effectiveness as a creator of the tangible conditions of civilisation; but these periods have been briefer, & their actual degree of democracy much less, than is commonly supposed. The "democracy" of Greece was upheld by the submergence of a vast slave population outside the radius of the verbal principle; & in modern nations the same thing is true under other names—the equivalent of the slaves being an industrial class with only theoretical privileges. Democracy can be a real force only in very small & very young countries—early New England forming a classic example; in which, however, the democracy went when the youth & simplicity went. The empty name & catchwords of democracy, of course, long survive the real article—veiling in most cases an indirect & invisible yet highly powerful government by financial & industrial interests. Certainly, the changes in America (& for that matter, elsewhere) resulting from modernisation are not by any stretch of the optimistic fancy to be welcomed. All that can be said for them is that they are absolutely inevitable. Everything in modern existence is a direct & absolute corollary of the discoveries of applied steam power & of large-scale applications of electrical energy; & there is no possible way to unmake a discovery once it has been stumbled on. It was so when the principle of agriculture was first stumbled on some 20,000 years ago or slightly less. Before that time all mankind were simple nomads, hunting & tending flocks. That accident created civilisation—a whole new way of life—& many doubtless regretted the change at the time. Actually, no one way of life as naturally evolved is very much better or worse than any other. What we hate is simply *change,* as such. And very naturally & reasonably, since most of the zest of life comes from illusions depending on stable backgrounds & continuity in traditions & folkways. In a century or two everybody will be used to the newer methods & ideologies, & will regard them as the old were once regarded. The special misfortune of those now living is that they form a transition generation, with too great a disparity between memories & actualities to feel at one with any attainable milieu. A "U.S. of Europe" would be merely a customs union. With nations so racially & culturally divergent, an actual federal super-nation like the American republic of 1790 would hardly be imaginable.

Thanks very much for the loan of *Poetry Review* & *Carillon,* which I return under separate cover. *The Carillon* has a very high standard, & ought to furnish useful concrete examples of genuine contemporary trends.

In again expressing my appreciation of the taste & workmanship of the Easter card, I must not fail to mention how enthusiastically my aunt Mrs. Gamwell appreciated those which I passed on to her. She thought them all exquisite, & led her list, qualitatively, with them. ¶ With best wishes, & hoping the spring may bring vigour & literary encouragement, I remain

    Yrs most sincerely
                    H P Lovecraft

Notes

1. John Macrae (1867–1944) spent fifty-nine years at E. P. Dutton, beginning as an office boy in 1885 and rising to president (1923–44). His son, Elliott B. Macrae, ran the company from 1944 until his death in 1968.

[39]   [ALS]

Brooklyn, N.Y.,
July 19, 1931

Dear Miss Toldridge:—

Yours of 1ˢᵗ inst. reached me in New York after considerable forwarding, for I have been detained here—far beyond my originally planned schedule—through the hospitality of several friends. I was unable to make any stopovers after Richmond on my way north, having (as I did last year) previously exhausted my cash. The South fascinates me so that I find myself always trying to remain in it as long as possible, even at the sacrifice of other parts of a contemplated trip. My Hudson River detour is now, of course, out of the question. Am dead broke except for my fare home—& shall start back rather soon now. I wish I had as many chances for visiting at length in Charleston as I have in New York!

All the cuttings are highly interesting, & I am duly grateful for them. Certainly, an astonishing lot of new data regarding the prehistoric American Southwest is being steadily unearthed.

St. Augustine was perhaps the all-around high spot of the trip; though for a long sojourn I think I would prefer Charleston, with its continuous Anglo-Saxon tradition & 18ᵗʰ century survivals. Still—only in St Augustine can one see actual 16ᵗʰ century houses & quasi-mediaeval fortifications. My stay in Florida has surely brought the Spanish colonial tradition much closer to my imagination. I have now touched all four of the great colonial civilisations of North America—English, French, Dutch, & Spanish. Dunedin & the Florida west coast agreed with me climatically, but rather bored me through lack of antiquities. Key West was a high spot—actually the West Indies in all but name. I was bitterly disappointed at not being able to get over to Cuba, but a lean purse is an unanswerable argument. I shall make every effort to get to Havana next year. Miami did not produce much of an impression, though some excursions out of it had their points of interest. I saw a Seminole village on the edge of the Everglades, & sailed out over a neighbouring coral reef in a glass-bottomed boat which allowed one to see the picturesque tropical marine fauna & flora of the ocean floor. On the return trip I stopped off at St Augustine for another week, but finally reëntered the old American South. It was like a homecoming to see old Georgian doorways & steeples again—& I explored Savannah for the first time. Then Charleston—though waning cash forced me to cut my stay short. I could only glance briefly at Richmond— then straight back to N Y, where my hosts eliminate food & lodging expenses. The south gave me, this spring, what I have never before experienced in nearly 41 years of existence—namely, 2 solid months of continuous comfort. I shall have to move down there some day—for obviously, it is the only climate in the U.S. physically suited to me. I do not, however, find any *weirdness* in the scene.

Others do, but I can't. All my sense of landscape-terror centres in the more remote & rocky regions of New England.

Glad you are having things in London Poetry Review[1] &c. Also that Miss
Radcliffe has won an honourable mention. This is my own bad luck season—
115-page novelette rejected by Weird Tales, & Putnam's giving my collected
MSS. what amounts to an urbane shelving.

Trust the photograph-colouring may prove an interesting & in time lu-
crative thing. Naturally it must be rather slow going at first, but I feel sure
(judging from your delicate technique in card illuminating) that you will soon
find it especially suited to your talents.

My elder aunt has been unusually well—for her—this summer, so that I
shall try to get her outdoors more upon my return home. Hope the autumn
will not be an early one.

With best wishes—& renewed thanks for the cuttings—

Yr most obt Servt

H P Lovecraft

Notes

1. No contributions by Toldridge in the *Poetry Review* have been found.

[40]   [ALS]

[31 August 1931]

Dear Miss Toldridge:—

Yrs. duly received—& many thanks for *Poetry Review*,
which I am returning after an appreciative perusal. Thanks also for the poetic
supplement—which, though naturally uneven in contents, contains some excellent material. That long poem of old Salem was especially interesting.[1] I am
retaining this item with much gratitude. The cuttings, as usual, are highly interesting—particularly the one on the source of the alphabet. The headline
writer was a bit confused in saying "Semitic, *not* Phoenician"—for the Phoenicians are one of the most typical races of the Semitic group! What was
meant, is that the newly indicated source involves *another* Semitic group—
more nearly akin to the Arabs than to the Phoenicians.

As for the Putnam venture—they returned the MSS., hence I doubt if
anything further will develop despite the hedging mention of later discussion.
They also returned a MS. of Long's. On the opposite side of the ledger—
Long & I are both pleased to see stories of ours (his "Visitor from Egypt" &
my "Music of Erich Zann['])" included in the new weird anthology, "Creeps
by Night", edited by Dashiell Hammett & about to be published by the John
Day Co.

I reached home late in July, & have since been overwhelmed with various tasks including revision. The trip surely formed a memorable one, & it will be long before I can afford to take another such. Next time I hope to be able to make more stopovers, including Washington—also to get down to Havana. No—I have never seen the West Indies; Key West being my farthest south just as Quebec is my farthest north. St. Augustine was very quaint—& is of course the most ancient place I have so far seen—but has not the massed feel of living antiquity that characterises Quebec. It was, in the first place, never so large as Quebec; & in the second place it has been too much exploited as a tourist centre to have the aspect of unmixed & spontaneous traditionalism that Quebec has. I wouldn't mind seeing Bermuda some time—also Jamaica, Barbadoes, the Virgin Islands, & other points in & near the West Indies. The Everglades probably have a good deal of rather spectral atmosphere in their tangled interior, & I regret that I lacked the cash to take a long boat trip into them from Miami. The trip over the coral reef was surely well worth the price—though of course the submarine vegetation in situ was not quite so dramatically impressive as the carefully arranged & lighted displays found in large museums.

About Knopf as a publisher—of course it is one of the best-known of the modern firms, but I have an idea that it usually favours material with a modern & sophisticated angle; hence you ought not to feel too disappointed if your book MS. does not ultimately land. This is the firm, as you doubtless know, which handles Mencken's *American Mercury*.[2] It is solid & reliable enough, & if it *does* extend any hope of acceptance one may rely on it. Perhaps it is not so fixed in its general trend as superficial observation seems to indicate. I hope very much that your various story MSS. (as well, of course, as the poetry) will find ultimate book publication; but 1931 is about the most unfavourable time for such a thing that can well be imagined. Incidentally, I hope that your MSS. will be returned in good condition. Putnam's mussed & tore mine so ruthlessly that I feel like suing them for damages!

Too bad the photograph-colouring is such drudgery—& so repugnant to your artistic sense. Unfortunately most remunerative pursuits—including revision & popular fiction-writing—have both of these qualities to a discouraging degree.

I was glad to see your rondel in the Charleston paper—it is a very delightful piece of work, & the public it will reach is a highly cultivated & discriminating one. Charleston is in many respects one of the most really civilised towns on the North-American continent—with an aesthetic life of surprising vigour & tenacity in view of its small size. This "Choir Practice" column appears to have a gratifyingly high standard—far, you will notice, above that of "The Circle."[3] Some of the mediocre stuff that gets in there would obviously have no place here. I return the cutting in case it is your only copy. Many thanks for the glimpse. If I were you I'd send a good deal of material there—for it would be certain to appear in good company & to command a really appreciative audience.

Sorry to hear that Miss Radcliffe is still in poor health. My aunt has had another relapse of her spinal neuritis; though not so severe a one, I think, as last year's. I think the dampness incident to lack of furnace heat in the house is responsible for these attacks, for they almost always come in the middle of summer.

As for social, economic, & political outlooks in England & elsewhere—one may only regret that one happens to be living in a period of major transition. Such periods are inevitable at certain intervals—when great changes in actual living conditions come too suddenly to be dealt with by preëxisting systems of organisation & tradition—& the only thing to do about them is to wait a century or so till things can have a chance to recrystallise. With good luck, one may hope to see old forms evolve gradually into new—in accordance with the actualities of today, yet without unnecessary breaks & harshnesses. But this evolution can never be altogether painless; for the generation in power is not used to the new conditions, & always clings blindly to the no longer applicable forms of the age amidst which it was reared. There will never be equilibrium or contentment in any country until the whole basis of economics is changed in such a way as to minimise the accumulation of profits on a large scale, & to give the government power to oversee such things as employment conditions & the coördination of industries. This has been made necessary by the advent of machine production, & the consequent growth of a complex, inescapable system of industrial interdependence which paralyses all previous laws & methods & leaves a vast proportion of the population without means of survival except through special measures outside the familiar cycle of old economic laws. Much may be learned from Soviet Russia, though no one would like to see the complete system of that country—with its discouragement of pure aesthetics & its arbitrary restriction of the individual—adopted in the western world. The choice is between chaos & reorganisation, & the wise man chooses the latter. Whether the new system will be as satisfying to mankind as the old, no one can say. That is merely an academic question anyway, since it will form the only possible system, whether one likes it or not. Meanwhile it is of course a melancholy sight for people used to the old order to watch its inevitable decay.

Some of the cuttings of the second batch are extraordinarily interesting—especially those about the sharpened submarine cable ends & about the petrified redwoods beneath Philadelphia. The new estimate of the earth's age is also of extreme interest.

With best wishes—

Yrs most sincerely,

H P Lovecraft

Notes

1. *Poetry Review* 22, No. 4 (July–August 1931) had a "Poetry Review Supplement" containing a number of poems by various authors. No poem on Salem appeared there, so HPL must be referring to a separate item.

2. H. L. Mencken and George Jean Nathan founded the *American Mercury,* published by Knopf, with the January 1924 issue.

3. Ellen M. Carroll (see letter 79, n. 2) edited the column "Choir Practice" for the *Charleston* [SC] *Post.* She edited *Unison: A Selection of Poems from Choir Practice* (Atlanta: E. Hartsock, The Bozart Press, 1930), *The Choir Practice Anthology: A Collection of Poems . . .* (Charleston: Paebar, 1932), and *The Choir Sings: A Collection of Outstanding Songs from "Choir Practice"* (Siloam Springs, AR: Bar D Press 1939).

[41]   [ALS]

Octr 9[, 1931]

Dear Miss Toldridge:—

Found the verses on my return from Hartford, & am hastening to comment on them before becoming engulfed in the job of book-revision I have undertaken. Both poems are very fine, & eminently worthy of a place in the permanent collection. The only debatable point is the one you have yourself cited.

As to this—if the only trouble with the rhyme were the secondary accent of both syllables, one might be tempted to let it go; for of course such liberties are occasionally condoned. In this case, however, there is the additional drawback of *exact identity* in the rhymed syllables—which rather magnifies the problem. Of course, many things of this sort do undeniably "get by"—but I would make every effort to change it if possible. Could you not say—

But this was very long ago . . . .
For even my locks had silver's trace,
And hers were like the driven snow
Above the flowering of her face.—

or something like that? I don't see that such a change disturbs any of the essential images. But of course, use your own judgment.

Sorry your copyist has been having such a hard time, & hope easier days lie in store for him. Glad that your story MS. was not lost. Such losses are sometimes major calamities, & indicate the advisability of great care with all MSS of which no duplicates exist.

As for the constellations visible at midnight in this time of year—the following diagram may give an idea. It roughly represents the night sky Octr 15 at midnight. For an earlier hour—or earlier time in the month—all the groups (except Ursa Minor at the pole & Ursa Major under it) would appear farther to the left (east), while for a later hour or date they would be farther west. All this can be perceived much better with the aid of a revolving planisphere—which most high-grade stationery stores carry in stock. No need to go out on the roof to use a planisphere! A good book to read for constellation lore is Garrett P. Serviss's "Astronomy With the Naked Eye."

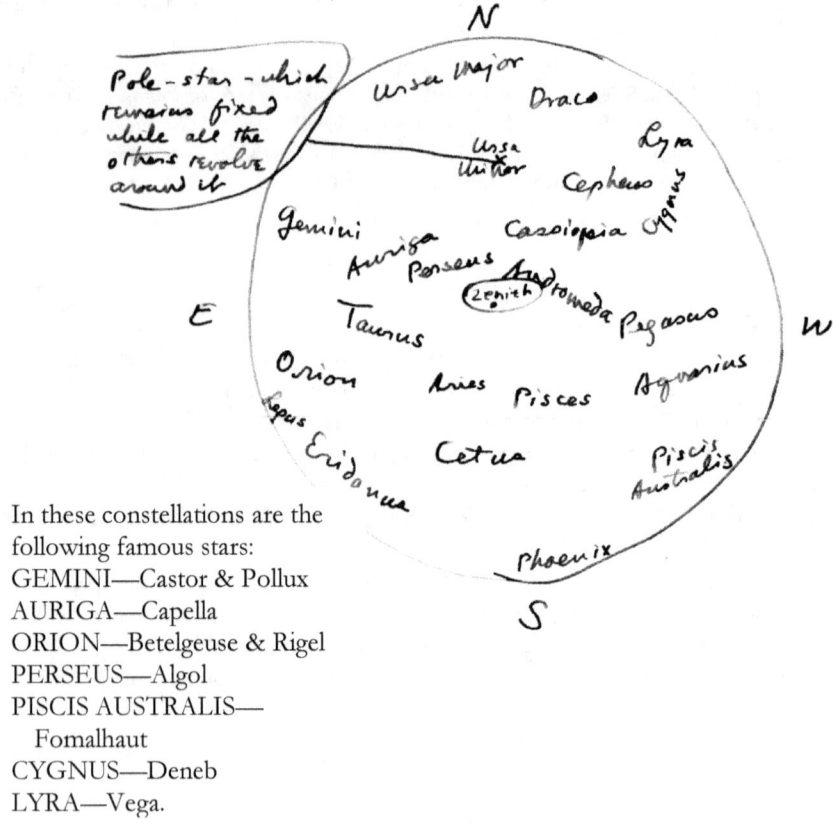

In these constellations are the following famous stars:
GEMINI—Castor & Pollux
AURIGA—Capella
ORION—Betelgeuse & Rigel
PERSEUS—Algol
PISCIS AUSTRALIS—
   Fomalhaut
CYGNUS—Deneb
LYRA—Vega.

Thanks for the cuttings, all of which are very interesting. Also for the *Poetry Review,* which I shall return presently.

I combined sightseeing with business on the Hartford trip, for I had never seen central Connecticut before. Returned indirectly—via Norwich—through a region of astonishing scenic beauty. Warm weather added to the pleasure. The book I am handling is a long history of Dartmouth College,[1] & I may have to make a short trip to Brattleboro Vt. before it goes to press.

With best wishes, & congratulations on the excellence of the poems;
I remain

Yr obt Servt

H P Lovecraft

P.S. It would be rather a good idea to make one two-part poem of these verses.

Notes

1. See letter 31, n. 2.

[42]   [ALS]

[31 October 1931?]

Dear Miss Toldridge:—

Your poem "The Voice" is a vivid & delightful piece of work, & I surely hope it may find an appropriate typographical haven. The only changes I would suggest are such as would help to eliminate trite & needless archaisms. Line 2 had better read:

"Must answer it; the *gulfs between* the stars"

The contraction "twixt" is hardly justified in good contemporary verse. In line 4 the *hath* had better be changed to *has*. Line 6 had better be recast altogether to eliminate the extremely hackneyed *Aurora* allusion. "Aurora", like "Sol," "Phoebus", "fair Luna", "radiant Hesper", &c. &c. &c., is a stilted "poeticism" so obvious as to be automatically barred from further use in serious poetry. Better adopt a new image—here is one which does not interfere with the existing rhyming scheme—

"Stirring the young dawn's delicate-hued cimars"

If the readers hesitate at the word cimars, they can consult Webster's Unabridged. And that seems to conclude the list of desirable changes. It is an excellent poem, & ought to win general appreciation.

Thanks for the cuttings, which are very interesting. The destruction of the Verplanck house gave me a jolt, for I know it well. It was one of the best-preserved Dutch houses of the Hudson Valley—one of the few still inhabited in undecayed prosperity by the direct line of the original builder. I hope the Dutch folk catch the incendiary & burn him alive in his own kerosene! The dialect cutting was highly interesting. I find marked speech variations in New York, & even in various parts of New England. Rhode Island is generally conservative—retaining forms & meanings after they have changed elsewhere. Our use of *tenement,* for instance, is the original British use—the New York & New Jersey usage being a provincial corruption not a century old. Rhode-Island is the only state in which certain oft-duplicated place names are pronounced as in

England. Of all the "Greenwiches" in America, Rhode Island's pair, East & West, are the only ones to call themselves "Grinnidge". Elsewhere the sound tends to be "Grenitch". Our *Warwick* is pronounced "Warrick", as in England; but outside Rhode Island the raw & literal *War´-wick* is widely heard. Also the name *Olney*—alone or in combination with "ville". We pronounce it *Ō´-ney*, but elsewhere the awkward & unjustified *Ŏl´-ney* is used.

Putnam's isn't so bad. I partly agree with one of their bases of rejection—that of an over-explanatory element in many of my tales. Hope your MSS. fare well with Knopf, but it isn't well to be overanxious one way or the other. As for your poems—surely I'll be glad to look the collection over when it is assembled, though my preferences ought not to count as absolute criteria.

My aunt is better again—coming down stairs occasionally. But the place has been in a turmoil for weeks owing to the installation of steam heat—work is impossible amidst the clatter & invasion, so I take everything to the vacant apartment of my younger aunt (now vacationing in Maine) when the weather does not permit outdoor sessions. I escaped going to Vermont by convincing the Stephen Daye Press that revision can be done successfully by mail. W. Paul Cook, by the way, is getting stabilised psychologically & industrially—& has a position in Boston. His health is precipitously better—though I entertain no hopes as to his immediate resumption of publishing activities. He was here recently, & I am now about to go to Boston to see him. He rooms in an old Georgian house in the lee of Beacon Hill.

As for New England as a seat of *weirdness*—a little historic reflection will shew why it is more naturally redolent of the bizarre & the sinister than any other part of America. It was here that the most gloomy-minded of all the colonists settled; & here that the dark woods & cryptic hills pressed closest. An abnormal Puritan psychology led to all kinds of repression, furtiveness, & grotesque hidden crime, while the long winters & backwoods isolation fostered monstrous secrets which never came to light. To me there is nothing more fraught with mystery & terror than a remote Massachusetts farmhouse against a lonely hill. Where else could an outbreak like the Salem witchcraft have occurred? Rhode Island does not share these tendencies—its history & settlement being different from those of other parts of New England—but just across the line in the old Bay State the macabre broods at its strongest.

As for the extent of the present transition in the world—it will possibly rank as one of the greatest to date, (at least in geographic extent) though in the end it may not involve so vast a total of change as the upheaval attending the dissolution of the Roman World—A.D. 400–800. The points of change are different, but when totals are added up I think the earlier upheaval is likely to come out ahead. We do not realise today how vast that change was, because we have—since 1450–1500—regained a great many of the classical elements which were then lost. But the difference between A.D. 400 & A.D. 900 was absolutely stupefying—almost everything was lost—language, literature, standards of living, habits of thought, &c. Today we are far more like a Roman of the days before the downfall, than like a denizen of the ensuing mediaeval world. The extent of the coming upheaval cannot yet be predicted—nor can we determine with certainty just what direction it will take. But it is very unlikely that any of the major languages will perish, or that there will be any sudden loss of the dominant appurtenances—mechanical or scholastic—of civilisation. Even in Russia a tremendous amount has been salvaged. However, I don't think any "golden age" is due—indeed, I think that future cultures may be more monotonous & emotionally unsatisfying than earlier ones. I doubt greatly if any culture will equal that of Athens around B.C. 450.

Too bad the photograph-colouring is such dismal drudgery—much, no doubt, like revising dull MSS. or trying to write popular fiction to order.

My "Music of Erich Zann" was written a decade ago & published in W.T. It concerns a steep ancient street in Paris, at whose top lived a sinister 'cellist whose strange music called to nameless things across unimaginable voids.[1] I have used "Atlantis" in a tale of an undersea temple . . . . in which a light gleamed. No—I never even heard of the Holland Magazine.[2] Cheap magazines pay 25¢ per line for verse, making a sonnet $3.50. As for the Alderson poem—"The Circle"—I did not think it a very remarkable piece of work. Rather hackneyed & platitudinous theme, & wholly undistinguished treatment. Still, it was by no means crude.

Frederick & other places in Maryland must be well worth visiting— indeed, I hope some day to explore the central tier of states—Pa-Md-Va— more fully. As yet, I have explored only the coastal areas. The gem of Maryland, so far as I have discovered, is ancient *Annapolis*—which I visited in 1928 but have not been able to get to since.

Too bad about the obliteration of Mardale. The same thing happens in America—examples being the Ashokan countryside in N.Y. & the Scituate region in Rhode Island. In a few years a new Massachusetts reservoir will wipe out many a quaint village south of Athol.[3]

With best wishes—

Y^r most ob^t Servt

H P Lovecraft

Notes

1. HPL's mention that Erich Zann was a "'cellist" suggests that the instrument he is said to have played, the viol, is the Renaissance instrument played between the legs; the term was not meant as an abbreviation for "violin."

2. Apparently a reference to *Holland's Magazine* (later *Holland's: The Magazine of the South*) (Dallas, TX, 1876–1953).

3. In 1929, construction began on a dam to create a reservoir to provide water to Manchester, England, thereby obliterating the nearby village of Mardale. Athol was not flooded, as were other nearby towns, by the creation of the Quabbin Reservoir.

[43]   [ALS]

[3 December 1931]

Dear Miss Toldridge:—

"Midnight Sky" (original version) is vivid & excellent, & I trust may find congenial placement. Of the three changes I might suggest, two would have to do with the omission of the article where it is obviously called for—a "poeticism" which sounds somewhat strained in contemporary verse. These two are both in Stan. 2, which I'd recommend to read as follows:

> Life all forgot, a stark self stood,
>> A frozen statue, in the place;
> The swift earth held a stiller mood
>> Than others in the race.

The remaining point is the elimination, if possible, of the artificially "poetical" *vasty* in St. 3, l. 2. I suggest *titan* as an alternative, but that is only tentative. Stan. 4, l. 2 contains an *inversion,* but it is not conspicuous enough to demand elimination. Altogether, the poem seems to me highly meritorious, & full of a convincing sense of the cosmic. Glad a majority of my remarks on the other verses proved acceptable. As for being 'classic & erudite'—that's the last thing in the world demanded by good poetry. *Simplicity* is the *sine qua non;* & even when classic erudition looms in the background, its externals should be minimised.

Thanks exceedingly for the cuttings, all of which were of great interest. Archaeology in the southwest is surely assuming astonishing proportions—revealing exact data in fields where only ignorance & conjecture have hitherto existed.

Have finished the book job & sent off the MS., but don't know yet whether or not I'll have to go to Brattleboro before the thing goes to press. It was quite a task because of the author's chaotic usage. Steam heat still uncertain & experimental—but the piping at least is over. I don't think I like it as well as the old hot air furnace. My aunt hasn't yet ventured outdoors except once, for Thanksgiving dinner—but may try it once or twice more before the cold weather brings on a general hibernation. Up to now the autumn has been commendably mild on the whole.

As for current changes in civilisation—surely no individual need worry in the least about any of them, unless active in some field directly affected. The majority of persons today will probably see very few striking & sudden changes in daily life, because (barring an upheaval like the Russian one) such things are invariably very gradual. *Ideas* & *mental perspectives* change swiftly—but after all, most people are doing about the same general kind of things (albeit somewhat differently proportioned in the case of the younger element) that they were doing thirty or forty years ago. Even the necessary social-economic readjustments in western governments will not mean a revolutionised set of folkways. Instead—their chief object will be to preserve existing folkways & institutions as far as possible under the mechanised conditions of the present & future. I hate to see picturesque old objects & customs vanish—but I don't let the matter keep me awake nights. As a matter of fact, a fair majority of the existing colonial architecture & a very large part of the existing cultural tradition will long survive me.

Glad you are benefited by a suspension of the photograph-colouring, & trust the card-painting may not form too arduous a substitute labour. At least, it must be much less exasperating. Glad the copying of your MSS. continues.

I visited around Boston with W. Paul Cook during the Hallowe'en weekend, & saw a fine exhibit of Poe MSS. & first editions at the public library. We also visited many ancient towns in the north of Boston region—including Portsmouth, N.H., & Newburyport, Mass. Both are typical early-American cities preserved without change by a conservative & far from wealthy citizenry. I enclose two or three typical views of the regions involved. Of course we had to take in good old Salem & Marblehead.

The amended versions of the poems all seem adequate to me. I would *not* eliminate the first stanza, but in the the [*sic*] second would say "like a cold statue" instead of "like frozen statue." There is really no justification for the suppression of the article in places like this. And in Stan. 3 I again advise the elimination of that artificial-sounding "vasty." "Little Stitches" is excellent & appealing. In "Magic Chorus" I would retain "hoariest" as in the text.

Holland's seems to be quite a publication, though I have never seen it or previously heard of it. I doubt it would care much for any of my stuff.

Thanks very much for the second set of cuttings—some of which are of especial interest just now, since I heard Prof. de Sitter lecture here Nov. 9 on "The Size of the Universe."[1] One of the most spectacular of recent astronomical developments is the growing conviction that the visible cosmos is in a state of constant expansion—as if it were scattering its contents into empty space. Probably all cosmic events have a similar history—forming through the accidental aggregation of wandering atomic clusters, subsequently going through a series of typical readjustments based on the electrical properties of matter, & ending in a final disintegration & dispersal. De Sitter is not the first proponent of this view of the cosmos—which perhaps originated with Dr. V. M. Slipher's[2] spectroscopic work at the Lowell Observatory in Arizona (which proved that all spiral nebulae & external galaxies are retreating rapidly into outer space, but he is the first to make it the subject of a mathematical test in the manner of Einstein. It will also be interesting to see how well de Sitter's theory of the origin of the solar system (through actually colliding stars instead of merely closely passing stars) will stand comparison with the views which have been dominant since 1905 or 1906. De Sitter is a pleasant-looking little old man with bald head, fringe of snowy hair, & snowy full beard. He speaks excellent English, but has not a very great vocal carrying-power, so that those in the rear of his audiences are distinctly out of luck. He is extremely clever in bringing the outlines of an abstruse subject within the layman's grasp, & shews great acumen in choosing illustrative lantern-slides.

The third set of cuttings—for which thanks—has some very interesting material. Thanks for *Poetry of Today*[3] & *Review*—the latter of which I shall return presently. Glad that more of your poems have been having a cordial reception in quarters whose opinion is of value.

Trust your colouring work will not be prosecuted too arduously. I am about to revise one novel & criticise (in detail, but without revision) another—a prospect which I do not welcome any too enthusiastically. Have a somewhat long story in rough shape, but lack the time to finish it.

With best wishes—

Yrs most sincerely,

H P Lovecraft

Notes

1. Willem de Sitter (1872–1934), Dutch mathematician and physicist who, in 1932, collaborated with Einstein in devising the theory of "dark matter."
2. Vesto Melvin Slipher (1875–1969), American astronomer, who hired Clyde Tombaugh (the discoverer of Pluto) to work at the Lowell Observatory. His brother Earl C. Slipher, also an astronomer, was the director at Lowell.
3. Presumably an issue of the periodical *Poetry of To-day* (London, 1919–48).

1932

[44]   [ALS]

10 Barnes St.,
Providence, R.I.,
Jany. 16, 1932

Dear Miss Toldridge:—

Let me thank you most sincerely for the cards—including the delightful New-Year one—which you really ought not to have spared from your remunerative stock. Many have gone forth from here, while my younger aunt has used others. The work on all is exquisite, & I especially appreciated the Georgian doorway. It is too bad that so many cards are cluttered with insipid rhymes. As usual, I bought the bulk of mine at Woolworth's, but the assortment was vastly better than at any other time I can recall. Your individual card—which arrived after the majority—is splendidly tasteful. I am not sure whether the silvery designs are of your workmanship or not. The later red & gold one is also splendid.

Many thanks also for the backlist of 18th century music—in which I am glad to see your song listed. It must afford you some satisfaction to be included in historic material of this sort. This brochure will make a fine item in my Georgian archives, & I am exceedingly indebted for it. I reënclose the latter, together with others. I doubt I could write anything acceptable for the Washington poetry contest. I vastly admire Genl. W. as a typical Virginia gentleman of the country's best period, & a person of high integrity & ability; but I do not applaud his choice of sides in the unhappy differences betwixt these colonies & their lawful sovereign & motherland.

Many thanks for the cuttings & pictures. The group from the rotogravure is magnificent, & reminds me that I must some time see the U. of Va. The note on Genl. Washington's ancestry was a real surprise to me—though I suppose many of the great Virginia houses have a line or two descending from those cargoes of wholesale-imported wives. I think I had heard of his descent from the Huguenot Maritan.

The Tolman mathematical data on the universe are of great interest, since the notion of a running-down or dispersing universe obviously needs amplification.[1] What we now see can be no more than a fragment of a complex rearranging process without beginning or ending.

About the so-called "Spite House"[2] at Marblehead—the name is merely the result of a cheap local wish to manufacture spurious local colour . . . . as if any fake colour were needed in a village so teeming with the real thing! The pseudo-legend alleges that an enemy of the old Fountain Inn's landlord erected the house to cut off the view from that hostelry—but anyone knowing the terrain realises that the Inn (long burned down) stood on vastly higher ground, so that this house could have no effect whatever on its view. Regarding the nature of heraldic stars—in arms & national flags—I have always understood that they are technically "mullets"—of marine origin.

Sorry to hear of the death of your friend, & of your own recent spell of indisposition. Glad the latter was brief, & trust it may not recur. I succeeded in getting my aunt out again to a Christmas dinner, & she seems none the worse for it. Hope her confidence in her travelling ability is now so much restored that she will attempt occasional excursions without the excuse of a holiday. Thanks for the New Year greetings. I doubt if 1932 will be much worse than 1931 for the majority, though there's no reason to think it will be much better.

I didn't have to go to Brattleboro, but spent some time around the new year with W. Paul Cook in Boston. We did all the museums in Cambridge—Germanic, Semitic, Peabody, (anthropology) Agassiz, (Nat. Histr.) & Fogg (art). The enclosed view is of one of the brand new Georgian buildings at Harvard—really splendid reproductions of the old style. A steepled church of 18th century architecture is also going up.

On Jany 8th I heard a lecture by Raymond M. Hood, foremost skyscraper architect of the country & native of Pawtucket, R.I. He spoke of the large area being developed in N Y as "Radio City", & shewed slides of the monumental group of related structures to be erected there. It will surely be an impressive & exotic place—& perhaps even beautiful to those who like the modern architectural aesthetic. Hood himself is an enthusiastic modernist.[3]

As for current political & social change—I don't believe the present tendencies indicate any more than closely analytical people (which, of course, excludes superficial business men & bombastic politicians) have always expected since the wide application of machinery to industry & transportation. Certain causes produce definite effects—& Marx & other sociologists outlined more or less inevitable consequences since the middle of the 19th century. Moreover, all cultures perish sooner or later through sheer collective senility—& the more dynamic they are, the quicker they go. Comparing the life of the existing Western civilisation with those of the Persian, Greek, Carthaginian, Roman, & other civilisations of the past, we see that it is about time for the early stages of decline to become manifest, even without the invention of machinery. But of course the beginning or decline does not mean the last chapter. Decay is usually a slow process, & in our case may extend from 500 to 1000 years. What would mark the *end* of the civilisation would be a relapse into a feudal or tribal state, with the later emergence of a new group of freshly mixed race-stock, newly metamorphosed language, & basically novel set of folkways & institutions. None of the existing changes is really basic. Empires are always temporary things with shifting boundaries & varying political systems. The Hellenic world had no unity or stability whatsoever during its greatest period—& that was the foremost civilisation our planet has yet seen. What is happening today is simply a necessary readjustment of institutions to fit a radically different set of actual living & working conditions & a tremendously enlarged world of knowledge. It is very probable that in 50 to 100 years a new approximate equilibrium will have been reached—the forms of civilisation being once more brought into relationship with the realities. It was so after the fall of Rome, after the Renaissance, & after the French Revolution. There is no need of worrying about civilisation so long as the language & general art tradition survive. As for India—it really does not matter what becomes of it so long as no outside power gets hold of it & makes it a menace to Western civilisation. The Hindoos themselves are too static & inert to do any harm outside their own boundaries. But it would be well for the Western world to leave India out of consideration as a stable economic reliance. All we can reasonably expect is to keep it *harmless*—i.e., out of Russian or Japanese hands. In many ways the readjustment of civilisation is to be welcomed, for it will eliminate a great deal of absurd pretence, insincerity, & obscurantism, such as always pile up after a culture has outgrown its forms.

Trust your literary arrangements will continue to progress smoothly—though you must remember that it is only the *creation* of art which is important. What becomes of it after it is evolved is of relatively little significance—& I'm sure I never expect to see my junk in collected form. For inexpensive publication I think you might well investigate the Driftwind Press—Walter J. Coates, North Montpelier, Vermont. Coates seems to have some new & better type, & could undoubtedly turn out a creditable & accurate job, even if not as de luxe a job as the Stephen Daye or Tuttle Co. could produce. In price he probably undercuts all competitors by a wide margin. I doubt if Cook will ever get into settled publishing again. In these times a real financial recovery is rare—& Cook is reluctant to tie himself down to any one place or enterprise again. He is disposing of his library, & has thoughts of going to Arizona.

De Sitter's view of the universe is extremely interesting & significant. Probably the expansive effect now perceived is in part illusory & in part due to one phase of a general pulsation of alternate expansions & contractions. In general, there seems to be no reason for regarding the cosmos as other than a self-contained & unchanging field of force—a basic condition of entity which always has existed & always will exist, & whose substance involves a rhythmic & perpetual rearrangement of parts in the manner of a kaleidoscope. The new explanation of the solar system advanced by Dr. Gunn[4] is of great interest as reviving the possibility that organic life is less of a rarity than it has been thought to be for the last thirty years. If accepted, it would restore the perspective which prevailed before the disproof of Laplace's old nebular hypothesis.

Glad you are rid of the photograph colouring work. You had previously sent one of the very tasteful "Mother" folders. If you like, I will return the duplicate—or give it to someone who can put it to its intended use. The design is extremely attractive & well-executed, & forms a very appropriate accompaniment for the text.

I duly received the Scottish Annual, & am perusing its contents with interest. Thanks very much for sending it. I am keeping it safely, & will return in good condition if (as I imagine) you wish to preserve it. It certainly sheds much light on the state of Caledonia feeling today, & reveals a tenacious attempt on the part of Scots to preserve some echo of their ancestral customs & appurtenances.

Weather here has been remarkably mild this month, but I fear colder is in store.

Best wishes—

> Yrs most sincerely,
>
> H P Lovecraft

Notes

1. Richard C. Tolman (1881–1948), American physicist and chemist, challenged Einstein's theory of an ever-expanding universe.
2. A spite house is a building constructed or altered to irritate neighbors or parties with land stakes. It typically obstructs light or access to neighboring buildings, or

serves as a flamboyant symbol of defiance. The ten-foot-wide Old Spite House (1715) on Orne Street is believed by some to have been built to obstruct a tavern's view of the sea. The more likely reason for its sobriquet is that each of the brothers who first lived there built his own section.

3. Raymond Mathewson Hood (1881–1934) was a celebrated architect born in Pawtucket, RI. He was involved in the Chicago World's Fair of 1933–34, A Century of Progress International Exposition.

4. Ross Gunn (1897–1966), American physicist, had suggested that there may be many more solar systems like ours scattered throughout the universe.

[45]   [ALS]

> 10 Barnes St.,
> Providence, R.I.,
> Feby. 26, 1932

Dear Miss Toldridge:—

Thanks for the cuttings—archaeology certainly is bringing unexpected things to light, & fancy the next few years will surpass even the immediate past in this respect. Thanks also for the Poetry Review loan.

Hope your book of poems can find a suitable publisher in the course of time. As for its possible readers—I fancy the same kind of persons who form the clientele of poetry circles & small poetry magazines would form the leading purchasing element. It would be well to advertise in some of these magazines—*Voices, Driftwind,* &c. Sorry to hear that the affairs of the Poetry Circle are unprosperous, but that is only natural during an interval of economic depression. It will pick up again when times improve—or, possibly, when people get used to the idea of their not improving. The arts are stimulated in one way by economic prosperity, but they also profit by any kind of stability admitting leisurely reflection. It would undoubtedly be good for the general aesthetic standards of the country if the money-worshipping attitude of the 1920's were never regained. With crude acquisitiveness dethroned as a standard of quality & goal of achievement, there would be more of a chance for the restoration of older & sounder standards based on intellectual & artistic values. Thanks for the "Choir Practice"—& congratulations on again appearing in this choice medium. Most of the other verses are also delightful. Providence has lately had a very good series of poetry lectures & readings at Brown University—I attended two, hearing Prof. S. Foster Damon[1] of this city & the more celebrated Stephen Vincent Benét. The latter made some very acute & pertinent comment.

As for the times—I don't see that they're getting any worse. They're merely not getting any better. It may be a good lesson for the "rugged individualists" to see the bankruptcy of their cherished pre-machine principles—for sooner or later they will have to begin building on a basis with greater chances for stability & permanence. Some would like to see a war with Japan because of the stimulus to munition & other industries & the disposal of surplus population—& also, because such a war will probably be necessary in any case sooner or later in order to ensure Anglo-Saxon security in the Pacific. But I rather doubt whether such will materialise just yet. Japan is doing to China only what all the other nations have been doing ever since the 1840's, & I fancy the Western powers will be content to hold off as long as there is no danger of Japan's getting full control of China. It would be the latter step—at once limiting Western trade in China & making Japan a dangerously powerful foe in the Pacific—which would cause Great Britain & the U.S. to consider a Japanese war. But before that time Japan may be heavily crippled by its virtually inevitable war with Soviet Russia. Japan got a late start, hence is doing its high-handed aggression today—whereas the other nations did theirs in the past & are now ready (having got what they want) to set back loftily & preach 'high ideals' to younger & less established nations. Many thanks, by the way, for the song. The words seem well-calculated to win popularity, & some time I may have a chance to get the music played & see what it is like. The sheet has a very tasteful & dignified appearance, & I am glad it secured mention in the bicentennial booklet. As or the question of the unfortunate division of the Empire in 1775–83—one generally takes sides according to one's basic system of philosophic human values. Those who think in terms of economics can make out quite a case for the rebels, but I do not belong to this school. In my opinion the paramount things of existence are those mental & imaginative landmarks—language, culture, traditions, perspectives, instinctive responses to environmental stimuli, &c—which give to mankind the illusion of significance & direction in the cosmic drift. Race & civilisation are more important, according to this point of view, than concrete political or economic status; so that the weakening of any racial culture by political division is to be regarded as an unqualified evil—justifiable only by the most extreme provocation. Greece suffered from lack of unity—Athens & Sparta, Syracuse & Thebes, &c. &c., being all separate city-states which acted together only under the most exceptional conditions. They managed to stand unitedly against Persia, but could not do it against Rome. Rome itself, on the other hand, was always admirably united—hence stood firm against all comers till dissolved by internal decay. The English civilisation has so far stood up successfully on both sides, & with good luck can probably continue to do so; but whenever an external menace appears one wishes that a coördinated defence by Britain & America were firmly guaranteed instead of merely probable. In addition, the state of culture in America would have been greatly improved by continued solidarity with Great Britain. It is unlikely that the vulgar financial & quantitative ideals of the American majority today would have been quite so paramount had the region remained true to its rightful sovereign—nor would the spirit of lawlessness have been so general & deep-seated. Some foreigners would have entered, but probably not in such vast quantities; & the machinery of assimilation would have been better. The policy of inviting "oppressed" races is fatal to national welfare, since these elements are almost always biologically inferior & therefore unfit to uphold the institutions established by elements of greater stamina. When a race or group is oppressed, it is usually because of its own inherent inferiority—& we do not want a nation of inferior cringers on the soil settled by sturdy Englishmen. I think the "melting pot" delusion is about played out, & doubt if any immigrants of non-Nordic stock will ever be welcomed on a large scale again. To fancy that the posterity of Slavs, Jews, & Latins can approximate the instinctive emotional life of sturdy, fighting Teutono-Celtic peoples is to subscribe to a fatal fallacy. A small quota of these aliens can do no harm, but any wholesale influx is gravely disastrous. Regarding the trouble of 1775—much was due to the greed of colonists who wanted something for nothing: Imperial defence against the French, Spanish, & Indians, but no tax obligations in return. Other elements resented the interference of His Majesty's officials in such typical frontier activities as piracy, smuggling, & counterfeiting. Yet on the opposite side it may be said that the home government did deal tactlessly & arbitrarily with the provinces, & that the general greed of human nature was manifest in British as well as colonial politics. From 1760 onward it was clear that a difficult problem existed—a problem of forming a permanent & equitable adjustment between colonies & motherland—& the best minds naturally recognised this as a complex matter requiring long years of gradual negotiation & experiment, with many temporary compromises, & the exercise of a general system of trial & error. No one was satisfied with the status quo; but the thoughtful man who reflected in terms of racial unity & cultural welfare rather than in immediate pounds sterling, Spanish milled dollars, & Portugese moedares was willing to bear any amount of immediate hardship rather than arbitrarily cut himself off from his own King & country. Probably only about half the colonists were infected with the germ of sedition, & of these ¾ were probably greedy plebeians with an eye for the main chance whilst the other quarter were misguided idealists who worshipped the eikons of "liberty & independence" [things which have a real meaning only under vastly different conditions, or in relation to actually foreign governing forces] in their emptiest & most meaninglessly rhetorical forms. But herd manias are contagious, & little by little a small majority were swept into the hysteria of rebellion—& finally into the tragic advocacy of complete secession. In the north, most of the cultivated towns—especially Portsmouth, N.H., Newport, R.I., New York, & Philadelphia—were predominantly loyal to the King. Newport, indeed, was so loyal that all the best families left when the Royal forces evacuated it in 1779—most going to St. John, New Brunswick, where the churchyards are full of old Newporters. In the South Williamsburg was largely loyal, while Charleston tended toward the rebels—probably because of the influential French Huguenot element. The fact that one-third of the whole population left the country after the war—forfeiting all their possessions voluntarily rather than abjure our rightful Sovereign—shews how vast was the basic sentiment of loyalty. If this third actually went to the extreme of accepting exile rather than submitting to the victorious rebel government, we may imagine how many more persons privately favoured the old government but outwardly took the rebel oath for reasons of expediency or through sheer geographical attachment to the physical soil & architecture of their native regions. New Englanders largely went to Nova Scotia—especially the mainland part previously little settled, but in 1784 erected into the separate Province of New Brunswick. New Yorkers & Pennsylvanians tended to settle in the newly opened region of Upper-Canada, now the Province of Ontario. To this day the best stock of the Canadian maritime provinces is of New England origin, & in Ontario the exile element continued to dominate until the middle of the 19th century, when high-grade stock from Great Britain came in equal & greater numbers. Southerners generally went to Bermuda, the Bahamas, & the West Indies—Nassau being virtually settled by Virginians & Carolinians, as well as by the Floridans evicted through the recession of Florida to Spain. Thus was blasted the finest culture that North America ever had a chance of achieving. Of all regions, Charleston was least affected; so that the colonial culture really functions down to this day. Virginia, being largely rural & self-sufficient, also came out well. In Philadelphia & New York the quality of life was measurably lowered, while New England was the hardest hit of all. Boston in particular fell into a detestable rut of Puritan narrowness, from which it emerged in the 1830's as the intellectual tradition of the 19th century evolved. This tradition, however, had a great deal of grotesqueness, puerility, & extravagance from which the colonial tradition was happily free. The country as a whole shewed a steady decline in taste as soon as the colonially bred generation began to die off. Up to 1820 there were enough colonially bred people alive to keep up the externals of a rational & cultivated civilisation, but after that the cruder younger generation & the newly-elevated lower classes began to reflect their influence. Andrew Jackson, elected in 1828, was the first President who stood distinctly outside the ranks of gentlefolk; & his influence (greater by far than any executive's influence could be today) was incalculably bad. From the 1830's onward until the 1890's or 1900's American life is seen to be distinctly grotesque & ridiculous—& while part of this is involved in the general world slump best described as "Victorianism", a very large share (especially in architecture & manners) is purely local & traceable to the separation from the British main stream. Buildings like the old Smithsonian Institution, or the State, War, & Navy Bldg., in Washington could never have been tolerated in England—nor could the tobacco-chewing & other quaint mannerisms which reached into surprisingly high strata of the American people. In the long pull back toward mature civilisation the South led, because it had slumped least. New England was next—with a certain upward trend beginning almost as soon as the slump of 1830 was complete—while New York never recovered. There was something strident, parvenu, & garish about New York culture even to the last—when it perished altogether beneath the 20th century flood of foreignism. And all this stems from the rash & tragic declaration of 1776. In the light of that declaration it is grimly amusing to see how the northern colonies turned in their traces over 80 years later & coerced the southern states when the latter sought to exercise the right of withdrawal established by the original revolt & specifically guaranteed by both Articles of Confederation & Constitution! To favour the rebellion of 1775–83 & to oppose the perfectly legitimate secession movement in the South in 1860–61 is a height of sublime absurdity & inconsistency which one seldom sees even in as comic a record of stupidity as the annals of mankind as a whole! No wonder certain Northerners like ex-President Franklin Peirce [*sic*] of New Hampshire refused to subscribe to the cant & hypocrisy of the general Northern position. New Hampshire—with a really extraordinary sense of underlying balance—was not only a very loyal colony in 1775–83, but was less rabid in its abolitionist mania & coercion sentiment than any other of the Northern states. N.H. & R.I. are the only two of the New England colonies to remain largely outside the snivelling Puritan influence of the Massachusetts-Bay. Meanwhile I myself remain in the position of those who reluctantly took the oath of abjuration in 1783. I am too attached to my native soil to leave it bodily, yet am unreconciled to the result that separated it from a Sovereign & national main stream to which I cannot but feel a continued personal allegiance. I may yet move to Jamaica or Barbadoes or some other tropical colony in order to die under the old flag.

I don't think Cook will really get to the point of going to Arizona—& I find that his touch of malaria was not permanent. He is not, however, likely to do any more publishing. Incidentally—I have just learnt that the printed sheets of my "Shunned House" are not lost but transferred to storage in N.H. They will, however, be unlikely to see binding & issuance. For inexpensive publication, the 'best bet' is now by all odds the Driftwind Press—conducted by Walter J. Coates, North Montpelier, Vermont. The Meador Pub. Co., 470 Atlantic Ave., Boston, Mass. is also worth investigating.

New Georgian buildings are very common in New England—in fact, virtually all of the public edifices of Providence erected within the past decade conform to this general type. It is obviously the one logical school of architecture for the Anglo-American colonies in relation to their history, & its sole formidable opponent is that raw "functionalism" which proclaims itself as the normal architecture of a new & rootless machine civilisation. I can understand the theoretical basis of the modernist position, but am unwilling to witness the unresisted replacement of the historic civilisation by a new one based wholly on machinery & quantity. The new will probably triumph in the end; but I like to see the old put up a good fight & keep alive the memory-filled background (whose loss will really mean a vast imaginative impoverishment) as long as possible. Undoubtedly shreds of traditionalism will last for more than a century beyond the lifetime of even the infants of today—for it takes hundreds of years to accomplish a transfer of civilisations. Washington is lucky in being specifically committed to a classical style of architecture. The skyscraper is not essentially novel; tall buildings having been common in mediaeval Italy, while Gothic towers approximate the same atmosphere. Modernism is manifested in certain proportionings based on the new structural materials (steel frame & concrete) employed & on the practical purpose of the edifices concerned. A skyscraper (following Gothic lines or employing classical ornament) can be traditional, while a one-story building (abjuring traditional ornamentation & proportion) can be modernistic. Europe—especially Germany & Scandinavia—has more modernistic buildings than America, & the greatest advocate of modernistic building & city-planning is the Frenchman Le Corbusier. I don't especially like the Empire State Bldg.—but it's the design & not the height which alienates me. I like its tall & fantastic neighbour ten blocks north—the needle-pointed Chrysler. When buildings reach this level of height their minor differences in altitude are not striking to the eye near the ground—I can't say that either Chrysler or Empire State *looks* any taller to me than the old Woolworth. I intend to go up in the Empire State this year. Last summer I was too broke to spare the dollar admission to the tower.

As to cycles in civilisation—of course, a little knowledge is carried over each dark age between collapse & revival, but new fundamental moods & perspectives govern. Knowledge will not suffice to keep a culture alive beyond a certain stage of senility, because people begin to be weary of the tame security & comfort which they purchase at so high a price as measured in sacrifice of individualism. The repression, conformity, & complex technological application necessary to keep a highly evolved material civilisation running is so basically galling to the free human spirit that ennui & revolt are inevitable sooner or later. People begin to think that the game isn't worth the candle—they'd rather do without electric power & plumbing than bother with the restrictions & concentration needed to keep such things going, & had rather run the risk of being stabbed than uphold the standard of law & order which prevents them from stabbing those whom they want to stab. The game of refinement is played out for the time being, & the general impulse is to return to the primitive & begin over again, as a child knocks over a tower of blocks & starts building another. The only kind of a culture which can last indefinitely is one of extreme liberality & non-material values—a culture of *ideas* rather than of *things*, in which there is no complex interlocking fabric to keep up, & which does not need to exert much pressure on the individual. Such cultures are common in Asia—& the Chinese is probably the highest example. In spite of all conquerors there will be a virtually unchanged China for generations after the present European world is forgotten. Only ruthless external force in repeated waves can extirpate such a deep-seated & self-sufficient way of life—it took the successive alien influences of Persia,

Greece, Rome, & Islam to wipe out the Cyclopean Pharaonic civilisation of primal Egypt. If China survives unchanged—as the chances are 999 to 1 it will—it will be due to historic determinism & not to any fine-looking signatures on paper. The comic-opera League of Nations has always made me laugh, because no promise ever yet restrained any individual or group whose wish to do a certain thing exceeds certain limits. When anybody wants anything badly enough, he'll reach out for it in spite of all prior preachments—& conversely, those who are ostensibly pledged to restrain him will be mighty slow to back up their pledge with real force unless the reacher's plans happen to interfere with their own personal advantage. Leagues & all that are very pretty on paper—but they never mean anything when the crucial moment really comes. That's human nature—a fixed biological condition which no fine talk or high-flown aspiration can ever change. Good old Teddy Roosevelt recognised this—but we haven't any men of that calibre today. Still—it does no harm for the little idealists to play around in the sand with their tin pails & shovels. Probably it amuses them & keeps them out of mischief. And of course, there are a few sorts of treaties based on real mutual advantage which have a greater holding power than the majority, & which undoubtedly prevent enough minor clashes to make them worth negotiating. But in the long run the only guarantee of national security is a large, well-trained, & well-equipped army & navy.

As for cosmic matters—I think a little reflection will shew you that the absence of any beginning or ending is not only not difficult to grasp, but that *the opposite conception is absolutely impossible either to grasp or seriously believe.* If all entity had a beginning & will have an ending, then *what began it, & what began the beginner* at one end, & *what will non-entity be after its conclusion?* These assumptions of finiteness are all puerile & arbitrary, & based on the mythology of the past. In the absence of any information beyond relatively narrow limits, the only reasonable adult assumption is that the space-time continuum represents a fixed & basic condition. It is all there is, has been, or will be anywhere. It is the primal essence of reality. It is fundamental entity, infinite & eternal; whose patterned rearrangements are an integral part of its properties, & of which the visible universe & human life are a negligible quasi-atom casually spawned for an instant & soon to be as though they had never been. But probably life as a basic principle is not peculiar to this part of space—though we might not recognise many of its other forms as being life at all.

If you have any stories you wish looked over I'd be glad to do it in the course of time. No—I don't think a tale is wasted if no one ever sees it. It is pleasant to have things praised, but the artist really creates merely for the pleasure of the process & for the satisfaction of preserving for himself a hitherto fleeting & unstable impression.

Best wishes—
      Sincerely—
                     H P Lovecraft

P.S. My aunt's health continues on a reasonably encouraging though scarcely active level.

[On separate page: P.]P.S. Looking at the MS., I see you use a pseudonym— "Barnet Toldridge."[2] I wouldn't advise doing that, for there's no conceivable advantage or point in so doing. On the other hand, it would merely puzzle those familiar with your work in the periodical press.

[P.P.P.S. on envelope] Just recd. the floral anticipation of summer. Many thanks! Wish the outdoor gardens were full of such right now! Cuttings are very interesting—thanks!

Notes

1. S[amuel] Foster Damon (1893–1971), Harvard graduate who since 1927 was a professor in the English department at Brown University. He was also for many years the curator of the Harris Collection of American Poetry and Plays at the John Hay Library. He accepted HPL's papers from RHB.
2. Toldridge used this pseudonym in several works published in the 1890s. See Bibliography.

[46]   [ALS]

                                   10 Barnes St.,
                                   Providence, R.I.,
                                   April 20, 1932

Dear Miss Toldridge:—
            Your poem, "Washington," is extremely fine, & I am sure it ought to receive favourable consideration if sent to any bicentennial contest. The only change I'd suggest is the expansion of l. 2 to normal pentameter length. You might say

            Is torn to travail & the night to stars.

But the later revision's *Awakes* is even better.

      Sorry the early March cold spell bothered you. It was duplicated here, but the new steam heat (plus a little gas stove assistance) coped with it admirably; so that my aunt & myself did not suffer.

      Thanks exceedingly for the sections of the Sunday Star containing the antiquarian material. I appreciated it greatly, & have placed it in my files. Thanks also for the cuttings, many of which are of extreme interest. The ghost story in the second batch goes into my files.

As for the final Washington line—of course it is really hyperbolical on analysis, but I fancy it is not more so than most of the material written around Genl. Washington. There is a deifying Washington myth just as there is a cognate Lincoln myth. Actually, the general was a man of good ability, entire honesty, & the luck to be the head of the winning side of an illegal venture which happened to gain spectacular success. Without indulging in any idolatry, I have a sincere respect for Genl. W. as an honourable Virginia gentleman of steady competence, aristocratic sincerity, truly English determination, & general good taste. What I deplore is his choice of sides in the unfortunate business of 1775–83—a mere accident of circumstance; since if his mother had let him join the Royal Navy in youth, there is little doubt but that he would (being broadened by travel & by the influence of the regular service) have remained loyal to his rightful King & served capably in Britain's sea forces under Lord Howe. However—apotheosis is the prevailing fashion, & there is no need to object to your final line when one correlates your truly powerful & excellent poem with the current usage.

Thanks for the tasteful Easter cards—though as I have said, you really ought not to waste your professional stock on 'deadheads'! Ordinarily I never send cards except at Christmas—but this time I put one of the Paschal pasteboards to immediate use in reciprocating an unexpected card from W. Paul Cook. Too bad you had to bother to mail them again—I have sometimes almost addressed outgoing letters to "Providence". The designs & colouring on these cards are really splendid; the most thoroughly artistic specimens, I think, being the pair last sent—with considerable black as well as gold & other colours in the design.

That Einstein–de Sitter item is certainly of the greatest significance, since this collaboration of the two foremost mathematico-physicists means a clearing-away of many obscurities.[1] Between them, they may be able to evolve in time a more permanent conception of the universe than has hitherto existed. Yes—the picture of de Sitter looks much as he did last winter. I note that the paper has rendered his first name erroneously—giving the German "Wilhelm" instead of the correct Dutch *Willem*. That grotesque head exhumed at Washington is indeed a fascinating & imagination-provoking thing. Thanks, incidentally, for the stamps—although there was not the slightest need of sending them. When I lend anything I never think of defraying return postage.

As for The League of Nations—it always seemed to me more or less of a joke, because founded on expectations unjustified by biology & sociology. In 1919 I was amused alike by those who preached of the boons to be derived from membership, & by those who ranted about the perils of participation.[2] Its record is about what I predicted—it hasn't done any particular good, or any particular harm except for the financial waste of maintenance. However—that is not to say that diplomatic negotiations designed to eliminate minor clashes of national interests ought not to be facilitated. Some sort of permanent machinery for international discussion—like the Hague Tribunal, for example—is indeed highly desirable, for it is capable of smoothing out many details which might otherwise grow into sources of war. The trouble with the League is its absurd pretensions to more than forensic powers, & its naive expectations of the international enforcement of penalties. For it may as well be realised that nothing whatever can stop a war when the motives become too strong & the possibility of physical success exists on one side or the other. In the Sino-Japanese matter considerable inside information is now leaking out. It appears that Chiang-Kai-Shek & the Nanking group were secretly apathetic in their defence, perhaps *preferring* Japanese dominance if it could be made to *seem* that they had opposed it. This was because they fear the communistic tendencies of that element which most vigorously opposes Japan both in Manchuria & in China proper. The 19th route army acted almost against orders in defending Chapei; & only reluctantly, & at the last moment, did the central government grant them support. But all this was to be expected—for China has never been united except accidentally or by imperial authority. The only surprise of the incident has been the relative lack of strength & brilliancy in the Japanese operations.

As for your poems—you certainly ought not to entertain any doubt concerning their merit, for readers seem quite unanimous in recognising their great charm, poignancy, delicacy, & musical cadence. I'll be glad to indicate those I think would best form a first book. I have a good many MSS. on file here, & you probably wouldn't need to send the newly typed copies unless it happened to be very easy to do so. I surely hope you can arrange for a volume sooner or later; though as I have said, it is the original creation—& not the subsequent career—of a work of art which constitutes its primary significance & justification. Don't bother about your audience—one never can tell who reads a thing once it's printed.

As for the new version of "Magic Charms"—a really delightful poem—there is a *noun* "firstling", which means the first-born of any animal species. It occurs in Shakespeare. Whether it can be strained into the meant adjectival-vegetable usage depends on the latitude of poetic symbolism. I think it is all right—& quite effective. *Immemorial* does not preclude the idea of a beginning—only that of a *remembered* beginning. *Chorals* vs. *wonders* in sestet leaves little room for preference. I think *And as we listen* is all right. One can't carry fastidiousness about repetition too far. Let the *and whose spell* line be as it is. The Holmes piece is delightful, & quite effective in its original form. This metre lends itself especially to mild variations.

As for the arrangement of material in a possible book—it is well to begin & end with things of maximum importance. Just what such would be in the given volume depends a great deal on the plan of selection. It would be hard to decide till one had picked all the contents. Whether a publisher would consider a volume containing both stories & poems remains to be seen. The two categories are not often mixed in a single book nowadays. If such a combination is adopted, the poems ought certainly to come first. As before stated, I'll be glad to look over the material whenever you wish—& you can decide whether to send the typed MS. or a list of titles. I don't know just how large a proportion of the material I have on hand here.

My aunt, though not going outdoors, has had no relapses of acute trouble during the winter. Cook seems to be in relatively excellent health. Long is busy with revision & popular magazine tales, so has had but little time for poetic pursuits of late. Sechrist—the bee expert—is now stationed in Davis, California. I've written a couple of tales since November, but am not attempting much marketing.[3] The Vanguard Press asked to see some of my stuff & I sent them 4 tales, but have no idea that they'll do anything about them. This is no time for book publishing—nor am I at all anxious to have a book published.

The present spring certainly has been provokingly backward so far. Hope next month will shew an improvement & make outings possible. I am now starting for Boston to spend a week with Cook. Best wishes—

    H P Lovecraft

P.S. No—the *him-hymn* rhyme in latest W. is *not* permissible. Sound is identical. Of last lines, I think "Is symbol of our everlastingness" is permissible. Of course, no nation is everlasting, but all pretend to believe they will be.

[P.P.S. on envelope:] Just rec'd. latest note & enclosures as I depart for the Boston coach. ¶ In Washin[gton]—change in line 4 all right. L. 5, better say "Travail & star *be carried* rim to rim", or something like that. *him* clashes with *rim*. The *him-hymn* rhyme is *not* permissible. *Must* be removed. Best last line— "is symbol of our everlastingness."

¶ In Magic Chorus I prefer "That Earth" to "Old Earth." Yes—on the whole I guess "most immemorial spring" is best. No choice at all regarding last line. Use your own preference. Yes—this is an exceptionally appealing poem.

Glad to look over the book MS. when I get back. I think quite a number of the Christmas, Easter, & Mother verses might go into a picked volume, if they did not overbalance it. Your plan of classification seems good as you describe it. Yes—I fancy you'd better send the MS. instead of relying on a list, for there seem to be some I haven't here. I'll give my opinions, though you oughtn't to rely on them except in conjunction with the opinions of many others. Above all, don't do any worrying about the matter.

Notes

1. See letter 43, n. 1.

2. See HPL's essay "The League" (1919); in *CE* 5.

3. Actually, HPL had written only one tale, "The Dreams in the Witch House" (February 1932), after completing "The Shadow over Innsmouth" (November–3 December 1931). He refused to submit either story to *WT*.

[47]   [ALS]

May 4[, 1932]

Dear Miss Toldridge:—

Send the book of MSS. along any time.* If I can't finish classifying the verse before starting on my trip, I'll take it along & mail from N.Y. or elsewhere. I don't yet know how much of a journey I'll be able to make. The Boston jaunt was not part of the main trip—for Boston is in the opposite direction from N.Y. I don't think there's any especial hurry about getting the MS. to publishers, for they consider books at *all* seasons. I suppose you had the Christmas trade in mind—but the chances are it would be too late for that anyway, since acceptance by the first publisher would be an almost unheard-of thing. Indeed, *any* acceptance of a poetry volume except on an author's expense basis at this time is very doubtful. The publishing business is at its very lowest ebb—magazines retrenching & failing, & book houses taking only such items as are virtually sure-fire in point of salability. However—I'll go through the MSS. as quickly as possible; giving a sort of rough gradation of all the items in such a way that the desired contents of both a small & a large book will be indicated. The *very best*, of course, could form the contents of a small volume—with second-best items added if something larger is desired. Of course—*all* are good enough for publication if you could manage a full-sized volume.

As for your fear of a too large number of sonnets reflecting the march of the years—I think it is wholly groundless. This theme is probably the most significant one in all life & literature, & there is hardly any such thing as overdoing it. One needn't worry too much about subject-matter so long as such matter lies within the domain of the genuine (as distinguished from the artificial, the sentimental, & the affected) & is treated with intensity & sincerity. You might even have a subtitled section of the book devoted to "Time" or "Years". I also wouldn't worry about the mathematical apportionment of verse-forms—so many sonnets, & so on. Good verse is good verse. Let it stand on its own merits, with its form as a secondary consideration. And don't regret *simplicity*. Simplicity is the highest attribute of classical art—all one needs to avoid is triteness, commonplaceness, & false or artificial sentiment. I don't believe "Shadows" & "Poor Little Pictures" are too long—but as I have said before, beware of the mood which expresses itself in such words as "dear", "little", "poor", &c. This

---

* P.S. The MS. has just arrived. Will survey it at earliest possible moment.

mood verges close upon artificial false sentiment—namby-pamby Victorian stuff—hence has to be watched & delimited with care. Yes—I guess the French forms are all right. I wouldn't worry too much about exact definitions of ballad form. Pedantry in such matters is a bit obsolete. I guess all the specimens will pass. As for mood—*of course* truth is the only goal to be aimed at. It doesn't matter a hang whether a poem is cheerful or sad so long as it's poignant & authentic. Also—don't worry about condition of MS.—erasures, &c. If the text is legible, that's all you need to consider. I'll file your letter with the MSS. & consult when I go over the text.

Many thanks for cuttings, which include some highly interesting material. Had a rather good time in Boston—doing several museums & climbing Bunker Hill Monument for the first time since 1897. Explored for the first time the Gardner Italian Palace or Museum of Renaissance Art in the Fenway. Great place—with a marvellous patio or interior court full of terraced flower-beds & statue-bordered pools.

Best wishes—& will report on poems as soon as possible.

Yrs sincerely,

H P Lovecraft

[48]   [ALS]

10 Barnes St.,

Providence, R.I.,

May 11, 1932

Dear Miss Toldridge:—

I am glad to say that I have had an opportunity of going carefully over your book MS. prior to my departure on the projected trip. Your assembled poetry really makes a splendid shewing; & as I remark in my notes, the whole thing as it stands is quite suitable for publication—title, arrangement & all. You certainly have reason for pride in this substantial body of achievement, & I believe that all critics will agree in pronouncing the volume replete with poetry of the most genuine & delicate sort.

In expressing opinions on the various poems I have tried to use as broad & objective a judgment as I can command, & I hope that my dicta may be found to have some usefulness. At the same time let me urge you not to be guided by the opinions of any one commentator. Seek different people's opinions & make a synthesis of them all. I trust I have covered all your queries in the enclosed notes.

Still in doubt as to how much of a trip I can make—but have one faint hope of getting to New Orleans, which I have always wanted to see. Certainly, I hope I can get out of the chilliness of this northern spring—whose backwardness is savagely compensating for the mild winter.

Hope you'll have good luck with the MS.—though of course you realise how slim the chances of placing any poetical volume are, especially at this season of depression. Don't worry about corrections in the text. Anything that is legible is good enough—for it's a false idea to suppose any standard of immaculateness is necessary.

Again wishing you the best of luck, & congratulating you on the excellence of the collection, I remain

> Yrs most sincerely,
> H. P. Lovecraft

[49]   [ANS postcard][1]

[Postmarked New Orleans, LA,
6 June 1932]

Glad to hear that work on poems passed satisfactory. Am now at the far end of my trip, & enjoying every minute. Tennessee . . . . the Mississippi seen for the first time . . . . Vicksburg . . . . Natchez . . . . & now ancient New Orleans, paradise of the architect & antiquarian. Right in the same class with Charleston & Quebec. Here for over a week, then Mobile, Ala. Am uncertain about rest of programme. Very faint hope of Charleston, & about 50-50 chance of stopping in Washington. Life is long but cash is short![2] Best wishes—H P Lovecraft

Notes

1. *Front:* Court Yard and Prison Rooms in the Cabildo. New Orleans, La.
2. HPL once wrote to August Derleth (7 May 1930) "Via longa, pecunia brevis!"; "The road is long, money short"—a parody of the Latin tag *Ars longa, vita brevis* ("Art is long, life is short").

[50]   [ALS]

[30 July 1932]

Dear Miss Toldridge:—

I am sure you can excuse the inadequacy of the present epistle when you hear of the melancholy circumstances attending its writing.

My return to Brooklyn was carried out according to schedule—but upon my 6th day there I received a disastrous telegram which sent me hastening home on the first train, & caused 1932 to take its place as a black year for this household. It told of the sudden sinking of my semi-invalid aunt, whose decade-long neuritic & arthritic pains had produced an unexpected weakening & collapse of the general organic system. Hope of survival had been abandoned—though the pains themselves, after a burst of extraordinary acuteness, had mercifully subsided. When I reached home—8 hours after receiving the telegram on the morning of July 1st—my aunt was in a semi-coma out of which she never emerged. The next day shewed no visible change, though the doctor thought

214 # Letters to Elizabeth Toldridge and Anne Tillery Renshaw

she was weaker & had but 24 hours to live. Sadly enough, his prophecy was correct; for the end came at 1:20 p.m. Sunday the 3d—so peacefully & imperceptibly that I could not for some time believe that the dread change had actually taken place. Services were held on the 6th—for traditional reasons, according to the ancient Anglican ritual, though my aunt had no more belief in childish theology & immortality-myths than I have—& interment took place in the Clark lot in old Swan Point Cemetery, (in another lot in which I shall be buried among the groves of Clark ancestors extending back to 1711).[1]

The vacuum created in this establishment is easy to imagine, since my aunt was its presiding genius & animating spirit. It will be impossible for me to get concentrated on any project of moment for some time to come—& meanwhile there intervenes the painful task of distributing my aunt's effects . . . . . whose familiar arrangement, so expressive of her tastes & personality, I dread to disturb. The family is now reduced to my younger aunt—living a mile from here—& myself.

I was very glad to be able to pause in Washington last month, & wish my stay could have been longer. Your mention of Mansfield ancestors is very interesting, & (because of the Connecticut locale) convinces me that the branch in question cannot be remote from the Mansfields (of New Haven) in the lineage of my young friend Long. His maternal grandmother was of that family. Pray convey my compliments to Miss M. when you see her.

I am grateful, as usual, for the cuttings—which contain some highly interesting material. The convention sidelights were of additional interest to me because I heard some of the shoddy, insincere, & long-winded oratory of that pompous emotional orgy over the radio while at Loveman's in Brooklyn. Thanks also for *The Poetry Review*, which I have just finished & am returning under separate cover.

With every good wish—
Yrs most sincerely—
H P Lovecraft

[P.S.] Was in Newport recently—a needed relaxation from the current strain. Old houses & bold oceanward cliffs are a tonic to me. Here are some views of what I saw.

[P.P.S. on envelope] Yrs. of the 28th recd. Many thanks for the cuttings. You can see by the adverse news within why I haven't been able to attend to much correspondence. I'm now endeavouring to straighten out my accumulated obligations. ¶ Yes—your city has surely seen some excitement of late.[2] Trouble like this will probably occur sporadically until something is done toward relieving the present situation, but I think the existing forces will suffice to preserve order for a long time—long enough, I hope, for the legislators to start some programme designed to relieve the tension. Probably nothing but a threat of this sort—perhaps many of them—could ever arouse the vested interests from their policy of blind & selfish complacency. But anyway—as I said—I doubt whether even a successful revolution would produce a bolshevik regime with profound upheaval. I don't think anybody wants such a thing—that is, no great numbers do. ¶ Sorry to hear you haven't been well, & hope you won't have any recurrence of the indisposition. ¶ A musician in Los Angeles—Harold Farnese, Asst. Director of the Inst. of Mus. Art (Grad. of Paris Conserv. & winner of latter's 1911 prize for comp.)—has just said he wants to set my weird verses "Mirage" & "The Elder Pharos" to music. I'm telling him to go ahead.

Notes

1. HPL was interred at the Phillips family plot, beside his parents and grandparents.
2. Presumably an allusion to the Bonus Army, a large group of impoverished World War I veterans who had come to Washington, DC, in the spring and summer of 1932 to demand early payment of bonuses that were to be paid in 1945. The army marched on the Capitol in 17 June. On 28 July the Washington police, in attempting to remove the veterans from government property, shot two of them, who later died. Later that day, Gen. Douglas MacArthur led troops and tanks to remove the veterans.

[51]   [ALS]

10 Barnes St.,
Providence, R.I.,
Aug. 12, 1932

Dear Miss Toldridge:—

Yrs. of the 2nd et seq. duly arrived, & I appreciate very keenly the sympathy you extend regarding my recent loss. The sense of vacancy resulting from the bereavement is of course very considerable, but one has to realise the inevitability of such events. Please extend my gratitude to Miss Mansfield for the condolences expressed through you.

Let me thank you for the cuttings, which included much of interest. The matter of dark nebulae is not altogether new, & I do not think you need to worry about its invalidating effect on your "Midnight Sky." In addition to those black spaces caused by the interception of starlight there are also many places in the sky where the stars actually thin out very strikingly, so that we are not denied the spectacle of vast cosmic abysses.

Thanks exceedingly for the always-interesting *Poetry Review,* & for your kind instructions not to return it. However, unless you have abandoned your custom of keeping a file of the magazine, I may ultimately venture to contravene those instructions—since it is always a pity to create gaps in a solid collection.

The Newport trip was indeed enjoyable, & I repeated it several times—taking advantage of the radically reduced boat fare. Newport is one of the most completely archaic towns in Rhode Island—quite in the class of Salem,

Charleston, Natchez, & other fascinating backwaters. Last week a friend was here for several days, & I took him to Newport as the chief event of the visit.

I hope to get north of Boston—in the totality zone—during the eclipse of August 31, but am not sure whether I shall bother to go to Maine for the zone of maximum duration. It really matters relatively little whether an amateur sees the totality for half a minute, or for a minute & a half, so long as he does see it. Even a momentary flash gives the full benefit of the corona. In 1925 (when I was in New York) some of us tramped up into the cold of northern Yonkers to see the January eclipse, but Long (judging from his description) seems to have seen as much from the roof of his apartment house in 100th St.

After the eclipse I have a vague hope of getting up to *both* Montreal & Quebec—since the B & M.R.R. has just announced a *$12.00* excursion including the two cities. This is of course incredibly & unprecedentedly cheap. It will not allow much time in either town, but Montreal is not as quaint as Quebec (I am told), & could probably be superficially inspected in a single day. Quebec, of course, I know well from my 1930 trip. I have never seen Montreal.

The other day I had a letter from a not unknown composer—Harold Farnese of Los Angeles, Asst. Director of the Inst. of Mus. Art, & graduate of the Paris Conservatory (whose 1911 prize for composition he won)—asking permission to set two of my "Fungi from Yuggoth" ("Mirage" & "The Elder Pharos") to music. I felt quite complimented by his request & accompanying comments, & gladly gave the desired permission. I shall be curious to see what he does, in a musical way, with my fantastic images. Another thing that rather pleased me recently was the appearance of an article on fiction writing in *The American Author,* in which the work of Clark Ashton Smith & myself was singled out for citation & quotation in connexion with the handling of narrative elements.[1]

The twilight is now getting too dim for writing—this being indited on Prospect Terrace, a small park not far from 10 Barnes, on the crest of the steep hill overlooking the spires & domes of the lower town outspread to the west 200 feet below. The view from here is especially alluring & mystery-suggesting at sunset, & I not infrequently bring my work hither at such—& other—times.

With best wishes & renewed expressions of appreciation, I remain

Yr most oblig'd & obdt Servt

H P Lovecraft

Notes

1. J. Randle Luten, "What Makes an Author Click?," *American Author* 4, No. 4 (July 1932): 11–13; rpt. in *A Weird Writer in Our Midst: Early Criticism of H. P. Lovecraft,* ed. S. T. Joshi (New York: Hippocampus Press, 2010).

[52]   [ALS]

10 Barnes St.,
Providence, R.I.,
Aug. 24, 1932.

Dear Miss Toldridge:—

Let me congratulate you & Miss Radcliffe on the inclusion of your poems in the Gabelle anthology! The praise from Markham is especially to be valued—& I don't think you need mind the recommendation to 'work hard'.[1] As a matter of fact, the only way even the greatest of poets continues to produce good material is by 'working hard'—in the sense of exerting constant care in technique, & being always on the alert to prune out anything of lessened poignancy & sincerity in his products. Your poem is without question one of the very finest in the collection. It is not easy to be really original, inspired, & distinctive on so widely treated a subject (for this reason poets laureate always seem commonplace when they revert to the familiar & overworked strains called for by their post), but you have succeeded to a remarkable degree. Abundant thanks for forwarding the anthology, which I am reading with the utmost interest & appreciation. It is exceedingly tasteful, & contains a marvellous array of material.

The reason I don't plan to invade Maine for the eclipse is purely financial. I may possibly get as far as Portsmouth, N.H. (I'll discuss that with W. Paul Cook, who will accompany me), but Newburyport seems to be the present choice. The difference in fare is considerable, & I am saving everything for the Montreal–Quebec jaunt whilst Cook is so nearly broke that every penny counts. I know a hill in Newburyport from which the view of sky & landscape will be especially fine. One can watch the approach of the shadow in a very interesting way if there be a good spread of landscape available. After all, the exact duration of the totality is a relatively minor matter. It is doubtful whether a few additional seconds of the phenomenon would produce on the consciousness an image any more powerful than that which a half-minute could produce. Dark filters for use in observing the eclipse are being sold at the Woolworth stores—rather more ingenious devices (with apertures for each eye) than those sold in 1925. Cook & I will equip ourselves with these.

Many thanks for the attractive cards of Mt. Hood. I wouldn't mind seeing some good-sized mountains sooner or later—my mountainous experience having been confined to a single excursion (1927) to New Hampshire's White Mountains. On that occasion I took the cog-wheel railway up Mt. Washington, but was deprived by sudden mists of a view from the summit. Still, it was spectral up there—with no sign of the earth below, & cosmic winds sweeping by from out of the unknown depths of space. I felt more isolated from the planet—& more potentially in touch with the unplumbed abysses of outer ether—than on any other occasion. The image lingers, & I may make fictional use of it sooner or later.

Thanks for the many cuttings. The one about the new version of Turkish history is amusing—for it is only an extreme form of what every nation does in dealing with its own past. As for the anthology—you really ought not to take the trouble & expense of sending me a permanent copy. Moreover—if any permanent copy *were* sent, the present one would be good enough—for the spot on the flyleaf is the merest trifle. I was pleased to see, at the head of the *prose* extracts, a bit by my good old friend Morton[2]—whom I think I mentioned as a visitor here Aug. 2–6. He is a trifle old-school & spread-eaglish in his oratory, but eloquent & sincere for all that—& a great old boy generally. He is the grandson of Rev. S. F. Smith, author of "My Country, 'tis of Thee."

In the latest lot of cuttings I was interested to see an allusion to the alleged landing of the Norse in Minnesota. This is not very generally credited—the text of the alleged Runic rock being as uncertain as that of the famous Brighton Rock in Massachusetts. The later item regarding the Georgia mummies is also highly interesting. Certainly, several racial variants were present in North America—though it is likely that all were of the mongoloid stock we call 'Indian', plus an infusion of the Polynesian.

About the eclipse—undoubtedly the partial spectacle in Washington (89%) will be highly interesting. To save you the trouble of borrowing smoked glass, here's a neat little device from Woolworth's which will be better still—& which you can save for the next eclipse. Similar things were sold at the time of the 1925 eclipse.

With all good wishes—

     Yrs most sincerely,

         H P Lovecraft

P.S. Am returning anthology & (despite instructions to the contrary) Poetry Review. The latter is unusually interesting—especially the article on Blunden—with whom a friend of mine has corresponded.[3]

[P.P.S. on envelope] Thanks tremendously for "Cries of London", just received. You really ought not to have given them away unless you have duplicates. They are full of the quaint atmosphere of the late 18th and very early 19th century, & form a valuable item in anyone's collection. To me they are of especial interest, because I have a little illustrated book of street cries—owned by a great-grandfather—published in N.Y. about 1830.[4] Again let me tender my profoundest & sincerest thanks! I presume you know of the artist of these famous & fascinating views—Francis Wheatley, 1747–1801.[5]

Notes

1. Beatrix Reynolds and James Gabelle, ed., *George Washington in the Hearts of His Countrymen: An Anthology.* Markham must have made his comment about Toldridge in a personal letter to her.

2. James F. Morton. "Washington in History," p. 11.

3. Frederick T. Wood, "On the Poetry of Edmund Blunden," *Poetry Review* 23, No. 4 (July–August 1932): 255–74. It is unknown which of HPL's colleagues had corresponded with Blunden (1896–1974), a leading British poet of the period.

4. Most likely *New York Street Cries in Rhyme* (New-York: Mahlon Day, 1825), and most likely from the library of Stephen Place, Jr.

5. W[illiam] Roberts, *The Cries of London* (London: The Connoisseur, 1924), with engravings by Francis Wheatley.

[53]   [ALS]

10 Barnes St.,

Providence, R.I.,

Septr 21, 1932.

Dear Miss Toldridge:—

Yr letter with appreciated enclosures reached me just as I was about to leave for my combined eclipse–Canadian expedition. Hope you had good luck with the partial phenomenon as visible in the D.C. The eclipse was a success for me, though many places in the totality zone were clouded. Cook & I picked ancient Newburyport as a post of observation; & although there were clouds in the sky, the sun & moon were entirely clear of them at the climactic moment of totality. We reached Newburyport long before the eclipse started, & chose a hilltop meadow with a wide view—near the northern part of the town—as our observatory. Naturally the clouds made us anxious, but the sun came out every little while & gave us long glimpses of all stages of the phenomenon. The landscape did not change in tone until the solar crescent was rather small, & then a kind of sunset vividness became apparent. When the crescent waned to extreme thinness, the scent grew strange & spectral—an almost deathlike quality inhering in the sickly yellowish light. Just about that time the sun went under a cloud, & Cook & I commenced cursing in seven different languages! At last, though, the thin thread of the pre-totality glitter emerged into a large patch of absolutely clear sky. The outspread valleys faded into unnatural night—Jupiter came out in the deep-violet heavens—ghoulish shadow-bands raced along the winding white roads—the last beaded strip of glitter vanished—& then the pale corona flickered into aureolar radiance around the black disc of the obscuring moon. We were seeing the real shew! Though Newburyport was by no means close to the line of maximum duration, the totality lasted for a surprisingly long time—long enough for the impression to sink ineffaceably in. It would have been foolish if we had gone up to the crowded central line in Maine or New Hampshire. The earth was darkened much more pronouncedly than in the eclipse of 1925, though the corona was not so bright. There was a suggestion of a streamer extending above & to the left of the disc, with a shorter corresponding streamer below & to the right. We absorbed the whole spectacle with utmost impressedness & appreciation.

Finally the beaded crescent reëmerged, the valleys glowed again in faint, eerie light, & the various partial phases were repeated in reverse order. The marvel was over, & accustomed things resumed their sway. I may never see another, but it's not everyone who has witnessed two total solar eclipses! Enclosed is a view which I picked up at a Woolworth store in Montreal, & which illustrates the phenomenon as seen from the belt of totality. Other enclosed views illustrate my Montreal-Quebec trip, which was a most decided success. Montreal is more British than Quebec, & does not seem at all foreign except in the French section east of St. Lawrence boulevard. It is a highly attractive city, well set off by the towering slope of Mt. Royal, which rises in its midst. The ancient part is that closest to the southern waterfront. Montreal would seem much like any high-grade American city but for the profusion of horse-drawn vehicles. I explored it thoroughly, & also visited the neighbouring Lachine rapids. But I was glad to get to old *Quebec* at last, for that is utterly unique among the cities of this continent. As in 1930 I revelled in the atmosphere of massed antiquity—& I also took a 'bus excursion around the neighbouring Isle d'Orleans, where the old French countryside remains in a primitive, unspoiled state. There were endless brick farmhouses with curved eaves, wind & water mills, wayside shrines, & quaint white villages clustering around ancient silver-steepled parish churches. Nothing but French is spoken, & the rustic population live where their ancestors have lived for 200 years—seldom even visiting Quebec. I hated to go home—& when passing through Boston eased the transition by making a side trip to ancient Marblehead. Since returning to Providence I have been kept on the run by successive guests—first Carl Strauch, a brilliant young Pennsylvanian poet, & then my young friend of many years—Donald Wandrei, the weaver of weird prose & verse. I took both of these youths over the Harris Collection of Poetry in the library of Brown Univ.—the greatest collection of American verse in the world. Now I am trying to catch up with my neglected work & correspondence. Days are getting shivery of late, so that most of my work has to be indoors. Hibernation will begin soon!

Best wishes—

Yr obt Servt

H P Lovecraft

P.S. Enclosed is a brochure of criticism which may interest you. Keep it—I have a good supply.[1]

Notes

1. *Further Criticism of Poetry,* by HPL.

[54]   [ALS]

10 Barnes St.,
Providence, R.I.,
Oct^r [28?], 1932.

Dear Miss Toldridge:—

Yes—last month's trip was certainly a remarkably en-
joyable one, & I wish it could have been longer. While in the Boston zone I
called on Charles A. A. Parker, editor of *L'Alouette* & publisher of poetic brochures, & what he shewed me of his equipment & specimens convinces me
that he could handle a job of small book publishing better & more economically than anyone else except Cook in his heyday. He could quote very low
rates, & yet could furnish work incomparably more tasteful in mechanical appearance than anything the Driftwind Press could furnish. I trust you'll keep
him in mind (address 114 Riverside Ave., Medford, Mass.) whenever you feel
able to indulge in publishing.

Glad you had as good an eclipse view as geography would permit. Yes—
Cook & I used the same kind of dark transparency, & found that it was vastly
superior to the common overexposed film—of which we also had specimens
for purposes of comparison. The inhabitants of Newburyport had all sorts of
devices, both regular & makeshift; & the shops sold completely out shortly
before the phenomenon started. When the long-awaited hour actually came,
all business closed down—a very easy thing to manage in a sleepy & picturesque backwater like Newburyport.

No—Cook could not accompany me on the Canadian trip. Possibly it
was just as well that I was alone, since my rate of travel usually proves exhausting to those less moved with exploratory enthusiasm than myself. To
save time & hotel bills I travel by night whenever I can—& on this occasion
cut out two successive nights of rest, spending them on trains.

Glad that little critical brochure proved of some interest. The somewhat
pompous title is not of my selection—I fact, I had no title at all, since the
matter was written as a routine report for the N.A.P.A.'s critical bureau. The
thing was so tediously long that the chairman didn't wish to inflict it on the
official organ—*The National Amateur*—where such stuff is usually published,
but decided to issue it as a separate publication of the critical department. His
business connexion with the printing firm of Fetter enabled him to do this at
a merely nominal cost. Its appearance is surely very fine—deceptively so, in
view of the elementary routine criticism contained within.

Thanks for the cuttings—all of which are of interest, & one of which I'm
sending to young Long for discussion. As for the planet Venus—fiction writers are beginning to awaken to its habitable possibilities, & to choose it as a
scene for extra-terrestrial adventures.

And I must thank you most especially for the fine & immaculate copy of
the Washington anthology which reached me Sept. 30th. As I said before, this

is an exceedingly interesting & delightful collection; & I am glad indeed to have it on my shelves. But really, you ought not to have gone to the extravagance of procuring an extra copy. Your own contribution is among the finest items on the table of contents, & you have every reason to take pride in the venture. My friend Parker—in Medford—knows James Gabelle, & thinks very highly of him. Gabelle, he says, was rather sorry that the conditions of his editorship did not give him a fuller authority over the contents of the volume. He, alone, would have eliminated all the more trivial & clumsy items—such as J. Milton Swartz's "George Washington, We Honour You." Again let me express my thanks for the welcome & attractive volume.

Sorry you've had eye trouble, & hope it'll soon be over. I wouldn't work on the exacting Christmas cards if I were you. I hope the juvenile books fare well with Longman's—but remember that placing is very difficult in these times. About eyes—muscular trouble often mends considerably, as mine did. In the winter of 1916–17 my eyesight was very bad & jumpy—everything would go black & indistinct now & then—& I had some new glasses (my present ones, which I wear very rarely for middle-distance vision as in theatres or at illustrated lectures) which I had to wear constantly except for close-range reading. As time passed, I needed them less & less; & in the winter of 1925–6 I left them off for general vision. Some two years ago I had returning tugs at the left eye—my worst one always—but my stay in Florida in 1931 seemed to cure the trouble. I don't yet know whether I'll ever have to return to glasses for constant use.

As for radios—I doubt if I shall ever get one, but of course one can often obtain entertaining material over them. My aunt in Slater Ave.[1] has one now, & I sometimes "fish" for distant stations when over there—for there is a fascination in the uncanny bridging of space. I have had stations as far off as Richmond, Cincinnati, Chicago, Detroit, & Montreal (the latter largely French), but have not been able as yet to get Charleston, New Orleans, or Quebec. If I had one I'd probably waste valuable time monkeying with it!

The outdoor season is about over for me, though I did take one final excursion to Salem & Marblehead Oct. 9—a splendidly warm day, with autumn colour beginning to appear in the foliage. Both old towns exerted their usual fascination, & only the coming of darkness drove me home.

As for puzzles & games—I have not the faintest interest in them, & have not had for 35 years or more. I begrudge the time & mental energy wasted upon them, since I always feel that I could be doing something else far more entertaining.

About the Harris Collection of Poetry at Brown—it's really no honour to be in it. It includes everything indiscriminately—good & bad—for purposes of historic record. Among the contents are the pathetic brochures of some of my very 'dumbest' revision-clients—including that immortal itinerant lecturer David V. Bush.

That cyclopean desert figure illustrated in the cutting you sent is certainly fascinating. It is probably only Indian work—but there ought to be a story in it!

As for political matters—with so many factors on either side, I'm about neutral. There is nothing in the basic policy of the Republican party (or Democratic either!) to provide for that slow redistribution of wealth which intensive mechanisation is gradually making imperative as an early measure—& yet the lack of a chance to inaugurate any farther-seeing policy at present makes one wonder whether it would be worth-while to go through the motions of a change that means little. Possibly it would be worth any amount of inconvenience & present confusion to have an entering wedge for a more potentially enduring system—anything to break down the artificial rigidity of the absolute existing forms. Roosevelt has a farther-seeing & more flexible outlook than Hoover, but is not as efficient in a narrow, immediate way. Norman Thomas sees farther than either—though all parts of his programme might not be necessary. As between the two with a real chance of election, there's not much to choose. After all—it is not the president but the heterogeneous array of puppets called Congress which has the real say in the moulding of external political policy. I don't spend much time bothering about the matter—for the real forces of social & political evolution are blind, hidden drifts recognised only by a few academic thinkers.

With best wishes—

Sincerely yrs

H P Lovecraft

[P.S.] Yes—the replacement of buildings in Washington has its unfortunate aspect. One must be thankful, though, that the new edifices are classical & traditional—as distinguished from hideous modernistic experiments (almost as bad as Victorian stuff) elsewhere.

Notes

1. Annie E. P. Gamwell lived in a flat at 61 Slater Avenue.

[55]   [ALS]

10 Barnes St.,
Providence, R.I.,
Decr 14, 1932

Dear Miss Toldridge:—

That rainy day you spoke of developed into an actual flood along the Pawtuxet River in R.I.—so that boats & canoes were used in the streets of some of the villages. Thanks exceedingly for the cuttings—which include some highly interesting things. The amount discovered about prehistoric America in the last five years—Esquimau "ivory culture", "basketmaker" race, pueblos timed by tree-rings, &c.—is truly astonishing.

I note the letter from Longmans with much interest, & hope that the agency chosen may prove useful. Many writers seem to find literary agents a vast help, & R. E. Howard & E. Hoffmann Price now depend very largely on them. I haven't had time to write anything new lately—& indeed, my recent things have been received so indifferently that I am glad to pause & take stock of things preparatory to a fresh start. As for anthologies—the only one I know of that I'm due (possibly) to appear in is the one which Price is planning. He's still in doubt as to what story he wants. (Probably "The Picture in the House".)[1] I suppose I mentioned "Creeps by Night", out last spring, which had my "Music of Erich Zann." Incidentally—although O'Brien doesn't mention me this year, the O. Henry Memorial Prize Annual gives my "Strange High House in the Mist" a first-class rating, & my "In the Vault" a second-class rating. By the way—I'm glad to hear that your eyes are better. Don't worry because you aren't constantly writing poetry. All aesthetic production comes by fits & starts. And I wouldn't attempt too much card-painting if I were you.

As for the election—it was so much of a foregone conclusion that I didn't even wait up for returns. There was really no other course to adopt—although, amusingly enough, the vast horde of voters who caused the change did not act from any intelligent reason. As I have been convinced for a number of years, the Republican principle of laissez faire, & the sacrosanct safeguarding of unlimited property-grabbing, cannot be successfully applied to the basically altered conditions of a highly mechanised age—depression or no depression—hence the only sensible thing to do is to substitute a party with longer-sighted & more flexible ideas. The Democrats share many of the fallacies of the Republicans, but in lesser degree—& of course there was no real choice outside the two major parties—hence they were the logical element to vote in. Now we shall see what—if anything—will get started. Too bad Pres. Hoover's ordinarily great independence hasn't as yet caused his mind to break free of the obsolete "profit & property" fetish. He is one of the greatest practical-detail administrators living—but unfortunately his high abilities seem to be all committed in a direction essentially wrong for the future of the nation. As Davies points out in that cutting you sent, the present depression is only part of the grave general problem before the statesmen of the next hundred years. I hope Hoover will have a chance to exercise his unique special gifts under some leadership of more liberal & philosophic tone—he is assuredly sincere & conscientious in the extreme, & has done admirably well according to the somewhat outmoded lights by which he has been steering. Yes—I think Ramsay MacDonald has risen to remarkable heights of statesmanship. He surely has no sinecure at present, with "hunger-marchers" & other knotty problems to cope with.

Yes—my surviving aunt & I spent a joint Thanksgiving, obtaining an adequate feast at the quiet restaurant which we usually patronise on such occasions.[2]

I was depressed two weeks ago last Saturday at learning of the death of Henry S. Whitehead, my delightful Florida host of 1931. He had written me very cheerfully—& with mention of future plans—as lately as Nov. 14, hence the bad news formed a double shock. He had long suffered from a gastric trouble, but during recent months it had seemed to be yielding to medical treatment. This will be a bad blow to his father—aged 84—& all of Dunedin will be in mourning for one who was its veritable idol. Whitehead was born in 1882, & graduated from Harvard in 1904, in the class with President-Elect Roosevelt. I have never met a person more brilliant, courageous, generous, learned, attractive, witty, & altogether admirable. Besides being an author he was an Episcopal clergyman—rector of the Church of the Good Shepherd in Dunedin. He always tried to minimise his illness—& even now it is difficult to believe that death can have overtaken one so brisk, active, & optimistic.

As for poetry—there is no reason at all why you should not send more poems around, including those submitted to Knopf. Magazine publication never interferes with *book* publication—especially if you specify that book rights are reserved. I'd keep right on sending things to as many poetry magazines as possible—for there is always an appreciative element among the readers of these periodicals.

Too bad your favourite radio station has been drowned out. I've never been able to get Washington on my aunt's machine, although there's a station in ancient *Alexandria* which comes almost as clearly as a local station. Baltimore is dependable, & Richmond, Roanoke, Charlotte N.C., Nashville, Tenn., & others are extremely distinct.

As for the international debt question—I believe it will eventually be worked out without a disastrous crisis—though not without great effort, perplexity, & compromise. It seems to me clear that anything like full repayment is, in view of the worldwide economic collapse, nothing less than a grotesque & absurd impossibility. It ought to be plain even to a dense & provincial congressman that impossibilities cannot be demanded—& I really think that some degree of common sense will be used when the actual facts of the case are further emphasised. It would be a disaster for American finance if the structure of British finance were imperilled—& this is the kind of argument which appeals to the large business interests & their political mouthpieces.

Thanks for the interesting cutting anent the hunger-marchers—who surely must be rather a nuisance around Washington. I recall how sullen & depressing the bonus army looked last June. T. R. Henry writes ably on these themes. Demonstrations of this sort are far from ornamental, yet would seem to be unavoidable in a period of inevitable transition. Those agitators are no more irrational in their demands for change, than the Hooverites are in their insane complacency & fatuous confidence that the mechanised future can be faced with now-meaningless formulae & methods evolved in the dead, non-mechanised past. What is needed is a middle course between the grotesque & suicidal reaction of the plutocrats & the more or less irresponsible & destructive programme of the communists. If human beings were by nature rational, the government would devise a liberal policy without intimidation from outside; but since they are not, it is probable that only the increasing threats of armed proletarian groups can start them into action. Then, in fear of their precious necks & moneybags, they will begin to think of remodelling governmental policy into some kind of conformity with present needs. The communists won't be likely to howl for their full demands once they are assured of the decent security which the government of the future must give or perish. If the Czar's government had been less stiff-necked, the bolsheviks would not have been in the saddle today.

When you assume the "rightness" of the dying civilisation you can hardly mean more than that it was roughly adequate to the special conditions of the bygone age which evolved it. No civilisation can have any "rightness" or other meaning apart from the conditions to which it is related. The obsolescent western culture was the product of a life hinging on agriculture & handicraft. In a machine age it has no meaning—for it is not able to offer the bulk of the population a chance to live adequately—or live at all, for that matter. Old-fashioned economics take no account of machine industry, & break down under the realities of a machine age. They are far more impracticable than even bolshevism—because they will not work at all! Something absolutely *must* be changed. The question is no longer "whether or not" but simply "what & how."

Christianity cannot be taken seriously. It is naive & unscientific to blame the world for not conforming to it—since it is a chimerical & poetic illusion to which human nature is utterly alien. It is meaningless—because no race or nation ever could or ought to conform to it. The only blameable thing is the stupid stubbornness with which people have continued to pretend belief in this irrelevant & unworkable Oriental importation. Had it been cast overboard long ago, the western world would have had all the earlier start toward a rational system of administration based on the actual needs of actual people. All that has enabled European mankind to survive in the past is the ignoring of the theoretical Christian doctrine & ethic. Very amusingly, the Christians of the 3d & 4th centuries A.D. were in exactly the same position as the ragged hunger marchers of today. Then *they* were the surly bolsheviks, ignorant & intolerant of civilisation, & arrayed against the prevailing vested interests & the surface of law & order. Then a political accident put them on top—& they forthwith became the vested plutocrats themselves, prepared to oppress others as they had lately been oppressed. They never had half the justification of the modern hunger marchers, for the latter are fighting for the right to live—a basic right which no one can deny. Nor would these marchers establish a wholly chaotic regime if they won by force. Modern Russia is far from a total chaos, although its material conditions—& most of its aesthetic conditions—at present would seem uncomfortable to us.

However—as I have said repeatedly—I do not think that the U.S. or England will experience a disruptive social revolution. There will of course be *threats,* but we are more adaptable than the Czarist Russians or Bourbon French. Common sense will dictate a gradual letdown & liberalisation amidst which no really important cultural element will need to perish—& which no one need regret, since it will be only an inevitable response to the equally inevitable conditions of anthropological evolution. Various phases or incidents may be more or less unpleasant—but that's a long way from such chaos as Russia & France have been through. No person, I believe, need have any fear of massacres or enthroned barbarism. Those extremes are usually the result of a too dogged clinging to the dying order by its fanatical upholders, but in the present case it seems impossible that the plutocrats will not themselves realise the impossibility of their position before it is too late. Scientific surveys of the industrial energy conditions in the U.S.—like that of the very competent & scholarly "technocrat" group—are becoming too conclusive, intelligent, & disinterested to be passed over lightly, even by people as pathetically self-blinded as the Hoover individualists. Physicists & engineers are getting down to hard quantitative details in estimating the displacement of man by machinery; & are shewing that the traditional relationship between men & industry is absolutely meaningless, irrelevant, & unworkable in the face of a world which can produce with a trifling human personnel all the material mankind can use either normally or forcedly. No man is now necessarily an asset to the industrial structure as he was most emphatically before 1800, moderately before 1900, & conceivably before 1920. The average man, no matter how able & willing he is, has ceased to have any *guarantee* of a living in exchange for his services. Out of all the population, only a few have any chance of supporting themselves in the future—no matter how great "business prosperity" may be—under the present system. The Republican conception of prosperity is merely a free exchange of money & goods among the few who have any to exchange. Meanwhile more & more persons have to starve or accept charity. In five or ten years more even a Hooverite will have to admit that the ancient relationship between the individual man & the social group—based on unmechanised man as the dominant unit in energy-application—has become utterly & unavoidably impracticable & obsolete. There is no getting around this, hedge as one may. We can't stop the use of machinery—& if we have automatic production machinery under a system of traditional finance & unregulated private property we shall have increasing unemployment, decline, & chaos. There will have to be a "new deal" in a wider sense than even the moderately liberal Roosevelt would now be willing to admit. Industry must be under governmental control, so that the slight amount of human work to be done may be distributed in such a way as to keep the whole population alive; & in order to accomplish this the whole system of profit & property-holding will have to be changed. For the first time there will have to be a planned survey of natural resources & production, & a deliberate policy of seeing that stocks of goods are placed where they are needed—irrespective of profit. Bursting grain elevators in Minneapolis & starving men in Boston form a paradox which a rational & stable society cannot permit. Probably orthodox finance with its gold (or other) standard will have to go—the "money" of the future consisting of permits to draw upon a governmentally controlled energy & material supply. But none of this need mean any overturn of non-economic folkways, aesthetic standards, or even living-standards except those of the ultra-luxurious. With the exercise of reason all the needed transitions might be pacifically accomplished without any change in the main cultural stream.

Thanks exceedingly for the very tasteful Yuletide cards—though you ought not to try our eyesight too severely on such work. The waits do indeed form a delightful motif.[3] I am gratefully & expectantly harbouring the "not to be opened till Christmas" envelope until the proper season. Yes—I wish I had Dunsany's artistic skill. He has always dabbled in some plastic art as a side line. Weather here is snowy, but not as bitterly cold as it might be.

With every good wish—

Yrs sincerely—

H P Lovecraft

P.S. [on envelope:] You will find an excellent account of the findings of the "technocracy" group (vide infra) in the New Outlook. It began in the Nov. issue, is continued in December, & will run in later numbers.[4]

Notes

1. The book was never published.
2. A place called Brennan's.
3. *Waits* are street singers of Christmas carols.
4. Wayne W. Parrish, "The New Technocracy," *New Outlook* 161, No. 2 (November 1932): 13–17; "Technocracy's Question," 161, No. 3 (December 1932): 13–17.

1933

[56]   [ALS]

10 Barnes St.,

Providence, R.I.,

Jany. 24, 1933

Dear Miss Toldridge:—

All envelopes received & contents read with interest. You really ought not to have given away so many of the painstakingly coloured cards—though I surely appreciated & used them. That cold spell—Dec. 15–17—was certainly vicious in the extreme. Of course I had to stay in (I can't safely go out under +20°), but with things ordered at the market that was no drawback. Too bad you had to go out—but hope the glasses are all right again.

Many thanks for cuttings—which include interesting specimens. Incidentally—apropos of one of them—an American boy *did* once become Lord Chancellor of England. When the eminent painter Copley—loyal to our rightful King & Parliament—set sail for London from Marblehead in 1775, he took with him his 3-year-old son, John Singleton Copley, Jun., born in Boston as he himself had been. Later on that child, learned in law & raised to the peerage, became Lord Lyndhurst—the Lord Chancellor! He died in 1863 at the ripe age of 91.

Heard a fine lecture on Spinoza—whose contributions to philosophy I appreciate more & more as I get older—at Brown just before the cold spell. It was delivered under the auspices of the newly founded R.I. Philosophical Society—a thing I may join if I find membership worth the annual dollar—by Prof. Emeritus Walter G. Everett, a rather well known philosophical writer, even outside Providence.[1] I shall attend later lectures in the course—all dealing with aspects of philosophy, & like the series I attended a year ago.

And now let me thank you most profusely for the Circle Anthology which duly reached me before Christmas. It is really an excellent number, & I am glad to see your work well represented. Miss Radcliffe's poem also appears to advantage, though the typographical error is regrettable. I am digesting the contents slowly & appreciatively, & adding it to the row of previous numbers on my shelves. But you really ought not to have gone to the expense of sending anything so substantial in these lean times. Again, abundant thanks! That enclosed card of St. Elizabeth from the Mother Land is, by the way, tremendously artistic & appealing. On Christmas day I duly opened the envelope marked therefor, & was delighted by the thoughtful & tasteful array therein. About the anthology preface—I dare say there are many for whom such a warning might be necessary. I noted an amusing misprint—"cli*n*ches" for *clichés*.

Many thanks for the New Year cards. I had a very pleasant holiday season including *two* Christmases & a rather unexpected trip. Sunday the 25th I dined with my surviving aunt—but that night, at the invitation of the parents of my friend Long, I took the 'bus for N.Y. to pay the young 'Man from Genoa' a surprise visit of a week, with Christmas dinner Monday the 26th. The event proved highly pleasant, & the surprise to my youthful 'grandson' was complete. I also saw others of the "gang"—including Donald Wandrei, who is still lingering in the east. We did the various museums—including the newly housed Mus. of Modern Art which has Whistler's famous portrait of his mother as a temporary loan exhibit from the Louvre.[2] The Brooklyn Mus. has two fine new Dutch rooms (circa 1650—from Holland), & the Metropolitan has a splendid archaic Greek Apollo acquired last autumn. All my available time for 8 days was busily crowded—my return taking place Jany. 3d.

Many thanks for The Carillon, which always contains verse of merit & interest. Of course no periodical has an uniformly excellent contents. It is enough if there are a few notable high spots.

By the way—I don't think poetry magazines, where no professionalism is concerned, demand the typing of MSS. as universally as ordinary magazines do. A short poem, plainly written in ink in a fairly large script, ought to stand a good chance of consideration in any of the purely aesthetic publications. It is well, though, to own a machine if possible. Second-hand specimens come very cheaply. And as I said before, don't mind temporary lulls in production. No one can write spontaneously *all* the time, & the wise poet simply rests on his oars when nothing suggests itself. It is the mediocre writer who insists on forcing himself to turn out a daily grist—a large part of which might much better have remained unwritten.

No—I couldn't write detective stories—I can't even read them any more, for they merely repeat artificial formulae. There is no life or sincerity in them. I disagree entirely with Miss Reese[3] regarding modern fiction—for the fact is that the newer novels are vastly superior to the older ones in that they actually deal with real human traits & motives and conduct. A few, of course, shew dispro-portion here & there; but for the most part they are honest & straightfor-ward—which Victorian "literature" never was. Of course a person saturated with the false taste of Victorian times, & reluctant to see life sincerely por-trayed, would naturally balk at many phases of modern literature—but that's the fault of Victorian insincerity, not of modern literature. There is nothing to regret in the passing of Victorian hypocrisy & namby-pambyness. Basically, it is not so much life that has changed, as mere manners & standards of expression. And since a large part of these changes have been in the direction of greater honesty, I think there is much more to commend than to deplore about them. Of course, it is unfortunate that a certain amount of amenity & considerateness had to perish along with the unctuous hypocrisy, but in the long run I fancy the gain predominates. There *never was* any "sweet old natural way of life"—but merely a perfumed whitewash of false sentiment & convention plastered over a world of blind stumbling much like the present world in essentials. Many of the ideals by which things were judged were so false & empty that perpetual mal-adjustment & increased hypocrisy resulted; while the fatuous standard of polite delicacy gave rise to an insincere mode of expression which virtually nullified the merit of the prevailing artistic effort. The only advantageous features of the age were on the surface—a certain smoothing-out of appearances which made life pleasant for some types who either thought little or saw little of the world. All who thought deeply or analysed the texture of life were sickened & repelled by the falsity & shallowness of the prevailing attitude. Thus Samuel Butler wrote "The Way of All Flesh" in disgusted protest against the hollow state of things he saw around him. On a humbler plane, I myself was so disgusted with the simpering affectation of the Victorian age that I turned back to the 18th cen-tury with its rational outlook & instinctive candour. We overvalue the Victorian age because it happened to be the last phase of the non-mechanised world. Of course, when we compare 1870 with 1933 we find in the former a security & repose which the latter lacks—yet the valuable thing lost is not the mock-refinement of 1870, but simply the permanent adjustment of race to environment which was common to 1570, 1670, 1770, & 1870. 1870 was so rotten with triviality & hollowness that I actually prefer 1933 to it. The *real* loss which mechanised chaos has brought is that perceived by contrasting *1770* with 1933. As for changes in one's thought & sympathies as time passes—that is a matter for congratulation, not regret. It implies an intelligent mind assimilating new data & discarding fallacious perspectives in favour of perspectives closer to reality. Only a fool preserves the ignorance & gullibility of his infancy. The only important thing in life is honestly to grasp the real "is-or-isn't-ness" of the universe, while making the most of whatever available beauty may happen to exist in it. But nothing in all this is antagonistic to the production of poetry. The rhythms & harmonies of the visible world certainly don't depend on the discarded affectations of one insignificant bygone period!

As for moving—I certainly wouldn't advise it unless financial considerations made it absolutely necessary. When one is well-adjusted to a place, the adjustment itself is a valuable asset worth paying for. And it is foolish to sacrifice familiar & cherished objects—furniture, pictures, &c—for whatever slight saving smaller quarters might afford. The worst experience I ever had was losing my birthplace, & I dread the thought of the day when still worse circumstances may force me out of my present comfortable quarters—where I have all my old things around me. But even if I had to seek a cheaper habitat, I'd never give up accustomed furniture & accessories if I could help it. I'd rather live in a tumble-down stable with my lifelong-known possessions than in a luxurious hotel with unfamiliar things.

Speaking of possessions—a fellow to whom I was lately able to do a literary favour has just given me a crystal radio set—which will perhaps unite with the set over at my aunt's in wasting my time! It was some time before I could get the thing to work, but at last I figured out the best aërial & grounding contacts & obtained fair results. It will get only the principal local station—whose power is so great that it drowns others out or encroaches on them in an instrument of this sort. I don't know how much the thing cost—but I have an idea that it is a cheap device even for a crystal set. You spoke of yours as being a crystal, yet capable of getting many stations—which argues a much better outfit than mine. Another recent gift which I have greatly appreciated is from W. Paul Cook—& is nothing less than a 3-volume copy of Maturin's splendid old horror novel "Melmoth, the Wanderer", written in 1820. This copy—of the 1892 reprint—formed part of the fine library which Cook began to disperse when his affairs crashed in 1930. He ought not to scatter his possessions so—but since he's determined to do it, I'm naturally grateful for such items as come in my direction!

I recently heard an interesting reading—by a Brown professor—of the poetry of James Stephens & Walter de la Mare. It is one of a series—in which

Robert Hillyer will read from his own work next Sunday. Later Leonard Bacon & the celebrated T. S. Eliot will be heard in person.[4]

Weather has remained remarkably mild—nearly 60° yesterday. I surely hope that the latter half of the winter will not have a compensating severity!

With every good wish, & renewed thanks for holiday cards, anthology, Carillon, newspaper cuttings, &c., I remain

Your most oblig'd & obt Servt
H P Lovecraft

Notes

1. Walter G. Everett (1860–1937), professor of philosophy at Brown and author of *Moral Values* (1918) and *The Life of the Spirit in Contemporary Civilization* (1935).
2. James McNeill Whistler (1834–1903), "Arrangement in Grey and Black: Portrait of the Painter's Mother" (popularly known as "Whistler's Mother") (1871), Musée d'Orsay, Paris.
3. Lizette Woodworth Reese (1856–1935), American poet. During the 1920s, she became a prominent literary figure, receiving critical praise from H. L. Mencken and others.
4. HPL refers to the British poets James Stephens (1882–1950; on 15 January) and Walter de la Mare (1873–1956; on 18 January) and American poets Robert Hillyer (1895–1961), Leonard Bacon (1887–1954), and T. S. Eliot (1888–1965) on 19 February. He attended all three readings.

[57]   [ALS]

10 Barnes St.,
Providence, R.I.,
March 25, 1933.

Dear Miss Toldridge:—

All the various envelopes safely arrived, & I wish to thank you especially for that Japanese note—which presented quite the most artistic bit of stationery I have ever seen. My admiration of Japanese art—dating from the days when my infant eyes rested upon various screens, fans, & bits of pottery at the old home—has always been prodigiously keen, & this stationery embodies some of its most attractive characteristics. The combination of utter simplicity, perfect harmony, & civilised repose is quite irresistible—& forms something which could never be duplicated outside Japan. The Japanese carry the spirit of art into the smallest details of life more fully than any other people since the Greeks—& it will be an irreparable loss if their newer generations lose the old spirit in an effort to assimilate western traditions. Hybridism never pays. Many in Japan realise this, & staunchly oppose westernisation. Old Nippon is a nation worth watching, because in my opinion it will form the next of the dominant world civilisations—though not, I hope, till after several more centuries of Anglo-Saxon dominance. One exquisite thing about that stationery is the *wave* motif at the bottom. Nothing has ever captured the inmost spirit of sea-foam as perfectly & vividly as Japanese art.

Thanks, as usual, for the generous array of cuttings. That theory of rock carvings 150,000 years old certainly is fascinating in the extreme—even though it presupposes the evolution of man to have begun at a period somewhat earlier than is usually assumed. If the existing species *homo sapiens* was already fully evolved 150,000 years ago, then its separation from the general primate stem which later produced such stunted specimens as *homo Neanderthalensis* & the like must have occurred at an incredibly early date—well back in the tertiary period. And the mind reels at the enormous gap of unrecorded history (what cities, arts, books, sciences, inventions, wars, modes of life, historic crises, cataclysms, & what not in those aeons of alternate tropic luxuriance & glaciation?) intervening betwixt the days of these carvings & the prodigiously later day—only 10,000 years ago—when the dawn of agriculture brought the first *known* stirrings of civilisation in the regions around the Persian Gulf. It is not likely that any continuous civilisation (granting that elder civilisations *did* exist) survived to influence the present chain of civilisations—except perhaps in vague, fragmentary, & largely discredited legends of forgotten elder worlds. Such legends float persistently around India & are taken up by the theosophists, & only the other day my New Orleans friend E. Hoffmann Price (who, by the way, is going to Soviet Russia as a technical expert in April) discovered an intensely picturesque mythcycle dealing with the earth's early aeons, the lost continents of Kusha (Atlantis) & Shâlmali (Lemuria), & the peopling of the earth from elder planets. There is talk of a secret book in some Eastern shrine, parts of which are older than the Earth. All this sounds amusingly like the synthetic mythology I have concocted for my stories, but Price assures me it is actual folklore & promises to send further particulars. All of our group may use this myth-cycle as a background for future stories. As for sunken continents—the one real probability is that a great deal of land once existed in the Pacific which exists no longer (whether a large continuous area or separate islands we can't say), & that it supported a much more advanced culture (as witness the Easter Island images & the cyclopean masonry on Ponape & Nan-Matal) than any of the Polynesian groups now possess. My friend Sechrist (the ex-Washingtonian bee expert) lived in Tahiti for years—close to the natives—& studied their folklore in detail. Among their legends is that of the "Wars of Tané", which includes the following:

> ". . . At one time he [Matai, God of Wind & Storm] was so wrathful that a great part of Mother Earth was submerged, & much of the dry land disappeared forever. These are the names of those who submerged so much of the earth: Terrible-Rain, Long-Continued Rain, Fierce-Hailstorm, Mist, Heavy-Dew, & Light-Dew; & these together left projecting only small parts of the earth above the sea."[1]

As for Roman stories—I might arrange the antiquities somehow if weird subject-matter were involved, but I have no gift for any kind of fiction outside the weird. No—Edward Lucas White has not, so far as I know, written any Roman tales since "Andivius Hedulio" & "The Unwilling Vestal." I wish he would—for I'd certainly be the most eager of readers. His are the only stories of Rome which are absolutely faithful to the Roman spirit. Regarding Miss Reese—her poetry is certainly genuine & poignant within its range. To be a minor poet of such accomplishments is no mean distinction. Baltimore has certainly contributed its quota to American letters.

As for radios—I dare say I am fortunate, for the one station (WSAR) which my feeble gift set is able to receive is in the National Broadcasting chain. Evidently crystal sets are really good only for the most powerful local station—whatever that may be. I would not want a loud-speaking tube set, however, since in a rooming establishment it would make me a conspicuous nuisance.

As for the poetry readings—Leonard Bacon was very good. Probably you know of him—for although a thorough & ancestral Rhode Islander, he has a wide reputation as an intelligent satirist. I have I [*sic*] always liked his stuff, since to me it seems to have something of the 18th century in it. T. S. Eliot was highly interesting—he read from "The Waste Land" & other poems not very comprehensible to the majority—including myself. There have also been some other interesting lectures hereabouts lately—including one by Prof. Ogburn of the government's committee for investigating social trends, & another by S. K. Ratcliffe.[2]

Glad to hear of the successfully published translation by your friend. Don't worry about lulls in your own writing—sooner or later ideas will come around with a force which will compel expression on your part.

Thanks enormously for the Washington postcards, which I am adding to my files with much appreciation. 18th century echoes always have a homelike & pleasing atmosphere. Special thanks also for the newspaper covering the inauguration. The ceremony must have been impressive indeed—it quite enthralled my aunt even as heard over the radio. I couldn't listen in—had been working two days without sleep & simply had to sleep through Saturday. Roosevelt so far impresses me very favourably. He seems to have the flexibility & directness needed at this time. The bank holiday did not incommode me, although future prospects are dismal. I may have to give up 10 Barnes & double up with my aunt in a cheap flat.

You mention wanting an "Alice in Wonderland" with the Tenniel illustrations. The A. L. Burt "Home Library" reprint—widely sold 30 years ago & probably on the market even now—has these illustrations in a very clear form, & ought to answer your purpose. These H. L. books used to sell for 50¢. Probably they're nearer a dollar now, if sold at all; but even at that figure they would be reasonable. I have a copy of this edition, & would be glad to lend it if you merely wish to *read* it. If you wish to *own* it, I think a diligent search among bookshops would certainly bring it to light sooner or later. Or you could write the A. L. Burt Co., 52–58 Duane St., N.Y. City, for information.

A fortnight ago a job took me to Hartford—to help a client do some re-search at the Athenaeum there.[3] As I said on the occasion of my one previous visit—Oct 1931—Hartford itself is not a highly interesting city; but this time I had a chance to explore the splendid colonial suburbs of Farmington & Wethersfield. Farmington is certainly one of the most beautiful villages in the U.S.—situate in a rolling countryside full of magnificent vistas, & adorned with magnificent elms. Most of the houses are colonial—some being of the 17th century gabled type with 2nd story overhang. I stopped at an inn of ram-bling construction, the nucleus dating back to 1638 (the year of Farmington's founding) & no part being newer than about 1790. The local church—white & steepled—was built in 1771. Wethersfield is rather different in aspect, but scarcely less interesting. It lies in a flat region, & has an enormously wide vil-lage common shaded by the largest elms east of the Rocky Mountains. The houses are mostly colonial, exhibiting the special marks of Connecticut-Valley architecture. In one of them—the Webb house—Gens. Washington, Ro-chambeau, & other rebels & Frenchmen planned (in May 1781) the campaign which was to end with the disaster of Yorktown in the following October. The brick church at Wethersfield, with a fine Georgian steeple, was built in 1763; it then being accounted the finest church in New-England outside Bos-ton. The view from its belfry was highly praised by the French officers who passed & re-passed through the town in 1781. The surrounding country was in those days famous for onion-growing, & still is, so far as I know. It was at Wethersfield that the Pequot war of 1637 first broke out.

Just now I am all tangled up with work—2 revision jobs going at once, & a novel of 80,000 words to revise looming in the offing. I had done 7½ pages of my collaborated story with Price[4] before this avalanche descended, but now heaven knows when I'll be able to get on with the thing. Incidentally—next July the magazine *Weird Tales* will print the first new story of mine (writ-ten, however, a year ago) which it has printed in 2 years. I hadn't intended to submit it, but a friend (young A. W. Derleth) to whom I had lent it for copy-ing shewed it to the editor, & the latter offered $140. for it.[5]

Spring is here at last—by the calendar—but in this latitude it doesn't mean much. Washington, I fancy, is a little ahead of us in having decent weather—at least, I recall being there as early as April 12 & finding the foliage all out, which it never is here at that date. And in Charleston I suppose things are really comfortable by this time.

With all good wishes—

Yrs most cordially & sincerely,

H P Lovecraft

Notes

1. Sir George Grey, *Polynesian Mythology* (London: John Murray, 1855), p. 8.

2. William Fielding Ogburn (1886–1959), professor of sociology at Columbia (1919–27) and director of the Committee on Social Trends (1930–33). Samuel Kerkham Ratcliffe (1868–1958), British journalist and writer on politics and sociology.

3. Actually, he appears to have gone to Hartford at the urging of his ex-wife Sonia; see her *Private Life of H. P. Lovecraft* (1992 ed.), p. 22: "I took a trip to beautiful Farmington, Conn. I was so enchanted with this beautiful Colonial city that I wrote to Howard at once to join me there which he did." It was their last meeting.

4. "Through the Gates of the Silver Key."

5. "The Dreams in the Witch House."

[58]   [ALS]

March 30[, 1933]

Dear Miss Toldridge:—

Your sonnet "Land of Lands" strikes me as splendid—highly adequate & impressive in both language & imagery—& am certain it ought to achieve a notable place in the contest for which it is designed. You *did* give the first 2 lines correctly in the original copy. I think the existing title is really quite sufficient, though the addition of "America" would certainly do no harm. The only change I could possibly suggest would be where lines 3 & 4 join. You have the rhetorically condensed construction:

". . . . . . till there came [those]
Who raised a cross . . . ."

—but this seems to me a trifle too far from plain speech. Somehow or other, the non-relative pronoun ought to be saved from suppression. How would it be to let the lines run something like this?

". . . . . till ⎰ they ⎱ came
                    ⎱ those ⎰
Who raised a cross . . . ."

I'll try to get this suggestion to you quickly, so that you may consider it (for whatever it is worth) in time for the contest. With such a fine specimen as this coming from your pen, you certainly ought not to complain of any decline in your poetical inspiration!

Thanks exceedingly for sending the *Poetry Review,* but don't hesitate to ask for the return of both the new & the preceding number. Possibly you may reconsider your decision not to keep a file. Incidentally—I fear I shall have to sacrifice a great deal of filed material in case of the threatened moving. It would take very commodious quarters to accomodate all I have accumulated & fitted into appropriate corners here.

Thanks also for the interesting cuttings, & for the highly attractive postcards. The Torquay view is especially fascinating.

I return the melancholy cutting about Sir Alexander Macdonald, which I am certainly very sorry to see. The baronetcy is correctly described*—all Scottish baronets being technically Baronets of Nova Scotia. Just as the baronetcies of England were created in 1611 to raise money (at least nominally) for the reduction of Ulster (as a result of which, baronets add the Red Hand of Ulster to their arms), so were the baronetcies of Scotland, established in 1625, created to raise money (in theory) for the reduction of Acadia—or Nova Scotia—in New France. The name "Baronet of Nova Scotia" refers to this purpose, & does not imply that the Scotsman receiving it is a Nova-Scotian. Today the name is merely antiquarian & historic—for since the act of union in 1707 there has been no distinction betwixt English & Scottish baronetcies. The age of Sir Alexander is correctly given—for I see in "The House of the Isles" (which, together with "The Fortunes of a Family", Lady Macdonald very kindly sent me after you had forwarded her parts of my praise of the books) that he was born in Sept. 1865—making him 67 last September. I am glad that the heir is a man well-fitted to carry on the illustrious traditions of his lineage. One error—a minor detail—in the cutting is the manner of spelling the name. I see by Lady M's book, which presumably had the benefit of her own proofreading, that the family follow the solid & unbroken form *Macdonald* instead of the more etymologically traditional "Mac Donald".

As for "wills"—I don't think you need to be worrying about such matters at present. Indeed, your prospective legatees may all be dead while you still flourish! My advice to everybody is to enjoy everything possible oneself, & to leave as little as possible of the enjoyment or performance of others. I'd suggest that, if you have anything convertible into poem-publishing cash, you do it now & enjoy the sight of the printed volume. Of course, anything like an heirloom is hard to part with—but a neat book of verse is a thing of dignity & fitness not unworthy of the bequeathers of the heirloom . . . . a purpose to which those bequeathers would be proud to see it put. As I have said, there are many opportunities nowadays to get fine printing done very reasonably—especially in connexion with *Charles A. A. Parker, 114 Riverside Ave., Medford, Mass.* If anything were left to me, even nominally, for the publication of poems, those poems would be published—but it would be a great deal better to have them appear while you can enjoy the favourable response which they will undoubtedly gain. Incidentally, though, let me say that I appreciate your idea most profoundly. If the Knopf firm are slow in acting on your MS., you certainly ought to hurry them up. Enough time has elapsed to make such a reminder eminently in order. You don't need to be peremptory, but it would be well to suggest, courteously, that the MS. be returned unless there is a possibility of a favourable decision on it. You surely ought to have

---

*although it was rather naive of the newspaper writer to dwell on the N.S. phase of the title

it on hand as a nucleus around which to group such other poems as you may select for a definitive volume. Don't hesitate to write—it can't do any harm, & firms often need prodding. You certainly ought to have a book of poems published sooner or later, & I am quite confident that you will. Why not write Parker & make inquiries about his terms? He is really greatly interested in assisting poets—& although himself poor, is not in the least mercenary in spirit.

The change from 10 Barnes seems imminent—my aunt & I make many expeditions in quest of possible quarters. So far we are trying to see whether we can't get something cheap without sacrificing a good neighbourhood. Our hunt has so far been confined to the ancient hill on whose crest I now dwell, & some of the houses investigated have been colonial. One is part of a brick row (late Georgian) that looks exactly like a London street, while another is a yellow cottage with a delightful Colonial doorway—slender pillars & fan carving. I have never lived in a colonial house despite my fondness for them. If I could land in one, I would feel at least partly repaid for the upheaval & the loss of familiar walls.

I am making haste to get this to you before you send "Land of Lands" to the contest. Don't feel obliged to act on my suggestion unless it seems sound to you. Individual taste may differ on condensations of the kind involved, but I always feel a distinct vacancy when important sentence-elements are suppressed.

No very springlike weather yet—but of course the really devastating cold is over. I don't think we have the hardy early butterflies described by Mr. Peattie in New England.

With best wishes, thanks for cards, Review, &c., & hopes for your success in the contest,

I remain,

Yr most oblig'd ob^t Servt

H P Lovecraft

[59]   [ALS]

10 Barnes St.,

Providence, R.I.,

April 29, 1933.

Dear Miss Toldridge:—

I am very glad my opinion of "Land of Lands" proved pleasing & encouraging to you, although there was really no need for you to distrust the merit of the sonnet. That point you mentioned in l. 8—*burn* instead of *shine*—impressed me as an advantageous one. The sense of *incandescence* struck me perfectly even before I read your comment. Incidentally—as I urged once before—don't harbour the idea that *simplicity* is a defect. It isn't—indeed, it is the *very reverse*. It is the best asset, apart from imaginative strength, which a poet can have. The symbolic language of poetry demands a complete simplicity which shall involve the basic words & constructions overlaid with the greatest number of familiar associations. When a poet becomes elaborate & involved he ceases to be a poet & encroaches on the domain of prose. You have no need to worry about the calibre of your poetry, & I surely hope the long-wished volume will be possible. I suppose the MS. is safe at Knopf's—you can use your judgment about requesting return. Certainly, this is the worst possible period for professional publication.

Moving prospects are still indecisive, though my aunt & I are still looking. So far we are still limiting our search to the ancient hill. I shall certainly hate to break up my quarters here—but if I get the right sort of room, the new place will look about the same. My place is so stuffed with furniture, & the walls so covered with bookcases & old pictures (mostly paintings by my mother, late aunt, & grandmother), that after all most of the familiar things I look at from day to day are the personal possessions which will go with me.

Abundant thanks for the new *Poetry Review*—of especial interest to me because of the space allotted to my favourite, Walter de la Mare.[1] As directed, I am not returning it—but I repeat that I shall be glad to send both it & the preceding number if you decide after all not to abandon your file. Thanks also for the interesting cuttings. I wish I could see Chatham at Fredericksburg.[2] As it is, I have felt like intruding on the private grounds—& not much of the house can be seen from outside them. I have doubtless seen those Georgetown houses, but did not identify them. It is interesting to know that one of them was the abode of Miss Radcliffe's grandfather.

Many thanks for the delightful Easter cards. Sorry the card-provider is ill, & hope she may soon recover. My aunt appreciated very highly the ones suggested for her, & sent them to some of her most critical friends.

I am returning with many thanks (for I fancy you will wish to preserve it as long as the paper holds out) the *Hall Times* with the notice of Sir Alexander Macdonald's funeral which you so kindly sent. He surely was suitably appreciated in the region of which he formed so important a part. Glad to hear that Lady M. is bearing the bereavement with fortitude. The new heir, from his picture, looks like the solid & dependable sort of person needed to meet the responsibilities of his position. Yes—the *Times* reflects a neighbourly, agricultural flavour not easy to duplicate in the U.S. It bespeaks a population close to ancestral soil, & sharing a well-understood scheme of settled life—so different from the nervous restlessness of a nation in a state of flux, with no real adjustment betwixt soil & population, & no common body of experience or background to knit the various elements into a coherent & self-comprehending fabric. In America no paper of the size & territorial scope of the *Times* could retain so personal & pastoral a character—though approximations to it can doubtless be found amongst the rural weeklies of the still unspoiled reaches of Northern New England & the South.

I am now trying to get my work wound up for the nonce—preparatory to moving. The Price story is done—& incidentally, Price is doing so well at fiction that he seems to have postponed his Russian trip indefinitely. This tale will be of novelette length—perhaps 13,000 words. Price is typing it, & I shall go over it once more. As to a *Vermont* story—I haven't written any since 1930. That one—"The Whisperer in Darkness"—was published in 1931, but I am sure you would not like it. If, however, you ever wish to read it I'll be glad to lend the carbon copy—if I can find it amidst the chaos of my files.

Hope you did not find the medical lecture too boring, & that the sage who delivered it can ultimately help to banish your ills completely. I have attended a number of more or less interesting lectures during the past winter, though the local season for such is now fast drawing to a close.

No—of course the A. L. Burt edition of "Alice" has no bibliophilic value, but the perfect reproductions of the Tenniel drawings make it very pleasant for one who does not possess one of the earlier editions. It is really most unfortunate that your own cherished copy is beyond recovery.

As for the future of civilisation—as I have often said, I do not see any evidence for anticipating any sudden crash. Of course, all periods of transition involve considerable hardship & bewilderment, but total collapses require factors which do not seem to exist in the present Western World. Social & political institutions must change vastly in order to adapt themselves to the realities of a fully mechanised world, but *gradualness* seems to be the probable mode of metamorphosis. The enclosed cutting illustrates about what I mean. Regarding currency inflation—of course it would inconvenience the user of a fixed income just as any rise in commodity prices would, but I doubt if—in the U.S.— it would ever tend to cause a collapse of the dollar equivalent to the post-war collapse of the German mark. Probably the inflated prices would not be as high as those to which we became used during the war. It is, admittedly, a drastic remedy; but it may be the only practicable one. Very often the only way to heal a bad wound is through a process of painful cauterisation.

Very little good spring weather here—when it's warm it's rainy, & when it's fair it's cold. But I am in such a turmoil that I couldn't appreciate good weather if I had it. Moving will probably begin within a fortnight, & the probabilities favour a joint household with my aunt in the yellow colonial house on the crest of the hill which I spoke of. We shall decide as soon as we can see the interior—the present tenants do not vacate till May 1. This will be only $40 a month with heat, & has 5 rooms. Another possibility—in case I don't combine with my aunt—is a small $5 a week apartment down the hill in Benefit St.—in the old Seagrave mansion where the noted astronomer F. E. Seagrave dwelt & had his private observatory until 1914.[3] I hope very much that you will not have to leave the flat where you are so comfortably settled.

With all good wishes—
                    Yr most ob^t Servt
                        H P Lovecraft

Notes

1. Frederick T. Wood, "On the Poetry of Walter de la Mare," *Poetry Review* 24, No. 2 (March–April 1933): 91–114.

2. Chatham Manor, a Georgian-style home completed in 1771 by William Fitzhugh, after about 3 years of construction, on the Rappahannock River in Stafford County, VA, opposite Fredericksburg. For more than a century, the center of a large, thriving plantation.

3. Frank Evans Seagrave (1859–1934). The observatory, headquarters of the Skyscrapers, a local astronomy club, is now located at 47 Peeptoad Road, North Scituate, RI. Formerly it was located at 119 Benefit Street.

[60]   [A.Ms]

                    H. P. Lovecraft   after May 25,
    10   ~~Barnes St~~   66   College St.
                                            Providence, R.I.
                                            May 14, 1933

Dear Miss Toldridge:—
                    Yes, my aunt & I *did* decide on the yellow colonial house on the ancient hill, & we are now on the brink of the indescribable chaos involved in moving into it from two different points. I think I said that the rent was finally quoted as low as $40.00 per month. On May 1st it was vacant for inspection—& one glimpse of the interior was enough to decide us. The edifice—which, with the differences peculiar to New England, is of the general type of the old Georgetown & Alexandria houses—lies on the crest of the hill in a quaint grassy court just off College St.—behind & next to the John Hay Library of Brown University (which houses the unparallelled Harris Collection of American Poetry), about half a mile south of 10 Barnes. The fine colonial doorway is like my book-plate come to life, though of a slightly later period (circa 1800),[1] with side lights & fan carving instead of a fanlight. In the rear is a picturesque, village-like garden at a higher level than the front of the house. The upper flat we have taken contains 5 rooms on the main (2nd) floor, plus 2 attic storerooms—one of

which is so attractive that I wish I could have it for an extra den! My quarters—a large study & a small bedroom—are on the south side, with my working table under a west window affording a splendid view of the lower town's outspread roofs & of the mystical sunsets that flame behind them. The interior is as fascinating as the exterior—with colonial fireplaces, mantels, & chimney cupboards, curving Georgian staircase, wide floor-boards, old-fashioned latches, small-paned windows, six-panel doors, rear wing with floor at a different level, (3 steps down) quaint attic stairs, &c.—just like the old houses open as museums. After admiring such all my life, I find something magical & dreamlike in the idea of *living in one* for the first time. I have obtained 3 new bookcases & a cabinet to file papers in. All this does not sound like an economy measure, but it is just that. The whole thing will cost only what I have been paying for one room & alcove alone at 10 Barnes. Steam heat & hot water are piped from the adjacent John Hay Library. The house is owned by the university.

That lecture session surely must have been arduous, & I am glad it is now over with. Hope you will not have to move—your rent surely ought to come down in these times. By the way—the astronomer Seagrave, whose old home I *almost* moved into, is still living. What he did in 1914 was to move out to the open country of western Rhode Island in order to secure better observing conditions. Serious astronomical observation (which has come now to be largely photographic) is virtually impossible in a populous city with dust, smoke, electric lights, & kindred obstacles.

Thanks very much for the interesting cuttings—especially the one about the radio signals from *outside*. Also for the delightful Japanese postcard. Yes—I heard Pres. Roosevelt's speech over the radio very distinctly, & thought its substance eminently sensible. He is certainly a speaker of extreme grace & fluency.

E. Hoffmann Price is leaving New Orleans, but seems to have dropped or postponed his plan of migrating to Soviet Russia. After a stop in St. Augustine he will settle for a time in New York, incidentally making a side-trip to Providence to repay that 25½ hour call.

Tomorrow the final blow of moving falls. I have already carried over some of my more fragile things in baskets, but now comes the great upheaval. I don't know when I'll ever see daylight again!

With best wishes—

> Yrs most cordially,
> H P Lovecraft

Notes

1. Actually, the Samuel G. Mumford house at 66 College Street (now moved to 65 Prospect Street) dates to c. 1825.

[61]   [ALS]

> 66 College St.,
> Providence, R.I.
> June 8, 1933.

Dear Miss Toldridge:—

> Yrs. duly received, & many thanks for the cuttings.

The household at #66 is gradually taking form, & it really surpasses my highest expectations. The charm of this old house is prodigious—it is positively dreamlike to come home through a colonial doorway & sit beside a Georgian mantel gazing out through small-paned windows over a sea of ancient roofs & greenery. The effect is so much that of a museum that I half-expect some guard to come around & evict me at 5 o'clock closing-time! I moved in May 15, but could not get my books settled till over a week later. My aunt moved in June 1st, & her quarters are now approaching settlement. Our household effects—of which we have naturally chosen the least Victorian specimens— fit splendidly into the new abode, creating an atmosphere curiously akin to that of our original home. Many articles dispersed since 1904 among separate households, or stored for lack of space, are now reunited & exhumed. Paintings & statuary brought by my grandfather from Europe now have a suitable setting once more, & over the staircase hangs an immense canvas (Rocks at Narragansett Pier) painted by my late elder aunt—who I wish could have lived to see it on display again. For 29 years it has not had a place to hang. The grounds & garden are highly pleasing, & my aunt plans to train up the facade a slip of ivy from the Washington estate at Mt. Vernon. The secluded situation of the house—in a grassy court—makes the modern world seem very far away, & the spirit of Georgian days hangs benignly over everything. Men with periwigs, knee-breeches, & three-cornered hats have actually dwelt in this abode! Each hour the chimes of many belfries resound musically—& the old Unitarian steeple (1816) & Brown University Clock Tower are visible from our windows. I can soon shew you a picture of the ancient hill in which the house is plainly visible. It occurs in a brochure issued by the State Educational Commission, & I am sending for extra copies. Near the house are some remarkable contrasts. Down the hill lies the modern business district of skyscrapers—yet only a half-square away is a crisscross of unpaved hillside lanes which you would vow could not exist in anything larger than a village of 1500 inhabitants! Settling was a frightful job—& my aunt & I both feel as if we had survived an earthquake. It has utterly disrupted my programme. Well—I hope I can hang on here as long as possible . . . . . there is no guarantee of absolute permanence, since my finances are accursedly shaky & since there is a dark possibility that the future enlargement of the John Hay Library may imperil the house. But it's great while it lasts! In the lower part of the house is a friend of my aunt's—a high-school teacher[1]—to whom we are really indebted for learning of the advantages & availability of this place.

We have had a few warm days at last—in fact, I am now out on my favourite wooded river-bank—which is not so much farther from #66 than from #10. I fear I cannot take a southern trip this year, though W. Paul Cook & I may attend the N.Y. Convention of the National Amateur Press Association early in July. I expect a number of guests this summer, including E.

Hoffmann Price, now uprooted from New Orleans. To accomodate these occasional sojourners, I have just purchased a cheap folding camp cot.

Best wishes—

Yr most obt hble Servt

H P Lovecraft

P.S. My booklets with the picture of this house have just arrived. Am sending one under separate cover. This house, with its rear wing, shews up very plainly—& you can also get a fine idea of College St. & the whole ancient neighbourhood. The vast Georgian court house is just completed—shewing how Providence sticks to its old traditions. ¶ Please return at your leisure— absolutely no hurry.

Notes

1. Alice Sheppard.

[62]　　[ALS]

66 College St.,

Providence, R.I.

June 25, 1933.

Dear Miss Toldridge:—

I am glad that my account of my new quarters proved interesting. Keep the brochure as long as you like—indeed, if it is of any permanent value for your files there is no need of returning it at all. The charm of 66 College St. persists, & as the days go by it looks more & more settled. Securing a place so completely suite[d] to my lifelong tastes was certainly a most singular piece of luck—a coincidence too apt & perfect to seem plausible in fiction. After this it would be difficult to live in a Victorian house again! The two rooms (in addition to the attic overflow & the relegation of all dietary paraphernalia to the dining-room) certainly form a boon, & allow me to display my things in a way impossible when confined to a single room. Incidentally—I am very glad that you will not be compelled to move. It takes a very great improvement indeed to make the exhausting experience of migration worth going through.

The spell of warm weather from June 8 to 12 was a vast boon to me, & I spent most of the time taking long walks in an especially idyllic bit of countryside (north of the town & west of my favourite Quinsnicket region) which I had never previously explored. I averaged about 12 miles each day, & was delighted by the exquisite nature of the scenery—green rolling hills, winding roads, ancient farmsteads with gnarled hillside orchards, rambling stone walls, fringes of deep, mystical woodlands, glimpses of blue lakelets, & impressive vistas of leagues of outspread slopes, forests, & meadows. The temperature ascended to 90° & 94° on certain days, which put new energy into me. I hated to see cooler weather come—though the majority doubtless welcomed it. I wish that Providence had a tropical climate!

It was undoubtedly wise to get rid of the burden of the Circle presidency, & I am sure that in the end Mrs. Green-Leach will become reconciled to the step. I abhor administrative work of any sort, & was never more bored & harassed than when President of the United (1917–18) & National (1922–3) Amateur Press Associations. Literature itself is much more interesting than the organisations which cluster around literature. Your sonnet, by the way, is extremely delightful; & I do not wonder that its subject was enthusiastic about it. I hope it will appear in print in due course of time. The other day I received from Coates of *Driftwind* a copy of his new anthology called "Harvest," & noted his inclusion of my "Canal"—one of the "Fungi from Yuggoth." To the best of my recollection this is the first time that any *verse* of mine has ever appeared between the covers of a book—except for certain tributes to a 92-year-old poet which were included in a book of his in 1923.[1]

Yes—I heard the King June 12 on my aunt's radio, & was delighted by the sound of his voice. It was the greatest thrill I had received since being on the still-loyal soil of Canada. His presentation of a portion of his message in French lent an added interest to the proceeding—reminding one of the days when our Sovereigns also claimed the throne of France, & had the fleur-de-lis quartered on the Royal Arms. As for the outcome of the economic conference—it is rather early to predict what it will be. Nothing brilliant can be looked for unless the U.S. will consent to a drastic revision of war debts—& it will take the president a long while to convert the stubborn backwoods congressmen to a rational attitude on this point.

Thanks very much for the cuttings. I envy Mr. Peattie his detailed & intelligent knowledge of nature—I could never keep so much in my head! In all these nature-notes I observe with envy the evidences of a slightly warmer climate in the Washington region than here. Washington, however, is still a long way from the real subtropics.

Just now settlement at #66 has been interrupted by a most painful accident—my aunt having broken her ankle while descending the stairs on June 14. The injured member was set at once at the R.I. Hospital—where she has since been. It is in a plaster cast, hence the patient is not yet able to get about. She will probably return home with a nurse very soon—& meanwhile I am constantly shuttling forth betwixt the house & the hospital. There is no danger; but the ordeal of lying still & waiting for amendment is very boresome & irritating, while the expense is a nervous disease all in itself! On account of this accident even my short trip to the N.Y. Convention will be cancelled.

Enclosed is the circular of a brochure of tales[2] by my friend Clark Ashton Smith, whose volumes of weird verse I think I once lent you. Possibly these would interest you less than the poems—but I send the circular anyway.

I am enclosing one to each of my correspondents in the hope of promoting the sale of the venture. He is having it printed at his own expense, & hardly expects to do more than cover the cost. The phantasies are splendid bits of weird prose-poetry—all rejected by editors because of an alleged lack of popular appeal. By the way—that "Shunned House" booklet of my own, so long delayed, will probably be issued during the present year by Coates of *Drift-wind,* who has taken over the unbound sheets from Cook.

Have just recd. advance sheets of my story which will appear in the July *Weird Tales.* Several very provoking misprints, including two of the trickily *misleading* sort—"magical LOVE" for "magical LORE," & "HUMAN element" for "KNOWN [chemical] element."

All good wishes—

Yr moft oblig'd, moft ob^t Servt

H P Lovecraft

Notes

1. See letter 4, n. 3.
2. For *The Double Shadow and Other Fantasies* (1933).

[63]   [ALS]

66 College St.,

Providence, R.I.,

July 22, 1933.

Dear Miss Toldridge:—

Yrs. duly received—& many thanks for the interesting assortment of cuttings. The account of progress on the Williamsburg restoration makes me eager to revisit that ancient capital—I was last there in 1930; & nothing had been done toward restoring the Capitol & Governor's Palace, though the Raleigh Tavern was just finished. The Wren building of the college was covered with scaffolding—in the midst of restoration. This work is exciting great interest in the North—my friend Cook saw a highly ingenious illustration of it, with models & pictures, at the Boston Public Library.

My aunt has now returned home with a nurse, though she is still confined to bed except for brief easy-chair periods. It will be fully two weeks more before the cast can be removed—which will mean the beginning of the crutch period. Naturally I have been kept very busy—having to be on duty each afternoon while the nurse is out—was not able to attend the N.A.P.A. convention in N.Y.

However—I had a sort of substitute convention right here just prior to my aunt's return, centreing in the long-heralded visit of E. Hoffmann Price. He arrived unexpectedly in his 1928 Ford Juggernaut on June 30, & during the next four days festivities were plentiful. Cook stopped in on his way to the N.Y. Convention, & young Harry Brobst (a correspondent from Pennsylvania who came here last year to take a position in a local hospital) was over twice—on one occasion staying all night for a session of triangular literary & philosophical discussion punctuated by a trip to an ancient churchyard (known to Poe in the 1840's, & completely hidden from all highways by bank walls & centuried houses) on the hill at about 3 a.m.

On July 2 Price brought his Juggernaut into the service of antiquarian exploration by taking me to a Rhode-Island region which—despite my lifelong residence less than 30 miles from it, & my 1/3 ancestral connexion with its ancient families—I had never (through lack of public transportation facilities) seen before. This was the historic "South County" or "Narragansett Country" west of the bay, where before the Revolution there existed a system of large plantations & black slaves comparable to that of the South. The scenery of this territory is ineffably fine, as I had long realised from reading, though none of the choicest areas can be glimpsed from the main trunk highways. On this occasion we began with the marvellously unspoiled colonial seaport of Wickford, & worked southward through the magical land of yesterday. We saw the rambling old snuff-mill where Gilbert Stuart was born in 1755, & the vast Rowland Robinson mansion (1705) amidst its gigantic centuried willows. The lone, deserted Ferry Church on a windswept headland claimed our notice, nor did we neglect the abandoned "Glebe" or rectory of the Rev. James MacSparran (1727), now spectrally overgrown with a lush profusion of vines & briers. We climbed a hill to the well-known "Hannah Robinson's Rock" (around which revolves a pathetic story)[8] & enjoyed what is probably the finest landscape vista in Rhode Island, if not in all New England—winding blue river far below, green meadows & woodlands, white headland church in the distance, & the remote gleam of the half-glimpsed sea. But the real climax was the wholly unspoiled colonial village of Kingston—ancient county-seat of King's [now Washington] County, & virtually unchanged since the days when men in knee-breeches & periwigs congregated there for the quarterly assizes. The well-kept, centuried houses, the enormous shade-trees, the venerable court building, & the quaint 1746 inn, all remain as of yore to fascinate the beholder. And to think I had never seen this gem of antiquity before!

Weather has been variable hereabouts. Some days delightful—up to 94°—but others detestably cool. However, I have had my old oil heater repaired (no gas connexion here except for the kitchen range), so that I manage to keep alive through the frigid interludes. I do my writing outdoors whenever possible—being now on Prospect Terrace, with the sunset expanse of the lower town outspread before me.

By the way, I am glad you did not fail to receive that booklet with the picture of #66 in it. I was apprehensive because at least one other correspondent didn't get it. I fear the envelopes I used were too loose for perfect safety. It is certainly rather extraordinary to have one's own abode shewn so perfectly in a chance public picture—& to have the whole locality so well displayed. The street which sweeps up from Market Square & is visible in the foreground is College St. This house, as you can see, stands back from the street at the end of a little unnamed court—although it is numbered as if in the street. College St.—so called since the original College Edifice was built in 1770—is a very old thoroughfare, & has borne several names in succession . . . such as Rosemary-Lane, Presbyterian-Lane (from the old meeting-house), later a Town Hall, which stood at the former Benefit St. where the upper half of the new Georgian courthouse now stands), & Hanover St. A majority of the houses which line it are colonial, & in its lower half—on the north side, not well shewn in the picture—are *two* of the ancient inn-yards, with archways through the houses to admit vehicles, which are becoming so uncommon in America. I know of only *one* other outside Providence, & even that is boarded up . . . . this being in N. 2nd St., Philadelphia. It is tragic to reflect that this lower row of ancient buildings (going back to 1750 or so) is probably doomed—the land being owned by the R.I. School of Design, which proposes some time to extend its own buildings over the site.

I hope you will not be disappointed with the result of your investments in fantastic fiction & poetry. Smith's work is really very fine—& highly enjoyable to anyone with a taste for the bizarre. Of the tales in his brochure I think I prefer "The Double Shadow", "A Night in Malneant", & "The Maze of the Enchanter." You'll find another story of his—"Ubbo-Sathla"—in the magazine. Hope my "Witch-House" won't repel you with its horror. There are six misprints, two of which are especially annoying—"magical *love*" (should be "magical LORE") on p. 92, & "*human* element" (should be "KNOWN element") on p. 101. In the same issue there is another story—"The Horror in the Museum"—which I re-wrote for a revision client until it is virtually my own work. Robert E. Howard, who has a story in, is a very picturesque Texan & a good correspondent of mine. I have met Seabury Quinn—a very pleasant person—who lives in Brooklyn. The reprint "Green Tea" is by a very well-known Anglo-Irish author of Victorian times.[1]

About your poems—I think you are too particular about their mechanical appearance. Any of the small poetry magazines, I feel sure, would take an untyped poem (especially if short) if plainly written in ink. Or I'd be glad to type a sonnet for you now & then—my hatred of the machine being a serious factor only when sizeable jobs of typing are concerned.

As for politics & economics—they are certainly a tangled mess, yet I feel that the present administration is doing the very best that can be done at this juncture. No one knows just what to do; & with the difficulty of overcoming the obstacles of a diffuse representative government, nothing better than what has been done would seem to be possible. I do not think that currency inflation will be allowed to reach disastrous proportions. Of course, accidents & unforeseen circumstances are always possible; yet with wise management it looks as if the depreciation of the dollar could be kept within proper bounds—restoring a price-level about the same as that of 1926—neither the ruinous high prices of 1919, nor the equally ruinous (to merchants & producers) low prices of 1932.

It is indeed provoking that you cannot get out to see the countryside & the unspoiled beauties of nature. Are there not parks in fairly accessible places, even though getting to & from them may be a bit cumbrous?

Thanks exceedingly for the *Carillon,* which seems to me to maintain as high a standard as any of the small poetry magazines.

Next Monday & Tuesday I shall have an outing, thanks to the nurse's willingness to stay in on those days. I shall visit my friend Long & his parents at Onset, near Cape Cod, where they are spending a short time. They (as well as a friend of Clark Ashton Smith's from California) recently passed through Providence en route for Massachusetts.[2]

With all good wishes—

Yr most ob^t Servt

H P Lovecraft

Notes

1. The stories in *WT* for July 1933 were Howard's "The Man on the Ground," Quinn's "The Hand of Glory," and "Green Tea" by J[oseph] Sheridan Le Fanu (1814–1873).
2. Helen V. Sully of Auburn, California.

[64]   [ALS]

Prospect Terrace

Aug. 28, 1933

Dear Miss Toldridge:—

Yrs. duly received, & thanks as usual for interesting enclosures. I wish I could see the ancient estate of "Makepeace"—the Eastern Shore must have a great deal of primitive material, but I have never been able to get over there. The editorial on the capitol dome is rather fascinating—though I honestly believe that Rhode Island's marble state house offers a strong rival to the Washington specimen. Our dome is relatively modern—1898—& designed by the famous firm of McKim, Mead, & White, but it follows the best Renaissance tradition & has a glamour all its own as it looms up on Smith's Hill, overlooking the civic centre of Providence. It is visible across the valley from my own ancient hill—& is before my eyes at this moment as I write from the eyrie of Prospect Terrace. From points farther north on the hill it can be seen against the sunset in a peculiarly picturesque juxtaposition with the Gothic tower of St. Patrick's church—also on Smith's Hill.[1] It is not this dome, however, which dominates the city skyline—that distinction being possessed by the still newer copper dome of the great Christian Science church atop my own ancient hill, about half way betwixt 66 College & 10 Barnes. Except for the business district on the west, Providence still has a traditional skyline of spires & domes. The little Japanese sketch is interesting—& I was glad to note in one of the cuttings that Japan's culture impresses at least one competent observer as proof against decay. Glad the College St. article interested you. Yes—College is the steep street in the foreground of the picture I sent. This house (facing south) is not directly on the street, but at the rear of a quaint grassy court leading off of it on the north side near the top. The court is level—ground being cut down to the level of its western edge—& the garden behind the house is also level, though at a higher elevation—ground being filled to the level of the eastern edge. Thus one has to climb a flight of steps to pass from the level court & front garden to the level rear garden. This whole arrangement of levels makes for great picturesqueness.

My aunt's cast was removed Aug. 3d, but the doctor forbids her to be very active as yet, even on crutches. Accordingly the nurse is still here, & I am still very much tied down. Have a New Hampshire invitation which I may be obliged to decline. Price's visit was indeed a pleasure. He is now staying with a friend who conducts a boys' school at Irvington, N.Y.—in the Sleepy Hollow country—& he may possibly come here again before going south for the winter. He has virtually decided to winter in Florida instead of New Orleans.

Latterly I have had some short trips—including two boat sails to Newport. I spent 2½ days at Onset, near the base of Cape Cod, with Frank B. Long & his parents; & have since had my friend James F. Morton (Curator of the Paterson Museum) as a guest—taking many rural walks & one Newport trip with him. Ancient Newport never changes, but always remains a trim bit of the 18ᵗʰ Century.

Glad my story did not bore you—& that you also liked Smith's material. Last week I had a letter from the Knopf firm, asking me to send a few stories for consideration as a possible book venture. I sent some—but realise how little a request of this sort actually means. The stuff will undoubtedly come back sooner or later with polite regrets. Incidentally—a new magazine called *The Fantasy Fan* has just started, & Smith & I are giving it all our old rejected MSS.—which it will print without pay, though giving us a generous supply of free copies. Three more weird magazines are also scheduled to appear—though I am not certain whether my material will suit them. Incidentally—I'm glad that Miss Mansfield saw the "Witch House", since her Salem background enables her to visualise the scene & psychology.

Let me thank you separately & especially for the splendid coloured postcards of Salisbury & Penshurst scenes. The charm of these things is indescribable, & I can scarcely resist an impulse to stow away on a liner & get one glimpse of the ancestral world at any cost! Both batches are tremendously fascinating, & go at once into my choicest files.

Glad you're started on another poem—but don't hurry it unduly or feel constrained to write more than you wish. Productivity naturally comes by fits & starts, & you will be almost unconsciously weaving verse after verse when the mood strikes. Don't get the idea that poetry must deal with the age & its troubles. That is really far from the essence of the art. What the world situation needs is more intelligent economics & philosophy, & poetry can hardly be expected to provide that! It is a mistake—& a sentimentality—to assume that poetry has a "mission". Art has no ulterior end—it is an end in itself, though by chance it often serves additional ends. Poetry is simply a reflection of beauty—not a panacea for social disorders. If it sometimes leads toward a state of mind in which social adjustment becomes more feasible, that is purely an incidental—or accidental—circumstance.

Clark Ashton Smith is writing less poetry now that he specialises in fiction, though occasionally he turns out some impressive verse. He greatly appreciates your ordering both "Ebony & Crystal" & the new brochure. Incidentally—he lately killed a rattlesnake which had almost crept upon him as he sat writing in the yard of his home. It has been 108° & 109° in Auburn recently—just my kind of weather!

As for Cape Cod—parts of it are very lovely, especially the steepled village of Sandwich, but the whole region has been greatly overrated as compared with other parts of New England. Not much is left of the original quaint folkways, since self-conscious artists & tourists have overrun the land. Scenically & atmospherically I prefer Vermont & New Hampshire, & the seacoast north of Boston.

It is possible that I can get to *Quebec* Septr. 1–6—the matter depending on whether friends can arrange to stay with my aunt afternoons during the period in question. I certainly hope I can manage it—for I long to see the citadel & ancient city walls of the mighty stronghold of the north, & to tread again a soil still loyal to our rightful King. This year's cheap excursions offer a choice of Quebec or Halifax. I have not seen Halifax, hence at first had a strong temptation to choose it instead of Quebec—but on second thought I incline again toward my old favourite, since I know that Halifax cannot possibly be as picturesque. There is much in Quebec & environs that I still wish to see—& of course I can never get enough of the parts I know thoroughly. If all goes well I shall start from Boston (where I'll see W. Paul Cook) Friday night at 8:45, arriving at Quebec Saturday noon. All that day in the ancient town, & the two days following. Also Tuesday up to 4 p.m., when the return train starts for Boston. I shall try to see the archaic & unspoiled Isle d'Orleans again if the 'bus rates are in any way reasonable. It rained torrents when I was there last year. I'd also like to see the Huron Indian village of Lorette, which I've never visited. When in Boston on the return trip I shall probably try to see Salem & Marblehead. My aunt rather laughs at me for liking to see the same places over & over instead of searching out new ones—but when a scene appeals to my imagination I cannot become sated with it. I enjoy new places just as much, though—& want very much to investigate *Nantucket* later on. That is on an island, & very expensive to visit despite its relative nearness. Indeed, my Quebec trip will probably cost less than a Nantucket jaunt would.

About "Green Tea"—it was written in the 1850's.[2] The Victorians went in strongly for weird fiction—Bulwer-Lytton, Dickens, Wilkie Collins, Harrison Ainsworth, Mrs. Oliphant, George W. M. Reynolds, H. Rider Haggard, R. L. Stevenson & countless others turned out reams of it. Its period of decline was around 1910 or so—but even then there were many representatives. It reflects a permanent mood of human nature, & will probably never become wholly extinct.

  Best wishes—
     Yr most ob[t] Serv[t]
      H P Lovecraft

[P.S.] Experimenting with new tales—don't know how they'll turn out.

Notes

1. St. Patrick's Catholic Church, on 224 Smith Street.
2. Actually, "Green Tea" was first serialized in *All the Year Round* (23 October–13 November 1869) and reprinted in Le Fanu's collection *In a Glass Darkly* (1872).

[65] [ANS postcard][1]

          [Postmarked Quebec, Canada,
             3 September 1933]

Having a magnificent time—fine hot weather so far. Saw Cook in Boston & looked up an old house—1637—in Boston suburbs that I'd never seen before. On the return trip shall try to do Salem & Marblehead. ¶ Quebec is just as ever—a fantastic dream—a picture into which one can walk bodily & actually touch the wonders of time & space delineated! Have only 4 days, but am keeping them crowded. Today largely suburbs. Nothing changed since last year—& the ancient citadel is undergoing careful repair—a project using the unemployed. The church shewn on this card commemorates the repulse of New England expedition (mostly Massachusetts men) under Phips in 1690. It was begun 2 years before but dedicated to the victory when finished.

  Best wishes—
H P Lovecraft

Notes

1. *Front:* Notre Dame De Victoire, Quebec. [HPL corrected "De Victoire" to "Des Victoires" and added the date "(1688)" at the end.]

[66]   [ALS]

66 College St.
Providence, R.I.,
[5 October 1933]

Dear Miss Toldridge:—

Thanks exceedingly for the various items. The Japanese print has the characteristic grace & delicacy of its school. The Witch-House views are highly interesting—especially since I have been all over the building in question. Please transmit my sincere thanks to Miss Mansfield. As she may have told you, this building was the home of the magistrate Jonathan Corwin, who in 1692 examined many persons suspected of witchcraft. Some of these examinations were conducted at his residence, in the second-story corner room at the extreme left of the pictures. In former years this house was assigned a great antiquity (1635) & was said to have been the home of Roger Williams during his Salem stay, but these legends have been wholly demolished through the researches of the Essex Institute. The building probably does not antedate 1650, long after Mr. Williams had become the founder of Providence. Originally it possessed many gables, like other Salem houses of its period; but these were removed in the early 1800's. The addition of the drugstore wing which protrudes from the front occurred about 1880, & was a great defacement. It really ought to be removed. The house proper is now an antique shop, & is open to visitors. I have a very attractive bas-relief of the old Witch House hanging above my table—together with a companion piece depicting the ancient gambrel roofs of Marblehead; both the work of the ingenious sculptor Sarah Symonds of Salem[1]—of whom Miss Mansfield would undoubtedly know.

My aunt is making very good progress these days—being all around the house on crutches, outdoors 3 times & probably being almost ready to graduate to a cane. Of course she cannot go downstairs except very slowly, but we have installed an electrical device to open the front door from the second floor—a virtual necessity when I am not available. We dispensed with the nurse two weeks ago—having my aunt's meals sent in from the boarding-house across the back garden.

I extend my sympathy regarding the painting & papering siege—such upheavals are certainly devastating; almost as much so as moving. However, you may find the freshness of the renovated apartment a sufficient compensation. Don't let it overawe you!

Price did not get here a second time after all. He did, however, get to see some of the gang in the N.Y. region; having an especially interesting triangular session with Long & Morton. He is now back in New Orleans—where he will spend the winter.

My trip was extremely pleasant—the whole Quebec sojourn being marked by fine hot weather. The ancient northern fortress was as fascinating as ever, & I visited all my favourite spots besides coming on several objects new to me.

On one afternoon I walked to the neighbouring village of Sillery, whose quaint church on a headland in the river is a fascinating object for miles around, & at another time I took a trolley trip to Montmorency Falls—seeing the fine Georgian mansion built by Gen. Sir Frederick Haldimand in 1781 & later inhabited by the Duke of Kent—Queen Victoria's father. The house is, alas, largely spoilt by additions & modernisations—being a summer hotel at present. As usual, I climbed to the citadel many times, & took several walks along the top of the great city wall. Quebec is the only walled city on the North American continent. The most inspiring sight of all was the Old Flag—the Union Jack—floating from the lofty citadel & the towers of the houses of Parliament.

I saw W. Paul Cook in Boston on both outbound & inbound trips, & also did some antiquarian exploring in Massachusetts. On the outbound trip I looked up the ancient Deane Winthrop house in a Boston suburb. This was build in 1637, & is one of the oldest in the country.[2] It is a simple farmhouse, but very well & solidly built. In the base of the colossal brick chimney is a secret room—of a sort very common in Massachusetts houses of the 17th century. The edifice is owned by a society, & is in very good condition.

On the inbound trip I explored my beloved Salem & Marblehead—coming on some interesting new sights in the former place. For one thing, I succeeded in getting inside the old Richard Derby house (1762) for the first time. This was the first brick house in Salem, & is finely panelled in a style which was somewhat old-fashioned even when the house was built. The Derbys were one of the foremost lines of Salem ship-owners & merchant princes—being virtually the originators of the East-India trade. Another interesting object was the perfect reproduction of a gabled house of 1650 recently built on the grounds of the Pequot Mills. I went through it with vast interest, & could hardly believe it was a modern fac-simile. Every detail of 17th century work is duplicated with scholarly fidelity. But the climax of all was another reproduction—that of the pioneer Salem settlement of 1630, carefully constructed & laid out in Forest River Park. This consists of a generous plot of ground at the harbour's edge, painstakingly landscaped & covered with absolutely perfect duplicates of the very earliest huts & houses—dwellings of a sort which have utterly vanished. All the early industries are also reproduced—there being such things as an ancient saw-pit, blacksmith shop, salt works, brick moulder, fish-drying outfit, & so on. Nothing else that I have ever seen gives so good a picture of the rough pioneer life led during the first decade of New England settlement. Marblehead possessed its accustomed charm—though my inspection of it was broken by several showers.

By the way—speaking of sightseeing—Providence now has a service of "rubberneck wagons", one of whose circulars I will enclose. To my mind, the typical sights are fairly well selected—though there are many others I would like to add. I must ask the return of this folder (though in no haste at all), since I can't seem to locate any more. I grabbed a few at the Union Station a few days ago, but the supply is exhausted now. By the way—"Prospect Terrace" is *not* another name for College St., but is a small park several blocks north of here, & situate like this house on the crest of the hill. It commands a peerless view of the lower town & of the purple hills of the open country beyond the town—& forms a magnificent place to lounge at sunset, when the sky flames red behind the great State House dome & the Gothic tower of St. Patrick's on Smith's Hill. It is an old haunt of mine—being not only near here, but on my direct route downtown from 10 Barnes St. I very frequently take my reading & writing out there. Yes—there is a very distinct similarity between Providence & Quebec—not only because of quaintness & antiquity, but because of the great hill or cliff which divides each into two separate worlds—"Haute Ville" & "Bas Ville". Newport lacks the striking differences in level, but is really far quainter than Providence. It is three years younger—founded 1639 instead of 1636—but has kept more of its ancient material. There are houses which must be as old as 1650 or 1660, whereas Providence has nothing older than 1735. Providence, however, surpasses both Newport & Quebec in some particulars—especially the presence of unsuspected bits of village garden or surprising remnants of rural lanes near the very centre of the main district.

I doubt if anything will come of the Knopf book business—although the firm did go so far as to ask the magazine *Weird Tales* about possible help in the advertising & marketing *if* they *should* publish the collection. It is very possible that they will hold on to the MSS. for a while in a tentative way—as they are doing with your poetry. As for the *Fantasy Fan*—I've just sent them an enlarged edition of my history of weird fiction (brought to date, the original having been written in 1926), which they intend to use (without remuneration, of course) as a serial. *Another* non-paying weird magazine has just been founded (so Smith tells me)—*Unusual Stories,* edited by one William Crawford of Everett, Pa. ¶ EXTRA—A definite rejection from the Knopf firm has just arrived—precisely as I expected.

Yes—I certainly hope I can get over to the mother land some time before I finally disintegrate. But once there, I don't believe I could ever tear myself away without a painful wrench. And it would be execrably tantalising to see a little, & not have the cash to see other things *almost* within reach—as when I was in Key West (in 1931) but lacked the cash to make the remaining 90 miles to Havana.

Your idea of a sonnet sequence seems to me excellent, & I trust you will act upon it in the near future.

Here are a few more Quebec views—including some of the ramparts & common which may supply the place of the mislaid one.

Yes—your own accident makes you very well able to sympathise with my aunt at present. The parallel is quite close—even to the fact that she was looking forward to a festive function at the time of the debacle. She was answering the doorbell—the caller being our downstairs neighbour (a teacher of

German named Miss Sheppard), who had come to invite her to the President's reception at the Brown Univ. commencement. She evidently mistook 2 steps (an isolated pair, before the staircase turns for the main descent) for one, & landed with a disastrous thud. For a time she thought the trouble was only a sprain, so that she simply sat still on the staircase talking with her caller & waiting for the ache to subside. At last, however, the pain caused her to summon a physician "just to be on the safe side"—& he, diagnosing the matter at once, imparted the bad news & turned her over to a specialist. I fancy the patient will be walking on her own feet by Christmas—though twinges & awkwardness will probably persist much longer.

As to the "mission" of poetry—of course, by chance certain poems may put certain individuals in moods favourable to social evolution or welfare; but that is not the function of the art, nor is it likely that poetry is sufficiently read & assimilated by the executive majority to make it in any way an effective influence in remodelling the times. The world is too complex to be aided by the *general* & inclusive moods which poetry stimulates. The idea of thinking of social problems in terms of *general* moods or emotions is an essentially obsolete one— shewn to be superficial & inadequate in the light of what we now know about human motives & relationships, & their infinitely diverse & largely hidden sources. Nothing can help society but hard, cool reason & prodigiously intricate scientific planning. All our modern problems hinge on *detail* & *quantity* instead of on general principles. They are a job for the economist & the statesman— not the poet, preacher, or self-styled prophet. As for prospects—I see no reason to feel less encouraged than one felt last spring & summer. No person could sensibly have expected miracles or quick results in the matter of economic recovery—for it will take 50 to 100 years to reorient society as a whole to an intensive machine economy. All one could have hoped for is a removal of immediate revolutionary prospects & a breaking-down of the vicious plutocratic recalcitrance typified by the Hoover administration. That was *enough* to hope for as one year's progress—& it seems to have been pretty well realised. There is much less revolutionary talk, & every step which has been taken is in the right *direction*, however slow an advance it may be. The old laissez-fair fallacy seems to have been fairly well shattered—notwithstanding the feebly peppery letters about "our sacred constitution" & "American individualism" which bewildered old gentlemen write to the editors of reactionary Republican papers. What more could have been expected in the first 6 or 7 months of the administration—with all the handicaps inherited from a stubbornly mistaken regime? As for lawlessness, &c.—this kind of thing is inseparable from ages of transition. When the *basic* problems (i.e., economic) are settled, this will also settle down. In the international field, I doubt if an early general war is as inevitable as pessimists predict. Hitler is not as bad as he is painted–you can't accept the opinion of a chronic reformer like Wells. He is of course crude & ruthless, but there are many worse alternatives to which Germany could turn. However—

the present age is surely a very unpleasant one to be living in.

    All good wishes—

Your most ob[t] h[ble] Servt

H P Lovecraft

P.S. As for my small radio—I haven't set it up, since my aunt's large tube set is in the living-room. I may later, though, in order to have independent material on tap at all hours. It will, however, be less easy to find good grounding connexions in the most convenient places.

[On envelope: P.]P.S. A man in the state of Washington has just broached the subject of reprinting my "Colour Out of Space" as a booklet.[3] ¶ Your P.S. just recd. Am enormously sorry to hear of your new foot trouble, & hope it will speedily vanish. My aunt can amply sympathise with you! Thanks for the added cuttings. Those migrating squirrels ought to be in R.I. by this time!

Notes

1. Sarah W. Symonds (1870–1965) was widely known for her bas relief plaques and figurines of historic sites throughout New England

2. See HPL to August Derleth, [September] 1933: "This is probably the 2nd oldest house of English origin in the U.S., & is tremendously interesting" (*Essential Solitude* 607).

3. F. Lee Baldwin (aet. 20) proposed the edition, but it was never published.

[67]   [ALS]

Oct. 17, 1933

Dear Miss Toldridge:—

    I must hasten to drop a line in appreciation of your splendid sonnet-sequence, which impresses me as one of the best poems you have ever produced—the real stuff, & worthy of submission to the very foremost magazines on your sending-list! My emendatory suggestions are very few. It might be just as well to have the title simply "Poetry" (the present form has the faintest Victorian, quasi-mediaeval savour). In #4, I think l. 10 is a bit redundant in syllables. How about simply omitting the *and?* It is perfectly complete without. In the next line remember that Frankenstein (in the novel, a Swiss medical student, Victor Frankenstein) means *the creator of a destroying monster*—not the monster itself. If you have that intention, it's all right. If you mean the monster itself, better change to *hydra-shapes* or some equivalent. But the whole thing is splendid stuff. Congratulations.

    Glad your new trouble is on the wane. My aunt's very much better—we take sizeable local walks now, & the other day went half way down the hill to the School of Design art museum to see the new formal garden in the inner court. A fascinating place—I enclose a rotogravure view, which please return.

Also enclose account of a gorgeous rainbow we saw. Best I ever saw in my life—positively apocalyptic! Lately my aunt has been taken on two fine long motor rides through the autumnal countryside. I went on both, & one took me through a magnificently unspoiled scenic region in Mass. that I never saw before—Westwood, Medfield, W Medway, Franklin. Have also taken pedestrian trips in picturesquely deserted regions N. of Prov. End of season—not much more outdoor reading & writing. So you read "The Festival". It is a bit crude & overcoloured, I fear—I wrote it exactly 10 years ago, almost to a month. Of course *Marblehead* is the prototype of Kingsport. Glad Miss M. found it impressively unwholesome! Other items in the magazine worth reading are Smith's "Seed from the Sepulchre" & Prout's "House of the Worm." Long's "Black Dead Thing" is a bit diffuse, but not bad.[1]

Thanks, as usual, for the interesting cuttings. Here is the proof of an article of mine[2] which may be of interest—from the coming issue of the Holland Socy's publication *De Halve Maen* (name of Henry Hudson's ship = the Half Moon), of which my friend W. B. Talman is editor. As you see, N E is not without trace of Dutch influence. Please return this sometime, though there is no hurry. I shall get extras of the paper, but want to circulate several copies.

Also enclosed with a request for ultimate return are 3 snaps of my present ancient abode—taken with a #2 Brownie which I bought 26 years ago—in far-off 1907. A sturdy two dollars' worth! You can see the fan-carved doorway with my aunt in it, also a full view of the house (slight distortion of perspective inevitable), plus a would-be artistic study of the eastern edge framed by the high marble wall of the college library. Later I shall attempt the more difficult task (time-exposure) of photographing bits of the *interior*—especially the colonial mantels in my study & my aunt's living-room.

The Asotin, Wash. man still thinks of bringing out my "Colour". New magazine *Unusual Stories* will print 2 of my old tales when it appears.[3]

I'll hasten to get this in the box in order to let you have suggestions on the sonnets. Again let me congratulate you on the force, eloquence, & music of this splendid series. You have no need to worry about your work!

All good wishes—

Yrs most cordially & sincerely,
H P Lovecraft

Notes

1. The stories mentioned were in the October 1933 issue of *WT*. HPL's story appeared in the magazine previously in January 1925. Mearle Prout's story was clearly inspired by HPL's tales. Long's story was later titled "Second Night Out."

2. "Some Dutch Footprints in New England."

3. HPL "Celephaïs" and "The Doom That Came to Sarnath" instead appeared in Crawford's companion publication, *Marvel Tales*.

1934

[68]   [ALS]

66 College St.,
Providence, R.I.,
Jany. 25, 1934.

Dear Miss Toldridge:—

Yrs. of the 9th, with its interesting enclosures, reached 66 College the day after I did. Glad to hear your wound is healing, & trust you will not become discouraged because of the slowness of the process. Destroyed tissue delays the healing, but does not make the ultimate recovery any less complete & permanent. I ought to know, since in 1907 I had nearly the whole under side of the 3d finger of my right hand burned off with phosphorus through an accident in my laboratory. Immense amounts of tissue were destroyed, & the thing took a long time to heal (I learned to write, after a fashion, with my left hand during the siege)—but within six months the finger was free from bandages, & it is now virtually as good as ever except for looks. Sorry to hear that Miss Mansfield is under the weather, & hope she will soon be back at maximum strength. Cook, I think, is improving vastly in nervous equilibrium. The quiet & simplicity of Vermont life, & the influence of Coates, are distinctly good for his psychology. He helps greatly with the Driftwind Press, & may yet evolve some joint publishing arrangement with Coates. For the present, however, he is only an assistant—though of course his presence makes itself felt in a perceptibly improved typographical standard. He has just written & printed (under the Driftwind imprint) a very clever booklet of socially & economically ironic comment,[1] which proves that his last summer's threat of "intellectual vegetation" was no more serious than Long & I thought it was. He is too brilliant to vegetate, even when he sets out to do so!

Glad to hear that my own social & economic comment proved interesting & encouraging to you. Let me assure you that the attitudes expressed are by no means original with me. I merely summarised & echoed what others have said much more forcibly & effectively—defining a position which I believe to be the general one among such conservative Anglo-Saxons as escape the influence of the plutocratic tradition. I do not think I differ greatly in theory from the more liberal elements of the present national government—& I shall certainly watch with the keenest interest the struggles of the government with the increasingly stubborn recalcitrants of the old economic order.

As my recent cards have apprised you, my visit to Long did finally materialise as a pleasant & fortnight-protracted reality. After a home Christmas including fireside decorations, surprise gifts, a turkey dinner at the boarding-house across the back garden, & a stroll half-way down the hill to hear the carol-singing* at the old Truman Beckwith mansion,[2] I took the midnight coach & arrived in Manhattan the next morning—in time for a duplicate Yule at the Long hearth. Mrs. Long is not quite recovered, & all the household were united in absorption in Belknap's new hobby—tropical fish. These sprightly finny citizens—whose ideas anent temperature are much like my own—form quite a heavy responsibility; since their diet, aëration, & heat have to be regulated with the strictest care. Their infinite variety, however, makes them much more interesting than goldfish; so that I fancy the present fashion for them will prove reasonably permanent.

I saw all of our group, & several interesting persons who were new to me—including Wandrei's younger brother, a weird artist whose talent probably surpasses that of all the rest of us put together. Watch for the name of Howard Wandrei in the art world—you'll hear of it most emphatically before many years elapse. I also met T. Everett Harré, the anthologist who reprinted my "Cthulhu" in "Beware After Dark." He has a glorious cat—a huge black & white fellow named William—which engrossed a large part of my attention. Another interesting person was the well-known weird author A. Merritt (of "Moon Pool" fame) whom I met for the first time. He took me to dinner at the Players' Club, which occupies the old home of Edwin Booth in Gramercy Park. It flattered me to learn that he has long known & liked my work—I have been an admirer of his ever since I read the "Moon Pool" in 1918. I saw the old year out at Samuel Loveman's—where one of the guests was the mother of the hapless poet Hart Crane, who committed suicide in 1932. Loveman quite overwhelmed me by giving me several objects for my collection of antiquities—a real Egyptian *ushabti* (small funerary statuette) 5000 years old, a Mayan stone idol of almost equal antiquity, & carved wooden monkey from the East Indian island of Bali.† Another correspondent I met was H. C. Koenig—who has for some time been lending me books on witch-craft from his remarkably extensive library. I managed to take in most of the museums—seeing at the Metropolitan the new Assyrian objects (including a pair of Lagard's colossal winged bulls—palace gate pylons), the colossal Etruscan Mars statues in terra-cotta, & the recently acquired Greek statues from the Lansdowne collection—an Amazon & a Diadumenos, both magnificent, though extensively restored. As I said on my card, subways helped me to beat the cold spell—while the second half of my visit was marked by unusu-

---

*I enclose a cutting anent carol-singing in Boston. The same custom exists in Providence—under even more traditional conditions.

†He also gave Long a splendid little Egyptian sphinx statuette which I wish I could get hold of!

ally warm weather. Upon my return to Providence I was confronted by an appalling accumulation of work—with which I have ever since been struggling.

Sorry to hear of the second injury & of its slow healing, but am glad it is not as severe as the first. For both, of course, plenty of time is needed. Removal of the tooth—while quite a trying burden at such a season—may help your general health in such a way that the injuries will heal more quickly.

Thanks extremely for all the various shipments of cuttings. I had that item about Rathesmere's fascistic turn ready to send you—but you got ahead of me. The O'Ren reference to the Loch Ness monster amused me, since Clark Ashton Smith & I are having quite a debate over this matter—Smith being inclined to take the bizarre entity quite seriously!

Heard an interesting Poe programme over my aunt's radio Jany. 19— when the cottage in Philadelphia was dedicated. Best speaker was Prof. Phelps of Yale.[3] Also heard broadcast from Byrd antarctic expedition— couldn't distinguish words, but the idea of desolation was itself exciting. Jan. 22 my aunt & I heard an interesting lecture by Prof. C. E. M. Joad of London—"Is Progress a Delusion"?[4] The speaker agreed, of course, that it is a delusion unless the human race can become less childish in its mentality than it has been in the past.

Glad you have been getting out, even briefly—& hope that longer trips will soon ensue. In two months it will—at least technically—be spring . . . a highly cheering thought!

All good wishes—

Yrs most sincerely,

H P Lovecraft

P.S. *Unusual Stories* is delayed, but subscribers will lose nothing thereby.

Notes

1. Apparently *A Day in the Life of Willis T. Crossman* ([North Montpelier, VT: Driftwind Press, 1934]), dated 1 January; reprinted in *W. Paul Cook: The Wandering Life of a Yankee Printer*, ed. Sean Donnelly (New York: Hippocampus Press, 2007), 175–88.

2. The Truman Beckwith House (1826, John Holden Greene, architect; now the Providence Handicraft Club) at 42 College Street, only a few doors west of the final residence of HPL and his aunt Annie Gamwell at 66 College St. Annie Gamwell had lived there since at least in 1927.

3. William Lyon Phelps (1865–1943), professor of English at Yale and a leading critic and scholar of the period.

4. C. E. M. Joad (1891–1953), British philosopher and lecturer.

[69]　　[ALS]

66 College St.,
Providence, R.I.,
Feby. 12, 1934.

Dear Miss Toldridge:—

Glad to hear that *Unusual Stories* has begun to arrive. Crawford seems to have encountered a good many difficulties, but I hope he will get a smooth-running programme in the end. Glad also that the cuttings were of interest. No—they were not to be returned. I fared very well through the late-January cold spell—not going out, of course, for its three days of rigour. This house heats admirably under all conditions (& 24 hours a day!), although one naturally keeps hall doors closed in sub-zero weather! The worst minimum of *that* spell was an even zero—5° worse than Washington. But the *next* one!!!

Thanks as usual for the interesting cuttings. That about the lizard people opens up all sorts of imaginative vistas; while the new theory of many planetary systems would seem to restore the ideas prevalent in my youth. Hope the 10-story building won't go up in Whitehall! Especial thanks, by the way, for the very interesting cards—of Shakespeare's birth-room & of old Mystic. I have often ridden through Mystic, & have admired its winding streets, quaint houses, picturesquely steep hill, & crowning white steeple. Some day I must pause & explore it on foot—I don't know Connecticut as well as I'd like to. That Pen & Brush card is delectably quaint—especially the cats.

I surely hope you can connect up with the new poetry magazine that pays. Certainly you can send any of the verses now in Knopf's hands; for magazine & book publication don't conflict. In sending anything to a magazine you might make sure by writing "First North American Serial Rights Only" in the upper right-hand corner of the MS. That makes it plain that you have a right to sell the MS. again to a book publisher. (This use of the word "serial" sounds odd because we tend to associate it with instalment publication, but its meaning here is different. It implies merely that one publication after another of the same piece constitutes a *series*.)[1]

The very latest cold spell broke all records for Rhode Island—Providence sinking down to *17 below*, the worst minimum in the history of the local weather bureau. The only approach to such a temperature in the memory of living persons was during the horrible winter of 1917–18. A closer parallel—perhaps worse because more protracted—was the appalling winter of 1778–9, when Narragansett Bay froze over, & his Majesty's troops in Newport nearly perished of cold—being forced to cut down all the neighbouring woods & even demolish some old vacant houses in order to get fuel enough to keep alive. This notwithstanding that many were Hessians, & used to the bitter winters of interior Germany. Naturally, I stuck closely to the house amidst the recent chill—the temperature *indoors* never getting below 83°! Surely the college heating plant is a priceless boon!

Yes—my trip certainly did contain an unusual number of points of varied interest. No—the art of the younger Wandrei cannot be said to be basically modern. He is at bottom a traditionalist of the main line; & his fantastic conceptions suggest Beardsley, Doré, John Martin, Rops, Goya, Fuseli, & other elder masters at the same time that they also embody a strongly original vision & execution. He never employs the modern geometrical conceptions of form, or the attempt to visualise abstractions. What he draws are delirious horrors that one might see if they existed. There is a certain amount of conventionalisation & decorativeness, of course, but in general the semblance of natural proportions remains. The power & technique of the drawings are marvellous—& there can be no question of their creator's brilliant future.

I enjoyed that Poe ceremony very much, & especially appreciated Phelps' reference to "Anthony Adverse" because somebody has just lent me that prodigious tome! I own Hervey Allen's life of Poe, which is the best yet published. Allen is also a splendid poet, as you doubtless know.

All good wishes—

Yr obt h^ble Servt

H P Lovecraft

[P.S.] I'm hustling this off briefly in order to assure you that it's all right to send the Knopf-book poems to a magazine. Hope you can land a goodly number remuneratively!

Notes

1. Actually, "serial" in the phrase in question refers to the fact that the item in question is being sold to a "serial" (i.e., a periodical), as opposed to a collection or anthology.

[70]   [ALS]

66 College St.,
Providence, R.I.,
March 29, 1934.

Dear Miss Toldridge:—

Various items duly received, & I must thank you for all of them—including the *Circle* with your brief & appealing poem[1] (do you wish it returned?), the singularly captivating Japanese material, & the many engrossing & well-chosen cuttings. I well recall "Prayer" from a previous manuscript perusal. Those Japanese designs haunt one—I'm not sure but that Japan has the greatest *living* art tradition in the world today. If only the vitiating influence of Western art & "modernistic" decadence can be excluded!

There has been some warmer weather hereabouts, so that overcoatless trips downtown are becoming far from uncommon. The record-breaking snow of Feby. 26th melted with gratifying swiftness. Before long I hope to take a few preliminary walks in the slowly awakening countryside—& I hope your own outdoor programme can also be resumed presently. You will have balmy days before we do up here—I recall the delicious warmth of April 12, 1925, when I first beheld Washington. It is barely possible that I can get to Florida this spring to visit a friend in De Land (young Barlow, whose tales you have seen in the *Fantasy Fan*), though financial considerations have so far kept the prospect from being really probable. Which reminds me that Sechrist—the ex-Washingtonian bee man—expects to go to Tahiti in the South Seas for the rest of his life. He is to retire from government service next June, & hopes to devote all his time to writing. He & his wife both speak French fluently, so that they can fit admirably into the society of Papeete—the Tahitian capital. Sechrist already knows Tahiti well, having lived there years ago while studying the folklore of the natives. He is a firm believer in a vanished Pacific civilisation (perhaps on a now-sunken continent), of which the peculiar institutions of the Polynesians are a survival. Climatically I would like Tahiti myself, though historically, architecturally, & scenically I think I'd prefer the West Indies. If I get to Florida this year I shall try somehow to scrape up extra cash enough to see Havana for a few days. Wish I could run into some mild revolutionary excitement there!

As for the small poetry magazines—as I have said before, I think they are distinctly encouraging, & that therefore they fulfil a useful function. It is absolutely impossible to get more than a small portion of one's verse published professionally, even if one is a widely recognised & well-received poet; & these humble booklets form an excellent means of preserving & diffusing items which would otherwise be confined to manuscript existence. As you are aware, some of the small magazines contain verses by the most celebrated of contemporary bards. It certainly does *not* harm one to have been a steady contributor to these non-professional & semi-professional verse media—for the situation is entirely different from that pertaining to prose. But of course, there is no advantage in telling professional markets of the reputation one has gained in private circles. They are more or less indifferent to such matters.

Sorry you are having to economise so closely—yet you are really highly fortunate to have any dependable source of income in these days. A reliable annuity of modest size is something whose continuance can be virtually guaranteed under any political system which the country would be likely to adopt—nor do I believe that any currency inflation would strain its purchasing power even nearly as badly as during the war & just afterward. The price level to be expected is, I think, something like that of the middle 1920's.

Unusual Stories is having a very hard time indeed—poor Crawford is paying for his utter inexperience in dealing with printers. At present he is trying to buy a press & do the printing himself—instructed by a friend who knows something of the typographical art. The size of the magazine will have to be smaller than originally planned—but the editor will do his best. He attempted too much in the first place. It would have been far wiser if he had planned something humbler & more practical, like the unassuming *Fantasy Fan*. But I fancy the subscribers will get something for their money if they'll be patient.

I surely hope to see Mystic some time. I know Norwichtown (a suburb of Norwich) from my one visit of 1931—it is a drowsy, delightful place full of fine old houses.

As for insect-domination as a story theme—it is a good one, but has been used to death in all the science-fiction magazines. I recall a splendid tale of the sort by Murray Leinster in an early *Amazing Stories*[2]—though most specimens tend toward hackneyedness. Incidentally—the biologist Julian Huxley (grandson of the famous Thomas H.) has shewn that, in actual fact, insects can never be expected to exceed a certain size upon the earth.[3] The mechanical & gravitational factors connected with their structure would make excessive bulk impossible. However, even within the possible range of size they can certainly be a formidable enough menace! Intelligence is already highly developed in many species—& who can say what a few hundred thousand years may bring about? Of all forms of animal life, insects are best adapted to the conditions of this planet. An outsider from some alien galaxy, if asked to select the *typical* fauna of Solar Planet #3, would undoubtedly name the articulata.

By the way—let me thank you exceedingly for the delightful Easter cards—both the individual one & those for re-sending. My aunt was exceedingly grateful for the latter, for she sends quite a number at this season—though I myself send greeting cards only at Yuletide. Those with your own poem are especially fine—though it was a bit small of the manufacturer to charge you for them after you had presented the verses free. Glad to hear that "Prayer" has been suggested for an anthology. These anthological opportunities—that is, high-grade ones such as this—are not wholly to be despised, since they argue a certain recognition of one's work, & (if accepted) often bring material before appreciative readers who might not otherwise see it. There are, of course, low-grade commercial anthologies which constitute mere rackets—the editor of Driftwind often warns against them—but the conductor of "Choir Practice" would certainly never stand sponsor for anything not of the best quality.

The advent of Spring—even technically—is surely pleasant to think of. I've had two glimpses of the countryside so far—one on March 5, when a warm day sent me splashing through the mud & melting snow of the fields & woods, & another on the 18th, when my aunt & I were treated to a motor ride toward Worcester. Despite the hard winter, many oak forests have retained their withered leaves—giving to the vernal landscape a curiously *autumnal* appearance. I never before saw the ponds & brooks so high—& when I crossed the broad gorge of the Blackstone on the 5th I found the lower banks completely overflowed; with the great trees & cottage roofs projecting above an aqueous expanse like reliques of sunken Atlantis. No real floods like those of 1927 are expected.

Have just read Machen's new book—"The Green Round"—his first weird production in 17 years. It is really extremely interesting—with something of that persistent sense of unreal worlds impinging on the real world which many imaginative persons possess. In the casualness & unexplainedness of the phenomenon represented, it recalls some of Machen's queer prefaces to his earlier books. However—it is marred by a certain rambling diffuseness, tameness, & over-use of typical stylistic mannerisms.

Some excellent temporary art exhibits at the local museum. Egyptian tomb paintings (following the Etruscan I spoke of before), Staffordshire china, Chinese textiles, & now one of the most important displays of modern Spanish art ever exhibited in the country. All these are accompanied by suitable lectures—I shall know something about art before it's all over!

Regret to hear that you have been somewhat under the weather, & hope that something like real spring will soon be here to restore vigour all around. My aunt slowly & steadily improves—never using a cane around the house, & sometimes omitting it even on short neighbourhood trips.

Again thanks for the delightful cards—a thanks which my aunt specifically echoes.

All good wishes—

> Yrs most sincerely,
> H P Lovecraft

Notes

1. "A Prayer."
2. Possibly "The Red Dust," *Amazing Stories* (January 1927).
3. Julian Huxley (1887–1975), British biologist and philosopher. His views on insects are found in *Ants* (1929) and other works.

[71]   [ALS]

> Y M C A—
> Charleston,
> April 29, '34

Dear Miss Toldridge:—

As usual, I am extremely grateful for the cuttings—which contained many things of phenomenal interest. I shall send Sechrist the ones about the Polynesians. There is certainly a fascinating mystery about this stock—& their cyclopean ruins & cryptical colossi. I suppose you have seen the titanic Easter Island images at the Smithsonian. The Fraser* article was of vast interest. Doubtless you are aware that Fraser's teacher—the celebrated Edward Greene Malbone—was a Rhode Islander who migrated to Charleston because of his health.[1]

Driftwind is a magazine—a monthly poetry journal which welcomes all contributions of merit but does not pay for them—& the Driftwind Press is the one-man "company" (Walter J. Coates, North Montpelier, Vermont) that issues both the magazine & occasional books of poetry. I have several times recommended Coates as probably the cheapest reliable publisher for a poetic brochure who could possibly be discovered. He has always been accurate & conscientious, & in recent months the artistic quality of his work has shewn marked improvement. Of course he handles no work except at the author's expense—no small publishers do. He has been having a very hard financial struggle—but just manages to keep above water. During the past winter Cook has been helping him typographically (hence, I fancy, the improved quality of work!) in exchange for food & lodging. Aside from that, he does all his printing himself—besides keeping a country store & (being a retired Unitarian clergyman) occasionally filling rural pulpits. Actually, Coates has done a marvellous service to Vermont literature by reviving interest in the figures of the past & giving an outlet to the figures of the present. His researches into the history of Vermont literature are extensive, & he hopes to publish them some day. Vermont is in many respects one of the most interesting states of the union— still essentially Anglo-Saxon, highly individual, & oddly reminiscent of the early American scene.

I was interested in the Maryland stamp—yrs. of Apr 9 being the first letter I received with it. It is really a highly artistic production, & a great credit to your commonwealth. Providence will probably have a tercentenary stamp in 1936. I note that the new stamp is *red* despite its 3¢ denomination. Perhaps 3¢ postage is to be so permanent that it is thought well to give the familiar old colour to the stamp in most constant use.

As you have already perceived from the postmark & date-line of this epistle, my southern trip *did* materialise. Had a pleasant week in N.Y. with Long & all the old group, & then shot down by 'bus to my favourite of all cities—the ancient & mellow home of "Choir Practice." Reached here at dawn Tuesday. Am stopping at Y M C A & absorbing colonial atmosphere as usual. Marvellous place—it certainly excels any other city I have ever seen, even Quebec. And the climate is superb. I have three times the energy I ever have in the north. Full summer here—rich green vegetation, hot days, straw hats, & all. On to Savannah May 1st, & in De Land, Fla. May 2 unless plans change. Temporary address for a fortnight or so—c/o R. H. BARLOW, BOX

---

*I have long been familiar with Fraser's house—a fine old brick colonial mansion in lower King St.—not far from the famous Brewton-Pringle house.

88, DE LAND, FLORIDA. But I hate to leave old Charleston! On my return trip I may be able to stop off in Washington—I hope so, but can't tell. Finances are embarrassingly tight—I never before attempted to cover so much distance on so little cash! A friend in Macon, Ga.[2] wants me to visit him, but I doubt if I can do it.

My prospective host is a delightful young fellow—book collector & embryonic weird author. You've probably seen his stuff in the *Fantasy Fan*. His household includes 5 cats & 6 infant *opossums* (whose mother was slain by a motor) which he feeds with a medicine-dropper!

By this time you've doubtless received the first real issue of Crawford's magazine—now renamed *Marvel Tales* & printed on his own amateur press. I knew he meant to come through with the venture, though many of his subscribers grew justifiedly impatient.

Hope you're enjoying the belated Washington spring. I noticed the delicate green leafage as I passed through—your season is far in advance of New England's & New York's, for it was still wintry up there when I left last Sunday night. Why *do* people live in the North? Best regards—

H P Lovecraft

Notes

1. HPL refers to the American painters Charles Fraser (1782–1860) and Edward Greene Malbone (1777–1807), both of whom worked in Charleston as miniaturists.
2. John Milton Samples, amateur journalist, editor of the *Silver Clarion*.

[72]   [ALS]

c/o Barlow, Box 88,
De Land, Fla.
May 22, 1934.

Dear Miss Toldridge:—

Never mind a case or two of bad luck in placing poems—in all such matters there are inevitable ups & downs! I like "Thoughts" & "Voices" immensely. In the latter I do not think there is any need of removing the word *croons* . . . . the modern abuse of which has not in any way permanently impaired its value. As for the matter in Stanza I—I think *Such* is preferable. Let us hope that good luck will attend both pieces in their respective encounters with the outside world. It is of course more or less unfortunate when one's verse cannot reach a suitable audience—but after all, to write it for one's own satisfaction is the important thing. Congratulations on these splendid new specimens!

Glad you saw the cherry blossoms—I, as usual, was too late for them. Thanks infinitely for the material dealing with them, as well as for the other material. The legends are indeed interesting & appealing. There is no denying the greatness of the Japanese civilisation, & I wish a way could be found to avert a war betwixt Japan & the Western World. I think that all Europeans & Americans should keep out of China, leaving it to the Japanese, in return for Japan's strictly keeping hands off the territories of the white nations—California, Australia, &c.

Glad you like "Celephaïs"—though the printed text had many abominable misprints, including some which seemed to present me in an illiterate light. The tale is an old one—obviously influenced by Dunsany & embodying the fragments of several actual dreams. I have not yet seen a copy of *Marvel Tales* (Barlow lost his before I reached De Land), but hope Crawford will be able to keep the venture going.

Yes—Machen wrote no weird fiction between 1917 ("The Terror") & 1933 ("The Green Round"). The new story is tamer than the earlier ones, but is still well worth reading. I was certainly sorry to read of White's suicide, & cannot imagine what could have caused it—though he had had trouble with publishers, & was probably in difficult financial circumstances.[1] The late Dr. Whitehead was in close touch with him. I shall never forget the power & realism of "Andivius Hedulio", which made old Rome live again.

No—the contemporary Spanish art shewn in Providence was not of the erratic sort known as "modernistic". Artistically, the modern Spaniards (except Picasso) seem to be healthily & refreshingly conservative.

Though I hated to leave Charleston, the post-Charlestonian phases of my trip have been very pleasant. I had 8½ hours in Savannah—a town of which I am very fond, though it cannot compare with Charleston in quaintness. It is restful—with tall palms & luxuriant, moss-draped live-oaks, innumerable parks, & a profusion of late-Georgian mansions of about a century ago. Florida proved as attractive as usual—its lush subtropical scenery having a singular fascination, while my health is braced up enormously by the vivifying warmth. De Land is a pretty town, & nearby is De Leon Springs—with an old sugar mill dating back to the Spanish period before 1763. The Barlow place—spacious, landscaped, & with a fascinating lake in the rear—is 14 miles west of the village, out of sight of any human habitation. Young Barlow—the son of a retired army Colonel—is an infinitely bright boy, & possesses innumerable accomplishments. He is very unfortunately handicapped by poor eyesight. He expects to be in Washington in the autumn—consulting oculists. He & I are having a splendid time—motoring to various points, rowing on the lake behind the house, & having reading, writing, & discussing sessions all over the nearby countryside. His collection of books & magazines pertaining to the weird is valuable & unusual. Not long ago Barlow shot a giant snake, whose skin he is going to use for binding books. The cats & 'possums are delightful!

Interested to see the "Choir Practice" address. I didn't look up Mrs. C. when in Charleston. Sorry her household has encountered difficulties. An interesting person whom I did meet in Charleston was Miss Eola Willis, Chairman of the local Art Commission & author of the standard history of the 18th century Charleston stage—a gentlewoman of ancient Carolina stock, aged about 70, who dwells in her hereditary mansion in unspoiled & colonial Tradd St.[2] Miss W. is not only an erudite historian & antiquarian, but a watercolour artist of great power, whose views of Carolina scenery are vivid & beautiful.

Took a trip to New Smyrna, Fla., & saw the ruins of a large Franciscan mission of 1696, & also site (& original canal) of Dr. Turnbull's plantation of 1768.

All good wishes—

Yrs most cordially,

H P Lovecraft

[P.S.] I didn't know the designer was dissatisfied with the Maryland stamp as printed. Have received a few of the stamps with picture of Whistler's mother, which are exceedingly artistic.

Notes

1. Edward Lucas White (b. 1866) committed suicide on 30 March 1934.
2. "Mrs. C." is Ellen M. Carroll. Eola Willis (1856–1952), *The Charleston Stage in the XVIII Century, with Social Settings of the Time* (Columbia, SC: The State Co., 1924).

[73]   [ALS]

St. Augustine, Fla.,

June 21, 1934.

Dear Miss Toldridge:—

My stay in De Land was surely protracted, but the cordiality of my hosts was not to be overcome. Barlow is a delightful boy—as you will discover for yourself when he is in Washington next autumn for ocular treatment . . . . . that is, if you would like to have him call. The state of his eyes is most unfortunate, & I surely hope that it can eventually be remedied.

My route north is still a bit uncertain—depending on whether or not I decide to pay a visit in Macon, Ga. I hope I can include Savannah & Charleston, but am not sure. Richmond is on the schedule—with a side trip to Williamsburg if I have the cash—& I must see Fredericksburg. If all goes well I shall stop off in Washington—giving your telephone a ring & seeing whether you are receiving callers. A young friend of mine—named Morse[1]—is now in the capital, acting as secretary to a professor-uncle who is doing some research work at the Library of Congress.

The cats at De Land were all prospering when last I saw them; though one—Jack—has been through a trying experience. He was missing for a day, & when he turned up again he seemed curiously ill. All sense of balance was gone, & he lurched & staggered like a feline toper! As he grew stronger, he seemed anxious to visit a neighbouring clump of palmettoes near the lake—where, it was discovered, lay a small snake . . . dead, & with a somewhat tooth-mangled cranium. Undoubtedly Jack had chosen this reptile for his prey, & had become poisoned by his ophidian feast. He's coming out all right, though. Of the little 'possums, only one managed to survive for any length of time, & even he succumbed in the end. He received the name of Henry, & graduated long before his demise from medicine-dropper nutritive methods. At another place in De Land I saw the most exquisite black kitten—a tiny atom, but wildly playful—that can be imagined.

Thanks exceedingly for the cuttings, which abound in interest. My young host was especially interested in the ones about interplanetary travel, Shakespearian folios, & giant lizards. I shall have to see the latter—I saw the short-lived specimens at the Bronx zoo in 1926, which now exist in stuffed form in the Am. Mus. of Nat. Hist. Thanks also for the very artistic Mother's Day stamp. I was greatly interested in the picture of the Tunis painting from which the Maryland stamp was taken.[2] Too bad a more faithful reproduction was not made.

I was very glad to see your new poem—"Late, Late"—& can really suggest no improvement unless you could somehow find an adequate equivalent for the rather well-worn *stars-bars* rhyme in st. iv. The lines are tremendously poignant & graceful, & I hope they may find publication in a medium of appropriate merit. Yes—*Driftwind* is a fairly well-known poetry magazine. The Vermont renaissance has been going on for 7 or 8 years now. Naturally some of the local literature is provincial, but it springs from a deep-seated background. You can get an idea of early Vermont literature from the opening article in that *Recluse* which I sent some years ago—if you still have it.[3]

Early in June I visited a most impressive spot—Silver Springs, some 60 miles from De Land. Here is found a series of placid lagoons whose floor is riddled with vast pits 30 to 60 feet deep, & covered with curious marine vegetation. In many places divers have encountered the huge bones of prehistoric animals, & one pit contains the remains of a weed-grown ship's boat—associated by local legend with the early Spanish explorers. I saw these varied wonders from a glass-bottomed boat. Out of the lagoons flows the Silver River, as typical a tropic stream as the Congo or Amazon, with tall palms, trailing vines & moss, & bending cypresses along the swampy banks. Alligators, turtles, & snakes abound, & on either side the jungle stretches away uninterruptedly for miles. It is here that the cinema of "Tarzan" was photographed. I took a 10-mile launch trip on the river, & could easily have imagined myself in the heart of Africa. ¶ Am now in ancient St. Augustine—

at the same quaint hotel I patronised in 1931. Staying a week—an utterly fascinating town! Best wishes—

    H P Lovecraft

Notes

1. Richard Ely Morse.
2. Edwin Burdett Tunis (1897–1973), artist, illustrator, muralist and author. He designed the Maryland Tercentenary Commemorative Postage Stamp (1934).
3. The *Recluse* (1927) contained "Study List: Vermont Poets and Poetry" (pp. 1–2) and "Early Vermont Minstrelsy" (pp. 3–14), both by Walter J. Coates.

[74]   [ALS]

           66 College St.,
           Providence, R.I.,
           July 27, 1934.

Dear Miss Toldridge:—

           I was surely glad to be able to stop in at the Farragut during my trip, & regret that I was limited to a single evening. The next day I explored the interior of the Capitol & Pan-American Bldg., visited Rock Creek Park, saw the furnished interior of Arlington mansion, & ascended the Washington monument—all for the first time in my life! The view from the monument is magnificent beyond description; while Arlington—as restored—forms one of the most fascinating plantation homes I have ever seen. I stopped a day in Philadelphia—visiting Germantown & the Wissahickon, & inspecting for the first time the newly restored & opened Poe cottage in N. 7th St., where the poet lived from 1842 to 1844. This shrine is furnished exactly as in Poe's day—even with one or two things he actually owned—& is full of interesting & significant reliques. I think I mentioned hearing the dedication of this place over the radio last winter. In N.Y. I found Long & his parents about to depart for Ocean Grove, N.J. for the week-end, & went along with them—having a very enjoyable time. I was too broke to see many of the old group in N.Y., & came home July 10th—running into a beastly cold spell which lasted 3 days.

    Glad to receive your note with interesting enclosures & the accompanying *Circle* with your excellent & captivating "Thoughts".[1] This issue as a whole seems to me distinctly above the average. Do you wish it returned? It is safely preserved. I note your change in "Late, Late", & believe it is thoroughly advantageous & advisable. I shall be glad when the poem receives appropriate placement.

    The cuttings, as usual, include intensely interesting material—that on prehistoric Florida races being especially timely. But I must thank you especially for those exquisite examples of Japanese stationery. Their delicate beauty is so vast that I doubt whether I can bear to use them for their avowed purpose & send them away! Rather shall I keep them on hand as art items.

One thing I found upon my arrival home was an utterly delightful coal-black kitten at the boarding-house across the back garden. He was just a furry handful—still a bit uncertain on his feet, but beginning to play. In aspect he was like a graceful bear cub of paperweight size. He constantly grows in size, strength, & playfulness, & I borrow him as often as I can. Another thing awaiting me was a veritable library of illustrated books on Old England, sent by a lucky friend now travelling there. Among them was a splendid London volume with etchings by Joseph Pennell.[2] Also a fine contemporary map of London.

By this time you have doubtless received the new Marvel Tales & Fantasy Fan. Both seem to be rather good issues as such things go—the former being especially an improvement on the preceding number. Long's story is quite powerful, it seems to me.[3]

Went over to the Historical Society (only a block from #66) the other day & saw a highly important local find—a huge tree-trunk dugout used by the Nipmuc Indians before the coming of the white man. It is in excellent condition, & is the largest Indian dugout ever discovered in the U.S. It was found by small boys at the bottom of the so-called Ponaganset Reservoir in Glocester, R.I. last month, & was later raised & brought to the Hist. Soc. Museum. The reason it lay so long undiscovered is that the pond formerly had a vastly higher level, so that it was under nearly 100 feet of water instead of about 10 as now. When changes were made in the reservoir system, the level of the water fell—& then an archaic mystery was brought to light.

I expect James F. Morton (curator of the Paterson Museum) to visit me August 2–3–4, & anticipate some highly interesting conversations. Hope I can get my work programme reasonably under control by then, for as it is I am utterly inundated by unperformed tasks. So rushed to death am I, that I have not yet even fully unpacked my valise from the trip!

A ray of hope—at last—of the publication of my friend Moe's "Doorways to Poetry", albeit in rather humble form, as an exercise book. I shall see that you get a copy if it comes out. Moe is resuming activity to some extent in the world of amateur journalism.

E. Hoffmann Price is off again to Auburn to visit Clark Ashton Smith. Robert E. Howard lately went through the Carlsbad Caverns in New Mexico, & writes with impressive vividness of them. If he is right, they must form one of the most stupendously impressive spectacles that this planet has to offer.

Two new kittens down in De Land—& Jack's neck is almost straight again. Barlow is making some experiments in trick photography with his new camera—with a view to producing weird & monstrous effects.

I trust you have been as well as usual, & that you have succeeded in getting outdoors now & then.

All good wishes—

Yr most oblig'd & obt Servt

H P Lovecraft

Notes

1. *Circle* (July–August 1931).
2. Joseph Pennell (1857–1928), American graphic artist and illustrator, noted for landscapes and architectural scenes. The volume in question may be *Haunts of Old London* (London: T. N. Foulis, 1914), consisting of 25 of Pennell's etchings. Sidney Dark's *London* (London: Macmillan, 1924; *LL* 220) also had illustrations by Pennell.
3. Frank Belknap Long, "The Dark Beasts," *Marvel Tales* (July/August 1934).

[75]   [ALS]

Nantucket, Mass—90 miles from 66 College St.

Providence, R.I.,

Aug. 31, 1934

Dear Miss Toldridge:—

Yes—I did manage to cover a bit of ground in Washington, for the genial warmth (96°) released & conserved my maximum energies. The cooler weather up here is far less bracing to me—though as yet only the evenings are really uncomfortable in their chill. Sorry your energies have been below par, & hope you may soon be fully recuperated. Thanks vastly for the cuttings—all of which interested me extremely. I saw that Pierce Mill dam in Rock Creek Park. The cutting about a multiplicity of solar systems—independently confirming the theory of Prof. Alter[1]—was absolutely new to me, & proved highly absorbing. Yes—the postage was fully prepaid on all envelopes.

Glad you liked "Through the Gates of the Silver Key"—which still fails to satisfy me. It is virtually my own work as it stands. Price wrote a crude sequel to my old "Silver Key" (1926),[2] but it was so false to the spirit of the original that I scrapped almost all of it & wrote the present thing in its place. All that is left of Price's work is the mathematical theorising in the middle of the story—plus the scene with the pedestals. And even this has been put into my language. The voyage to Yaddith is entirely my own, in idea & language alike.

Had an enjoyable visit from James F. Morton (curator of the Paterson Museum) August 2–3–4. We visited many local points of interest, & spent the final day at ancient Newport—seeing the U.S. fleet in the harbour, exploring the venerable streets, & walking & resting on the famous ocean cliffs. Morton is getting to be a mighty genealogist, & has just traced the one line which we hold in common (Perkins) back to the year 1380 . . . Chaucer's time! He is now in Maine, & will be circulating around New England till early October.

Of my own recent vacational activities a card & a folder have doubtless apprised you. The visit around Boston was highly interesting despite the anxiety caused by Cook's nervous collapse & sudden return to Vermont; but *Nantucket* of course forms the climax. It would take volumes to describe the place—through pictures may help. I enclose a few more. More than Salem, Newport, Marblehead, Portsmouth, or any other town I have ever seen, it represents a typical Yankee seaport of 1790 or 1800 absolutely as it used to be. Horses still numerous—main street paved with huge round cobblestones—skyline dominated by ancient belfries & white steeple—old windmill on the highest hill—gardens & picket fences everywhere—95% of the houses built before 1840 in Georgian style, perhaps 80% antedating 1810 & 40% being pre-revolutionary—narrow winding lanes here & there—knockers & doorplates & horse-blocks & hitching-posts . . . . . the antiquity is complete! A combination of insular isolation, commercial collapse, & artistic appreciation has ensured this felicitous survival. Summer visitors & artists now dominate Nantucket, & have done much to preserve its elder-world charm. The town proper has magnificent trees, but the bulk of the island has lost its forests & consists of rolling grassy meadows. I've seen about everything there is to see—houses, street vistas, windmill, whaling museum, Historical Society, &c. I guess I mentioned seeing Saturn at the Maria Mitchell observatory. Am looking up local history & traditions at the Athenaeum (now a public library), & have bought 2 books on the subject. The anecdote about the Salt Box house type & Job Macy's father which you sent is very timely—I've seen the house in question! The worst trouble with this visit is the beastly *cold*, which occasionally becomes so great as to hamper my activities. No heat in the houses yet—& on one day I couldn't write. At this moment I have a heavy blanket draped toga-wise over my suit! And yet my aunt—warmer-blooded than I—is going up to Ogunquit, Maine, for a fortnight as soon as I get home! I wish I were in Florida!

I certainly hope you can get on some sort of outing next summer—I think it would pay you even if the actual transportation involved some inconvenience. Young Barlow will be going to Washington very soon now, & will probably give you a call on the telephone. You'll find him, I think, a very interesting boy. I surely hope his eyes can be benefited. He has just finished a fortnight's visiting at Daytona Beach.

Thanks vastly of the Bath & Stratford cards—all replete with charm. I surely hope I can get to the old land sooner or later!

As for little Sam Perkins—you ought to see him *now!* Bless Grandpa's bones, what a little black dynamo of ceaseless sportive energy! Of all little imps of Beëlzebub . . . . & how he can purr! I have him over at 66 nearly all the time, but his folks don't seem to mind!

Well—I trust your health will stay mended this time, & that you will take care not to overdo. With every good wish, & thanking you again for enclosures,

I remain

Yr most oblig'd, most ob^t Servt

H P Lovecraft

Notes

1. Dinsmore Alter (1888–1968), American astronomer and meteorologist, and director of the Griffith Observatory in Los Angeles.
2. "The Lord of Illusion." First published in *Crypt of Cthulhu* No. 10 (Yuletide 1982): 46–56.

[76]   [ALS]

66 College St.,

Providence, R.I.,

Octr 6, 1934.

Dear Miss Toldridge:—

I am indeed glad that you found the Nantucket material of interest. My week there ended as pleasantly as it began—& toward the last I explored some of the environs of the town on a hired bicycle . . . . the first time in 20 years that I had been on a wheel. Riding was quite as easy & familiar as if I had last dismounted only the day before, & it seemed marvellously exhilarating & rejuvenating to be spinning along just as in the old times. The place is certainly all that the folders shew—& more. Never had I realised that so fascinating a haven of the past could exist only 90 miles away. The secret of its distinctiveness & preservation is, of course, its insular isolation. It is a little world in itself—Daniel Webster once called it (when he went there to try some cases in the 1830's) "The Unknown City in the Sea".[1] Nowhere else do the actual feel & substance of the past exist so perfectly & unbrokenly. I enclose a couple more cards, plus a map of the town & island which may prove interesting. The names & details in these maps can be well brought out by a reading-glass of moderate power. It was pleasant to be able to see Saturn through a good telescope. I have an astronomical telescope with 3" object-glass myself; but its portable mounting is crude, & its performance leaves much to be desired. I have, however, looked through the 12" telescope of the local Ladd Observatory—an adjunct of Brown University. E. Hoffmann Price has lately been making a round of California observatories, & gazed through the Lick Observatory's celebrated 36" refractor. I hope you will be able to get a sight of some choice celestial objects through a telescope before long. Does not Washington afford such opportunities? It seems to me that the U.S. Naval Observatory at Georgetown—with a fine 26" refractor—must sometimes be open to the public. I'm glad to hear, by the way, that your health is better; & trust you will adhere faithfully to the prescribed diet. I'm eating rather carefully myself, having had a touch of indigestion. My aunt enjoyed Ogunquit immensely, as she always does. She has made trips thither on & off for years—stopping at The Lookout. As your friend has probably told you, Ogunquit is a place of rather impressive cliff scenery—with a walk along the edge of the cliffs called the "Marginal Way." It is not far from the quaint old towns of Kennebunk & Kennebunkport—which I would vastly prefer to it. I have never been there—except to ride through its centre on the 'bus when I visited Portland in 1927.

Let me thank you exceedingly for the generous fund of enclosures—especially that delectable series describing the minutiae of life in old Washington. I have read this with the most extreme interest, & shall file it permanently with other antiquarian material. It is pleasing & curious to note the little obscure details of bygone periods—the sports, the songs, the cheap fiction, the manners, the idioms, the prevailing popular interests, & so on. Nothing of this sort is so trivial that it ought not to be preserved, since only by the careful study of such material can the genuine texture of the past be reconstructed by the historian. America was very neglectful of this kind of thing until a decade ago, but is now making up for lost time. Even the most absurd of old-fashioned dime novels are now carefully guarded in the principal libraries as important historico-sociological source-material. I also enjoyed the cutting about the restoration of Delphi—as well, indeed, as all the rest. Doubtless you realise that the mention of "Theodoric" as the suppressor of the oracle was erroneous. *Theodosius* was the emperor (& he was not merely a Byzantine emperor, either—he ruled both halves of the empire) responsible for this, & for the suppression of the schools of philosophy. Theodoric was an Ostrogothic king who ruled in conquered Italy a century later, after the fall of the Western Empire. The account of Stobi & its exhumed antiquities was a complete surprise to me—I had never heard of the discovery before![2] I hope it will receive more notice in the press, & that pictures of the excavations will appear in the rotogravures. By the way—I am vastly indebted for those views of old Washington—at least one of which represents a house I have never seen. I seem to be finding new things in the capital each year—only last July I found an ancient house (The Maples—once a country-seat) in the southeastern section that I had never seen before. These new views go at once into my files. No—my files are by no means orderly or well classified, but consist of very rough divisions scattered in different places—some in a metal cabinet, some on closet shelves, some in cabinet drawers, & so on. It is a wonder I ever find anything! Incidentally, I trust you'll eventually come across your poem "The River & the Boat."

Cold weather appears here off & on now—but the steam is going idyllically 24 hours a day! During the transition period I depended on my oil stove. Sunsets still blaze—& through a framework of foliage incipiently autumnal. Getting too late for outdoor reading & writing—my last trip of that sort was Septr. 26, when I cleaned up some revision in 2 places—first on a stone wall at a high point of the Breakneck Hill Pond (in my favourite countryside N. of Prov.), & then atop a rocky cliff beside a glassy tarn in the midst of deep woods. From the first site I had a marvellous vista of verdant valley & distant steepled hill. The leaves had just begun to turn—but despite the pallor of the sunlight the landscape was still predominantly aestival. Yes—the Morton who visited me in August is the one who contributed to the Washington anthology. Gabelle is a great friend of his. Cook is, I think, rather better, though not feeling rather energetic. Haven't seen anybody lately, though I expect a call from the brothers Wandrei as they pass through Providence in the course of their present motor tour. They are now in Montreal. Also, my host of last August in Wollaston—E. H. Cole—may come down some week-end for Rhodinsular exploration. No—I haven't come across any interesting Providence literati, though there are such without doubt. I seem to find the most interesting persons scattered about from Vermont to Florida, Texas, & California!

Nearly sunk with a wretched job of novel revision—but I'm shifting the worst of it on to someone else in sheer self-defence. Haven't had a chance for any original fiction. The only recent thing I've written is an elegy for a recently deceased member of the amateur journalist circle—a rather stilted & mediocre composition which would have been not quite so bad if I had not written it to order in a hurry for C. W. Smith.[3] I'll enclose Smith's booklet containing it—which you needn't bother to return. The bad typography & misprints are lamentable.

You may see Barlow before long. Too bad he can't arrange to see Dr. Wilmer, but I doubt if he could afford it. He has the services of army specialists free as long as he is a minor—since his father is a retired army colonel. The doctor he consults is in that ugly State, War, & Navy Bldg. near the White House.

It is with grief that I record the news of my little black friend Sam Perkins—for, just as I was most garrulously proclaiming his graces & virtues to all my correspondents, he pranced & pattered away to the fields of eternal catnip! He was found lifeless one morning amidst his favourite shrubbery, & now he sleeps beneath the grasses with which he loved to play in life. No cause for his early passing could be discovered—but it was probably a recurrence of a trouble which he had early in August, when he was inexplicably ill for 3 days. Blessed little Piece of the Night! He lived but from June to September, & will never know what the savage rigours of winter are like! The grave, whiskered elders of the Kappa Alpha Tau stare wistfully from the clubhouse roof, & mew in elegiac numbers:

> The ancient garden seems tonight
> A deeper gloom to bear,
> As if some silent shadow's blight
> Were hov'ring in the air.

> With hidden griefs the grasses sway,
> Unable quite to word them—
> Remembering from yesterday
> The little paws that stirr'd them.[4]

Your new sonnet "Poetry" strikes me as powerful & delightful, & I do not think you need feel dissatisfied with any of the points you mention. *Giant* is not only a permissible adjective through common usage, but is officially recognised as such by Stormonth's highly conservative British dictionary—the one I habitually go by. The rise in intensity in the latter part is a desirable quality—adding to the climactic effect. It seems to me that this piece ought to fare very well indeed in the Circle contest . . . . though such contests are not always adjudicated impartially & intelligently. All too often devotion to one particular school or another causes a judge to miss vital points of absolute merit in some of the entries, while overpraising mediocrity in others. Watching the laureateship awards year after year in the National Amateur Press Association is enough to disillusion anyone regarding the significance of contests. Still—it's always pleasant to win one! I have tried to avoid serving as verse critic in the National Assn. this year, but fear I shall have to do so for lack of a willing successor. The new administration—largely hustling youths with real literary ambitions—is trying to improve the quality of the members' writings; & it would not do to leave them critically short-handed at the present juncture. By the way—some time ago, in answer to a request, I prepared an article for one of the amateur papers which may interest you when it comes out—an account of each of the houses in which Poe ever lived, with a description of those still standing.[5] I'll send you a copy when it appears. Naturally, the most extensive descriptions are of the Fordham cottage & the newly restored Philadelphia house which I visited last July. ¶ With all good wishes, & congratulations on the genuine excellence of "Poetry", I remain

Yrs most sincerely,

H P Lovecraft

Notes

1. The quotation is found in William Francis Macy (1867–?), ed. *The Nantucket Scrap Basket: Being a Collection of Characteristic Stories and Sayings of the People of the Town and Island of Nantucket, Massachusetts* (Nantucket: The Inquirer and Mirror, 1916; *LL* 585), 79. The actual quotation says "ocean" rather than "sea." HPL's own essay on Nantucket is titled "The Unknown City in the Ocean."
2. Stobi (now Gradsko; Ancient Greek: Στόβοι) was an ancient town of Paeonia, later conquered by Macedon, and then turned into the capital of the Roman province of Macedonia Salutaris (now in the Republic of Macedonia). The Museum of Belgrade investigated the city from 1924 to 1936.
3. "Edith Miniter."

4. HPL never titled the poem, but it is generally known as "Little Sam Perkins."
5. "Homes and Shrines of Poe."

[77]   [ALS]

66 College St.
Providence, R.I.,
Nov. 14, 1934.

Dear Miss Toldridge:—

Your messages duly received—& I certainly hope that some miracle may enable you to stay along at the Farragut! The prospect of moving is always a disconcerting one—& when one has grown as used to a place as you have to your present quarters,[1] a transfer is little short of a tragedy. Possibly your physician may be able to exert enough "pull" to avert the catastrophe—I really don't see why at least *one* residential apartment couldn't be allowed to remain in what is otherwise a medical building. Well—one may only hope for the best. If you *do* have to move, have you ever thought of looking for quarters in ancient & picturesque Georgetown! That is the section I should try to live in if I were a Washingtonian. But possibly you wouldn't care to be so remote from the centre of things. And I know that one grows tremendously used to certain neighbourhoods.

Sorry to hear you've had another accident—though fortunately this one appears to be rather slight. I trust that all effects of it may soon be dispelled. If by any chance it leads to some arrangement letting you stay at the Farragut, you will probably think it well worth undergoing!

I can imagine the upheavals of old papers, &c. incident to the threat of moving. That's just what I went through a year & a half ago! However, I ended up by keeping nearly everything—which was practicable, since I have more space here than I had in Barnes St. I'd surely be glad to file any new poems which you may send. I have quite a file of your work as it is—MSS., cuttings, & bits on cards . . . besides items in anthologies & numbers of *The Circle*.

Nantucket surely was magnificent, & I hope extremely that I can get there again next summer. The present autumn has not been very genial, on the whole; so that rural trips have been fewer than last year. However, owing to a fortunate opportunity, I did secure some of the finest autumn vistas in all my experience during the week-end of October. 19–21—when I again visited Edward H. Cole in Wollaston & was taken on sundry explorations in his well-heated Chevrolet.

On the 20th we invaded a section of north central Massachusetts which I had never before visited, & in which I saw the best autumn foliage & landscape panoramas that I ever beheld. The focus of the trip was West Townsend (see enclosed card), where we lunched at a rambling old tavern built in 1774, & pattonised the quaintest general store that I've seen in 30 years.

Nearby is the Willard Brook State Forest, where we revelled in wooded hills, rock waterfalls, & leafy gorges of indescribable picturesqueness. From nearly every point the distant bulk of Mt. Wachusett loomed up, & once we had a splendid view of a steepled village in a valley. We returned via Leominster, Bolton, Sudbury, & Waltham—at the first-named place momentarily crossing the path of former travels of mine. On the 21st Cole & his wife brought me back to Providence in the car—picking up my aunt at #66 & setting out for the ancient Narragansett Country which Price & I explored last year. We visited venerable Wickford with its drowsing wharves & elm-shaded main street, & later struck inland to the gorgeously lovely spot where Gilbert Stuart's birthplace—a snuff mill built in 1750—broods beside the Pettaquamscutt or Narrow River. As I mentioned in 1933, this ancient structure has been fully restored—wheel & all—so that it can grind snuff as well as it did when Stuart's father ran it 180 years ago. The caretaker always starts the great wheel for visitors, allowing them to see the wooden cog-wheels & grinding machinery in action. The mechanism is in the basement, with the water-wheel outside controlled by a rope & lever. In restoring the 18th century machinery it was necessary to send to England & Scotland for some of the parts—no artisan in the United States now being able to fashion them. The countryside around the mill—winding river with wooded banks, grassy slopes, & narrow, rutted roads bordered by vine-grown stone walls—was doubly beautiful in its autumnal splendour of red & gold; & Cole insisted on some adventurous explorations which resulted in our getting partly lost. It surely was a great trip—proving afresh that a heated car is a great aid to sightseeing in weather like this. Cole has some idea of coming again before winter—but the landscape will have lost its charm in another week. The Wandreis have not shewed up so far—possibly they have eliminated Providence from their itinerary. My last card from them was from Montreal. Barlow is now in Washington, & you'll doubtless see him shortly. His eyes are now under expert observation, though I don't yet know what the verdict will be. He is taking an art course at the Corcoran Gallery—a light one, since the oculist will not sanction anything heavier. Price is now in Oakland, California—his family home. He has twice called on Clark Ashton Smith—in Auburn.

Many thanks for the various cuttings—including the "Choir Practice" with your delightful "Magic Charms" . . . . which is a favourite of mine. I shall add this to my collection with appreciation. This column is surely a great institution, & speaks much for the judgment of its conductor. I did not know that Mrs. Carroll was herself a poet till Miss Radcliffe mentioned her new book.[2] I must get a look at the latter. It ought to be delightful, if its author's taste in selecting others' poetry is any criterion. And meanwhile I trust that your own sonnet "Poetry" may prosper in the coming contest.

Sorry you didn't find "The River & the Boat", but glad that other long-lost MSS came to light. Too bad, though, that you threw everything away—

unless indeed you felt absolutely convinced that it did not come up to your standard. I've dumped a number of my effusions, but usually keep them in reserve—so that I can incorporate parts of them into other things later on.

I am tremendously obliged for the cards—all of which are extremely welcome acquisitions for my collection. The two Bath specimens help to give me an excellent variety covering that ancient town—for you had sent some before, while a travelling friend sent a voluminous folder of Bath photographs last summer. The so-called "Sally Lunn" bun or tea-cake, which is common in New England, was indeed named from a noted pastry-cook of Bath who flourished in the late 18th century. She was accustomed to carry her wares in a basket & cry them aloud on the streets, & I am not certain whether she ever actually kept a shop. The recipe for her buns, however, was bought by one Dalmar, a baker, who composed a song about these wares—a song once having much popularity. Possibly the shop shewn in the card is meant to be his.

The cuttings are extremely interesting—especially the one about early Washington, which I shall add to the group previously sent. The hearth in Henry's law office is quaint & pleasant—I have a picture of the house in my files, & am very glad of this interior view to supplement it. The lines "To the Night-Sky", by Edgar Kemler,[3] undoubtedly possess a certain power, though they also have a tendency toward abruptness & even obscurity which does not seem to me altogether an asset. It is clear that the author has tried very hard to break away from conventional images—& for this he is to be congratulated. Still, it is only with caution that the general style of the sonnet should be emulated.

Recently my next-door neighbour—the marble John Hay Library—held an exhibition of books & other reliques associated with Thomas Holley Chivers of Georgia—the obscure weird poet of the 1840's who influenced & was influenced by Poe. As a poet, Chivers was extravagant & often childish; but he had a certain curious quality which makes him worth mentioning as a landmark in American letters.[4]

Well—I surely hope that you can manage to stay at the Farragut somehow. But if not, there must be many other pleasant places available, once you discover them. ¶ All good wishes

——Yrs most sincerely

—H P Lovecraft

Notes

1. Toldridge had lived at the Farragut for thirty years.

2. Ellen M. Carroll, *Lonely Shores* (1934), a volume of poetry.

3. Edgar Kemler (1916–1960), American critic best known for *The Deflation of American Ideals* (1941) and *The Irreverent Mr. Mencken* (1950). No published poetry by him has been found.

4. In December HPL heard a lecture on Chivers (1809–1858) by S. Foster Damon of Brown University.

[78]   [ANS postcard][1]

[Postmarked Providence, RI,
20 November 1934]

Congratulations on securing such pleasant quarters in your own neighbourhood. Once the nuisance of moving is over, I'm sure you'll like the new place as well as the old. There will be compensating factors to replace anything not duplicated—for example, that west window sounds ideal! And the kitchen is an enormous asset. I am dropping Barlow a card telling him to call either before Thanksgiving at the Farragut, or considerably after that event at the La Salle. He is in a fever of activities—I've had nothing but a postal signed "frantically yours" in the last 3 weeks! ¶ Thanks as usual for the interesting cuttings. Rediscovery of Roman Carthage (which was close to the older & wholly destroyed Punic city of the same name) is certainly an event of the highest importance. In the late imperial age it was second only to Rome itself in the western world. ¶ Shall be delighted to see the Carroll book—but you must not send it *permanently* if you have the slightest use for it in your own library. ¶ Splendid warm weather for the past 4 days—have been out quite a bit. ¶ Expect to go to Boston Friday to see W. Paul Cook, who is there for a week. ¶ Well—I hope the moving ordeal won't prove arduous. Certainly the reality won't be as bad as the anticipation! ¶ All good wishes—
Yrs most sincerely—
H P Lovecraft

Notes

1. *Front:* Benedict Temple of Music, Roger Williams Park, Providence, R.I.

[79]   [ALS]

66 College St.
Providence, R.I.,
Dec. 29, 1934.

Dear Miss Toldridge:—

I am indeed glad to hear that your moving has been safely accomplished—but sorry your dusky coadjutor has been indisposed. Her absence must have made the readjustment process—difficult enough at best—doubly trying. Hope she is now thoroughly mended & able to play her accustomed part in household affairs. It is unfortunate that the Farragut had to be transformed, but I fancy you will become fond of the La Salle in course of time. Let us hope that this haven will remain unchanged! It will—

incidentally—seem much more homelike when all the lighting effects are perfected. I am very dependent on good lighting—indeed, I've rejected many an hotel room because of too dim illumination. Lights are the first things I look to in securing quarters.

Glad little Bobby Barlow has been dropping in. He mentioned in a note how much he enjoyed his calls. His photographic work is surely remarkable in the extreme. Has he shewn you any of his reproductions of Howard Wandrei's weird drawings? Indeed, he is astonishingly clever in every way—drawing, painting, clay modelling, writing, & general craftsmanship. His bookbinding jobs—in which he sometimes uses the skins of snakes he has shot—are masterpieces in their way. I hope the improvement in his vision will be permanent—for without the active use of his eyes he is left utterly stranded. Everything he enjoys involves the heavy use of eyesight.

Yes—the gang surely are migratory by nature. Donald Wandrei has been out to California visiting Clark Ashton Smith, & is now in New York again—for how long, I am not yet certain. Price is still in Oakland, & is thinking—at the moment—of buying a lot in San Carlos (south of San Francisco in San Mateo Co., east of the bay) & building a very cheap house on it. If you still receive the *Fantasy Fan* you've doubtless noticed the interview with Price. (If not, I can send you recent issues—one dedicated to me.)[1]

Your sonnet was surely delightful, & I trust it will receive appropriate recognition. As for very short poems—they do seem to be rather frequent of late, but I wouldn't worry about following fashions. The thing to cultivate is a sort of independent, timeless style. Of course it is necessary to avoid what is hackneyed, & to eschew such forms of the past as are recognisably artificial & ill-founded in aesthetics; but that does not imply any need of suiting transient & capricious whims. Sorry the methods of the Paebar anthology have proved disappointing.[2] Yes—Coates of *Driftwind* has often complained of anthologies whose methods seemed lax, piratical, & non-conscientious. He mentioned the Paebar—& also Henry Harrison last October. Anthology editing seems to be quite a racket—but probably the missing volume will appear sooner or later. The delay, however, is indeed unfortunate.

Yes—I fancy it is wise to keep the kitchen usable as such, since restaurant meals can seldom be as cheap as home-prepared ones. However, you could probably disguise or conceal the stove & sink with screens, so as to give the room a sort of residential character. It might serve as a useful overflow for furniture, books, & pictures which the main room cannot accomodate.

Early this month I attended an unusual number of lectures—closely grouped together as part of the local observance of "Art Week." One of them was a demonstration of painting by two of the city's foremost artists—a landscapist & a portraitist—who executed a picture apiece in full view of the audience.[3] It was really a fascinating thing to watch. Another feature was a display of the choicest of the 717 Japanese prints just acquired by the local museum. As you know, these things form quite a hobby with me—& I enjoyed the exhibit enormously. This acquisition puts Providence more or less in the running with Boston, whose Museum of Fine Arts specialises in Japanese art. Still another "Art Week" feature was an exhibition of the new aesthetic form—the correlation of shifting projected colours with music. It must have been highly interesting, but I had to forgo it—since the weather was too cold to permit of my going out. Enclosed is a catalogue of the Japanese exhibit.

Thanks—as usual—for the cuttings, & let me express a particular & delighted gratitude for the generous variety of Christmas cards, which both my aunt & I appreciate enormously. You really ought not, though, to be so liberal now that you do not get cards in a professional way. The designs are splendid—of the dignity & appropriateness so hard to find in the shops—& I keenly appreciated the feline specimens! What a pair of recruits for the Kappa Alpha Tau fraternity[4] which meets on the shed roof across the garden! Would that little Sam Perkins might have seen them! The large 18th cent. storm scene is magnificent!

And—climax of all—"Lonely Shores"! How can I convey even a fraction of my gratitude for this delectable volume? But really, you ought not to have given it *permanently!* The poems are exquisite—things like "Dolor", "Strange Beauty", "Japanese Prints in Winter", "Late Winter Evening", &c. Mrs. Carroll is surely as gifted in original creation as in selective taste, as indeed I felt sure she must be after following "Choir Practice[?"] for a number of years.

My aunt & I had an exceptionally pleasant Christmas, & I hope the same is true of yourself. We had a *tree* for the first time in over a quarter of a century. All our old-time tree ornaments were long ago dispersed; but I laid in a new & inexpensive stock at Woolworth's & Kresge's—tinsel star & rope, globular baubles, set of lights, stand, & abundant shreds of tinsel to hang from the branches like the Spanish moss of the far south. The result was really delightful & impressive, & I've spent considerable time admiring & gloating. We had numerous though inexpensive presents—my best one from my aunt being a picture of the oldest house in Providence (the Stephen Hopkins house—1742—only a block & a half from our door), drawn by a local artist & simply framed. We began the day most auspiciously by listening to the great British Empire broadcast—which I hope you did not miss. Etheric conversations between London & the uttermost reaches of our Dominions—Australia, Tasmania, Canada, India, South Africa, & so on—with other messages from Scotland, Ireland, Liverpool, & a country place in the Cotswolds . . . . & finally an address by the King. I don't know when I've ever had a greater imaginative stimulus. After it was over I turned face down the dollar bill that was tied on top of one of my gifts . . . . . I couldn't bear to see the features of one who was instrumental in the cruel tearing of these colonies from the Empire in whose fabrick they rightly belong! Later in the day came a turkey feast at the boarding house across the back garden (home of the late Sam Perkins), a general unveiling of gifts, & a session of conversation & contemplation by candlelight & tree-light. At the boarding-house Mrs. Spotty (little Sam Perkins' mother) received a catnip mouse as a Christmas gift, & seemed very well pleased with that traditional feline delicacy. I couldn't locate any of the members of the Kappa Alpha Tau—the weather being inauspicious for sessions atop fence & clubhouse—but trust they all partook of ample Yuletide cheer.

Well—unless something goes wrong, the New York convention season will open Monday morning—the last day of 1934. Barlow hit the metropolis Christmas Day, & is staying at a rather luxurious hotel in 102nd St. which Long found for him. His tastes in lodging are so sumptuous & sybaritical that he couldn't get about the country as cheaply as I do! He & Long find each other tremendously congenial, as I knew they would. On Thursday Wandrei put in his appearance—& tomorrow night I shall myself take a stage coach for Manhattan, arriving at the Long headquarters in time for breakfast. It certainly ought to be quite a gathering—with other local gang-members likewise on hand. Don't know how long I'll stay—probably a week or more. The weather will be a troublesome factor, but in N.Y. the subway system forms a convenient way of getting around without much exposure. Barlow has not seen N Y since his infancy, so that all the museums, book shops, &c. will be new to him. Doubtless Long will be taking him about this week—& what he doesn't shew him, I will next week.

By the way—in obtaining some minor Yule-gifts at one of the numerous emporia of Mr. Frank Winfield Woolworth, I came across something so interesting that I am recommending it to everyone in the least fond of old-time British things. It is a series of 64-page booklets composed entirely of pictures (simple line drawings) illustrative of Britain's history in all its phases—architecture, costumes, familiar utensils, vehicles, famous houses & personages, typical scenes, &c. &c. ad infinitum. I suppose it is really designed for school children, but I am near enough to my second childhood to revel unashamedly in it. It is really of tremendous value to anyone in gaining a quick idea of the exact scenes & objects & costumes characterising every period. There ought to be seven in the series, but the last one (dealing with the Empire) has so far been unobtainable in Providence. I have the other six[5]—one giving Britain's whole story rapidly, & the other 5 treating each period in detail, from prehistoric times to the age of Sir Oswald Moseley & the National government. If you ever pass a Woolworth's, I heartily recommend this series (published in England by Sankey, Hudson, & Co. of Manchester) as an investment you won't regret. I shall look for the Empire booklet in N.Y. ¶ With all good wishes & renewed thanks—

Your most oblig'd, most obt Servt—

H P Lovecraft

[P.S. on envelope:] Just received the splendid New Year greeting, with its vivid presentation of a spirited elder scene. It is truly magnificent—a subject for framing, & a fine companion print to a gorgeous view received last year. Most abundant thanks!

Notes

1. Fred Anger and Louis C. Smith's "An Interview with E. Hoffman [*sic*] Price" appeared in *Fantasy Fan* 2, No. 4 (December 1934): 60–61. The October 1934 issue was dedicated to HPL.

2. Paebar published *The Choir Practice Anthology: A Collection of Poems* (1931) edited by Ellen M. Carroll.

3. Hezekiah Anthony Dyer (1872–1943); John Robinson Frazier (1889–1966).

4. Because 66 College Street was on Brown University's fraternity row, HPL devised the Greek name K.A.T. (standing for Kompson Ailuron Taxis, or "band of elegant [or well-dressed] cats") for the array of cats at the boarding house.

5. The books are by C. W. Airne; see Bibliography. The seventh book in the series (actually the first one published) appears to be *Our Empire's Story Told in Pictures* (Manchester: Sankey, Hudson & Co., 1934). There is no evidence that HPL procured this volume.

1935

[80]   [ALS]

66 College St.,
Providence, R.I.,
Jany. 22, 1935

Dear Miss Toldridge:—

Sorry to hear that the new place is so difficult to get adjusted to, but believe you will gradually become acclimated & even attached to it. It will, of course, take considerable experimentation to work out the best possible furnishing & lighting arrangement. You speak of the uncomfortable chairs—does this mean that your accustomed chairs *seem* uncomfortable in the altered locale, or that you really have a new set? I had assumed that your furniture was your own, & that both the Farragut & La Salle apartments were rented unfurnished. I could never become used to new furniture—wherever I have been, I have always had the same old chairs, tables, bookcases, & pictures around me. Well—in any case, I feel sure you can soon adjust the new quarters to your liking. Glad the faithful Alice is beginning to grow useful again. It is curious about the radio—I found that I couldn't make my small crystal set (which I had at Barnes St. in 1932) work in this locality. Nowadays I depend on my aunt's ordinary loud-speaking set. If you want a set with ear-phones yet do not wish to risk another crystal outfit, I think it would pay you to investigate a new *one-tube* variety which has lately come on the market at a price of something like $5.00. I'll send you an advertisement of one—later if I can't find it in time to enclose in this letter. A local hardware firm advertises it off & on. Glad you have a new lamp—I am very dependent on good lighting, & can understand how important a part it plays. Regarding shops on the ground floor—nowadays that is something one has to expect if anywhere near a business section. Young Long's home is thus situated—not the front in 97th St., but the side in Broadway. The family had hard work getting used to it when they moved from West End Ave. in 1927, but they now accept it as a matter of course. In colonial times residences above shops were common—such was the custom in European cities in the 18th century & before, even the palazzi of the Italian nobility occasionally housing trade on the ground floor. That, too, was a custom in ancient Roman times—many of the finest homes being situate in the *rear* of shops. The entrance to the home would be a long, tunnel-like passage between shop fronts. The majority of the residences unearthed at Pompeii & Herculaneum are of this type—which was also common in Rome itself. The great Roman apartment houses of many stories—*insulae,* so-called—were similarly arranged on the ground floor. The fact is, that strictly residential districts in compact towns form a comparatively new idea—not much more than 200 years old. In mediaeval & ancient times a town house was not very highly regarded—being merely a sort of stopping-place to occupy when one was not at one's country-seat. It was on the latter that all real care & expense were lavished. The first strictly residential districts were half-rural suburbs, with houses of more or less rural architecture. I can't recall any really fine *compact* residence neighbourhoods till the settling of London's West End after 1700. It was then that the Georgian town-house as we know it evolved. The La Salle certainly forms a city within itself—I don't believe Providence has any apartment-house of comparable capacity. In general, we have fewer than any other large city of the north . . . the individual or at most two-family house being still overwhelmingly predominant. Great rows of apartments, such as are seen in Washington, N.Y., & Boston, are unknown here—indeed, the physical aspect of Providence is much less like that of a large city than like that of a small town. A Providentian would feel much more at home in Salem or Portsmouth or Fredericksburg or Annapolis than in any average modern metropolis. The one largish city comparable to Providence in this respect is Richmond—though I suppose New Orleans (whose architecture, however, is very different) ought to be reckoned also. Providence has some *small* apartment houses (with only 12 apartments) which closely resemble private houses & have all the homelike features—green lawns with trees, &c.—which preserve the traditional quality of a residence section. It was in one of these that my aunt dwelt before coming to 66 College St.

I am glad you had a pleasant Christmas, with the perennial tree suitably illuminated. About those booklets with Britain's story—if I can find a set I'll send it along, although I have not seen any on sale since Christmas. I doubt if they could be obtained except at Woolworth's, since the publishers appear to have some exclusive marketing arrangement with the Woolworth chain both in England & the U.S. By this same token, they ought to be obtainable the year round instead of merely at Yuletide. We shall see.

Curious that the F F no longer reaches you. If you paid a dollar at the outset, you ought to have received the magazine for 18 months according to Editor Hornig's special offer of Sept. '33. That would make your subscription extend until February 1935—next month. What is the *last* issue you received from Hornig? I'd advise you to drop him a line anent the matter—or I will. Meanwhile I enclose the issue dedicated to me, plus the Dec. issue with the reprint of my Poe chapter. These need not be returned, since I have duplicates. I also enclose a catalogue of a rather interesting exhibit at the college which my aunt & I have just been to see. The Javanese puppets are of the most grotesque aspect conceivable—much like some of little Barlow's drawings. Another interesting current exhibit—at the art museum—is of 18th century French wall paper—much of which adorned the Georgian homes of colonial America. There was an interesting lecture on this last Sunday.

I continue to read in "Lonely Shores" with interest & appreciation. Regarding your own poetry—don't force matters, but simply write when the mood strikes—meanwhile keeping the bulk of your work well classified for possible book publication. It is possible that young Barlow might want to issue a collection of yours if certain plans of his—relative to printing facilities—materialise.

Yes—as you probably gathered from the youthful delegate—we surely did have a very congenial convocation in New York. It was all Belknap & I could do to stop Bob from spending his return fare on books & pictures— but we finally bundled him on to a Washington coach without too disastrous a trail of indebtedness behind him! He revelled in the Metropolitan Museum, public library, & various bookstalls—& incidentally picked up some enviable bargains. We had several congenial gatherings—at the largest of which 15 were present. The Wandrei brothers were both on hand, & have taken a joint flat in the Greenwich Village section. On one occasion Samuel Loveman shewed us his collection of from 300 to 400 Clark Ashton Smith drawings— which I had seen in 1922 (in Cleveland, before Loveman came to N.Y.), but which were wholly new to Long, Barlow, & the Wandreis. The weather in general was quite favourable—only 2 days being so cold as to give me inconvenience. I returned home Jany. 8, & have since been trying to catch up with the tasks which accumulated during my absence.

Let me thank you exceedingly for the envelopes of cuttings—one of which reached me, through forwarding, in N.Y. Sorry you have trouble getting the paper delivered, & hope a satisfactory scheme can shortly be worked out.

I've just indulged in a rather badly-needed extravagance—bought 2 dark-walnut sets of drawers for filing purposes. My files have been getting almost out of control. Expect delivery today—but haven't quite decided how I'll arrange them. I may pile one atop the other & thus have a single tall cabinet. The total of 10 drawers will do much toward bringing order out of my present chaos. Got the cabinets at a fire sale—$4.44 each. Long recently acquired something similar.

All good wishes—

Yr most ob^t h^ble Servt

H P Lovecraft

[81]   [ALS]

66 College St.,
Providence, R.I.,
Feby. 12, 1935

Dear Miss Toldridge:—

I hasten to acknowledge the batch of delightful poems just received—for which abundant thanks—& to make a suggestion or two in time for embodiment or adaptation (in case of acceptability) in whatever copies you send for publication.

All of the verses are really splendid—especially "The Queer New Slant", "Death Lifts the Gates", & "Spangled Dark". Most of them need no changes whatsoever, but there are three places where I think a slight touch or two might be beneficial. In "On Reading Certain Plaints"—in the fourth stanza, a syllable (one-won) is rhymed *with itself* despite the different spelling. This can easily be eliminated if the word *battling* can be spared—as I think it can because of the idea of *war* so implicit in the preceding stanza (conquer . . . drum or fife). Thus line 1 could read:

Warms him, like morning's sun,

The other two suggested changes are in that especially delectable piece— "Spangled Dark." Here the expression "Ought other hour" has a slightly artificial sound—in addition to which there is a slight ambiguity in meaning. That is—is it meant that there is at evening a quiet dower *such as earth can never know at any other hour,* or a quiet dower *which makes it seem as if no other hour had ever existed on earth?* What revision to suggest depends entirely on which your meaning is. Accordingly I am suggesting alterations for either case:

(a)   An evening rim of sky . . . .
          Such quiet flowers————(verb, not noun)
     As earth can never know
          At other hours.

(b)   An evening rim of sky . . . .
          Such quiet dower

> As if earth never know
> Another hour!

The final suggestion touches the last stanza of the same poem. Here the rhyme is out of pattern, as I shall forthwith demonstrate. These short lines are *iambic dimeters*—composed of 2 iambic feet each—as the earlier ones plainly indicate:

> ˘   ‾   ˘   ‾
> So peace/ful—still . . . .
> ˘   ‾   ˘   ‾
> Man's day / is done

Therefore the rhyming syllables must be the final ones of the second foot— that is, the *fourth* syllables of each line if the metre is regular. Well— recognising this, & therefore assuming that *single rhyme* is intended in the last stanza (since the short lines still contain only four syllables), we find the final rhyme to be erroneous—a -*ly* being rhymed *with itself*. Besides, it is usually unwise to rhyme *two secondarily* accented syllables [cheer"-i-*ly´*—drear"-i-*ly´*]. Now as I look at these words, I notice that—accidentally or otherwise— *cheerily* & *drearily* are words which *would* make an acceptable *triple* rhyme *if* they occupied the right metrical *positions* (i.e., of course, with the rhyming or primary [non-identical] syllables as the second syllables of the second feet) in the given lines. But you must realise that they do not now occupy such positions. To make a real triple rhyme, the syllables *cheer* & *drear* would have to form the fourth syllables of the lines, with the identical or "weak" syllables running over . . . so that these lines would have 6 syllables each. Thus:

> But woman's has no end:
> ˘   ‾   ˘   ‾
> And calm | and *cheer* | ily
> Sets she the evening lamp
> ˘   ‾   ˘   ‾
> Or sad | and *drear* | ily?

You can easily appreciate what I mean by looking at pieces of verse where single & double (or triple) rhymes are indiscriminately mixed. Here you will always see that it is the *first* (or accented & non-identical) syllables of the double or triple rhyme which corresponds to the one syllable of the single rhyme—so that when a double or triple rhyme is used the lines containing it always exceed the corresponding singly-rhymed lines in number of syllables. There is no such thing as having the first (& really rhyming) syllables of a double or triple rhyme come earlier in the lines than the metrical place where the syllables of a single rhyme would ordinarily come. If this were done, then the syllables falling where the rhyme ought to be would be *identical*—& therefore no rhyme. Also, the coincidence of sound earlier in the lines would grate harshly. We crave rhymes *where we expect them*, & rather resent them elsewhere. When we come on a double or triple rhyme we expect the first (really rhyming) syllable to fall where the single rhyming syllables have been—with the extra (identical) syllables as a lightly breathed aftermath. This is not the case in the last stanza of "Spangled Dark"—hence the present comment. Here let me quote, as an illustration, a typical bit of double rhyme occurring in the midst of single rhyme. Note that the *first* syllable of the double corresponds to the usual single, & that the double-rhymed lines run over the common syllabic length:

(Beginning of Keats's Endymion)

ᵕ ‒	ᵕ ‒	ᵕ ‒	ᵕ ‒	ᵕ ‒	ᵕ
A thing	of beau	ty is	a joy	for ev	er
Its love	li ness	in creas	es; it	will nev	er
Pass in	to noth	ing ness;	but still	will keep	
A bow	er qui	et for	us, &	a sleep	
Full of	sweet dreams,	& health,	& qui	et breath	ing.
There fore,	on ev´	ry mor	row, we	are wreath	ing
A flow´	ry band	to bind	us to	the earth,	
Spite of	des pon	dence, of	th' inhu	man dearth	

Well—I fancy this point is now clear. To return to "Spangled Dark"— viewing it as a whole, I do not think this poem really ought to have any double rhymes. The wistful, delicate cast of the theme appears to me ideally suited to the single-rhyme plan followed in the earlier stanzas. You can see by scanning the sample of a triple-rhymed last stanza on the preceding page that an ending of this sort is distinctly jarring. Therefore let me suggest something like the following—which carries out the plan of the earlier part:

> But woman's has no end:
>> With spirits high
> Sets she the evening lamp,
>> Or with a sigh?

Of course, you may think of something apter than this—but this gives the general idea. Incidentally—at this writing I am looking out the window into a sunset so mystically glamourous as any which could have inspired the poem . . . . . orange, rose, & *green* all curiously mingled in wavy lines behind a pair of ancient church towers, with a distant needle like [*sic*] steeple (on a hill 2 or 3 miles away) in the far distance. And some of the lights of the lower town are winking on . . . . as my desk light will have to do very shortly if this script is to remain even partly legible!

Later—lights on

I waited to watch the rest of the sunset—utterly magnificent! The rose & green gave place to crimson & orange—one vast sea welling up from the violet horizon. And the evening star blazed over the city's tallest tower. To continue—thanks immensely for the cuttings. Those anent Jamestown & the weather go into my permanent files. Did I mention, by the way, that I have a new addition to my filing facilities—two dark walnut chests of drawers picked up cheaply at a fire sale? Piled one atop the other, they form a single tall cabinet which fits finely into my old-fashioned furnishing scheme without disturbing any previous item. Though new, they are of a plain colonial design which makes them look a couple of centuries old.

Wretched weather hereabouts—the snowstorm of Jany. 23–4 paralysed local traffic for days, & has not yet melted off. Cold days in continuous succession—so that I've been outdoors only on rare occasions. I did, though, manage to attend two of the poetry readings by authors at the college— Susanna Valentine Mitchell (now of Prov.)[1] & Archibald MacLeish (author of "Conquistador"). Both were excellent—& MacLeish comes about as near to a major poet as this hemisphere can now boast. Hope Hornig is straightening out your F F subscription—I dropped him a line about it. Which reminds me—did I send you the amateur paper containing my "Homes & Shrines of Poe"? If not, let me know, & I will do so. Little Barlow, by the way, has just sent me a fine edition of Poe's tales with fantastic illustrations by Harry Clarke.

E. Hoffmann Price has bought a cottage atop a wooded hill near Redwood City California—in sight of the southern part of San Francisco Bay. He has also acquired a marvellous white cat—a mighty hunter who claws gophers out of their holes & brings them for his master to see before devouring them. Price has appropriately named him Nimrod.[2] He simply strayed in one day & shewed an inclination to remain . . . previous history unknown!

Again, congratulations on the excellent poems—& I hope the accompanying suggestions are helpful. ¶ Yr obt Servt
H P Lovecraft

Next day—Feby. 13

This letter was held over because the weather was too cold for an outward venture (sunsets aren't always as warm as they look!), & I am now in receipt of yours of yesterday—with the two splendid additional poems. "I Am Kin to the Stars" is exquisite & elusive—& I can't think of any advisable change. "The Unconquerable" is majestic & powerful, & replete with vivid images. Both of these ought to be welcomed appreciatively by suitable publishers.

I'll suggest a few changes, on technical grounds, in "The Unconquerable". Well along on p. 2 there is a line ending in *gain,* with the next line having *Again* at the beginning. This juxtaposition of similar sounds halts the ear a bit, so I would suggest eliminating the *again* altogether & letting all the nouns depend directly on *conquers* in unbroken sequence—inserting *weakness* to replace *again*. Thus the line in question would read:

> Weakness, disloyalty, & biting pain

The next suggestion touches the second line after this. The word *emprise* is accented properly on the *last* syllable—*em-prize'*—hence cannot occupy its present place in the line. I suggest substituting *valour*—or any dissyllable accented on the first syllable. Later—on p. 3—we find a passage where the same rhyme—*ize*—is used twice in immediate succession, & where you have some question-marks regarding certain lines. I would suggest the following version of the whole passage—which removes the repeated rhyme & attends to the debatable points:

> Relentless ambush—source of man's despair,
> That strikes his pride to earth & pins it there;
> That ties him hand & foot, & binds his eyes
> Till ghostly glories only he descries;
> That wraps him in a cloud; that swathes his ears
> To sound—have shadowy anthems of the spheres.

Of course you can probably think of some improvement on this version—but it may form a sort of guide in the right direction. The final suggestion concerns the third line from the end of the poem. There is no verb *to shapen*—*shapen* (= shaped) being merely the past participle of *to shape*. As an alternative—wholly suitable, I think—I would recommend *To fashion*. But these of course are all minor points. The poem is splendid, & I hope it may achieve suitable publication. There is no need of lamenting any lack of "scholarliness" which it may possess. As I have remarked before, erudition really has no place in true poetry. Simplicity & directness are the keynotes of real power & classical form.

Many thanks for the additional cuttings—all of interest. I have three or four family albums (& drawers & boxes full of daguerreotypes & other ancestral pictures), though I don't keep them on the table in Victorian fashion for the delectation of the casual visitor. The cutting about first editions ought to interest our young friend Barlow—since bibliophily is his dominant & outstanding weakness. Glad the F F proved of interest. I think I can complete your set if you'll let me know the last number you received. If you sent a dollar in the summer of 1933 you ought to receive the magazine for *18 months* in accordance with Hornig's special offer of that period. That would make your subscription last until March of this year—next month. I am jogging Hornig's memory on this point. Here is the *January* issue. Have you *September?* I have almost a dozen of that number to spare. The hardest issue to get will be November—dedicated to Clark Ashton Smith—but I can certainly secure you a copy in the end if Hornig himself doesn't "come across". And by the way—let me know if I failed to send *The Californian* with my "Homes & Shrines of Poe". I have several spare copies of that.

Sorry the La Salle is hard to get adjusted to—but I fancy it will seem more homelike as time passes. That patch of western sky ought to be quite a compensation. Too bad the rent is higher—but all landlords are pirates who hold up their victims for as much as they can get! Glad you can get glimpses of the moon. This study has some fine moon-vistas—last week I caught the infinitely thin crescent in the west just after new moon. Last Sunday evening I was all ready to watch the occultation of the Pleiades, but clouds malignly intervened.

Well—again let me congratulate you on the delightful assortment of recent verse—which I am sure others will join with me in praising. Hope the foregoing emendatory suggestions may seem helpful rather than merely pedantic. Glad Little Bobby drops in now & then. A truly brilliant kid! ¶ All good wishes—

　　　　　Yr obt Servt H P L

P.S. I hope the verses will all find appropriate publication . . . . in "Choir Practice", *The Circle,* or some other suitable medium. A poet I knew has placed things in *Spirit.* That might make a good medium.

[P.]P.S. If by any chance your F F subscription was only for 6 months—expiring *last* Spring—I can send you several of last year's earlier issues. I have dozens of some of them.

Notes

1. Susanna Valentine Mitchell, author of the poetry volumes *Journey Taken by a Woman* (1935), *In the Bright April Weather* (1952), and *Make New Banners* (1954). Her *Collected Poems* appeared in 1966.
2. In the Bible, a mighty hunter and king of Shinar who was a great-grandson of Noah.

[82]　　　[ALS]

　　　　　　　　　　　　　　　　　　　　　　　　Feby. 27[, 1935]

Dear Miss Toldridge:—

　　　　　　　　　　I was glad to learn that my comments on the poems proved helpful, & trust that no difficulty will be encountered in deciding on a final form. Regarding exactness of technique—there is no advantage in bending the familiar & naturally evolved rules so long as the system behind them is followed at all. It is perfectly legitimate to experiment in entirely new media; but when one adopts a pattern of definite type, which causes certain usages to be expected, it tends to halt the reader if these usages are capriciously disregarded.

Of course some points of usage are less deeply seated than others. Thus one may sometimes vary the *vowel* sounds in a rhyme (as was commonly done prior to the middle 19th century) without greatly affronting the ear. But certain other points—like the final consonant in a rhyme, or the proper number & location of the accentual beats in a line—are much more basic, & must be heeded lest the reader feel a harshness & disappointing quality in the result. Much recent verse is curiously ineffective because it tries to ride two horses at the same time—to cling to basic traditional patterns in theme, feeling, & major technique, & yet to disregard the lesser niceties of the chosen medium. This is really a great mistake, for when a certain effect is planned & prepared for, it ought to be carried out in a manner harmonious with the preparation. If something more ragged & flexible is wished, an entire medium of less traditional pattern ought to be chosen. Technique ought to be imperceptible—so thoroughly absorbed & unconsciously used by the poet that the reader notices nothing at all about the form. Regarding a rhyme of *cheerily* & *drearily*—it is indeed a very musical one, but must of course come in such a way that the *stress of rhyme* will fall on the *cheer-drear* syllables. In practice, the one dominantly appropriate place for such triple rhymes is *dactylic* verse—verse where one accented syllable is followed by two unaccented ones. Since a triple rhyme *is itself a dactylic foot,* it can be used to end a dactylic line without any "overflow" such as the two unaccented syllables must form when the same rhyme is used in iambic verse. *Two* syllables is really an excessive overflow for any ordinary piece of serious verse—the general effect subtly tending toward the comic. Indeed, in my opinion the triple rhyme in iambic verse is suited only to satire & comedy. In dactylic verse all is different—as witness Hood's famous "Bridge of Sighs"

$$- \; \smile \; - \; \smile \; -$$
—One more un | fortunate
Weary of breath
Rashly im | portunate
Gone to her death[1]

Note that the *rhyme* syllable (-ort) in the long lines corresponds to the rhyme syllable (-eath) in the short lines[;] that is, rhyme-syllable corresponds to rhyme-syllable, irrespective of whether it is at the end of a line or not. We can either take the short lines as a type & call the unaccented syllables (-ŭnăte) an overflow, or take the long lines as a type & say that the short ones have two syllables amputated.

$$- \; \smile \; - \; -$$
One more | unfort . . . .
Wear y | of breath

Thus the *cheerily-drearily* rhyme ought to be in some poem of this general cast—either as a terminal rhyme or as an internal rhyme in specimens of more elaborate & intricate cast. Just as a sample—you might construct something like this—comparing ignorance or delusion to blindness:

> ‾ ˘ ˘ ‾ ˘ ˘
> Sun shining | cheerily,
> Rain falling drearily,
>
> ‾ ˘ ˘ ‾ ˘
> Noontide or night:
> All are the same to him—
> Only a name to him—
> Sunder'd from sight.

———

> ‾ ˘ ˘ ‾ ˘˘
> Chaos & | clarity,
> Likeness, disparity,
>
> ‾ ˘ ˘ ‾
> Fine & u | couth:
> Mix themselves hazily
> When we lag lazily
> Sunder'd from truth.

Anyhow—the point is that a *cheerily-drearily* rhyme ought not to be used in iambic verse (unless comic), & in general ought to be where the emphatic nature of the rhyming syllables (cheer-drear) is sufficiently provided for in the pattern. As to the "other hour" stanza—the possible *ambiguity* was even more of an objection than the quasi-archaic *ought*. I see that the version

> Such quiet flowers
> As earth can never know
> At other hours

is the one intended—& trust that this text, or something equally clear, will be decided on. Regarding "The Unconquerable"—the primary objection to the word *shapen* was not its archaism but its use in an erroneous way. *Shapen* is a *past participle*—& never was anything else. The expression *to shapen* or *I shapen* or *we shapen never was* possible. One can say that a figure *is shapen*, but not that a man can *shapen* a figure. It is just like the case of *do* & *done*. We try *to do* (not *to done*) a thing; but the thing itself *is done*. The grammatical status of *shapen* & *done* is precisely similar. Participles like *shapen, been, done, gone,* &c. are all in the same class. Probably it was the resemblance of the form to *sharpen* which caused the slip—but this of course is a false parallel. As you realise, *sharpen* is *another sort* of a word—with *sharpened* as a past participle. On the other hand, *shapen* is merely the participial form of *shape* . . . I *shape, to shape,* &c. In this especial line, the word *fashion* is probably about as good as any. As for another verb to replace *conquer*—transitive, & of 2 syllables with the accent on the first—the only one I can think of at the moment is *master.* However, there is such a thing as intentional rhetorical repetition; & I am not sure but that the reiteration of *conquer* has its advantages. Concerning the lines I re-cast—it is perfectly all right to use them. Literature is full of parallel cases—many lines of Goldsmith's "Deserted Village" were retouched or supplied by Dr. Johnson, while in the autumn sections of Thomson's "Seasons" there is an entire 12-line passage interpolated by Pope. And in Pope's own translation of the Odyssey whole books were supplied by Broome & Fenton.[2]

Glad you found the F F enjoyable. Under separate cover I am sending the Sept. & Nov. issues—which ought to complete your file. If any issues are still lacking, let me know—for I think I can supply any of the recent ones except July. I have an almost comical surplus of June issues. I am also sending the paper with my Poe house article—plus an art museum bulletin which I think will interest you. This month there was a splendid lecture & special exhibition pertaining to my favourite Hokusai, & the entire quarterly bulletin was devoted to the subject of Japanese prints. The article was so fine, & the illustrations so graphic, that I could not resist getting several extra copies to send to especially appreciative persons. Note *one* mistake—on p. 19, with illus. on p. 22—where a *Hokusai* fan print of hibiscus flowers is erroneously attributed to *Hiroshige.* I wouldn't have spotted this if I had not seen the original prints & their authentic labels in the museum. Another lecture at the School of Design was on contemporary art in Soviet Russia—with abundant lantern-slides. It seems that the Russians are doing better than they are commonly thought to be doing—& producing some fine work in spite of their theories that art should be subordinated to some social purpose. Oddly enough, they are far freer from freakish & decadent tendencies than are the modern (or "modernistic") artists of the western world.

I hope your adjustment to the La Salle may gradually become more & more comfortable. If I were you I'd have all the chair-cushions I wanted, regardless of possible guests. I don't pretend to keep my study immaculate for company. Papers & books have to be scattered about, & those who come to see me have to take the place as they find it. Glad you have had such resplendent sunsets. Only one recent sunset here has quite equalled all the splendours you describe.

Thanks immensely for the cuttings. Thomas R. Henry's column is absolutely the best account of scientific progress for the average reader that I've seen anywhere. I was interested in the note on the Julian Hawthorne novel,[3] which I've vainly tried to locate at various times. Another fascinating thing was the account of the new Maya discoveries.

A few days ago I had a letter from Loring & Mussey of N.Y. asking to see some of my stuff with a view to possible book publication. Since this is the 5th time I have received such a request, with no tangible results to date, I'm not as naively excited about the matter as I might otherwise be. However—just to leave no stone unturned, I sent them a fairly representative array of MSS.

There are four coal-black little brothers of the late Samuel Perkins at the boarding-house across the garden—13 days old. I fervently hope at least one will be retained! ¶ Glad Barlow gets around now & then, & hope he'll keep a wise watch on his health. ¶ I'll hasten to get this mailed in order to have all the poetry comment on record. Best wishes—

Y^r most obt Servt

H P Lovecraft

[P.S. on envelope:] Rumour has just arrived that the F F has failed!

Notes

1. Thomas Hood the Elder (1799–1845), "The Bridge of Sighs" (1844), ll. 1–4.
2. HPL refers to the British poets William Broome (1689–1745) and Elijah Fenton (1683–1730).
3. Evidently a novel by Julian Hawthorne (1846–1934). Several of his novels have elements of weirdness—including *Archibald Malmaison* (1879) and *The Professor's Sister* (1888)—so HPL could be referring to one of these.

[83]   [ALS]

66 College St.,

Providence, R.I.

March 25, 1935.

Dear Miss Toldridge:—

Sorry to hear there is so much difficulty in getting things mailed, & trust an improved system may ultimately be devised. I was sorry, too, to read of good old Justice Holmes's death—for I had hoped he would round out a century & more after being freed from judicial cares. It makes me feel my own years to realise that he was the *son* of the original O. W. H. . . . . whom I might have recalled had my memory been more acute in 1893.[1] The funeral must have been impressive—& deservedly so, since Justice Holmes was really a great figure in his own right, no matter how much his father's fame may have eclipsed him in popular consciousness. In a changing era he was one of the very first to perceive the reality & far-reaching ramifications of the change—at a time when lesser men were blindly clinging to externals which his keen mind recognised as obsolescent. It is gratifying to reflect that he lived to see his own liberal philosophy become dominant in the nation—so that today his side of a court decision would be more likely to be a majority than a dissenting verdict. What a pageant of history he lived through—his first memories of the white-steepled, classic-columned Poe period of the 1840's, with the tension of the civil war issues increasing—then the war itself, with himself in an active role—then the flamboyant, decadent "flash age" of the '70s, with parvenu grotesqueness & extravagance rampant, & with private capitalism laying the foundations of the present crash—then the precieuse, mincing '80's, the "daring" [']90's & the Spanish War, & the smug, hopeful Theodore Roosevelt era of reform & expansion—then the world war & its hectic aftermath, with changing standards & folkways—& finally the smashup & the first experimental steps toward recovery & a saner order. All in one lifetime! Yet many have lived longer without seeing a millionth as much change. It is the *period* more than the individual span—for even young people today have outlived the world they were born in. Little Bobby Barlow, for all his scant 16 years, can remember a world & a phase of civilisation—the feverish, thoughtless, reckless age of the 1920's—which is today as dead as Tyre & Babylon!

Glad the various things I sent were of interest. Is your F F file now complete up to January? As I said in an exterior postscript, the little magazine has found it impossible to continue, so that the February issue is the last. I'm enclosing a copy of that farewell number herewith. Evidently my Sup. Hor. in Lit. will never be completed! Some of the features of the F F will be taken over by a similar publication called *Fantasy Magazine*—in which a biographical sketch & portrait of me will appear in April.[2]

I thought that Japanese print bulletin especially delightful—you may recall that Hokusai's "Cranes on Snow-Laden Pine" was one of the things I especially liked in the exhibition last December. I was glad to get so good a reproduction of it. Another captivating print is the one of the cat watching the butterflies—which reminds me that the local feline family is now narrowed down to the mother & *one* coal-black kitten . . . a delectable duplicate of the lamented Sam Perkins. He's going to be a spirited little imp—he *hisses* manfully if a finger is poked too familiarly at him! I am calling him John Perkins—though perhaps his real owners will apply some other name to him. He'll make a good member for the Kappa Alpha Tau—which reminds me that the elders of that society have begun to sun themselves on the clubhouse roof in encouragingly vernal fashion. I had a long conversation with the tiger vice-president the other day!

Many thanks for the interesting cuttings—the sunset item is especially interesting. I have seen some fine sunsets of late—with Venus & the thin crescent moon adding charm during the early March evenings. My outing season of 1935 is already under way—unusually early for me. March 2–3 I had a very interesting visitor—the 22-year-old son of an old friend of mine in Milwaukee. The young man—Robert Ellis Moe—graduated from the U. of Wis. with high honours in electrical engineering in 1933, & stepped at once into a good position with the Gen. Elec. Co. Lately he was transferred to Bridgeport, Conn.—which puts him within a cruising radius of Providence (130 m) & New York (60 m). I had not seen him before since he was 11—& he certainly has grown. He came in his car, & I shewed him all the colonial sights of Providence & of the quaint little seaports down both sides of Narragansett Bay—Warren & Bristol on the east shore, East Greenwich & Wickford on the west shore. The weather was very favourable, & I certainly welcomed the sight of the countryside after so long an hibernation. My guest seemed very appreciative, & expects to come again. My first *pedestrian* outing occurred March 6, when the temperature went up to *65°*. On this occasion I took a 12-mile walk in the countryside north of Providence, & felt much the better for it. A later excursion—March 9, when a relative took my aunt & me to ride—extended through the terrain east of Providence, just across the line in Massachusetts. We had some excellent vistas of woods & fields & village spires, & could feel the atmosphere of coming spring on every hand.

The other night I saw a very interesting illustrated lecture on the recently uncovered 9th & 10th century mosaics in the great church of St. Sophia in Constantinople—by Thomas Whittemore, who had charge of the uncovering.[3] Now that the building has been wisely transformed to a museum, the modern trappings are being cleared away—leaving it as it was in its prime. This edifice has always fascinated me—a product of Rome's final decay (A.D. 532–8), yet embodying the majority of Roman design in one titanic swan-song. It has, of course, the subtle Oriental touches which had begun to develop as Byzantine architecture—& these mosaics, installed 300 to 400 years later, are utterly Byzantine in their technique. The building is one of the best preserved of all the large structures which have come down from the edge of classical antiquity. When it was erected, Latin was still the language of Western Europe & North Africa, & the Roman people had not yet begun to realise that the occidental half of the Empire had irrevocably fallen. Justinianus brought the Eastern Empire to its apex of power—even reconquering Italy for the time being. People in that age must have felt somewhat like people today—with impending change in the air—yet nothing really radical happened. It was over a century before the Moslem wave swept the Mediterranean littoral, & 400 years before the lowest point of the Dark Ages was reached.

I've just picked up a book which I highly recommend to anyone with a couple of dollars to spare—the new one-volume Modern Encyclopaedia, revised to 1935 & published by Grosset & Dunlap for $1.95. It is sold at all the Liggett Drug Stores & elsewhere. Marvellously comprehensive—& with all the *new* material not to be found in any other volume of the sort. I've needed such a thing for ages—my newest other encyclopaedia being of 1914. This one includes things as late as last September. In getting the book, be sure to select a perfect copy—it is of course cheaply printed, & some of the copies have slight defects. I exchanged my first one. My present one has a crease or two, but I am keeping it because any other would probably be no better. The original edition came out in 1933 at $3.50, & was quite widely advertised.

Excellent lecture March 11 at the college by Prof. W. F. G. Swann of the Franklin Institute—on the cosmic rays.[4] With the aid of slides & instruments, the speaker gave a rather clearer idea of the latest aspects of the subject than I had ever had before.

Glad *Marvel Tales* safely arrived. The format is much improved, though the contents are mediocre. My "Sarnath" is an old piece—1919—& is badly misprinted. By the way—there is a new semi-professional magazine called *The Galleon,* published by L. A. Eshbach, 1337 Good St., Reading, Pa., which has a very high standard & would welcome poetical contributions. No remuneration, however. The editor used to be with *Marvel Tales.*

Your "Half Minute Flights" are all exceedingly graceful, & certainly ought to be acceptable to some paper or other. Hope you'll come across an appropriate place for them—they would go well in either a daily or a weekly. Yes—I made up those lines illustrative of the use of triple rhyme in dactylic verse.

Glad Barlow is finding his art course helpful & enjoyable. His bookbinding lessons must be pretty advanced, since he has long been highly skilled in that art. Existing specimens of his work have a quite professional look. I've seldom encountered a brighter or more promising boy, & I certainly hope he'll be careful of his eyesight & general health. As a Floridan, he ought to be interested in the ending of the century-long Seminole war mentioned in one of the cuttings! It certainly does make history doubly vivid to encounter such a tangible link with the past! I have seen the grave of Osceola at Ft. Moultrie, Charleston—& the cell in Ft. Marion, St. Augustine, where he was first imprisoned. Also the Dade monument in St. Augustine.

Those cuttings anent juvenile "literature" are going into my permanent files of Americana. Which reminds me that I have just extended the system of cabinets whose beginning I described in January. My new acquisition consists of *six* small cabinets of a kind just on the market—papier-maché with wood frame, in imitation brown grained wood finish. Each $22 \times 13 \times 9\frac{1}{2}$" in size, & having four drawers, each $12 \times 8\frac{1}{4} \times 4\frac{3}{4}$". I got them at a special sale for only a dollar each, & they have proved a marvellous help in disposing of odd piles of pamphlets & envelopes of cuttings. They are so small that they can be tucked neatly in various corners without disturbing the general furnishing scheme in the least. I think they were intended to be *shoe-boxes*—but this humble purpose does not make them any the less valuable in my eyes.

Now as to the "Foundations" contest—in which I hope you'll have the very best of luck—I will hasten to make such comments as I can upon your delightfully graceful entry. It seems to me thoroughly excellent, & ought to stand a good chance of winning. My few suggestions have to do mainly with the earlier lines of the poem.

First, a *tower* with *roots* is undeniably a mixed metaphor. Could you not sacrifice the root idea & change *roots* to *base* in line 2?

Second, the syntax in l. 4 is a trifle elliptical & confusing: "(naught) . . . shall shake, nor it be brought". Could you not change the line to read as follows".

> "_ – —————naught
> Can make it sway, nor can its walls be brought"

Third, the language in lines 5 & 6 tend toward a slight cumbrousness. Could not the following be substituted?

> "To nothingness . . . being built on rock beneath,
> And pois'd as firm as any brow-borne wreath."

It seems especially desirable to change from *light* to *firm,* since a thing *lightly* resting may easily be blown away. Of course, these are only suggestions, & you may think of another version better than any of the previous ones.

The *fourth* point I would tend to bring up is very trivial & debatable—a mere matter of smooth flow, in which there may be excellent arguments on the other side. This is in line 15, where I would substitute *sources* for *beginning.*

I trust that at least one or two of these suggestions may prove helpful, & that this bulletin may reach you in due season. Barring accidents, it will be mailed Monday the 25th, reaching you the following day. As before stated, I think the poem is truly excellent, & certainly hope it will meet with good fortune in the contest.

Well—I will close in haste to ensure early mailing. With all good wishes, I remain

Yr most oblig'd & ob^t Servt

H P Lovecraft

Notes

1. Justice Oliver Wendell Holmes, Jr. (b. 1841), an Associate Justice of the Supreme Court, died on 6 March 1935. He was the son of the poet and man of letters Oliver Wendell Holmes, Sr. (1809–1894). HPL was told that Holmes had dandled the two-year-old Lovecraft on his knee when he was visiting his friend, the poet Louise Imogen Guiney, in the winter of 1892–93.

2. F. Lee Baldwin, "H. P. Lovecraft: A Biographical Sketch," *Fantasy Magazine* 4, No. 5 (April 1935): 108–10, 132. The first page contains a linoleum cut of HPL by Duane W. Rimel. "Supernatural Horror in Literature" was to be continued in Willis Conover's *Science-Fantasy Correspondent,* but ultimately was not.

3. Thomas Whittemore (1871–1950), American archaeologist who devoted himself chiefly to Byzantine and Coptic art.

4. William Francis Gray Swann (1884–1962), British physicist and director of the Franklin Institute (1927–59).

[84]   [ALS]

66 College St.,
Providence, R.I.,
April 22, 1935.

Dear Miss Toldridge:—

Glad my suggestions regarding "Foundations" proved useful. The new version which you so kindly enclosed is by far the best yet—indeed, I don't see how it could well be improved upon. The improvement over the preceding versions is really spectacular—& it seems to me that the poem ought to stand an excellent chance of a prize in any contest to which it is submitted. Here's wishing it the best of luck!

Regarding the late lamented F F—if you will send me a list of all the issues you have, I think I can complete your file. The first was *Sept. 1933,* & no month was skipped. If you did not receive all the issues for which you subscribed, Editor Hornig must be made to supply the missing ones. Look carefully & see if you can't find the *December* issue (1934)—which I *seem* to recall sending you. That was the issue devoted to *Poe.* Or is it the *Dec. 1933* issue which you lack? In any case, let me know the ones you *have*—& I think I can unearth the others somehow. The discontinuance of the magazine was a great disappointment to all devotees of weird fiction—for humble though it was, it filled an unique special want. My Sup. Horror in Lit. was published complete in 1927 in W. Paul Cook's *Recluse.* Did I not send you a copy of that? If not, I will lend one later. The present serial reprinting contains several changes of text—bringing the facts down to date. Many important weird books have been published—or discovered by me—since the original printing 8 years ago.

Little John Perkins continues to prosper, & bids fair to develop into a redoubtable warrior. He is a diminutive streak of furry black lightning, & will certainly be a very frequent & welcome guest at #66 during the months (& I hope years!) to come.

Yes—transitional periods are always hard to go through . . . because new conditions have to be met by repeated experimentation, trial, & error, & because so many people retain from the past a hampering body of prejudices, standards, & psychological attitudes which are meaningless & even dangerous in the light of present necessities. However, so far as the Anglo-Saxon world is concerned, I think there is no likelihood of any such explosion as Russia's—or even any such eccentric regime as Germany's. The struggle is developing about as one might have predicted. It is being demonstrated that stronger remedies are needed—but the ice has already been broken for their non-violent adoption in successive stages. If the blind & fatuous Hoover Republicans had hung on, there would have been no precedent for National change. No public relief, no intelligent coördination of industries, no rescue from financial panic & violent revolution. Now, however, the machinery is limbered up, & the government knows it must band in the direction of public need. The constant application of irritants like Huey Long & Father Coughlin is really a good sign—a sign of adherence to legal methods instead of violence. While it is unlikely that the plans of either of these agitators would work, the pressure they exert performs a valuable function in forcing the government to consider some radical *but workable* step. That step, of course, is the public operation (& probably ownership in the end) of the larger industries & utilities. Only by public control—with its policy of non-profit operation for service only—of industry, can the massed resources of the nation be sufficiently released to permit of the rational redistribution which the overwhelming mass of the people insistently—& rightly—demand. All this, of course, is much further than the present administration is now willing to go—but this administration will be likely to respond to pressure better than its insanely bigoted predecessor ever could have done. The elections of 1936 will be very tense & important—& if the Democrats are wise, they will move sharply toward the left in order to retain what otherwise may be a third-party vote. There will, of course, be unpleasantness. Old-time "let 'em starve" conservatives will howl, & large-scale private business will create as much trouble as it can. But these influences no longer have the power they once had. A steady trend toward rational socialistic planning may be expected, & only some unforeseen obstacle would be likely to release any violent or culturally subversive forces. The most that may be expected in the direction of a revolution is some vigorous coup d'etat like Mussolini's march on Rome in 1922, or the Spanish overturn of 1931. And even this sort of thing is less probable than a "revolution" of ballots only, such as that which seated the Nazis in 1933. Nor need it be even as much as that if the present administration will break further with capitalism & continue in the bold pioneering course of its first half. The fact is, that no important element in America or England *wants* any major upsetting of the general ways of life. All that any responsible person wants is a restoration of the virtual certainty that a livelihood can be obtained in exchange for services. The desired adjustment is *purely economic*—not cultural. Such changes in culture-values as would eventually result from the needed shift would be very slow & subtle—& in an *unqualifiedly desirable* direction . . . i.e., a direction of lessened emphasis on property & wealth & acquisitive ability, & greater emphasis on personal excellence. The major evils of the newer age will probably be those common to all new ages—clumsiness, inexperience, & inefficiency. These must be expected until a new industrial-economic-governmental technique can be worked out & established as part of the national folkways. Naturally this means a tedious & gruelling period ahead—but one ought to be thankful that no worse need be expected. When one reflects on the horrors of violent revolutions, one can appreciate the good luck of a nation likely to get off with mere *discomfort*. The present age, it seems to me, is most distinctly *not* one of "peril" or "menace" or "cataclysm", as some loose-mouthed sensationalists insist. It is, rather, one of *discomfort, bother, hardship, fumbling, bewilderment, disappointment, stagnation, & slow transition.* It is much more like the gradual readjustment of the Western World after Rome's fall than like the destruction of Babylonia before the Persian hosts, or the extinction of classic culture in North Africa by the Moslems in the 7th century.

I surely hope that you may be able to arrive at some satisfactory & permanent housing arrangement—too bad you missed the chance for that lower-priced apartment. That hold-up in the La Salle must have seemed rather exciting when you read of it—but in view of his small pickings, I fancy the bandit will seek richer fields hereafter! Trust Barlow will be around with usual frequency in future—he certainly does crowd himself with manifold activities, even though he has resigned the (non-paying) photographic job.

About Osceola—what he has in St. Augustine is not a *monument,* but a life-size wax figure in the museum section of the old fort where he was imprisoned. The nearest thing to a monument is the tablet at his grave at Ft. Moultrie in Charleston. The monument I spoke of in St. Augustine is to the American soldiers massacred during the Seminole war—a low pyramid in the military cemetery. I wish I could get down to those regions this year, but am rather doubtful about the possibility.

Thanks as usual for the interesting array of cuttings—including the 3d. article of the juvenile literature series. I now have 3 articles—the *first* (in an issue whose despatches are dated Mar. 16), the *third,* & the *concluding* (in an issue with items dated March 20). Nowhere does it say how many articles the series was to contain—but it could not have been long. Five at the very most. Don't think of bothering to unearth the missing numbers! The account of the restoration of the old Warren house is fascinating, & I wish I could see it sometime. The historic old manor-houses & churches of the south are rather hard to get at if one has no private transportation facilities, since they tend to be rural & isolated. The return of the house on the Eastern Shore is interesting to note. A youth of my acquaintance[1] lived for some time in Salisbury, Md., & is very familiar with the territory. Extremely glad of the article on Robert Mills—whose work in Charleston & elsewhere I have always admired. He is undoubtedly one of the greatest of all the American classic-revival architects.

The Easter cards are extremely appealing—& your rhymes are both highly graceful, clever, & appropriate. Thanks enormously—my aunt was quite captivated by them, & is using them with vast appreciation. I note with interest that one of them was printed in Providence.

Finally, let me thank you tremendously for the copy of the anthology with your extremely graceful & effective "Prayer". It pleases me vastly to have the lines in this neat & ample setting—though you ought not to have been so generous with a thing as presumably costly as the book. As yet I have only cursorily scanned the other contributions, but seem to find a number of excellent things (besides some more mediocre material) & several familiar names. The format of the book is gratifyingly tasteful, & I believe you are to be congratulated on having your work represented therein. Again—abundant thanks! ¶ With best wishes—

Your most oblig'd & ob^t Servt

H P Lovecraft

[P.S.] Interested to note the sale of the Macdonald paintings—though sorry the family is obliged to part with them. ¶ That magazine—*The Galleon*—to which I recommended your sending verses has just taken 2 of my "Fungi from Yuggoth" & an old prose fantasy called "The Quest of Iranon."[2]

Notes

1. J. Vernon Shea.
2. The *Galleon* took "Background" and "Harbour Whistles" but published only "Background."

[85]   [ALS]

66 College St.,

Providence, R.I.

June 2, 1935.

Dear Miss Toldridge:—

Let me acknowledge with gratitude yours of May 20—& the previous note of April 23—laden with interesting enclosures. I was especially glad of the picture of Gadsby's Tavern—which I have seen many times in Alexandria, & the ball-room woodwork of which is preserved in the Metropolitan Museum of N.Y. Thanks, too, for "Choir Practice" with your delightful little poem "Forsythia". I have been very grateful to forsythias this "spring" for letting me know that winter is at least technically over! But for them—& now, for the tardy & reluctant verdure—I would be inclined to doubt the advent of the nominally vernal season! I note with interest the review of my friend Parker's anthology.[1]

Glad little Barlow continues to drop in, & sorry he'll have to be leaving soon. Yes—he is urging Grandpa to attempt another De Land visit, & I shall accept with pleasure if I can find any way of financing it. I shall, however, be obliged to forego most of the intermediate stops—most of which mean at least one night's hotel bill. I may (if I can go at all) shoot directly down, & make the few stops I can (St. Augustine, Charleston, Washington, Philadelphia) on the return trip. I surely expect the pleasure of at least one call at The La Salle—or its successor, if you find better quarters between now & the time in question. Regarding quarters—have you thought of ancient Georgetown? That is the place I'd try for above all others if I had occasion to live in Washington. Perhaps, though, the rent in all of its desirable neighbourhoods is high. Miss Radcliffe might be able to give you some idea of prices & conditions.

Under separate cover I am sending the Nov. F F, which you mentioned lacking. If you will—after a final inventory—let me have a list of *all* the numbers in your files, I'll see how well I can complete the set. I'll lend the *Recluse* as soon as my copy is returned. Don't worry about the juvenile literature cuttings—there are so many excellent features of the sort that one series can well be endured in incomplete form! The *Galleon* with my sonnet "Background" came some time ago. My prose sketch "The Quest of Iranon" (1921) will appear in the next issue.

Sorry the prize in that contest was so (apparently) capriciously bestowed. Appraising verse is a delicate business, & I suppose all verdicts are condensed in some quarter or other. I've just had to serve as a juror in two poetry contests, & in one case it was ticklish work estimating 2nd & 3d choices. Oddly—in both of these cases the *best* poem was unmistakable . . . so plainly superior that I presume all the jurors will agree. Glad Barlow is helping you get verse typed. He seems to rattle the keys partly by touch, so I doubt whether the process hurts his eyes.

As for politics, economics, & sociology—I fancy that in Washington (as, for other reasons, in N.Y. City) one gets somewhat overemphasised pictures of existing twists & future crises. One is in the midst of legislation & debate—the struggles of partisans, the turmoil of special interests, & the ramifications of rumour—& thus hears extreme estimates & oratorical prophecies which exaggerate the magnitude of coming changes. Actually, I don't think any violent European system like bolshevism or Nazism has even a chance to get started. No substantial group in England or America either want what such systems offer, or believe the assumptions on which they are based. Changes will come— but in America they will come from native & agricultural sources rather than from the European radicals of our eastern cities. The northwest—Olsen in Minnesota & the La Follettes in Wisconsin[2]—is worth studying as a possible source of American political & economic development. Here we see the problems of a mechanised nation discussed by people of essentially the same sort as those who established the national tradition centuries ago—cautious farmers, villagers, & small-town men of north-European Aryan ancestry & settled institutions. They know as well as the swarthy-faced Jewish & Italian agitators of the east that the old laissez-faire system can't last—but unlike those swarthy aliens, they have no sympathy with schemes which would destroy their familiar adjustment (an adjustment essentially akin to that of all old-Americans) to the general customs of the past. And of course it is clear that these native Nordic liberals vastly outnumber the hook-nosed & olive-skinned Marxists of the Eastern seaboard. Northwestern Farmer-Labour elements, Wisconsin Progressives, Corn-Belt followers of Milo Reno,[3] California experimenters, Coughlinites, & even Huey Long partisans are all regular Americans with regular American wishes regarding the future. They may be ignorant & inept, & may do some fearful bungling before they force the reluctant plutocrats to yield to the necessary extent; but not for a moment would they sanction the aesthetic heritage destruction preached by the bolshevik fringe. With this element active & increasingly well-organised, one has very little of a cataclysmic nature to fear from the popular so-called "radicalism" of America. Things may become rather inconvenient for the wealthy commercialist—but that isn't much to worry over as compared with the extremes found in Europe & Asia. If little things are symbols of larger attitudes, a significant story is conveyed by the sartorial habits of victorious radicals in Russia & England or America. In Russia the leaders cry out not only against the *economics* of aristocracy but against its very *costume*. Thus Stalin & other executives wear workmen's blouses on all occasions. In England, on the other hand, a Labourite elected to Parliament generally adopts the top hat & morning coat of his elder colleagues from the gentry. We have an instinct of the *continuity of custom* which central & western Europeans lack. Even Huey Long—despite some weird extremes of sportiness—at least keeps shaved & wears clean collars!

The present so-called "spring" is surely one of the tardiest I can remember—& yet I had one good two-day outing a month ago, when genial weather felicitously coincided with a visiting & exploring session. The occasion was that of the second visit of young Robert Moe—whose early March visit I described in a previous letter. As before, he came in his 1928 Ford—& once more we managed to keep that vehicle busy.

The guest arrived on the morning of Saturday April 27, & we at once started out to visit venerable Newport. We went by way of Fall River to avoid the heavy tolls of the Mt. Hope Bridge, & followed the east road down the island of Aquidneck to our destination. En route we stopped to photograph a highly idyllic scene—an ancient windmill atop a grassy knoll, with farm buildings, stone walls, & a flock of sheep near by. I enclose a print. Before entering the city proper we visited "Whitehall" (1724), where the famous philosopher Berkeley lived during his brief but memorable new world sojourn. Also saw the Hanging Rocks where Berkeley used to sit reading, writing, or meditating—& the great rock cliffs called "Purgatory", where the sea pounds thunderously in. Entering Newport on the side opposite to that encountered in a boat trip, we visited the great cliffs & descended the celebrated "40 steps" to the water. Then—at last—the ancient town—with 1698 Quaker Meetinghouse, 1726 Anglican church, 1739 Colony-house, 1749 library, 1760 Market house, 1763 Jews' Synagogue, & private dwellings as old as 1675. It was a glorious hot day—up to 82° in Providence, though not quite so good in Newport. On the return trip—made over the west road in the twilight—we saw the ancient Overing house, where in 1777 a small rowboat party of rebels made a prisoner of Genl. Prescott of His Majesty's regulars. Also saw another of the ancient windmills for which the island is famous. It is the lack of vigorous water-power which made flat lands like Holland, Nantucket, Cape Cod,

Long Island, & this island of Aquidneck or Rhode Island (from which the whole colony eventually took its name) take so completely to windmills.

Sunday the 28th we went to ancient New Bedford—Nantucket's successor as the world's great whaling centre, whose last lone exemplar of the industry put to sea only 11 or 12 years ago. The marine museum was closed—but after a tour of Johnnycake Hill (with the Seaman's Bethel & Mariner's Home mentioned in "Moby Dick") & the centuried waterfronts we set off southward to sample something still better. This was the Round Hills estate of Col. E. H. R. Green (son of the celebrated financier & miser Hetty Green) in South Dartmouth, where the old whaling barque *Charles W. Morgan* (built 1841) is preserved at a realistic-looking wharf—but solidly embedded in concrete as a permanent exhibit. We went all over the vessel—which is tremendously fascinating—& snapped some pictures of it. That is, Moe snapped several, & I snapped one. I enclose a print of the latter. Also on the Green estate is an ancient windmill moved from Rhode-Island. We then explored a region—where southern Mass. adjoins southeastern R.I.—which I had never seen before in my life. Splendid unspoiled countryside with rambling stone walls & idyllic white-steepled villages of the old New England type. Of the latter the two best specimens—Adamsville & Little Compton Commons—are both in Rhode Island. Adamsville contains the world's only known monument to a *hen*—perpetuating the fame of the Rhode Island Red, a breed evolved in that village from East Indian & Chinese gallinaceous forbears. At Little Compton Commons can be found the home & grave of Elizabeth Alden Pabodie—daughter of the famed John Alden & Priscilla Mullins of Plymouth, & first white woman born in New England. This region was once the seat of the Sakonnet Indians—whose squaw-sachem Awashanks was persuaded by the noted old warrior Capt. Benjamin Church not to join King Philip's conspiracy in 1675. It was settled from Plymouth around 1673, & (like Barrington, Warren, & Bristol) came into the Massachusetts-Bay in 1691 & into Rhode-Island (where a boundary dispute was settled by H. M. George II) in 1747. Capt. Church lies buried not far from Little Compton Commons. Well—at last we turned north through Tiverton, where on our left we had some marvellous vistas of low-lying fields & blue water. Here we passed the home of the navigator Capt. Robert Gray, who in 1792 discovered the Columbia River in the far-off Oregon country—naming it after his staunch Rhode-Island brig. Then back home via Fall River (an ugly mill city across the line in Massachusetts) & ancient Warren . . . at which latter place we paused at the famous Maxfield's (a rendezvous of Morton, Cook, & other visitors of mine) for a dinner consisting entirely of ice cream—a pint & a half each. (6 varieties—Moe: chocolate, coffee, caramel, banana, pistachio, ginger. HPL: chocolate, coffee, caramel, banana, lemon, strawberry.) Finally back to #66—after which I regretfully guided the guest out of town on his way to Bridgeport, & took a 4-mile rural & suburban walk before returning home. Quite a session, all in all! I am enclosing the principal snap shots which I took during the proceedings. You may keep them if they are of any permanent interest.

The next week-end—May 3–4–5—I visited Edward H. Cole in the Boston zone, but cold weather seriously interfered with our sightseeing. We did, however, explore many byways of ancient & perennially fascinating Marblehead. That forms the entire list of major outings to date. This is no climate for outdoor life!

Cook may go to St. Louis to investigate a possible printing situation—but he is also considering one in Weston, Vermont. Neither prospect is very promising.

Have just learned with sorrow that *another* row of ancient buildings in this vicinity is about to feel the vandal's hand. You probably recall my rage at the destruction of the S. Water St. warehouses (1816) in 1929. This time the scene of devastation is College St. itself—the doomed row being that huddle of quaint houses & archways reaching from Benefit St. downward to the foot of the hill—on the same (north) side as the court leading to #66, but beginning ¾ of a block lower down. Included in the cataclysm are the houses of the first president of Brown (1771), a fine 1750 specimen, & one of those rare old archways leading under parts of a building to inner courtyards . . . . of which the only perfect survivors in America are those on Providence's ancient hill. (There is a bricked-up specimen in Richmond, & a boarded up specimen in Philadelphia) On the site will ascend the new main building of the R.I. School of Design. Two palliating & consoling factors exist: (a) the preservation, restoration, & incorporation in the new building of the bottom (& only brick) house of the ancient row—the old Franklin House, with its quaint inn-yard archway. Thus the survival of *one* of the archways is assured. And (b) the choice of a splendid Providence-Georgian design for the new edifice. The structure's lower units will harmonise with the surviving Franklin House, while the upper units will blend in pattern with the residential buildings higher up in the hill. One part will even have a "monitor roof" like #66—a form especially typical of Providence in the 1790–1810 period. The  architect is F. Ellis Jackson, who also designed the new Providence-Georgian court house (1928–1933) across the street from the proposed structure. The change is regrettable, yet it is fortunate that the character of the new building will be the same. Obviously, Providence is remaining dominantly true to its traditional Georgian heritage, & avoiding the "modernistic" epidemic from which even Boston is not quite immune.

On May 25 I had an interesting visit from young Charles D. Hornig, erstwhile editor of the *Fantasy Fan*. He is a very prepossessing youth—pleasant & intelligent—& seemed to appreciate the archaic charm of venerable Providence. I shewed him most of the historic high spots—including the hidden churchyard on the ancient hill, which I have probably described in previous epistles.

With all good wishes—
Yrs most cordially & sincerely—
H P Lovecraft

Notes

1. *Threads in Tapestry: An Anthology of Verse,* compiled and edited by Rachel Hall, Marcia A. Taylor, and Charles A. A. Parker (Medford, MA: Charles A. A. Parker, 1934f.). The anthology was published in two annual volumes (1934 and 1935); either the 1934 or the 1935 volume was being reviewed at this time.
2. Floyd B. Olsen (1891–1936), governor of Minnesota (1931–36), belonging to the Farmer-Labor party; Robert M. La Follette (1855–1925), governor (1901–06) and U.S. senator from Wisconsin (1906–25), and his sons, Robert M. La Follette, Jr. (1895–1953), U.S. senator from Wisconsin (1925–47), and Philip La Follette (1897–1965), governor of Wisconsin (1931–33, 1935–39), all from the Progressive party.
3. Milo Reno, agrarian radical, president of the National Farm Holiday Association.

[86]   [ALS]

c/o Barlow, Box 88,
De Land, Florida.
July 9, 1935.

Dear Miss Toldridge:—

I am indeed grateful for yours of July 1st, with its plenitude of interesting enclosures. The percentage of important material in those cuttings is gratifyingly high—such things as the blood classification of mummies, the evolution of birds, the doomed tavern (alas!) at New Market, the frigate in the York River, & the prehistoric Kentucky mines being especially absorbing.

We continue to have a splendid time down here, & I am profiting enormously by the warm climate . . . . feeling prodigiously better than I ever do in the north. Bob's brother Wayne has returned to his duties as 2nd Lieutenant at Ft. Sam Houston, Texas, & his genial presence is missed. There is, however, still plenty to do. Bob's cabin across the lake is virtually finished, & last week I cut a roadway from the landing to the cabinward path. This edifice is ideally located in a picturesque oak grove—not the live-oak of the south, but the old-fashioned, traditional oak of the north & of Old England. On this account I am tentatively calling the place *Druid Grove* (without any intention of infringing on Baltimore's "Druid Hill")—& Bob seems inclined to accept the designation. The press, desk, & other Barlovian accessories are now moved over, & work on the first printing project is begun. This consists of a thin book of Frank Belknap Long's poems—those excluded from "A Man from Genoa" or written since—which we intend to issue *secretly* & present to the gifted author as an *absolute surprise.* We shall call the volume "The Goblin Tower"—after one of the poems included in it. Later on Bob aims to publish an amateur magazine of high quality—connected with the National Amateur Press Association. (an interesting nation-wide organisation which I believe I have mentioned to you before.) Eventually Cyrus & Darius—together with their young master—will probably move across to the cabin—so that Bob will come to the house only for his meals. But all that is in the future.

No—the Florida temperature never gets up to 100 in the shade. It hasn't been over 90° since I've been in De Land—80° to 88° or so is the usual summer range. Being between two bodies of water, Florida has what amounts to the equable climate of an island. It isn't as hot as the north at the latter's summer maximum, but it *stays* warm when the north has cold days sandwiched in. Such an *absence of cold*—rather than any spells of extreme heat—is what keeps Florida mild & genial & permits of the flourishing of such subtropical flora as palms, live-oaks, & the like. Farther south in Florida the weather averages warmer, but 100° is seldom reached. At the extreme south Key West (on an island) has a general range from 60° in winter to 95° in summer.

On June 17 we visited an interesting place—Black Water Creek, a typical river near the Barlow estate where the lush scenery suggests the Congo, Amazon, & other exotic streams found in history & legend. It winds through a steaming jungle of tall, moss-draped cypresses, whose grotesque, twisted roots writhe curiously at the water's edge. Palms lean precariously over the brink, & vines & creepers strow the black, dank earth of the bordering forest aisles. Sinister sunken logs loom up at various points, & in the forest pallid flowers & leprous fungi gleam whitely through a perpetual twilight. It is much like the river at Silver Springs of which I wrote you last year—though I enjoyed it even more because of the more leisurely observing conditions. At Silver Springs I was whizzed ahead in a launch; this time we (Bob, Wayne, & I) went along slowly in a rowboat. Each bend of the tortuous stream brought to light some unexpected vista of tropical luxuriance, & we absorbed the spectacle to the full. Snakes & alligators were somewhat in evidence—though none came near our boat. I hope for more trips of this kind, since I am especially sensitive to the beauty of subtropical scenery.

The duration of my visit still remains indefinite. I never saw a household so super-hospitable as the Barlows, & each suggestion for departure that I make is promptly vetoed. At present it looks as if I might stay across the line into August.

Glad you found *The Californian* of interest—it is an excellent representative of the better side of "Amateur Journalism"[.] Bob's story therein is really tremendously clever.[1]

I've told Barlow of your work on your two new poems, & he (as do I) wishes you the best of luck. I shall be very glad to look them over whenever they are ready for such inspection. Later on Bob may ask permission to publish a small volume of your shorter poems—& I trust you'll view the plan favourably. By that time he will have had enough practice with his press to turn out a really good-looking book. Don't judge his ultimate finished work by the book of Long's poems (a copy of which will be presented to you when it is finished), since this venture is frankly experimental.

Our friend Clark Ashton Smith (whose poems you have seen) has recently taken up a new hobby—that of *sculptural carving* in talc, rhyolite, *dinosaur bone* (a deposit of which exists near his home in Auburn, Calif.), & other appropriate materials. Specimens sent to Bob & me are really impressive. The technique of this *carving* is wholly different from that of the *modelling* in which Bob so brilliantly excels.

Enclosed are 2 or 3 cards which may be of interest. Pardon me if I repeat any previously sent. Best regards from Bob & myself.

Yr most ob^t h^ble Servt

H P Lovecraft

Notes

1. Probably "'Till A' the Seas'" (revised by HPL), *Californian* 3, No. 1 (Summer 1935): 3–7.

[87]   [ALS]

66 College St.,

Providence, R.I.,

Octr. 25, 1935.

Dear Miss Toldridge:—

Let me thank you sincerely for the cuttings recently received—which include many new & highly interesting matters. The account of the very important Dubois discoveries is the clearest I have so far seen—& I also welcomed fresh light on the Kadish discoveries. Hope the old Annapolis house will fall into good hands—I recall it vividly. That Lindblad hypothesis of the solar system may revolutionise many astronomical concepts.

Sorry there are mailing difficulties at the La Salle, & hope Barlow will get his card. You'll probably hear from him before long. And incidentally, I hope the lower-priced flat with the westward view will soon be available.

I'm slowly getting my programme under control, & have at last read up the accumulated papers & magazines. This process has been interrupted by three outings—one a visit to E. H. Cole Sept. 20–23; another a trip to New Haven with my aunt Oct. 8th, & the third a trip to Boston with Samuel Loveman Oct. 16–18.

The Cole visit was marked by many side-trips to interesting rural regions in Massachusetts. We saw rocky Nahant & ancient Marblehead, & traversed the exquisitely picturesque hills of the Connecticut Valley—winding up with a day around Cape Cod & its gleaming beaches. I was surely glad of this ample & representative glimpse of New England scenery after so long an absence among subtropical landscapes.

The New Haven trip was very welcome, since I had never before been off a moving vehicle in that lovely & historic town. The present trip allowed me 7½ hours for exploration while my aunt visited a friend. The day was ideally sunny (though I could have wished it warmer), & the ride through autumnal Connecticut scenery (100 miles = 2½ hours) delightful. New Haven is not as rich in colonial antiquities as Providence, but has a peculiar charm of its own. Streets are broad & well-kept, & in the residential sections (some of which include hills & fine views) there are endless stately mansions a century old, with generous grounds & gardens, & an almost continuous overarching canopy of great elms. I visited ancient Connecticut Hall (1752—the oldest Yale college building, where Nathan Hale of the class of 1773 roomed), old Centre Church (1812, with an interesting crypt containing the grave of Benedict Arnold's first wife), the Pierpont house (1767), the historical, art, & natural history museums, the Farnam & Marsh botanic gardens, & various other points of interest—crowding as much as possible into the limited time available. Most impressive of all the sights, perhaps, were the great *new* quadrangles of the University—each an absolutely faithful reproduction of old-time architecture & atmosphere, & forming a self-contained little world in itself. The Gothic courtyards transport one in fancy to mediaeval Oxford or Cambridge—spires, oriels, pointed arches, mullioned windows, arcades with groined roofs, climbing ivy, sundials, lawns, gardens, vine-clad walls, & flag-stoned walks—everything to give the young occupants that massed impression of their accumulated cultural heritage which they might obtain in Old England itself. To stroll through these quadrangles in the golden afternoon sunlight; at dusk, when the lights in the diamond-paned casements flicker up one by one; or in the beams of a mellow Hunter's moon; is to walk bodily into an enchanted region of dream. It is the past—& the ancient mother land—brought magically to the present time & place. The choicest of these quadrangles is Calhoun College—named for the Great South Carolina statesman (whose grave in St. Philip's Churchyard, Charleston, I visited only 2 months ago), who was a graduate of Yale. Nor are the Georgian quadrangles less glamourous—each being a magical summoning-up of the world of two centuries ago. Many distinct styles of Georgian architecture are represented, & the buildings & landscaping alike reflect the finest taste which European civilisation has yet evolved. Lucky is the boy whose formative years are spent amid such scenes! I wandered for hours through the limitless labyrinth of unexpected elder microcosms, & mourned the lack of further time. Certainly, I must visit New Haven again, since many of its treasures would require weeks for proper inspection and appreciation.

But even the New Haven trip did not quite end my 1935 travels. Oct. 16 at 6 a.m. my friend Samuel Loveman arrived in Providence on the N.Y. boat, & after a brief session at 66 we both started out for Boston to absorb books, museums, & antiquities. Stayed 3 days—stopping at Technology Chambers in Irvington St.—but had no time to look up Cole or any of the local group.

Last week I received Barlow's *Dragon-Fly*, & was delighted with it in every way. Of course the typography is largely practice work—but in spite of all crudities one can clearly appreciate the taste of the editor. The graceful lines on p. 7 form a pleasing sample of the quality of the whole![1]

About your poetry—don't hurry, for everything done at leisure is better than things done under pressure. Spontaneity & ease are the foundation stones of artistic expression.

With every good wish—
Yrs most sincerely—

H. P. Lovecraft

P.S. No—my aunt didn't meet your friend in Ogunquit, having been there only briefly this year.

[P.P.S.] ¶ Saw the cinema "Clive of India" the other day.[2] Magnificent spectacle—full of the spirit of the 18th century & of the British fire that conquered a whole Oriental empire. Historically condensed in the interest of drama, but correct in large essentials—& in costume & architecture.

Notes

1. HPL refers to Toldridge's poem "Expectancy."
2. *Clive of India* (20th Century Productions/United Artists, 1935), produced by Darryl F. Zanuck, directed by Richard Boleslawski; starring Ronald Colman, Loretta Young, and Colin Clive. Based on the novel by R. J. Minney.

[88]   [ALS]

66 College St.,
Providence, R.I.,
Dec. 15, 1935

Dear Miss Toldridge:—

I was indeed glad to receive your letter & interesting cuttings. I believe I mentioned that the John Hay Library is next-door to #66—although I haven't yet dropped in on any cinematic projections of books! There are, though, frequent exhibitions there (books & reliques of literary or historic interest) which I usually see. Not a very long trip to take! That Salmon River expedition in Idaho was quite an event. A correspondent of mine in that region[1] sent me some long illustrated local accounts. The unidentified rock drawings are very curious, though not unlike other Indian pictures. All the voyagers agreed that the scenery includes some of the most impressive in America. Again, thanks for the varied material!

I think you are wise in remaining in 632—for the trouble & expense of an upheaval would probably annul any advantage gained. The present place is really delightful—& the *view* a vast asset in itself. I would miss my present westward view tremendously if I were to lose it. Of course, all places have their drawbacks, but they have to be viewed comparatively.

Glad the travel notes & cards proved of interest. I surely was lucky to obtain such a varied pageant of New England scenery before the advent of cold weather. New Haven was a genuine high spot—I never suspected the haunting charm of the town from my previous hurried dashes through its central portions. The Yale quadrangles really form one of the finest architectural achievements of modern times—absolute poems in brick & stone—or crystallised fragments of dreams. I ought also to have mentioned the magnificent Gothic campanile on the old main campus—the Harkness Tower—whose summit I had previously seen from 'buses.

The sessions with Loveman were also delightful. No—his collection of poetry is not yet issued, although final proofs have been revised. It is scheduled for publication early in 1936.

Autumn lasted remarkably well—but coldness arrived at last. 66, however, heats as well as ever. Mr. John Perkins is indeed flourishing—a huge black giant whose little white necktie is more visible than it was in his infancy. His coat is the glossiest, most flawlessly black piece of fur that I've seen in many a day. He is a very musical gentleman—indeed, only two felines of my acquaintance (one of them Bobby's yellow Cyrus) can excel him in volume of purring. He spends a good deal of time here, alternately playing, drowsing, & sprawling in catnip, & is one of the most companionable beings alive. He has three little brothers now—for all of whom good homes have been found. As for the Barlovian Persians—at last accounts they were as flourishing as ever. I appreciated the picture of Timmie & his canary friend—especially since Timmie looks exactly like my friend Peter Randall, president of the furry fraternity which meets on the shed roof beneath my window.

Glad your copy of Belknap's book has arrived. I had meant to shew you my copy on my return trip, but absent-mindedly packed it in a home-bound bundle in St. Augustine. Barlow will surely appreciate any word of commendation you may bestow. The printing suffers from being his *first* job, but the binding is more representative. Long himself was delighted & astonished—the existence of the book having been kept a perfect secret till a completed copy was mailed to him. This programme of printing & bookbinding is probably helpful rather than exhausting to Barlow. It eases his nerves, while the trips across the lake to his cabin give him outdoor air & exercise which he wouldn't otherwise get. Florida is certainly about the most healthful setting he could have.

Glad the sonnet in *The Galleon* wears well. I have written one weird story of late,[2] but have not yet sent it to a magazine. However, two of my older stories—novelettes written respectively in 1931 & last February—were lately ac-

cepted by *Astounding Stories* & will appear in the course of time.[3] This acceptance was very encouraging to me. I don't go in much for essays—a few articles on widely scattered topics being all I have ever done in that line outside
of letters.

As for your poetry—you'll be turning out some new specimens before
you realise it. Gaps always occur in cycles of production. I wrote no stories in
either 1929 or 1934. Sorry to hear of Miss Mansfield's illness, & hope she will
soon be better. That prize offered by the Conservation Society ought to
tempt the poetic genius of both yourself & Miss Radcliffe.

Thanks extremely for the delightful Thanksgiving card, which my aunt &
I greatly appreciated. We passed the holiday very pleasantly—dining with
friends at the house across the garden where Johnny Perkins lives. Hope your
own holiday was a festive one.

Every good wish—

> Yrs most sincerely,
> H P Lovecraft

Notes

1. Duane W. Rimel. HPL refers to the National Geographic Society's Salmon River
Expedition of 1935.
2. "The Haunter of the Dark."
3. *At the Mountains of Madness* and "The Shadow out of Time."

[89]   [ALS]

> 66 College St.,
> Providence, R.I.,
> Dec. 20, 1935.

Dear Miss Toldridge:—

Again I must thank you for some highly interesting
enclosures—& for the tasteful & generous batch of cards, which did indeed
arrive safely, & which both my aunt & I appreciate most profoundly. That
scintillant Christmas-tree one is surely captivating—with a particular appeal
of its own. Glad to see your verses on one of the cards.

Recent cuttings include some things of especial interest—especially the two
T. R. Henry articles on super-galaxies. New information about the larger units
of the cosmos comes in so fast that one can scarcely keep track of it. I must get
hold of that new book by Moulton—"Consider the Heavens"—which is
probably as good a summary of contemporary astronomical knowledge as is
obtainable anywhere. Another fascinating thing is that description of the two
prehistoric forests near Washington, whose reliques are just turning up.

You'll probably hear from young Barlow before long. He has been very
busy with various things, & has had a debilitating touch of malaria—from

which he is now emerging. He'll be glad to receive your card. Just now he is beginning to print my "Fungi From Yuggoth" as a small book like "The Goblin Tower"—though I tell him he ought not to waste his time on such trivialities. It will, of course, proceed at a leisurely pace—but you'll receive a copy in course of time.[1]

Harking back to the enclosures—that account of the Horace lecture reminds me that my aunt & I heard a very pleasant discourse on the perennial bard Dec. 13 at the college—by Gordon J. Laing of the U. of Chicago.[2] There is also an interesting exhibit of books &c. connected with Horace at the John Hay Library next door to 66.

Weather has not been unduly cold for the season here, though naturally this is a distinctly indoor period. No—I have noticed no recent rainbow, but in any case these phenomena are narrowly local, so that the occurrence of one in Washington (or more narrowly still, in your part of Washington) would not mean that such a thing was visible elsewhere. The existence of a rainbow depends on a certain precise state of the atmosphere—with water-vapour in just the right state to refract the horizontal beams of a low-lying sun in a particular way—& such a specialised condition would not be likely to extend over more than a square mile or so at a given time.

Glad the sun will presently be travelling northward. By the way—owing to the paradoxes of our regularised calendar (which seeks to make time-intervals absolutely regular despite irregularities in the earth's orbit & motion) the *afternoons* began to grow longer after *Dec. 15*—although the *day as a whole* continued to grow shorter until the 21st. because of the greater shortening of the mornings. The *earliest setting* of the sun occurs during the week whose central point is around Dec. 10. By the 21st a gain of 2 minutes in the length of the afternoons has occurred. Washington's more southerly latitude makes its variations in day-length less extreme than Providence's . . . just as ours are less extreme than London's. By *local mean time* the Washington sunset on the shortest afternoon is 10 minutes later than Providence's (4:38 to our 4:28), while the arbitrary rearrangements of *Standard Time* increase the discrepancy to 32 minutes (Washn. 4:46; Providence 4:14)

Yes, indeed,—Johnny Perkins is far stronger than little Sam ever was. In the first place, of course, he is much older than Sam ever lived to be—but even when younger he had more energy . . . despite a severe illness last summer while I was in Florida.

Our Christmas tree arrived yesterday, but will be kept in a cool closet to prevent deterioration until the 24th. I'm saving your sealed envelope to open with other parcels for the 25th—& must again thank you for the thoughtful message. Sorry there was anxiety about the mailing, but for once the elevator boy stands vindicated. He did his duty!

Well, I surely hope that the weather will be warmer around the holidays. Glad you have a tree, albeit a small one, & trust your Yule will be festive &

pleasant. With every good wish—
    Yrs most sincerely

H P Lovecraft

Notes

1. RHB had begun typesetting *Fungi from Yuggoth*, then decided he wanted to publish a book containing it and other poems by HPL, but HPL scotched the new, more ambitious concept. They settled on two separate books, but in the end, neither appeared.

2. HPL refers to a lecture on the Roman poet Horace (Q. Horatius Flaccus) by Gordon J. Laing (1869–1945), a classical scholar and director of the University of Chicago Press (1909–40). With Paul Shorey, he coedited Horace's *Odes and Epodes* (1919).

1936

[90]   [ALS]

66 College St.,
Providence, R.I.,
Jany. 31, 1936

Dear Miss Toldridge:—
            Communications duly arrived—& many thanks for the generous plenitude of cuttings in each. The first was forwarded to me in N.Y., where I visited the author of "The Goblin Tower" from Dec. 30 to Jany. 6. My visit was highly enjoyable, & included glimpses of all the old group. Loveman shewed me his new book of poems, just out, of which I read the proofs last September. Enclosed is a circular describing it. I surely hope it will receive favourable reviews. On two occasions I visited the new Hayden Planetarium of the Am. Museum, & found it a highly impressive device. It consists of a round, domed building of 2 storeys. On the lower floor is a circular hall whose ceiling is a gigantic orrery—shewing the planets revolving around the sun at their proper relative speeds. Above it is another circular hall whose roof is the great dome, & whose edge is made to represent the horizon of N.Y. as seen from Central Park. In the middle of this upper hall is a projector (that looks like a "space ship" or like one of the armoured Martians in "The War of the Worlds") which casts on the concave dome a perfect image of the sky— capable of duplicating the natural apparent motions of the celestial vault, & of depicting the heavens as seen at any hour, at any season, from any latitude, & at any period of history. Other parts of the projector can cast suitably moveable images of the sun, moon, & planets, & diagrammatic arrows & circles for explanatory purposes. The effect is infinitely lifelike—as if one were outdoors beneath the sky. Lectures—different each month (I heard both Dec. & Jan. ones)—are given in connexion with this apparatus. In the annular corridors on

each floor are niches containing typical astronomical instruments of all ages—telescopes, transits, celestial globes, armillary spheres, &c.—& cases to display books, meteorites, & other miscellany. Astronomical pictures line the walls, & at the desk may be obtained useful pamphlets, books, planispheres, &c. The institution holds classes in elementary astronomy, & sponsors clubs of amateur observers. Altogether, it is the most complete & active popular astronomical centre imaginable. It seems to be crowded at all hours—attesting a public interest in astronomy which did not exist when I was young. Enclosed is a postcard reproducing one of the paintings in the upper corridor.

Speaking of astronomy—sunrise & sunset are never the same in different latitudes, except around the time of the equinoxes, March 21 & Sept. 22, when the day is equal to the night nearly everywhere. At the poles, there are alternately 6 m. of continuous light & 6 m. of continuous darkness. At the equator, the days & nights are always equal—12 hrs. each. Between those two extremes conditions vary. The nearer the pole, the more *unequal* the day & night. North or south of lat. 66½ the sun does not rise at midwinter or set at midsummer. In London the days & nights are more unequal than in Providence—December daylight being very brief, & June darkness likewise short. In Washington the inequality is less than in Providence. Your winter days are longer than ours, & your summer days are shorter. This equality is still greater in Charleston—& even more so in Florida. Well—I'm surely glad you have a good western horizon to enjoy.

Glad your Christmas was pleasant. My own surely was. I think I mentioned that we had a tree again. Your cards, as I said before, were enormously appreciated. Barlow's surprise—"The Cats of Ulthar"—did not arrive till I had left for N.Y., but I saw Long's copy there.[1] I surely appreciated Bobby's thoughtfulness & industry! His health, by the way, seems to be much better—so if I were you I would notify him about the change in your poem. He is now working on another *Dragon-Fly*.

Hope all your poetic plans will develop smoothly—but don't worry because material doesn't get published in book form. The primary function of all art—including poetry—is simply to please its creator. And then, of course, it is quite probable that you will have a book or two sooner or later. Have you seen the *Californian* with your poems?[2]

Glad that old Annapolis tavern is to be restored. I recall it very well—as a bank building. Few towns are more thoroughly fascinating than the ancient colonial capital on the yellow Severn. Here is a cutting shewing how extensive the Annapolis restoration plans are.

I was certainly grieved at the news of the King's death.[3] Few sovereigns have been more kindly & honourable, & more truly representative of the virtues & aspirations of the Anglo-Saxon race. There can be no doubt, however, but that his successor is keenly alive to the responsibilities of the throne, & resolved to discharge his duties in a fashion worthy of his ancestors. It surely gives me a venerable feeling to realise that I have now lived under *four* reigns—of Victoria, the Seventh Edward, George, & now the Eighth Edward!

Heavy snow around Poe's birthday—& since then a wave of devastating cold. Yet—taking it from the beginning, the winter has not averaged a severe one.

Yrs most sincerely

H P Lovecraft

P.S. Yours of the 30th just arrived—& thanks vastly for the many interesting enclosures. Those Japanese prints are exquisite, & I am adding them with extreme gratitude to my permanent collection. ¶ I'm sure Barlow would appreciate the windmill cutting. Incidentally, thanks for that of the old Cape Cod mill, which I saw just before its removal to Michigan.

[P.P.S. on envelope]

"The Moon" just recd. A splendid poem! Vivid & full of imagination. In publishing it you might add a footnote about the Jeans theory that the moon will eventually break up into a quasi-Saturnian ring. Other theories hold that it will break up into larger fragments, some of which will crash into the earth & exterminate whatever life-forms remain there. I don't see any astronomical mistakes in your text. ¶ In line 12, since *de-sires´* is a disyllable, couldn't a change be made to even up the metre? Something like

‒ ˘   ˘ ‒   ˘ ‒   ˘ ‒   ˘ ‒

Æons | of prayers | & wish | es weigh | it down

However—the existing version is all right so far as *stresses* go, & some might even prefer it. Many critics object to my kind of syllable-counting. ¶ I think it really would be better to eliminate the "yon" in the last line & substitute *that*. See how well the line would look—

With that bright living world, earth's counterpart!

By the way—I presume you use the word *counterpart* in a very elastic sense. Of course the moon is only ¼ as large as the earth (diam. 2162 m as against Earth's 7918). The *real* "counterpart" of the earth is Venus, with a diameter of 7816 m. [Incidentally, I am now revising a story with the scene laid on Venus.][4] ¶ Congratulations on this very excellent poem, which I hope will appear soon in print. ¶ Your use of *infinitesimally* is practically if not mathematically admissible. Let it stand. *Sensate* is all right in a figurative, imaginative sense.

Notes

1. RHB published *The Cats of Ulthar* (Cassia, FL.: Dragon-Fly Press, 1935) as his "'35 Christmas card" (HPL to W. F. Anger, 2 September 1936; postcard, University of Minnesota) in an edition of 42 copies.

2. See letter 92.

3. George V (b. 1865), king of England (1910–36), died on 20 January 1936.
4. "In the Walls of Eryx."

[91]   [ALS]

Feby. 10, 1936

Dear Miss Toldridge:—

Yours of the 8th with new poem & interesting cuttings duly recd. I am hastening to reply because of something I *forgot to correct* in my earlier hasty survey of that delightful moon poem. I hope you can pardon this prior oversight.

It is in line 5—where the phrase *light-years away* occurs. This expression cannot be applied to lunar-terrestrial matters, since it is a *unit of distance*—& one so vast (the distance traversed by light in a *year* at its rate of 186,000 miles per *second*) as to be applicable only to the stupendous abysses of the *stellar universe*. The moon is only 262,000 miles from the earth, & the future ring (if mathematicians guess aright) will be even nearer than that. What you really wish to convey, I have an idea, is *time* rather than *distance**—in which case some chronological rather than spatial expression will be needed. Could you say:

Of semi-luminous parts, *vast ages hence?*

That would suit the sense perfectly, if it seems linguistically appropriate to you. I like the added lines extremely, & believe the poem as a whole is one of your best—which is saying a good deal!

Thanks for the new poem, "When Earth & Sky are One." This is vivid & powerful indeed, & perfectly captures the elusive spell & sense of mystery in the perennial wonder of sunset. I think the presence of the word *mystic* is quite permissible—there being in this case no perfectly adequate synonym.

I hope that both poems may appear advantageously in print—& am sure they will be appreciated as soon as seen. Hope this reaches you in time to have the matter of Moon, l. 5 straightened out before the text is submitted for publication. It surely was stupid of me not to see this point before!

Thanks immensely for the cuttings. I am saving that supposed early poem of Poe's—& will be eager to hear what various critics & biographers think about its authorship. To me it really seems to have the characteristic Poe note.[1]

Wretched snowy weather still—& a discouraging amount of continuous cold. I haven't been out of the house since Jany. 13.

---

*If, after all, you wish to suggest the wide space between earth & its future ring, you might say *"vast leagues away"*

But I must hasten to get this in the mail.
Best wishes—

Yrs most sincerely,
H P L

Notes

1. The poem in question is "Impromptu—To Kate Carol." It is not in fact an "early poem," having been written in early 1845. The poem was first included in J. H. Whitty's edition of Poe's *Complete Poems* (1911), but the attribution was disputed by John Grier Varner, "Note on a Poem Attributed to Poe," *American Literature* 8, No. 1 (March 1936): 66–68; Varner maintained that the poem was written by Frances S. Osgood. T. O. Mabbott, in his edition of Poe's *Complete Poems* (1978), accepts the attribution to Poe.

[92]   [ALS]

66 College St.,
Providence, R.I.,
March 15, 1936

Dear Miss Toldridge:—

I am indeed sorry to learn that you have been ill, & hope most profoundly that you are now back at your usual health-level. My sympathy is all the more acute & concrete because *this* household has been hard hit by illness. No sooner had I recovered from a late-January touch of grippe than my aunt came down with a far severer version of the same malady[1]—so that ever since mid-February I have been a sort of combined nurse, secretary, market-man, butler, & errand-boy. Complications have prolonged the case, & now it seems likely that my aunt will have to spend some time at an hospital—perhaps transferring to a less formal nursing home after a fortnight, but not returning to #66 for a month or so. It is certainly a very trying thing for her—but I hope she will be fully on her feet again in time to enjoy the late spring & summer.

As usual, I am extremely grateful for the cuttings. That Dingle theory of a "sealed universe" is intensely interesting—& offers the imagination infinite possibilities.[2] It is this uncertain—almost adventurous—quality in modern astronomy which has helped so much to increase the popularity of the science. There is more than a coincidence in the building of vast planetaria—each a popular astronomical centre—at this especial stage of history. I believe I mentioned that, in addition to the New York one, there are planetaria in Philadelphia, Chicago, Los Angeles, Munich, & perhaps elsewhere. One is being discussed for Boston, though its financing is still doubtful.

About differences in time of sunrise & sunset—500 miles in a north-&-south line is enough to produce quite a discrepancy. East & west distance doesn't make so great a difference because time is reckoned in different belts, & the *relative* rising & setting of the sun is always the same in the same latitude. Thus, the days in Rome, Providence, Chicago, Vladivostok, Khiva, & Constantinople are of about the same length, because the latitude of all these places is around 41° or 42° N. The exact hour of sunrise or sunset in the time of the region concerned depends—so far as *longitude* is concerned, on the position of the given place in relation to the meridian whose time it uses. Thus the *clock* hour (not the *absolute* hour) of sunset in Providence is the same as that in Mountain City, Nevada (a place in the same latitude which has the same distance east of its time-meridian [the 120th] that Providence has east of its own time-meridian [the 75th]), but different from that in Salisbury, Connecticut . . . . since the latter is nearer its time-meridian than Providence. When a city chooses to go by the time of a very remote meridian, the result is very peculiar. If the chosen time-meridian is far to the east, the clock time is pushed ahead of the sun time so that something like daylight-saving time results. This is what has happened in Chicago since March 1st, when the city abandoned Central Time (90th meridian) & turned to Eastern (75th meridian) in order to be identical with the East. Chicago & Providence now have the same absolute clock time—when it is 6 p.m. in Providence it is also 6 p.m. by the clocks in Chicago. But because Chicago is really 15° of longitude west of Providence, the *sun time* is always an hour different. Thus at 6 p.m. the sun is setting in Providence—while in Chicago at the same clock hour (since March 1) it is still high above the horizon. Before March 1st, when Chicago was on Central Time, her clocks were an hour behind ours & her sunset occurred at the same *clock time* as in Providence.

Being able to see the sunset from one's window is surely a great privilege, & I am glad you now have it. That one thing ought to do much toward reconciling you to the La Salle.

About *Weird Tales*—too bad you bothered to send for copies, since weird fiction really isn't in your line. I could have lent you copies of any of my tales. If the magazines haven't arrived by this time, I'll drop a line to Wright & ask what the trouble is. Another tale of mine—"At the Mountains of Madness", with an antarctic scene—is running as a serial in *Astounding Stories,* the final instalment being on the stands today. Still another tale—"The Shadow out of Time"—will appear in *Astounding* in June. My "Shadow Over Innsmouth" will be brought out as a booklet by the publisher of *Marvel Tales.*

Sorry to hear of Gov. Ritchie's death, though I think his political & social vision did not include quite all the needs of a changing era.[3] Sorry, too, that his cousin whom you knew could not have lived longer.

Glad you have set more of your poetry in motion—but I hope you will include the new as well as the old in this circulation, for some of your best specimens are of very recent date. Don't be so particular about the *form* of your MSS.—they are all right so long as they are legible, & in the case of short poems plain handwriting is often accepted in lieu of typing. Hope you make a good shewing in the sonnet contest—if, indeed, this Marshall enterprise is a contest. As for the Circle—I don't believe your resignation will close any useful avenues to your verse, though there may have been a certain pleasure in membership. Odd that you haven't heard from Mrs. Green-Leach—for she surely must appreciate your services in founding one of the leading branches of her organisation! By the way—I hope you will let Barlow & me place your name on the membership list of the National Amateur Press Association—the society I have occasionally mentioned to you, & with which *Causerie, The Dragon Fly,* & *The Californian* are connected. The organisation is attempting a qualitative renaissance after a long slump, & work such as yours is eagerly sought & keenly appreciated. Any work sent to Barlow will eventually be placed in some N.A.P.A paper of suitable calibre—there are so many different journals that one can't always tell at first just which one of them is the most suitable receptacle for a given specimen of verse. *The Californian* (the large issue of which, with "Poetry" & "The River & the Boat", I trust you duly received) is especially in need of *long* contributions, either in prose or in verse. Barlow has certainly done well with his publishing programme, & speaks of a forthcoming second issue of *The Dragon Fly* with something of yours in it.[4] Glad you received *Causerie,* which is one of the best papers of the season. Edkins is perhaps the most brilliant person ever connected with amateur journalism. He was intensely active from 1882 to 1897, & is now returning after a long period of silence. I feel very proud of having been instrumental in effecting his return.

I have indeed heard of Benjamin Musser,[5] & am very glad you are contributing to his St. Francis anthology. He certainly cannot fail to appreciate the poem you are sending, & I don't believe he would make acceptance conditional upon your purchasing the book—although this is the custom with some anthologists.

The cold spell here broke about the middle of February, & there have since been some very mild days. Last Tuesday the mercury reached 64°, & on the following day it was 62°. However, there'll be many a cold day before spring actually arrives—even though the sun crosses the theoretical vernal equinox next Friday. I hope to get outdoors locally, though the illness of my aunt will probably prevent my taking any long trips until late summer. I hope your own plans for walking outdoors duly materialised—& that such a walk was not the cause of the illness mentioned in your later note. Very soon the climatic difference between Washington & Providence will begin to shew itself—you will be having breaths of mild air & budding boughs while Rhode Island is still bleak & wintry. And of course *Charleston* is ahead of both—warm days & blossoms being even now at hand.

Mr. Perkins is indeed flourishing—& so is his younger brother Gilbert John Murray Kynymond Elliot, 4th Earl of Minto. Lord Minto was born in

September, & is still very playful. He was named by one of his friends in the boarding house who spends the summer in New Brunswick & was a great admirer of the 4th Earl during his governor-generalship of Canada. The feline Gilbert is black & white, & presents a very graceful aspect. He was intended to be given away, but at the last moment the boarding-house decided to keep him. I am surely glad of his continued presence in these parts, for the local feline element has just been depleted by the removal from the neighbourhood of two of my favourite furry patriarchs—whose human family migrated else-where. ¶ With every good wish for restored health—

Yrs most sincerely
H P Lovecraft

Notes

1. Annie Gamwell in fact was to have a mastectomy for breast cancer.
2. Presumably Herbert Dingle (1890–1978), British physicist and president of the Royal Astronomical Society (1951–53).
3. Albert Ritchie (1876–1936), governor of Maryland (1920–35), died on 24 February.
4. "Locusts and Wild Honey."
5. Benjamin Francis Musser (1889–1951) was a friend of Robert E. Howard. His book, *Canticles for St. Francis* (Manchester, NH: Magnificat Press, 1936), contains Toldridge's "Sweet Francis."

[93]   [ALS]
66 College St.,
Providence, R.I.,
March 27, 1936

Dear Miss Toldridge:—

Despite the chaos engulfing me, I will try to make haste in commenting on the delightful poem which came yesterday. Let me say that my aunt is doing very well at the hospital—now taking good meals, & sitting up each day a little. Yesterday morning she was wheeled on the sun porch for a glimpse of the park-like grounds. I call on alternate days, but so far she has received no other visitors. She still has, of course, much discomfort—digestive stress, sleeplessness, & the irritation of reclining in one fixed position. The length of her stay is not yet certain—but she likes this hospital so much better than the one where she was in 1933 that she has not the same nervous anxiety to get away. Her present abode is on the same grounds as the other hospital, but is a wholly different building—only remotely connected with the R.I. Hospital proper. It is a select institution—the best hospital in the state—called the Jane Brown Memorial, & was recently honoured by the presence of the president of Brown University, who underwent an appendicitis operation.

My route over there & back is of course the same as in 1933, & I am getting reacquainted with the geography of a section I have not visited in the interim!

Both the poem & the corrections safely arrived, & I believe all the changes are for the better. By all means keep *broken* in Stan. II, l. 1. In the 3d line of the same stanza I think *prisoned* is the best word. The coined word *prismed* (there is no verb *to prism*) has a certain picturesqueness, but I think a more normal construction is preferable. The word *pinioned* has not quite the right overtones, since it implies a sort of constraint or binding distinctly uncomfortable. *Prisoned*, on the other hand, has a potentially cheerful secondary meaning—implying *held* in a pleasant sense—hence is perfectly applicable to the present case. Coming to stanza III l. 3—I note the new version, but think the line ought to have another unaccented syllable to even up the metre. How would this do?

> Peace kisses earth, whose *vesture*
> Is tinted like a flower.

The rhymes of *before* & *door* & *hour* & *flow'r* are all right. The whole poem is splendid, & I surely hope it wins the coveted prize. In any case, I hope eventually to see it in appropriate print.

Thanks extremely for the many interesting cuttings—I have just sent the one about Prof. Goddard's rocket experiments to a youth intensely interested in this phase of research, who has witnessed many of the demonstrations of the Am. Rocket Society in N.Y.[1] And let me add a word of most extreme gratitude for the two additional Bath cards, which I am adding most delightedly to the file containing the others. This series has a particular charm—an apparent artlessness which is really the acme of art.

I was surely sorry to hear of your illness, & am glad you are now well out of it & taking at least brief excursions in the genial spring air. I doubt if your indigestion indicates anything more serious than a need of dietary readjustment. Every now & then many persons need such a readjustment. My aunt does—having been benefited by a new proportioning of food elements some 5 years ago, & being about to have a still newer nourishment programme worked out. Milk is always good for one—although I don't like it except in coffee or in connexion with other foods. I get my own meals very largely— even when my aunt is here—picking up something good at a delicatessen, or using the increasing variety of good things which come in cans.

Glad you liked *Causerie*, & that you'll let us put your name on the N.A.P.A. list. Don't frown on the word *amateur*—remember that the primary sense is not that of an unskilled beginner, but of a person who follows an art *for its own sake* . . . like a gentleman rather than a tradesman . . . . instead of for hire. Glad you saw the stories in W T & found them readable.

Yes—there is no question but that the sonnet is a form particularly suited to your type of genius. It interests me greatly to learn that your work was once surveyed by Maurice Francis Egan,[2] & that he advised you to specialise in the sonnet. That advice surely attests to a sound critical judgment . . . & his later remembrance of the incident shews that the work must have made a genuine impression on him.

Well—I shall try to get this directly in the mail in order that you may receive the comments on "Sundown" as soon as possible.

Wishing you the best of health—

Yrs most sincerely,

H P Lovecraft

Notes

1. Robert Hutchings Goddard (1882–1945), American physicist and inventor, launched the first liquid-fuel rocket in 1926. From 1926 to 1941 he launched a variety of rockets, designed both for space travel and for use in warfare. The American Rocket Society was founded in 1930. The "youth" referred to is Kenneth J. Sterling.

2. Maurice Francis Egan (1852–1924), American diplomat, Catholic journalist, literary critic, and novelist. His most popular novel was *The Wiles of Sexton Maginnis* (1909).

[94]   [ALS]

66 College St.,
Providence, R.I.,
May 8, 1936

Dear Miss Toldridge:—

Yrs. of April 23d with appreciated enclosures duly arrived, & I must thank you for the cuttings—& for the very interesting cactus card. Here, indeed, appear more varieties than the Barlow lawn ever dreamed of! It is the "prickly pear" type which predominates in Florida.

Sorry your indisposition was long in disappearing, but trust it is all gone now. Glad you were able to make the trip in quest of the apple-blossoms you glimpsed from afar. Spring is creeping along at last—even up here—& I imagine Washington has more of it than Providence. We had no good weather till last week, but since then there have been days warm enough to write outdoors. Leaves & flowers are out, & the local landscape is truly an exquisite spectacle.

My aunt's improvement has continued, & on April 21 she returned to 66 College. Each day shews some increase in strength, though she still requires some coöperation in household tasks. She takes walks each sunny day—& on April 30 we were treated to a delightful motor ride through the country to Westport Point, Mass. I have so far been too busy to take long rural walks, but hope to begin before long. Barlow has invited me down to De Land again, but I have my doubts as to whether I can go. Duties here, & lack of finances, make the outlook rather dim.

The Dragon Fly is indeed a N.A.P.A. venture, & I hope its young editor will soon finish & mail the second issue. It interests me to know that you shewed

Causerie to an author as versatile as Mrs. Stoddard.[1] If she would care for a copy, I can send you another. Edkins will have a second issue out before long. In the near future you will begin to receive other N.A.P.A. papers—both good & bad—& I trust you can excuse the crude & childish ones for the sake of the more substantial specimens. Hope everything will go well in the contest—& that both you & Miss Radcliffe will win honours. Yes—Miss R's work would certainly be welcomed in the N.A.P.A., & I think she may join it in due course of time. About the sonnet sequence—I'm sure you'll hear from them eventually.

I was interested to hear of your early contributions to *Harpers,*[2] & of the floral tribute connected with it. Incidentally—my friend James F. Morton met the stepfather of that tribute's donor in Richmond some years ago. Mr. Valentine was a great & venerable figure, & recalled having seen Poe when he was a boy.[3] It is unfortunate that you did not follow up that first *Harpers* contribution with others, for I'm sure later stories would have been just as good as their predecessor.

Mr. Perkins & Lord Minto disport as usual about the garden, & occasionally pay visits to 66. And according to latest reports Cyrus & Darius are still flourishing in De Land.

About card-painting—I hope you will not attempt any programme which would be likely to overtax your eyesight. It surely is delicate work—& you must put especially conscientious care into it in order to secure the splendid results that you do.

Last Monday the R.I. Tercentenary observances began—with parade in colonial costumes which started at the college gate only a stone's throw from #66. The marchers descended College Street hill, at the foot of which they were joined by Gov. Green in a genuine colonial coach. The party then proceeded to the ancient colony-house (1761), where they reënacted—in the selfsame room—the tragic sessions of the rebel legislature held May 4, 1776, when the treasonable hotheads disavowed the lawful authority of our Sovereign & Parliament. In this mock-session the parts of the old deputies were taken in each case by their direct lineal descendants—Gov. Green representing his ancestor Col. Arnold, who presented the rebel resolutions 160 years ago. This 175-year-old building was too small to admit many spectators, but I was lucky enough to get in & secure an excellent vantage-point. Costumes & procedure were so well-arranged that the illusion was perfect. I could almost imagine the calendar turned back, & had hard work not to hiss the rebels & applaud the loyal minority who stood firmly by his Majesty's government. Later in the day—at a State House ceremony which I did not attend—Gov. Curley of Mass. presented to Gov. Green a copy of the recent revocation of Roger Williams's banishment in Oct. 1655. After 300½ years, I am sure that Roger highly appreciates this mark of consideration!

With all good wishes, & hoping you are much better,
        Yr most obt hble Servt
                H P Lovecraft

Notes

1. Presumably Mary Handel Stoddard, a poet in Toldridge's poetry circle.
2. See "The Timid Heart of Lizzie" in the Bibliography.
3. Edward V. Valentine (1838–1930), later a noted sculptor, saw Poe on at least one occasion in August 1849, two months before Poe's death.

[95]   [ALS]

66 College St.,
Providence, R.I.,
June 5, 1936.

Dear Miss Toldridge:—

Recent chronicles & cuttings duly arrived, & I am as usual grateful. My aunt continues to improve (though hampered by a dental siege), & is increasingly active in various ways. Mr. Perkins & the Earl of Minto call now & then (I especially enjoy having them both at once), but my programme remains in a state of considerable congestion & chaos. Several warm days have improved my health considerably, & I have managed to be outdoors now & then. I very much doubt my ability to get south this year despite young Bob's generous invitation—indeed, I fancy my amount of travel in 1936 will not be great.

Mr. Valentine of Richmond *saw* Poe when a small boy, but never met or spoke with the poet. He was over 90 when Morton met him—& a delightful conversationalist, full of mellow reminiscences. I *almost* met him in 1931,[1] when the curator of the Poe shrine suggested my calling on him; but before I went I learned that he was ill & abandoned the project. Incidentally—I feel sure that Mrs. Ingle would be delighted to hear from you again.

Sorry "The Moon" didn't capture prizes in the contest, but am glad that Miss Radcliffe's entry received some mention. It is hard to pick out any central principle of selection governing such competitions—so much depends upon the individual theories & biasses of the various judges. "De gustibus non disputandum est" is the truest of adages!

Regarding R.I. Tercentery events—there may be some more historic spectacles comparable to that of May 4, but I look forward chiefly to the opening of certain ancient houses (one of which will become a public museum) for public inspection. The other day my aunt & I attended an exhibition of drawings & etchings of old Providence houses & street scenes by an artist especially skilled in that line—Henry J. Peck, who lived on the ancient hill just below us. He captures the spirit of old Providence about as well as any artist I can think of.

Apropos of the historic atmosphere—I stumbled on an interesting *genea-logical* discovery recently, when I learned for the first time that I am a great-great-great-great-great-great-great-great-great-grandson of the Elizabethan *astronomer* who introduced the Copernican theory into England! For one who has been a lifelong amateur devotee of the heavens, this was indeed a gratifying find! Ordinarily I am a very sluggish genealogist, being content to take what existing charts tell & carry the matter no further. The other day I encountered a caller of my aunt's—a lady related to us in the Field & Wilcox lines—& she mentioned how proud I ought to be of our common forbear, *the astronomer John Field or Felde.* That rather bewildered me, since our charts carried the Field line back only to the original Providence settler John Field, who died in 1686, & I knew he was no star-gazer. Soon, however, it turned out that the ancestor of this settler has been known for ages among genealogists, though I had no inking of it. The 16th Century astronomer (whose 1557 Ephemeris contained the first English account of the Copernican system, & who has been called "The Proto-Copernican of England") was the Prov. colonist's *own grandfather*—hence *my* 9-times-great-grandfather. It vastly elated me to acquire a real man of science for my pedigree—which in general is overpopulated with clergymen but short on realistic thinkers. [Even so, this new discovery has added *one more* divine to the list—for the Prov. colonist's maternal grandfather was the Rev. John Sotwell, Vicar of Peniston in Yorkshire.] Later I looked up the standard Field genealogy at the library & found out all about the line. It comes from Sir Hubertus de la Feld [of the family of Counts de la Feld, seated near Colmar in Alsace], a follower of William the Conqueror who took lands in Lancashire in 1069; the Prov. stock springing from the Yorkshire branch centring around Sowerby, Ardsley, & Thurnscoe in the West Riding. I have copied an abundance of notes & now have my Field lineage straight back—in exactly 20 generations—to one Roger de la Feld of Sowerby, born in 1240. But it is the *astronomer* who chiefly interests me, & about whom I am anxious to learn more. I have a triple allotment of Field blood, being descended from no less than three of the Providence settler's grandchildren.

Had a tremendous file-cleaning the other day, & threw away about a ton of old letters & papers. My files had become absolutely unmanageable, so that I had to take time off & set them in order. I've adopted a new system of conveniently shallow cardboard boxes for small cuttings such as "Stars, Men, & Atoms", which makes it vastly easier for me to find a given item. ¶ All good wishes—

Yr most obᵗ humble Servᵗ

H P Lovecraft

Notes

1. HPL likely means 1930. James. F. Morton met Valentine in 1929.

[96]   [ALS]

66 College St.,
Providence, R.I.,
June 25, 1936.

Dear Miss Toldridge:—

Very pleased to receive your recent bulletin & cut-
tings. Thanks, as usual! It delighted me to see that Charleston's splendid
"Vanderhorst Row" is in shape again after its long years of desertion. It remained in the same family down the years, & was finally owned by a collateral
descendant who let it go to ruin—a curious kind of miser who lived to be 95
or more. Last year I rejoiced to see the long-delayed reconstruction going
on—though the interior required almost total replacement. Glad to know that
so much of the original woodwork could be put back. The brick walls, of
course, are not changed. They are supremely graceful—in a late-Georgian
tradition of universal type rather than in the especial local tradition of
Charleston. It is one of the few Charleston buildings which would be equally
at home in Georgetown, Annapolis, Providence, Salem, London, or Bath.

My aunt, I am glad to say, continues to gain strength—& is resuming her
usual activities more & more. Those lines which you found & have placed
with your mother's picture surely are of singular grace & appropriateness.

The new filing system certainly has helped things greatly. I always appreciate the T. R. Henry articles—& imagine that those with a biological theme (recent discoveries in heredity—about the effect of radiation on genes, &c.—may
double or treble our knowledge of what life is & how its existing forms came to
be) must be scarcely less interesting than the anthropological, palaeontological,
astronomical, &c. ones. As for the reliques of Lady Macdonald which you
mention—certainly I would be glad to file them (as adjuncts of the books
which she so considerately sent me) if you did not wish to retain them yourself;
but I really think you ought to retain them, for surely they cannot take up a
great amount of room. If you were to send them elsewhere you would probably
miss them. Deciding what to keep & what to eliminate is always a problem, but
I generally lean toward the keeping side. A doubtful item if kept can always be
discarded later, but an item once discarded is generally past regaining!

I shall send that Persian rug cutting to E. Hoffmann Price, who is a specialist in that field. Persian art has an unique & distinctive beauty which is becoming more & more recognised in the western world.

Glad Barlow is about to send out the new *Dragon Fly*—with your delightful poem.[1] By this time the second issue of *Causerie* should have reached
you—let me know if it fails to do so. A *National Amateur* & *Californian* will
also be along soon. About voting for officers & amendments in the
N.A.P.A.—enclosed are two postcards which indicate what seems to be the
best way to vote this year. Bradofsky should be elected editor to atone for the
persecution he has endured as president.

Glad the sunsets are so delightful, & wish the La Salle could somehow come down in its rental. The high rates prevailing in Washington are really lamentable.

Very recently two of Providence's most notable colonial mansions—the John Brown & Edward Carrington houses—were thrown open as public museums . . . albeit at exorbitantly high admission rates. Yesterday afternoon I explored both of them, & was not disappointed. The Brown house excels in sheer magnificence any mansion I have ever explored—from Quebec on the north to St. Augustine & New Orleans on the south. The closest parallel, perhaps, is the Brewton-Pringle house in Charleston. I enclose a folder, of which I obtained a large supply. The Carrington house (built 1809) is less classical in its symmetry, but is remarkably homelike. With its stables, courtyard, coach-houses, & extensive grounds it forms one of the finest domestic units of the Early-Republic period now on exhibition. This estate has been given to the R.I. School of Design by the last of the family (who lives in another colonial mansion coming down through another ancestral line) as a permanent museum . . . with all its original furniture, china, &c. undisturbed. I could not obtain any pictures of the place, though I am told that some will be available later. Recently I was informed of a new historical map of R.I. meant to be published in connexion with the the [*sic*] state's tercentenary, & shall endeavour to secure copies of it. I am now reading the very excellent life of Roger Williams by Emily Easton—a work which possesses particular value because of its ample delineation of its subject's London background. Aside from its depiction of colonial history, it sheds a fascinating light upon Jacobean England.

Wretched weather hereabouts—I am now shivering over an oil heater. 1936 bids fair to be a year without a summer! Best wishes—

Yrs most sincerely,
H P Lovecraft

Notes

1. I.e., "Locusts and Wild Honey."

[97]   [ALS]

66 College St.,
Providence, R.I.
July 31, 1936.

Dear Miss Toldridge:—

Let me thank you, as usual, for the many interesting enclosures—although you must never feel compelled to bother with clipping & sending them. I hate to impose responsibilities—& you ought never to trouble with searching out any items which are not immediately at hand &

ready to be spared. Furthermore—never send away anything which you might enjoy keeping in your own files.

The N.A.P.A. election is now over, so there is no need about bothering with ballots till next June. I am glad to say that the preferable candidates (those listed on the card I sent) won. As to the office of Executive Judge— which I had in the term just closed—let me say that it is one of the worst nui- sances in amateur journalism. I wouldn't accept it again under any circum- stances. All three of the hapless incumbents were kept busy working on absurd & frivolous complaints from members—in many cases motivated by personal malice—& you can see from our long report in the N.A. what com- plex messes we generally had to deal with. In some years—when general harmony reigns—these judgeships are sinecures; but just at present they are nightmares because of the warfare going on among certain of the members. Incidentally—one of the chief combatants in these hostilities, Edwin Hadley Smith, is a resident of your own city.[1]

About that "Director of the Providence Observatory" business—it is a *pure joke*. There never was such an observatory, & I've never been the director of anything! It all arose when the editor of one of the "fan" magazines saw a childhood amateur paper of mine—the *Rhode Island Journal of Astronomy*, which I issued on a hectograph when I was 12 & 13 & 14 years old. In those days I childishly called my own set of astronomical instruments "The Providence Observatory", & named myself as "director". The "fan" editor, not realising that the paper was a "kid" venture, published as an item that I was once "Di- rector of the Prov. Observatory"—a thing which evoked many laughs until I officially explained & contradicted it.[2] Your fellow-Washingtonian E. H. Smith happened to see the item—hence his spoofing way of addressing me.

I have not read the *Californian* yet, but it looks like an excellent issue. Glad you have the second *Dragon-Fly*. Have you the *second* issue of *Causerie*? If not, let me know, & I can supply you. It is quite the best paper of the season, even though the editor attributes a famous Latin quotation (which, by the way, ought to begin "certum est" instead of "credo", although the latter ver- sion is widely quoted) from Tertullian to Origen—who wrote in *Greek*.[3]

The recent spell of warm weather helped me greatly—making me feel really active & vigorous for the first time in 1936. I made the most of it & succeeded in getting more work done in a *week* than I can ordinarily get done in a *month*. Also took an interesting trip to Newport by boat—enjoying the ancient town, & getting considerable writing done on the rocky oceanward cliffs.

July 18–19 I had an enjoyable visit from my old friend M. W. Moe (poet- teacher-N.A.P.A. member—from Milwaukee) & his gifted son Robert (the latter—now of Bridgeport Conn.—the youth who was here with his car in the spring of '35.). It was my first sight of Moe in 13 yrs, & I fancy he found me more changed than I found him. His son brought him in the car, & we covered quite a bit of scenic & historic ground in the all-too-brief span of 2 days. Weather favoured us—warmth & sun throughout.

July 22 I saw the new Peltier comet from the Ladd Observatory of Brown University (on high ground a mile N. of here), which I used to haunt in youth. In the 12" telescope it shewed a tiny disc with fanlike luminous haze spreading form it. I could have seen it in my own small glass but for the obstructed nature of the northern sky in this neighbourhood.

Of the *latest* pleasant news you are probably aware already, since the visitor who creates it paused to see you in Washington. Little Bobby arrived here July 28, & I was so glad to see him that I forgave him the fierce moustache & side-whiskers! He has taken quarters at the boarding-house across the garden, & is surely a most congenial neighbour! Hope I shan't bore him shewing him sights! Just now he seems intent on buying up all the old books in Providence's myriad shops. All good wishes—

  Yrs sincerely—

  H P Lovecraft

[P.S.] Almost simultaneously with R H B came a loan-exhibit of Clark Ashton Smith's grotesque miniature sculptures. It includes some magnificent items— as Barlow & I agree.

Notes

1. HPL addressed the feud in *Some Current Motives and Practices*.
2. HPL to Donald Wollheim, c. October 1935; in *Phantagraph* 4, No. 2 (November–December 1935): 3: "Your statement that I was once director of the Providence Observatory flabbergasted me a bit, insomuch as there has never been any 'Providence Observatory'! Then afte[r] a moment, it dawned on me that you must have seen one of my kid publications of 30 or more years ago—when I used to call my own small telescope & other astronomical apparatus 'THE PROVIDENCE OBSERVATORY' & publish [by hectograph or typewriter] important-looking 'bulletins' & 'annuals'. Thus do the exaggerations of youth bear misleading fruit in old age."
3. HPL refers to Tertullian's celebrated quotation "Certum est quia impossibile est" (It is certain because it is impossible; from *De Carne Christi* 5). It is often misquoted as "Credo quia impossibile est."

[98]   [ALS]

  66 College St.,
  Providence, R.I.,
  August 27, 1936.

Dear Miss Toldridge:—

  I surely was pleased to see young R H B when he breezed in—although I think he'd look a lot better minus the whiskerage. I'm an advocate of the 18th century clean shave. We've been seeing all the local sights & museums, & have done some research on the New England lines in the visitor's ancestry. It appears that Barlow & I are *6th cousins*—our lines of descent from a common ancestor being as follows:

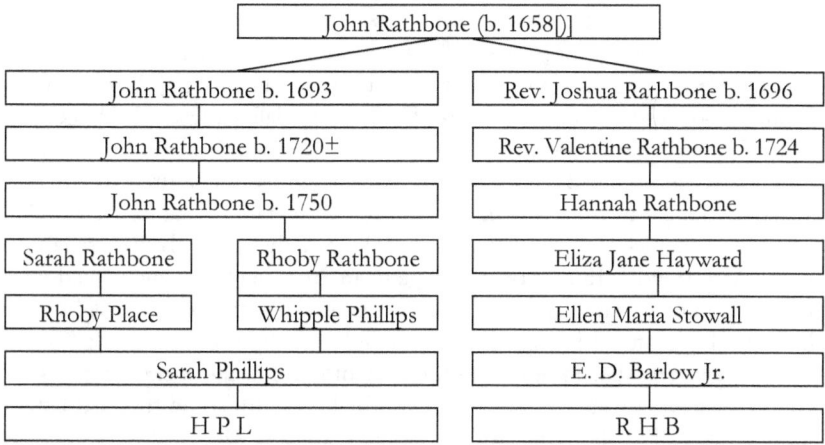

John Rathbone (b. 1658[)]

John Rathbone b. 1693	Rev. Joshua Rathbone b. 1696
John Rathbone b. 1720±	Rev. Valentine Rathbone b. 1724
John Rathbone b. 1750	Hannah Rathbone

Sarah Rathbone — Rhoby Rathbone | Eliza Jane Hayward
Rhoby Place — Whipple Phillips | Ellen Maria Stowall
Sarah Phillips | E. D. Barlow Jr.
H P L | R H B

From August 6th to 10th our local literary group had a *third* member in the person of Dr. Adolphe de Castro, one-time friend & biographer of Ambrose Bierce, & later a revision client of mine. He took in a good many local sights, & on one occasion we all gathered in the hidden hillside churchyard just north of #66—a sequestered spot where Poe used to wander while on visits here 90 years ago—& composed rhymed acrostics on the name *Edgar Allan Poe*.[1]

Thanks so much for the cuttings. R H B & I both appreciated the ones on cats. This reminds me of the sad news from the house across the garden—a melancholy event indeed! I have lost my two best friends, for about a month ago both Mr. Perkins & the Earl of Minto succumbed to some obscure epidemic (seemingly digestive in nature) which has been ravaging the feline population hereabouts. The resultant feeling of desolation is very great—& I hope that future brothers of the departed may some day help to compensate for the loss. But nobody could quite replace Mr. John Perkins with his sharp Egyptian nose, long legs, & eloquent tail. He will be long & fondly remembered!

Sorry to hear that you are feeling restless & dissatisfied with Washington. Actually, there are few more beautiful or comfortable places than the national capital—although it has not quite the fascination of Charleston. Quebec is as fascinating as Charleston, but several factors might make it less homelike & comfortable. For one thing, the winters are savagely cold—temperatures of 20° below zero being common. Spring is late—snow being on the ground until the middle of April—& autumn is early; October being bitterly frigid, & November bringing the snow. I've been in Quebec only in summer, & could not possibly survive there the year round. Moreover, the fact that *French* is the dominant language might make the city less homelike to some. English is generally understood in shops & the street, but it is not the principal language. Only about 5% of the population is of other than French origin. However—Quebec is a great place for all that. The landscape setting & architecture make it the most *intrinsically beautiful* city on this continent—& the better classes of the population have an admirable stateliness & courtesy. Some of the surrounding countryside is extremely lovely, having typical French cottages with curved eaves. This is especially true of the largely unspoiled Isle d'Orleans—now connected with the mainland by a bridge. But Quebec certainly means close hibernation for those not inured to the cold. Washington, for most, is an infinitely more comfortable place to live in.

Many thanks for that series of articles on the Crow Indian rehabilitation—with the description of the "American Stonehenge", which I had never heard of before. This latter must be a tremendously impressive sight. I am keeping this material in my files for possible literary use. Barlow & I took a sail to Newport Aug. 15, enjoying the ancient town & the rocky sea-cliffs. On Aug. 20 we went to ancient Salem & Marblehead with some friends,[2] exploring the original of the House of the Seven Gables & seeing other 17th & 18th century interiors. Glad *Causerie* duly arrived. Edkins is quite ill at present, but expects to be in better shape in September.

Barlow will probably be moving along toward Kansas City Sept. 1st, & he hopes to be able to manage a stop in Washington—in which case you will see him again, whiskers & all. His health seems to have been pretty good during the past month, & I hope it will continue so.

All good wishes—

Yr most obt Servt

H P Lovecraft

Notes

1. The three acrostics were HPL's "In a Sequester'd Providence Churchyard Where Once Poe Walk'd," RHB's "St. John's Churchyard," and de Castro's "Edgar Allan Poe." These, and others written later by M. W. Moe and Henry Kuttner, appear in David E. Schultz, "In a Sequester'd Churchyard," *Crypt of Cthulhu* No. 57 (St. John's Eve 1988): 26–29.

2. Of two friends mentioned in various letters, HPL names only Kenneth J. Sterling.

[99]   [ALS]

66 College St.,

Providence, R.I.,

Octr. 6, 1936.

Dear Miss Toldridge:—

Abundant thanks for the Navajo articles & other cuttings. This material is really tremendously interesting, & contained much that was new to me. The Desert of the Black Blood is one of the most strikingly weird things I have ever seen described outside fiction, & would make an ideal setting for a fantastic story.[1] The suggestion of primal ruins is especially appealing. The Navajos themselves form a highly interesting study. I read Oliver La Farge's work about them—"Laughing Boy"[2]—some years ago. I enjoyed the article about old George Town books, & wish I could have seen the exhibition which evoked it.

Edkins liked your *Californian* contributions very much, & regards you as one of the few real poets now in the N.A.P.A. I probably mentioned that he was quite ill & scheduled to undergo a second serious operation. This operation is now over, & the patient is recovering steadily. When his convalescence is complete, he'll probably feel the best he has felt in many years.

Sorry Barlow couldn't stop in Washington on his return trip, but I fancy the group in New York—Long, Sterling, Koenig, &c.—kept him there so long that he had to hurry through the later stages of his journey. He left here Sept. 1st—& his next permanent address will be *c/o H. M. Langworthy, 810 W. 57th St. Terrace, Kansas City, Mo.* (an aunt's). His health is certainly much better than it has been for several years, & I hope it will continue to be so. He is one of the most brilliant youths I have ever met; & as soon as maturity enables him to centralise his abundant scattered energies in one definite field (& I tend to think more & more that *literature* is the one best adapted to him, despite his many other aptitudes), he will begin to produce notable work.

Glad you have been feeling somewhat better of late, & hope you will be able to work out some satisfactory residential decision. Except for the troublesome economic factor, the La Salle seems admirably adapted to your needs—& I hope you will be able to arrange for the signing of another lease. Regarding the relative merits of cities—unless one is intent on some specific thing like the climate of Key West or the scenery of Quebec or the architecture of Charleston, I really don't think Washington could be bettered. In all the *general* factors which go to make a place residentially desirable, it certainly stands very high. It has a classic architectural beauty unexcelled on this continent, it has all the facilities of a metropolis, it has a mild & generally desirable climate, it has (in Georgetown) an abundance of historic quaintness, & it is close to some of the finest scenery in the country—to say nothing of picturesquely ancient towns & historic sites. It has always been one of my favourite cities, & if I domiciled there I should certainly be very slow to think of breaking away.

Since Barlow's departure I have been making up lost time with work & fighting the cold weather with my oil heater. (Though the steam is now on.) Had a pleasant visit from my friend Morton (curator of the Paterson Museum) Sept. 11–12–13, during which we visited the colonial village of Warren down the bay. Revisory duties have been heavy—especially one job for your fellow-Washingtonian Mrs. Renshaw, (a text book for use in the School of Expression) on which I became greatly delayed.

October weather has put a stop to my outdoor reading & writing sessions, but I still take rural rambles on pleasant days when I can spare the time. Recently I've been concentrating on Neutaconkanut Hill—the great ridge west of the city, which I can see in the distance from my window—& have explored some weirdly fascinating woodlands & valleys beyond the crest which I never before visited. It is curious how one discovers new regions close at hand—even late in life. I had often been up Neutaconkanut Hill in the past—for the sake of the magnificent eastward view of outspread town, countryside, & bay—but had never realised how extensive the woods beyond the crest are. I had thought they were merely a fringe abutting on privately owned farms. As it is, I have discovered almost a new world at my doorstep—a region of great oaks, hidden meadows starred with autumnal flowers, & crumbling remnants of colonial stone walls—which I shall probably use sooner or later in some fictional attempt. This region is much nearer the city than my favourite Quinsnicket woods, & I shall probably visit it often in future—though of course the present year's rambles will not be likely to outlast October. I hope the coming winter will not be severe, despite numerous predictions that it will be. But in any case the abundant steam heat in this house will solve the indoor problem.

Hoping that your health continues to improve, & that you can somehow be able to solve the residence problem, I remain

Yrs most sincerely

H P Lovecraft

Notes

1. HPL to Earl Peirce, 28 November 1936 (ms., State Historical Society of Wisconsin): "Then there have been newspaper accounts of an incredible place in New Mexico—in Navajo's country—called 'The Desert of the Black Blood.' This is a ghoulish & desolate area of broken lava which is rifted by great chasms & which has probably never been penetrated beyond a few miles by any white man—or any living Indian for that matter. Aëroplanes, flying over it, have spied what look like ruins at its very heart; & local legends tell of an ancient & mysterious city whose crumbling walls now harbour carnivorous dragons. Yes—the southwest is surely a place for the connoisseur in strange horror to visit—though one would need a guide to help one find the genuine high spots with a minimum of wasteful wandering."

2. The novel won the Pulitzer Prize in 1930.

[100]   [ALS]

66 College St.,

Providence, R.I.,

Oct. 29, 1936.

Dear Miss Toldridge:—

Sorry to learn in yours of Oct. 8 that your "Statue of Liberty" verses arrived too late, but am glad they were so keenly appreciated when they did arrive. Glad also to hear that the N.A.P.A. material continues to come. You will probably receive a request for poetry for *The Californian* before long, & I trust you will have something on hand to send. Pleased to know that you've heard from Little Bobby Barlow—who seems to be getting fairly well acclimated in Kansas City. He was sorry that he could not make more stops on his journey west from here.

Thanks as usual for the many interesting cuttings—& for the new King Edward stamp. This is the first specimen of the stamp that I have seen, & I really like it exceedingly. It has an admirably artistic balance & simplicity. One misses the familiar type of design usually associated with postage stamps— but since stamps are after all a comparatively modern innovation, less than a century old, the violation of tradition can scarcely be called an extreme one. I can't sympathise with those who attack the new stamp so violently. The cuttings included some extremely absorbing material—especially the one suggesting that the peninsular part of India is of recent geologic origin—2600 B.C., within historical times. The account of the old Indian graveyard near Washington reminds me of that discovered at St. Augustine two years ago— which I saw upon its first opening to the public. The zoölogical & palaeontological items are likewise of great interest—I had not known of this matter of the dying "wisents"—so-called, & of their cross-breeding with the American bison. So far as I can see, these animals are what we have always called the *aurochs* (*urus* in Caesar's Commentaries), & which I thought were rather carefully guarded on private preserves in Lithuania. Where the name "wisent" comes from, I'm sure I don't know! I'm glad steps are being taken to strengthen the breed, for I knew the aurochs was approaching extinction. In classical antiquity the word *bison* (Gr. Βισον) was generally applied to the aurochs, notwithstanding Caesar's use of a different word. Pliny uses the form *bison*. When the New World was discovered, the term of course became transferred at once to our "buffaloes"—which are superficially identical with the aurochs.

Yes—political thunders are raging, but I hope nothing will occur to block the reëlection of the present administration, & thus check the long-needed social evolution now so slowly getting under way. Plutocrats & blind reactionaries are desperately struggling, & using every art of slander, propaganda, & insidious suggestion; but I still feel hopeful of a good New Deal majority.

Your new poem is delightful, & I am very grateful for the copy. There are only two changes I would suggest—one in line 7, where the noun *firstling* seems somehow not as good as a frankly adjectival phrase such as *first bold;* & one in the line after that, where the word *au-gust'* seems to get accented on its first syllable. For *august* one might substitute *towering*—or any dissyllable with the accent on the first syllable. Hope these lines will appear in print before long. You surely have no reason to be discouraged about your poetry—& incidentally, it is undoubtedly read by more persons than you realise.

Yes—my poet-friend Jonathan E. Hoag lived to be 96½, & would undoubtedly have become a centenarian but for the accident which caused his death in 1927. Did I ever send you his book of poems? He was a correspondent of mine for over eleven years, but of all our group only James F. Morton ever met him in person.

Pres. Roosevelt was here Oct. 21, & I had several fine glimpses of him. He spoke from the terrace of the state house to an audience of about 60,000.

October 20 & 21 were phenomenally warm—& just as I had become resigned to immediate hibernation! I went exploring both days—& found a magnificent forest only 3 miles from here *which I had never seen before!* The place—of which I had heard vaguely, but which happens to be between my usual routes of exploration—is called the "Squantum Woods", & lies down the east shore of the bay, in the town of East Providence. It is now a State Reservation, & was made accessible by the cutting-through of the Barrington Parkway. Great oaks & birches—steep slopes & rock ledges—& a gorgeous sunset beyond the trees on both occasions. Then glimpses of the crescent moon, Venus, & Jupiter—& the lights of far-off Providence from high places on the parkway. Another goal for rustic rambles! On my expedition of the 20th a particularly congenial bodyguard or retinue attended me through the sunlit arcades of the grove—in the persons of *two tiny kittens,* one grey & one tortoise-shell, who appeared out of nowhere in the midst of the sylvan solitudes. Blithe spirits of the ancient wood—furry faunlets of the shadowy vale! I wonder where their mother was? Judging by their diminutiveness, they could not have been long separated from her side. Probably they appertained to an hospital whose grounds are contiguous with the mystical forest. Both were at first very timid, & reluctant to let Grandpa catch them; but eventually the little grey fellow became very purr-ful & amicable—climbing over the Old Gentleman, playing with twigs & with Grandpa's watch-charm, & eventually curling up & going to sleep in the grandpaternal lap. But little brother remained suspicious & aloof—clawing & spitting with surprising vehemence on the one occasion when Grandpa caught him. He hung around, however, because he didn't want to lose his brother! Not wishing to wake my new friend, I carried him about when I continued my ramble—little tortoise-shell brother tagging along reluctantly & dubiously at a discreet distance in the rear. When the grey faunlet awaked, he requested to be set down; but proceeded to trot companionably after Grandpa—sometimes getting under the old gentleman's feet & considerably retarding progress. Thus I roamed the venerable forest aisles for a hour & a half—till the ruddy disc of the sun vanished behind the farther hills & treetops. As I emerged from the wood, I feared that my faithful retinue might follow me on the parkway & incur the perils of motor traffic—& was considering expedients for discouraging their further attendance—but I discovered that they were not without native caution. Or perhaps they were wholly genii loci, without real existence apart from their dim nemorense habitat. At any rate, Little Grey Boy paused at the edge of the grove with a mewed farewell—& naturally Little Tortoise-Shell had no great eagerness to follow. I bade them a regretful & ceremonious adieu—& on the next day looked for them in vain.

I am indeed sorry to hear that you have been feeling less vigorous than usual of late, & hope you will soon be up to the usual level again. No doubt you will be as the autumn advances—for I believe your reactions to the weather are the opposite of mine. In any case don't let a brief spell of indisposition give you a pessimistic outlook, or cause you to fear that you will not be seeing all your friends again! A few weeks more of rest & good weather will have you in the best of condition (allowing, of course, for the accident which so provokingly interferes with your walking), & a decade hence is likely to see you writing as busily & as pleasantly as ever! So don't talk of disposing of worldly goods, or anything like that! As I said once before, I would of course appreciate deeply the thoughtfulness & graciousness implied in the sending of the ring you mention, & would cherish such a work of esteem with the utmost gratitude. But at the present time you have no need to be thinking about later recipients of things. You are here to use & enjoy them *yourself*, & will be for a long span of years! Don't let my good old friend Mr. Hoag outdo you—or our fellow amateur "Tryout" Smith, who was 84 last Saturday but is as active & forward-looking as a boy! Temporary bad health will pass, & you'll have a lot of comfort ahead in spite of that troublesome accident & its consequences!

Which reminds me that I'm very glad to hear you've renewed your lease at the La Salle. So scarce are housing accomodations in Washington, that I doubt whether you could have done better—& your present quarters certainly do seem extremely comfortable & congenial with their glamorous sunset view. I only hope their retention does not involve too great a financial strain. You are surely lucky to have the coöperation of the dusky Alice (whom Barlow recalls most pleasantly—& whose pension I hope can be successfully arranged), & of the "landlady" who does so much to promote the smoothness of the meals programme. I imagine you will find the new fishes extremely companionable, & hope your heating system is sufficient to keep the temperature always high enough for the little fellow. Tropical fish are rather like *me* as regards climate. If the thermometer ever falls below a certain point (I forget just what that point is—perhaps it's different for different species), they perish. *Guppies* are *very* small tropical fish. Any expert could tell you whether or not your small dark friend belongs to that species. Young Long was a great tropical fish enthusiast a year or two ago, & I learned from him all that I know about the subject. He had two or three aquaria, with electric heating-irons to leave in the water in order to maintain the temperature even when the room becomes cool. Latterly Belknap hasn't been so much interested in his fish, so that his father has very largely taken over the care & proprietorship of the various Long aquaria.

Genealogy surely is an interesting pursuit, although I could never spend as much time & energy on it as my friend Morton does. It did please me to discover last spring my connexion with the Elizabethan astronomer John Field. Sorry your accident has prevented you from continuing your own library researches in recent years, & trust you'll find various opportunities now & then. The discovery of your British cousins must have been a delightful & dramatic event—giving you a particularly concrete & tangible link with the ancestral sod. By the way—since you speak of lacking a *Dragon-Fly* to send them, I am mailing you a copy under separate cover. Thanks to the generosity of my bewhiskered young guest of last August I have several duplicates to spare. I'm sure they will appreciate the delicate & distinctive charm of "Expectancy".

Well—I am *still* working on that Renshaw text-book. The manuscript, considerably abridged, came back once more for revision, & now I am reading the printer's proofs & catching a number of errors therein. The job is being handled by the Standard Press of 930 H. St., N.W.—perhaps you know of it. It will have to be done & delivered by Nov. 5th, since the course involving the book opens on the 6th. Haste has made this job more difficult than it would otherwise have been.

Amateur journalism seems to promise a fair-to-middling year. I was extremely glad to see your poem "Peace" in *The Southern Amateur*—which is, by the way, becoming a remarkably fine little paper. Edkins' contributions form companions worthy of your own—& you will, incidentally, be glad to hear that their gifted author's recovery progresses steadily. On Nov. 4 he will leave for Florida—whose climate ought to complete his restoration to full health. Whether he will feel able to issue another *Causerie* this year remains to be seen. It is possible that he can't manage it financially, since his long illness & two operations have about emptied his purse. Only the advantageous & providential sub-letting of his house (in Highland Park, Ill., near Chicago) enables him to get South this winter. Glad the bulk of the amateur magazines now reach you. Some are pretty crude, but there are enough good ones to make membership worth retaining. Wish Little Bobby could get his press out to Kansas City & issue another *Dragon-Fly!* By the way—your fellow-Washingtonian Edwin Hadley Smith recently put me vastly in his debt by sending a vast bundle of bygone issues of the *National Amateur*—carrying my file back scatteringly to 1883—plus a reprint of the very first issue (1876). It certainly gives me a clearer idea of the amateurdom of the past than I ever had before. I've just finished a critical report for the N.A., but I don't know when it can be used.[1] I'm doing prose for the most part instead of verse this year; since there is a shortage of prose critics, while Rheinhart Kleiner can handle the verse better than I.

As for stories—I have one in *Weird Tales* this month (the issue dated December), but it isn't especially good.[2] I doubt whether you'd care much for it. The illustration is by the new W.T. artist Virgil Finlay—a highly remarkable youth who is also a poet of no mean calibre. Good drawing intrinsically, but not an accurate depiction of the scene it is supposed to illustrate. The book edition of my "Shadow Over Innsmouth" seems to be taking shape at last— at least, I read proofs of the final section last week, & received sample pages of another section of the finished text the other day. But my hopes are not too high, since Crawford's capacity for delay is infinite & inexplicable!

Thanks extremely for the attractive Japanese postcard. I surely would like to see Japan some time—few lands can be as thoroughly beautiful.

I was certainly sorry not to be able to get south this year, but my financial situation is appalling. I'm lucky to be able to eat & have a roof over my head . . . & I haven't had a new suit of clothes since 1928. If ever I get hold of more cash, the south will see a lot of me! This northern climate is simply murderous.

All good wishes, & thanks for enclosures—

Yrs most sincerely—

H P Lovecraft

Notes

1. I.e., "[Literary Review.]"
2. "The Haunter of the Dark."

[101]   [ALS]

66 College St.,
Providence, R.I.,
Dec. 4, 1936.

Dear Miss Toldridge:—

Thanks as usual for recent cuttings—including the delectable black cats. I was greatly interested in the Devon article, because that county forms the source of over half the lines in my paternal ancestry. One of my great-grandparents was a Mary Fulford,[1] indirectly connected with the Great-Fulford line mentioned in the article, so that the keepers of England's last jester were undoubtedly my lineal ancestors. I'd like to see old Devon.

Yes—the Roger Williams lecture was highly interesting. Of the intellectual precursors mentioned, the principal one was the little-known Sebastian Castellio, rector of the University of Geneva in the 16th century, who protested long & eloquently against John Calvin's ruthless consignment of the famous "heretic" Servetus to the stake in 1553. His books, "Concerning Heretics" & "The Art of Doubt",[2] were suppressed, & it is doubtful whether Williams ever saw them; but he had the same general libertarian attitude which characterised the founder of Providence in the next century. He said, among other things, that "To burn a man alive does not defend a doctrine, but merely slays a man." In the end Castellio was himself condemned to the flames by Calvin, but chance granted him a natural death before the sentence could be carried out. A biography of Castellio by Stefan Zweig has lately been published—a timely thing in an age when intellectual liberty is again challenged over half the European continent—& it is probable that the next generation will know him better than those of the last two centuries have known him.

The paintings in that recent local exhibition surely included some grotesque specimens—yet both Sullivan & Kaufer are very competent artists in the academic as well as the radical tradition.[3] That "Weekly wash in the graveyard" picture was undoubtedly an attempt to embody a vaguely ironic concept—a contrast of mankind's pompous pretenses & inflated utterances with the prosaic substance of life. Sullivan really lacks the complete & studied irrationalism of the true surrealists whose externals he imitates.

Regarding the poem—I am sure that *early* or *earliest* forms a good substitute for *firstling*. Sorry there has been delay about preparation.

Glad the extra *Dragon-Fly* duly arrived, & that you've written the bewhiskered young editor. I assume that you have the *second* issue safely. No—it isn't *necessary* to acknowledge *Causerie* by letter, although Edkins always appreciates & feels cheered by a personal acknowledgment. Don't take the trouble to write if any real effort is involved—but if a word seems easy in some spare moment, you can reach the now comfortably convalescent editor at *San Sebastian Hotel, Coral Gables, Florida.* Needless to say, I envy him his present whereabouts!

I was certainly delighted with the outcome of the election. There was no doubt in my mind as to the general nature of the result, but the *extent* of the landslide was a pleasant surprise. It forms a splendid & specific answer to the doubts of radicals & reactionaries alike as to what the American people want!

My outings kept up remarkably late in the year—even over the line into November. Since my last letter I have opened up one more realm of fascinating terra incognita—the region west of the Neutaconkanut Hill which I previously mentioned, & the western slopes of that eminence itself. On Oct. 28 I penetrated a terrain which took me half a mile from any spot I had ever trod before in the course of a long life. I followed a road which branches north & west from the Plainfield Pike, ascending a low rise which skirts Neutaconkanut's western foot & which commands an utterly idyllic vista of rolling meadows, ancient stone walls, hoary groves, & distant cottage roofs to the west & south. Only 2 or 3 miles from the city's heart—& yet in the primal rural New England of the first colonists! Just before sunset I ascended the hill by a precipitous cart-path bordering an ancient wood, & from the dizzy crest obtained an almost stupefying prospect of outspread countryside, gleaming rivulets, far-off forests, & mystical orange sky with the great solar disc sinking redly amidst bars of stratus clouds. Entering the woods, I saw the actual sunset through the trees, & then turned east to cross the hill to that more familiar cityward slope which I have always known. Never before had I realised the great extent of Neutaconkanut's surface. It is really a miniature plateau or table-land, with valleys, ridges, & summits of its own, rather than a simple hill. From some of the hidden interior meadows—remote from every sign of nearby human life—I secured truly marvellous glimpses of the remote urban skyline—a dream of enchanted pinnacles & domes half-floating in air, & with an obscure aura of mystery around them. The upper windows of some of the taller towers held the fire of the sun after I had lost it, affording a spectacle of cryptic & curious glamour. Then I saw the great round disc of the Hunter's Moon (2 days before full) floating above the belfries & minarets, while in the orange-glowing west Venus & Jupiter commenced to twinkle. My route across the plateau was varied—sometimes through the interior, but now & then getting toward the wooded edge where dark valleys slope down to the plain below, & huge balanced boulders on rocky heights impart a spectral, druidic effect as they stand out against the twilight. I did not begin to cover the full extent of the plateau, & can see that I have a field for several future voyages of discovery. Finally I came to more familiar ground—where the grassy ridge of an old buried aqueduct gives the illusion of one of those vestigial Roman roads which traverse the woods & meadows of old England—& stood once more on the well-known eastward crest which I have gazed at since the age of three. The outspread city was rapidly lighting up, & lay like a constellation in the deepening dusk. The moon poured down increasing floods of pale gold, & the glow of Venus & Jupiter in the fading west grew intense. Then down the steep hillside to the car line (too cold for enjoyable walking when there's no scenery to compensate for shivers!) & back to the prosaic haunts of man.

I saw the January *Weird Tales* lately, & was greatly pleased with Finlay's illustration for my "Thing on the Doorstep". Finlay has genuine imagination—something all too rare among recent illustrators. Which reminds me—last week, in a letter, Finlay was lamenting the disappearance of the old Renaissance & 18th century custom of writing verses on current works of art & literature. In my reply—just to shew him that I still belong to the 18th century—I concocted the following macabre bit—referring to a very fine & very bizarre drawing of nameless elder fiends of outer space which he made for a W T story last May:

To Mr. Finlay, Upon his Drawing for Mr. Bloch's Tale, "The Faceless God".

> In dim abysses pulse the shapes of night,
> Hungry & hideous, with strange mitres crown'd;
> Black pinions beating in fantastic flight
> From orb to orb thro' sunless voids profound.
> None dares to name the cosmos whence they course,
> Or guess the look on each amorphous face,
> Or speak the words that with resistless force
> Would draw them from the hells of outer space.
>
> Yet here upon a page our frighten'd glance
> Finds monstrous forms no human eye should see;
> Hints of those blasphemies whose countenance
> Spreads death & madness thro' infinity.
> What limner he who braves black gulfs alone
> And lives to make their alien horrors known?

Speaking of weird art—possibly you know that our bewhiskered young friend Barlow is taking a course at the Kansas City Art Institute. And out in California Clark Ashton Smith will have an exhibition of his grotesque sculpture at the Crocker Art Gallery in Sacramento next month—the chief piece being an 11-inch statuette called (after an entity in one of my stories) "Cthulhu's Child."

My "Shadow Over Innsmouth" is out at last, but makes a rather sorry appearance—with slovenly format, amateurish-looking binding, & 34 bad misprints. The one redeeming feature is the set of 4 illustrations by Frank A. Utpatel, one of which is also reproduced on the book's jacket.

Fanciful Tales arrived the other day, & I have so far counted 59 bad misprints in my story "The Nameless City." That is surely something of a record!

Wednesday night I heard a highly interesting illustrated lecture on the Williamsburg restoration by the son of the landscape gardener in charge of that phase of the project. I must see the completely restored town some day.

All good wishes—

Yrs most sincerely—

H P Lovecraft

Notes

1. Kenneth W. Faig, Jr., points out that the wife of the emigrant Joseph Lovecraft (1774-1850) was actually Mary Full (1782–1864), not Mary Fulford. The claim that Rev. Francis Fulford was her father is false.

2. Sebastian Castellio (1515–1563), French theologian, an early proponent of religious toleration and freedom of thought. The works referred to are *Concerning Heretics* (*De Haereticis,* 1554) and *The Art of Doubt* (*De Arte Dubitandi,* 1563).

3. J. Banigan Sullivan (1905–1970) and Waldo Glover Kaufer (1906–1972).

[102]   [ALS]

66 College St.,

Providence, R.I.,

Dec. 12, 1936.

Dear Miss Toldridge:—

Yours of the 11th arrived this morning, & I must thank you for the attractive cards & interesting cutting enclosed. Your verses on that coaching card are especially delightful, & would go well in print on cards of that type. The *kittens* are captivating!

I was extremely sorry to note the fate of the Musser anthology containing your St. Francis verses, & hope most strongly that the missing edition will eventually turn up. It seems as if a large shipment like that ought to be ultimately traceable. If any of the contributors helped to finance the volume, Musser ought certainly to return their remittances unless he can produce the edition. But in any case the incident is unfortunate—like that of Poe's first small book "Tamerlane", the bulk of the edition of which was lost or destroyed without ever having been distributed. Another albeit humbler case is that of my "Shunned House"—whose unbound sheets have been drifting from pillar to post since 1928, & which is now stranded in storage in De Land. However—a *few* copies of "Tamerlane"—& the "Shunned House"—did get into the hands of readers.

Speaking of books—yesterday I sent you a copy of my "Shadow Over Innsmouth", with the errors corrected as neatly as I could manage. Not a very impressive affair—though Utpatel's illustrations are good (even if he does represent a long-bearded nonagenarian as smooth-faced in one of them). The story may or may not prove amusing, but in any event it is this first book (if one can call it that) of mine to attain circulation. I believe you already have a "Shunned House", thanks to Little Whiskerando.

By this time you have the letter in which I acknowledge—most gratefully & appreciatively—the delightful & memory-surrounded ring which arrived on Thursday. It is pleasant indeed to know its history, & the source of that attractive [']'planetary system" of diamonds. Let me repeat my thanks for this honour of custodianship—& my assurances that the heirloom is at your complete disposal whenever you with to have it with you again.[1] I am sure that the kinsfolk in the mother land will appreciate most profoundly the other reliques sent to them—although in this case also you really ought to have retained the articles for your own enjoyment. No apologies are necessary for the 'un-shined' state of the ring—indeed, I always prefer a certain appearance of mellowness in any object to utter, sapolio-suggesting spic-&-span-ness.[2] So once more let me attest my sincerest appreciation & gratitude!

I heard King Edward's farewell message over my aunt's radio yesterday afternoon, & thought it one of the most moving & impressive messages ever shared by the general public.[3] One may measure the tremendous changes in custom & popular orientation brought about by the machine age when one reflects how wild & fantastic would have seemed the notion, 25 years ago, of the whole world's hearing a personal recital of a royal tragedy in the actual voice of the chief figure—the man occupying a central place in current history. Truly, the times change—even though certain circles stubbornly refuse to admit the fact, or at least to admit some of its more important social implications.

The entire incident fills me with great sorrow, though at the present stage it may have been wise for King Edward to acquiesce as he did. For centuries ago Henry the Eighth—the only other *VIII*th on our throne—shewed no such complaisance toward those who sought to interfere in his domestic affairs. Today I presume King Edward thought ahead & decided that a constitutional struggle would have dangerous possibilities for British & Imperial unity which did not exist in the tightly-knit little England of the 1500's. Of the wisdom of the romance behind the struggle not so much may be said, but even here a superficial judgment would not be wise. King Edward is the product of his times & circumstances, & not everyone so situated could fall as easily into staid 19th century patterns as did the Duke of York. Now, in middle age, there seems to be a focussing of Edward's domestic ambitions which did not exist before. One might wish that the object were a more suitable one, yet to condemn even the existing romance in comparison with the dozens of far more sordid royal romances tolerated in the past is a piece of irritating hypocrisy & impertinence. In the light of history, interpreted through the realism of the present, there is no real reason why King Edward should not have been permitted to make Mrs. Simpson the Queen. His refusal to accept domestic dictation is creditable, & indicative of a truly royal stature. The attitude shewn in his farewell message is one of genuine nobility, & I believe the sincerity, simplicity, & naive pathos of that speech give it a quality closely akin to literary greatness.

But regret for what has happened should not be allowed to cloud the respect due to the new Sovereign. Of George VI one may well say, as did his abdicating brother, 'God Save the King'! ¶ All good wishes

Yr————

H P Lovecraft

Notes

1. See HPL to RHB, 11 December 1936: "Yesterday I received from Aunt Lizzie that heirloom ring which she's talked so much about. I had tried my best to stop her sending it—she ought to snap out of that 'not long for this world' attitude. Hope you drop her occasional cheering letters. I try to do so" (*O Fortunate Floridian* 384). Ironically, HPL himself was "not long for this world," for he died only two and half months later.

2. Sapolio was a brand of soap noted for its advertising.

3. Edward VIII (1894–1972), king of England, after having succeeded George V on 20 January 1936, abdicated on 11 December, ostensibly because he refused to give up his plan to marry the American divorcée Wallis Simpson. After his abdication, he became the Duke of Windsor and married Simpson on 3 June 1937.

1937

[103]   [ALS]

The Ancient Hill
—Jany. 7, 1937.

Dear Miss Toldridge:—

I was glad to hear that the copy of "Innsmouth" reached you safely, & that it seemed acceptable despite its multitudinous crudities. I tried to correct all the errors, but an eagle-eyed young friend has lately found eight more—hence I am herewith enclosing a list which you can either keep in the book, or use in correcting the text (as I did) with penknife & sharp pencil.[1] I dare say there are even more—but if these are rectified the version will be at least moderately correct. It is unfortunate that the story had to be published in so slovenly a way.

Meanwhile I am indebted to you for still more cards—all of which were appreciated by myself & my aunt. The unused ones were gratefully used— either by one or the other of us—& the others have been filed with equal gratitude. I liked especially the doorway, black kitten, wreath, & later feline card. Thanks also for the red King Edward stamp with very light cancellation . . . the best I've yet received. The green ½d. & brown 1½d. have come in my mail, but I haven't yet seen the blue one of higher denomination. These stamps, I believe, will be issued for some time—until a new George VI issue is designed. Australia, on the other hand, has just suppressed a half-printed but not-issued King Edward series, hence will change directly from the 5th to the 6th George without intermediate record—as will, indeed, all the rest of the Dominions, where no replacement of the George V stamps has yet occurred.

The ring is still receiving appreciative admiration. My aunt thinks it espe- cially exquisite, & wore it to a dinner on the evening after Christmas. Really, that central sun & its eight little planets form a delightful system of sparking orbs! You were truly altogether too generous in sending it—& whenever you think you'd like a reminiscent look at it, it is always available!

Our Yuletide was commendably festive—including a turkey dinner at the boarding-house across the garden, with Mrs. Spotty Perkins (mother of my late friends Samuel & John Perkins, & the Earl of Minto) meandering pur- ringly among the tables & finally jumping up on the window-seat for a nap. We had a tree in front of the hearth in my aunt's living-room; its verdant boughs thickly festooned with a tinsel imitation of Charleston's & Florida's best Spanish moss, & its outlines emphasised by a not ungraceful lighting sys- tem. Around its base were ranged the gifts—which included (on my side) a hassock tall enough to let me reach the top shelves of my bookcases, & (on my aunt's side) a cabinet of drawers for odds & ends, not unlike my own fil- ing cabinets, but of more ladylike arrangement & aspect. Of outside gifts, a miniature sleeping cat modelled & black-enamelled by Little Bobby Barlow may be noted. More distinctive, though, was perhaps the gift which came quite unexpectedly from young Willis Conover (one of the weird "fan maga- zine" editors) of Cambridge, Maryland, down on the Eastern Shore. For lo! when I had removed numberless layers of corrugated paper & excelsior, what should I find before me but the yellowed & crumbling fragments of *a long- interred human skull!* It came from an Indian mound not far from the sender's home—a place distinguished by many archaeological exploits of Conover & his young friends. Its condition is such that its reassembling will form a very delicate task—so that I may reserve it for the ministrations of some expert mender like Young Whiskerando upon the occasion of some future visit. Reflective fancy strives to evoke the image of him to whom it once belonged. Was it some feathered chieftain who in his day oft ululated in triumph as he counted the tufted scalps sliced from coppery or colonist foes? Or some crafty medicine-man who with mask & drum called forth from the Great Abyss those shadowy Things which were better left uncalled? This we may never know—unless perchance some incantation droned out of the pages of the dark & dreaded Necronomicon will have power to draw strange emanations from the lifeless & centuried clay, & raise up amidst the cobwebs of my ancient study a shimmering mist not without power to speak!

Glad to hear that you had a tree with an appropriate circle of gifts around it. Sorry, though, that your "landlady" has had to move away—thus depriving you of those excellent meals. Have you, as an alternative, thought of the possibilities of goods in cans—or of the varied products of the delicatessen? These, I feel sure, are both reasonable in price & deliverable at your apartment. They now form my own staple diet, for I dislike more & more the bother of going down the hill to lunch rooms.

Abundant thanks, as usual, for the cuttings—those on Troy being of especial interest. The recent identification of the 7th instead of 6th level as the Homeric one is surely a dramatic archaeological achievement. The Basques surely are a mystery—& no light seems to fall on the nature & affiliations of their language as the years pass. The recent speculations on the source & date of the Indian migrations are particularly interesting, & ought to be remembered in connexion with estimates of the antiquity of certain Central American artifacts. Mexican historians & archaeologists seem inclined to assign man too high an antiquity in the western hemisphere. The remarks on London architecture filled me with dismay. Not that modernistic buildings are any worse than the most grotesque Victorian monstrosities, but that any new ugliness is to be deplored.

About the kind of *sphere* shewn on the arms of the astronomer John Field—it is what is known as an *armillary* (AR´-MIL-LA-RY) sphere; a collection of metal rings set up to represent the imaginary circles (like latitude & longitude, &c) of the sky. The word comes from the Latin *armilla*, an *armlet*, because the various metallic rings or hoops composing the apparatus vaguely suggest a collection of armlets on an enlarged but thinner scale. It is something of this sort which is, according to the cutting you sent, about to be set up in Washington's Meridian Park.

I saw that cutting about the death of Roger Williams' oldest known descendant—or rather, I saw the corresponding item in the local paper. The honour now falls to a Mr. Peck of this city (age 89), former principal of our classical high school, & still active in many fields. My aunt knows him & his family—his sister was the famous mountain-climber Miss Annie Peck, after whom a peak in Peru was recently named.

An alliance of the nations of the western hemisphere would be a highly useful thing if it could be held together. It might not be able to stop a European war, but it might enable the Americas to preserve neutrality until such a time as intervention might seem necessary. It would likewise form a bulwark against the European penetration of South America—such as the long & persistent efforts of Germany to colonise & dominate Brazil.

Hope the fishes will continue to prosper—even if you have to get them a larger aquarium. There are often some striking bargains in aquaria—at least in New York. I recall Long's acquisition of a surprisingly capacious rectangular specimen for about a dollar a year or two ago.

Glad the lines to Finlay seemed adequate. Here is a similar tribute which I recently inscribed to good old Clark Ashton Smith—whose fantastic stories, verses, pictures, & miniature carvings need no introduction. The name "Averoigne" occurring in the text is that of an imaginary region in mediaeval France where many of Smith's weirdest tales are set:

To Klarkash-Ton, Wizard of Averoigne[2]

A time-black tower against dim banks of cloud;
Around its base the pathless, pressing wood.
Shadow and silence, moss and mould, enshroud
Grey, age-fell'd slabs that once as cromlechs stood.
No fall of foot, no song of bird awakes
The lethal aisles of sempiternal night,
Tho' oft with stir of wings the dense air shakes,
As in the tower there glows a pallid light.

* * *

For here, apart, dwells one whose hands have wrought
Strange eidola that chill the world with fear;
Whose graven runes in tones of dread have taught
What things beyond the star-gulfs lurk and leer.
Dark Lord of Averoigne—whose windows stare
On pits of dream no other gaze could bear!

Hope your health continues to improve. I was a bit under the weather last week with a slight touch of the prevailing grippe, but this is now on the wane. The winter has so far been surprisingly mild, & I only hope it will keep on being so. Heard an interesting lecture Sunday on Peruvian antiquities, & was astonished to learn of the amount of pre-Inca architecture which has been unearthed in the coastal region. Lantern slides & specimens of recently-excavated pottery supplemented the address.

All good wishes—

Yrs most sincerely,

H P Lovecraft

Notes

1. The lengthy errata sheet for the book contained even more errors.

2. HPL typically titled the poem, in correspondence, "To Clark Ashton Smith, Esq., upon his Fantastic Tales, Verses, Pictures, & Sculptures."

Letters to Anne Tillery Renshaw

Anna Tilley Renshaw

Letters to Anne Tillery Renshaw

[1]   [AHT]

598 Angell Street, Providence, R.I.,

August 24, 1918

Estimable Mrs. Browning-Lover:—

Permit me to apologise for my harshness toward your favourite bard in the recent UNITED AMATEUR.[1] I am most distinctly not a Browning-lover—in poetry and philosophy alike I am the direct antithesis of this gentleman in thought—but I should not like to do him an injustice. I tried to be fair, but I find it hard to assume a liking when I have it not. Browning sums up everything I dislike—if I tried to conceal this sentiment in affected admiration, I should be a hypocrite. However, I recognise B's place in literature, and shall never try to attack or satirise him. No writer can arouse so much discussion unless he is really great in some way. But for mine own part, I adhere to Mr. A. Pope and his school;—except when I venture into the manner of the late E. A. Poe.

And now concerning Mr. Alfred Galpin, Junior, Sage, Singer, Scientist, born Nov. 8, 1901. Galpin is the son of an elderly man, a Civil War veteran at present seventy-seven years of age, and is therefore separated from his own father by a greater gulf of years than that which separated me from my favourite grandfather. The elder Galpin is himself a very remarkable character—a deep student of scientific and philosophical subjects, though rather bigoted in his hatred of religion. Galpin senior, delighted at the possession of a son in his latter days, gave all his time to the systematic training of the boy's mind, and certainly achieved marvellous results—though of course the native brain capacity of the child greatly assisted. Each question the babe would ask in his infantile curiosity would be answered by the father in such a way as to excite further questioning, hence from the first little Alfred was supremely *intelligent*. He did not stumble on things as other children do—he knew the reasons why he did things! His processes of thought were trained and clarified at an age when most boys are dully playing with blocks and iron locomotives. But Galpin senior was no fanatic, and he knew the value of even development; wherefore Alfred was not wholly confined to study. He had his blocks and locomotives *besides* the mental training—and is today a normal, healthy, well-balanced lad. As Alfred grew to grammar school age, he was noted mainly for his keen wit and humour, and a little disliked by his schoolfellows because his nimble processes of thought left them behind in conversation. He was twelve when Moe first knew him. Moe was called in to tutor him for an examination,

357

but soon found that the lad needed little help. At the very first session Galpin, instead of being taught, himself taught Moe a new way to extract cube root! When he entered high-school his wit was quite famous, and on account of his antics he was nicknamed "Charlie Chaplin" and called a "nut". But high-school made him a more serious thinker, & in his second year he was moved to deep study. The curriculum was too slow for him, & one assignment in class would by a chain of thought cause him to read volume after volume— allusions in everything he read being followed up to the limit. In this extensive reading he was aided by his marvellous acquisitive & retentive powers. He had but to glance over a page to become complete & permanent master of its contents. Naturally, he joined Moe's press club, but for some reason or other did not come into the United. About this time he formulated a system of philosophy really astonishing for one of his years—& which, interestingly enough, comes nearest to my own beliefs of any system I have ever known. He was not content to let mankind & his little earth serve as the centre of things—he recognised our insignificance in the midst of absolute eternity & absolute infinity. When a lad of fourteen or fifteen thinks vividly & imaginatively of these matters, he cannot justly be described as other than a prodigy. Always scribbling in prose, Galpin began versification early in his high-school life. His thoroughness here made itself manifest, for his earliest attempts shew a sound mastery of technique. In all his work I never saw a very bad line, and have detected only one false rhyme. ("ideal" and "feel".) He is the easiest person on earth to correct, for once told anything, he never forgets it. In his haste he has sometimes fallen into errors of spelling, especially in some of the uncommon polysyllabic words which his philosophical subjects compel him to employ. Yet one casual mention of a fault forever banishes it from his work. His utter lack of conscious effort in learning is wonderful. Galpin first dawned above my horizon a year ago, when as President I was looking about for a fourth vice-president to appoint. I had tried Joseph Harriman, then considered the brightest high-school boy in the Association, but he had graduated & gone to college, so recommended Galpin to me as a very likely candidate. I immediately wrote Galpin, expecting of course a hesitant, schoolboyish reply. To my surprise, there came back a sparkling letter, full of mature wit & polish, accepting the office, & expressing a desire to enter more fully into amateur journalism. Since then we have become the closest of friends & correspondents, averaging three long letters per week. On more intimate acquaintance, Galpin drops a bit of his mature gravity & shews the genuine boyishness in him—but I like him the more for it, since it takes me back to my own youth. Always a recluse, with no varied events of life to mark the transition from boyhood to manhood, I have retained more of the old juvenile point of view & sympathy than I would care to acknowledge publicly. I have grown up without knowing it, & am at times almost alarmed at the unbelievable fact that I am getting on in years. Wherefore Galpin seems like a breath of ancient naturalness—like an awakening to boyhood after a strange dream of growing up to be twenty-eight years old! It is so easy to take up the thread of youth again with a youthful correspondent, & no immediate visible signs of my advanced age. It is hard for me to realise that eleven years separate me from Galpin, for his thoughts fit in so well with my own. I am convinced that he has a mighty future. He is passing me already in the intellectual race, & in a few years will have left me behind completely. Moe recognises in him the signs of incipient greatness, and is trying to persuade him to attend the great University of Wisconsin instead of the small Lawrence College which he had had in mind. He will graduate from high-school next June. In poetry you would find much more in common with Galpin than with me, for he ridicules my eighteenth-century formality, and seeks in verse more of the emotional and impressionistic qualities which you so highly value. You would, however, deem him rather strict regarding technique; for he writes evenly and with care, heeding all the rules of regular composition. In person Galpin is tall and attractive, if I may judge from figures and photographs. He is six feet one inch in height, and has a splendidly earnest and intelligent face. At the same time, he impresses the casual observer not as a dryasdust pedant, but as a genuine, wholesome boy. He does not look more than his almost seventeen years, and is fond of sports and all normal amusements. He is a bit of a daredevil, and at the recent convention frightened the entire assemblage with his feats of rock-climbing and chasm-leaping. He fears nothing on earth—or in infinity, for that matter. Young as he is, Galpin's professional career is already begun. For a year he has been the APPLETON CRESCENT'S star reporter, working out of school hours, and has now been appointed Sporting Editor of that sheet—an uncongenial place, but one which satisfies him financially. The CRESCENT is a small paper, and not without some ill-repressed pro-German tendencies. It is Galpin's delight to slip in occasional patriotic paragraphs surreptitiously, with the connivance of the City Editor—a thorough American who detests the pro-German leaning as wholeheartedly as Galpin himself. The owner, Meyer—dares not remove these items once they are in, for fear of arousing sentiment in a definite way. I advocated (and secured) Galpin's election as first Vice-President this year, and have appointed him to the critical bureau. Next year I shall advocate him for the presidency. Moe gave him a large collection of amateur journals before leaving for Madison, and the boy is now more thoroughly conversant with ancient amateur history than I am. He has great plans for the recruiting programme, and is most enthusiastic as an amateur. I wish you might have had as able an assistant as he during your Vice-Presidential term. I fear I made but an indifferent V. P.[2] His immediate objective is a large Appleton membership, since he thinks local activity there will furnish an admirable nucleus. Since his advent to office he has generously appointed me to the recruiting committee, and has kept me busy writing recruiting letters to sundry literary Appletonians. That work reminds me of my former recruiting labours two or three years ago. In a short time Galpin will be well known throughout the fraternity, but I thought you might enjoy advance information. A large number of articles from his pen will appear in the next crop of magazines, and the public will have a better opportunity to judge of his brilliant style. This style is not yet perfected in all the finer points, but is far enough advanced to shew what it will evolve into as time passes. You will especially delight in his touch of mysticism, a thing most clearly shown in his parables. He has a positive genius for allegory—as you will see when you read his "Nolens Trahitur" in Mr. Samples' SILVER CLARION.[3]

You flatter me with your opinion of my lines on Alan Seeger. They were written in great haste—and with the immediate motive of complying with a request for a piece to fill up a vacant space in Smith's TRYOUT. However, when the request came, I had been planning a tribute to Seeger for some time. It surprises me that you should have thought the piece worth typing— had I known, I should have prepared a typed version myself. I am glad your friend likewise deems the lines worth preservation. Two of my pieces appear in THE NATIONAL ENQUIRER this week.[4] One, which I will give here, is on my birth month:

AUGUST

Come, mellow month, whose full-blown charms
    O'er mead and wood diffuse their grace;
Whose ardour all the valley warms,
    And glads the grateful mountain's face.

The waving corn in yonder field,
    Delighted, owns thy genial ray;
Whilst clover'd plains adoring yield
    The frankincense of new-mown hay.

The sky a lovelier blue puts on;
    The sun thro' Virgo proudly rides;
The lark sings sweeter at the dawn;
    The stream with purer crystal glides.

The grove with tropic plenty flow'rs,
    And summer reigns in regal state;
Precious the boons of earlier hours,
    Yet now doth each one culminate.

To youthful bards the spring I give;
    To sighing swains the June divine;
But I midst riper joys would live,
    And choose the August days as mine!   H. P. L.

Your enclosed poems are all exquisite, but with the privilege of a hardened old Critick I shall take the liberty of making a remark or two. In "Coming!", line 2 stanza 2 needs emendation for two reasons. (1) Because the expression "Such is an actual fact" is utterly prose-like and hardly adapted to poetry; and (2) because "fact" and "track" do not rhyme. I take the liberty of suggesting a new line, which will make the stanza read thus:

> "Happy sweet Living is coming again;
>> Verily hastening back;
> Happy sweet Living is coming when
>> My Love's on the homeward track."

"Back" does rhyme with "track", but T and K can never be so paired. In "Was It You", the rhyme of "me" with itself in stanza 3 is technically impossible. Rhyming syllables must have different initial consonants. I suggest that line 1 be thus amended:

> "A tender dream came a-winging free."

"free" and "me" do rhyme, but "me" and "me" do not, for they are the same. "Mountain Wonder" strikes me as the finest and most appealing poem of the present collection—and besides its basic merit it has not a single technical flaw. I wish you would send it to Mr. Cook for one of his magazines—or to Miss McGeoch for the UNITED AMATEUR.[5] If there were any hope for another CONSERVATIVE within a year, I would ask for it myself—alack—hope dwelleth not here! I shall probably issue nothing till July 1919.

"To a Friend" I perused with much interest, and judging that the dominant metre intended is the iambic pentameter quatrain, I took the liberty of framing the enclosed revised version, which conforms throughout to that measure. Pardon the elimination of double rhymes, but they are not strictly permissible in a piece of this sort, where the single rhyme predominates. Note also the following: Stanza 2 line 4—"do play" is not in the best taste, as Mr. Pope demonstrates in his Essay on Criticism:

> "While expletives their feeble aid DO join"[6]

In stanza 4, I have removed the "bank of credit" metaphor as too commercial an allusion for poetical purposes. Images must have the Aonian ambrosial smack. (Sm.) In the next stanza I removed an "insurance" allusion for like reason. In stanza 6 I changed the rhyme of 2nd and 4th lines because it is not well to rhyme syllables whose accents are merely secondary. Also—the "-ee" rhyme followed too closely after the similar rhyme in the preceding stanza. Going back to the 4th stanza (I forgot to mention this in order) I have removed the expression "and such"—which is too colloquial and even comic in its suggestions, for serious verse. Note that I used this exact expression my satirical epilogue to "Aletheia Phrikodes"[7]—relying upon it for a laughable effect:

"And thanks his stars—or cosmoses and such—"

Surely this is unsuited to a serious theme. Stanza 8 required a maximum of reconstruction, as you will see by the repeated versions I made. But I think my final revision will pass muster. No 9 is the best in the original version, and required only one or two insertions for metrical reasons. I trust you may not think this revision presumptuous—but I cannot help desiring to straighten out verse whose thought is marked by so much nobility. I wish I could convert you to my notion—for no poem is so effective in the rough, as when polished to euphonious urbanity.

    I subscribe myself

Yr most obedient humble servant

H. Lovecraft.

Notes

1. HPL [unsigned], "Department of Public Criticism," *United Amateur* 17, No. 6 (July 1918): 121 (now rpt. in *Lovecraft Annual 2013:* 156): "'Browning As An Asset,' a brief essay by Anny Vyne Tillery (Renshaw), presents forcibly and gracefully the best arguments in favour of the celebrated and somewhat cryptical bard. Though the poetry lover may condemn Mr. Browning for his harshness, and the philosopher censure him for his pragmatism, none may deny that this unusual character was a thinker, and a remarkably faithful thinker. Whether or not he was mistaken in his acceptance of subjective phenomena as a basis for a creed, he was valiantly striving for the truth, and through all his obscurity and affectation shines the gleam of the genuine poet. Mrs. Renshaw is a Browning lover, and makes the most of these points. Her essay is a pattern of nobility and a model of style." Tillery's "Browning as an Asset" appeared in *United Amateur* 17, No. 4 (March 1918): 64–65.

2. HPL first First Vice-President of the UAPA for the 1915–16 term.

3. John Milton Samples, editor of the amateur journal the *Silver Clarion,* which HPL declared to be an "exponent of . . . literary mildness and wholesomeness" (*CE* 1.198). Galpin's "Nolens Trahitur" appeared in the September 1918 issue (see *CE* 1.211).

4. "August" and "The Link" appeared in the *National Enquirer* (a temperance paper published in Indianapolis, IN) on 22 August 1918.

5. Verna McGeoch, Official Editor of the UAPA (1917–19) and hence editor of the *United Amateur.*

6. Alexander Pope, *An Essay on Criticism* (1711), l. 346.

7. "Aletheia Phrikodes" is itself part of "The Poe-et's Nightmare."

[2]   [AHT]

598 Angell St.,
Providence, R.I.,
Sept. 16, 1918

Cultor Musarum[1]:—

The Brisbane clippings were perused with due appreciation. Don Arturo has an eye to the masses, doubtless owing to his long connexion with Hearst; hence his tribute to Popery.[2] His powers of forcible and lucid expression are phenomenal, and I regret that he has so long been mixed up with such a yellow-souled traitor as the serpent Hearst. In these *Times* editorials he seems free from the Hearst atmosphere of disloyalty. Perhaps if Hearst does not amend his ways, Brisbane will leave his employ. In the *N.Y. Tribune,* the leading anti-Hearst publication, there is much speculation as to whether Brisbane or Hearst really controls the *Washington Times.* For years Hearst has preyed upon civilisation by catering to the base prejudices of the canaille with anti-English, seditious, half-anarchistic matter. Hitherto his shrewd subtlety has kept him clear of the law; but I fancy he will finally be restrained. Since America entered the war, a distinct public sentiment against him is developing.

I notice that Brisbane has something to say about the rideless Sundays. Presumably this new regulation somewhat curtails your enjoyment of the "Smith Flyer".[3] Since I am carless, I can look on the matter with a more philosophical detachment. As I remarked once before, it is remarkable how little war conditions touch a confirmed recluse and semi-invalid. Rhode Island responded nobly to the rule. In this city there are many placards on the telegraph posts—"If you use your car on Sunday, you are a Slacker!"

I remain yr most obt Servt
H P Lovecraft.

Notes

1. Latin for "supporter of the Muses."
2. HPL refers to the well-known American journalist Arthur Brisbane (1864–1936), who had long worked for William Randolph Hearst. HPL appears to allude to editorials on the Catholic church written in the *Washington Times,* of which Brisbane had just become the owner.
3. The Smith Flyer was an automobile manufactured by the A. O. Smith Co. of Milwaukee from 1915 to 1919. Laws in some states prohibited driving a car on Sundays.

[3]   [AHT]

598 Angell St.,
Providence, R.I.,
June 1, 1921

Dear Mrs. Renshaw:—

I am answering letters promptly these last few days,

because I lack the will & energy to do anything heavier. The death of my mother on May 24 gave me an extreme nervous shock, & I find concentration & continuous endeavour quite impossible. I am, of course, supremely unemotional; & do not weep or indulge in any of the lugubrious demonstrations of the vulgar—but the psychological effect of so vast & unexpected a disaster is none the less considerable, & I cannot sleep much, or labour with any particular spirit or success.

Despite my mother's nervous illness & presence at a sanitarium for two years, the fatal malady was entirely different & unconnected—a digestive trouble of sudden appearance which necessitated an operation. No grave result was apprehended till the very day before death, but it then became evident that only a strong constitution could cause survival. Never strong or vigorous, my mother was unable to recover. The result is the cause of wide & profound sorrow, although to my mother it was only a relief from nervous suffering. For two years she had wished for little else—just as I myself wish for oblivion. Like me, she was an agnostic with no belief in immortality, & wished for death all the more because it meant peace & not an eternity of boresome consciousness. For my part, I do not think I shall wait for a natural death; since there is no longer any particular reason why I should exist. During my mother's lifetime I was aware that voluntary euthanasia on my part would cause her distress, but it is now possible for me to regulate the term of my existence with the assurance that my end would cause no one more than a passing annoyance—of course my aunts are infinitely considerate & solicitous, but the death of a nephew is seldom a momentous event. Possibly I shall find enough interesting things to read & study to warrant my hanging on indefinitely, but I do not intend to endure boredom beyond a certain limit. It is better to be as one was in the eternity before he was born. My mother was, in all probability, the only person who thoroughly understood me, with the possible exception of Alfred Galpin. She was a person of unusual charm & force of character, accomplished in literature & the fine arts; a French scholar, musician, & painter in oils. I shall not again be likely to meet with a mind so thoroughly admirable.

I am interested to observe your present reaction to Kant, in view of what your ultimate reaction will probably be; for I am convinced that you will later discard theism. Kant is one of the long line of jugglers with metaphysical abstractions, whose tenuous sophistries fairly hypnotise the student whose feet are not firmly on the ground. In other words, he carries thought into regions wherein there is no basis whatever for thought; for thought is valuable and significant only when supplied with objects to classify and from which to deduce. Neither Kant nor anyone else can possibly furnish "absolute proofs" of a deity or moral governor; for later discoveries have fully removed the necessity for assuming a personality behind nature, whilst morals are no more than local expedients for harmonious living, embodied into tradition. Schopenhauer explodes Kant in vigorous fashion, saying:

"Kant's language is often indistinct, indefinite, inadequate, and sometimes obscure. . . . . He who is himself clear to the bottom, and knows with perfect distinctness what he thinks and wishes, will never write indistinctly; will never set up wavering and indefinite conceptions, compose most difficult and complicated expressions from foreign languages to denote them, and use these expressions constantly afterward, as Kant took words and formulae from earlier philosophy, especially Scholasticism, which he combined with each other to suit his purposes; as, for example, "transcendental synthetic unity of appreciation", and in general "unity of synthesis" always used where "union" would be quite sufficient by itself. Moreover, a man who is himself quite clear will not be always saying anew what has once been explained, as Kant does, for example, in the case of the understanding, the categories, experience, and other leading conceptions."[1]

And Friedrich Nietzsche, the greatest philosopher of them all, said among other things the following:

"The spectacle of the Tartuffery of old Kant, equally stiff and decent, with which he entices us into the dialectic by-ways that lead (more correctly mislead) to his "categorical imperative"—makes us fastidious ones smile, we who find no small amusement in spying out the subtle tricks of old moralists and ethical preachers".[2]

Heine said that Kant was a man designed by Nature to sell coffee and sugar over a counter, and pointed out that whilst he postulated a deity in his practical system, he exploded such a thing in his theoretical system. Heine whimsically adds that Kant invented his "proof" of a deity to console his old manservant Lampe, who was fearfully disconcerted by the truths of pure reason, and no doubt looked to his kind master to be saved from the rude shocks of truth.[3] Altogether, Kant is one whose name might be quite readily commenced with a lower-case "c". His value in stimulating thought & advancing philosophy need not be questioned, but in matters of detail he is simply an empty & exaggerated name—one of those figures who receive accretions of blind adulation until they become mere magic words—mystical abracadabras of classical tradition whose revered mouthings & dialectics would evaporate if examined without the deafness & blindness of irrational veneration. As sequels to Kant, I sincerely trust that you will read Schopenhauer & Nietzsche, in the order named; following these with the most modern rational work—"Modern Science & Materialism", by Hugh Elliot, (1919). To emerge from the artificial fog of empty, resonant, mystical words without a single real idea behind them, into the clear light of minds with actual conceptions, is a tonic to the intellect. Lest you fancy that I am making an idol of Nietzsche as others do of Kant, let me state clearly that I do not swallow him whole. His ethical system is a joke—or a poet's dream,

366 ❊ *Letters to Elizabeth Toldridge and Anne Tillery Renshaw*

which amounts to the same thing. It is in his method, & his account of the basic origin & actual relation of existing ideas & standards, which make him the master figure of the modern age & founder of unvarnished sincerity in philosophic thought. It is impossible to understand philosophy without Nietzsche—as Mencken says; like him or not, you cannot escape him.[4]

Dr. Sigmund Freud of Vienna, whose system of psycho-analysis I have begun to investigate, will probably prove the end of idealistic thought. In details, I think he has his limitations; & I am inclined to accept the modifications of Adler, who in placing the ego above the eros makes a scientific return to the position which Nietzsche assumed for wholly philosophical reasons. But to Freud is due the credit of discovering the basic principles of one dominating motive behind all psychological processes; establishing inductively what Nietzsche established deductively—the selfish, individual *wille zur macht* which is the only driving force in the organic world.

As I grow older, I lose much of the prejudice & shallow enthusiasm for empirical & accepted traditions which retarded my progress toward realism in earlier years. I have today not a single well-defined wish save to die or to learn facts. This position makes me eminently receptive, for a new idea no longer meets with any conflict from old ideas—I can change my theories as often as valid evidence is changed, or as my judgment improves through exercise in the province of philosophical reflection. I am, I hope, now a complete machine without disturbing & biassing volition; a machine for the reception & classification of ideas & the construction of theories. As such, I may say that the obsoleteness of religion & idealism as systems of enlightened thought is impressed upon me with redoubled force. If any thing is true, it is that these beliefs are soon to be finally extinct until some cataclysm shall wipe out civilisation & inaugurate a new Dark Age of myth & ignorance.

Believe me,

Yr most obedient Servt,

H P Lovecraft.

Notes

1. Arthur Schopenhauer, "Criticism of the Kantian Philosophy," usually printed as an appendix to *The World as Will and Representation* (1818). See the translation by R. B. Haldane and J. Kemp (London: Kegan Paul, Trübner, 1909), 2.21.

2. Friedrich Nietzsche, *Beyond Good and Evil* (1886), Part 1, Section 5.

3. Heinrich Heine's comments on Kant can be found in the fragmentary treatise *On the History of Religion and Philosophy in Germany* (1835).

4. See H. L. Mencken, *The Philosophy of Friedrich Nietzsche* (Boston: John W. Luce, 1908).

[4]   [AHT]

598 Angell St.,
Providence, R.I.,
Oct. 3, 1921

Dear National Chairman:—

[. . . ?]

But this is not all of my industrial activity! I am now a professional fiction writer—albeit in a very limited sense. The vociferous George Julian Houtain has attempted to found a piquant professional monthly—25¢ per copy, $2.50 per year—with the alluring title of *Home Brew;* & for this ambitious venture he has demanded of me a series of six gruesome tales, all with the same central character, at the munificent price of $5.00 each! At first I refused; for fiction written to order is not art, whilst any *series* involves forcing & repetition of the most unclassical sort. But upon the insistence of the jovial editor I have given in, & have embarked upon a most hideous succession of yarns & narratives bearing the generic caption "Herbert West—Reanimator". Houtain said, "You can't make them too morbid", & I have taken him at his word! The two already finished are entitled respectively "From the Dark" & "The Plague Daemon". Of the success of the magazine I have substantial doubts, but if it does succeed I shall have excellent opportunities for acquiring a reputation for sinister diabolism!

The human sub-treasury, Mrs. Sonia H. Greene of Ukrainia, Muscovy, & Brooklyn, was in Providence Sept. 4 & 5, & exhibited the most explosive interest in the United. Allowing for the emotional extravagance of the Slavonic temperament, Mrs. G. is really a person of the greatest refinement & keenest intelligence; & my aunt became positively lyrical in her praise. You have probably seen Mrs. G.'s paper—*The Rainbow*—ere this, and may judge her general amateur interest by it.[1] After her amazing pledge to the O. O. Fund[2] I do not know how tactful it would be to suggest recruiting funds immediately; but after a duly decorous interval I fancy the matter might well be broached. You might drop her a line of welcome, her address being 259 Parkside Ave., Brooklyn, N.Y. Mrs. G. is an agnostic & anti-religionist, as you may observe in *The Rainbow;* but is too Russian & emotional to share the biting cynicism of Galpin & myself. In amateurdom she will prove a valuable fighter on the side of pure literature as opposed to pallid Woodbeeism.[3] She has a plan of convoking a sort of convention of artists, pagans, & philosophers in New York during the last week in December & the first week in January; & has invited Galpin, Loveman, & myself to be present. If that child Galpinius actually goes, I will be there if I have to go on foot & return in an ambulance—for sight of him is something positively not to be missed! Otherwise, it is a question whether my traditional seclusion would not triumph over my more recent tendency to make brief observations of the circumambient world. My aunt, though, urges me to go.

Yr most obt Servt
H P Lovecraft.

Notes

1. Sonia Greene's amateur journal, the *Rainbow* (No. 1, October 1921; No. 2, May 1922) contained many contributions by HPL and his colleagues. See HPL's unsigned article, "*Rainbow* Called Best First Issue," *National Amateur* 44, No. 4 (March 1922): 44–46; in *CE* 1.

2. Greene had donated $50.00 to the Official Organ Fund, a fund collected to offset costs for printing the *United Amateur*. See *SL* 1.143.

3. HPL refers to the Woodbees, an amateur group based in Columbus, OH, led by Ida C. Haughton and others. HPL constantly feuded with them in regard to the literary direction of the UAPA.

[5]   [AHT]

Dec. 10, 1921

Dear Head Prof:—

I notice also the disarmament propaganda, & sincerely hope that you are *not* connected with this movement! For in sober truth, this "brotherhood" stuff is hardly the sort of thing to advance when *facts* are to be faced. Adults ought to know by this time that "brotherhood", "unselfishness", "love", sacrifice", & all the rest of the "bla-bla" are uncivilised dreams & myths. Wars will always exist, armament or no armament, because they are the one inevitable result of a certain frequently recurring arrangement of ineradicable human instincts—when a certain group wants a certain thing with sufficient intensity, it will burst through every restraint to get it. "World peace" is such a fallacious & unscientific illusion that I wonder anyone can entertain it. The present conference[1] amuses me—or rather, I am amused at what the superficial masses fancy it can do. It is one of many gatherings to adjudicate important international questions, but the armament side is relatively trivial. The naval cuts may go through, but they will do nothing more than avert tax increases for the nations concerned. They will have no influence on the making of war—for that comes from deeper causes & overleaps every barrier. To hear pacifists clamour for the *abolition* of this or that—submarines or poison gas—makes me laugh. What is not done openly will be done secretly except in the case of unconcealable capital ships! If submarines & poison gas are "abolished", the next war will find most of the nations in possession of a goodly supply of both. The nation—if any—that *does* keep faith, will be left at the mercy of the rest. And that is the reason all such pacifist wailing is silly. To disarm one nation or group will avert no evil, but will merely create the greater evil of delivering it as a prey to shrewder & less scrupulous alien forces.

The next war will probably be between England, France, & America on the one hand, & Germany, Japan, & Russia on the other. Of the potential enemy, only one nation is a member of the conference. Germany is finding innumerable ways to remain strong save as a sea-power, Russia has the most terrible army of human wolves in existence, & Japan will break faith in every way possible. Let facts be faced before the ignorant & unqualified masses try to adjudicate problems which are difficult enough for trained statesmen!

But this is not to say that warfare is not becoming a menace in view of destructive invention. All that is sadly sure—& the next war will probably end civilisation, or start the ultimate ending. The point is, that good or bad the thing cannot be helped any more than the winter which kills the summer, or the earthquakes, the waterspouts, & the tidal waves. We live in a decadent age like that of the later Roman Empire, & only the simple can find grounds to dodge the fact. But the old man rambles!

> Yr most obt subordinate,
> L: Theobald Jun.

Notes

1. The Washington Naval Conference of 1921–22, which proposed limitations in the naval arms race.

[6]   [AHT]

> Theobald Butcher-Shop
> May 3, 1922

Dear Mrs. Renshaw:—

April 6–12 I took the most extended trip of my monotonous existence, going for the first time to New York City to meet the illustrious Samuel Loveman, who was there in a futile attempt to secure commercial employment. We were guests of Mrs. Greene of *The Rainbow*, whose philanthropy went to the length of turning over her entire flat to us & stopping with a neighbour herself. Loveman is utterly delightful—refined, delicate, sensitive, & aesthetic; though he does his best to conceal his artistic predilections beneath a modest exterior of commonplace good-fellowship. He read two of his unfinished masterpieces,[1] & I cannot but pronounce him in my mature opinion the greatest poet amateur journalism has ever produced. To meet him in person was a delight I had hardly dared to expect— now I must meet that delectable little imp Galpin, & life will be complete! We were given the most agreeable hospitality by all the local amateurs, & took infinite pleasure in meeting that young wonder Frank Belknap Long, Jr., who will be one of the literary giants of the next amateur generation. Long is a slight, dark, exceedingly handsome, & altogether poetic lad of twenty. We dined twice at his house—his parents are delightful—& in his company visited the historic Fordham cottage occupied from 1844 to 1849 by the one real literary figure of America—*Edgar Allan Poe*. Kleiner & Morton also shewed us many sights, the most impressive of which was the almost dreamlike & Dunsanian city skyline as seen from Manhattan Bridge. One whole day Loveman & I roamed around the Metropolitan Museum of Art, drinking in classic beauty, & agreeing that real beauty perished utterly with the Graeco-Roman age. Everything since has been an inferior imitation. I enclose some snapshots which I took during my travels—and which you might ultimately return, though there is no hurry. I stood the trip remarkably well whilst it lasted, but was wholly laid up for a week and a half afterward. Still—it was worth it.

> Yr most obt Servt
> L: Theobald Jun.

Notes

1. Probably *The Hermaphrodite* (1926) and *The Sphinx* (1944), a prose play; in *Out of the Immortal Night*.

[7]   [AHT]

> 598 Angell St.,
> Providence, R.I.,
> June 14, 1922

My dear Mrs. Renshaw:—

David V. Bush is a short, plump fellow of about forty-five, with a bland face, bald head, & very fair taste in attire. He is actually an immensely good sort—kindly, affable, winning, & smiling. Probably he has to be in order to induce people to let him live after they have read his verse. His keynote is hearty good-fellowship, & I almost think he is rather sincere about it. His "success-in-life" stuff is no joke so far as finance is concerned; for with his present "psychological" mountebank outfit, his Theobaldised books of doggerel, & his newly-founded magazine, MIND POWER PLUS, he actually shovels in the coin at a very gratifying rate. Otherwise he'd never have a suite at the Copley-Plaza. He welcomed Old Grandfather Theobald with open arms—& mouth—& discoursed for many moments on all things beneath the solar orb; displaying an intelligent knowledge of current events which would do credit to anyone under ten years of age. What amazed me most of all is that he does not mispronounce badly. No doubt his wife, a former teacher, has corrected some of his original orthoepic creations; but from his verse one would never guess that he is so well able to make himself understood in his native tongue. He is very ambitious. Oh, dear, yes! With becoming modesty he announces his intention of revolutionising the country with his new gospel of dynamic psychology; which has all the virtues of "New Thought" plus a saving vagueness which prevents its absurdity from being exposed before the credulous public amongst whom his missionary labours lie. He means well, & undoubtedly believes much of what he preaches. I think I have before mentioned that David started life as a poor farmer's boy—his father could nether read nor write till after his marriage—coming to Philadelphia when six years old, & thereafter almost ruining his health selling loads of papers too heavy for him to carry, & lacking even a bed to sleep on. In school he was taunted as backward (they must have seen his verse!), & in later life he was buffeted from pillar to post—successively as a trick cyclist in a circus, a ten-twenty-thirty "ham" actor, a "Shakespearian interpreter" on the lecture platform, a "success" orator, a clergyman, and a "modern psychologist". What the fellow really can do is to fascinate people by sheer force of a pleasing manner. He is a natural orator—of that there is no doubt—a very fair actor, & an undeniably efficient organiser & business-man. His aesthetic crimes are due to a blind spot in his critical faculty—he makes a public ass of himself when others with no greater gifts cut a better figure through their knowledge of when to keep quiet. But he is not quite so blind to the inferiority of his work as would appear from his writings. He knows he's no Keats, & laments it. Aside from the trifling matter of reclaiming the world from all its folly & misery, Dave's prime ambition is to be a great actor—not the tank circuit sort he used to be, but the regular Mantell or Barrymore sort of thing. I say "ambition", though Dave wouldn't call it that, since he thinks he's it already! In fact, he questioned me very interestedly about the modern American stage (whereof his ignorance is perfect) in an effort to ascertain whether there is any outstanding dramatist capable of writing a play to order which may suit his exacting requirements. He wants a starring vehicle for himself, in which the extremes of comedy are combined with the extremes of tragedy— in short, he wants to play Hamlet and the Grave-digger all at once in the same play—& the play must have a conclusion which drives home the truth of the psychology Dave preached. I do not wonder that his search must be exhaustive—so mighty a paragon of mixed artistic & didactic dramaturgy do his requirements demand! When he asked me very pressingly for the name of America's greatest dramatist, I humbly spoke a good word for that promising young person Eugene O'Neill—whose "Emperor Jones", it developed, Davy had already seen without witting the author thereof. When I told him that Gene is James O'Neill's son, his face lighted with intelligence—for in sooth, the old boy was not unknown to the admiring David in days agone.[1] And when I had finished, Dave hauled out his inevitable note-book & took down O'Neill's name & address—with the happy intention of writing him very soon anent the job of making a nice tragic-comedy, with suitable moral, to order. (INTERMISSION FOR APPROPRIATE LAUGHTER) I'd give a whole dime to see O'Neill's face when he reads Dave's condescending request. I wonder if he'll have the humour to spoof the poor fish along! Probably he won't even bother to answer him—but he ought to get at least a faint, world-weary smile out of it.

My first session with Dave ended in little more than an hour, for I had to beat it for the North Station to catch the 2:15 Haverhill train. I duly caught it, was met at the Haverhill dee-po by the Littles, and participated in a call on honest old Tryout Smith. Good old boy—there's nobody else just like him on earth, and our planet is poorer for the fact.

The next day of the trip was spent at the old Sawyer place in Merrimac, Mass., which is a farmhouse of the 1730 period refitted in original style by the local historical society. It is rented by the day to parties of antiquarian inclinations, and my generous hosts engaged it out of regard for my eighteenth century tastes. There I dined amidst scenes which a Colonial traveller might have beheld two centuries ago, and in the afternoon went across the bridge to the village's broad, shady main street (that goes in upper-case, too!) to look up my new United recruit, Edgar Jacobs Davis, aged thirteen years. I landed Edgar after Smithy had shewed me an Haverhill paper with an account of his poetical activities. It looked promising, so I started with the age-old recruiting process and bagged my victim; incidentally noting that he was an amazingly bright and erudite infant for his years. When I found myself in his vicinity, nothing but a personal call would do; so I marched up to the spacious Victorian house at 16 Main St. and hailed as a true adopted grandson the sturdy, ruddy, tousle-headed, knickerbockered individual who admitted me. Edgar is, I may here remark once and for all, SOME BOY! I really think I have at last discovered a second Galpin; for the child amazes me more each time I hear from him. In person he is quiet and modest, but on paper he sometimes "lets out" pyrotechnically; shewing a veritably stupefying range of interests and command of language, ideas, and humour. He quotes Latin incessantly, writes facile impromptu verse on every subject under the sun with any or no provocation, and has that delightful impudence which means mental vigour and healthy iconoclasm and independence. He is distinctly of Galpinian cast, and I am now endeavouring to get him in touch with that superboy. Alfredus ought to find him an interesting kidlet to adopt, whilst he would find in Alfredus a maturer companion of inestimable value. They are marvellously alike—cynics, humourists, scholars, and always inquirers. Edgar's father owns a hardware store in Haverhill, whilst his mother is a former teacher. They all come of the best old New-England stock, and are substantial folk in their community. I think Edgar has a splendid future both in amateurdom and out—I am immensely proud to have recruited him. His interest in the United is extreme, and I hope he will be widely welcomed. You might drop him a note or card if you have the time—Edgar J. Davis, 16 Main St., Merrimac, Mass. Merrimac is a placid, sizeable village a few miles east of Haverhill. I hardly need say that Edgar is on our side of the United campaign. After receiving the last WOODBEE, he gave vent to an impromptu whereof the following is part—

"Leo Fritter
Is a queer old critter,
Full of the deuce,
He hain't got no use
For fellows who try
To mount to the sky."

This reminds me of the fruit of some recent musing of mine own—

There is a quaint fellow call'd Fritter;
An amiable sort of a critter.
    But when he slung lead
    At Old Theobald's head
The votes shew'd him up as a bum hitter!

The day after the Davis call, the Littles motored north to their summer camp on Lake Winnipesaukee, and took me as far as the last railway link with Boston—which was Dover, N.H. This is the farthest north I ever was in my life, and whilst on the journey I obtained my first glimpse of Maine—which I did not enter. To describe the scenic beauties of the ride would be impossible—New-England, beyond the immigration-tainted belt, is too lovely for poet to describe. This is why I make rhymes about it—

Wide rolling pastures, till'd by many a swain,
And teeming orchards scatter'd o'er the plain;
Unbounded prospects o'er the vales and hills,
With fat kine quaffing at the crystal rills.
SIMPLICITY! blest Nature's first ally!
Child of the balmy groves and lucent sky;
God of the dell, the thicket, and the slope,
And last kind guardian of declining hope![2]

The vistas of winding road, with ancient farmhouses nestling amidst old gardens and under centuried trees; the glimpses of villages in the vales, white steeples piercing canopies of dense billowing foliage—oh, the deuce! It would take Sechrist or some real writer to get it on paper! We passed through Exeter, seat of the famous academy—it is a dreamy old town; a perpetual twilight of delicate foliage with friendly ghosts of great white houses. Portsmouth is a Georgian city miraculously preserved till this decadent age—the streets of Colonial mansions are captivating. And then at one point we saw the sea— the broad, boundless, billowing British sea, which serves our mighty race as a fortress against base foes! God Save the King! There was a lone ship sailing south, and far out one could faintly glimpse misty suggestions of the half-fabulous Isles of Shoals.

Back in Boston, I called at the new Parker-Miniter establishment,[3] slept at the Brunswick, seat of last year's convention, & on the next day "did" the art museum & all the old graveyards. In the evening I attended one of Bush's lectures—& marvelled. Boston, with its predilection for transcendental nonsense, is the champion jay town of my limited geographical experience. Though Bush said the house was nothing as compared with his shouting, S.R.O. western audiences, it sure was some bunch for a Boston event—& was composed not only of the dumb-bells & coal-heavers one would expect, but also of many who bore the unmistakable stigmata of Bostonese culchaw. The subject was about the power of thought—oh, but thought is a wonderful thing! I never realised before—or since—just how wonderful a thing thought is! Bush told heaps of anecdotes—one about a gentleman who was burned to death because he wouldn't get a priest to give the last rites to his pore dyin' wife. At another time he attacked the local tramway service—which drew much applause. I applauded, too, having that day ridden in a crazy combination of the vintage of 1880—a couple of broken-down horse-cars spliced together & mounted on the wheels of some kid's discarded velocipede—or something like that. But the real gem—a gem because it had no connexion with the lecture—was Davy's very tragic portrayal of John B. Gough's delirium tremens.[4] This sure was a bird of an act—he had a red & green spotlight alternating, & made faces & clawed the air in fine style as he screamingly struggled with the pink snakes & other friendly beasties. If I were putting on a shew I'd be tempted to hire Dave as a Roman mob or something like that.—But no doubt Gene O'Neill will get ahead of me by furnishing that starring vehicle. The ordeal was over about ten-thirty, & I chuckled to see the victims pause at a table in the foyer & plunk down good money for bum verses I had tinkered up in past years. There were books, wall-cards, & all that sort of thing; & not one bally stanza whose final form didn't come from Grandpa Theobald's labouring pen. If Bush can sell the stuff like that, Morton & I would have to boost our rates! The jamboree, I may mention, was held at Convention Hall on St. Botolph St.—but stay! I'll chuck a circular in this letter. That will give you a recent mug of Davy— though in truth he doesn't look quite so bad as all that. After the show Dave wanted to dine with me at a cafe, but I had to beat it for the train, hence bade a cordial good-bye. After all, he's a harmless, likeable chap, & I fancy it will be a bit less impossible to do his work in the future. He enjoys life—as do all who are spared the curse of intelligence.

Yr. most obt Servt,
L: Theobald Jun.

Notes

1. James O'Neill (1847–1920), the father of Eugene O'Neill, was a well-known Irish actor.

2. Lines 5–8 are from HPL's "Simplicity: A Poem" (1922; see *The Ancient Track,* 246–47); the others evidently are original.

3. I.e., a residence jointly occupied by the amateurs Charles A. A. Parker and Edith Miniter.

4. John B. Gough (1817–1886) was an American temperance advocate and author of *Sunlight and Shadow* (1880), which HPL claimed converted him to the temperance cause (*SL* 1.35).

[8] [ALS]

66 College St.,
Providence, R.I.,
Feby. 24, 1936

Dear A T R:—

      I must not delay further in acknowledging yours of the 15th & 18th, with instalments of "Well-Bred Speech" copy. Unfortunately I was in a very tight place—with two prior tasks calling for immediate attention—but I managed to do some elementary work on the MS., & am forming an idea of what the rest will be like. I hope extremely that I shall not cause any disastrous delay—& I'll notify you very shortly if anything seems to augur against delivery by April 1st. In that case *Moe* might come to the rescue very successfully. My *new* handicap is the rather severe illness of my aunt with a grippe attack vastly worse than the one I had last month. For a week I've been rather closely chained as a sort of combined nurse, butler, & errand-boy—though I have a certain amount of time at my desk. It may be all right—& in any event I'll report on current progress & make a few enquiries as to the later stages of the job. Your replies to the latter will be as valuable to Moe (or anyone else whom you might choose) as to me if the completion has to be transferred.

      I see that the job is somewhat ampler than I had expected—involving the furnishing of original elements as well as the revision of a specific text. Rates can be discussed later—I fancy that any figure you would quote (with current precedent in mind) would be satisfactory. What I have done so far is to arrange the text in the order indicated in the table of contents, & go over the language & examples with care—smoothing out any hasty passages & rectifying a few points which seemed to need attention. I shall discuss some of the latter presently. In several places the exact *meaning* of the text seemed obscure or ambiguous—a possible result of haste, stenographic error, or extreme abstractness, sententiousness, & novelty of style. Wherever this occurs, I have given the passage whatever meaning I think was intended—& have made a note in the margin. It will be well for you to look sharply at any place so marked—making sure that I have not misrepresented what you meant to convey. In order to avoid building on an uncertain foundation, it is possible that I will—notwithstanding the extra postal expense—send along the copy at its present stage of revision for your approval or correction. I will decide this more fully after finishing this letter & seeing how many points can be settled without such a step.

First point—I assume that you do not wish any particular expanding of the continuous text except where you have specifically called for amplification. That is, you mean to have the bulk of the work in essentially its present language—allowing for corrections & clarifications & specified additions.

Second point—regarding the distribution of the contents of the *mimeographed leaflet* in the text: (1) Is the "List of Cultural & Economic Terms" to form the basis of Chapter IV—"Terms Which Should Own a Place in Your Conversation"? If not, where *is* this chapter, & where shall the list go? Is this list meant to be an appendage of such a chapter? Or do you wish me to write the chapter as a continuous text in imitation of your style, giving general observations on the subject of allusion & working in the list as an ingredient or supplement? Or have you written such a chapter & inadvertently omitted it from the MS.? Furthermore—just how do you wish this list *amplified?* Do you mean that the catalogue of terms is to be enlarged as a catalogue (if so, to what approximate length?) on its present plan, or that each term in the existing list is to be treated in detail, with current application or meaning ("denotation", as you term it) & literary, folklore, or historical source ("connotation") given in full? If the latter, could you give a concrete illustration by taking one or two terms & arranging the definitions & sources as you wish them to be in all cases?

I would need to have assistance in handling the abstruse & technical economic terms—many of which are bewilderingly recent & extremely rare in general literature. Several are obviously derived from the literature of economics, yet I am frankly ignorant of their original source. Of one or two—at least, in their present form—I don't even know the current direct application. This may be a shameful confession of illiteracy on my part—& yet I feel certain that in my day such a minute & exhaustively documented knowledge of advanced political economy was not expected of the average layman—even the educated layman. It would have been like expecting one to refer familiarly to the echinida of the oölitic system, to the lactones of monohydroxy-monobasic acids (γ & δ types) of the paraffin series, to De l'Isle's method of determining the solar parallax from a transit of Venus, or to the comparison of masses by acceleration-tests—all in the course of a homelike evening around the parlour hearth! However, I know that times change, & that today—in the face of greater impending economic changes than have ever been known to man since the discovery of agriculture—technical economics has come to occupy as prominent a place in general scholarship as Latin & Greek did when I was young. Therefore I don't doubt but that all the terms you list *ought* to be known—as regards both application & derivation—to every modern person who calls himself well-informed. The fault is mine—but I *don't* know them all, & will therefore (lacking the ability to make library researches during my present period of emergency duty as nurse-butler-errand-boy) have to ask some-one else to supply facts concerning the exact shade of meaning of "plane of competition", the original literary use of the phrase "Margin of Culture", & suchlike. I am an old man & don't know nothin'! Incidentally—if what you wish is merely an expansion of the list, have you any choice as to the *nature* of the added allusions? Mythology? English literature? history? the fine arts? the sciences? political economy? Or all of these in equal proportions? It is very hard to draw a line or set an *absolute* standard as to what shall be known famil-iarly. Astonishing ignorance is the rule, even among persons of good birth & approved formal education. A young friend of mine recently tried a question-naire of ten simple questions on about 50 persons of presumably non-plebeian status, & the results were appalling & incredible. Yet even I—for all my igno-rance—could readily answer all of these without head-scratching or Britan-nica-delving! (2) Is the section "After this Course, What Shall I Read?" to be blended into Chapter X (which is marked for amplification), or to form a sup-plement or appendix? Also, what is to be the disposition of the Reading List at the beginning of the leaflet? Is it to be preserved intact, or altered by omission & addition while remaining a table, or to be broken down into some sort of continuous text with comments? I note your request for additions to the read-ing chapter. Does that include changes in this particular list? Also—do you wish more suggestions for scientific, philosophical, &c. reading in the "After this Course" section? I notice you include few recent books. Do you wish me to cite more contemporary volumes on the rapidly-changing sciences? I ha-ven't kept track of all, but might have a few suggestions.

Third Point (proceeding with the main MS. in the proper order) Much change is advisable in the section relating to the history of language in general & of the English language in particular. If I decide to send back the MS. for approval or correction you will see what I have done. It would not be possi-ble to state that a "divine revelation" theory of speech is seriously considered today, for no reputable anthropologist could tolerate so primitive a myth. See any real authority—Boule, Keith, Lankester, Briffault, Money-Kyrle, G. Elliot Smith, Ratzel, Sir Arthur Evans, Sir H. H. Johnston, &c. &c. This, let me as-sure you, is no prejudice of mine, & has nothing to do with my own absence of supernatural belief. Many students of anthropology believe in the gods in one way or another, but simply do not adhere to the archaic notion that Zeus or Wotan or Yahwe or Brahma or Ahura-Mazda gave specific linguistic in-struction to the noble & aspiring race of *homo sapiens*. Of course, you will find many grandiloquent statements about divine pedagogy in the older & less sci-entific writers of the middle & early 19th century—good old Trench,[1] for ex-ample—but today that kind of thing could draw nothing but a laugh from an alert young audience. Therefore—all apart from the wider question of the ex-istence of cosmic consciousness, purpose, & direction—it is important not to echo any myth so universally abandoned by first-rate anthropologists. As you will see, my changes do not include or imply any attack on the conventional mythology. (2) More—in the absence of public library opportunities I have not been able to find any indication that English was ever thought to descend from Hebrew. It is true that certain English *words* were falsely assigned a He-brew etymology, but so far as I know there was never any clear notion that the whole syntactical structure was Semitic. On the other hand, its relation to other Germanic tongues was always more or less loosely recognised. I have given this passage an ambiguous phrasing pending my access to suitable books. At any rate, a clear recognition of the Indo-Germanic linguistic family begins in the late 18th century with the celebrated Orientalist Sir William Jones. (3). You have not given enough major language classes. There are at least 10—possibly more, if the Euskarian (Basque) falls into a separate cate-gory, & if the Tuareg is not truly Hamitic. And of course dozens of families are extinct. The main survivors seem to be (1) Aryan, (2) Semitic, (3) Hamitic, (4) Turanian (European Mongoloid—Magyar, Finnish, &c), (5) true Mongo-lian (including Chinese, Thibetan, &c. Japanese is a puzzling hybrid), (6) Bantu or negroid, (7) Dravidian (black races—not nigger—of southern In-dia), (8) Malay-Polynesian, (9) American Indian (distinct variant from Mongo-lian—Esquimau speech doubtful), & (10) Australoid-Tasmanian.

Fourth point—the list of common errors. Do you wish this greatly changed? And if so, in *what direction?* That is, shall I descend in the cultural scale & pay attention to such speech-habits as the repetition of "I said" & "he said" [or "I says," & "he says"] in narrating a conversation—or the use of "like he done" & "ain't got no"—or shall I ascend & pay attention to points which are relatively subtle . . . . defective parallelism of sentence elements, awkward overlapping dependence of clauses or phrases, "dangling" modifiers, &c. &c.? In other words, about how do you want lines to be drawn? One *could* fill any number of volumes with different typical mistakes & illustrations of them. What selective principles ought to be kept in mind? Or do you wish the exist-ing selection to remain substantially unchanged? I will now proceed to con-sider some of your individual specimen sentences, & indicate a few which I believe demand additional reflection. (a) Under "mistakes in number" you condemn the phrase "pains were taken". I find good authority for a plural verb in this case. May I substitute "His politics *are* liberal"—a sentence about which no doubt can exist? (b) are you sure that "necessity" (unless clearly per-sonified) cannot take *which* as a relative? (c) I believe that the section on the *subjunctive* ought to have quite a bit of reconsideration in the light of current use. Even Walker—a century & a half ago—spoke of the steadily narrowing province of the subjunctive, & the precise Victorian Rev. Stopford Brooke is still more specific about this.[2] Today a *too traditionally* **correct** use of the sub-junctive produces an inescapable suggestion of pedantry, & I believe current text-books will have to allow for it. I don't by any means condone that radical policy favoured by the National Council of Teachers of English three or so years ago—when they voted to approve things like "It is *me*", "*Who* are you looking for?", "None *are* expected", "More *quick*", "Try *&* get well", &c.—but I do believe in keeping an ear cocked for the daily living speech of well-born & cultivated persons, & in quietly ceasing to emphasise forms which depart too widely from such spontaneous usage. Generally what *seems* to be an innovation will be found to possess a long history of informal & increasingly tolerated usage—just as the Romance languages were not really sudden decay-products of classical Latin, but were rather mere risings to the surface of *colloquial* tendencies which had existed for centuries in the various regions concerned, side by side with the formal Latin of literature & oratory. The language had always been changing. Cicero did not follow all the precedents of Plautus, Apuleius differed from Cicero, & Boëthius differed from Apuleius. Thus I believe it would be wise to change the title of the subjunctive section to read:

> The subjunctive mood should—except when rendered obsolete by idiomatic usage—be used after IF, WHETHER, THOUGH, TILL, LEST, & UNLESS, & after other expressions which indicate indecision, a doubt, or a wish.

As for the examples: do you not think that the time for objecting to "Unless he has told you to stay you need not" is definitely past? Just pause & imagine the *oral* effect of the alternative precise form. Is there not something subtly *comic* in such over-precision? I have taken the liberty of substituting a sentence in which the absence of the subjunctive is still (except in the eyes of the National Council) a fault: "If I *was* to do this, I would be wrong." Do you endorse this change? Another change: for "Whether the book was ever published, I do not know" [a *correct* sentence by contemporary colloquial standards], I am substituting "he will arrive, though he *goes* slowly." Has this your approval? I would welcome your opinion on all these specific points—& especially on the general question of enlarging [& if so, in what direction] or not enlarging the entire list as it stands.

Fifth point—words frequently mispronounced. *Some* of these have more than one permissible pronunciation—see parallel tables in the front of Webster's Unabridged. Do you allow for this—or believe that of the permitted forms (*I* say "il-*lus'*-trate", but dozens of perfectly literate people say "*il'*-lustrate") one is so much preferable to any other that it ought to be exclusively recommended? Incidentally—do you wish this list amplified? It could be quite logically extended to the bulk of an entire volume!

¶ Such are the doubtful matters. I hope that I shall have things arranged in such a way as to let me get immediately at the work as soon as it comes back with specific instructions. Or if you wish to avoid *any* uncertainty, you could place it elsewhere at once—the present start being equally valid, no matter who goes on with it. In any case I shall see that it is done & delivered—by myself or by another (I *hope* by myself) on or before April 1st!

Thanks for the attractive brochure "This Way Out", which arrived early in the month. The A.A.V.W. programme is interesting indeed—& will surely keep you on the move if you attend many of the scheduled events! The postal announcement of the Ten-Weeks' Course looks highly alluring—& I hope it is drawing a goodly quota of new students for the school. I must take advantage of your kind invitation & see this institution some day when my present quasi-imprisonment is over!

In conclusion, let me apologise for my stupidity & seeming inconsiderateness in bothering you with these questions when you are so busy. I know you gave carte blanche—but I do think it is best to see at this point whether I am headed right. I'm sure you can pardon me in view of the excellence of my intentions. My intentions would pave Tartarus or build a sea-wall along both banks of Phlegethon! ¶ Awaiting instructions—& hoping for the best, I remain
                    —Yr most oblig'd & obt Servt
                    H P L

P.S. I have decided, after all, to send the whole MS. temporarily back for comment & suggestions. I think it is worth the extra postage to know whether everything is going in the right direction so far. Please read it carefully, & straighten out (if necessary) those places where marginal question-marks indicate originally doubtful readings. ¶ In clearing up the 5 specific points, you might return this letter which enumerates them if that would enable you to reply more briefly & easily.

Notes

1. Richard Chevenix Trench (1807–1886), British archbishop, poet, and essayist, and author of *On the Study of Words* (1851; *LL* 893).
2. See John Walker (1732–1807), *A Rhetorical Grammar* (1785; *LL* 915); Stopford A. Brooke (1832–1916), *English Literature* (1876) and other works.

[9] [ALS]

                                        66 College St.,
                                        Providence, R.I.,
                                        March 30, 1936
Dear A T R:—
            I ought to begin with several solid paragraphs of apology for my previous non-acknowledgment of your letter & MS. of Feby. 28, but you can perhaps pardon me when you learn the difficulties under which I am labouring. If I was completely sunk in February, I am now veritably buried beneath the ocean floor! All is chaos, since I am entirely without unworried

leisure, & am simply crushed to a pulp—like Giles Corey beneath his load of stones[1]—by the avalanche of varied & largely unperformable tasks heaped upon me. My aunt's illness has increased, necessitating her removal to the hospital—where, however, she is slowly but surely recovering. With a servantless house, unnumbered errands, & my aunt's correspondence as well as my own upon my hands, I can do no more than raise the white flag & cry "Kamerad!"[2] regarding a million neglected obligations. Many letters with a February postmark still remain unopened. Of all the messes I have ever been in, this comes close to taking the prize! And it *would* have to explode around me just as I was tackling a job which I wished to do promptly & well!

But, let me hasten to assure you, your large manila envelope is *not* among the unopened ones! On the other hand, I gave your revised MS. a close survey in odd moments as quickly as possible, & have since kept it constantly in front of me—jotting down necessary emendations whenever I could spare a second from tasks admitting of no delay. Naturally, I have not made even approximately the progress I *ought* to have made in a month; but on the other hand I feel that the time has not been wholly lost. The things I have done are all in the *right direction,* & will save just so much time for anyone who finishes the work. This applies especially to the straightening out of numerous items in the *familiar allusion* department. Here (if I may say so without the imputation of egotism) I have done some wholesale correction of historical, mythological, & other points which I doubt if the average reviser would be likely to have parallelled. Not that I am better informed than others, but that I have the dull, plodding patience to *look closely* for slips & make very sure that nothing erroneous or misleading remains. It is the fashion nowadays to be neglectful, slipshod, & inaccurate, but I believe that a text—especially if it is designed *for the specific purpose of instruction*—has no excuse for being other than just as accurate as normal scholarship can make it. Therefore I am not ashamed to be conscientious in the old-fashioned way, even though it gain me (as indeed it has!) the name of pedant. This matter salves my conscience to some extent; since despite my outrageous slowness—& even if I have to turn the ending of the job over to another—I can say with confidence that the trip of the MS. to #66 has not been wholly in vain. This fourth chapter is now complete—assuming that you wish no increase in the number of terms explained. In one or two instances I have intruded upon alien soil & placed question-marks opposite certain of the baffling economic terms . . . . where, without any real knowledge, I seem to have nebulous memories of meanings other than those given. These notations may expose me as a very great dunce, but I had rather be so exposed than to let any debatable point slip by.

Well—the one other thing I have done is to "proofread" the badly typed MS. *throughout,* & eliminate all the numberless textual errors. In many places the apparent omission of whole sentences—or parts of sentences—has thrown the text into meaningless chaos; & whenever this has occurred I have

382 ❊ *Letters to Elizabeth Toldridge and Anne Tillery Renshaw*

applied the principle of recension as intelligently as I am able. Several times—where my own pencilled text of last month is concerned—I must confess that the fault probably lay with my wretched handwriting . . . . . as, for instance, when your not-very-resourceful typist interpreted ORIENTALISTS as ORI-ANFOLOTS [or was I wrong—& was Sir William Jones a member of some esoteric order which gave him the name of *Orionfolot?* But anyhow, he was *also* an *Orientalist!*], & turned rhetoric to anthropology by rendering TRITE ALLU-SIONS as TRIBE ALLUSIONS! Now in this connexion—& in view of the large amount of my scrawling in Chap IV—let me say that I will always be glad to go over any passage transcribed from my text. If you will send me *both the typed version & my original scrawl* (so that I can duplicate the original wording) I will very carefully correct the text in neatly printed characters which will match the typing and leave no room for further misinterpretation.

Here, then, is the present state of the manuscript. No new or original matter yet supplied (except in correcting the familiar allusion section), but the whole text made correct & intelligible *as already developed.* This will be of great value to anyone continuing the work. Chapters II (Common Errors) & IV (familiar allusions) virtually complete—certain points (stenographic) in the former having been set right.

Does this seem pitifully inadequate? Well—nobody can be sorrier than I! As you see, I have chosen for performance those things which can be done perfectly well under stress & in odd moments—*mere correction & research* [i.e., the simple "research" of verifying my own corrections in the books in my own library. Under present stress I could not possibly undertake real research at the public library.]—& shall continue in the same way. My next step will be to double (as requested) your list of words frequently mispronounced—calling upon my recollections of characteristic slips both patrician[*] & plebeian to swell the grand total. The *real difficulty* will be in developing—under present conditions—those additions which require the exercise of *original taste & judgment* . . . . . a task seeming very formidable amidst the piled-up obligations & interrupted time-schedule of the moment. Had I your fund of active energy, I dare say there would be no trouble—but alas! this poor old head needs a certain amount of repose, leisure, & tranquillity if it is to function in more than a merely mnemonic or automatic way!

Now this brings up the question of whether I ought—in justice to your needs—to try to finish the job. Your kind extension of time to May 1st greatly helps—& the ruthless shelving of various other matters may operate in the same direction. On the other hand, the return of my aunt from the hospital will reimpose the duties of a nurse upon me, & thus operate adversely. As yet,

---

[*]the *conscious affection* by cultivated persons of certain fashionable but grotesque pronunciations (such as *har-rass'* for *har'rass*) angers me more than the naive & innocent blundering of the unlettered.

I do not know when this return will take place—or just how much care (in the way of meal-getting, &c.) my aunt will require at that time. The uncertainty adds to the perplexity of the situation.

Well—I believe that, subject to your veto, I will postpone a decision until April 7 or 8 . . . about a week, in which time I will know just a bit better where I stand. By that time—I hope—the word list will be complete, & I may have been able to dig up some further reading suggestions. Thus the job will be far enough advanced to enable any reviser *under normal conditions* to finish it in the remainder of the month. If I then think I can do it, I will (subject to your approval) try it. If I fear I can't, I'll pass it on to Moe or any other critic you may name . . . or (if requested) return it to 1739. Incidentally, be sure to instruct me clearly on what to do with the MS. in case I have to transfer its conclusion to another.

As for the proper amends to make for messing up & delaying everything— let me say that if I cannot finish the job I *will make no charge whatsoever for work already performed.* Thus (in view of the February work & of the really substantial corrections in Chapter IV) I believe I can adequately & honourably square myself for any trouble I may have caused by throwing (albeit innocently, regretfully & involuntarily) a monkey-wrench into your scholastic programme!

Commenting in order upon the points in yours of 28th ult.—the new form you have given the text indeed constitutes a vast improvement & simplifies the reviser's task. As to the matter of that early-Victorian "divine-instruction" theory—the sober presentation of such a thing in a book written later than 1860 illustrates the bad results of *non-coördination* among the different branches of knowledge. Where a small fragment of one science overlaps into the field of another (as, in this case, a small fragment of anthropology overlaps into philology or linguistics), the lesser authorities in the second science are woefully apt to be totally ignorant of the details or recent developments of the first one—which is not their specialty. Thus the estimable Professor Lockwood (whom I seem vaguely to recall as a collaborator with one Emerson in a rhetoric shoved at me in high school thirty years ago)[3] may be an excellent philologist, yet is obviously out of touch with those other sciences which touch philology only occasionally. It is not the business of the philologist to investigate the pre-grammatical beginnings of articulate speech. That is something for the anthropologist, psychologist, & biologist to handle. But one wishes that—if a philologist *insists* on referring to contiguous sciences—he would take the trouble to see what their reputable *contemporary* exponents have to say on the points of contact!

Incidentally—regarding that point about the old belief in a Hebraic origin of English, for which I said I could uncover no evidence—I have since (in the limited time I have had for searching . . . only in my own library, of course) found something which may shed a bit of light. It seems that in the later Middle Ages certain classical scholars—preëminently Guichard & Gebelin—did indeed waste a prodigious amount of energy trying to prove that *Greek & Latin* are descended from Hebrew. But since in those days no connexion between English (i.e., the Teutonic base. Of course, students *always* realised that the Norman-French element came directly from a debased Latin dialect) & the Greek & Latin tongues was recognised, this hardly affects the original point at issue. However—it is by no means impossible that the theory of an Hebrew-born English *did* exist, since this sort of unguided & fantastic speculation was rampant in mediaeval times. where did you find the reference? In Lockwood? And were there any further details given? The matter is certainly interesting. In early modern times—& almost up to the age of Sir William Jones—scholars recognised the kinship of English to Dutch, German, & Scandinavian (also ancient Gothic) speech, but had nothing to say about Hebrew save in connexion with certain words. It may be remarked that during the ages of Christian orthodoxy scholars felt under no necessity of tracing all languages to a common source, since they accepted the well-known myth of Babel, involving a total confusion of tongues—a fresh linguistic start from scratch!

About the chapter on vocabulary—a little more leisure may enable me to see just what it needs. But I hesitate to amplify the *voice* section, since I am so totally inexperienced in the theory & practice of elocution as distinguished from written language. I am all pen—no tongue! Chapter VII will take reflection—but ought not to be prohibitively difficult. Chapter VIII—the citation of additional stock expressions to avoid—will be easy as soon as I can get a moment to think in. And I certainly hope to concoct some book lists (not, I fear, as ample as I could concoct if I had time to spend at the library) in the near future—both in the literary & scientific departments. This is just the sort of a job I best like to do when I'm in shape for it! As for touches of humour—if any of that quality is left in me after the wringing which the early part of '36 has given me, I surely won't spare them! But not much can be absolutely guaranteed in that line!

Oh, yes—about that matter of words doubtfully pronounced, I seem not to have made myself clear. I didn't suggest marking the pronunciation of words. What I asked was this: how can we say that a word is frequently *mispronounced* when *both* of the commonly encountered versions possess a certain amount of sanction? Thus the word at the very head of your list—abdomen—has its secondary & less classical pronunciation (ab´-do-men) sanctioned by at least two reputable dictionaries prior to 1890's. However, I assume that when you enter a word on your list you refuse to recognise the less traditional pronunciation as proper despite the endorsement of certain lexicographers. [So do I, as a matter of fact. I couldn't possibly bring myself to say *ab´-do-men* or *con´-cen-trate* or *ad´-dress* or *ill´-us-trate*.] Some of the words you list* I have never heard mispronounced, but I assume that your wide experience with novices (*in*

---

arid, necessary, chorus, adjourn, &c.

person at the school—gawd knows I've *corresponded* with enough of 'em in amateur journalism! I suppose the speech of some of my rough-diamond correspondents would nearly floor me if I were to meet them face to face!) has given you ampler opportunities for judging certain grotesque verbal manhandlings as common & characteristic. Maybe I mangle a lot of words myself without knowing it! ¶ Such are the facts. I shall be ready for any sort of instructions, & meanwhile reiterate my profound regret concerning any bother my unavoidable tardiness may be causing. ¶ With best wishes & apologies—

      Yr most obt Servt—

        H P L

Notes

1. See Mary E. Wilkins Freeman (1852–1930), *Giles Corey, Yeoman* (New York: Harper & Brothers, 1893; *LL* 332), a play about the Salem witch trials. HPL purchased a copy in 1924 (*SL* 1.360).

2. A shout of surrender (Comrade!) used by German soldiers.

3. Sara E. H. Lockwood and Mary Alice Emerson, *Composition and Rhetoric for Higher Schools* (Boston: Ginn & Co., 1901).

[10] [ALS]

          66 College St.,

          Providence, R.I.,

          Septr. 19, 1936

Dear A T R:—

      Yours of Tuesday gave me a guilty start anent the really criminal slowness I have shewn in dealing with "Well-Bred English". As the accompanying MS. will attest, the work is done after a fashion; & yet the obvious need for consultation & condensation will make its readiness by Oct. 1st a tight squeak. Whatever I can do to atone for my seeming delinquency I will do. I will *now* be able to act *instantaneously* on the MS. when it returns after your possible changes, & ought to have it back in your hands at least five days after such a time as you may send it. In a final draught I will take care about having my script more legible. The present additions will be hard to read in spots, but whatever you decide to keep you can have typed with blanks left for undecipherable words. Then send me the typed sheets *plus my originals* (for I can't always recall what I said in a given place, & might not think of so good a word the second time), & I'll fill in the lacunae with neat* printing like this.

First let me give excuses. When I last wrote, my aunt was in a convalescent home—half-way stage betwixt the hospital & here. She returned to #66 April 21, but required so much coöperation that my programme remained

---

*pardon my egotism if the adjective is unjustify'd!

utterly disorganised. In addition, my own health was wretched—a state of nervous exhaustion bordering on breakdown, plus a troublesome digestive siege. Whatever I could do, could be done only in unsatisfactory snatches. The continuous concentration needed for effective work was impossible. Cold weather—for the New England spring came atrociously late this year— aggravated the trouble. In July I began to feel considerably better, & my aunt also recovered well. (She is virtually her old self now.) I now made some headway with my chaotic programme, & accomplished quite a bit on the book—completing the tables of mispronounced words, two-pronunciation words, & clichés, & augmenting & transposing various chapters—but re- served the *really* tough job of composing the balanced reading course for my native month of August—the understood deadline being some time in Sep- tember. Alas for the five-year-plans of muridae & hominidae! One evening as I came home from a writing session on Prospect Terrace (a favourite park of mine on the ancient hill just north of here), I found a youthful guest parked in the living-room & surrounded by a profusion of bags & baggage . . . . Little Bobby Barlow, my Florida host of '34 & '35, arrived for an indefinite stay & requiring a maximum of guiding, conversation, & time-consuming attention in general! Ædepol! the kid took a room at the boarding-house across the garden, but despite this degree of independence was a constant responsibility. He *must* be shewn to this or that museum or bookstall . . . he *must* discuss some new fantasy or chapter in his future monumental novel . . . . & so on, & so on. What could an old man do—especially since Bobby was such a gener- ous & assiduous host himself last year & the year before? Well—I did a lot of work in the small hours after the kid had retired to his trans-hortense cubicle (& then he thought it funny that Grandpa didn't get up till noon!), but what headway could such stolen snatches make against a schedule-congestion which had things *already* half shot to hades? And the child only lit out last week!! Results are what might be expected. Lacking *continuous* opportunities to work, I only just made the deadline—& that without having had the debat- able chapters discussed, as they should have been by this time. But I would have had the MS. in the mails this week anyhow. Of the MS. & its features much more anon.

It remains to say that despite its general nightmare quality the summer was not without its compensations. July 18–19 I had a very pleasant though regrettably brief visit from our old friend Moe*—who likewise did some shining at the Congress of Am. Poets in N.Y. He came with his son Bob (now located in Bridgeport, Conn. as I may have told you) in the latter's 1928 Ford, & we did quite a bit of sightseeing. I hadn't seen good old Mocrates in person since 1923, & found that time had in the interim aged him far less

---

*Since his return home he has had quite a breakdown—nervous & heat—but is now pulling around all right.

than it has aged me. Young Moe, by the way, is in Providence again today—the presence of a fair friend of his[1] as a graduate student at Brown making him less of a stranger than formerly to our thriving municipality. Barlow's visit, too, was extremely pleasant despite its somewhat exacting nature. I helped him trace out some of the New England lines in his ancestry, & found he is my *6th cousin* by virtue of common descent from one John Rathbone of Block Island who died in 1658 (old Jim Morton & I are *7th cousins* through common descent from one John Perkins Jr. [also an ancestor of F D R & of Sec. of Labour Perkins] of Upswich, who died in 1699 or thereabouts.) He appreciated all the local museums & kindred facilities, & I shewed him ancient Salem & Marblehead on Aug. 20—my 46th birthday. He may not return to Florida at all—for a domestic upheaval seems destined to land him & his mother with her relatives in Kansas, whither he is now winging his way. During his visit I also had another unexpected guest—old Adolphe Danziger de Castro, one-time friend of Ambrose Bierce & later a revision client of mine. He paused in Providence (at an hotel) for five days—en route to N.Y. from Boston, where he had been to perform the melancholy rite of scattering his late wife's ashes upon the sea in accordance with her final request. Old 'Dolph, now 77, is the same amiable charlatan as ever. I had not seen him face to face since '28, but (as in Moe's case) the years have aged him less than they have me. He tried to wish some insanely unprofitable revision jobs on me—but the obviously hopeless state of my programme enabled me to put him off without offending him. Meanwhile Bobby Barlow & I shew'd him around the town, & derived considerable enjoyment from his pompous reminiscences of the great. On one occasion we sat on a tomb in a hidden hillside churchyard just north of here & wrote rhymed acrostics (at Barlow's suggestion) on the name of *Edgar Allan Poe*—who 90 years ago wander'd through that selfsame necropolis whilst on visits to Providence.[2] Still later I had a visit from the expansive & omniscient James Ferdinand Morton, who came fresh from his winning of the crossword-puzzle championship at the Boston convention of the Puzzlers' League. We had the usual good time arguing—& one day celebrated our reunion by eating 2 quarts apiece of ice cream at noon, & a pint more apiece in the evening after a heavy spaghetti dinner. That's what we call reducing! And so it goes. For a constitutional hermit, I surely have been seeing young Moe a bit. Incidentally, your 1916 United recruit, the Rev. Eugene B. Kuntz, is now visiting a daughter in New York & taking side-trips of ambitious length (one to Montreal). Before he returns to the mesas, cacti, & pueblos of New Mexico I hope he'll get up this way (assuming that I'll remain too broke to hit N Y myself this autumn)—for I've never seen the good old boy in person despite a 20-year exchange of letters with him.

I am sorry to hear of your brother's cardiac attack—but glad he is now radically improved. Despite the rush & anxiety I hope your summer proved largely pleasant—I surely envy you the Mexican jaunt, since the antiquities of

Spanish America would undoubtedly move my archaically oriented soul to unseemly raptures. The Catskills, too, are an exquisite region—I visited in the ancient town of Kingston in '29 & '30, & was impressed with the pastoral charm of Ulster County. After all these pleasantly varied sights, I trust the approaching grind of scholastic labour does not seem too formidable.

Speaking of scholastic labour (after a properly Latin-American postponement of the business angle)—I now call attention to the accompanying manuscript. My orders—as collectively gleaned from yours of Feby. 28 & April 6—were to perform the following operations on the existing text. Let us see how well or ill I have done this.

1. Expand the list of words frequently mispronounced to a whole chapter on pronunciation, explaining about cases where more than one permissible pronunciation exists & indicating preference.
2. Correct errors in chapter on familiar allusions.
3. Amplify chapter on increasing vocabulary.
4. Await further expert suggestions before monkeying with chapter on tone-training, a subject about which I know absolutely nothing.
5. Amplify the chapter on conversational approaches.
6. Provide a list of 50 stock phrases or "bromides."
7. Add needed touches & transpositions throughout the text.
8. Expand the final chapter into a reading course covering literature, the sciences, & the arts, with mention of *recent* books in fields rapidly changed by discovery or development.
9. Preserve as light a touch as possible, & leave the book much longer than at present—perhaps doubled.

Considering the points in order: (1) I have provided the new chapter on pronunciation, & have enormously expanded the list of words often mispronounced by persons of fair education or better . . . also supplying a list of parallel pronunciations. You will probably like the chapter, but may wish the lists to be shorter. In that case simply strike out what you think ought to be excluded—an easy enough procedure. Since the compilation of these lists entailed considerable research—more than I expected—I would ask as a favour that they be returned to me for possible use in some future project if you decide to abridge them drastically for the book. And now a word about the manner of representing pronunciations in the second list. Owing to the popular nature of the present work, I decided that a simpler & more homely method than the full use of diacritical marks would prove most useful— hence the course followed. But I was not sure that you would prefer this— hence the occasional lack of uniformity. My idea was to let you decide for yourself, & then return the MS. to me for uniform adaptation to whichever system—a loose, graphic one (as en´-syne) or a strictly academic one (as ĕn-´sĭn)—you might prefer. I fancy there is still time to do this—unless you have time to do it yourself. [This same principle, by the way, applies to all the text. In many cases I felt that you might not like what I was doing; but not knowing your preference (& imagining you in various parts of this & adjacent countries, beyond feasible postal reach) I merely went tentatively ahead without too much regard for final form, trusting to be able to make quick final changes after you had seen the MS.]

(2) About the familiar allusion chapter. I think I had made a few badly needed changes before writing you last April, but I have made more since. I remarked at the time my lack of authority in the field of *economic terms;* but subsequent delvings have dispelled a few instances of that ignorance, so that I have been emboldened to act upon certain misgivings originally rather vague. Whenever I have made a change in an economic definition it is because of what seems to me convincing evidence as to the real meaning. I would be glad to discuss any point which may seem wrong to you. Regarding this whole chapter—I ardently wish that circumstances had given me more of a chance to discuss it with you at length. You somewhere stated that you did not wish it expanded or reproportioned as to subject-matter—but my original impression persists that a rather different selection of phrases (& probably a fuller one, although of course the pupil must in any case be referred to Brewer's "Dictionary of Phrase & Fable" or some similar work or works in the end) should have been made. The present selection certainly stresses the *economic* to an extent unlikely to be found in common conversation—while the vast battery of allusions drawn from *the sciences & the arts* seems unduly lacking in representation. I would have been glad (& would still be glad) to assist in the formulation of a reproportioned list of any desired length. Meanwhile I can assure you that *all the non-economic* allusions of the present list are now absolutely correct, & that whatever changes I *have* made in the economic ones are overwhelmingly *likely* to be in the direction of greater correctness. Which seems to dispose of Chapter IV for the present.

(3) I hope my additions to the vocabulary chapter will be found acceptable. So far as the original scope of this chapter is concerned, my principal new point is that relating to the need of care about the nature & quality of newly acquired words. But this chapter is also involved in a case of *transposition.* The later chapter on "Bromides" ended up with a great deal of generalised matter about habits & conditions of studying which certainly had nothing to do with stock phrases, & which obviously—because of its highly general & quasi-introductory nature—should have come earlier in the book. I have now taken the liberty of detaching this material & adding it to the vocabulary chapter—a change which certainly gives it a more appropriate & effective position in relation to the entire plan of the book.

(4) I have perforce—as an iggernant guy what don't know nothin' abaout elocutin'—let the tone-training chapter alone, though I'll be glad to act quick-

ly on any revised version you care to submit before the crossing of the utter, ultimate deadline.

(5) I think I have given the conversational approach chapter whatever points (largely on choice of topics) it may have lacked. Let the text speak for itself. Because of the close relationship of this chapter to the one on "Speech in Social Usage" (the two might well be fused into one with the title of the latter) I have thought it necessary to make them *adjacent*. This was fortunately a very easy & simple process, since the chapter which separated them—that on "bromides"—was one which ought in any case (because of its more *fundamental* nature) to have come before either of them. The table of contents tells the story. "Bromides" *now* forms *Chapter VI,* coming directly after the vocabulary chapter, while "Tone Training" follows it as Chap. VII. "Approaches" proceeds directly & logically from "Tone-Training" as Chap. VIII, whilst "Social Uses" continues without interruption from "Approaches" under its original numeration. I am confident that you will agree with me regarding these points.

(6) The chapter on "bromides", relocated & freed from its irrelevant final parts, has been augmented by a little discussion & a stupendously long list of common examples. It is not meant that this list should be retained in full—unless of course you wish to change your original plan. You asked for only *fifty* specimens—but it occurred to me that my lesser familiarity with varied types of every-day speech might cause me to pick the wrong or least typical fifty. Hence the present omnium gatherum—from which you may choose whatever you wish, rejecting the rest. Because of the time & care entailed in the preparation of this list, & because of its potential usefulness at some later date, I will repeat the request made in connexion with the pronunciation lists & ask that—as a great favour—you ultimately return it (after making your selections) unless you decide after all to use the curious hodge-podge entire.

(7) This point is covered in the discussion of the others.

(8) We now come to the main point—the reading course. Here is where the digging & searching & planning & plugging have come in! I said last winter or spring that I wished some really adequate & thoughtfully designed guide to contemporary reading—especially up-to-date study in the rapidly-changing sciences & constantly reinterpreted arts—could be made to exist. Well—if it doesn't exist now, I've at least done my damndest [*sic*] to make it! You can't imagine the intricacy & difficulty of the job of assembling so much *utterly heterogeneous* & *dizzily contemporary* data. The literature section wasn't so bad, since I knew about what I wanted to say or recommend. But the science section—boy! It certainly was a brisk chase for an old man to dig up those 1934 & 1935 titles—& I had to turn to an infinite variety of sources for really dependable dope. Verbal enquiries—hints in current science articles—names from recent textbook catalogues—first-hand verifications . . . . . & even in the end I couldn't rule all the old-timers out, since I found that certain of the

friends of my youth had touches of clearness & suitability for the lone student which most of the depression-age parvenus lack! I arranged the recommendations in an *order* whose careful (& I hope scientific) devising itself took the better part of a day. As a result of that session of planning I made for my own ease a table of the logical relationship of the various fields of learning—which may come in handy some day. But I'd better let the magnum opus speak for itself. Here it is—& if you can't read the script I'll gladly unriddle any passage which you may submit. It is a tragic fact that you *may* not want anything as full as this for your essentially elementary treatise. If so, I would suggest that you quickly outline your alternative needs & submit them to me together with the existing text. With the text as a guide, I could prepare a shorter course very promptly. Or you might do the same yourself. The great advantage of the present list—either as it is or as it could be abridged—is that it concentrates on really significant things as opposed to random choices. I thought damn hard before jotting down any title. With this guide, as with the pronunciation & cliché lists, I will present the same request that it (i.e. pages 55–73 of the MS.) be eventually returned for future use if nothing resembling it is included in the book. I would of course remove such sentences & paragraphs as are yours before appropriating it for other purposes. It was made for the book—& I would merely wish to salvage what isn't desired for that enterprise.

(9) It has not always been possible to preserve a light & humorous style; but where such a style would imperil clearness, concrete definiteness, freedom from ambiguity I feel sure you will approve my willingness to sacrifice. I have tried very carefully to preserve at least outward resemblance to the original style where (a) the text joined original portions directly or (b) occupied portions homologous to certain key parts of original text. I meant to conduct further experiments in recasting passages in a more colloquial vein, but am prevented by the imminence of the deadline. I will still be glad to alter any passages pointed out for alteration—the desired direction of change being indicated. Or if you wish to attempt the alteration yourself, I will be equally glad to look over your final version & iron out any point which may not perfectly convey what was meant to be conveyed. And remember that I am always ready to help in unriddling unreadable portions of my veritably lousy script. Regarding the element of *length*—when you see how much typing my various interpolations make, I fancy you'll agree that the virtual doubling has been accomplished—even if the reading-guide section be substantially slashed.

Well—I hope I haven't made too rotten a mess. As before indicated, I apologise grovellingly for my chronological sins, & offer as full a reparation as is possible at this late date. I certainly hope that what I've done is of some use, & that I didn't do you an unwitting injury in not passing up the job last winter when I saw how badly I was going to be situated during '36. ¶ With suitable obeisances, then, & awaiting whatever further orders may be forth-coming, I remain

Yr most obt, most humble Servt

H P L

P.S. Here is a summary of the parts of my added material which I wish you'd return in the end *if* you can't use them in anything like their existing form:

1. List of mispronounced words—p. 15
2. List of words with dual pronunciation—pp. 15a–15e
3. Catalogue of clichés—pp. 38e, 38f
4. The complete reading guide—pp. 55–73.

Notes

1. Eunice French.
2. See letter no. 98 to Elizabeth Toldridge and n. 1.

Appendix

Poems by Elizabeth Toldridge

Expectancy

Our eyes are feasted on the browns and greens
Of hoary woods and fields where winging song
Has perfect place; and on the bauzy sheens
Of rolling mists that to the seas belong!
And lifted eyes discern dim etchings made,
Upon grey skies, of chimney-pot and spire
And slim beseeching boughs with fingers laid
Together as for prayer, and straining higher!
While up, and out, and on—the feast is spread:
An orient—like a lady rich and proud—
In gold brocade with many a crimson thread.
And silver, wrought in flower-and-leaf of cloud!
Yet all these beauties are but happenings—
Not even reflection of—the other things. . . . .

I Know a Forest Dark and Deep

(Rondel)

I know a forest dark and deep—
    The way to it no man may tell!
    No guidepost and no beckoning bell—
Or, whether it lies by plain or sheep!
Yet, what of need to climb or creep
    When all have wings that herein dwell?
I know a forest dark and deep—
    The way to it no man may tell!
Here, tired old dreams have fallen asleep.
    But young dreams stir beneath the spell
    Of singing shadows, and stars that fell,
Long, long ago, for us to keep!
I know a forest dark and deep!

Locusts and Wild Honey

I hear the locusts shrilling down the ways. . . .
I see an older skyline, violet-gold.
A magic branch. A rose with fold on fold
Of pinky velvet, sweet as incense-rays.
I meet again, starred nights and sunswept days
Whose flocks of timid dreams are meekly bold—
Triumphant things that earlier choral told,
Its dying bars, an ecstasy of praise!
If there befell what blurred the face of joy,
And winds of fate that shattered like a blow
The hopes Life fostered till it taught to sigh:
Such riches of deprival never cloy—
And this old heart may still enjoy a show. . . .
The glory of its youth is passing by!

Poe

Mid shadowy wonders all his own—he wrought
    His wild dark fancies on the rock of Time!
    With brooding power he cut his tragic rhyme
So deep—it shall endure while thought be thought.
Dreams of unearthly beauty, too, he brought,
    Enshrined in music, bearing many a chime
    Of sweetness indescribable; sublime
With grievings; and with mourning echoes fraught.
To us—late listeners his magic binds
    With strange sad melodies of soul and star—
        'Tis as he were a god dispensing these;
The whispered desolations of all winds,
    The lonely throbbing of all hearts that are,
        The inconsolable sobbing of the seas!

H. P. Lovecraft

He calls us not (as modern craftsmen do)
    To scenes attained, where sin's hideous scars
On human souls are gilded—no—but to
    The far, pure, foamy glaxies of stars!
Terrors he brings and things not known before,
    From lone and dismal haunts of old dead suns.
Yet are our spirits outward-drawn—to soar
    Through vastnesses where a stainless Wonder runs!

Mist

And what is mist? A softly luminous thing,
    A wraith-like shade that haunts the mountain-side;
    That now essays the valiant trees to hide—
The timid bushes lightly covering.
O that again its slivery scarves would fling
    To the world's edge and there for whiles abide,
    Toward brave mesas, starred, sky-wide,
That it may earth and heaven together bring.

Impalpable, yet real as time and tears . . .
    And life itself? A mist it might well be,
        That hangs beneath the blue, and only strays
To screen from us—wide earth's pale joys and fears
    Far, other beauties that we fain would see—
        Then breaks. . . . Eternity no more delays!

Ephemera

And is our day the longer, valiant one?
Not even do we stay from sun to sun!
At dawn, we shake out gauzy wings that beat
And beat, where misty ways are sweet;
We touch the Noon's high paths; eve's level bars
And then the night comes on (all deep with start)
To find we are but empty shells and still
Ghostily clinging to life's window-sill. . . .

Midnight Sky

By Elizabeth "Barnet" Toldridge

Light years away, stars flash about
    Down titan paths that look to be
Of dusty-silver beaten out
    On bleak immensity. . . .

Far universes spend their gleams,
    Huge blacknesses their shadows fling,
A horror hides where nothing seems. . . .
    Yet little near-stars sing!

Capella croons a mystic word,
    And Vega chants its haunting note,

While Rigel, like an earthly bird,
　　Drops music from its throat!

But those dread gulfs—(Where Something strays
　　The boldest may not dare defy)
Along the dusty-silver ways,
　　Unsearchable, they lie....

Divinity

To H. P. L.

It is your mind that is of kin to me.
　　Yet, of the mind, some make a thing but borne
　　Of juggling forces, atoms blent or torn
Apart—electrons, whirling dizzily!
You look at me with eyes that seem to see
　　The dreams of all the ages men have worn
　　So proudly; eyes that pity the forloen,
That cannot hide your spirit, strong and free.
And so I hug my simple faith. I know
　　My needs great answer lies within my reach:
　　　　A light that shines in darkness all the while . . . .
Nothing evolved from nothingness could show
　　Such splendours as are hinted in your speech,
　　　　Such glories as are shadowed in your smile.

Toldridge's Poetry Manuscripts at JHL

Alpha and Omega
  My Mother
  Thanksgiving
Ave Maria
  The Greatest Thing in the World
And Mystery Wakes
Baby Clothes
Ballads of Life and Death
Beauty
Beauty
The Birth of Eros
  Pandora's Gift
Birthday Roses
The Blue, Blue Sky
The Blue, Blue Sky
  The Gathering Years
  Illusion
  Stars
The Blue, Blue Sky
A Calling's Cost
  A Birthday
  Death
  Defeat
  Kinship
  A Man
Cherry Bloom
  The Road of Life
  The Robe
  When Music Breaks
Christmas Day
The Christmas Star
  Chistmas
  The First Christmas
  Light o' Christmas
Compassioned
  Cameo
  Hold Fast

Keep Sweet
Crusade
  The Convert
  Other Things
  Ships
The Cry of the Daughter
Dahlia
Dahlia, Dahlia
Death
Death—Lift the Gates
Death Lifts the Gates
Destiny
Divinity
Divinity
Divinity
Divinity
Drought
The Eagle
  Disappointment
Earth Speaks
The East to the West
The East to the West
  Rashjudgment
Easter
  The Wonderful Star
Easter
Ephemera
Expectancy
Failure
Forsythia
Foundations
Foundations
Foundations
Fulfillment
  Pain

Locusts and Wild Honey

Magic Chorus

Oh, Sweetest Word

Oh, Sweetest Word

Oh, Sweetest Word

What make the grave . . .

Printed

A halo glimmered

Man is a warrior . . . [pages two to four only]

New York [by Mina Barret: ms. in Toldridge's hand]

Contents of Winnings (ms., New York Public Library)

The River and the Boat

The Unconquerable

When Souls Strike Fire

Rashjudgment

Peace

The Moon

Smoke, and a Hospital Window

The Old Fashioned Door

Shadows

The Voice

America

Locusts and Wild Honey

Expectation

Pigeon Flight

The Long, Long Years

The Lady Poetry

I am Kin to the Winds

Voices, Voices

Ships

The Gift of Years

Prayer

Thoughts

The Lightnings and the Thunders

Drought

Sundown

Midnight Sky

World-Discontent

The Talking Tree

Flag of My Home and Heart

Late, So Late

Woodrow Wilson

The Leader

Wilson: 1917

The Land

The Sea

Lilt and Lure

Ephemera

Intercession

Life

In His Likeness

The Acolyte

In the Park

Letters by Elizabeth Toldridge

The Farragut
Washington, D.C.

To
Mr. Alfred A. Knopf,
730 Fifth Avenue
New York City.

Dear Mr. Knopf,

This letter, with small box of data—a picture or two, letters and some family notes—will be sent to you at my death, if not before. In my "Last Will and Testament," I am leaving "Winnings" to you, absolutely and forever, with all that might accrue from it, if ever published by you.

The relics may be destroyed. I only thought you should know a little bit about me; and if dear Mrs. Knopf would care to keep the most cheerful picture of me, she would do me an honor.

Having been a clerk in the United States Treasury for a long while, I worked evenings with a unit there, during the war, and with my church unit, receiving a Certificate for Service, signed by President Wilson—my proudest possession! I am a Promoter in the Apostleship of Prayer and a member of the Sodality, St. Matthew's Church. I was a Charter (artist) member of The Arts Club of Washington, and of the International Association of Art and Letters; a member of The League of American Pen Women and of The American Poetry Circle, I having been asked to organize a group of the latter in Washington, which still flourishes! I "joined" them all to keep the glorious Cause of my Lady Poetry—but I have never had the courage to stand upon a platform and recite my *own* poetry!!

If only one story, one poem, could find a little place even on the outermost confines of literature! I should not care whether my name were there or not—as only the thing itself were real—and I believe that I should know about it in the Great Hereafter——

In the firm belief that you and your dear wife prevented my dying of grief by your heavenly kindness in holding the manuscript,

I am,

Forever gratefully and faithfully,

(Elizabeth) Barnet Toldridge

January 1934

The Farragut
Washington, D.C.

To
Mr. Alfred A. Knopf,
    730 Fifth Avenue,
      New York City

Dear Mr. Knopf,

    As I have written more than once, I now give to you the little book "Winnings" to be your own, absolutely and forever. I should not dare to be so presumptuous, did I not feel that there might be some little bit of *reality* to it, somewhere—because of the way it came (out of life itself) and because of my years of laboring——

    Wishing for you and your dear wife all blessed fortune,
    I am,
        Faithfully and gratefully,

Legal name	–	Elizabeth A. Toldridge
Pen name	–	Barnet Toldridge

October 27, 1934

Washington

Dear Mr. Knopf,

    I am writing at this time because it seems to me, now, the part of wisdom to attend to one or two things near to my heart *while I am here* – as I am very far from "young and strong" and have no family. So I am sending with this, with your kind permission, one or two bits of family data, one or two messages I prize—

    Having written, years ago, regarding some clan matters of the McIntyres—I discovered Lady Alice Macdonald of the Isles to be a very lovely person, so I am sending you this little book of hers, wishing an accident had not happened to one of the flyleaves! Sir Alexander, her husband, died a year or two ago, and their only son, Godfrey, now bears the title.

    The "family data" may be destroyed, as I have no one to leave it to—although as I said in the letter in the little box, I should be honoured if dear Mrs. Knopf would care to keep the most cheerful of my pictures!

    Feeling that "Winnings" belongs to you will help me "die happy"—so you know I am grateful.

    Begging every joy for you both, I am,
        Faithfully,
           Barnet Toldridge

The letter in the box was written some time ago and I have not reread it. It was to have been forwarded after I had left for the stratosphere—or even farther! B.T.

Unpublished parts of Well-Bred Speech *as written by H. P. Lovecraft*

CHAPTER III
WORDS FREQUENTLY MISPRONOUNCED

Correct pronunciation is one of the chief factors in well-bred English. Nothing, perhaps, is more unpleasantly conspicuous than a mispronounced word. Because of the large part played in life by oral speech, bad pronunciation is far more likely to be noticed than is bad spelling; and because of its quicker recognisability in common conversation, it tends to attract attention much more often than does equal carelessness in grammar. It would pay one, then, to guard his accents and phonetic values very closely; following the custom of the most cultivated speakers, and always being ready to consult the dictionary when doubt arises.

Never let an unfamiliar pronunciation by a competent speaker go neglected. Always look it up in the best dictionary obtainable. While the speaker may, like all mortals, have erred, there is a greater chance that the hearer has always harboured a wrong pronunciation of the word in question. The average person has never been in a position to have his pronunciation of all the obscurer words of the language tested, and as a result all of us retain certain latent errors. Some of these will probably always be with us, but if we are alert we may happen on many opportunities for correction.

Listening to good speakers and checking up on their pronunciation whenever it differs from ours is one way. Another way is reading good poetry and looking up any unfamiliar pronunciation when it seems to be indicated by some rhyming sound, or by the accent of some word as determined by its place in the metre. For example, if we have been mispronouncing the word *trow* to rhyme with *plough,* we may learn our error when we come upon some such couplet as

"it . . . and well I *trow*
Why thou demand'st that taper's *glow.* "

Or if we have been accustomed to accent *indissoluble* erroneously on the third syllable, we are corrected when we encounter and verify the accent indicated by the metre in Thomson's line:

"As with | a chain | *indis* | *solu* | *ble* bound."

Still another excellent practice is to take a leisure hour for the reviewing of all the words one knows but does not habitually use. Almost invariably there will be dozens met commonly in print but seldom uttered, which we shall realise we actually do not know how to pronounce. All of these should be looked up in a reliable dictionary. Some, of course, we shall find we have guessed right from the spelling or from various analogies; but many others will present features which we did not suspect. In connexion with this matter we would do well to study very carefully the particular set of diacritical marks employed by the dictionary we consult. Different dictionaries sometimes employ different systems, but each may be mastered in a short time if we note very carefully the illustrative words on the bottom of the pages, where the meaning of each arbitrary symbol attached to various vowels, diphthongs, consonants, and combinations in the phonetic representation of the main vocabulary is plainly shewn by some universally understood example.

There are, of course, many cases where a word has more than one pronunciation in good usage—a confusing but inevitable result of the natural, spontaneous, and haphazard growth of language. Sometimes these differing pronunciations represent the usage of different regions or classes or occupational or scholastic groups, while sometimes they seem to occur indiscriminately in all regions and among all types of persons. When usage is definitely divided among well-educated and cultivated persons, we have to grant all the variants a more or less legitimate status; although we may indicate a general preference based on past custom and on the history and nature of the words in question. All dictionaries recognise variant pronunciations, and some give long parallel columns of them in prefaces or appendices. Each dictionary usually indicates preferences in usage, although no two are likely to have the same preference regarding any given debatable word.

In practice it is not well to follow any one dictionary slavishly, for even the best authorities are not free from local or personal bias, imperfect observation, pedantic purism, and other influences leading toward questionable judgment. Compare the preferences of several good dictionaries—the Merriam Webster, the Standard, the new Oxford, and so on—and supplement this with close attention to the daily speech of cultivated persons, such as lecturers with a sound traditional and academic background.

When usage seems quite evenly divided, let certain points of common sense turn the scales. Choose the pronunciation which seems to be general rather than local, traditional rather than parvenu, mellowly cultivated rather than merely "smart" or fashionable, and normally historic (in harmony with the nature and history of the word in this and ancestral languages, as indicated by the etymological notes in dictionaries) rather than arbitrary or capricious. Thus, in general, *con-cen´-trate* is to be preferred to *con´-cen-trate; ab-do´-men* to *ab´-do-men; ensign* to *ensin; profeel* to *profyle;* and so on. A table of suggested preferences occurs at the end of this chapter.

Oddly enough, the words we most frequently mispronounce are not always the obscure ones. Certain very ordinary expressions contain pitfalls into which we stumble surprisingly often, so that a list of the proper pronunciations of our most commonly used words would shew most of us as erring much oftener than we would like to admit. We are especially apt to shift accents, to give a wrong quantity to vowels and certain consonants, to suppress sounds or even whole syllables, to add unjustified sounds and syllables, and to transpose certain sounds (as in saying "irrevelent" for *irrelevant*). In the following list will be found words often mispronounced by persons of good or average education. Each is worth looking up in the dictionary. No one person mispronounces them all, but there are few of us who do not mispronounce several. Among them all general types of error are represented, though certain regional or class usages (like the New York interchange of *oi* and *er*, the illiterate flat *a*, the redundant Bostonese broad *ä* where short *a* is called for, etc.) are omitted as too well known to need illustration. Where a dual usage exists, the supplementary table of parallel pronunciations will help to piece out the dictionary.

Words frequently Mispronounced*

abdomen	critique	inexorable	real
abstinence	culinary	inexplicable	recess
access	cupola	inquiry	recompense
acclimate	curator	insidious	refutable
acclimatize	deaf	instinct (adj.)	repartee
accompaniment	debonair	integral	repertoire
accurate	debris	interesting	research
acumen	debut	intrigue	respiratory
address	debutante	inversion	respite
adept	decade	irrefutable	retain (v.)
adjoin	demise	irrelevant	robust
adjutant	demonstrative	irreparable	roil
admiralty	despicable	Italian	romance
adult	desultory	javelin	roof
adverse	detail	jewel	root
aesthete	detour	jocund	route
aggrandize	diaeresis	joust	sacerdotal
Alexandrine	dilute	jowl	sacrilegious
alias	dinosaur	jugular	salaam
alien	diphtheria	kettle	sapient
alienate	dirigible	kiln	sarsaparilla
ally	disaster	lamentable	scalene
almond	distich	larynx	secretary

* [if this full list is not used, please return original to HPL for other uses]

[certain minor differentiation betwixt s and x, and betwixt the x and gz sounds, omitted in this and the following table]

alternate (adj.)
alternately
amenity
apotheosis
apparatus
applicable
Arab
Arabic
Arctic
Armistice
Aspirant
Associate
Automobile
Aversion
Aviation
bade
been
Belial
bestiality
biography
bouquet
bowsprit
brigand
brooch
brusque
buccaneer
buoy
bureaucracy
business
Calliope
Cantonment
caramel
carotid
centrifugal
cerement
chagrin
chiropodist
chivalric
clandestine
clique
column
combatant
comely

Doric
duty
dynasty
egoist
eligible
elm
environment
Epicurean
Erato
erudition
evidently
excursion
exemplary
expert (adj.)
exquisite
extraneous
extraordinary
falcon
faucet
faux pas
February
fecundate
film
finance
flaccid
forehead
formidable
foyer
fragmentary
frontier
fulcrum
fulsome
genealogy
genuine
gesture
gladiolus
gondola
government
gratis
grimace
grease (v.)
guardian
halfpenny

leisure
library
lilac
literature
loathsome
loyal
lyceum
machination
magazine
marquis
mercantile
Michaelmas
mineralogy
mischievous
mongrel
moustache
naive
necessarily
nomad
nouveau riche
obesity
objurgate
obligatory
obsolete
occult
often
palimpsest
panegyric
paraffin
pariah
parochial
patron
peremptory
periphrasis
Persia
petrel
pharmacopoeia
pianist
pianoforte
pilaster
piquant
plebeian
precedence

simile
shone
simultaneous
sinecure
solecism
sonorous
soporific
spaniel
squalor
static
statue
strata
subside
subtle
succinct
suicidal
suite
supine
supple
synod
tenacious
tergiversate
Terpsichore
textile
Thalia
theatre
thither
threepence
tirade
topographical
tortoise
toward
transmigrate
travail
tremendous
tribune
trombone
trow
unfrequented
univocal
usage
vagary
valet

comparable	harass	preface	valuable
complaisant	have	presage (v.)	vaudeville
couch	heinous	prescience	vehement
concentrate	highwayman	presentation	verbatim
condolence	horizon	presentiment	version
conduit	hospitable	pretence	viscount
confiscate	hygienic	primarily	visor
conjugal	hyperbole	prism	volute
connoisseur	hypocrisy	profile	Warwick
constable	idea	programme	was
construe	ideal	promenade	Westminster
consummate (adj.)	illustrate	promulgate	xylophone
contemplative	immediate	pulchritude	zodiacal
contour	impious	purport	
contrite	improvise	pyrites	
conversant	incognito	quay	
coup d'etat	incomparable	rapine	
coupon	indicatory	ration	
creek	indissoluble	rationale	

List of Words with More than One Accepted Pronunciation, Giving two usages and indicating a reasonable preference.*

Word	Preferred Pronunciation	Secondary Pronunciation
ABDOMEN	ab-do´-men	ab´-do-men
ACCESS	ak-sess´	ak´-sess
ACOUSTIC	a-kow´-stic	a-koo´-stic
AERIE	ee´-ry	a´-ry
AGAIN	a-gen´	a-gane´
ALCOVE	al´-cove	al-cove´
ALKALINE	al-ka-lyne	al-ka-lin
APRON	ā-prun	ā´-purn
ALMOND	ah´-mond	al´-mond
ALTERNATE (v.)	al´-ter-nate	al-ter´-nate
ARISTOCRAT	a-ris´-to-crat	ar´-is-to-crat

---

*[Note—if this table is retained I'll prepare a more uniform and scientific set of phonetic renderings.]

[Please return this table if you don't want it for the book. I could use it myself in some other project.]

BALLET	băl-lay (even accent)	băl´-let
BEEN	bin	bean
BRUSQUE	broosk	brusk
CANINE	kay-nine´	kay´-nine
CEMENT	se-ment´	sem´-ent
CONCENTRATE	kon-sen´-trate	kon´-sen-trate
CONFISCATE	kon-fis´-cate	kon´-fis-cate
CONGENER	kon-je´-ner	kon´-je-ner
CONTEMPLATE	kon-tem´-plate	kon´-tem-plate
CONTENTS	kon´-tents	kon-tents´
CONTOUR	kon-toor´	kon´-tour
DECOROUS	de-co´-rous	dek´-o-rous
DEFILE	de-file´	de´-file
DEPOT	day´-po	dee´-po
DEMONSTRATE	dem´-on-strate	de-mon´-strate
DETAIL (n.)	de -tale´	dee´-tale
DIPHTHONG	dif-thong	dip-thong
DIVERSE	di-verse´	di´-verse
DOCILE	dos´-sil	do´-sil
DRAMA	drah´-ma	dray´-ma
DURESS	du-ress´	du´-ress
DYNASTY	di´-nas-ty	din´-as-ty
ECONOMIC	e-co-nom´-ik	ek-o-nom´-ik
EITHER	e´-ther	i´-ther
ENSIGN	en´-syne	en´-sin (Am. Mil.)
ENVELOPE	on´-ve-lope	en´-ve-lope
ENVIRONS	en-vi´-rons	en´-vi-rons
EPOCH	e´-pok	ep´-ok
EXTANT	ex-tant´	ex´-tant
EXTIRPATE	ex-tir´-pate	ex´-tir-pate
FAÇADE	fa-sahd´	fa-sade´
FOETID	fe´-tid	fet´-id
FRACAS	frah-kah´	fray´-kass
GAPE	gape	gäpe
GOUGE	gowj	gooj
HOSTLER	os´-ler	hos´-ler
HUMBLE	hum´-ble	um´-ble
HUMOUR	hu´-mer	you´-mer
HYGIENE	hy´-gi-ene	hy´-gene
IDEOGRAPHIC	id-e-o-graph´-ic	i-de-o-graph´-ic
ILLUSTRATE	il-lus´-trate	il´-lus-trate
INCREASE (n.)	in´-crease	in-crease´
INFANTILE	in´-fan-tyl	in´-fan-tyle

INNATE	in-nate´	in´-nate
INTERSTICE	in-ter´-stis	in´-ter-stice
INVALID (n.)	in´-val-id	in´-va-leed
IRREFUTABLE	ir-re-fu´-ta-ble	ir-ref´-u-ta-ble
ISOLATE	i´-so-late	is-o-late
KORAN	ko´-ran	ko-ran´
LANDAU	lan-do´	lan-daw
LEAPT	lept	leept
LEGEND	lej´-end	1ee´-jund
LEVER	lee´-ver	lev´-ver
MAMA	ma-mah´	mah´-ma
MARITIME	mar´-i-time	mar´-i-tym
MAUNDER	mawn´-der	mahn´-der
MEDIAEVAL	med-i-e´-val	me-di-e´-val
MEMOIR	mem´-war	mem´-war
MOBILE	mo´-bil	mo-beel
NEITHER	nee´-ther	nye´-ther
NEMEAN	ne-me´-an	nee´-me-an
NEPHEW	nev´-yew	neff´-yew
NEPOTISM	nep´-o-tism	nee´-po-tism
OASIS	o-a´-sis	o´-a-sis
OBEISANCE	o-bay´-sance	o-bee´-sance
OBLIQUE	o-bleek´	o-blike´
OMEGA	o´-me-ga	o-mee´-ga
ORNATE	or-nate´	or´-nate
PACIFICATION	pa-sif´-i-ca´-tion	pas´-i-fi-ca´-tion
PAGEANT	paj´-ent	pay´-gent
PANORAMA	pan-o-rah´-ma	pan-o-ray´-ma
PANTHEON	pan´-the-on	pan-th-e´-on
PAPA	pah-pah´	pah´-pa
PARQUET	par-kay´	par-ket´
PATENT (n.)	pat´-ent	pa´-tent
PECULIARITY	pe-cu-li-ar´-i-ty	pe-cul-yer´-i-ty
PECUNIARY	pe-cu´-ni-a-ry	pe-cun´-ya-ry
PEDAL (adj.)	ped´-al	pe´-dal
PERFECT (v.)	per´-fect	per-fect´
PERFUME (n.)	per´-fume	per-fume´
PERMIT (n.)	per´-mit	per-mit´
PERUKE	per-uke´	per´-uke
PHALANX	fay´-lanks	fal´-anx
PHTHISIS	thi´-sis	ti´-sis
PINEAL	pin´-e-al	pi´-ne-al
PLACARD	plak´-ard	pla-kard´

PLAGIARISM	play´-ji-ar-ism	play´-ja-rism
PLEIADES	ply´-a-deez	plee´-a-deez
PLETHORIC	ple-thor´-ic	pleth´-o-ric
PORTENT	por´-tent	por-tent´
POSSESS	poz-zes´	pos-sess´
PRAYER	pray´-er	prair
PRELUDE	prel´-ude	pre-´lude
PRESAGE (n.)	pres´-age	pre´-sage
PRESTIGE	pres-teezh´	pres´-tij
PRETEXT	pre-text´	pre´-text
PROCESS	pros´-sess	pro´-cess
PROFILE	pro-feel´	pro´-fyle
PROGRESS (n.)	prog´-ress	pro´-gress
PROLIX	pro-lix´	pro´-lix
PRONUNCIATION	pro-nun-si-a´-tion	pro-nun-shi-a-´tion
PROTEAN	pro-te´-an	pro´-te-an
PROVOCATIVE	pro-vok´-a-tive	pro-vo´-ka-tive
PRUSSIC	prus´-sik	proo´-sik
PSALMIST	sahm´-ist	sal´-mist
PSALMODY	sahm´-o-dy	sal´-mo-dy
PUERILE	pu´-er-il	pu´-er-ile
QUININE	kwi-nine´	kwi´-nine
QUOIN	koin	kwoin
RABBI	rab´-bye	rab´-by
RATHER	ra´-ther	ray´-ther
RATIONS	ray´-shuns	rash´-uns (Am. Mil.)
RECOGNISABLE	rek´-og-ni-sa-ble	re-cog´-ni-sa-ble
RECONDITE	rek´-on-dite	re-con´-dite
RECUSANT	rek´-u-sant	re-ku´-sant
REMEDILESS	rem´-e-di-less	re-med´-i-less
REPTILE	rep´-tyle	rep´-til
REQUIEM	rek´-wi-em	ree´-kwi-em
RETCH	rech	reach
RETROCEDE	re´-tro-cede	ret´-ro-cede
RETROGRADE	ret´-ro-grade	re´-tro-grade
RETROSPECT	ret´-ro-spect	re´-tro-spect
REVEILLE	re´-val-ya	rev´-a-lee
REVOLT	re-volt´	re-volt´
RHYTHM	(th as in that)	(th as in thing)
RICOCHET (n. & v.)	rik-o-shay´	rik o-shet´
RIGHTEOUS	rit´-yus	ri´-chus
RONDEAU	ron-do´	ron´-do
RUFFIAN	ruf´-fi-an	ruf´-yan

SACRIFICE (n. & v.)	sak´-ri-fyce	sak´-ri-fyze
SALINE	say´-line	sa-line´
SAPPHIRE	saf´-fire	saf´-fer
SATIRE	sat´-ire	sat´-ter
SATYR	sat´-er	say´-ter
SAVAGERY	sav´-a-ger-y	sav´-aj-ry
SCATH (n.)	skath (th as in thing)	skath
SCATHE (v.)	skath (th as in that)	skath (th as in thing)
SEAMSTRESS	sem´-stress	seem´-stress
SENTIENT	sen´-shi-ent	sen´-shent
SERIES	se´-reez	se´-ri-eez
SHIRE	shire	sheer
SHONE	shon	shon
SIBYLLINE	sib´-bil-line	sib´-bil-lin
SIMULTANEOUS	si´-mul-ta´-ne-ous	sim´-ul-ta´-ne-ous
SLIVER	sliv´-er	sly´-ver
SLOTH	sloth	sloth
SMALLPOX	small-pox´	small´-pox
SOJOURN	so´-journ	so-journ´
SOLDER	sod´-der	sol´-der
SOPORIFIC	so´-po-rif´-ic	sop´-o-rif´-ic
SOUGH	suf	sow
SPHEROID	sfeer´-oid	sfer´-oid
SPLENETIC	sple-net´-ic	splen´-e-tic
SQUIRREL	squir´-rel	squr´-rel
STALWART	stahl´-wart	stawl´-wart
STEELYARD	still´-yard	steel´-yard
STIRRUP	stir´-up	stur´-rup
SUFFICE	suf-fice´	suf-fize´
SUGGEST	suj-jest´	sug-jest´
SUMACH	su´-mak	shu´-mac
SUPERCILIOUS	su-per-sil´-i-ous	su-per-sil´-yus
SURTOUT	sir-too´	sir-toot´
SURVEILLANCE	sir-vayl´-yance	sir-vayl´-lance
SURVEY (n.)	sur´-vey	sir-vay´
TALISMAN	tal´-is-man	tal´-iz-man
TANTIVY	tan-tiv´-y	tan´-ti-vy
TAPIS	tah-pee´	tay´-pis
TARTUFFE	tar-toof´	tar-tuff´
TAUNT	tawnt	tahnt
TEDIOUS	te-di-ous	teed´-yus
TELEOLOGY	tel´-e-ol-o-gy	te´-le-ol-o-gy
TENET	ten´-et	te´-net

TETRARCH	tet´-rarch	te´-trarch
THEREFORE	thair´-for	thir´-for
THOMIST	to´-mist	tho-´-mist
THRENODY	thren´-o-dy	thre´-no-dy
TIRADE	ti-rade´	ti-räd´
TMESIS	tme´-sis	me´-sis
TOMATO	to-mah´-to	to-may´-to
TOUPEE	too-pay´	too-pee´
TRACHEA	tra-ke´-a	tra´-ke-a
TRAIT	tray	trayt
TRAMONTANE	tra-mon´-tane	tram´-on-tane´
TREATISE	tree´-tiss	tree´-tiz
TREMOR	trem´-or	tree´-mor
TRIO	tree´-o	try´-o
TRIPARTATE	try-par´-tite	trip´-ar-tite
TRUCULENCE	truk´-u-lence	trook´-u-lence
TUBEROSE	tu´-ber-oze	tube´-roze
TURQUOISE	tur-koiz´	tur-keez´
VACATE	va´-cate	va-cate´
VALET	val´-let	val-lay´
VASE	vayze	vahze
VEDA	vee´-da	vay´-da
VERTIGO	ver´-ti-go	ver-ti´-go
VIGNETTE	vin-yet´	vin´-yet
VIRTU	vir-too´	vir´-too
VISNE	vee´-nee	veen
VITALITY	vi-tal´-i-ty	vi-tal´-i-ty
VITUPERATE	vi - tu´-per-ate	vi -tu´-per-ate
VULPINE	vul´-pine	vul´-pin
WALNUT	wawl´-nut	wol´-nut
WALRUS	wawl´-rus	wol´-rus
WANT	wawnt	wont
WARRIOR	wor´-ri-er	wawr´-yer
WAYLAY	way-lay´	way´-lay
WOUND	woond	wownd

CHAPTER IV
TERMS WHICH SHOULD OWN A PLACE
IN YOUR CONVERSATION

If the words, terms, names, and places [here] mentioned [and described] are familiar enough to you to own a place in your after-dinner conversation, you may boast of a good general education. [Do not, however, overwork the habit of allusiveness, or drag in learned references on slight pretexts. Knowledge of these background-landmarks is chiefly valuable in helping us understand the occasional allusions in what we read. They should figure more sparingly in ordinary conversation.] Do you know both the denotation and the connotation [of these expressions?]

Louvain

A city in Belgium—before the World War, a center of art and culture. It was the seat of a great University and Library filled with irreplaceable manuscripts and art treasures. No one dreamed that the Germans would destroy these priceless works as they marched across the country, but they did—ruthlessly. It belonged to the world and the world is helping to rebuild it. The term is used now to mean "ruthless destruction".

Armageddon

[A table-land in Palestine—also called the Plain of Esdraleon—which for strategic reasons has been a scene of repeated battles since prehistoric times. It marked several decisive struggles recorded in the Old Testament, and] made such an impression on racial consciousness that it came to symbolize all conflict. The book of Revelation calls the final conflict between good and evil Armageddon. Theodore Roosevelt [used the term in describing the struggle against economic greed launched by his "Bull Moose" movement in 1912, and not long afterward it became applied to the World War and its attendant issues.]

River of Doubt

Geographers were in doubt as to whether a certain river, the Rio Dubito, in Brazil is a tributary of the Amazon. Soon after the defeat of the Bull Moose movement, Theodore Roosevelt went on an exploring expedition and proved that this stream is a tributary. The river is now called Rio Roosevelt. Reporters joked about Teddy's discovering a river of doubt in politics. When some leader makes a wrong move politically he is said to have discovered a River of Doubt.

Philanderer

[From the Greek φίλανδρος (philandros = man-loving), a word meaning "loving men" or "loving one's husband", which by transferrence became applied to a male flirt.] It is never used to designate flirt of the female sex, she is termed a coquette. The verb "philandering", meaning to trifle with the affections, should be used with the masculine gender only. [The popularity of this expression was perhaps promoted by Ariosto's use of the name *Philander* for a coquettish masculine character in "Orlando Furioso".]

A Pair of Sixes

The highest throw in playing dice. One may be said to have thrown a "pair of sixes" when he has put over a successful deal, been lucky on the market or won in a contest.

Terpsichore

The goddess of the dance. Anything pertaining to the grace, beauty, and rhythm of the dance may be referred to as terpsichorean art.

William Tell

William Tell[, in popular legend,] was a famous Swiss marksman. Gessler, an Austrian tyrant, set his cap on a post and admonished all who passed to salute it. Tell refused and received this sentence: to bring his only son and one arrow to the place and to shoot an apple from his son's head at one trial. Tell succeeded. Gessler, noticing a second arrow, asked the reason, only to be told that if he had failed, the second arrow was to be for Gessler's heart. Later Tell freed Switzerland from the Austrians, and virtually carried out his determination to use this arrow for Gessler's heart. It signifies the fight for Swiss freedom which took place 600 years before our own Revolutionary War. [The myth of William Tell (see Fiske's "Myths and Myth-Makers" and Baring-Gould's "Curious Myths of the Middle Ages") is a variant of a very ancient Aryan legend, probably based on the struggle between darkness and the shafts or rays of the sun. Other versions occur in Scandinavian, Finnish, and Russian mythology.]

Madam Butterfly

An opera based on the love of an American Naval Lieutenant and a Japanese maiden—Pinkerton and Cho-Cho San. It deals with their romance, betrothal and wedding, the departure of Pinkerton to America promising to return. But he forgets his Japanese wife, and marries an American girl. In the meantime Cho-Cho San patiently and loyally awaits his return, teaching the little one who has arrived to love the American Flag. Pinkerton finally comes, bringing his bride, having no idea of the loyalty of his Japanese butterfly. Upon her discovery of his faithlessness she takes her life. It signifies that there can be no understanding or marital happiness between the East and West.

Dante

One of the world's great epic poets. His "Divine Comedy" tells the story of the glory of God's love for man. The first part, the "Inferno", is known more widely. Other great tragedies which have depicted the triumph of some phase of love are: Shakespeare's "Hamlet", the love of son for father; Goethe's "Faust", the love of woman for man; Aeschylus' "Prometheus Bound", the love of man for mankind; the book of Job, the love of man for God.

Will O' the Wisp

Where decaying vegetable matter exists[,] a ball of phosphorescent light may be seen over marshy places. This [is] especially true of the chalk cliffs in England, and here a legend originated of a feeble-minded boy, Will, who followed this wisp of light until it led him over the cliff into the sea. Hence the following of any lure that might lead to destruction may be called [following] a Will O' the Wisp.

Fourth Estate

[Under the monarchy] France had [recognised classes or "]estates["—]the Nobility, the [Clergy, and the Commons. The "Tiers Etat" (Third Estate) or Commons had been recognised and given a position in the "States-General" or constitutional representative assembly since 1302, but the actual common people suffered increasingly as time went on. In the eighteenth century the peasant and artisan classes] were taxed heavily but owned nothing, [and] possessed no privileges. Rousseau [and others] saw the injustice of this and began the agitation which resulted in the French Revolution. [When the last summoning of the States-General occurred, just before the revolution in 1789, the part played by the Third Estate was widely discussed; but the eminent British statesman Edmund Burke, remarking the presence of a gallery full of newspaper reporters capable of moulding public opinion, remarked: "Yonder sits the *Fourth Estate*, more important than them all." Thereafter the phrase "Fourth Estate" as applied to the press became popular, so that today a member of the journalistic profession is said to belong to the "Fourth Estate".]

Herculean Labors

Hercules, a legendary hero, was adopted as the Greek patron of strength. [Through an act of jealousy among the gods, he was at birth bound to servitude under] Eury[s]theus, King of [Mycenae and Tiryns in] Argolis, [a sentence later confirmed by the Delphic oracle.] Eury[s]theus gave Hercules twelve difficult tasks to perform. He accomplished them all. Any task that requires superhuman strength is called a[n] "Herculean Labor". [The seventh labour of Hercules was to clean the filthy stables of King Augeas of Elis in a single day, a task which he accomplished by turning the waters of two rivers through them. "Cleaning the Augean Stables"] is another way of speaking of clearing up some nearly hopeless muddle [of unsavoury character.]

Machiavellian

Machiavelli, statesman and historian, was [Second Chancellor and] Secretary of the Florentine Republic during the [expulsion] of the Medici family. [Sent in 1502 as an envoy to the camp of] Cesar[e] Borgia[,] who was trying to unite all Italy under [the banner of his father] Pope Alexander VI, [he formed a profound admiration for the wily and devious tactics of that prince.] Machiavelli was [driven from public office when the Medici returned to power in Florence in 1512.] He spent the remainder of his life in literary endeavors and wrote "The Prince", a classic on statecraft [in which Cesare Borgia and his shrewd unscrupulousness are held up as models.]

Cesar[e] and his father, Pope Alexander VI[,] were the real rulers of Italy. They were crafty, shrewd, dissolute and sinister, and through intrigue and unscrupulous means gained their ends. Machiavellian tactics are those which arrive at an end by any means whatsoever. "The end justifies the means", is his motto.

Florence Nightingale

The first woman in England to do army nursing. During the Crimean War she promptly offered her services and organised a band of nurses. She was consulted by persons in high places and admired and respected by all for her womanly qualities and high merit. At first she had to overcome bureaucratic opposition. She was adored by the wounded.

Mrs. Grundy

Dame Rumor[, or more particularly, *conventional opinion*. Taken from Morton's "Speed the Plough".]

Pharisaic

The Pharisees were a sect among the ancient Jews noted for strict formalism, pretentious and superior sanctity. Any self-righteous person or one with a holier-than-thou attitude may be said to be Pharisaic. It refers to hypocrisy.

Philistine

[The Philistines were a powerful people, probably of Minoan or Cretan race-stock, who settled on the coast of Canaan about the same time that the Hebrews invaded the region. The name Palestine is derived from them. They formed the Hebrews' chief rival for possession of the land.] Returning from one of their captivities the Jews wished to build a temple and the Philistines offered aid. But in return they requested the privilege of worshipping their own idols in the building. This so horrified the priests that they forbade all association and spoke of their neighbors as outlaws. So the term Philistine came to mean one who is [unorthodox, ill-behaved, or an outsider. In the ceaseless town-and-gown warfare between German university students and non-student bourgeois youths, the latter came to have the appellation "Philisters" or "Philistines"; and from this practice the name spread to all narrow-minded, unimaginative, non-intellectual, inartistic, commercial-spirited, sheep-like persons—of the sort which Mr. H. L. Mencken attacks as "boobs" and "Rotarians". The first authoritative literary use of "Philistine" in the present sense was by Matthew Arnold in the nineteenth century.]

Mrs. Harris

The story of Martin Chuzzlewit by Dickens contains the character of Sairey Gamp, who uses an imaginary person, Mrs. Harris, as a club over friends and foes. Her own wishes and demands were conveyed by crediting them to Mrs. Harris. It was her method for establishing her own ideas of propriety.

A Sop to Cerberus

The domain of Pluto, the King of the Underworld, was guarded by a three headed dog, Cerberus. The only means of gaining an entrance [unharmed] was by diverting the attention of the dog. [Among the Greeks and Romans it was a funeral custom to place in the hands of the deceased a small cake, which when offered to Cerberus would keep him so busy that he would let the newcomer pass without molestation. This cake was called "a sop to Cerberus"—the word sop perhaps referring to the cake dipped in honey and drugs with which the Sybil pacified the dog when leading Aeneas into the-nether world. Analogous to this custom was that of the coin—to pay the infernal ferryman Charon—placed in the mouth of the dead. Both customs survive to this day among the rustics of Greece, despite the opposition of the Christian Church. In general, to bribe a sentinel may be said to be throwing "a sop to Cerberus".]

Peter the Hermit

—preached the first crusade. There were eleven such attempts to take the Sepulchre of Christ. The two most miserable failures were the Crusade of the Virgins and Children's Crusade.

John Barleycorn

A name given to intoxicating liquors. It was used many years ago in England.

The Golden Horn

[The narrow curved inlet of the Bosporus on which Constantinople is situated. So named, in all probability, from its shape and general beauty. The name (in Greek, Chrysoceras) was also applied to the land promontory or neck bearing the city. A possible parallel source of the name was the immense amount of commerce and wealth which flowed through it. In modern times it has been linked with the gilded mosques built since the Turkish conquest in 1453, which now picturesquely greet the eyes of those approaching by sea. On account of its strategic position as guardian of Black Sea commerce, there is a perpetual struggle among nations for its control.]

The Lake Poets

In the beautiful lake region of England lived and worked three famous poets, Wordsworth, Southey and Coleridge. The first two were poet laureates. Their writings were inspired by the beauty and harmony of their surroundings. At first they were ridiculed by the term—lake poets—later it became a term of praise.

Sophocles

One of three early Greek trag[ic dramatists], the other two being Euripides and Aeschylus. They belong to the Golden Age of Greece.

Shelley

Percy Bysshe Shelley, [a leading] lyric poet of England. Unappreciated and unhonoured in his day, but now one of the world's best loved poets. He was greatly admired by Browning, who derived much inspiration from his poetry.

Gret[na] Green

A village in Scotland, just over the border from England, a haven for young couples wishing a quiet and speedy marriage. Any community today has its Gretna Green. Rockville serves for Washington.

Cassandra

[Daughter] of King Priam of Troy. She was given the gift of prophecy [by Apollo in exchange for a promise, but because she failed to keep this promise the god (unable to recall his original gift) added the proviso that none of her prophecies should ever be believed. Foreseeing the fall of Troy, she sought to warn her countrymen but was disregarded—hence roamed about wringing her hands and weeping. Anyone today who frantically warns the nation of possible evils to come may be called a "weeping Cassandra".]

Sour Grapes

One of the most famous of Aesop's fables.

Sir Philip Sidney

During the reign [of Elizabeth], Sir Philip Sidney [the poet and romancer] was considered the ideal English gentleman, a model of chivalry. He was [a cavalry] general during the war [against Spain] in Holland. Wounded and dying in the field, he gave his last cup of water to a dying [soldier]. Beau Brummel[l] is spoken of as the model of dress[,] and Lord Chesterfield as the model of manners.

The Oxford Movement

A movement in the Church of England against the liberalism of the day. A call for more ritualism, more of the High Church formalism. Bishop Manning and Bishop Newman left the Church of England, through this movement, and were made Cardinals in the Church of Rome. The movement originated among the "dons" of Oxford University.

Crossing the Rubicon

When the political heads of Rome wished to be relieved of a disturbing leader they [often] sent him into one of their colonies as [a governor]. Julius C[ae]sar was [governor] of the colony of Gaul, and was constantly being urged by his friends to return to rule Rome, [then in the hands of a corrupt aristocratic party dominated by Pompeius. Between Italy proper and the domain governed by Caesar lay the little river Rubicon. If he crossed into Italy with his army, he would be starting a civil war, and there could be no turning back—but eventually he did cross, taking the decisive step which led to his victory and dictatorship.] Thus when one makes a difficult decision, from which there is no recall, we say "he has crossed the Rubicon."

Pan-Germanism

[In general, the principle of uniting all Germanic peoples in one compact fabric. Loosely used to mean an attempt to extend Germanic influence throughout the world, or at least throughout a definite zone.] For years before the World War, Germany put forth every effort to make herself super[ior]. She tried to educate the world to turn to Germany for the best in everything— medicine, education, economics. She hoped to gain complete control of Central Europe. She established a sphere of Teutonic influence from Berlin to Bagdad.

Chauvinism

Chauvin, a [character in French literature, was a typically blind idolator of Napoleon and of the belligerent nationalistic ideals for which he stood.] His slogan was "All for France". We find many Americans inclined to be Chauvinistic about their own country.

Sancho-Panza

In Cervantes' satire on chivalry, "Don Quixote", we find the hero riding on an old, dilapidated horse, but with his head always in the clouds. His faithful bodyguard, Sancho-Panza, who humbly rides on a donkey, is a philosopher of the commonplace, and constantly tries to call his master back to this mundane sphere.

The Three Rs

The fundamentals of education—meaning to include reading, (w)riting, and (a)rithmetic. [The phrase was popularised in a toast by Sir William Curtis. By transferrence, the term "Three R's" has come to signify the essential practical rudiments of any branch of scholarship, or the basic, essential phases of any line of endeavour.]

Moliere

The Shakespeare of France. [Eminent dramatist who lived from 1622 to 1673. His character of *Tartuffe* is the standard symbol of hypocrisy.]

Unearned Increment

Any increase of value produced by forces independent of the person who receives it. One which comes from enhanced value of an article. A great percentage of such gain [should logically be] taken by the government[, and is to an increasing extent.]

Unscrambling Eggs

This term has reference to the merging of two or three companies (that is[,] exchanging stock and becoming one). It is next to impossible to restore such a merger to its original status. Literally, eggs cannot be unscrambled.

Invisible Imports

The law permits a person returning from abroad to bring back $100 worth of goods on which he pay no customs duty. Such goods would be one form of invisible imports. Another form of invisible imports is goods which are smuggled in, such as laces and diamonds. A great many things are brought into the United States free of duty. No record is kept of them and they are also invisible imports. Also more subjectively we may speak of talent, genius, and strange doctrines as invisible imports.

Hedging

Selling securities against previous purchases of other securities to avert possible loss or, conversely, to buy against previous sales. Example: a person might buy 100 shares of Anaconda copper on the margin and put up as collateral 100 shares of something else which he had not paid for. Making one thing serve for another, neither being paid for. In other forms of business it might be making stock represent profits and at the same time represent capital. Sharp business practices [involving this principle] are called "hedging".

Laissez-Faire

The let-alone principle. In economics, absolutely uncontrolled industrial and commercial competition. Derived from the French phrase "laissez faire et passer le monde va de lui-meme"—"let it alone; the world revolves of itself". Policy of running things as they were; not changing them.

Compensated Dollars

Yesterday the dollar bought $1.50 worth of goods. Today the dollar is worth fifty-nine cents. So the dollar is not properly compensated.

Collective Bargaining

[When the employes of a company do not negotiate individually with the owners or managers regarding salary and working conditions, but band together and collectively negotiate—through a representative or group of representatives—for terms and conditions which shall apply impartially to all.]

Neo-Malthusianism

A new [application in modified form] of the theory expounded by Malthus—suggest[ing] artificial limitation of birth as one means of improving social conditions. Malthus did research in the field of economics. He wrote the "Essay on Population" and in this book, which is today a classic[,] he advanced the idea that population tends to increase faster than the [food supply or general necessities of life]. His theory has been proved false [in certain essentials] because of his lack of ability to foresee an age of invention [and intensive food production. The prefix "neo" (new) signifies that the new doctrine is based on the old theory.]

Regional Reserve Banks

Banking system inaugurated during President Wilson's administration. These are not banks of general deposit, but are super-banks established in twelve important industrial centers of the United States. Member banks, of which there are many[,] may deposit with the Reserve Banks. The chief purpose in the establishment of the Reserve System was the stabilization of banking conditions in order to avoid panics. It is advisable to deposit in a bank which is a member of the Federal Reserve Banking System.

Vicarious Leisure

Vicarious means "substitute". Anything vicariously done is done by substitute or proxy. A change of occupation is sometimes spoken of as "vicarious leisure".

Sympathetic Strike

A strike originated by [a] certain labor organization which may have just cause for striking and later joined by certain other organizations of labor in sympathy with the striking union.

Industrial Efficiency

During the World War the Taylor Efficiency Methods were introduced into the United States Government. This system sought to introduce methods whereby all waste would be eliminated[,] and [the] duties of all employees performed with maximum speed and efficiency. This system had been tried and found successful in the business world. It proved of immense benefit, the only difficulty being that it was hard to apply to human beings[,] since one man may be physically and mentally able to do considerably more than one or more of his fellow-men. It can be worked out approximately but not accurately with human beings. It can be accurately applied through machines. Industrial efficiency must alway[s] be considered from the approximate rather than the absolute angle, when the human element is involved.

Fabianism

Fabius was a Roman General who adopted a policy of postponing a battle until he wore his enemy out. He won his war by postponement. General Foch, in the World War, used the Fabian tactics, which amounts to a postponement, retrenchment or competition until a competitor or enemy is worn out.

A Just Price

A just price is one in which the dollar buys one hundred cents worth of commodity value. A "just price" can not be applied to the professions, being applicable only to things involving commodity value. When a profession is involved it is considered a fee for service performed and serve is intangible, not having a commodity value.

Due Process of Law

Working things out by "due process of law" means going through all [applicable] legal machinery [including] equity. Criminal courts solve problems between citizen and state. [Civil] courts solve problems between citizens. [Courts of equity decide fine points demanding expert individual interpretations of laws whose application is not superficially obvious.]

"The Public Be Damned"

"The Public Be Damned" is a quoted policy. Some years ago Cornelius Vanderbilt was trying to get a franchise to run a railroad through a certain portion of New York City. The citizens did not wish the franchise granted because it meant condemning their property without properly compensating them. A certain newspaper reporter was sent to interview Mr. Vanderbilt and called his attention to the fact that public opinion was against the proposition. The reporter called while Mr. Vanderbilt was having breakfast and found him in none too good humor. The reporter stated that public opinion was against his proposal to run the railroad through this portion of New York and Mr. Vanderbilt said, "The Public Be Damned". The young reporter hurried back to the newspaper and spread the remark in broad headlines across the front sheet of his paper. Since then the phrase has come into common use and is supposed generally to be the policy of [all great utility companies—and thence, by extension, of] all rich men. It has often been spoken of as the policy of the Republican Party: "The Public Be Damned" is the policy now in strong use by large corporations.

Survival of the Fittest

This quotation comes from [Charles] Darwin['s] theory [of organic evolution, which shews] that only those [individuals and] species which are [best adapted to their environment survive. The common significance is that only the strongest individuals survive and succeed. When applied] to modern business it means "cut throat competition". The little man goes to the wall. It might be said that the policy of the chain stores against the small store is an example[,] although the chain stores defend their policy on the strength of the statement that the small dealer, particularly the grocery dealer, is bound to go to the wall anyway in five years.

The Domestic System

The monetary system of a country varies according to the type of money or coins used. Ours is based on dollars and cents; the English on pounds and shillings.

Crusoe Economics

Robinson Crusoe, from whom this expression originates, was cast away on an island. It therefore became necessary for him to invent means of providing food and shelter for himself[; and conversely, he was not forced to consider others in planning his own acts and welfare. Those who advocate a policy of laissez-faire or "rugged individualism", with every person or group using individual initiative to secure private advantage and gain, and disregarding the ultimate effect of such practices on the general social fabric, are said to preach "Crusoe Economics". In a rather different sense, one might apply the term to that sort of national policy—now existing in Nazi Germany—which demands that a country be economically independent and self-sufficient, and able to get along without any foreign imports or exports.]

Sabotage

In Holland and some sections of France there are boggy lands and peasants wear wooden shoes which are called by the French "Sabots". Northern France does much lace making with delicate expensive machinery. Some of the socialist workers[,] in order to accomplish their demands without striking[,] decided to stay on and receive their wages but to do everything they could to ruin the companies. They started by throwing wooden shoes into the machinery[, causing damage] which took months for repair. At the present time the term refers to any method which is used to destroy industry from within.

Joint Costs

Expenses shared by two or more groups in establishing a certain business enterprise. A Realty Company and a Transportation Company could share the cost of opening a new subdivision.

Peaceful Picketing

A scheme evolved by trade unions for bringing about a picketing system in which no effort is made to do anything destructive to person or property.

A Complete Merger

A combination in which every bit of the property of two or more concerns is merged for the benefit of the parties to the merger.

Liquid Assets

Property which can be turned into money at once, such as Government bonds.

Gary Dinners

Judge Elbert Gary, General Manager of the United States Steel Corporation, gave several dinners at which new policies or dividends were announced. Gary dinners became important in the financial world as showing trends in the prices of steel and influenced the whole stock market.

The New Freedom

[Title of a book by Woodrow Wilson, indicating the increased freedom accorded to mankind through the evolution of society and government. The term has recently been used in a narrow colloquial sense to mean the freer and easier status of women under modern civilisation—especially the increased freedom of entry into all lines of endeavour.]

The Iron Law of Wages

"The Iron Law of Wages" means that wages always ascend after the cost of living increases, that is they follow the cost of living instead of preceding it. It also means that wages are determined by the law of supply and demand.

Social Organism

"Social Organism" means the structure of the society in which we live, embodying law, order, policies, etc.

A Court of Equity

A court which settles [obscure and debatable points of law not clearly covered by any visible clause in the written statutes. In common with other *civil* courts it] differs from a criminal court in that [the latter] settles the principle of violated law between citizen and state.

A Holding Company

One organized to take care of the promotion of another company and to hold its stock[,] thus evading responsibility or suit.

Lombard Street

Lombard Street is to London what Wall Street is to New York—the financial district of London. [It derives its name from the Lombard or North Italian bankers and money-lenders who first transacted business there.]

Living Wages

Are supposed to mean a sufficient income to provide the necessities of life, some recreations and an old age reserve and partial support of state—that is, contributions to the support of the state through taxes.

The Plane of Competition

Is the basis upon which rival companies are competing.

Milling in Transit

"Milling in Transit" amounts to this: A large wholesale grocery company in New York City orders from a grain elevator in Minnesota so many barrels of flour[. The grain dealer then orders the necessary amount from the] wheat-fields[, directing that it be milled into flour at the proper place] and then shipped to New York. Therefore, the wheat would be milled in transit [between the fields and] New York.

The Economic Man

[A term applied to the political economist's abstract conception of a human being as merely an economic factor—that is, a man considered only in his economic aspects as producer and consumer, without reference to his instincts, emotions, traditions, and personality in general.]

Social and Industrial Justice

Means an equal opportunity to earn a living. We believe in this principle in America—in equal opportunity for all—colored and whit[e] alike.

A Greenback

At the close of the Civil War a great many greenbacks or dollar bills were issued by the Government to pay the soldiers without [the existence of any reserve of authorised precious metal behind them]. When Grant took office one of the planks of his platform was that he would not repudiate [these] greenbacks. [The term greenback has since come to mean any piece of paper money which has no reserve metal to back it, and which therefore may be worth only a small fraction of its face value. Greenbacks are "fiat money" or "inflated currency"—like the Continental currency issued by the United States during the Revolution, and the worthless German marks of the postwar period.]

The Margin of Culture

The margin of culture is very narrow indeed, especially in the economic field. The greed for self-preservation is so primitive and near the surface that[,] striking a man's pocketbook[,] you see the man of the jungle come snarling at you. Men lose their finer feelings over dollars. Men who think of money only become [un]interested in the [art] of living [and the culture which renders life worth living.]

CHAPTER V
INCREASING YOUR VOCABULARY

["How may I increase my vocabulary?"] Teachers of English are often asked this question by students who are becoming word-conscious. So many answers are suggested by the exponents of various systems that we find it almost as confusing as the question of how to improve one's health! [The need of an ample and well-assimilated vocabulary in place of our usually meagre and overworked word-supply is too obvious to require emphasis. No adequate expression is possible when our choice of words is limited to a few common and hackneyed terms, each of which has to be monotonously repeated within single paragraphs or sentences, used clumsily and even erroneously to cover meanings for which the correct word is not known, and set in awkward and fumbling constructions in order to express ideas which more appropriate words could express clearly, directly, and gracefully. We may take it for granted that proper and forceful expression depends absolutely upon our easy and thoroughly understanding command of a wide range of words—a reservoir from which we may select terms as needed to give variety to our speech, to express exact shades of meaning and association, to secure simple and graceful grammatical constructions, and to make our speech musical and harmonious through the avoidance of harsh sound-combinations and unpleasant rhythms.]

The average well-educated person possesses three vocabularies—one each for reading, writing and speaking. The largest number of words—perhaps five thousand—is recognized in reading. One may be vaguely familiar with ten thousand words, but most of us recognize promptly and distinctly only about half that number as we come upon them suddenly in books and periodicals. In writing we use even fewer—while the speaking vocabulary of this same individual will probably run around thirteen hundred words.

In England the oldest and best families have [tended] to furnish a standard of speech. In America the cultivated and academic elements in the older regions and elsewhere perform a kindred function. The best usage is codified in dictionaries, and we should never fail to consult them in any case of doubt. Get the dictionary habit, and learn to understand fully the diacritical marks which show the pronunciation of words. Never let a word pass you until you have mastered its pronunciation, dictionary definition and associational meaning. In other words, be familiar with both the denotation and the connotation of a term.

Fall in love with words. Take joy in their origin and cultivate their precise application. Study their background. Make yourself wholly familiar with the meaning of a word and use it three times properly; after that you will feel that you are an authority on the subject. Although Lincoln's [systematic studies were distinctly limited—giving rise to the common legend that he had mastered] only the dictionary and the Bible[—]he was able to prepare an address so vital and so fundamental that it continues persistently to stir the reader. Its simplicity and sincerity are remarkable and spring from the writer's perfect knowledge of the exact value and application of every word he used.

Reading is [the great] open sesame to vocabulary building. If you will look intently at the words you meet in your reading, and sensitize yourself to their emotional atmosphere, you will develop a genuine accuracy in usage which will mark you as an educated person. The intent perusal of good books will provide a fine discrimination in the use of words.

Since speech is continuously growing, it is not possible for it to have a crystallized form as a whole. Certain words remain permanently in the language, but many of them change more or less subtly with the introduction of new inventions, new customs, and new fads, and with the shifting ideas of the generations. [Beware, however, of accepting an apparent change too soon.] The daily newspapers must not be your guide in this matter. Hurried and careless writing corrupts the language, [and saddles it with ugly and awkward usages which are neither called for by any real need, nor justified by principles of etymology and rhetoric. Some degree of permanence is essential to the speech of any civilised people. A constantly shifting language is a mark of a very low cultural level—as illustrated by those African tribes whose dialects change so rapidly that grandparents and grandchildren have difficulty in understanding each other. When unsettled usage seems to exist, always choose the form sanctioned by sound tradition and exemplified in the best works of literature.

One of the best] methods of improving the vocabulary rests upon association with cultured persons, persons who speak correctly, and who usually command attention. It should be easy for you to recognize such individuals. Engage them in conversation as often as possible. See and hear certain actors in standard plays. The Barrymores, Hampden, Ruth Chatterton, have devoted years to the training of speech and voice. Lecturers today provide some excellent examples of good speech.

[Let us notice—parenthetically—the need of care in pronouncing and enunciating our new verbal acquisitions. In this matter the speech of competent actors, lecturers, and cultivated persons in general is doubly valuable.] During these active, exacting post-war years many persons who possess an ample general education have become acutely conscious of various defects in voice, accent, and conversational quality. Such defects disturb one's sense of fitness, and remedial agencies will grow in number as their recognition increases. Many of our words are pronounced with throaty sounds or with slovenly enunciation. The careful joining of words in such a way as to avoid the dropping or slurring-over of syllables should have particular attention. Americans are particularly guilty of lip-laziness. The lips should be very flexible and responsive for the careful carving of each word before it is emitted.

The practice of writing sentences calling for discrimination in the use of synonyms is another method of improving one's vocabulary. A thesaurus or a book of synonyms should be at your elbow constantly, and attention should be paid to fine gradations of meaning or association. [The great incentive to vocabulary-building in writing is the constant need of synonyms in order to avoid ungraceful repetitions of the same word within a limited space. The beginner, in seeking the variety necessary to good expression, is constantly sent to the thesaurus for different words of parallel meaning—and before he knows it has commenced to acquire an apt and usable stock. The fact that the additional words are sought for a special purpose and must stand the test of immediate use makes this one of the most truly practical and directly helpful of all methods.

However, certain other methods are not to be despised. More than one successful author has spent idle hours in the fascinating pastime of merely browsing through dictionaries, thesauri, and books of synonyms, and noting words which seem to have a peculiar vividness and charm. Of course, this pastime entails a certain amount of waste, and brings to light many words for which no immediate use can be found; but it also helps one now and then to stumble upon some term of surprising aptness and paramount value. Naturally, every new word thus acquired should be thoroughly investigated in the best dictionaries, and watched for in the reading of the best literature. One should also try to work it into some experimental composition, in order to assimilate it as soon and as thoroughly as possible to one's regular working vocabulary.

Be cautious, though, about the public use of a new word—all the more so if it has been haphazardly acquired. Never air a recent acquisition merely for the same of shewing off. Take] plenty of time to develop the impression behind a word before you hasten into utterance with it. Since words are symbols of ideas all care must be taken both to choose a word perfectly fitted to your idea, and to see that the idea is duly conveyed to the mind of your listener. Be careful, too, that your tone and words of utterance make plain your own perfect grasp of what you are conveying. Impression must definitely and eternally be associated with expression.

[But most of all cultivate the dictionary—for in the long run the bulk of your acquisitions will come through the verification of strange words seen in reading or heard from good speakers. Whenever you run across a word that is hazy in your mind, stop at once and confirm its meaning, pronunciation, and precise usage.

Nor must your building of a vocabulary be a merely quantitative matter. Additional words are of no value—are, in fact, an actual liability—unless they are the right words used in the right way. Good literature and good speakers supply words with the associations needed to guide you in their later use. Be careful to adhere to the usage thus indicated. While always seeking variety, be equally resolved to seek simplicity. Do not use obscure or unusual words when common words (always the best ones because of their rich cargo of associations) will convey your meaning with equal accuracy and grace. The only excuse for esoteric, scientific, or academic language is the need for technical precision when certain abstract or complex subjects are under discussion. Beware of the bizarre, and shun the 1890-ish fondness for "purple passages". One of our best imaginative writers sadly weakens his prose through his fatal addiction to words like *fulvous, orgillous, plenilunal,* and *chryselephantine.* Don't pick words because of their impressive looks. Remember that a word is only a means to an end—that of expression. Choose as your models the direct, pointed, animated, and crystally clear prose writers of the early eighteenth century—Addison, Steele, Swift, and Defoe. Avoid in particular the bombastic, pseudo-scientific jargon of the popular press, whose cheap hollowness has recently been so cleverly exposed in A. P. Herbert's book "What a Word!"

Yet the opposite extreme of laboured over-simplicity and artificial naïveté is equally to be avoided. An adult need not be expected to write in monosyllables or keep to the vocabulary of a five-year-old. Much that is said about preferring Saxon-derived words to Latin-derived words is simply non-sense—as we must realise when we reflect that fully five-sevenths of our normal literate vocabulary is of classical origin. It is true that the common names of certain basic objects, emotions, and relationships tend to be Saxon, yet we find that infinitely more of our commonest words are of Latin ances-try. The wise thing is simply to forget—for the moment—all about the ulti-mate source of a word, and to choose it purely on the strength of its present and traditional associations in our own language. If we stick to this rule, we shall be right more often than we would if we bothered to sift the Saxon from the Latin. English usage must be our guide. In writing poetry we cannot use quite the same vocabulary as in writing prose, since the language of exact statement, argument, and scientific exposition is out of place in verse. But careful study of the best models will shew us what is or is not appropriate in the various branches of writing.

We must learn by reading and experience what words are appropriate in certain places, and what general classes to avoid. Slang cannot be ruled out, but it should be used with a proper recognition of its informal, semi-humorous, and grotesquely metaphorical character, and applied only to situa-tions which call for a distinct element of piquancy or an emphatically free-and-easy atmosphere. No spectacle is more pitiful than that of the illiterate person solemnly using cheap and hackneyed slang for a simple statement, in perfect unconsciousness of the fact that he *is* using anything but normal speech. Worse than slang is the all-too-popular class of words known as *bar-barisms*—vulgar imitations of words which have no real existence, but which have been coined by ignorant journalists or have filtered up from the realm of parody, colloquial, regional, or plebeian dialect. *Burglarize, thusly, enthuse, donate, emote, disgruntled, proven,* and *stomp* are examples of this sort of word. And more—we should guard against using words twisted out of their proper meanings, like *transpire* for *happen, intrigue* for *fascinate,* and so on, as against words which have been cheapened by overuse, or cheap or pedantic use, like *meticulous, galore, outstanding, reaction* (for response), *awful* (for extremely), *contact* (as a verb), *wonderful* (for rather good), and similar offenders.

Shun likewise the unassimilated foreign words and phrases with which self-consciously cultivated persons in the nineteenth century used to air their schol-arship or fashionable training. There are certain rare instances where, as used by a very thorough scholar, some imported expression will catch a meaning which eludes the native idiom. Also, there are a few exotic words and phrases, like *dil-ettante, faux pas, magnum opus,* etc., which have become almost assimilated to our language; the words becoming naturalised English words, and the phrases rec-ognised as traditional adjuncts. All this, however, does not justify the 1880 ped-ant's lavish sprinkling of his pages with such classicisms as *caeteris paribus, stans pede in uno, seriatim, onus probandi,* and so on; the pompous Victorian politician's spouting of *fiat justitia, vox populi, audi alteram partem, commune bonum,* and the like; or the Gallicist gush of the belles and dandies of the Rutherford B. Hayes period, who prattle of *soirées* which *tout le monde* attend and where everything was *comme il faut,* although certain *soi disant beaux esprits* to whom one has to listen *bon gre, mal gre* were *très difficile.* The mania for French jargon among the fashionables of yesteryear rivalled the mania for Greek tags and scraps among the corresponding classes of Romans in late republican and imperial times. Let us leave the custom in its well-earned grave.

But in order to grasp and apply these various principles of taste in speech we must put ourselves in the right mood and form the proper habits of constant alertness and faithful study. We must learn to analyse and discriminate, and take an intelligent notice of what we say and write.

Many defects of speech are due to confused attention. Two of the leading faults are obtrusively visible precision and extreme slovenliness.] Between these two poles lie most of the other difficulties. Most every day speech is slip-shod. Try to avoid common mob phrases such as "see", "you bet", "sure thing", "you said it", "listen", "hear", and "yeah".

Effective study will go far toward improving one's attention to speech difficulties. Often students say, "I just have never known how to study properly." This is a good place for a few condensed hints.

First, keep yourself in good physical condition. Interference from defective eyesight, bad teeth and other obstructions should be removed as soon as possible by medical attention.

Get the right environment for proper study, such as adequate light, [suitable] temperature, easy clothing, and a comfortable position at the desk or in the chair.

Form a place-and-time-for-study habit. The actual rewards of such a habit are ample and satisfactory.

Give up the idea that you are making your efforts merely for the teacher. Let the incentive come from within.

Ask for help only when you have to. Give most of your time and attention to your weak points, and try to solve the problems of expression yourself. A solution obtained through your own efforts is usually more thorough and more deeply impressed than any secured with external aid.

Be sure to interrupt each hour with ten minutes' complete change. [Mark] a pathway of attention through your books. Don't hesitate to underline when you are impressed[—though shunning the immature egotistical habit of annotating various authors with pseudo-profound reflections and critical comments.]

Committing to memory may be far more effective if done through emotionalizing. Test all of your impressions with some form of both written and spoken expression. Complete knowledge lies in impression plus expression.

CHAPTER VI
"BROMIDES MUST GO"

Thanks to Gelett Burgess and his pamphlet, "Are You a Bromide?", we have taken over into colloquial use the term "Bromides" as a synonym for hackneyed expressions. Nothing is more indicative of mental staleness and inertia than the habitual use of clichés. These fixed phrases, no matter how apt some of them may have been when used for the first time with reference to specific objects or situations, have long ago become utterly devitalized and worn out through endless repetition and careless, indiscriminate, inaccurate application. They are no longer associated with thought and wit, but have become cheap, shoddy substitutes for these things. They are marks of a thinker so slovenly that his ideas call for no original dress—these things being so hazy that he fancies he is brilliantly expressing them when he parrots the left-over and largely irrelevant phrases of others. Stale bits from the daily press like "taken into custody" or "ferocious canine"; forced synonyms and linguistic flourishes [like "watery element" or "grand finale";] trite allusions like "the [Muses]", or "the light fantastic"; [worn-out similes and metaphors like "cold as ice", "pretty as a picture", or "fine as silk";] and overworked quotations such as "China to Peru", "footprints on the sands of time", "I am the captain of my soul", or "the moving finger writes"—how really pathetic all these are!

[May] we not expect [in contemporary utterance phrases and expressions far fresher, more individual, and more distinctive than] "feathered songster", "budding genius", [or] "sadder but wiser"? Attractive speakers [and writers] have originality[; they choose new images and groupings of words to express the new ideas and pictures created by their intellects and imaginations. They may, of course, now and then consciously employ an apt quotation or familiar idiomatic phrase; but in such cases they do so sparingly and knowingly, and with no wholesale, irresponsible substitution of second-hand thoughts and imagery for their own conceptions and diction. It is one thing to borrow an old expression like "one fell swoop" to give a homely and semi-humorous touch to a certain bit of described action, but quite another thing to pepper the whole length of a discourse or composition with "bated breaths", "psychological moments", "supreme sacrifices", and "floral tributes".

Our trite expressions have come from varied sources; some from the lore of the past, and some from the colloquialism or written speech of more recent times. The Bible and Shakespeare—those prolific parents of conscious quotations—have been equally fecund in populating the realm of unconscious allusions. Shakespeare is probably the greatest single source, and the poets of the past in general seem to outdo modern sources. Some of these clichés are generally recognised as quotations, while others are less frequently linked with their origin. In many the original text is more or less garbled, being sometimes traceable only with difficulty. In more cases than not, these figures and phrases were powerful and vivid in their pristine setting. In other cases—especially those of expressions springing from modern speech or from the florid and bombastic newspaper English of the nineteenth century—the sources themselves were tawdry.

We are here subjoining a list of stock phrases culled at random and set down in no particular order. All of these are things to be avoided in speech and composition, except in the very sparing, conscious, and quasi-humorous way dictated by a mature taste. It is safer for the beginner to eschew them entirely. A study of this list will tend to familiarise one with the earmarks of the class, and to help him avoid the use of these and kindred expressions.*

---

* [I may or may not have duplicated stuff in the famous Burgess book—which I've never seen.

[If you use only a small part of this list, you might return the original in the end for possible future use. Collecting all this junk took so much time and recollection that I'd hate to see the result wasted!]

fearfully and wonderfully made

pillar of the church

end is not yet

take the stump

fleshpots of Egypt

over and above

apple of his eye

salt of the earth

sounding brass and tinkling cymbals

by leaps and bounds

confusion worse confounded

music hath charms

as the twig is bent

slowly but surely

it goes without saying

first fine careless rapture

conspicuous by its absence

pearl of great price

open road

drop in the bucket

even Homer nods

sweat of his brow

sleep of the just

nature's sweet restorer

skin of his teeth

whited sepulchre

cup that cheers

lead a charmed life

fallen from high estate

counterfeit presentment

man after my own heart

blue Empyrean

jaundiced eye

that way madness lies

yeoman service

coals of fire

led to the slaughter

young idea

thorn in the flesh

lily hand

wife of his bosom

more sinned against than sinning

ministering angel

beggars description

cribbed, cabined, confined

deep calls unto deep

household words

still waters run deep

end of his rope

witching hour

worm turns

Mother Earth

Mother Nature

Old Sol

Fair Luna

embarrassment of riches

distance lends enchantment

that is another story

add insult to injury

pile Ossa on Pelion

livelong day

die is cast

mount Pegasus

pink of perfection

smells of the lamp

what's in a name

days are numbered

fair means or foul

all things to all men

genius is near to madness

sought my downy couch

wee small hours

cynosure of all eyes

wood-notes wild

hold the mirror to nature

last straw

all Nature smiles

dulcet strains

bright and early

labour of love

briny deep

vasty deep

bounding fine

bounding billows

terrible in its intensity

tumultuous applause

down at the heel

wish was father to the thought

took the words from my mouth
westward the course of empire
deep-dyed villainy
order is heaven's first law
a collation was served
Solomon in all his glory
hold a candle
coward dies a thousand deaths
mischief for idle hands
more than meets the ear
last but not least
sadder but wiser
tired but happy
easier said than done
last infirmity of noble mind
ills that flesh is heir to
scotch the snake
full of sound and fury
river like a silver ribbon
tower of strength
more honoured in breach than observance
mad as a wet hen
airy nothings
fragrant weed
succulent bivalve
in the words of the poet
free, white, and twenty-one
sublime to the ridiculous
guide, philosopher, and friend
scholar and gentleman
perfect gentle knight
made of sterner stuff
budding genius
humble cot
one touch of nature
filthy lucre
led to the altar
wending his way
paint the lily
comparisons are odious
more in sorrow than in anger
barren ground
melancholy days

pearls before swine
too much of a good thing
sea-change
haunts of man
strange bedfellows
laughable if it were not tragic
carpet of green sward
into the thin air
stuff that dreams are made of
sun sinks to rest
sober as a judge
nine days' wonder
on his last legs
bitter end
call a spade a spade
happy accident
exception proves the rule
ill wind
leave no stone unturned
golden mean
midnight oil
silence is golden
bark worse than his bite
plain as a pikestaff
silence gives consent
broad acres
smell a rat
strike while the iron's hot
tried and true
perfumes of Arabia
make night hideous
rouse the echoes
memory is green
make the welkin ring
Gorgons and Hydras and Chimae-
  ras dire
king of terrors
free and easy
arose as one man
stars fought in their courses
fly in the ointment
faithful unto death
raven locks
better half

simple faith
millstone around his neck
better part of valour
majesty of the law
dim religious light
play fast and loose
purple hills
world is his oyster
fury of the elements
gall and wormwood
curry favour
cool, refreshing draught
fit for a king
pomp and circumstance
appeal from Philip drunk to Philip sober
suit the action to the word
let the word serve for the deed
in solitary state
bulwark of liberty
tissue of lies
figment of the imagination
breath of scandal
finger of suspicion
hand of the law
has seen better days
through a glass darkly
silvery moon
clothed in autumnal beauty
world's mine oyster
villainous smell
make the angels weep
whose name is legion
uneasy lies the head that wears a crown
meat and drink to me
forever and a day
words fail me
dull sickening thud
wines of the wind
fine frenzy
injured innocence
cannon's mouth
wolf in sheep's clothing

take a back seat
caudal appendage
in on the ground floor
brown study
Daniel come to judgment
childish treble
apparel oft proclaims the man
course of true love
sere and yellow leaf
prophetic soul
haven't scratched the surface
passing fair
seething mass of humanity
completes the picture
Hobson's choice
sermons in stones
beginning of the end
primrose path
unconsidered trifle
vault above
leap in the dark
silent as the tomb
velvety lawn
laid on with a trowel
goes against my stomach
Grand Old Man
break a lance
local habitation and a name
goes against the grain
wise saws
in our midst
we die but once
love is blind
devil can quote Scripture
as Oscar Wilde said, "too utterly utter"
damask cheek
discourse sweet music
needs no recommendation
busy bee
toothsome viands
old familiar faces
he that hath ears
wars and rumours of wars
meat and drink to me

clinging vine
beat swords into ploughshares
land of the living
heave a sigh of relief
work like a Trojan
still, small voice
indite a masterpiece
scene lay before us
in cold blood
signs of the times
nothing new under the sun

eat, drink, and be merry
iron entered his soul
midsummer madness
method in his madness
forever and a day
cut the Gordian knot
great unwashed
milk and honey

CHAPTER X
WHAT SHALL I READ?
[HPL's additions in brackets]

Cultured speech requires a background of literature, general science, philosophy, [history,] and sociology. Books afford the greatest access to such material. Naturally, no one can lay down a hard and fast rule for reading, but a few suggestions will awaken your appetite. Your own tastes must guide you somewhat, although you must not limit yourself by your present appreciations. As you become better acquainted with the contents of excellent books you will find your ideals and tastes changing within certain limits.

Vari[e]ties of style, author, and content will act like hot and cold applications to your intellect. You will find increased stimulus therefrom. But be sure that you talk to someone about your reading. Pass it on as soon as feasible. Give it away and you will keep it. True knowledge relies upon your impression plus expression. Learn also to give personal reactions to your reading rather than mere reports.

One of the most understanding books written about a mother is J. M. Barrie's "Margaret Ogilvy". You are probably familiar with his popular play, "Peter Pan".

When reading Bacon's Essays take them in small doses—but be sure to sample such wisdom.

A modern scientist, Beebe, has a way of bringing his own adventures agreeably into your own mind. Try his "Arcturus Adventure". You must not eschew poetry, so delight for an evening in Rupert Brook[e]'s poems and Elizabeth Barrett Browning's "Sonnets from the Portuguese". Her husband nicknamed her the "Little Portuguese", hence the title. His poems may be a bit abstruse for a beginner, but find someone who can read them to you understandingly. What food for thought is there!

Perhaps, with the Soviet experiment insistently clamoring for attention, you would like something from Russian literature. Dostoievsky's "Crim[e] and Punishment" and "Brothers Karamazov" will afford you more than one grim evening. Or read Tolstoi's "Kreutzer Sonata" for a horrible confession. Maxim Gorki is the [leading] representative of modern Bear Land.

It is necessary to know what and where this earth is on which you live. Flammarion's Astronomy is a good simple book. Or try Ball' "Story of the Heavens."

Read several books at once, for each book opens up a new part of the mind. So why not try a good book on geology? Try some book published since 1934. This geology will tell you what has happened to the earth during the hundreds of millions of years that it has been spinning around the sun.

Wallace's book on Darwinism will inform you on evolution, about the development of the animal life on the earth, and how you have gradually arisen to an erect position, and learned to study the stars instead of studying ways to kill and eat your neighbor.

Now that you understand about the Universe in which your earth is a little traveller, something about geology and evolution, then read a good book on psychology and learn something about yourself, how it becomes possible for your brain to see and understand the world around you and the distant suns. Prof. James has written an admirable book on psychology. Get it. Or try Alfred Adler's What Life Should Mean to You.

Now you are ready for philosophy, which means the history of human thought and abstract speculation. Philosophy represents the effort of man to explain things to himself, as religion represents man's effort to believe. The history of philosophy written by George Lewes, husband of George Eliot, is easy and pleasant to read, and sufficiently, although not perfectly accurate.

Meanwhile neglect not your Shakespeare for at least fifteen minutes every day. Other books feed different parts of the mind. Shakespeare feeds the entire brain. Read a little at a time and change from one book to another.

Bacon was [perhaps] one of the world's three greatest thinkers[, yet] he died in [relative] disgrace[—]which shows that intellect is sometimes apart from character. So take time out to read his Essays.

For your children's sake, you want to know something about education so read Herbert Spencer's book on "Education" and Rousseau's "Emile".

To know something about yourself and your kind, read the lives of a few (12 to 20) of the world's important men; for instance, Socrates, Alexander the Great, Aristotle, Caesar, Napoleon, Voltaire, Michelangelo, Leonardo Da Vinci. If you can't read their lives, at least look them up in a first-class encyclopedia.

The aim of [good] reading is instructive. It will surely speed the hours but the primary function is self-awakening. It will utterly change your relations with others. It will act like hot and cold applications on the intelligence. It will produce quickened perceptions and new arrangements of concepts. In other words—you will discover many new possibilities within and without yourself.

Glossary of
Frequently Mentioned Names

Baldwin, F[ranklin] Lee (1913–1987), weird fiction fan who came into epistolary contact with HPL in 1933. He wrote an early biography, "H. P. Lovecraft: A Biographical Sketch" (*Fantasy Magazine,* April 1935).

Barlow, R[obert] H[ayward] (1918–1951), author and collector. As a teenager he corresponded with HPL and acted as his host during two long visits in the summers of 1934 and 1935. In the 1930s he wrote several works of weird and fantasy fiction, some in collaboration with HPL. HPL appointed him his literary executor. He assisted August Derleth and Donald Wandrei in preparing the early HPL volumes for Arkham House. In the 1940s he went to Mexico and became a distinguished anthropologist. He died by suicide. HPL's letters to Barlow have been published as *O Fortunate Floridian* (Tampa, FL: University of Tampa Press, 2007).

Blackwood, Algernon (1869–1951), leading British writer of weird fiction who gained celebrity with *John Silence—Physician Extraordinary* (1908), *Incredible Adventures* (1914), and other volumes. HPL considered his novella "The Willows" (1907) the greatest weird tale in literature.

Brobst, Harry K[ern] (1909–2010), late associate of HPL who moved to Providence in 1932 and saw HPL regularly thereafter.

Bullen, John Ravenor (1886–1927), amateur poet from Canada. HPL edited his poems, *White Fire* (1927), for posthumous publication.

Bush, (Rev.) David Van (1882–1959), prolific author of inspirational verse and popular psychology manuals, many of them revised by HPL.

Clark, Franklin C. (1847–1915), husband of HPL's aunt Lillian, a physician and writer on medicine and local and natural history. He translated Homer, Virgil, Lucretius, and Statius into English verse. HPL possessed Clark's translations of the *Georgics* and *Aeneid* of Virgil and mentioned on several occasions his desire to see the work published.

Clark, Lillian D[elora] (1856–1932), HPL's maternal aunt. She married Dr. Franklin Chase Clark in 1902. From 1926 to her death she shared quarters with HPL at 10 Barnes Street.

Coates, Walter J[ohn] (1880–1941), friend of W. Paul Cook and editor of *Driftwind.*

Cole, Edward H[arold] (1892–1966), longtime amateur associate of HPL, living in the Boston area. Editor of the *Olympian.*

Conover, Willis (1921–1996), weird fiction fan who edited *Science-Fantasy Correspondent* (1936–37) and was a late correspondent of HPL.

Cook, W. Paul (1881–1948), publisher of the *Monadnock Monthly*, the *Vagrant*, and other amateur journals; a longtime amateur journalist, printer, and life-long friend of HPL. He first visited HPL in 1917, and it was he who urged HPL to resume writing fiction after a hiatus of nine years. In 1927 Cook published the *Recluse*, with HPL's "Supernatural Horror in Literature."

Crawford, William L[evy] (1911–1984), editor of *Marvel Tales* and *Unusual Stories* and publisher of the Visionary Publishing Company, which issued HPL's *The Shadow over Innsmouth* (1936).

Daas, Edward F. (1879–1962), amateur journalist who recruited HPL into the movement in 1914.

Davis, Edgar J., young amateur journalist with whom HPL explored New-buryport and other locales in New England.

de Castro, Adolphe (Danziger) (1859–1959), author, co-translator with Ambrose Bierce of Richard Voss's *The Monk and the Hangman's Daughter*, and correspondent of HPL. HPL revised his "The Last Test" and "The Electric Executioner."

de la Mare, Walter (1873–1956), British author and poet who wrote occasional weird tales much admired by HPL for their subtlety and allusiveness.

Derleth, August W[illiam] (1909–1971), author of weird tales and also a long series of regional and historical works set in his native Wisconsin. After HPL's death, he and Donald Wandrei founded the publishing firm of Arkham House to preserve HPL's work in book form.

Dunsany, Lord (Edward John Moreton Drax Plunkett) (1878–1957), Irish writer of fantasy tales whose work notably influenced HPL after HPL read it in 1919.

Dwyer, Bernard Austin (1897–1943), weird fiction fan and would-be writer and artist, living in West Shokan, NY; correspondent of HPL.

Edkins, Ernest A[rthur] (1867–1946), amateur journalist associated with the "halcyon days" of the National Amateur Press Association (1885–95). He came in touch with HPL in 1932.

Eshbach, Lloyd Arthur (1910–2003), science fiction writer and publisher who edited the *Galleon* and published some of HPL's poems and stories in the magazine.

Farnese, Harold S. (1885–1945), musical composer who set some of HPL's poems to music. He corresponded sporadically with HPL from 1932 to 1933.

Finlay, Virgil (1914–1971), one of the great weird artists of his time and a prolific contributor of artwork to the pulps; late correspondent of HPL.

Galpin, Alfred (1901–1983), amateur journalist, French scholar, composer, and protégé, then longtime friend, of HPL. He lived in Appleton, WI.

Gamwell, Annie E[meline] P[hillips] (1866–1941), HPL's younger aunt, living with him at 66 College Street (1933–37). She had been married (1897–1936) to Edward F[rancis] Gamwell (1869–1936).

Goodenough, Arthur H[enry] (1871–1936), amateur poet who resided in Brattleboro, VT. HPL visited him there on several occasions.

Green-Leach, Leacy Naylor (1862–1936). Poet and editor. Founded and edited the Baltimore-based literary magazine, the *Circle*, which ran from 1923 until 1938. In 1923, established the Baltimore literary group, the American Poetry Circle.

Greene, Sonia Haft (1883–1972), HPL's wife (1924–29). Born Sonia Haft Shafirkin in Ichnya (near Kiev), in the Ukraine. Settling in the United States, she eventually joined the amateur journalism movement, publishing two lavish issues of the *Rainbow* and becoming president of the UAPA (1924–25). After her divorce from HPL, she moved to California and married Dr. Nathaniel Davis. Her memoir of HPL has been published as *The Private Life of H. P. Lovecraft* (1985; rev. 1992).

Houtain, George Julian (1884–1945), amateur journalist who established the semi-professional humor magazine *Home Brew*, for which he commissioned HPL to write "Herbert West—Reanimator" (1921–22) and "The Lurking Fear" (1922).

Howard, Robert E[rvin] (1906–1936), prolific Texas author of weird and adventure tales for *Weird Tales* and other pulp magazines; creator of the adventure hero Conan of Cimmeria. He and HPL corresponded voluminously from 1930 to 1936. He committed suicide when he heard of his mother's impending death.

Kirk, George [Willard] (1898–1962), member of the Kalem Club. He published *Twenty-one Letters of Ambrose Bierce* (1922) and ran the Chelsea Bookshop in New York.

Kleiner, Rheinhart (1892–1949), amateur poet and longtime friend of HPL. He visited HPL in Providence in 1918, 1919, and 1920, and met him frequently during the heyday of the Kalem Club (1924–26).

Koenig, H[erman] C[harles] (1893–1959), late associate of HPL who spearheaded the rediscovery of the work of William Hope Hodgson.

Kuntz, Eugene B. (1865–1944), Prussian-born poet, Presbyterian minister, and amateur journalist. HPL edited Kuntz's slim collection of poems, *Thoughts and Pictures* (Haverhill, MA: "Cooperatively published by H. P. Loveracft [*sic*] and C. W. Smith," 1932), probably revising the poems in the process.

Long, Frank Belknap (1901–1994), fiction writer and poet and one of HPL's closest friends and correspondents. Late in life he wrote the memoir, *Howard Phillips Lovecraft: Dreamer on the Nightside* (1975).

Loveman, Samuel E. (1887–1976), poet and longtime friend of HPL and Hart Crane, and associate of Ambrose Bierce, Hart Crane, George Sterling, and Clark Ashton Smith. He wrote *The Hermaphrodite* (1926) and other works.

Machen, Arthur (1863–1947), Welsh author of weird fiction whose work influenced HPL significantly after he read it in 1923.

McNeil, Everett (1862–1929), author of historical and adventure novels for boys; member of the Kalem Club.

Merritt, A[braham] (1884–1943), writer of fantasy and horror tales for the pulps. His work was much admired by HPL in spite of its concessions to pulp formulae. His late novel, *Dwellers in the Mirage* (1932), may have been influenced by HPL.

Miniter, Edith (1867–1934), amateur author who also professionally published a novel, *Our Natupski Neighbors* (1916) and many short stories. HPL was guest at her home in Wilbraham, Massachusetts, in the summer of 1928.

Moe, Maurice W[inter] (1882–1940), amateur journalist, English teacher, and longtime friend and correspondent of HPL. He lived successively in Appleton and Milwaukee, WI.

Moe, Robert Ellis (1912–1992), one of Maurice W. Moe's two sons (the other was Donald), who began corresponding with HPL in 1934 and met him on several occasions.

Morse, Richard Ely (1909–1986), poet, librarian at Princeton University, and correspondent of HPL.

Morton, James F[erdinand] (1870–1941), amateur journalist, member of the Kalem Club, author of many tracts on race prejudice, freethought, and taxation, and longtime friend of HPL. See *Letters to James F. Morton* (Hippocampus Press, 2011).

Munn, H[arold] Warner (1903–1981), contributor to the pulp magazines, living near W. Paul Cook in Athol, MA.

Orton, Vrest (1897–1986), a late member of the Kalem Club. He was for a time an editor at the *Saturday Review* and later the founder of the Vermont Country Store. He compiled an early bibliography of Theodore Dreiser, *Dreiserana* (1929).

Price, E[dgar] Hoffmann (1898–1988), prolific pulp writer of weird and adventure tales. HPL met him in New Orleans in 1932 and corresponded extensively with him thereafter.

Sechrist, Edward Lloyd (1873–1953), amateur journalist and beekeeper. HPL met him on several occasions, especially during visits to Washington, DC.

Smith, Charles W. ("Tryout") (1852–1948), longtime amateur journalist, editor of the *Tryout,* and friend and correspondent of HPL.

Smith, Clark Ashton (1893–1961), prolific California poet and writer of fantasy tales. He received a "fan" letter from HPL in 1922 and corresponded with him until HPL's death.

Sterling, Kenneth (1920–1995), young science fiction fan who came into contact with HPL in 1934. They collaborated on the science fiction story "In the Walls of Eryx" (1935). Sterling later became a distinguished physician.

Strauch, Carl Ferdinand (1908–1989), friend of Harry Brobst and correspondent of HPL. He later became a distinguished professor and critic.

Talman, Wilfred Blanch (1904–1986), correspondent of HPL and late member of the Kalem Club. HPL assisted Talman on his story "Two Black Bottles" (1926) and wrote "Some Dutch Footprints in New England" for Talman to publish in *De Halve Maen,* the journal of the Holland Society of New York. Late in life he wrote the memoir *The Normal Lovecraft* (1973).

Wandrei, Donald (1908–1987), poet and author of weird fiction, science fiction, and detective tales. He corresponded with HPL from 1926 to 1937, visited HPL in Providence in 1927 and 1932, and met HPL occasionally in New York during the 1930s. He helped HPL get "The Shadow out of Time" published in *Astounding Stories.* After HPL's death he and August Derleth founded the publishing firm Arkham House to preserve HPL's work. For their joint correspondence, see *Mysteries of Time and Spirit.*

Wandrei, Howard (1909–1956), younger brother of Donald Wandrei, premier weird artist and prolific author of weird fiction, science fiction, and detective stories; correspondent of HPL.

Whitehead, Henry S[t. Clair] (1882–1932), author of weird and adventure tales, many of them set in the Virgin Islands. HPL corresponded with him and visited him in Florida in 1931. HPL wrote a brief eulogy of Whitehead for *Weird Tales.*

Bibliography

A. Works by H. P. Lovecraft

Books

The Ancient Track: Complete Poetical Works. Edited by S. T. Joshi. San Francisco: Night Shade Books, 2001. Rev. ed. New York: Hippocampus Press, 2013.

The Annotated Supernatural Horror in Literature. Edited by S. T. Joshi. New York: Hippocampus Press, 2000 (rev. ed. 2012).

At the Mountains of Madness and Other Novels. Edited by S. T. Joshi. Sauk City, WI: Arkham House, [1985]. [*MM*]

The Cats of Ulthar. Cassia, FL: Dragon-Fly Press, 1935. (*LL* 547)

Collected Essays. Edited by S. T. Joshi. New York: Hippocampus Press, 2004–06. 5 vols. [*CE*]

Dagon and Other Macabre Tales. Edited by S. T. Joshi. Sauk City, WI: Arkham House, [1986]. [*D*]

The Dunwich Horror and Others. Edited by S. T. Joshi. Sauk City, WI: Arkham House, [1984]. [*DH*]

Essential Solitude: The Letters of H. P. Lovecraft and August Derleth. Edited by David E. Schultz and S. T. Joshi. New York: Hippocampus Press, 2008. 2 vols.

The Fiction. New York: Barnes & Noble, 2008 (rev. ed. 2011). [All fiction save revisions and collaborations.]

The Horror in the Museum and Other Revisions. Edited by S. T. Joshi. Sauk City, WI: Arkham House, [1989]. [*HM*]

Letters to Rheinhart Kleiner. Edited by S. T. Joshi and David E. Schultz. New York: Hippocampus Press, 2005.

Letters to James F. Morton. Edited by David E. Schultz and S. T. Joshi. New York: Hippocampus Press, 2011.

O Fortunate Floridian: H. P. Lovecraft's Letters to R. H. Barlow. Edited by S. T. Joshi and David E. Schultz. Tampa, FL: University of Tampa Press, 2007.

The Shunned House. Athol, MA: Recluse Press, 1928 (printed but not bound or distributed until 1959–61).

Stories

At the Mountains of Madness. Astounding Stories 16, No. 6 (February 1936): 8–32; 17, No. 1 (March 1936): 125–55; 17, No. 2 (April 1936): 132–50. In *MM*.

"The Call of Cthulhu." *WT* 11, No. 2 (February 1928): 159–78, 287. In *Beware After Dark! The World's Most Stupendous Tales of Mystery, Horror, Thrills and Terror,* ed. T. Everett Harré. New York: Macaulay, 1929, pp. 223–59. In *DH*.

The Case of Charles Dexter Ward. *Weird Tales* 35, No. 9 (May 1941): 8–40; 35, No. 10 (July 1941): 84–121 (abridged). Complete text in *Beyond the Wall of Sleep*. Sauk City, WI: Arkham House, 1943. In *MM*.

"The Cats of Ulthar." *Tryout* 6, No. 11 (November 1920): [6–11]. *WT* 7, No. 2 (Feb. 1926): 252–54. In *D*.

"Celephaïs." *Rainbow* No. 2 (May 1922): 10–12. *Marvel Tales* 1, No. 1 (May 1934): 26, 28–32. In *D*.

"Dagon." *Vagrant* No. 11 (November 1919): 23–29. *WT* 2, No. 3 (October 1923): 23–25. In *D*.

"The Doom That Came to Sarnath." *Scot* No. 44 (June 1920): 90–98. *Marvel Tales of Science and Fantasy* 1, No. 4 (Mar.–Apr. 1935): 157–63. In *D*.

The Dream-Quest of Unknown Kadath. In *Beyond the Wall of Sleep*. Sauk City, WI: Arkham House, 1943. In *MM*.

"The Dreams in the Witch House."' *WT* 22, No. 1 (July 1933): 86–111. In *MM*.

"The Dunwich Horror." *WT* 13, No. 4 (April 1929): 481–508. In *DH*.

"The Festival." *WT* 5, No. 1 (January 1925): 169–74. *WT* 22, No. 4 (October 1933): 519–20, 522–28. In *D*.

"The Haunter of the Dark." *WT* 28, No. 5 (December 1936): 538–53. In *DH*.

"Herbert West—Reanimator." *Home Brew* 1, No. 1 (February 1922): 19–25 ("From the Dark"); 1, No. 2 (March 1922): 45–50 ("The Plague Demon"); 1, No. 3 (April 1922): 21–26 ("Six Shots by Moonlight"); 1, No. 4 (May 1922): 53–58 ("The Scream of the Dead"); 1, No. 5 (June 1922): 45–50 ("The Horror from the Shadows"); 1, No. 6 (July 1922): 57–62 ("The Tomb-Legions").

"The Horror at Red Hook." *WT* 9, No. 1 (January 1927): 59–73. In *You'll Need a Night Light*, ed. Christine Campbell Thomson. London: Selwyn & Blount, 1927, pp. 228–54. In *D*.

"The Lurking Fear." *Home Brew* 2, No. 6 (January 1923): 4–10; 3, No. 1 (February 1923): 18–23; 3, No. 2 (March 1923): 31–37, 44, 48; 3, No. 3 (April 1923): 35–42. *WT* 11, No. 6 (June 1928): 791–804. In *D*.

"The Moon-Bog." *WT* 7, No. 6 (June 1926): 805–10. In *D*.

"The Music of Erich Zann." *National Amateur* 44, No. 4 (March 1922): 38–40. *WT* 5, No. 5 (May 1925): 219–34. In *Creeps by Night: Chills and Thrills*, ed. Dashiell Hammett. New York: John Day Co., 1931, pp. 347–63. In *Modern Tales of Horror*, ed. Dashiell Hammett. London: Victor Gollancz, 1932, pp. 301–17. *Evening Standard* (London) (24 October 1932): 20–21. *WT* 24, No. 5 (November 1934): 644–48, 655–56. In *DH*.

"The Nameless City." *Wolverine* No. 11 (November 1921): 3–15. *Fanciful Tales* 1, No. 1 (Fall 1936): 5–18. In *D*.

"The Outsider." *WT* 7, No. 4 (April 1926): 449–53. *WT* 17, No. 4 (June–July 1931): 566–71. In *DH*.

"Pickman's Model." *WT* 10, No. 4 (October 1927): 505–14. In *By Daylight Only*, ed. Christine Campbell Thomson. London: Selwyn & Blount, 1929, pp.

37–52. *WT* 28, No. 4 (November 1936): 495–505. In *The "Not at Night" Omnibus,* ed. Christine Campbell Thomson. London: Selwyn & Blount, [1937], pp. 279–307. In *DH.*

"Polaris." *Philosopher* 1, No. 1 (December 1920): 3–5. *National Amateur* 48, No. 5 (May 1926): 48–49. *Fantasy Fan* 1, No. 6 (February 1934): 83–85. In *D.*

"The Quest of Iranon." *Galleon* 1, No. 5 (July–August 1935): 12–20. In *D.*

"The Rats in the Walls." *WT* 3, No. 3 (March 1924): 25–31. *WT* 15, No. 6 (June 1930): 841–53. In *Switch On the Light,* ed. Christine Campbell Thomson. London: Selwyn & Blount, 1931, pp. 141–65. In *DH.*

"The Shadow out of Time."*Astounding Stories* 17, No. 4 (June 1936): 110–54. In *DH.*

The Shadow over Innsmouth. Everett, PA: The Visionary Publishing Co., 1936. In *DH.*

"The Shunned House." *WT* 30, No. 4 (October 1937): 418–36. In *MM.*

"The Silver Key." *WT* 13, No. 1 (January 1929): 41–49, 144. In *MM.*

"The Statement of Randolph Carter." *Vagrant* No. 13 (May 1920): 41–48. *WT* 5, No. 2 (February 1925): 149–53. In *MM.*

"Strange High House in the Mist." *WT* 18, No. 3 (October 1931): 394–400. In *D.*

"The Temple." *WT* 6, No. 3 (September 1925): 329–36, 429–31. *WT* 27, No. 2 (February 1936): 239–44, 246–49. In *D.*

"The Thing on the Doorstep." *WT* 29, No. 1 (January 1937): 52–70. In *DH.*

"The Tomb." *Vagrant* No. 14 (March 1922): 50–64. *WT* 7, No. 1 (January 1926): 117–23. In *D.*

"The Very Old Folk." *Scienti-Snaps* 3, No. 3 (Summer 1940): 4–8. In *MW.*

Revisions and Collaborations

Bishop, Zealia Brown Reed. "The Mound." *WT* 35, No. 6 (November 1940): 98–120 (abridged). In *HM.*

Sterling, Kenneth. "In the Walls of Eryx." *WT* 34, No. 4 (October 1939): 50–68. In *HM.*

Price, E. Hoffmann. "Through the Gates of the Silver Key." *WT* 24, No. 1 (July 1934): 60–85. In *MM.*

Essays and Miscellany

"An Account of a Trip to the Antient Fairbanks House, in Dedham, and to the Red Horse Tavern in Sudbury, in the Province of the Massachusetts-Bay." In *CE* 4.

"An Account of Charleston, in His Maj[ty]'s Province of South-Carolina." In *CE* 4.

448 ❧ *Letters to Elizabeth Toldridge and Anne Tillery Renshaw*

[Autobiographical Notice.] In Edward J. O'Brien, ed., *The Best Short Stories of 1928, and the Yearbook of the American Short Story.* New York: Dodd, Mead, 1928, p. 324. In *CE* 5.

"Commonplace Book." In *CE* 5.

"For Official Editor—Anne Tillery Renshaw." *The Conservative* 5, No. 1 (July 1919): 11-12 (unsigned). In *CE* 1.

Further Criticism of Poetry. See "Notes on Verse Technique."

"Homes and Shrines of Poe." *Californian* 2, No. 3 (Winter 1934): 8–10. In *CE* 4.

"[Literary Review.]" *Californian* 4, No. 3 (Winter 1936): 27–33.

"Metrical Regularity." *Conservative* 1, No. 2 (July 1915): 2–4. In *CE* 2.

"Notes on Verse Technique." Published as *Further Criticism of Poetry.* Louisville, KY: Printed on the Press of George G. Fetter Co., 1932. In *CE* 1.

"Poetry and the Artistic Ideal." *Acolyte* 1, No. 3 (Spring 1943): 3–6. An extract from HPL's letter to Elizabeth Toldridge of 3 September [1929].

"Sleepy Hollow To-day." In Sterling A. Leonard and Harold Y. Moffett, ed. *Junior Literature: Book Two.* New York: Macmillan, 1930, 1935, pp. 545–46. An extract from "Observations on Several Parts of America." In *CE* 4.

Some Current Motives and Practices. [DeLand, FL: R. H. Barlow, 1936.] In *CE* 1.

"Some Dutch Footprints in New England." *De Halve Maen* 9, No. 1 (18 October 1933): 2, 4. In *CE* 4.

"Suggestions for a Reading Guide. In *The Dark Brotherhood and Other Pieces,* ed. August Derleth. (Sauk City, WI: Arkham House, 1966). In *CE* 2.

"Supernatural Horror in Literature." *Recluse* No. 1 (1927): 23–59. Rev. ed. in *Fantasy Fan* (October 1933–February 1935). In *D, CE* 2.

"Symphony and Stress." *Conservative* 1, No. 3 (October 1915): 12–14 (unsigned). In *CE* 5.

"Systematic Instruction in the United." *Ole Miss'* 2 (December 1915): 4–5. In *CE* 1.

"The Unknown City in the Ocean." *Perspective Review* (Winter 1934 [Fourth Anniversary Number]): 4–8. In *CE* 4.

"Vermont—A First Impression." *Driftwind* 2, No. 5 (March 1928): [5–9]. In *CE* 4.

"The Vers Libre Epidemic." *Conservative* 2, No. 4 (January 1917): 2–4. In *CE* 2

Poems [all poems are in *AT*]

"Aletheia Phrikodes." See "The Poe-et's Nightmare."

"The Ancient Track." *WT* 15, No. 3 (March 1930): 300.

"August." *Tryout* 4, No. 8 (August 1918): [3]. *National Enquirer* 6, No. 21 (22 August 1918): 10. *Californian* 5, No. 1 (Summer 1937): 25.

"Autumn." *Tryout* 3, No. 12 (November 1917): [3–5]. [Providence] *Evening News* 51, No. 125 (5 November 1917): 3; *National Enquirer* 9, No. 4 (23 October 1919): 7.

"Ave atque Vale." *Tryout* 11, No. 10 (December 1927): [3–4].

"The Dead Bookworm." *United Amateur* 19, No. 1 (September 1919): 1 (as by "John J. Jones").

"The East India Brick Row." *Providence Journal* 102, No. 7 (8 January 1930): 13.

"Edith Miniter." *Tryout*, 16, No. 8 (August 1934): [5–6].

Fungi from Yuggoth.

    XVIII. "The Gardens of Yin." *Driftwind* 6, No. 5 (March 1932): 34.

    XXI. "Nyarlathotep." *Weird Tales* 17, No. 1 (January 1931): 12.

    XXII. "Azathoth." *Weird Tales* 17, No. 1 (January 1931): 12.

    XXIII. "Mirage." *WT* 17, No. 2 (February–March 1931): 175.

    XXIV. "The Canal." *Driftwind* 6, No. 5 (March 1932): 34. In *Harvest: A Sheaf of Poems from* Driftwind, ed. Walter John Coates. North Montpelier, VT: Driftwind Press, 1933, p. 33.

    XXVII. "The Elder Pharos." *WT* 17, No. 2 (February–March 1931): 175.

    XXX. "Background." *Providence Journal* 102, No. 91 (16 April 1930): 13; *Galleon* 1, No. 4 (May–June 1935): 8.

"A Garden." *Vagrant* [Spring 1927]: 60. The issue of the *Vagrant* was long delayed and should have emerged as early as 1923.

"In a Sequester'd Providence Churchyard Where Once Poe Walk'd." *Science-Fantasy Correspondent* 1, No. 3 (March–April 1937): 16–17. *WT* 31, No. 5 (May 1938): 578 (as "Where Poe Once Walked: An Acrostic Sonnet"). In *Four Acrostic Sonnets on Poe* (1936), ed. Maurice W. Moe.

"[Little Sam Perkins.]" *Olympian* No. 35 (Autumn 1940): 36.

"A Mississippi Autumn." *Ole Miss'* No. 2 (December 1915): 5–6 (as by "Howard Phillips Lovecraft, Metrical Mechanic").

"The Outpost." *Bacon's Essays* 3, No. 1 (Spring 1930): 7. *Fantasy Magazine* 3, No. 3 (May 1934): 24–25. *O-Wash-Ta-Nong* 3, No. 1 (January 1938): 1.

"The Poe-et's Nightmare." *Vagrant* No. 8 (July 1918): [13–23].

"Recapture." *WT* 15, No. 5 (May 1930): 693. (Later sonnet XXXIV of *Fungi from Yuggoth.*)

"The Smile." *Symphony* No. 12 (July 1916) [3–4].

"To Alan Seeger." *Tryout* 4, No. 7 (July 1918): [1–2].

"To Clark Ashton Smith, Esq., upon His Fantastic Tales, Verses, Pictures, and Sculptures." *WT* 31, No. 4 (April 1938): 392 (as "To Clark Ashton Smith").

"To Mr. Finlay, upon His Drawing for Mr. Bloch's Tale, 'The Faceless God.'" *Phantagraph* 6, No. 1 (May 1937) (as "To Mr. Finlay").

"To the Members of the Pin-Feathers on the Merits of Their Organisation, and of Their New Publication, *The Pinfeather.*" *Pinfeather* 1, No. 1 (November 1914): 3–4.

B. Works by Elizabeth Augusta Toldridge

Books

Mother. Chicago: J. Raymond Howe Co., 1919. A broadside.

Mother's Love Songs. Boston: Richard Badger/Gorham Press, 1911. *Contents:* The Little Dream-Mother; What Was It Made Me Love You Sweet; My Little White Rose; When She Comes and Goes; So Beautiful and Good; Sweetheart-Mother; My "Beauty Rose"; Mother's Pansies; In April; The Mother Angel; My Love Lady; Mother's Flower; My Lady-Love; My Riches; Home and Love; The Mother-Deeps; Robin Time; The Meaning of It All; There Is Nothing Too Sweet for Mother; A Fairy I Know; A Birthday; Mother's Day; The Forever; Guardian Mother; Immortality; Love Names; My Mother; The Wonder of It; A Wreath of Arbutus; Companioned; Mother; A Birthday; The Heritage of the Noble One; The Miracle; The Cry of the Daughter; The Lullaby of the Leaves; All Mothers.

The Soul of Love. New York: Broadway Pub. Co., 1910. *Contents:* The Greeting; The Parting; Memory-Glow; The Rock of Vision; Love's Highest Note.

Poems

"Beauty." In *The Choir Practice Anthology*, ed. Ellen M. Carroll. New York: Paebar, 1932, pp. 44–45.

"Betrothal." In *American Poetry Circle Anthology*. New York: Leacy N. Green-Leach, 1930, p. 111.

"A Calling's Cost." *New England Magazine* 32, No. 5 (July 1905): 578.

"Cherry Bloom." *Circle* 8, No. 1 (January–February 1931): 10–11.

"Christ's Masterpiece." *Catholic World* 60 (March 1895): 768 (as by "Barnet Toldridge").

"Dawn." *Circle* 3, No. 3 (1926): 45.

"The Eagle." *Circle* 7, No. 1 (January–February 1930): 20.

"Ephemera." *Leaves* No. 1 (Summer 1937): 63.

"Expectancy." *Dragon-Fly* No. 1 (15 October 1935): 7.

"Flag of My Home and Heart." *The Tower Light* 6, No. 1 (October 1932): 38.

"The Gathering Years." In *American Poetry Circle Anthology*. New York: Leacy N. Green-Leach, 1932, p. 116.

"H. P. Lovecraft." *Leaves* No. 1 (Summer 1937): 63.

"In the Woods." *Circle* 2, No. 3 (1925): 39. *Penwoman's Bulletin* (unseen). In *American Poetry Circle Anthology*. New York: Leacy N. Green-Leach, 1928, p. 133.

"Locusts and Wild Honey." *Dragon-Fly* No. 2 (15 May 1936): 41 (as by "E. Toldridge").

"Mist." *Leaves* No. 1 (Summer 1937): 34.

"Mother." In *American Poetry Circle Anthology*. New York: Leacy N. Green-Leach, 1928, p. 134.

"The Mother Love." *Christian Science Monitor* (24 October 1903).

"Neglected Gifts." *New England Magazine* 32, No. 6 (August 1905): 691.

"Noblesse Oblige." *The Circle* 7, No. 4 (July–August 1930): 76. In *American Poetry Circle Anthology*. New York: Leacy N. Green-Leach, 1930, p. 111.

"Poe." *Circle* 3, No. 2 (1926): 24.

"The Poem Called Life." In *American Poetry Circle Anthology*. New York: Leacy N. Green-Leach, 1929, p. 103.

"Poetry." *Californian* 3, No. 3 (Winter 1935): 102–3.

"The Poetry Path." *Californian* 5, No. 2 (Autumn 1937): 68.

"A Prayer." *Circle* 11, No. 1 (January–February 1934): 6.

"The River and the Boat." *Californian* 3, No. 3 (Winter 1935): 72.

"The Road of Life." *Circle* 2, No. 6 (1925): 87.

"The Robe." *Poetry of Today* (unseen). In *American Poetry Circle Anthology*. New York: Leacy N. Green-Leach, 1932, p. 116.

"S.O.S." *Circle* 7, No. 5 (November–December 1930): 100.

"Stars." In *American Poetry Circle Anthology*. New York: Leacy N. Green-Leach, 1929, p. 103

"Sweet Francis." *The Anthonian* (October 1921). *Poetry Review* (September–October 1926). In *American Poetry Circle Anthology*. New York: Leacy N. Green-Leach, 1928, p. 133. In *Canticles for Saint Francis*, ed. Benjamin Musser. Manchester, NH: Magnificat Press, 1936, p. 214.

"Thoughts." *Circle* 11, No. 3 (July–August 1934): 64.

"Unmothered." *Troubadour* 2, No. 1 (June 1929): 34.

"Washington." In *George Washington in the Hearts of His Countrymen: An Anthology 1732–1932*, ed. Beatrix Reynolds and James Gabelle. [Ridgewood, NJ: Garen Publishing Co., 1932], p. 81.

Short Stories

"The Greeting." In *The Soul of Love*, pp 13–17.

'Joanna's Crowning Sorrow." *New England Magazine* 32, No. 1 (March 1905): 79–84.

"A Little Picture of Mirandy." *International* 10, No. 4 (April 1901) 276–77 (as by "Barnet Toldridge").

"Love's Highest Note." In *The Soul of Love*, pp 77–104.

"Memory Glow." In *The Soul of Love*, pp 47–54.

"The Parting." In *The Soul of Love*, pp 31–43.

"The Rock of Vision." In *The Soul of Love*, pp 57–73.

"The Timid Heart of Lizzie." *Harper's Weekly* 38 (11 August 1894): 751 (as by "Barnet Toldridge").

D. Works by Anne Tillery Renshaw

Addressing the Public: A Manual for Professional Speakers. Washington DC: The Renshaw School of Speech, 1937.

Moods, Mystical and Otherwise. By Anne Vyne Tillery. Boston: Sherman, French & Company, 1914. *Contents:* Dusk Veils; A New Time; My Kinsmen; Mr. Spring Sunshine; Dancing Grasses; Balm of Pine; Willow-weeds; The Cut in the Road; A Song of Summer; Cotton Fields; Corn Song; When the Brook Says "Hush"; A Violet Grown Old; Withered Lilies; Bailey Blessings; Little Wet Flowers; Such a Day; A Love Fancy; To Emilie; Like Thee; Night Visions; A Little Farewell; Good Night, Love; Romance; Life; A "Melody in F"; The Dust That Is To Be; Little Teakettle; "Doin's"; Song of the Bullfrogs; Ghosts; Fancy; Pines Moonlit; The Burial of Dreams; Could We but Know; Paths; On the Life of Things; My Life Gift; To the World Silent; As I Pass; Heart of Hunger; Being Blue; A Void; Eyes of Error; Child Heart; Down the Glen; Life's Trinity; A Way of Thinking; Mexico; At Buena Vista; The Net; Immigrant; A Prayer; Pure of Heart; A Hope Song; Purity; Prayer Sympathy; Mine Host.

Salvaging Self Esteem: A Program for Self-improvement. Washington DC: The Renshaw School of Speech, 1937.

Well Bred Speech: A Brief Intensive Aid for English Students. Washington, DC: Standard Press, 1936.

This Way Out: A Concise Plan for Focusing Your Seven Latent Abilities . . . Washington DC: The Renshaw School, 1936.

"The Horizon of Dreams." *Conservative* 1, No. 4 (January 1916): 2 (poem).
"Our Friend, the Conservative." *Ole Miss'* No. 2 (December 1915): 2–3 (essay).

A review under the auspices of the Pen Women's League of *Lincoln,* by Nathaniel Wright Stevenson. Mentioned in *The Washington Post,* Washington DC. "Radio Programs, " Monday, December 1, 1924, Eastern Standard Time. WRC Radio Corp. 4 p.m.

E. Works by Others

Airne, C. W. (1889–). *Britain's Story Told in Pictures.* Manchester: Sankey, Hudson, & Co., [1935]. (*LL* 15)

———. *The Story of Hanoverian and Modern Britain Told in Pictures.* Sankey, Hudson & Co., 1935. (*LL*)

———. *The Story of Mediaeval Britain Told in Pictures.* Sankey, Hudson & Co., 1935. (*LL*)

———. *The Story of Prehistoric & Roman Britain Told in Pictures.* Sankey, Hudson & Co., [1935].

————. *Story of Saxon and Norman Britain Told in Pictures.* Sankey, Hudson & Co. [1935].

————. *The Story of Tudor and Stuart Britain Told in Pictures.* Sankey, & Hudson & Co., 1935. (*LL*)

Alden, Abner (1758?–1820). *The Reader: Containing the Art of Delivery, Articulation, Accent, Pronunciation,* [etc.]. 1802. 3rd ed. Boston: Printed by J. T. Buckingham for Thomas & Andrews, 1808. (*LL* 16)

Allen, Hervey (1889–1949). *Anthony Adverse.* New York: Holt, Rinehart & Winston, 1933.

————. *Israfel: The Life and Times of Edgar Allan Poe.* New York: George H. Doran Co., 1927. 2 vols. (*LL* 18)

American Poetry Circle Anthology. New York: Leacy N. Green-Leach, 1928. (*LL* 24)

American Poetry Circle Anthology. New York: Leacy N. Green-Leach, 1929. (*LL* 25)

American Poetry Circle Anthology. New York: Leacy N. Green-Leach, 1930. (*LL*)

American Poetry Circle Anthology. New York: Leacy Naylor Green-Leach, 1932. 120 pp. (*LL* 26)

Baudelaire, Charles Pierre (1821–1867). *Baudelaire: His Prose and Poetry.* Ed. T. R. Smith. New York: Boni & Liveright (Modern Library), [1919]. (*LL* 69)

Bayne, Samuel G. (1844–1924). *The Pith of Astronomy (without Mathematics): The Latest Facts and Figures as Developed by the Giant Telescopes.* New York: Harper & Brothers, 1903.

Boswell, James (1740–1795). *The Journal of a Tour to the Hebrides with Samuel Johnson, LL.D.* 1785. (*LL* 982)

————. *The Life of Samuel Johnson, LL.D.* 1791. London: J. M. Dent; New York: E. P. Dutton (Everyman's Library), 1910. (*LL* 113)

Brewer, Ebenezer Cobham (1810–1897). *A Dictionary of Phrase and Fable.* London: Cassell, 1870.

Bridges, Robert (1844–1930). *The Testament of Beauty.* Oxford: Clarendon Press, 1929.

Buchan, John (1875–1940). *Witch Wood.* Boston: Houghton Mifflin, 1927.

Bullen, John Ravenor (1886–1927). *White Fire.* Edited by H. P. Lovecraft. Athol, MA: Recluse Press, 1927 [actually January 1928]. (*LL* 131)

Byrne, Donn (pseud. of Brian Donn-Byrne, 1889–1928). *Destiny Bay.* Boston: Little, Brown, 1928.

Carroll, Ellen M. *The Choir Practice Anthology: A Collection of Poems.* New York: Paebar, 1932.

————. *Lonely Shores.* Atlanta: Bonner Press, Emory University, 1934. (*LL*)

Carroll, Lewis. *Alice's Adventures in Wonderland; and Through the Looking-Glass.* 1865/1871. With Ninety-two Illustrations by John Tenniel. New York: A. L. Burt, [19—]. (*LL*)

Davis, William Stearns (1877–1930). *A Friend of Caesar: A Tale of the Fall of the Roman Republic, 50–47 B.C.* New York: Macmillan, 1900.

454 ❦ *Letters to Elizabeth Toldridge and Anne Tillery Renshaw*

Doyle, Sir Arthur Conan (1859–1930). *The Maracot Deep and Other Stories*. London: John Murray, 1929.

Dunsany, Lord (Edward John Moreton Drax Plunkett, 18th baron) (1878–1957). *The Blessing of Pan*. London: G. P. Putnam's Sons, 1927. (*LL* 270)

———. *The Book of Wonder* (1912) [with *Time and the Gods* (1906)]. New York: Boni & Liveright (Modern Library), [1918]. (*LL* 271)

———. *Don Rodriguez: Chronicles of Shadow Valley*. New York: G. P. Putnam's Sons, 1922. (*LL* 272)

———. *A Dreamer's Tales and Other Stories* [*A Dreamer's Tales* (1910) and *The Sword of Welleran* (1908)]. New York: Boni & Liveright (Modern Library), [1917], [1919], or [1921]. (*LL* 273)

———. *Fifty Poems*. G. P. Putnam's Sons, 1929.

———. *The Gods of Pegāna*. London: Elkin Mathews, 1905.

———. *Time and the Gods*. London: Heinemann, 1906.

Easton, Emily M. *Roger Williams, Prophet and Pioneer*. Boston: Houghton Mifflin, 1930.

Eberlein, Harold Donaldson. *The Architecture of Colonial America*. Boston: Little, Brown, 1921. (*LL* 290)

Eddington, Sir Arthur S. (1882–1944). *The Nature of the Physical World*. Cambridge: Cambridge University Press, 1928.

Elliot, Hugh (1881–1930). *Modern Science and Materialism*. London: Longmans, Green, 1919.

Flecker, James Elroy (1884–1915). *Hassan: The Story of Hassan of Baghdad and How He Came to Make the Golden Journey to Samarkand*. New York: Alfred A. Knopf, 1922.

Fort, Charles (1874–1932). *The Book of the Damned*. New York: Boni & Liveright, 1919.

———. *New Lands*. New York: Boni & Liveright, 1923.

Frazer, Sir James George. *The Golden Bough: A Study in Comparative Religion*. London: Macmillan, 1890 (2 vols.). Expanded ed. London: Macmillan, 1900–1915 (12 vols.).

Griswold, Rufus Wilmot (1815–1857), ed. *The Poets and Poetry of America*. Philadelphia: Carey & Lea, 1842. (*LL* 380)

Gummere, Francis Barton (1855–1919). *A Handbook of Poetics, for Students of English Verse*. Boston: Ginn & Co., 1885.

Hoag, Jonathan E[than] (1831–1927). *The Poetical Works of Jonathan E. Hoag*. [New York: Privately printed], 1923. (*LL* 425)

Ingram, John H. (1842–1916). *Edgar Allan Poe: His Life, Letters, and Opinions*. London: J. Hogg, 1880. 2 vols. (*LL* 457)

Johnson, Samuel (1709–1784). *A Dictionary of the English Language*. 1755. 12th ed., corr, & rev. with Considerable Additions from the 8th ed. of the Original. Montrose, 1802. (*LL* 465)

Jeans, Sir James (1877–1946). *The New Background of Science*. Cambridge: Cambridge University Press, 1933.

Joshi, S. T. *I Am Providence: The Life and Times of H. P. Lovecraft*. New York: Hippocampus Press, 2010.

———. *Lovecraft's Library: A Catalogue*. 3rd ed. New York: Hippocampus Press, 2012.

Juvenal (D. Junius Juvenalis) (60?–140?). *The Satires of Decimus Junius Juvenalis*. With a Literal Interlinear Translation on the Hamiltonian System by Hiram Corson. With a Life of Juvenal by William Gifford, Esq. Philadelphia: D. McKay, [1868]. (*LL* 489)

Kimball, Gertrude Selwyn (1863–1910). *Providence in Colonial Times*. Boston: Houghton Mifflin, 1912.

Kittredge, George Lyman (1860–1941). *Witchcraft in Old and New England*. Cambridge, MA: Harvard University Press, 1929.

Krutch, Joseph Wood (1893–1970). *The Modern Temper: A Study and a Confession*. New York: Harcourt, Brace, 1929.

La Farge, Oliver (1901–1963). *Laughing Boy*. New York: Houghton Mifflin, 1929.

Long, Frank Belknap (1901–1994). *The Horror from the Hills*. *WT* (January and February–March 1931). Sauk City, WI: Arkham House, 1963.

———. *The Man from Genoa and Other Poems*. Athol, MA: Recluse Press, 1926.

———. *The Goblin Tower*. Cassia, FL: Dragon-Fly Press, 1935.

Longfellow, Henry Wadsworth (1807–1882). *Poems of Henry Wadsworth Longfellow*. Boston: Houghton Mifflin, 1887. (*LL* 544)

Loveman, Samuel (1887–1976). *The Hermaphrodsite: A Poem*. Athol, MA: W. Paul Cook, 1926. (*LL* 529)

———. *Out of the Immortal Night: Selected Works of Samuel Loveman*. Edited by S. T. Joshi and David E. Schultz. New York: Hippocampus Press, 2004.

———. *The Sphinx: A Conversation*. [North Montpelier, VT:] W. Paul Cook, 1944.

Macdonald, Alice Edith (Middleton), Lady (1861–1935). *All the Days of My Life*. London: John Murray, 1929.

———. *The Fortunes of a Family (Bosville of New Hall, Gunthwaite and Thorpe) through Nine Centuries*. Edinburgh: Printed by T. & A. Constable, 1928. (*LL* 565)

———. *The House of the Isles*. Edinburgh: T. & A. Constable, [1925]. (*LL* 566)

Machen, Arthur (1863–1947). *The Green Round*. London: Ernest Benn, 1933.

———. *The Hill of Dreams*. 1907. (*LL* 572)

———. *The House of Souls*. 1906. New York: Alfred A. Knopf, 1923. (*LL* 573) [Contains: "The White People."]

MacLeish, Archibald (1892–1982). *Conquistador*. Boston: Houghton Mifflin, 1932.

Matthews, Brander (1852–1929). *A Study of Versification* Boston: Houghton Mifflin, 1911.

Maturin, Charles Robert (1782?–1824). *Melmoth the Wanderer.* 1820. London: Richard Bentley & Son, 1892. 3 vols. (*LL* 599)

The Modern Encyclopedia: A New Library of World Knowledge. Edited by A. H. McDannald. New York: Grosset & Dunlap, 1935. (*LL* 613)

Morton, James F. "Washington in History." In *George Washington in the Hearts of His Countrymen: An Anthology 1732–1932,* ed. Beatrix Reynolds and James Gabelle. [Ridgewood, NJ: Garen Publishing Co., 1932], p. 11.

Moulton, Forest Ray. *Consider the Heavens.* Garden City, NY: Doubleday, Doran, 1925.

Minnigerode, Meade (1887–1967). *The Fabulous Forties: 1840–1850.* Garden City, NY: Garden City Publishing Co., 1924.

Musser, Benjamin Francis (1889–1951), ed. *Canticles for St. Francis.* Manchester, NH: Magnificat Press, 1936.

Newcomb, Simon (1835–1909). *Astronomy for Everybody.* New York: McClure, Phillips & Co., 1904. (*LL* 647)

O'Neill, Eugene. *The Emperor Jones.* New York: Stewart Kidd, 1921.

Pater, Walter (1839–1894). *Greek Studies.* London: Macmillan, 1895.

———. *Marius the Epicurean: His Sensations and Ideas.* 1885. New York: Boni & Liveright (Modern Library), [1921]. (*LL* 677)

———. *Studies in the History of the Renaissance.* London: Macmillan, 1873, 1877 (as *The Renaissance: Studies in Art and Poetry*).

Poe, Edgar Allan (1809–1849). *Tales of Mystery and Imagination.* Illustrated by Harry Clarke. 1919. New York: Tudor Publishing Co., 1933. (*LL* 701)

———. *Tamerlane and Other Poems.* Boston: Calvin F. S. Thomas, 1827 (as by "A Bostonian").

Raymond, George Lansing (1839–1929). *Poetry as a Representative Art: An Essay in Comparative Aesthetics.* New York: G. P. Putnam's Sons, 1886.

Reynolds, Beatrix, and James Gabelle, ed. *George Washington in the Hearts of His Countrymen: An Anthology 1732–1932.* [Ridgewood, NJ: Garen Publishing Co., 1932.] (*LL* 728)

Russell, Bertrand (1872–1970). *Our Knowledge of the External World as a Field for Scientific Method in Philosophy.* London: Open Court Publishing Co., 1914.

Santayana, George (1863–1952). *The Life of Reason; or, The Phases of Human Progress.* New York: Scribner's, 1905–22. 5 vols.

———. *Scepticism and Animal Faith.* New York: Scribner's, 1923.

Serviss, Garrett P. (1851–1929). *Astronomy with the Naked Eye.* New York: Harper & Brothers, 1908. (*LL* 780)

Seymour, G. S., ed. *A Bookfellow Anthology.* Chicago: The Bookfellows, 1925–36. 12 vols. (*LL* 786) [HPL had only Vol. 1 (1925).]

Shapley, Harlow (1885–1972). *Starlight.* New York: George H. Doran, 1926.

Sienkiewitz, Henryk (1846–1916). *Quo Vadis.* Tr. Jeremiah Curtin. Boston: Little, Brown, 1896.

Smith, Clark Ashton (1893–1961). *The Double Shadow and Other Fantasies.* Auburn, CA: Auburn Journal Press, 1933). (*LL* 810)

———. *Ebony and Crystal: Poems in Verse and Prose.* Preface by George Sterling. Auburn, CA: [Auburn Journal,] 1922. (*LL* 811)

———. *The Star-Treader and Other Poems.* San Francisco: A. M. Robertson, 1912. (*LL* 814)

Stormonth, James (1824–1882). *A Dictionary of the English Language.* 1871. The Pronunciation Carefully Revised by the Rev. P. H. Help. New York: Harper & Brothers, 1885. (*LL* 850)

Summers, Montague (1880–1948). *The Geography of Witchcraft.* London: Kegan Paul, Trench, Trübner; New York: Alfred A. Knopf, 1927.

———. *The Vampire: His Kith and Kin.* London: Kegan Paul, 1928.

———. *The Vampire in Europe.* London: Kegan Paul, 1929.

Wandrei, Donald (1908–1987). *Dead Titans, Waken! and Invisible Sun.* Edited by S. T. Joshi. Lakewood, CO: Centipede Press, 2011.

———. *The Web of Easter Island.* Sauk City, WI: Arkham House, 1948.

White, Edward Lucas (1866–1934). *Andivius Hedulio: Adventures of a Roman Nobleman in the Days of the Empire.* New York: E. P. Dutton, 1923. (*LL* 942)

———. *The Unwilling Vestal: A Tale of Rome under the Caesars.* New York: E. P. Dutton, 1918.

Wilde, Oscar (1854–1900). *Fairy Tales and Poems in Prose.* New York: Boni & Liveright (Modern Library), [1918]. (*LL* 954)

———. *The Picture of Dorian Gray.* 1890. New York: Boni & Liveright (Modern Library), 1918. (*LL* 956)

Wilder, Thornton (1897–1975). *The Bridge of San Luis Rey.* New York: Boni, 1927.

Wood, Clement. *Hints on Writing Poetry.* Girard, KS: Haldeman-Julius, [1924].

Woodberry, George E. (1855–1930). *Edgar Allan Poe.* Boston: Houghton Mifflin, 1885. (*LL* 970)

Zweig, Stefan (1881–1942). *The Right to Heresy: Castellio Against Calvin.* Translated by Eden and Cedar Paul. New York: Viking, 1936.

Index